Gender and Education

Readings on the Economy, Polity and Society

This series of readers is meant to introduce university students and research scholars to important research that has been published in the *Economic and Political Weekly* in specific areas. The readers draw on the large number of research articles that has been published in *EPW* over the decades. Each set of readings is compiled by a senior academic who has also written an introductory essay for the volume. *EPW* is grateful to the authors of the articles included here for permission to reproduce them. This series with two titles published every year between 2016 and 2019 has been produced with the help of a grant from the Tata Trusts. *EPW* is grateful to the Tata Trusts for supporting this venture.

Published

Economic Reforms and Growth in India, ed. **Pulapre Balakrishnan** (E-book)

Environment, Technology and Development: Critical and Subversive Essays, ed. **Rohan D'Souza**

Village Society, ed. **Surinder S. Jodhka**

The Adivasi Question: Issues of Land, Forest and Livelihood, ed. **Indra Munshi**

Women and Work, ed. **Padmini Swaminathan**

Decentralisation and Local Governments: The Indian Experience, ed. **T. R. Raghunandan**

Higher Education in India: In Search of Equality, Quality and Quantity, ed. **Jandhyala B. G. Tilak**

The Problem of Caste, ed. **Satish Deshpande**

Social Policy, ed. **Jean Drèze**

Water: Growing Understanding, Emerging Perspectives, eds **Mihir Shah and P. S. Vijayshankar**

A Handbook of Rural India, ed. **Surinder S. Jodhka**

Gender and Education

Edited by

Vimala Ramachandran
and
Kameshwari Jandhyala

TATA TRUSTS

Orient BlackSwan

GENDER AND EDUCATION

ORIENT BLACKSWAN PRIVATE LIMITED

Registered Office
3-6-752 Himayatnagar, Hyderabad 500 029, Telangana, India
e-mail: centraloffice@orientblackswan.com

Other Offices
Bengaluru, Bhopal, Chennai, Guwahati, Hyderabad,
Jaipur, Kolkata, Lucknow, Mumbai, New Delhi,
Noida, Patna, Visakhapatnam

First published by Orient Blackswan Pvt. Ltd. 2019

ISBN 978-93-5287-740-9

Typeset by
Le Studio Graphique, Gurgaon
in Adobe Garamond Pro 10.5/12.5

030249

Printed in India at
Yash Printographics, Noida

Published by
Orient Blackswan Private Limited
3-6-752 Himayatnagar, Hyderabad 500 029, Telangana, India
e-mail: info@orientblackswan.com

CONTENTS

Section III

Pedagogy, Curriculum and Textbooks

Tables, Figures and Maps

Tables

Figures

Maps

Abbreviations

AICTE	All-India Council for Teacher Education
AMC	Ahmedabad Municipal Corporation
ANM	Auxiliary-Nurse Midwife
AWC	Anganwadi Centre
BC	Backward Castes
BRC	Block Resource Centres
CEDAW	Convention on the Elimination of all forms of Discrimination Against Women
CL	Casual Labourers
CRC	Cluster Resource Centres
CSDS	Centre for the Study of Developing Societies
CSR	Corporate Social Responsibility
DPEP	District Primary Education Programme
EBB	Educationally Backward Blocks
EC	Education Commission
EG	Excluded Groups
EGS	Education Guarantee Scheme
EM	English Medium
FC	Forward Castes
FGD	Focus Group Discussion
GC	General Caste
GE	Generalised Entropy
GER	Gross Enrolment Ratios
GNP	Gross National Product
GPS	Government Primary School
GT-IMPI	Global Theme on Institutions, Markets, Policy and Impacts
HE	Higher Education
HRM	Human Resource Management
ICDS	Integrated Child Development Services
ICRISAT	International Crop Research Institute of the Semi-Arid Tropics
IDPAD	Indo-Dutch Programme on Alternatives in Development
IG	Included Groups
ILER	India Labour and Employment Report
JRF	Junior Research Fellow/Fellowship

KDF	Kernel Density Function
KGBV	Kasturba Gandhi Balika Vidyalayas
LSMS	Living Standard Measurement Survey
MHRD	Ministry of Human Resource Development
MM	Marathi Medium
MS	Mahila Samakhya
MSK	Mahila Shikshan Kendra
NAAC	National Assessment and Accreditation Council
NCERT	National Council of Educational Research and Training
NCF	National Curriculum Framework
NES	National Election Study
NET	National Entrance Test
NFHS	National Family Health Survey
NIEPA	National Institute of Educational Planning and Administration
NIOS	National Institute for Open Schooling
NPE	National Policy on Education
NPERC	National Policy on Education Review Committee
NSS	National Sample Survey
NSSO	National Sample Survey Office
NT	Nomadic Tribe
OBC	Other Backward Classes
OLS	Ordinary Least Squares
PAF	Phule-Ambedkarite Feminist
PMIS	Project Management Information System
POA	Programme of Action
PRI	Panchayati Raj Institutions
PWD	Public Works Department
RMSA	Rashtriya Madhyamik Shiksha Abhiyan
RSS	Rashtriya Swayamsevak Sangh
RW	Regular Workers
SBC	School Building Committee
SC	Scheduled Castes
SDMC	School Development and Monitoring Committee
SHG	Self-Help Group
SMC	School Management Committee
SSA	Sarva Shiksha Abhiyan
ST	Scheduled Tribes
TLM	Teaching-Learning Materials
TNTC	Tamil Nadu Textbook Corporation
TPR	Teacher-Pupil Ratio
UC	Upper Castes
UDHR	Universal Declaration of Human Rights
U-DISE	Unified District Information System for Education
UEE	Universalisation of Elementary Education

UGC	University Grants Commission
UNDP	United Nations Development Programme
UNICEF	United Nations International Children's Emergency Fund
VEC	Village Education Committee
VECC	Village Education Construction Committee
VLC	Village-Level Committee
VLS	Village-Level Studies

Introduction

How Much has Changed and What has Remained Unchanged?

Vimala Ramachandran and Kameshwari Jandhyala

Social Texture in India

It is often believed that the social texture of India is impervious to change and that caste and gender relations have continued to exert a strong influence on people's access to education and livelihoods. If we are to go by the current media reports on the situation of women and the predicament of Dalit or tribal groups, it looks as if social and gender relations have remained unchanged and are resistant to change. This is, though, far from the reality. Over the last century, India has witnessed considerable change. However, some spheres remain totally untouched—namely the all-pervasive son preference that leads to undervaluing girls in almost all regions and communities of India. Understanding and unravelling the complex interplay between modernity and tradition on the one hand, and between economic realities and social structures on the other, can be an exciting field of study. This introductory chapter explores the way the status of women has been changing, using the education domain to explain and illustrate this complex web with its multiple layers that need to be unravelled across a vast country.

Education of women and girls in India has been widely debated and discussed since the mid-1900s. Discussing the historical perspective on women's education in the chapter on 'Education and Development' in the iconic *Towards Equality* report, Vina Mazumdar said:

> Social reformers in India, whether they were modernising liberals or revivalists, also emphasised the crucial importance of education of women to improve their status in society. However, when we look at their justification for this departure from tradition then prevalent in the country, we notice certain significant omissions. According to the reformers the main purpose of educating women was not to make them more efficient and active units in the process of socio-economic and political development, but to make them more capable of fulfilling their traditional roles in society as wives and mothers... (GOI 1975: 179).

In the pre-Independence phase, women's education was positioned as a necessary driver of modernism, and the struggle was between the traditionalists who were concerned about its impact on social and familial relations and the modernisers, who argued for a modern/secular education. The concerns of the traditionalists were really unwarranted, as at the core, the modernisers too did not seek an education for women and girls that would challenge gender social relations.

Policies and programmes in independent India provide a fascinating story of how the ideological moorings on the issue of women's/girls' education have been framed and shaped. At the time of Independence, equality and equity were enshrined in the Constitution, with a commitment to creating conditions to ensure that the traditionally excluded Scheduled Castes and Tribes are brought into the ambit of education. The Five-Year Plans and the stated policies on education took this commitment forward, albeit in fits and starts. There was an expansion in the school system and infrastructure and the recruitment of women teachers as a means to bring girls into schools. The appreciation of the exclusionary nature of this expanding education system was yet to become part of public discourse and programming.

Globally, the 1980s witnessed international efforts to highlight the importance of women's equality. In India, the *Towards Equality* (GOI 1975) report of 1975 highlighted education as a critical terrain in the struggle for gender equality and gender justice. However, the response of the burgeoning women's/feminist movement was rather lukewarm. Barring traditional social reformers and missionaries,[1] political movements of all shades (including the women's movement), Dalit[2] and tribal struggles, the communist-inspired agrarian movements and trade unions did not flag universal elementary education on their agenda. They highlighted the plight of the poor and the marginalised, argued for greater employment opportunities and affirmative action to reserve a certain percentage of jobs and seats in educational institutions, etc. Universal elementary education, however, has never been high on the political agenda.

Interestingly, the mid-1980s heralded a churning in education with the publication of the *Challenge to Education* by the government (Ministry of Education, GOI 1985). This document was debated across the country and it culminated in the formulation of the New Education Policy of 1986. It was this policy statement that made a radical statement on the transformatory potential of education. Coming after the tumultuous 1980s, this policy acknowledged the need to address the roots of women's marginalisation, if the larger goals of gender equity and equality in education are to be realised. It also stated that:

> Education will be used as an agent of basic change in the status of women. In order to neutralize the accumulated distortions of the past, there will be a well-conceived edge in favour of women. The National Education System will play a positive, interventionist role in the empowerment of women. It will foster the development of new values through redesigned curricula, textbooks, training and orientation of teachers, decision-makers, administrators and the active involvement of educational institutions (GOI 1986, NPE: Para 4.2).[3]

This commitment was translated into a fascinating programme for women's equality and empowerment called Mahila Samakhya (started in 1987), which sought to create the conditions and environment for poor women to seek and ensure learning and education for themselves and their daughters. The National Literacy Mission also gained momentum in the country in the early 1990s when issues close to women's lived experience, such as alcoholism and violence, were brought into the teaching-learning processes and materials. From the early 1990s, the drive for universal primary education through the District Primary Education Programme (DPEP) brought gender issues to the fore in curriculum and textbook revision, gender sensitisation of teachers, and community mobilisation on girls' education, among others. The National Curriculum Framework 2005 gave a clear and succinct direction to gender, equity and equality in education.

Much has changed in India. The political and cultural environment today has a distinct fundamentalist and communal hue. This is reflected in the draft New Education Policy of 2016. In a recent critique of this draft, Ramamurthy and Pandian draw attention to major concerns:

> The new education policy, as proposed, chooses not to address the fundamental issues plaguing the education system but instead, it propagates a corporate, neo-liberal, neo-cultural, a Sanskritised, global and market-oriented education system which is governed by a wholly separate and centralised bureaucracy, where state government power and oversight is minimal (Ramamurty and Pandian 2016: 46).

It is too early to say if this draft will be accepted as policy and the kind of impact it may have. However, the trend is fairly clear. Privatisation is the preferred path of expansion at all levels (primary to higher/technical education). Socio-economic and gender equity issues have been put on the backburner. Social norms and practices are changing, partly because of economic change and partly due to greater exposure to the world, through the eyes of the media. The aspirations of young women and girls are changing alongside the expectations of their families. Having a working spouse/daughter is seen as an asset, especially among the poor and the middle classes. Expectedly, this has led to greater participation in education.

Let us start with some stark and contrasting data on women's education in India. While all-India figures say little about regional and other forms of inequalities, nevertheless serve to highlight the broad trends (Table I.1). In 1951, female literacy rate was 8.86 per cent and it went up to 39.29 per cent in 1991, to 53.67 per cent in 2001 and in 2011, it was 65.46 per cent. The initial spurt in literacy in the first four decades after Independence slowed down in the subsequent decades, suggesting the social complexity of educational participation. The regional variations are wide—at one end of the spectrum is Kerala with a female literacy rate of 92 per cent, followed by Mizoram at 89.4 per cent; and at the other end is Rajasthan with a female literacy rate of 52.7 per cent, followed by Bihar at 53.3 per cent (*Census of India 2011*). Let us take one of the most marginalised social groups of India—the indigenous tribes known as Scheduled Tribes. From a female literacy rate of 3.2 per cent in 1961, the female literacy rate among Scheduled Tribes was 49.4 per cent in 2011. Similarly, the female literacy rate among Scheduled Castes was 3.3 per cent in 1961 and it went up to 56.5 per cent in 2011.

TABLE I.1: All India Literacy Rate of General, SC and ST Population (1961–2011) (Figures in percentage)

Year	*All Social Groups*			*SC*			*ST*		
	M	*F*	*Total*	*M*	*F*	*Total*	*M*	*F*	*Total*
1951	27.15	8.86	18.31	na	na	na	na	na	na
1961	40.4	15.4	28.3	17.0	3.3	10.3	13.8	3.2	8.5
1971	46.0	22.0	34.5	22.4	6.4	14.7	17.6	4.9	11.3
1981	56.4	29.8	43.6	31.1	10.9	21.4	24.5	8.0	16.4
1991	64.1	39.3	52.2	49.9	23.8	37.4	40.7	18.2	29.6
2001	75.2	53.7	64.8	66.6	41.9	54.7	59.2	34.8	47.1
2011	80.9	64.6	73.0	75.2	56.5	66.1	68.5	49.4	59.0

Source: Registrar General of India, *Census of India*, Various Years.

Right from the time of Independence, in 1947, to the present (2019), social differences and inequalities have been discernible across geographical regions, terrain (forest, mountainous, desert, fertile plains), social groups (socially advantaged communities and those that are disadvantaged, like the SCs and STs, and so on), wealth quintiles and gender, which cuts across all these divides. Customs and traditions among some communities are stronger than others, and educational status, occupation, migration and location (rural/urban) also exert influence. Therefore, any discussion on women and education in India needs to be located within a specific social context. While generic figures (like the literacy data above) give an overview, it is not possible to understand the situation without placing the analysis within specific contexts.

A sensitive indicator of gender inequality in India is sex ratio. In 1901, the sex ratio was 972 (females per 1,000 males); it went down to 946 in 1951, 927 in 1991 and marginally up to 943 in 2011. Another sensitive indicator is the *sex ratio at birth (SRB)*[4], which points to the persistence of son preference in the country. Apart from the fact that there are significant differences between the north and some north-western states and the southern and eastern states of India, what is interesting is that urban-rural differences are *skewed in favour of rural areas*, with the child sex ratio in rural areas being 919 while it is 902 in urban areas (Census 2011). This is a telling statement on Indian society—that a greater number of years of education of men and women and a relatively better economic status do not improve the chances of survival of girl children. According to Census 2011, rural child sex ratio is higher as compared to urban areas in 26 states. The Census commissioner reports that, 'In rural India, there are 74 districts with CSR < 850 in 2011, whereas, there were 54 districts in this group in 2001. In 38 districts, the decline in CSR has been more than 50 points. In 51 districts, there is increase in CSR with 20 or points'. (MOSPI, GOI 2012: 30)

The data for sex ratio at birth is collected through the Sample Registration System (SRS), which records all birth and deaths. How many children who are born actually survive? S. Irudaya Rajan cautions us that the data from difference sources [Census, NFHS (National Family Health Survey), SRS and Civil Registration] may not always match; however, the broad trend across different data sources seem to be similar. He points out that the registration of births is below 80 per cent in states like Uttar Pradesh and Bihar, while in Tamil Nadu, 100 per cent of births are registered. Notwithstanding these caveats, most commentators agree that there are significant differences across states. He opines that:

> Between 2011 and 2014 several states... have witnessed a sharp decline in SRB. For instance, Gujarat, Himachal Pradesh, Karnataka, West Bengal and Tamil Nadu have recorded a decline in SRB... the source-dependent difference in SRB for Tamil Nadu, for example, is perturbing. According to the SRS, Tamil Nadu has experienced a decline in SRB from 905 to 834 between 2011 and 2014 on a 100% birth registration rate for the same period... However, other sources such as the SRS peg Tamil Nadu's SRB at 929 in 2007–09 and at 921 in 2012–14 in contrast to the NFHS figures of 896 in 2004–05 and 954 in 2015–16 (Rajan et al. 2017: 15).

The economically better-off and better-educated middle classes, in rural and urban areas, are known to practice female infanticide and sex-selective abortion. It was argued that the landed rural middle class did this to prevent the depletion of wealth (Kaur et al. 2016). It was also believed that non-landowning communities—especially the SC and ST—did not (traditionally) resort to these practices. However, the 2001 Census shows that this trend does not hold true any more and SC communities, especially in urban areas, also practice sex-selective abortion. Son preference is catching on among the SC, ST and OBC communities. Kaur et al. argue, 'Hence, while caste patterns might have been somewhat distinctive in an earlier period, there is much greater homogeneity currently in the behaviour of caste groups vis-à-vis gender discrimination...' (ibid.: 8).

The economic situation of people in India is changing rapidly. It is also believed that poverty levels are coming down slowly and educational levels are going up, with many more young people completing at least eight years of elementary education. Yet, son preference persists and is rapidly spreading to communities and areas where this was not so evident, or even in communities that were matrilineal. The question is whether higher levels of education and more wealth exert a negative or positive influence on son preference. The jury is still out, as most experts believe that the situation on the ground is rapidly changing and, given the huge diversity across regions, communities and economic wealth quartiles, *it is difficult to conclusively say what the national trend is.*[5] This changing landscape affects children's rights from the time they are born. Starting with breastfeeding, immunisation, health care and nutrition, to preschool education and schooling, communities and parents make choices. These choices adversely affect some children, especially girls and children born with disabilities.

On the other hand, recent surveys have thrown up some encouraging results. Child marriage has often been cited as a serious issue and deterrent—especially when it comes to a girl's education and well-being. 'Child marriage' is a phrase used for any marriage that happens before the legal age of 18 years for girls and 21 years for boys. However, it is important to distinguish between two phases—one marriage before the age of 14, and the other after 14 but before 18 years. This distinction, however, is not made in the national data. Analysis of recently released NFHS–4 data reveals that 28 per cent of women in the age-group 18–29 years and 17 per cent of men in the age-group 21–29 years were married before attaining the legal age of marriage (NFHS–4, 2016).[6] The incidence of child marriage for girls is highest in West Bengal (44 per cent), Bihar (42 per cent), Jharkhand (39 per cent), Rajasthan (33 per cent), Assam (33 per cent) and Madhya Pradesh (33 per cent) (NFHS–4). Child marriage for boys is highest in Rajasthan and Madhya Pradesh (28 per cent each), followed by Bihar and Jharkhand (27 per cent each). CBPS argues:

> NFHS survey also noted that prevalence of child marriage is higher in rural areas and for those with lower levels of education. Median age at first marriage for urban women in age group 25—49 years was 19.8 years as against 18.1 years for rural women. The median age for women in the age group 25–49 years with no schooling is 17.2 years as against 19.7 years for women with 10–11 years of schooling/education.... increases to 22.7 years for women with 12 or more years of schooling. Shift in the median age for first marriage clearly indicates a linkage between child marriage and education.... (CBPS 2018).

What is interesting is that, across India, social norms with respect to child marriage and early marriage are changing. At the same time, as we have noted in the preceding paragraphs, sex ratio at birth is more adverse in urban as compared to rural areas. Conversely, early marriage is more prevalent in rural than in urban areas. More in-depth qualitative studies many be needed to explain this difference. In a recent qualitative study conducted (Ramachandran and Saxena 2018), it was heartening to find that the incidence of child marriage has come down drastically in rural areas—meaning that in the four to five years preceding the qualitative study done in 2018—not one girl or boy was married before the age of 14 in the six sample villages of Uttar Pradesh and Jharkhand. With almost universal enrolment in elementary schools, almost all the children in the sample households were studying or had completed Class VIII before dropping out. We found a two-way relationship between secondary education and early marriage—higher levels of school education postpone the age of marriage and equally, when (for whatever reason) girls drop out, the chances of their getting married are also high. This phenomenon is affirmed through a number of sample surveys done over the past decade or more. There has been a significant decline in incidences of child marriage across India.

ISSUES RESISTANT TO CHANGE

Winds of change are blowing across India with some positive trends, but there is much that is grim and of grave concern. There are areas like child marriage or girls' participation in education where positive trends are visible (Table I.2), and there are areas that seem impervious to change and are very troubling—like strong son

TABLE I.2: Child marriage rates, India (marriage before 18 years for girls and 21 years for boys)

S No	State	Census 2001	Census 2011	DLHS–3 (2007–08)	NFHS–3 (2005–06)	NFHS–4 (2015–16)	Decline in child marriage %	
							Between Census 2001 and Census 2011	Between NFHS–3 and NFHS–4
	India	32.1	17.2	42.9	47.4	26.8	46.4	43.5
1	Andhra Pradesh	42	20.2	51.9	35.5	32.7	51.9	–
2	Arunachal Pradesh	23.7	14.3	26.2	42	23.5	39.6	44
3	Assam	24.5	16.5	40	38	32.6	32.6	14.2
4	Bihar	53	23	68.2	60.3	39.1	56.6	35.2
5	Chhattisgarh	32.5	15	45.2	55	21.3	53.8	61.3
6	Goa	5.6	3.2	19.1	11.7	9.8	42.7	16.2
7	Gujarat	18.6	12.1	35.4	38.7	24.9	35	35.7
8	Haryana	31	14.5	28	39.8	18.5	53.3	53.5
9	Himachal Pradesh	7.3	4.2	9.1	12.3	8.6	42.5	30.1
10	Jammu and Kashmir	14.7	6.9	24.6	14.4	8.7	53.1	39.6
11	Jharkhand	48.4	27.9	55.7	63.2	38	42.4	39.9
12	Karnataka	26	12.3	50.2	41.2	23.2	52.7	43.7
13	Kerala	10.1	6	15.5	15.4	7.6	40.7	50.6
14	Madhya Pradesh	46	22.5	53.8	53	30	51.1	43.4
15	Maharashtra	19.2	11.5	40.4	39	25.1	40	35.6
16	Manipur	11	6.7	24.7	12.7	13.1	39.3	-3.1
17	Meghalaya	16.8	12.7	34.3	24.5	16.5	24.5	32.7
18	Mizoram	10.7	7.9	23.7	20.6	10.8	26.2	47.6
19	Nagaland	13	8.6	--	21.4	13.3	33.8	37.9
20	NCT Delhi	14.7	7.4	24.2	22.7	13	49.7	42.7
21	Odisha	22.8	12.3	37.5	37.2	21.3	46.1	42.7
22	Punjab	8.7	4.3	15.5	19.7	7.6	50.6	61.4
23	Rajasthan	51.5	31.6	57.6	65.2	35.4	38.6	45.7
24	Sikkim	21.5	14.9	30.6	30.1	14.5	30.7	51.8
25	Tamil Nadu	14.7	7.1	24	21.5	15.7	51.7	27
26	Tripura	26.9	21.5	43.6	41	32.2	20	21.5
27	Uttar Pradesh	40.5	17.6	54.9	58.6	21.2	56.5	63.8
28	Uttarakhand	16.3	7.6	19.7	22.6	13.9	53.3	38.5
29	West Bengal	37.2	29.2	54.7	53.3	40.7	21.4	23.6

Notes: Pearson Correlation coefficient between: Child marriage from Census 2011 and NFHS–4 = 0.919 p value – .000 (n=29); decline in Census and NFHS = 0.405 p value – .032 (n=28).

Source: Kumar 2016.

preference, violence against women in the home, in society and in public spaces. The percentage of women who work outside the home and for wages also shows little improvement, in fact work participation ratios have been coming down in the last decade (Sudarshan 2018).[7]

A thorny web of factors influences gender relations/gender inequality across different regions, states, communities, income groups and religious groups. It is against this backdrop that one needs to look at women and education in India. Gender equality in education and girls' access to education are influenced by three interlocking sets of issues—(i) economy, society and culture, (ii) accessibility/availability to formal education, and (iii) gender norms. The interplay of socio-economic inequalities, physical infrastructure and connectivity, and gender relations creates a complex web that either promotes or impedes girls' ability to go through schooling.[8] While economic disparities and social inequalities are certainly important, a number of researchers argue that cultural beliefs and practices and regional characteristics play an important role (Colclough et al. 2000). Poverty, social inequalities and gender relations intersect in different ways in different regions of the country, with one reinforcing the other in some and offsetting one in others. Understanding and unravelling this is the biggest challenge today.[9] In this context, it would be valuable to recall that rural-urban differences in enrolment, attendance and completion are greater than male-female differences. Equally, disparities between very poor households (below poverty line) and the top quartile are much higher than gender, social and regional differences. Inter-community differences are often as severe as intra-community differences. As evident in Table I.3 below,

TABLE I.3: Graded Inequities in Literacy Rates

	Census 2001	*Census 2011*
Rural Female ST	32.4	46.9
Rural Female SC	37.6	52.6
All Rural Female	46.13	57.9
Rural Female Non-SC/ST	50.2	61.1
Rural Male ST	57.4	66.8
Rural Male SC	53.7	72.6
Urban Female SC	57.5	68.6
Urban Female ST	59.9	70.3
All Rural Male	70.7	77.1
All Urban Female	72.86	79.1
Rural Male Non-SC/ST	74.3	79.9
Urban Female Non-SC/ST	75.5	81.0
Urban Male ST	77.8	83.2
Urban Male SC	77.9	83.3
All Urban Male	86.27	88.8
Urban Male Non-SC/ST	87.6	89.7

Source: Adapted by Vimala Ramachandran from Lall and Rao 2011: 34.

gender differences are clearly evident, suggesting the deep patriarchal nature of discrimination and exclusion. This seems to supersede and cut across the social stratification of caste, which in itself is the most troubling aspect of Indian society.

This is best illustrated by a textured analysis of the census data of India on literacy and also a nuanced presentation of data on dropout rates in different stages of schooling in India.

School Education

Till the early 1990s, it was common to start any analysis of the gender gap in education with mapping the provision of schooling (access/supply) and the willingness of parents to educate their daughters. The main concern at that time in India's history was to ensure that all children have access to a functioning primary school within walking distance. It was believed that when access became easy, social attitudes towards daughters would change. Therefore, through the decade of the 1990s the government focussed on opening primary schools and setting a norm of providing a primary school within 1 kilometre of a child's residence. By the year 2000, the idea of universal elementary education gained greater acceptance and with the launching of a flagship education programme called Sarva Shiksha Abhiyan in 2003, the effort was to ensure that all children have access to at least eight years of schooling.

With globalisation and the rapid inroads made by the media, it was soon apparent that even the poorest and the most deprived families were ready to send their sons and daughters to school. Coupled with the nation-wide push for Right to Free and Compulsory Education in 2010 (as a campaign in 2004–09, when it was finally notified as a right by the government), it soon became quite apparent that availability and accessibility to government schools was indeed very important. There is widespread consensus that, in theory, close to 99 per cent of habitations have access to a primary school within a kilometre distance. They could be a fully functioning school with one teacher for each class, or a small school with one teacher teaching all classes. As late as 2016–17, 10.93 per cent of primary schools (Classes I to V) were single-teacher schools. Equally alarming is that 10.98 per cent of government-aided schools were also being managed by a single teacher. This phenomenon is not limited to primary schools alone. U-DISE (Unified District Information System for Education) data reports that there are single-teacher schools at the upper-primary level (9.8 per cent) and even among the higher-secondary schools (3.33 per cent). An overwhelming proportion of these schools are located in rural/remote areas (NIEPA 2018, U-DISE 2016–17). It is therefore not surprising that while universal enrolment may have become the norm, many children drop out. In 2000, 40.3 per cent of children who enrolled in Class I dropped out before they completed Class V—the percentage of girls who dropped out was 42.3 per cent. If we take Classes I to X as a continuum—22.13 per cent of children drop out of school at various stages (see Table I.4).

TABLE I.4: Dropout Rates in Classes I–V, I–VIII and I–X

Year	Class I–V			Class I–VIII			Class I–X		
	Boys	Girls	Total	Boys	Girls	Total	Boys	Girls	Total
1999–2000	38.7	42.3	40.3	52	58.0	54.5	66.6	70.6	68.3
2009–10	30.25	27.25	28.86	40.59	44.39	42.39	53.38	51.97	52.76
2011–12	23.4	21.0	22.3	41.5	40.0	40.8	48.6	52.2	50.3
2016–17	6.40	6.30	6.35	4.97	6.42	5.67	22.11	22.15	22.13

Source: Till 2011–12, SES/SSE (Various Years); for 2016–17, NUEPA, U-DISE.

If we are to look closely at the dropout rate of different social groups and by gender, a different picture emerges. In 2001–02, a shocking 82 per cent of all tribal girls who enrolled in Class I would have dropped out before they completed Class X, followed closely by tribal boys, and then SC girls and boys. This picture was not very different in 2016–17. While overall dropout rates have fallen significantly, children from socially disadvantaged communities (tribal and SC) still drop out (see Table I.5). However, since 2010, an interesting trend is discernible. The dropout rates of girls have come down at a faster rate than that of boys—across all communities/ social groups. This trend is particularly significant because, for several decades, the government was primarily concerned about gender gaps in enrolment and dropout rates, and therefore introduced several incentives to retain girls in school, like providing free uniforms, textbooks and school supplies; bicycles for girls after Class VI, scholarships/cash transfers to delay the age of marriage; residential facilities through RMSA hostels—to name a few. This has obviously had a positive result.

TABLE I.5: Dropout Rates of All Categories, ST & SC Students (1990–91, 2010–11)

Year	Sex	Classes I–V			Classes I–VIII			Classes I–X		
		All	SC	ST	All	SC	ST	All	SC	ST
2001–02	Boys	38.4	43.7	51	52.9	58.6	67.3	64.2	71.1	79.9
	Girls	39.9	47.1	54.1	56.9	63.6	72.7	68.6	74.9	82.9
	Total	39	45.2	52.3	54.6	60.7	69.5	66	72.7	81.2
2010–11	Boys	28.7	29.8	37.2	40.3	46.7	54.7	50.4	57.4	70.6
	Girls	25.1	23.1	33.9	41	39	55.4	47.9	54.1	71.3
	Total	27	26.7	35.6	40.6	43.3	55	49.3	56	70.9
								Classes IX and X		
2016–17	Boys	4.48	8.3	8.57	3.92	8.02	8.86	15.14	23.06	27.41
	Girls	4.96	7.86	8.51	4.72	8.01	8.9	16.27	21.99	26.51
	Total	4.71	8.09	8.54	4.3	8.01	8.88	15.68	22.55	26.97

Source: School education statistics, MHRD for 2001–02 and 2010–11, U-DISE Flash Statistics 2016–17.

What happens after a child enrols in school? Recent research on push out factors highlights the attitudes and practices of teachers in school and also of children from relatively forward social groups (Nambissan 1996, 2000 and 2001; Ramachandran and Naorem 2012). There is a recognition of the need to interrogate classroom practices, teacher/administrator attitudes and prejudices, and curriculum that may reinforce social biases/discriminatory practices and gender stereotypes (NCF Position Paper 3.2, NCERT 2005 b; Ramachandran 2004, 2012). At the same time, the educational achievement of children is more than just a combined effect of both supply and demand factors. Gender, caste, class, location, and the kind of school (single-teacher school/multi-grade schools), all affect learning outcomes. Equally, one cannot ignore the impact of children's experience of schooling, the role of the teacher and the overall school environment in the learning journey of children.

Sample surveys like ASER (2005 onwards) and the school-based National Assessment Survey, conducted by NCERT, reveal that children in rural and urban schools and in government and private schools are not learning as much as they are expected to. Learning has emerged as a huge challenge. This has led to a serious debate on whether India is facing a learning crisis (*Seminar*, June 2018). The consensus across the education community is that:

> When they complete 8 or 10 or 12 years of schooling our children are not equipped to negotiate the world they live in with confidence and with the requisite knowledge and skills to help them deal with the world from a position of strength....parents and children admit that the schools and colleges they attended did not add much value.... the 'social capital' that children bring into the school is an important predictor of 'success'—meaning that children who have educated parents, have access to books and other reading materials, have greater exposure to creative arts, media and live in resource-rich environments—seem to gain a lot more from the educational process as compared to those who come from resource-poor environment (Ramachandran and Rajagopalan 2018: 14).

During the course of the debate on learning, an interesting insight was that there are no major gender differences in learning outcomes—boys and girls across different levels are in the same boat.

Secondary and Higher Secondary

Gender and caste/community differences emerge sharply in secondary schools. For girls in particular, several issues come into play: greater restrictions on mobility, concerns of security, gendering of subject options and above all, costs of secondary schooling. A serious issue that affects girls' participation is distance to secondary schools. RMSA (Rashtriya Madhyamik Shiksha Abhiyan) guidelines state that secondary schools should be located within a reasonable distance (5–7 km) of any habitation and yet, in many villages and districts, students have to travel huge distances in order to go to a government secondary school in India. For e.g., in Baran and Barmer (Rajasthan), the nearest distance to secondary school is close to 10–15 km (Jandhyala and Ramachandran 2014). Increased distance means more adolescent girls drop out of schools due to safety concerns. Studies have reported that increased distance is a serious barrier to girls' enrolment. According to the UN Report on Women (2012), an increase of 0.5 km reduced the girls' enrolment rate by 20 per cent. Often, parents and adolescent girls fear sexual harassment and violence on the way to school, and when longer distances are coupled with non-availability of a safe public transportation system, it further pushes more girls to drop out of school (Jandhyala and Ramachandran 2014). Increased distance also means increased transportation cost that often affects girls more than boys, and children from disadvantaged families. In many parts of the country, girls' schools and schools located in tribal areas do not offer science or mathematics at the secondary/senior secondary levels. As a result, they are shut out of many career options.

Public under-investment in secondary education has resulted in the mushrooming of private secondary schools. Only 40 per cent secondary schools are run by the government, and the remaining are private unaided or aided (NIEPA 2016, U-DISE 2015–16). Unlike elementary school, where the costs of going to school are negligible, there are direct and indirect costs (such as admission fee, tuition fees, exam fee, books, stationery, lab fee, dress, sanitary napkins, etc.) attached with secondary and higher secondary education, which can constitute a significant portion of the family income. Studies have shown that the additional cost of attending private secondary school can be as high as 2.5 times the cost of government secondary schools (Siddhu 2011). Inability to access government secondary schools, compounded with higher costs of education, has serious gender and equity implications, because girls and children from disadvantaged groups are more likely to attend government secondary schools, while attending private schools continues to be a privilege reserved for boys and children from wealthier, upper-caste families (ASER 2016; Majumdar 2005; World Bank 2009).

Non-availability of girls' only secondary schools is a serious issue in some regions of the country—parents of adolescent girls in several areas of the country and from some communities are reluctant to send their girls to co-educational schools because of safety concerns. Often, girls have to negotiate harassment, sexual innuendoes and derisive talks, both in and outside the classroom, especially in co-educational schools; and due to a lack of girls' only schools, many end up dropping out altogether. Strong cultural and traditional values also play a significant role in girls' mobility, especially after they enter the pubescent stage. In his study, Siddhu (2011) reports that it is socially unacceptable for girls to travel alone after a certain age in Uttar Pradesh. Likewise, in Ajmer, it was found that Muslim girls would drop out if the secondary school was situated outside the Muslim neighbourhood (Jandhyala and Ramachandran 2014). The lack of women teachers has an important bearing on girls' participation, especially at secondary and higher secondary levels. In fact, the presence of female teachers not only aids enrolment but also helps in retention, because along with providing emotional and moral support to girls, female teachers can also have a positive influence on girls' education. However, the percentage of female teachers is 40.57 per cent at the secondary level (NIEPA 2016, U-DISE 2015).There is also a shortage of subject specific teachers. Nearly 40 per cent schools do not have a Mathematics, Social Studies and/or Language teacher and nearly one-third do not have a Science teacher (Sixth RMSA JRM report, 2015). The shortage of female and subject specialist teachers not only limits the options for students, but it also has a spiralling effect on the future availability of teachers and affects women's participation in the labour market.

Access is also a critical issue for marginalised groups, in particular for children from the SC/ST and Muslim categories, children from migrant families, and those living in remote or conflict areas. In a study, it was found that there is a disparity in secondary school availability between villages that have a high SC/ST population and those that have a lower SC/ST population (Visaria 2014). While more than 80 per cent villages with less than 25 per cent SC/ST population had greater access to secondary schools, only 4–6 per cent villages with more than 50 per cent SC/ST population had access to secondary schools. Likewise, the overall enrolment rate of Muslim students in secondary and higher secondary schools is 9.39 per cent (NIEPA 2016, U-DISE 2015–16), and information on the enrolment status of children from migrant families and children living in remote and conflict areas continues to be patchy.

The lack of functioning toilets is a deterrent for adolescent girls to attend schools, because it not only affects hygiene and privacy issues, but also causes inconvenience to girls when they are menstruating (Samson et al. 2007; Bandyopadhyay and Subrahmanian 2008). In some studies, the lack of a supportive environment and harassment (examples include humiliation, beating students with sticks, and sexual harassment) by teachers and/or members of staff has been identified as an important reason for dropping out of schools, especially for girls (Samson et al. 2007; Bandyopadhyay and Subrahmanian 2008). Growing violence against women, coupled with safety issues and a shortage of female teachers, creates an inhospitable environment, and therefore girls often drop out of the school system.

Gender difference in household expenditure on education, health and nutrition has been an important focus for several decades now. Even though the gender gap in terms of enrolment and literacy rate has reduced, there is significant evidence of gender disparity in household spending at every level of education. For decades now, researchers have presented robust evidence of the existence of a pro-male bias in household spending on education (Tilak and Chaudhury in Ramachandran and Saxena et al. 2018). As Chaudhari and Roy (2006) argue in Chapter 15, preference of the households to invest in the education of boys rather than girls is widely prevalent in India, and such a difference widens further as one goes up the education ladder—this being the highest in the case of higher education (Chaudhuri and Roy 2006; Kambhampati 2008). Using IHDS data, Azam and Kingdon (2013) have shown that gender disparities in educational expenditure are more prevalent in rural areas and in certain states. Households discriminate against investment in girls' education, due to their male bias.

Our recent qualitative study in Jharkhand and Uttar Pradesh (Ramachandran et al. 2014) confirms this trend. Gender difference in household spending on secondary education in Uttar Pradesh has increased from Rs 396 in 2007–08 to Rs 1,853 in 2013–14 (4.67 times), and from Rs 569 to Rs 1,768 in Jharkhand (3.10 times). At the all-India level, the increase was 2.8 times. At the higher secondary level, the gender difference in household expenditure has gone up from Rs 1,013 in

2007–08 to Rs 1,982 in 2013–14 in Uttar Pradesh (two times), and in Jharkhand from Rs 224 to Rs 1,726 (7.7 times). Importantly, pro-male bias in household spending is relatively higher in urban areas (with very few exceptions) than in rural areas, in both secondary and higher secondary levels of education in both the states, like it is in India as a whole.

What does educational expenditure entail? The 71st Round of NSSO categorises the expenditure as (i) course fee, (ii) books and stationery, (iii) transport, (iv) private coaching, and (v) other expenditure. During the course of our fieldwork, we found that parents were not as willing to spend on private coaching for girls, while they were willing to do so for their boys. Equally, we also found that parents preferred to enrol their daughters in government or aided schools—where the expenditure on fee, study material and other expenditures (lab fee) were lower. Interestingly, discrimination between the two genders was far more among very poor/poor families, while it was not so significant among the middle classes. This is not surprising, given that poor families also make economic choices that are driven by gendered social norms and perceptions, and often choose to spend less on girls.

THIS VOLUME

This collection has been drawn from articles published in *Economic and Political Weekly*, from the year 2000 to 2017. The selection has been presented in three sections. In Section I on Gender and Social Equity, we have brought together chapters that lay out and explain the different axes of inequality. The chapters range from exploring the life-cycle of education (Ramachandran, Jandhyala and Saihjee), girlhood (Krishna Kumar), notions of equality, inequality and transition (Sadhana Saxena, Jeemol Unni, Divya Vaid and Nandini Manjrekar), segregation of schools (Ramachandran and Saihjee) and women teachers (Jandhyala and Ramachandran). Section II encompasses chapters that explore the political, economic and social context of education. Starting with the impact of social conflict on girls' education (Sheth and Haeem), it explores gender gaps and gender relations (McDougall, Saigal, Singh Mehta and Shree, Chaudhuri and Roy), ending with globalisation, higher education and expectations from education (Chanana and Maertens). Section III of this volume focusses on pedagogy and curriculum through textual analysis of books (Bhog, Bharadwaj and Mullick), the hidden pedagogies (Ghose and Bhog) and feminist pedagogies (Rege).

As discussed in the introductory section of this chapter, the selection of 21 chapters was done with a view to highlight and showcase the debate that went on in the *EPW*. Most of the issues explored by the authors are as relevant today as they were in the year they were published.

Lori McDougall's (Chapter 11) argument—that gender differences can be attributed to location, socio-economic situation, economic development and overall infrastructure—remains relevant today. The chapter makes a compelling argument for region/context (sub-district/block/cluster) strategies to bridge gender gaps in education. While 'decentralisation of education invokes both risks and opportunities – including the danger of forced consensus by dominant social groups as well as the promise of greater public accountability', the hard reality is that in a country that is so diverse and unequal, no one model can fit all. This remains a huge issue today with the new Samagra Shiksha Abhiyan promoting a national model. Further, from the early 1990s, the drive for universal primary and then elementary education was led by the Centre, with the states playing a supportive role. In the recent past (2014 onwards) in the education sector, Centre-state relations have moved in the direction of greater devolution of financial and programmatic powers to the states, affirming the federal structure of India. In this context, the role of the Centre in influencing or directing education strategies and interventions is reduced. The assumption is that individual states would make context-relevant plans and allocate resources according to these priorities. At one level, this move away from a centralised approach seems pertinent, but the issues raised by McDougall loom large: of the voices/needs of the dominant social groups being the principal driver, with key social concerns and issues, such as gender and social discrimination, exclusion and equity, being glossed over.

Overcoming segregation and exclusion has been a part of much of education planning and the interventions of both government and non-government players. Ramachandran and Saihjee's chapter (Chapter 5) draws attention to the newer forms of segregation, what they call 'hierarchies of access', to describe the new segregation occurring in primary education. Based on field-based survey data on primary education, they argue that who you are, where you live, your family's economic status and your community/caste identity effectively determines which school you enrol in. Social stratification is not just reflected in schools, but is reinforced in it. Over the decades, not only have different kinds of government schools emerged, but the world of private schools is also equally diverse and segregated. These newer hierarchies and segregations are evident in the government public schools in which poor children, girls, and children with special needs are enrolled. Similarly, Ramachandran et al.'s chapter on the life-cycle of children explores the factors that facilitate or impede successful primary school completion. A complex interlocking of family, community and school-specific factors influences the ability of children from different socio-economic backgrounds to complete primary schools. The cumulative burden along the child-development continuum, which poor children and girls in particular bear, and the ways in which deprivation, health and education affect a child going to school, is clearly brought forth. The chapter argues for greater public awareness of health and nutrition as an important determinant in school participation and completion.

The question that Nandini Manjrekar raises in her chapter on contemporary challenges to women's education remains relevant even today. She observes that education has remained a peripheral concern of the women's movement. While feminist scholars have explored the intersection of race/caste, class and gender, the role of formal education in this intersection is often ignored. She asks, 'Is it worth considering whether the assumed instrumentalist nature of formal education, particularly in the post-independence era, has not inhibited more radical interpretations of what formal education means for girls, both in terms of self-perceptions as well as materially...?' This question is even more important today, when the quality and texture of formal education adds little value to the students, especially when they leave school with little knowledge, skills and cognitive abilities. In the same vein, Ambika Kohli's chapter, based on her work in urban slums in Delhi and Yamuna Nagar, is an interesting micro-study which demonstrates that education alone cannot help us achieve gender equality. Ultimately, education is not only embedded in the existing social structure but it is also deeply rooted in patriarchal values. Education cannot and does not stand alone, and, as Kohli argues, 'development, oppression, empowerment, equality, inequality and patriarchy exist together...'. As the discussions on sex ratio and sex-selective abortion in the introductory sections argue, education of girls and women is capable of entrenching patriarchal values. Yet, it also has the potential to become a transformative power, provided the content, process and pedagogies are transformed.

Balwant Singh Mehta and Mega Shree's chapter on inequality, gender and socio-religious groups strengthens the argument laid out in the opening sections of this chapter—that gender as a stand-alone category means little in India. Social and economic inequality magnifies the structure of inequality. This chapter points towards and concurs with the newer social hierarchies and exclusions referred to in Ramachandran and Saihjee's article in this volume. The situation of women in high-caste or well-off urban communities is a far cry from the situation of women who are socially, economically and geographically disadvantaged. They buttress their argument by highlighting the widening differences between marginalised groups in the labour market. Socially marginalised groups are not only in menial and low-skilled jobs, but are paid very little. They show that while the participation of women in high-skilled jobs has improved, this has not been the case for women from socially marginalised groups. They conclude that the main factors 'that contributed to income inequality in labour markets are education level, status of work (regular or casual), gender, and age or work experience...'. Investing in educating and enhancing the skills of marginalised groups—and of women among them—is critical to bridging the divide.

Divya Vaid's fascinating chapter on gendered inequality in educational transitions is based on a very unlikely data source: the National Election Study of 1996. She shows that the transition from one level to the next depends on a number of factors: caste, class, parents' education, father's income, and so on. As argued in the earlier section of this chapter, gender as a stand-alone category does not determine school participation. Other characteristics are equally, if not more, important. Parameters like caste gain greater importance at higher levels of education. Similarly, the parents' education is also significant. She concludes:

> Father's class has a consistently high parameter at all stages of the education process... the gender-odds ratio is the same for all four classes, which refutes the notion of a more egalitarian Indian middle-class... it is observed that higher castes fare better than the backward castes, where education for both boys and girls is concerned, but surprisingly caste does not appear to play as decisive a role in the decision to make a successive

> transition, as does father's class. The parameter for caste becomes insignificant in the last transition stages....

Her counter-intuitive findings are as relevant today as they were when the chapter was first published.

In contrast to Vaid, the chapter on educational expenditures across two genders by Kausik Chaudhuri and Sushmita Roy examines the gender gap in educational expenditure in two north-Indian states. This issue has received the attention of researchers for several decades now. However, the authors point out that empirical evidence of lower resource allocation for the education of girls is not very definitive, even though the discrimination in allocations to boys, as distinct from girls, is observed to be rampant. This lack of evidence has been attributed to inexact and inadequate analytical tools. The chapter addresses the methodological inadequacies to arrive at a clearer estimation of discrimination in financial allocations. Their analysis of household expenditure 'confirms the presence of a gender gap in education expenditure but also suggests that this gap become more important with a rise in the age of the child...' This difference is sharp in families that trade-off between expenditure and no expenditure; however, it is not so prominent in households that are already spending some money on the education of their sons and daughters.

Among the chapters that explore gender differentials, Jeemol Unni's is interesting, inasmuch as it comments on the capability approach. She examines how caste and religion mediate access and returns of men and women to education. She strengthens the argument explored in the introductory sections of this chapter by showing that:

> There is systemic curtailment of freedom by agencies operating in these communities to choose a way out of poverty through education. Besides belonging to the lower castes, the choice of education is further restricted by gender and location. Being a girl/woman living in rural areas, as well as belonging to the SC/ST community ensures that she is triply crippled....

She identifies the following factors as impeding equal opportunity and free choice: dropping out from school at different stages, poor reading skills and poor access to media and reading newspapers. The above effectively puts the children at a huge disadvantage, as they lack the 'social capital' or the 'capability' necessary to negotiate the educational maze from a position of strength.

Privatisation of education has been on the rise for over two decades, a result of the liberalisation of the economy. The implication of this process is evident in many sectors and clearly in the mushrooming of private primary schools. Despite better infrastructure and better trained teachers, the public-school system is often perceived to be dysfunctional and providing poor quality education. De et al.'s chapter on private schools for the less privileged is a timely reminder of the dangers of unregulated privatisation. Parental choice of government or low-cost private school, among the very poor/poor, is driven by dysfunctional government schools on the one hand and the desire for the English medium on the other. Notwithstanding this scenario, even when low-cost private schools do not teach English, parents still opt for it. De et al. argue that among the important equity issues are the persisting problems with government schools and the increasing reliance on private tuitions (which adds to the cost, even when children are in government schools). Before RTE (when this chapter was written in 2002), norms for opening schools were diluted so much that there was a sudden increase in the numbers of such schools. However, it may be interesting to see if the situation is different today (after notification of the RTE Act in 2010). Equally, the quality and functioning of government schools in an area determine the quality and functioning of private schools. Ironically, the 'benchmark' is set by government schools.

Another chapter that explores the impact of growing privatisation is Karuna Chanana's chapter on globalisation, higher education and gender. At one level, increased enrolment and secondary/higher secondary school completion has increased the demand for higher education. However, the last few decades have also witnessed the privatisation of higher education and rising costs. The numbers and spread of government higher education institutions have not kept pace with increasing demand and many more private players have entered the higher education space. Chanana argues:

> Due to the twin concern with equality and excellence, higher education in India was fully supported by federal and provincial governments. However, in spite of very low fees and 'reservations', or affirmative action, the connection between socio-economic status, merit and elite institutions, the women and disadvantaged groups have either been excluded from or had a negligible representation in the best public institutions.... However, since 1991, the policies of the government have dramatically changed the seemingly privileged position of higher education. The government began to talk of removing public support to higher education and to make it self-financing while privatising it.... (higher education is) characterised by a few high-quality institutions at the top, while the majority at the bottom was of poor and indifferent quality...

The last few decades have seen a significant increase in the number of women enrolling in higher education, though clustering around traditional disciplines—mainly in the humanities and, to a lesser extent, in basic sciences—with barely any enrolment in applied sciences and technical streams, or in what the author terms non-professional, non-market courses. The chapter raises a lot of questions; what it does not explore are the regional differences within India and the huge north-south divide in girls' access to science and related disciplines.

With many more girls enrolling in secondary and higher secondary schools, in an environment where sexual violence/harassment is evident both in society and inside schools, Jandhyala and Ramachandran argue that increasing the pool of women teachers is critical. Based on a qualitative study done in Rajasthan, the chapter discusses why having women teachers in all co-educational schools needs to be taken up on a priority basis.

Sheth and Haeem's chapter looks at the adverse impact of the communal violence in Gujarat on Hindu and Muslim girls, focussing on two municipal primary schools in Ahmedabad. Even after the immediate violence has ceased, communal tension continues to exercise a vitiating influence on citizens and everyday modes of existence. Religious identity has shaped girl's education in such a way that, after 2002, there has been a reversal of earlier trends. Where many more Muslim girls and boys opted for general education earlier, there has been a gradual shift to Urdu schools. Among the reasons cited by mothers is that Urdu schools are located in their own localities and they would make their daughters a 'better Muslim'. Probing deeper, the authors found that parents are not ready to pay for their girls' education, as the Urdu schools are free. This is also the case with the Dalit families interviewed. They show:

> [a] long-standing fear psychosis prevails among both Dalit and Muslim mothers of Rajpur, which has resulted in a reluctance to send girls to school outside the *moholla*, especially if the route to the school takes them through localities of the 'other' community.... Even when the girls go to the nearby municipal schools, they feel compelled to escort their daughters...'

The root cause of this behaviour change is fear of violence and the steady distancing of children of different communities from each other. The long-term impact is that girls cannot aspire to education beyond the upper-primary level, as they become constrained by the social environment, the neighbourhood, poverty and the onset of menarche. The authors show that welfare schemes for different social groups 'added a further dimension to the feelings of discrimination and separation'.

What do parents expect from education? To what extent do subjective expectations influence the choices they make and how much are they willing to spend? While a lot has been written about the supply side and the universal goodness of education, not many have explored the aspirations of people and why they make the choices they do. Annemie Maertens explores this issue in her chapter 'Does Education Pay Off?'. In some ways this chapter is dated, because a recent spurt in educational participation, especially since 2010, tells us that families have higher expectations today; however, the downside is that increasing unemployment, especially of the educated youth in both rural and urban areas, has raised a red flag on the returns to formal education. This chapter is important because it shows that parents—even the poorest—have some idea of the returns to education. While it may differ across caste/community, parental economic status, location and gender, the fact remains that people make rational choices not only about education, but also about marriage.

Sadhana Saxena raises a pertinent question on equality in education and points to the tension between the rights discourse and the provision of quality education. She examines the government scheme Kasturba Gandhi Balika Vidhyalaya, which offers residential school education at the upper-primary level for girls who drop out or are not part of the education system. This is a highly textured chapter that explores the notion of equality and then turns the spotlight on the KGBV programme. The question she poses is whether providing quality education to a select few disadvantaged rural girls is justified when the majority of girls are left out. This question was posed time and again, from when the first Navodaya Vidhyalaya was started to now, when there are various genres of model schools. How do these 'special schemes', which cater to a select few, distort the main system? All schools, she rightly argues, should have adequate infrastructure, qualified teachers and the basic wherewithal to provide good quality education. By creating small islands of excellence, the government is deflecting attention from the right of all children to education.

Krishna Kumar's 'Education and Girlhood' is a beautiful think piece that frames the inherent contradictions of the power of education to foster autonomy and agency on the one hand, and on the other, the agenda of the state to use education to get citizens to conform to dominant social values and gender relations. Children learn at home and in school and:

> [while] the home provides knowledge necessary for the child's induction into the social world and their adjustment to it, the school deals with different domains and kinds of knowledge that are not necessarily consistent with the knowledge acquired at home. While some kinds of knowledge acquired at school may promote acceptance—or even appreciation—of the social work the family presents, other kinds may sow seeds of dissatisfaction and questioning, thereby undermining the family's role in preparing the child to adjust to the social world, along with its norms and values.

Kumar points out that in today's world, the school functions as an institution of the state. Over the years, since colonial times, the school has sidestepped 'culture', thereby sending the signal that social values and social structures are a given and that questioning and challenging is not part of the schooling experience. This world—of separating knowledge and skills that schools are supposed to provide from values and practices—affects girlhood in many ways. Market and culture cannot be distinguished, as the two merge and send out similar messages. Kumar thus concludes by arguing that 'socialising the girl into an acceptable woman by facilitating her internalisation of the body project is an agenda shared by market and custom'. The school here is not just a mute spectator, but subtly strengthens this agenda.

The four chapters on pedagogy and the content of education take Krishna Kumar's insightful arguments further. The late Sharmila Rege was a prolific writer and a deep thinker. Her chapter explores how the historical homogeneity in classrooms has been challenged by the entry of students from historically disadvantaged sections of Indian society—leading not only to friction but also notions of standards and merit. This remains a highly contentious issue today and therefore Rege's chapter is a must-read in today's highly polarised society and polity. She brings to the fore the voices of the historically excluded social groups and how they have to constantly struggle to include their realities into existing educational pedagogies.

Dipta Bhog's chapter on 'Gender and Curriculum' starts with the pre-Independence tug of war between the traditionalists and those who promoted modern education. The quotes she uses to illustrate the common perspective speak volumes about the strong gendered notions of girls' education, such as: 'Nothing can be gained by anglicising our girls or teaching them to ape the ways of men...' Schools must not create an 'aversion to our domestic life... The education of girls requires to be improved in various directions to suit the conditions of the various classes of girls and make them well-equipped so as to enable them to become good housewives and good mothers...it would not be wise to impart such kind of education as would implant in them tastes which they would have no opportunity of gratifying in their afterlife (sic).' Bhog highlights the huge gap between what NPE 1986 propagated (education for women's equality) and the dilution of gender equality in NCF 2000. She argues that there is an absence of a critical perspective among textbook writers, who continue to portray women as the traditionalist did. This chapter was written before NCF 2005 was drafted. It may be interesting to see if the new NCF has any impact on textbooks and the portrayal of women, though the existing evidence on the analysis of post-2005 textbooks does not show any significant change in the portrayal of women.

Dipta Bhog et al. do that by analysing school textbooks (post-NCF 2005) from four states. This is a brilliant one-of-a-kind chapter that deep-dives into language textbooks and reveals the hidden curriculum. The takeaways from this analysis confirm our worst fears. Language emerges as an important site of national identity, with the promotion of a 'pure' language as being different from local dialects on the one hand, and the Hindi–Urdu binary on the other. Nation, national identity and nationhood emerge as key themes in language textbooks—all of which are portrayed in masculine terms. The inclusion of other identities and other realities, apart from the mainstream, does not seem to be a priority. What these kinds of textbooks do to minorities, tribal groups and socially marginalised communities is a question that begs attention.

Malini Ghose reiterates the same argument in her chapter on literacy, power and feminism. She rightly argues that the preoccupation in adult literacy was with skills to read/write and not much else. However, three examples of literacy initiatives from a women's empowerment programme demonstrated how they can empower and foster critical thinking through participatory pedagogies. She shows how engaging with the politics of language plays a critical role in 'constructing identities, determines what constitutes knowledge, ways of seeing the work and self-expression...' She also demonstrates how this was done by challenging existing hierarchies. When such literacy or educational programmes are run, the tension between the mainstream and the alternative comes to the fore. The state/government effectively marginalises empowering feminist pedagogies by relegating them to the realm of innovative short-term projects.

Notes

1. Social reformers in the nineteenth and twentieth century spearheaded efforts to establish educational institutions for women across the country. Their efforts have made a significant impact in various pockets across the country. The existence of islands of high female literacy in areas like Baroda in Gujarat and Jhunjhunu in Rajasthan was primarily due to the efforts of social reformers, the philanthropy of enlightened business people and erstwhile royal families.

2. The word Dalit refers to people from disadvantaged communities, namely those classified in the Indian Constitution as Scheduled Castes. Many sections of this community were considered untouchables in India for many centuries.

3. Jandhyala and Ramachandran (2014: 8)

4. Sex Ratio at birth denotes the number of female live births to 1,000 male live births.

5. Concluding an exhaustive literature review, Ravinder Kaur et al. summarise: 'There are, thus, two contradictory conclusions about the relationship between SRB and prosperity (or higher-class status). First, an optimist view that prosperity leads to an improvement in the SRB; the second, an opposite pessimistic view. The reasoning behind the optimistic view is supported by the observation that as people become richer and more educated, their ideas and perceptions of the value of girls and boys begins to shift towards becoming more gender equal. The implicit assumption made in the optimist view is that with a rise in prosperity, there is a rise in educational attainment as well. However, the pessimistic view is that sex selection will rise as socio-economic circumstances improve. A likely explanation for this phenomenon is that as the poor begin to move up the economic ladder, they tend to shape the composition of a smaller family through recently acquired means and access to sex selection technology, preferring more sons' (2016: 11).

6. NFHS-4, International Institute of Population Sciences, Ministry of Health and Family Welfare, Government of India, 2016 http://rchiips.org/NFHS/NFHS-4Reports/India.pdf (accessed: 24 July 2018).

7. 'Higher education is a route of social mobility as much as occupational mobility. Overall, there is a U-shaped relationship between levels of education and work force participation rates (WFPR)...men's level of participation is significantly higher; WFPR is high among the illiterate, falls with primary/secondary education, and increases again with education above secondary level. The fall could reflect mismatch between jobs sought and jobs available...The decline in work participation levels of women with an increase in their literacy...also reflects attitudes and a 'Sanskritisation' effect of women withdrawing from work as a signal of improved status...' (Sudarshan 2018: 221–242)

8. 'There are well-known substantial differences in well-being across social groups in India... Average per capita income of SC/ST at all-India level is about one-third lower than among other groups. Headcount poverty among other (non-deprived groups in 1999/2000) was 16%, 30% for minorities (Muslims), 36% for SC and 44% for ST... Deprived groups also have lower literacy than other groups... Ranking on neonatal, post-natal, infant, child and under-5 mortality indicators for socially-excluded groups are similar to those of other indicators (e.g. IMR for SC and ST are about 84 and 62 for non-deprived groups)' (de Haan 2004).

9. Kabeer and Subramanian highlighted the 'gender intensified disadvantage' wherein 'the specific forms of disadvantage faced by girls and not boys that it is also important to acknowledge and that related to roles for girls deriving from gender division of labour, their reproductive cycles and perceptions of risk and vulnerability to sexual violence. These gender-specific forms of disadvantages need to be identified and distinguished from those that are gender intensified in order to facilitate the identification of suitable social policies...' (Kabeer and Subramanian 1999).

REFERENCES

ASER. 2016. 'Study on Access, Provision and Learning in Secondary Education: A Two-Block Study in Hardoi (Uttar Pradesh) and Sambhalpur (Odisha)', End line Report. New Delhi: ASER Centre.

Azam, M., and G. G. Kingdon. 2013. 'Are Girls the Fairer Sex in India? Revisiting Intra Household Allocation of Education Expenditure'. *World Development* 42: 143–164.

Bandyopadhyay, M., and R. Subrahmanian. 2008. 'Gender Equity in Education: A Review of Trends and Factors'. Create Pathways to Access, Research Monograph No. 18, Project Report. Falmer, UK: Consortium for Research on Educational Access, Transitions and Equity (CREATE).

Census of India 2011. 2011. New Delhi. Government of India. Available at http://censusindia.gov.in/2011-Common/CensusData2011.html [Government of India website].

Colclough, C., P. Rose, and M. Tembon. 2000. 'Gender Inequalities in Primary Schooling: The Roles of Poverty and Adverse Cultural Practice'. *International Journal of Educational Development* 20 (1): 5–27.

CBPS. 2018. Secondary Education and Child Marriage in India, unpublished working paper, Bangalore: CBPS.

Chaudhuri, K., and S. Roy. 2006. 'Do Parents Spread Educational Expenditure Evenly across the Two Genders? Evidence from Two North Indian States', *Economic and Political Weekly* 41 (52): 5276–82.

de Haan, Arjan. 2004. 'Disparities within India's Poorest Regions: Why Do the Same Institutions Work Differently in Different Places?' Equity and Development: World Development Report Background Papers, World Bank, Washington DC.

Government of India. 1975. *Towards Equality: Report of the Committee on the Status of Women in India*. New Delhi: Department of Women and Child Development.

———. 1985. *Challenge to Education: A Policy Perspective*. New Delhi: Department of Education.

———. 1986. *National Policy on Education*. New Delhi: Department of Education, MHRD.

———. 2014. *Key Indicators of Social Consumption in India: Education*, 71st Round, January–June. NSSO: Ministry of Statistics and Programme Implementation, available at http://mospi.nic.in/mospi_new/upload/nss_71st_ki_education_30june15.pdf.

———. 2015. *Sixth RMSA Joint Review Mission Aide Memoire Report*. New Delhi: MHRD.

———. MOHFW. 2016. *National Family Health Survey – 4 India Report*, available at http://rchiips.org/NFHS/NFHS-4Reports/India.pdf. Accessed on 24 July 2018.

———. 2012. *Provisional Population Totals*. New Delhi: Office of the Registrar General and Census Commissioner.

Jandhyala, Kameshwari, and Vimala Ramachandran. 2014. 'Women Teachers and the Achievement of Gender and Equity Goals in Secondary Education: An Exploratory Study in Rajasthan'. New Delhi: MacArthur Foundation.

Kabeer, Naila, and R. Subramaniam. 1999. 'The Rationale for Gender Awareness and the Policy Process in Institutions, Relations and Outcomes: Frameworks and Tools for Gender Aware Planning'. Discussion Paper No. 357. UK: IDS Sussex.

Kambhampati, U. S. 2008. 'Does Household Expenditure on Education Depend upon Returns to Education in India?' Henley Business School Working Paper No. 060, University of Reading, UK.

Kaur, Ravinder, Surjit S. Bhalla, Manoj K. Agarwal, and Prasanthi Ramakrishnan. 2016. *Sex Ratio at Birth: Role of Gender, Class and Education*. New Delhi: UNFPA.

Kumar, Sanjay. 2016. 'Measuring Child Marriage from Census and Large Scale Data Systems in India'. *Demography India* 45 (1&2): 59–76. Available at http://demographyindia.in/article_document/17/283115.pdf.

Lall, Marie, and S. Srinivasa Rao. 2011. 'Revisiting the Equity Debate in India and the UK: Caste, Race and Class Intersections in Education'. In Marie Lall and Geetha B. Nambissan, eds, *Education and Social Justice in the Era of Globalisation: Perspectives from India and the UK*. New Delhi: Routledge: 34.

Majumdar, M. 2005. 'Schooling and "Skilling" of the Country's Youth: Secondary Education in Four Indian States'. *Economic and Political Weekly* 4: 2351–63.

Nambissan, Geetha B. 1996. 'Equity in Education? Schooling of Dalit Children in India'. *Economic and Political Weekly* 31(16–19), 20–27 April: 1011–1024.

——. 2000. 'Dealing with Deprivation'. *Seminar*, No. 493, September: 9.

——. 2001. 'Social Diversity and Regional Disparities in Schooling: A Study of Rural Rajasthan'. In A. Vaidyanathan and P. R. Gopinathan Nair, ed. *Elementary Education in Rural India: A Grassroots View*. New Delhi: Sage Publications.

NCERT. 2005 a. *National Curriculum Framework – 2005*. New Delhi: NCERT.

——. 2005 b. *NCF Position Paper 3.2 – Gender Issues in Education*. New Delhi: NCERT.

NIEPA 2016. *School Education in India: U-DISE Flash Statistics 2015–16*. New Delhi: NIEPA.

NIEPA 2018. *School Education in India: U-DISE Flash Statistics 2016–17*. New Delhi: NIEPA.

Rajan, S. Irudaya, Sharada Srinivasan, and Arjun S. Bedi. 2017. 'Update on Trends in Sex Ratio at Birth in India'. *Economic and Political Weekly* 52 (11): 14–16, 18 March.

Ramachandran, Vimala, ed. 2004. *Hierarchies of Access: Gender and Equity in Primary Education*. New Delhi: Sage Publications.

——. 2012. 'Evaluating Gender and Equity in Elementary Education: Reflections on Methodologies, Processes and Outcomes'. *Indian Journal of Gender Studies* 19 (2): 233–238. New Delhi: Sage Publications.

Ramachandran, Vimala, and Niti Saxena. 2018. 'Quality and Systemic Functioning of Secondary Education in India: A Qualitative Study in Uttar Pradesh and Jharkhand', Draft Report submitted to World Bank, New Delhi.

Ramachandran, Vimala, and Sridhar Rajagopalan. 2018. 'The Problem'. *Seminar*, No. 706, June: Are Our Children Learning: a Symposium on the Crisis in Learning Afflicting Our Schools.

Ramachandran, Vimala, and Taramani Naorem. 2013. 'What it Means To Be a Dalit or Tribal Child in Our Schools: A Synthesis of a Six-State Qualitative Study'. *Economic and Political Weekly* 48 (44), 2 November: 43–52.

Ramamurthy, S., and K. Pandian. 2016. 'A Comparative Critique with NPE 1986 and National Policy on Education 2016'. *Economic and Political Weekly* 52 (16): 46–53, 22 April.

Samson, M., A. De, and C. Noronha. 2007. 'Building Unequal Capabilities: Schooling of Delhi's Adolescents'. Paper presented at the IX UKFIET International Conference on Education and Development, Oxford, UK.

Siddhu. G. 2011. 'Who Makes it to Secondary School? Determinants of Transition to Secondary Schools in Rural India'. *International Journal of Educational Development* 31: 394–401.

Sudarshan, Ratna M. 2018. 'Higher Education and Gendered Norms: Enabling the 'use' of women's education'. In N. V. Varghese, Nidhi S. Sabharwal and C. M. Malish, eds, *India Higher Education Report 2016: Equity*: 221–242. New Delhi: Sage Publications.

Tilak, Jandhyala, and Pradeep Kumar Chaudhury. 2018. 'Public and Family Expenditure in Secodnary Education in Jharkhand and Uttar Pradesh'. In Vimala Ramachandran and Niti Saxena, eds, Quality and Systemic Functioning of Secondary Education in India: A Qualitative Study in Uttar Pradesh and Jharkhand, Draft Report submitted to World Bank, New Delhi.

Visaria, Leela. 2014. 'Population, Education and Development'. *Economic and Political Weekly* 49 (45):38–45, November.

World Bank. 2009. 'Secondary Education in India: Universalizing Opportunities', Human Development Unit, South Asia Region, New Delhi.

SECTION I

Gender and Social Equity

1

Through the Life-Cycle of Children

*Factors that Facilitate/Impede Successful Primary School Completion**

Vimala Ramachandran,
Kameshwari Jandhyala and Aarti Saihjee

In a recent qualitative research study funded by the World Bank, the Educational Resource Unit explored factors that contribute towards or impede successful primary school completion among children living in diverse poverty conditions.[1] The issue was approached from select vantage points across five social domains—the child, family, community, institutions (pre-school and primary school), and other services (health care, sanitation, water, transport, etc.). This domain approach helped to understand the causality as well as social processes implicated wholly or partially in children's full participation in schooling (e.g., poverty, class, gender, birth order, ethnicity, lack of schools or transportation, poor health, etc.).

We attempted to explore the critical intersection between sociological analyses of the identified domains and a life-cycle perspective on child development. The research focused on children in discrete age groups along the integrated child development continuum—conception to birth, 0–3 years, 3–6 years, and 6–11 years. The adoption of a life-cycle perspective helped us to highlight the cumulative impact of neglect of or support extended to a child along the continuum, and the different needs of children of varied age groups. The dual yet integrated focus on physical development, as well as the psycho-social factors framing it, enabled us to explore the continuous and cumulative nature of the social and economic exclusion

---

* Previously published in *Economic and Political Weekly* 38 (47) November 2003: 4994–5002. This chapter draws upon 'Snakes and Ladders: Factors That Facilitate/Impede Successful Primary School Completion', New Delhi: World Bank, 2003—a synthesis report by the authors of a qualitative research study funded by the World Bank. The views expressed in this chapter are that of the authors and not of the World Bank.

that poor children face from the moment of conception, and its possible impact on their ability to complete primary education.[2]

The study is based on detailed fieldwork conducted in both rural and urban areas between September–November 2002, in the three states of Andhra Pradesh, Karnataka, and Uttar Pradesh. This was primarily a qualitative enquiry that relied on detailed observation and formal and informal interviews to collect data. The study is exploratory and illustrative, focusing on children, their family, larger community, and the extant local education and health services, within the context of the larger socio-economic situation in the selected states and the specific study area. Six villages and urban settlements each were selected for the study to reflect diversity in terms of location, demographic characteristics, remoteness/accessibility, caste and community composition, and functioning of ICDS (Integrated Child Development Services) and primary education facilities. Hence, the study is not, and does not, purport to be an evaluation of existing programmes on the ground. Further, the sample is also skewed in favour of children living in diverse poverty situations—primarily focusing on the bottom quartile of the socio-economic ladder.

The chapter is based on the findings of our field study. Section I of the chapter briefly summarises what we actually observed in the field, regarding health, education, and nutrition status of the child, and the (dis)enabling role played by the family, community, the local infrastructure and service delivery system. Section II identifies the social, economic, and political factors that exert considerable influence on the ability of a child to complete primary education, individually and in tandem with each other, and as they play out along the integrated child development continuum. The concluding Section III explores the possible implications of these findings for policy-making, as well as implementation.

FROM CONCEPTION TO BIRTH

Children in this stage of development have been the focus of a number of health and family welfare programmes—ICDS programme since the mid-1970s, Maternal and Child Health (MCH) and Family Planning (FP) programmes of the 1980s, Child Survival and Safe Motherhood (CSSM) programme in the 1990s, and more recently, the Reproductive and Child Health (RCH) programme. Notwithstanding this, across the three states, few women took any special nutrition during pregnancy; if anything, most women reported that they consciously ate less in order to ensure a smooth delivery. Most believed that it was all right to eat less and have smaller babies, as it is easier to deliver them. Many women interviewed said that they 'fatten them (children) up' after they are born.

Nearly all deliveries across the three states took place at home, assisted by the '*dai*' (traditional birth attendant or TBA) or a relative/neighbour. Trained midwives were either not within their reach, or families did not think it important to access one. Even though macro data indicates a higher incidence of institutional and trained midwife-assisted deliveries in Karnataka and Andhra Pradesh, our research shows no significant difference across the states.[3] It is likely that as we go down the socio-economic ladder, interstate variations on key indicators of maternal and child health become minimal. Institutional delivery still remains uncommon.

Most women continue to breastfeed their children till the next child is on its way, even up to 24 months. Special nutrition during lactation was clearly a novelty for most women. Since most children began to eat food only when they were able to pick it up, or to take it from a person or another place, the activity could well be called eating and not feeding. Most women in the surveyed households were thin, anaemic, and ate once or at best twice a day. Given the severe drought situation prevailing during fieldwork, especially in Karnataka and AP, food was limited to rice/broken wheat, with salt and some chillies. Children were fed the same food. Many women reported that they were given iron/folic (IFA) tablets by the ANM (Auxiliary-Nurse Midwife). However, given the very low awareness about its benefits, consumption was irregular. Very few had taken pre-delivery tetanus toxoid injections, especially in Uttar Pradesh.[4]

Perhaps the most disturbing finding of the study relates to the low level of awareness about health, including antenatal care, immunisation, and nutrition during pregnancy. Despite the presence of the anganwadi worker (AWW) and monthly visits by the ANM, nutrition and health education activities are practically non-existent, at least vis-à-vis the poorest women in the surveyed villages and urban slums. While general awareness levels were certainly higher in urban slums, there was little difference in practice. Focus group discussions (FGD) usually revealed that the monthly visit of the ANM is limited to one specific area in the village, and that she rarely visits distant settlements inhabited by SC or ST groups. Similarly, in urban areas, recent migrants (especially those in the slums at the periphery) are often bypassed by service providers.

Not surprisingly, the workload of women in the poor households was fairly high, more so in the case of those engaged in daily wage labour, and there was no respite evident for pregnant women either. Many women also feared losing children due to several illnesses that could easily be prevented by vaccinations. Regarding birth control, very few women used IUD or Mala D (contraceptive pill), and the dominant measure was female sterilisation. The health situation of women and children, as evident by all indicators, is very poor.

The initial phase of child development is, without a doubt, dependent on the overall well-being of the mother. Given that mothers in our sample belong to poor families, the picture that emerges is rather dismal—of women having babies too soon, too often, and too many. While the average age of marriage in the different states as a whole is 19 (Uttar Pradesh), 20 (Karnataka), and 18 (Andhra Pradesh), the mean age of marriage in the profiled households is much lower, at 13, 15, and 15, respectively. Clearly, very poor households in all the three states record a much lower age of marriage than the state average (Table 1.1). The combination of low awareness and poverty of individual households contributes to both the poor health of mothers and low birth weight of babies. We could not ascertain the birth-weight, as most of the children in the surveyed households were born at home; however, the children appeared visibly small and malnourished. Our investigation confirms the macro finding that one-third of all babies in India are born with low birth weight (as compared to Bangladesh where the proportion is 50 per cent, and sub-Sahara Africa, where it is one-sixth (Ramalingaswami et al. 1996). This has important implications for the physical survival of children and their ability to grow and learn.

TABLE 1.1: Key Reproductive Health Indicators in Selected Households in UP, Karnataka, and Andhra Pradesh

	Uttar Pradesh	*Karnataka*	*Andhra Pradesh*
Number of mothers profiled	18	18	18
Average age of marriage	13.1	15.1	14.8
Average age of first conception	17.2	16.3	18.8
Average number of pregnancies per woman	6.2	5.4	4.3
Average number of successful deliveries per woman	5.9	5.3	4.1
Successful deliveries	89 out of 114 pregnancies	89 out of 92 pregnancies	65 out of 76 pregnancies
Abortions/miscarriages	3 out of 114 pregnancies	3 miscarriages reported	4 out of 76 pregnancies
Per cent children died under five years of live born	20.8 per cent	10.9 per cent	14.9 per cent
Average number of children per woman	4.7	4.5	3.5
Deliveries at home/assisted by *dai* (TBA) or relatives	109 out of 110	83 out of 89	68 out of 76
Deliveries in hospital	1 only	6 out of 89	8 out of 76

Source: Household survey data.

EXPLORING ZERO TO THREE YEARS

Families surveyed in Uttar Pradesh reveal that out of the 85 children in the 18 households, 13 were below the age of three and most of the 2-year-olds and below were still being breast-fed. They hardly ate any food—partaking in what was cooked in the house, mostly *roti* dipped in tea! As evident from Table 1.2, on the nutritional status of 6–60 months, mortality rates (in the surveyed households) for the under-five age-group were high in all the three states. Even though the sample studied is very small and statistically insignificant, we apprehend higher deprivation and vulnerability of the population living in urban slums in all states. In the case of Andhra Pradesh, contrary to experiences in Karnataka and Uttar Pradesh, the situation in the centrally located slum was far worse than the periphery, especially with respect to under five years mortality. Is it because of greater environmental pollution, abject poverty, and lack of coping mechanisms vis-à-vis the pressures of modern life, despite better access to health facilities?

Though there was no severe water shortage in most of the study areas, hygiene was poor, and most children were unclothed or unkempt, with uncombed hair, unwashed faces, and unbathed bodies. Running noses, skin rashes, and boils were a fairly common sight. Close to 64 per cent of children in Uttar Pradesh and 83 per cent children in Karnataka reported that they suffered from some ailment during the last three months. In Andhra Pradesh, 37 per cent children were suffering from some ailment during the field visit. The incidence of water-borne diseases is still high—despite the finding that a majority of the houses obtain drinking water from tubewells and protected water supply schemes. This could be due to lack of sanitation and poor personal hygiene, as indicated by the lack of good practices for water dispensing, hand-washing habits with soap at appropriate times, both at the household and school level. Exposure to smoke is very high in all the observed habitations, as firewood is the main fuel used, and there is no separate cooking space. These factors may also be contributing to low birth weights.

A shocking finding in Uttar Pradesh was that out of 36 children (a total from the families surveyed), 11 were partially immunised, 18 received only polio drops (50 per cent), and seven had received no immunisation! Regular child health and immunisation services were also non-existent. There was no discernible difference in the immunisation status of Muslim families profiled in Uttar Pradesh. The situation in Karnataka and Andhra Pradesh was somewhat better. While nearly all children had received polio drops, and approximately 40 per cent BCG shots, other vaccine preventable diseases (DPT, measles) did not seem to be on the priority list of service providers (Table 1.3). During discussions and interviews, it emerged that families do not resist immunisation services if they are provided within their hamlet, but they rarely go out of their way to get their children immunised. Awareness about the importance of vaccines in disease prevention is low, as is knowledge about the links between clean drinking water and proper sanitation and disease.

Ramrati of village two of Uttar Pradesh uses powdered 'Septran' (sulpha drug) tablets, bought in the village shop, to manage her 1-year-old son's fever (Mehrotra et al. 2003). In Karnataka, the medicine shop in village two stocks antibiotics and sulpha drugs—which the shopkeeper dispenses after ascertaining the symptoms. Small babies are also given powdered drugs dissolved in water (Krishnamurty and Periodi 2003). The situation was similar in Andhra Pradesh.

The impact of malnutrition is evident in the children, who are underweight and small, with unhealthy reddish brown hair and cracks at the edges of the mouth, indicating vitamin deficiency. The situation seemed particularly alarming in the tribal villages studied, where around 59 per cent of the children observed were suffering from some ailment.

Notwithstanding malnutrition, four out of six rural children and two out of the three urban children below three years in Uttar Pradesh (Muslim and Hindu families) attained age-appropriate development milestones—they were seen crawling, walking, running, communicating their needs, laughing and playing. The sheer joy of being a child and running free was visible in their bright eyes and shrill voices. It is heartening that children are in constant interaction with older siblings, and other neighbouring children and families. These experiences provide the children with a rich repertoire of communicative and social stimulation. While stimulation from parents—who are terribly overworked—may be limited, this seems to be more than compensated by siblings, and other people in the extended family and community.

When poor and weak mothers give birth to children in the absence of family, community, and institutional support, an intergenerational process of poor health, nutrition, and education is set in motion, in which a majority of Indian children are willy-nilly caught. These handicaps have a long-term effect, and become more evident in children who are further ahead on the child-development continuum.

PRE-SCHOOL YEARS

This phase in the life of a child is critical for physical, emotional, and intellectual development. Adequate nutrition, vital for children in this very important stage of development, is unfortunately deficient in poor households. While children are able to feed themselves, the inability of parents to provide a balanced diet, or even basic food at regular intervals, emerges as one of the important areas of concern in this age-group. This is also a period when the child becomes a little more independent, is able to eat by herself, to ask for food, and communicates her needs. At the same time, she is more susceptible to infections as she wanders around.

Measurements taken in the course of the study (Table 1.2 on nutritional status) showed that the majority of children observed in poor households seem to be moderately to severely malnourished. Though appropriate indicators for the rural and urban poor have still to be worked out, the children look underweight for their age or height, their skin is coarse/rough, their hair discoloured, and many of them (six months to four years) are pot-bellied, with extremely thin limbs. While children are very active and alert, playing and running around, it is apparent that greater attention needs to be paid to their overall nutritional status.

Most experts argue that a child can be positively prepared for schooling through supportive experiences in the home, neighbourhood, and community. However, our household observations suggest that there is little structuring by adults/parents of children's activities—whether it be play, language, or health. When it comes to participation in household activity, the care of younger children, economic participation, food processing, and other productive activity, though the parents' signals are unambiguous, assertive, directive, and sometimes even autocratic. Socio-economic participation in the household and productive activity seemed far ahead of age-expectations. Even young children are taking responsibility for a range of sibling care/household/farm/cattle care-related work (Sharma and Chaudhary 2003).

The children observed had little to eat and that too, only a few times a day. A limited number of children access ICDS services, with the location of the AWC (Anganwadi Centre) and the caste of the AWW determining access. Further, the quantity and regularity of distribution of supplements remains a major source of worry in Uttar Pradesh. While this does not seem to be a major issue in Karnataka and Andhra Pradesh, discussions with women revealed that only a fixed number of children are admitted; many of them were turned away because the centre could not accommodate more children. Fortunately in some areas, like the two villages visited in Karnataka, the government has responded by opening an additional ICDS centre in the village (one in the Golla community in village 1, and one in the SC community in village 2). Such was not the case in Uttar Pradesh.

TABLE 1.2: Nutritional Status of Children: Aged 6–60 Months

State	*Number of Children*	*Level of Malnutrition*	*Wt for Age Under-Nutrition*	*Ht for Age Stunting*	*Wt for Ht Wasting*
Uttar Pradesh	22	Severe (–3SD)	7	3	1
		Moderate (–2SD)-*	10	6	6
Karnataka	18	Severe (–3SD)	4	9	0
		Moderate (–2SD)-*	11	13	3
Andhra Pradesh	23	Severe (–3SD)	1	2	0
		Moderate (–2SD)-*	3	3	0
Total for 3 states	63	Severe (–3SD)	12	14	1
		Moderate (–2SD)-*	24	22	9

Notes: *Includes –3SD
The above 'Z' scores are obtained using NCHS (National Centre for Health Statistics) standards through 'EPINFO' package of WHO of measured anthropometrical measurements of height and weight and reported approximate age in months in AP schools.
Source: Household Survey Data.

TABLE 1.3: Immunisation Status of Children Observed

	BCG and Polio	*Only Polio*	*NA*
Uttar Pradesh (36)	11	18	7
Karnataka (25)	12	12	1
Andhra Pradesh (57)	28	23	6

Source: Survey Data.

Even in a relatively better performing state like Andhra Pradesh, children's access to AWC is far from satisfactory. For example, out of the 22 children in the 0–6 year age-group, there were seven children below 36 months and 15 in the 3–6 years age-group who did not avail the anganwadi services. None of the children below three years of age utilised the services of the anganwadi centres. In the 3–6 year age-group, of the 15 children, only 10 were enrolled in the anganwadi. This includes the one disabled boy in the urban-centre household. Of the remaining five children who were not enrolled, four were in the tribal village. It is worth stressing that enrolment does not automatically imply access to services. Some children are merely enrolled and are not necessarily benefitting from the ICDS programme.

The problem of irregular food supply was most acute in Uttar Pradesh. Our qualitative study confirms findings reported in larger surveys:

> According to the National Institute of Public Cooperation and Child Development (NIPCCD) report (1992), 27 per cent of AWC did not receive any nutrition supplement for over 90 days, i.e., the average disruption in their supply was for 63.7

> days...Similarly, the provision of double ration to severely malnourished children is often ineffective, because such children are often incapable of eating much at one go. Again the morning hours appear to be the time when pregnant and lactating women are busy with domestic chores and hence attendance at AWCs for accessing these services, especially supplementary nutrition, tends to be poor (Gupta 2003).

The above analysis was confirmed during our investigations. Discussions with AWWs revealed that there is no system for identifying the severely malnourished, to provide double rations. While we saw pregnant and lactating mothers coming to the AWC in Karnataka and Andhra Pradesh, we did not come across even a single woman who came to the AWC in Uttar Pradesh. Most distressing was that in Uttar Pradesh, the fortified '*dalia*' meant for the AWC was being sold in the local shops, with people buying it both for their own consumption and also to feed their cattle!

While recording the food habits of children in the three states, we were alarmed to see that in Uttar Pradesh, most often the children ate '*roti*' with salt, this in a region where a wide variety of green leafy vegetables are grown and are locally available. Consumption of meat and fish was at best sporadic, with boys getting a very small piece and girls making do with the gravy. Andhra Pradesh and Karnataka also reported that the main diet was polished rice with some chutney or diluted '*saru*'. It needs to be stressed that state averages camouflage extreme inequalities that prevail between and within communities. Since the study has focused on children in diverse poverty situations, our findings may appear far more alarming than indicated by state or national averages.

The pre-school education component of the ICDS programme, although evident on paper, was non-existent in reality. While we did find play material in most AWCs, it was locked up in cupboards. This seems to be the result of a fairly common belief that expensive (relatively speaking) and attractive things are too precious to be handled by children and need to be brought out for display only during inspections. The same was the case with library books in schools.

During our visits, children were usually sitting quietly in rows with a slate and chalk in their hands. In some villages, we could not interact with the children because they dispersed soon after the meal. The attitude of the teacher and the helper also leaves much to be desired—they were indifferent, if not shouting at and scolding the children. Only in Karnataka did we observe some pre-school play activities. Clearly the ICDS programme, as operational in the villages, did not seem to play a significant role in enhancing the preparedness of children to go to school—unless, of course, sitting quietly in rows with slate and chalk can be considered preparation!

The mother's committees were introduced to strengthen IEC activities (education and awareness) and make the AWW accountable to the community. In all the villages/slums surveyed, these committees are dysfunctional, even though they exist on paper. We also found that villages with other women's groups [Mahila Samakhya groups, SHGs (Self-Help Groups)] are more aware of the ICDS programme and what it is supposed to deliver, though this awareness, even here, rarely translates into active collaboration.

The visibility of the ICDS programme is high, both in the villages and in urban slums. People are aware of the AWW and the helper. Focus group discussions invariably turn spirited, in most cases leading to vocal criticism about the helper (who is expected to escort children to the centre), other services (looking after the children), the irregular supply of nutritional supplements (Uttar Pradesh) and timings of the centre. The ICDS programme, however, does not seem to enjoy the same importance as other schemes, more so in the eyes of the government. The status of the AWW, as compared to the schoolteacher or the ANM, is low. Consequently, even if the AWW is motivated and wants to be active, she has little space for demonstrating initiative. She also receives little support from her superiors.

Many AWWs (especially in UP) were not trained and essentially learnt on the job. They look upon the ICDS as a nutrition programme and their own role as one who distributes food and maintains records. Interviews with AWWs in all the areas revealed that record-keeping was seen as a key function.

The AWW does not make any conscious effort to enrol the most deprived strata. Though Karnataka and Andhra Pradesh have sanctioned additional centres in hamlets/settlements, this was not the case in Uttar Pradesh, where one ICDS centre caters to the entire village, regardless of the number of children in the appropriate age group. As a result, in Uttar Pradesh, only 40 children per centre are enrolled, and even this is not done on the basis of who needs the services. Caste is a serious issue with the teacher and the AW helper (AWH) (Table 1.4). If both are from the forward caste, then children from Dalit families have little access. Parents in the sample households felt that they could make no demands on the teacher, as she is upper caste. Almost all the families we interacted with expect the AWH to come and fetch the kids, which does not happen. Therefore, if the AWC is at some distance and mothers are overworked, the children do not reach the ICDS centre.

Table 1.4: Status of Children in Surveyed Households

	Uttar Pradesh	*Karnataka*	*Andhra Pradesh*
Children below 36 months	12	17	7
Children enrolled in AWC	1	3	None
Children 3–6 years	13	19	15
Enrolled AWC	5	13	10
Children 6–11 years	36	32	31
Enrolled in school	30	24	30
Dropouts	2	6	1
Never enrolled	4	2	–
Children in 11+ age-group	24	14	5
Enrolled in primary school	4	1	2
Dropped out before completing primary	5	NA	NA
Completed primary and dropped out	4	2	–
Enrolled in upper-primary	2	1	–
No information		–	3
Never enrolled/went to school	9	1	–

Source: Survey Data.

As children reach the pre-school age, education and access to education becomes a defining variable in framing their life-chances, along with health and nutrition. It is an exploratory phase on the child-development continuum, where pre-school exposure and adequate nutrition (as an integral part of service delivery) become essential inputs to further the holistic development of children. Evidence from the ground indicates a rather contrary picture, marked by erratic provision of nutrition by the state and a rather weak and ineffective pre-school component. Politics of caste identity and status also emerges as an important factor in denying children and parents access to the nutrition supplements and the effective functioning of the AWCs.

SCHOOL-GOING CHILDREN

In the 1990s, the issue of access to primary schools received considerable attention in all the three states. Most children in the surveyed households were enrolled. Many of them were also attending school, with varying degrees of regularity.

In Uttar Pradesh, the 18 poorest households selected for the study had a total of 85 children, of whom 60 were in the 6+ age-group. Of these, 40 children were in primary school or had completed primary education, 13 never went to school and seven had dropped out. An interesting pattern that emerged from the educational history of these families was that of the 36 children in the 6–11 age-group, 30 were in primary schools. This included all the children (including girls) in the 6–11 age-group from Muslim households. In the 11–14 age-group, there are 11 children, four of whom were currently in primary school. Of the six who have completed primary schooling (which included one Muslim girl and two Muslim boys), only two (one boy and one girl, both non-Muslims) had moved to the upper-primary level. Of the remaining 13 children in the 14+ age-group, only one had completed primary schooling, another was still in primary school and 11 never went to school or had dropped out. The families reported that the educational situation has significantly improved in the last five to seven years.

In Karnataka, out of the 30 boys and 30 girls in the 18 households surveyed, 57 children (29 girls and 28 boys) were either enrolled in the AWC or primary school. One boy had dropped out in Class IV and one boy and one girl were not going to the AWC. Discussions with mothers and adolescent girls and boys revealed that campaigns like 'Chinnara Angala' (to get children back to school), 'Ba Marali Shalege (Monday morning procession of children with songs and slogans, asking children to come back) and 'Pratibha Karanji' (encouraging creativity) have made a significant impact. Almost all the children in the village/urban settlements are in school. The state government also provides free uniforms, textbooks and school bags to all SC and ST children up to Class V and the same is extended up to Class X for children of Devadasis.

In Andhra Pradesh, out of the 58 children observed in the 18 households surveyed, 31 were in the 6–11 years age-group, of whom 30 were enrolled and attending schools. Only two of the five children in the 11+ age-group were in school.

Enrolment in AWC was low. Out of the 22 children in the 0–6 year age-group, none of the seven below three years were enrolled in the AWC, while 11 of the 15 in the 3–6 years were enrolled in the AWC.

Enrolment is obviously not a big issue any more: attendance, transition, completion and learning outcomes are emerging as bigger issues and it is these that are intimately related to our preferred proxy indicator of child development, namely completion of primary schooling. The cohort study, based on official school records in all the schools visited, gives a fairly positive picture. For example, in Karnataka, 71 per cent of the children who entered Class I in 1998, from six sample schools, reached Class V in 2002. However, once we moved beyond the 'official' records, conversations with teachers revealed a different and more complex picture. In all the three states, the teachers were reluctant to admit that children drop out, and hence many children are shown in the registers and some of them are marked as long-absentees. In some schools, they are also marked present, especially when the distribution of dry rations is linked to attendance! Teachers often become defensive when asked about dropouts or long-absentees.

Children from poor households are not very regular. They tend to absent themselves for a range of reasons. In Karnataka and UP, parents said it was difficult for them to 'force' their children to go to school, especially when nothing much happens there. Some parents said that they need their children at home for small chores, especially during the heavy/peak agricultural seasons, when a child is sick or when they have to migrate for work.

Many children above the age of six in the surveyed households and attending government schools reported that they work before as well as after school. The burden of work was most severe for the first-born, especially if she is the eldest daughter. There was no appreciable difference between Muslim/Hindu and tribal/non-tribal families. Apart from sibling care, children support their families with care of milch cows/goats, fetching fuel wood/fodder, water, running errands and looking after sick family members. As a result, children either get late for school or miss it altogether. The gender division of work and added responsibility of household work on older girls in the family was marked in all the three states. In Andhra Pradesh and Uttar Pradesh, we met boys who were in temporary bondage to pay off a loan taken by the parents. Engaging in full-time work during weekends and holidays is a fairly routine activity among children.

If such is the situation with respect to children and work, what implications does this have for primary schooling? The community is aware of the need to educate their children, yet the children are burdened with work before and after school, during holidays and vacations—both household/domestic and sibling-care related chores, and work outside the home or in home-based occupations. This obviously directly impacts on the learning abilities of children—especially when they put in long hours every day. Most children in poor households do not get time to revise/read their books, especially girls who are higher up in the birth order. Given the nutritional status of most poor children, energy levels are low and impact upon children's ability to concentrate in school. The impact of working and yet attending school needs to be examined, with reference to its impact on learning outcomes.

LEARNING OUTCOMES

In Uttar Pradesh, we observed that most children in Classes III, IV and V were neither able to read fluently from their textbooks, nor could they solve simple addition or subtraction sums. For instance, 11 (out of 18) children were attending the GPS (Government Public Schools) from the 18 households in the urban sample from UP. Five children attending Classes II, III and IV showed poor learning levels. Three children from Class II were unable to recognise letters or numerals. The two children in Class III were also unable to read, write or count, though they knew certain lessons by rote. 'Earlier Class II pass could read postcards, now they can't even write their names,' complained a father during the FGD in urban Sitapur. 'What is the use of sending him to school? I pulled him out after Class IV and he now helps me with my work.'

The situation was not dramatically different in Karnataka or in Andhra Pradesh. Yes, a few more could read, but on further investigation we realised that children with literate parents (especially the mother), or those who attend private tuition classes are the ones most able to read. Children who are first-generation school-goers barely manage to recognise letters in the alphabet and can, at best, read a few words. Group discussions in the community revealed that parents feel that the quality of teaching has declined, that the community and the teachers do not really care if the children of the poor learn to read. Also, teachers are not held accountable for the learning outcomes of children, especially in the primary and middle schools, where there are no board examinations. Other qualitative and quantitative research studies have also made similar observations (Jha and Jhingran 2002; Pratichi Trust 2002; PROBE 1999; Ramachandran 2002).

IS SCHOOLING REALLY FREE FOR THE POOR?

Today, there is widespread agreement that access to education has improved significantly in the last decade and even very poor parents want to send their children to school. There is also growing evidence of private schools mushrooming all over, and that children are being sent to private schools, if the parents can so afford. In some cases, parents decide to send their children to private schools even when they cannot really afford it!

In Uttar Pradesh, we found that the teachers collect 'fees'—official and unofficial. Community members and students reported that teachers in government schools often asked children to get Rs 5 to 10 during national festivals, for issuing of transfer certificates or for release of scholarship money. If payment for schooling is necessary, parents consciously opt for private schools. Perceived poor quality and poor learning outcomes in GPS often seem to be instrumental in the emergence of these private schools. In one study village in Uttar Pradesh, we came across a private school that did not expel children even if they did not pay the fees regularly—hence making it more attractive to parents.

Private tuition classes profiled in Karnataka were priced at around Rs 30 a month. Parents seem to believe that children learn fast and are able to cope with their studies if they are enrolled in tuition classes. One mother said: 'I send my child to a private tutor for two hours because it is better to have short time of concentrated learning than many hours of not learning at all!' Private tuitions, which collect unofficial fees and compel children to buy guidebooks, are gradually becoming more common. What is noteworthy is that such practices have become more widespread in the last decade, the period when community demand for perceivably good quality education has also grown.

Hunger in the Classroom

Discussions with children revealed that many of them do not eat anything in the morning, especially girls, who have little time, given their morning chores. In Andhra Pradesh, several girls said they only drink water before coming to school and eat only during the lunch break! Given that most poor households have to gather fuel wood, families basically cook two meals a day—mid-morning and after sundown. Where children do eat before coming to school, the staple diet seemed to be *roti* and salt (Uttar Pradesh), and a piece of *jawar roti* or rice with chilly chutney (Andhra Pradesh). On most days, almost 10–15 per cent of children (the majority of them girls) come to school without eating. When we explored this further and asked why few children ate in the morning, some girls said they did not have time to eat! Lack of an adequate meal before attending school, what has usually been referred to as short-term hunger, has an adverse impact on the child's performance in school, her ability to concentrate and learn new concepts. In such a situation, the provision of a hot mid-day meal becomes all the more necessary.

Incentives—Do They Make a Difference?

We heard conflicting statements. Some teachers, especially in Uttar Pradesh, argued that incentives like dry rations had little effect on retention or achievement levels, and that students who enrolled for incentives were regular only on the days prior to distribution. They were of the opinion that scholarships should be handed over at the end of the academic session to ensure that children did not drop out mid-term or attend classes at random intervals. The teachers did not think that rations for poor children ensured food security at home or prevented them from taking on extra work. The community and teachers were all praise for the mid-day meal programme in Karnataka and in Andhra Pradesh, which commenced on 1 January 2003.

Incentives like textbooks, uniforms and scholarships, though welcome, were also issues over which parents and teachers complained and argued. While we did not come across any case of delayed distribution of textbooks, the distribution of scholarships and uniforms leave much to be desired. In Uttar Pradesh, free textbooks mean little because most children purchase 'guide books' right from Class I. Parents insist that teachers forced them to buy these, while the teachers aver that parents buy them on their own. The fact remains that most children had them in their school bags and copy the question and answers in their notebooks—some of the children could not even read what they had written!

TEACHERS' ATTITUDES AND DEVELOPMENT OF SELF-ESTEEM

What value does education add to the lives of children? There is little disagreement over the role of education in enhancing the self-esteem and self-confidence of children. Yet, discrimination and/or differential treatment in school can and does affect the overall confidence levels and the self-esteem of children. Both children and parents are categorical that teachers treat poor children differentially, that they do not appreciate the predicament of children who have to work before and after school. Constant reinforcement of caste and community-based negative stereotypes also has a long-term effect on children, whereby they internalise these perceptions and see themselves as being solely responsible for their own situation. Hence, it is not surprising to come across parents and children alike who believe that their inability to be 'literate' or 'get an education' is more a function of their caste/community identity (for instance, Adivasis [STs] are backward and uncivilised, etc.), as opposed to the larger political economy. Casual and sometimes sarcastic comments on how worthwhile the education is in the lives of children who will 'end up' doing what their parents do—agricultural wage labour, sweeper, cobbler, etc.,—dampens a child's self-esteem and aspirations.

EMERGING ISSUES

As stated earlier, our sample is skewed in favour of the very poor; therefore, the observations need to be read contextually and may not be completely applicable to other socio-economic groups. However, this sample enables us to understand the situation with respect to the 10–15 per cent of the poorest households in a village or a slum, and provides insights into the ways in which children from these households continue to be deprived or marginalised. The rest of the section elaborates on the emerging themes that characterise the interplay of the proximal and distal factors in determining the educational outcomes of children living in diverse poverty situations, especially with specific reference to gender, caste, community and region.

Cumulative Impact on Child Development

The research, by focussing on children of different age groups along the integrated child development continuum, illustrates the continuous and cumulative nature of social and economic exclusion that children face from the moment of conception. Health, nutrition and education are no doubt the three main sectors that impact a child's development. However, as we have seen, the nature of impact of these sectors is not discrete or merely additive; rather, it is far more complicated, varying in its intensity and manifestation according to the sub-stage under consideration. The health and nutrition status of both mother and child is clearly significant in the early years. The continuous and cumulative nature of impact has also meant that, although the age groups are discrete in nature, the impact of non-attainment of appropriate developmental milestones, health and nutritional outcomes, or learning capacities implies that these necessarily accompany the child to the next stage, leading to more failures than successes and, in some cases, intergenerational transfer of these handicaps. This results in a downward spiral of poverty, ill-health, malnutrition and poor learning outcomes for children. Our research also indicates that, despite the potential, the current social policy is unable to effectively capture and tap the positive synergy of the different sectoral interventions. It is also unable to proactively harness the family and community in meeting its objectives of reaching the child, especially the poorest child, and creating a supportive environment for its development.

Intermeshing Poverty and Social Status

Poverty impacts the overall health status of children. Lack of easy access to water affects their overall hygiene. Even when poor families have access to safe water, storing practices and usage affect the quality of the water they drink. The level of poverty, significantly impacting on food and nutrition security, is closely related to availability of work.[5] During 'normal' times, most poor (below poverty line families) eat less nutritious food than households above the poverty line. Discussions on intra-household food distribution also revealed that adult men get precedence, followed by boys, then girls, and finally women.

Economic explanations per se rarely explain persistent bottlenecks in attaining universal primary education. The reality is that economic factors are inextricably entwined with social variables in determining children's ability to both access and continue in schools, often making it difficult to distinguish between the two. The in-depth study of elementary education of the poorest and other deprived groups by Jha and Jhingran (2002) provides perhaps one of the more exhaustive databases in recent years on the issue and sheds light on competing factors that frame educational decision-making in poor households. They argue that enrolment and attendance are not only determined by the economic situation, but also by the social status of groups.

The same is reflected in our study, where the caste and community of children influence educational participation and outcomes, along with economic status. While an improvement in the economic situation certainly makes a difference, this alone does not explain the lack of access or regularity of attendance in school, and probably explains why the SC, ST and other minority groups (Muslims in UP) in our sample emerge at the bottom of the educational ladder. The attitudes and prejudices of teachers and children regarding the social and community identities of marginal groups in the school also play an important role in defining educational outcomes for the latter. As a result, schools that cater to a specific disadvantaged group often record better attendance/performance of these groups, provided the quality of schooling is satisfactory. In many areas of the country, the teacher-pupil ratio and overall infrastructure/facilities in schools that cater exclusively to marginal groups are not comparable to the regular government schools that cater to mixed social groups. This phenomenon, known as hierarchies of access, has come to be accepted as a significant factor in explaining children's access to and the quality of schooling they receive, thereby influencing the ability of children to successfully complete primary schooling (Ramachandran 2002).

The interplay of gender with social and economic status adds another important dimension to the issue. Gender relations in the family, community and in the society exert significant influence on the ability of girl children to access services, nutrition, immunisation, healthcare (especially during bouts of illness) and schooling. The good news, however, is that if girls do reach school and are able to cross the initial barrier, they are highly motivated and struggle against all odds to remain in school. Similarly, if regularity can be assured, girls perform as well, if not better, than boys in school.

Another significant factor that emerged during the course of this study as well as previous quantitative and qualitative studies (Ramachandran 2002; Jha and Jhingran 2002) is one of changing social norms with regard to schooling. Discussions in rural Karnataka and Andhra Pradesh revealed that sending children to school has become a norm in the community. This transformation in social norms and practices has occurred in the last eight to ten years. Government-initiated campaigns (*Chinnara Angala, Ma Marali Shale, Chaduvula Pandaga*), intensive NGO-led mobilisation against child labour (notably, the contribution of the MV Foundation in Andhra Pradesh) and sustained efforts to make school a joyful experience (Nalikali and Kalinali of Karnataka) have made a major difference. The governments of Karnataka and Andhra Pradesh have ensured that teachers reach the schools and have tried to address cadre management concerns, so as to rationalise teacher deployment. Conversely, lack of sustained mobilisation and corresponding government efforts in Uttar Pradesh to ensure functioning schools is perhaps responsible for the persistent apathy with respect to education, especially for the poor, who rely on government schools.

Health, Nutrition and Education

The relation between health and education is often perceived as a one-way street, with most discussions focussing on the role education can play in facilitating health awareness and improving the health status of individuals and communities. Usually left out of the debate is the critical and reciprocal nature of the link between health and education, specifically in relation to children, whereby poor health and nutrition can actually prove to be a barrier to attendance and educational attainment/achievement. The most obvious medical evidence indicates that childhood disability, chronic illness and extreme malnutrition of children are a direct impediment to his/her participation in school. Further, the frequency, duration and severity of illnesses that affect a child also influences the regularity and attendance of an enrolled child. However, barring the polio drive, there is little energy in the health sector. What still remains fuzzy is the less than tangible link between endemic poverty, malnutrition and educational attainment/achievements.

Further, inadequate nutrition, manifested in short-term hunger syndrome, impacts on a child's ability to learn and retain new concepts.[6] Hence the common complaints by teachers that children lack the ability to concentrate, are listless, etc., take on a new urgency. Several studies, especially those on the Tamil Nadu mid-day meal programme, have stressed the benefits of a hot and sumptuous meal in school, particularly for children in poverty situations. As discussed earlier, dry rations seem to have little impact. No wonder the Supreme Court's judgment on serving cooked meals in school, instead of distributing dry rations, was welcomed by parents and children. The experience of Karnataka was quite impressive—not just in ensuring regularity in school, but in making a significant difference to children from the surveyed households.

The Way Forward

The School System

An important insight provided by this study is that a well-functioning and attractive school, with basic facilities and motivated teachers, makes a major difference in the lives of poor children. Access and quality have thus to be seen as being part of the same continuum—one without the other is meaningless. This is of particular importance in government schools that cater to the majority of poor children in rural and urban areas. The shift that we are seeking is that the school system has to gear itself towards ensuring learning outcomes of children. If this is taken as a non-negotiable principle, then the school needs to function as an integrated whole, where a range of inputs/activities converge, in order to create a non-intimidating and creative learning environment.

Equally, a well-run mid-day meal programme positively impacts on enrolment, retention, as well as learning. While Karnataka and Andhra Pradesh have a good programme, Uttar Pradesh is yet to implement it.

The teacher is the fulcrum around which an effective schooling system revolves. While this appears to be a cliché, the real task before us today is to break this down into doable steps, for instance making them accountable for measurable learning outcomes. Actual teaching time and teacher-pupil ratio (TPR) remain important areas of concern. In the schools visited in UP, the TPR in rural schools was high as 1:173, in one case, and the actual teaching time was less than one hour per class/per day! In the tribal school visited in AP, only one of the three teachers was present on any given day.

Another context-specific strategy worth exploring, especially in tribal areas, where it has not been easy to ensure posting and regular attendance of teachers, is to locate a school in a cluster (*mandal* in the case of AP) that is easily accessible and transport children from Class IV onwards to the school, rather than one school in every habitation. This recommendation is being made in light of evidence that the tribal and SC children studying in residential schools (*ashram shala*, residential school for SCs) come across as better equipped academically. This might enable the government to pool its resources, human and financial, and ensure that children from poor families and disadvantaged communities get good quality education. It would also facilitate good teacher-pupil ratios and also ensure regular teaching. In the same vein, residential condensed programmes for girls in the 11+ age-group could be particularly valuable in educationally backward regions.

The ICDS Programme

A major finding relates to the ineffectiveness of the pre-school education component of the ICDS programme in all (except one) centres observed. This has also been highlighted in recent studies (NCAER, ICDS Field Study 1999).

Our discussions in the community raised the question of whether the ICDS programme should indeed be the nodal point for pre-school education. One proposal worth considering is delinking the pre-school education component from ICDS and AWC and instead making it an integral part of primary schools. An important spin-off of this restructuring would be that children in the 3–5+ age-group could benefit from the universal mid-day meal programme, thereby improving their nutritional status. This is of particular importance for children from poor families. For example, the Government of Assam took a policy decision to open a pre-school section (Ka-Maan) for children under six. Similarly, the Shishu Shiksha Kendra in Madhya Pradesh caters to the pre-school education needs of children in the 3–5 age-group. There are several such initiatives from across the country, underscoring the importance of pre-school education in preparing children for primary schooling. Balwadis of Pratham (Mumbai, Delhi, etc.) and Uttarakhand Sewa Nidhi of UP are examples of successful innovations in the non-government sector.

This shift will enable the AWW to concentrate on the nutrition and health of children in the 0–3+ age-group, pregnant and lactating mothers, adolescent girls, and more importantly in nutrition education of the community. This will also ensure that nutrition supplements and other health interventions reach those who are most in need. Since not all poor children have access to the ICDS centre (especially in UP, where each village has only one centre), the government could consider making it a universal programme for all children in the appropriate age group, as also for all pregnant and lactating mothers in the catchment area of the ICDS centre. It is important to emphasise that provision of dry rations to pregnant and lactating mothers defeats the very purpose of supplementary nutrition. Given the precarious economic situation of the households studied, the supplement goes into the food kitty of the family.

HEALTH AND NUTRITION

Public education has received a setback in the last 30 years. It may be worthwhile to re-visit earlier nutrition education and preventive health programmes. One disturbing feature is that every new programme introduced tends to diminish the validity of earlier efforts. In all the three states, it was rather disconcerting that simple messages (kitchen gardens, eating leafy vegetables, universal planting of common fruits like guava/berries, nutritional value of coarse grains, etc.) that enable people to harvest whatever local resources they have to improve their nutritional status are no longer seen as being important.

More effective public education is needed to highlight the link between complete immunisation and disease prevention. Discussions in all the three states revealed big gaps in people's appreciation of immunisation. Unfortunately, as pointed out in the Mid-Term Review of the Ninth Five-Year Plan of the government (Planning Commission GOI 2001) routine, immunisation has suffered—this has serious implications for the health of children.

> It is a matter of concern that there has been a fall in routine immunisation. It is obvious that the target of 100 per cent coverage of all six vaccine preventable diseases has not been achieved. Several states have reported substantial decline in routine immunisation...Reported factors responsible for poor coverage range from vacancy at ANM level (40 per cent in Bihar), poor mobility, poor access, problem in distribution and storage of vaccines, lack of supervision and monitoring, poor cold chain maintenance and ongoing campaign mode programmes disrupting routine activities... (Planning Commission GOI 2000–01).

Role of Community Groups and Listening to Children's Voices

Today, there are multiple village-level groups and committees, with competing goals and overlapping roles. To seriously address crucial factors that facilitate/impede the overall development and growth of children, it is vital to re-examine the roles/ mandate of these committees and look for ways to empower specific groups of people to play a more positive interventionist role, to ensure that benefits accrue to those most in need. The enthusiasm with which these committees are constituted is rarely matched by resources/activities to educate and empower them. It is thus necessary to pay special attention to the process of constitution of committees and strengthen training/capacity building activities, which are necessary to give them the teeth to make the difference. This applies to all the committees established for primary education/child development at the village level.

Notes

1. We are grateful to Venita Kaul of World Bank for giving us the permission to publish an abridged version of the synthesis report.

2. Successful primary school completion requires not only completion of five years of schooling, but it also implies the ability to read and write with comprehension, be an active learner, as well as develop self-learning capacity, the ability to articulate/communicate, and to develop positive self-esteem and self-confidence.

3. Interestingly, the official statistics compiled by the Registrar General of India, from the records of ANMs or other sources and those collected by the NFHS from responses of women are at variance, as evident in Table 1.2. The households consistently report a much higher proportion of deliveries taking place at home.

4. NFHS-2 (1998–99) reveals that only 52.89 per cent rural and 76.34 per cent urban women were given iron folic acid tablets during pregnancy. If we are to look at Uttar Pradesh, only 32.91 per cent women received IFA tablets!

5. Jha and Jhingran (2002: 54–55) argue, 'The issue of acute food shortage faced by poor people in drought affected areas in the midst of gigantic "surplus" food stocks rotting

in godowns has been an area of debate and discussion.... What is important to point out in this respect is that the poor do not face food insecurity only during drought or drought-like situations. In many places, periodic food crises are an annual phenomenon, the intensity of the crisis and length of the period increases during years of bad or no crop.... Nearly one third of these families usually face a food crisis for more than four months in a year, the rest go through this for about two-three months'.

6. A review of literature on the subject notes that the capacity for processing, structuring and classifying information, the ability to ask and answer appropriate questions, short-term memory, and levels of alertness, attention and concentration, are some of the capacities which are crucial for success in school. These are known to be adversely affected by nutritional and health deficits, which therefore limit the ability of the child to benefit from classroom instruction or later learning opportunities (Levinger 1994; Del Rosso and Marek 1996, cited in New Concept 2003). Malnutrition, even in its milder form, can dull motivation and curiosity, reduce the child's exploratory play and interaction with caregivers and the environment, thus restricting the child's psychosocial development [Martorell (1997), cited in New Concept (2003)].

REFERENCES

Gaag, Jacques van der, and Jee-Peng Tan. 1998. 'The Benefits of Early Child Development Programmes: An Economic Analysis', Vol. 1. Education: World Bank.

Government of India. 2001: Mid-Term Review of the Ninth Five-Year Plan, New Delhi: Planning Commission.

Gupta, Devandra B. 2003. 'Studies of Existing Policies and Related Provisions and Schemes'. Draft Report of a study commissioned by the World Bank, New Delhi, April.

International Institute for Population Sciences. 1995. 'National Family Health Survey (NFHS-1)', 1992–93: IIPS, Mumbai.

———. 2000: 'National Family Health Survey (NFHS-2)', 1998–99 IIPS: Mumbai.

Jha, Jyotsna, and Dhir Jhingran. 2002. 'Elementary Education for the Poorest and other Deprived Groups'. New Delhi: Centre for Policy Research.

Kaul V., C. Ramachandran, and G. C. Upadhayay. 1993. 'Impact of ECE on Retention in Primary Grades, a Longitudinal Study'. New Delhi: NCERT.

Krishnamurty, Lakshmi, and Vani Periodi. 2003. 'Listening to Children', in Vimala Ramachandran, ed. 'Snakes and Ladders: Factors that Facilitate/Impede Successful Primary School Completion', unpublished and unabridged report submitted to World Bank, New Delhi.

Levinger, B., Del Rosso, and Marek. 1994. 'Early Childhood Care and Education in the Context of Education for All'. New Concept Information Systems Private Limited, New Delhi.

Martorell, R. 1997. 'Under Nutrition during Pregnancy and Early Childhood Consequences for Cognitive and Behavioural Development'. Unpublished paper made available by Venita Kaul of the World Bank, New Delhi.

Mehrotra, Nishi, et al. 2003. 'Against All Odds: A Study of Children in Poverty Situations', in Vimala Ramachandran, ed. 'Snakes and Ladders: Factors that Facilitate/Impede Successful Primary School Completion', unpublished and unabridged report submitted to World Bank, New Delhi.

National Council of Applied Economic Research. 1999. *ICDS Field Survey*. New Delhi: NCAER.

New Concept Information Systems Private. 2003. 'Integrated Child Development – A Conceptual Framework', January. New Delhi.

Pratichi (India) Trust. 2002. 'The Pratichi Education Report'. New Delhi: Pratichi (India) Trust.

PROBE, Report. 1999. 'Public Report, on Basic Education in India'. New Delhi: Oxford University Press.

Ramachandran, Vimala, ed. 2002. 'Hierarchies of Access: Gender and Social Equity in Primary Education in India'. New Delhi: European Commission.

____. 2003. 'Snakes and Ladders: Factors that Facilitate/Impede Successful Primary School Completion', unpublished and unabridged report submitted to World Bank, New Delhi.

Ramalingaswami, Vulmiri, Urban Jonsson, and Jon Rhode. 1996. 'The Asian Enigma, Progress of Nations', UNICEF, downloaded from www.unicef.org.

Sharma, Neerja, and Nandita Chaudhary. 2003. 'From Home to School: Circumstances in the Lives of Children from Poor Families', in Vimala Ramachandran, ed. 'Snakes and Ladders: Factors that Facilitate/Impede Successful Primary School Completion', unpublished and unabridged report submitted to World Bank, New Delhi.

2

Private Schools for the Less Privileged

*Some Insights from a Case Study**

Anuradha De, Claire Noronha and Meera Samson†

The post-NPE (National Policy on Education) 1986 era witnessed a spate of educational initiatives that were both national and foreign-funded, ranging from the Total Literacy Campaign and Operation Blackboard to DPEP (District Primary Education Programme) and Lok Jumbish. Attention was concentrated on building parental demand for education and on expanding and improving the government school system, especially at the primary level. Field surveys in the 1990s began to report a surge in parental demand for education and accompanying this was a new phenomenon—small, fee-charging private schools for the less privileged. It appeared that low-income groups not only wanted education, but were willing to pay for it. The new phenomenon was welcomed by education bureaucrats. The government system was struggling with both access and retention issues and many felt that the new private schools could be allies in achieving UEE (Universalisation of Elementary Education). However, even by the end of the 1990s, little research had been done on these schools or in fact on the private sector in schooling in general (De, Noronha, Samson and Majumdar 2002: 131, 133). Many of these schools were 'unrecognised' and were therefore even missing from statistical surveys (ibid.). This chapter is based on data from a small field-study, undertaken from October–December 1999, in order to understand these private schools.

Available macro-level data indicated that high private participation rates in elementary schooling existed in both prosperous and less prosperous states. For our survey, Haryana was taken as an example of the former and Uttar Pradesh of the

* This is the second part of a study on private schools. The first part was a desk study of secondary data on private schooling done by the authors, along with Manabi Majumdar. See 'Private Schools and Universal Elementary Education' in R. Govinda, ed., (2002), *India Education Report*, NIEPA and OUP.

latter. Rajasthan, in the same region, was also interesting. Evidence suggests that, in spite of the low level of private-sector participation in schools, the private unaided sector was absorbing most of the increase in enrolment in the state. Six locations were identified in these three states, one urban and one rural in an educationally disadvantaged district in each state. The sample districts were Bhiwani in Haryana, Rampur in UP and Dhaulpur in Rajasthan. In the three district headquarters, care was taken to identify two to four contiguous wards where the economically disadvantaged resided, and where there was a sufficient concentration of private schools. In rural areas, village clusters, located 10–15 kms away from the district headquarters, with high private school development were chosen. These became the sample areas. A census of all the schools in the sample area was undertaken and some basic information collected about each school.

In the next stage, about 12 schools were chosen randomly from the list for a detailed survey; care was taken to ensure the inclusion of different types of management, particularly private unaided schools. In addition, 50 households in each sample area, chosen through circular random sampling, were also surveyed. Since the survey intended to look at schooling issues, only families with at least one child enrolled between Classes I–VIII formed the household sample (a neighbouring household was taken where necessary). Data was collected on all the children in the household and more detailed information pertaining to the one child enrolled in Classes I–VIII. If the households had more than one child in this category, one was selected randomly for a more detailed survey.

All three sample districts had a largely agrarian economy and both rural Dhaulpur and rural Bhiwani samples were dominated by large and prosperous villages. The small, poor and backward villages of rural Rampur were a complete contrast. Urban Bhiwani was the most prosperous of the six areas and only here were elite private schools accessed by a few households in the sample. In both rural and urban Bhiwani, non-enrolled children were rare. Again, this was in complete contrast to rural Rampur, which had entire sections with no enrolled children. Female literacy, according to the 1991 Census, varies from the 35 per cent of Bhiwani to the 15 per cent of Dhaulpur and Rampur. Generalising from this small and diverse sample is difficult. We did not attempt to measure the incidence of private schools; instead we focussed on rural areas and disadvantaged urban areas, where many private schools had come up. We talked with parents, teachers and children to gain insights into schooling options for the disadvantaged in these areas.

The chapter is divided into two sections. Section I sums up the major findings. It deals with the striking features of the schooling scene, including the fall in government schools and the significant role played by the private unaided sector. It then focusses on the quality of the new private schools, their cost and their clientele. Next, we explore the reasons for the rapid growth of the private unaided sector and the nature of its growth. In the process, we have to look at the role of the government in this scenario. Section II looks at the issues that this situation brings to the fore, particularly with regard to the implications for UEE.

SOME SIGNIFICANT FINDINGS

School Development

Although the survey did concentrate on disadvantaged areas, it was interesting to find that the six samples varied greatly in terms of the educational facilities to which they had access. This is not obvious from secondary sources such as the SAIES, since district-level figures for schooling facilities are not easily available. Urban Bhiwani, with its ample provision of schooling facilities ranging all the way to the senior secondary level, is at the upper end of the spectrum and rural Rampur (also economically the poorest area), with no secondary school at all, is the worst-off (Table 2.1). Table 2.2 shows that school participation varies correspondingly—as many as 20 per cent of children in urban and rural Bhiwani were enrolled at secondary and higher secondary levels, while in rural Rampur, this came down to 2 per cent.

TABLE 2.1: Total Number of Schools in Six Sample Areas

	Urban			*Rural*		
	Bhiwani	*Dhaulpur*	*Rampur*	*Bhiwani*	*Dhaulpur*	*Rampur*
Primary	23	12	24	7	8	12
Upper-primary	9	18	9	9	8	1
Secondary/Sr. Secondary	14	7	1	3	2	0
Total	46	37	34	19	18	13

Notes: Schools with Classes I–V, I–VIII, I–X, I–XII may or may not have a pre-primary section.
Primary schools have Classes I–V, upper-primary have Classes I–VIII or VI–VIII, secondary or senior-secondary have Classes I–X, I–X, VI–X, or VI–XII.

TABLE 2.2: Number of Children Enrolled in Sample Households

No of Children Enrolled in:	*Urban*			*Rural*		
	Bhiwani	*Dhaulpur*	*Rampur*	*Bhiwani*	*Dhaulpur*	*Rampur*
Classes I–V*	74 (59.2)**	92 (67.7)	88 (63.8)	71(57.3)	79 (67.5)	104 (89.7)
Classes VI–VIII	26 (20.8)	32 (23.5)	29 (21.0)	32 (25.8)	24 (20.5)	10 (8.6)
Classes IX–XII	25 (20.0)	12 (8.8)	21 (15.2)	21 (16.9)	14 (12.0)	2 (1.7)
Total	125 (100)	136 (100)	118 (100)	124 (100)	117 (100)	116 (100)

Notes: * Includes children enrolled in the pre-primary classes.
** Figures in brackets indicate percentage.
Sample households had at least one child currently enrolled between Classes I–VIII.

In the last 10 years, no new government schools have been set up in urban areas. Even in rural areas, the proportion of new schools was very low (30 per cent), especially compared to the private unaided sector, which has been mushrooming rapidly. About 70 per cent of these schools have come up in the last 10 years.

In urban areas, many government schools functioned in rented buildings, and very old ones at that. Most buildings were dangerously old and dilapidated and all primary schools complained of an acute shortage of space. When the school could no longer operate from its rented space, both in urban Bhiwani and in urban Rampur, it simply moved into another school, so that three or four schools could operate from the same premises. In one large school building, for example, three rooms were occupied by one primary school, and two other primary schools occupied two other rooms. The rest of the building was unusable. In other words, the situation for government primary schools here is not zero growth, but negative growth. Children were often in unprotected spaces—in verandahs, with men playing cards near them (urban Bhiwani), for example. In urban Dhaulpur, a government primary school has been operating for 15 years under the '*chhatris*' (umbrellas) of a monument, unprotected from the sun and rain. To access the government schools, children had to walk long distances and cross busy roads. According to teachers, they did so for the dry rations, not for schooling. In rural areas, except for Bhiwani, children were crammed into one or two classrooms. On the whole, neither were the children comfortable, nor was the environment secure or conducive to learning.

During the survey, the pulse polio campaign was going on. It completely disrupted teaching activity in the primary schools, rural and urban, leading to the closure of schools for two to three days in some cases. Notwithstanding the overall casual atmosphere, the odd government primary school appeared to function well and we also met young children who were able to read.

Secondary-level government schools functioned much better and had better infrastructure. They were relatively few in number and generally had Classes VI–X or VI–XII. The government girls' secondary schools in both rural Bhiwani and rural Dhaulpur enjoyed an excellent reputation.

As we can see from Table 2.2 (the total number of enrolled children in the sample areas) and Table 2.3 (the numbers enrolled in private schools in all six sites), the majority of children in the urban samples were in private schools.[1] The proportion of those going to private schools is lower in the rural samples, but is still considerable in Bhiwani and Dhaulpur and somewhat less in Rampur. Enrolment in private schools attended by sample households was largely at the primary level, though there was substantial enrolment at the upper-primary level as well (Table 2.3). The pre-primary section had a high proportion of the enrolment.

TABLE 2.3: Number of Children Enrolled in Private Schools in Sample Households

No of Children Enrolled in:	*Urban*			*Rural*		
	Bhiwani	*Dhaulpur*	*Rampur*	*Bhiwani*	*Dhaulpur*	*Rampur*
Classes I–V*	53	64	65	38	40	34
Classes VI–VIII	19	18	16	18	9	2
Classes IX–XII	12	5	6	11	1	1
Total	84	87	87	67	50	37

Notes: *Includes children enrolled in the pre-primary classes.
Sample households had at least one child currently enrolled between Classes I–VIII.

About six of the 300 households could access schools that the middle class associates with the term 'private schools'.[2] These schools would run from Class I up to the secondary level; would have trained, often experienced teachers; and an adequate number of classrooms with sufficient air and light, a library, laboratories and grounds with play equipment. The general picture was quite different in our study. The heterogeneity of the private schooling scene and its uneven development across the samples and across schooling levels is easily observable in Table 2.4. There were aided and unaided private schools of different levels and among the latter, there were recognised and unrecognised schools.[3]

TABLE 2.4: Number and Type of Private Schools in Sample Areas

	Urban			*Rural*		
	Bhiwani	*Dhaulpur*	*Rampur*	*Bhiwani*	*Dhaulpur*	*Rampur*
Private unaided recognised	*14*	*24*	*15*	*3*	*5*	*2*
Primary	2	3	9	0	1	2
Upper-primary	4	16	6	3	5	0
Secondary/Sr secondary	8	5	0	0	0	0
Private unaided unrecognised	*14*	*4*	*11*	*9*	*3*	*6*
Primary	9	4	10	3	3	6
Upper-primary	5	0	1	6	0	0
Secondary/Sr secondary	0	0	0	0	0	0
Private aided	*6*	*1*	*1*	*0*	*0*	*0*
Primary	3	0	0	0	0	0
Upper-primary	0	1	1	0	0	0
Secondary/Sr secondary	3	0	0	0	0	0
Total	36	29	27	12	9	8

Notes: Primary schools have Classes I–V, upper-primary have Classes I–VIII or VI–VIII, secondary or senior-secondary schools have Classes I–X, I–XII, VI–X, or VI–XII.

A few points can be highlighted:

- Aided schools were few, found only in urban areas, and none less than 30 years old. The majority were in urban Bhiwani, at the secondary as well as primary level. Most of these schools belonged to an earlier philanthropic era, when private donations provided very good infrastructure. However, they were found to be charging high fees. The sole aided schools in Dhaulpur and Rampur had modest infrastructure and fees that were at government school-level. Aided schools were a valued good which was in short supply.
- Unaided schools set up in the late 1970s and 1980s were also different. Though they had less magnificent infrastructure, it was adequate and the schools also had different types of curricular activities. Such schools included the popular Adarsh Vidya Mandir of urban Dhaulpur and its counterpart in rural Dhaulpur, as well as a Muslim trust school in urban Rampur.

- No category or sub-category was homogeneous. Let alone unrecognised schools, even recognised schools could range from reasonable to disastrous. Nor was any category confined to one level, though primary-level private schools were most numerous in Rampur, upper-primary in Dhaulpur and higher levels in Bhiwani. None of the better quality schools in any category, not even those with modest fees, were accessed easily by the majority of our sample households. Most were enrolled in medium and low-fee schools, more like those described in the next section, although here too there is a spectrum.

New Private Schools

Quality

The new schools were often set up in a part of the owner's house. Even when the school had its own premises, and even in the recognised schools, rooms were small and congested. Sounds from one classroom impinged on others. A small courtyard could function as the playground for over 200 children. Little children—almost all private schools had a pre-school section—were also cooped up in small rooms. In urban areas, schools usually had desks and chairs rather than *durris*, a feature that parents appreciated. The unrecognised schools were often newer and had even poorer infrastructure. The exception was urban Rampur, where an unrecognised charitable trust school, running up to the upper-primary level, was functioning with community support; this school had excellent infrastructure.

Although the rooms were poky, private schools often looked more inviting than government schools, because maintenance was better. In the urban areas, especially, since schools often benefited from being in the owner's house, basic facilities like drinking water and toilet, electricity and fans were generally available. On the other hand, teaching aids were often missing and libraries non-existent, as were playgrounds.[4]

An important advantage of many of these private schools is the low pupil-teacher ratio. It is true that this is more by default than by design, because most of these schools are struggling to increase enrolment. The more successful schools have a higher pupil-teacher ratio. Multi-grade teaching is also common. The biggest disadvantage was that few schools had trained teachers. They were often so young and inexperienced that parents complained. Even the recognised schools saw a high turnover, that is, teachers rarely stayed long. A striking example comes from rural Bhiwani, which had the best developed private schooling system accessed by disadvantaged parents. In the two recognised schools, both around 10 years old, five of the nine teachers in one school and seven of the 12 in the other had been around for less than a year. These were both upper-primary schools, like the two best unrecognised schools in the area. In the latter schools, each with seven staff members, not a single one had any kind of training.

There is, however, no gainsaying the fact that private schools were generally hard at work with their charges. This sheer abundance of teaching time, whatever the competence of the teachers involved, would definitely have some impact. Many of these schools also scored points by increasing the number of working days, as compared to government schools. Homework and tests were a regular feature and are part of the better achievement associated with these schools.

The curriculum in the private schools was the standard curriculum of other schools, both government and elite private. In fact, much of the stress on English and on prescribing many textbooks came from imitating the latter group of schools. Teaching methods were conventional. Much emphasis was placed on rote-learning and written work. '*Kunjis*' (inferior guidebooks) were found in the schoolbags of older children. Schools took pride in their teaching of English—the nursery rhymes, the 'Good Morning' and the grammar. There was little stress on activities other than academic, although most schools claimed to have extra-curricular activities. Even inter-school competitions organised in rural Bhiwani private schools—and these were among the best of the new schools—were organised around doing better at the Class VIII examinations.

No formal achievement test was administered during this survey and perhaps these small private schools need to be assessed. The fact that the parents are spending money to send their children to the private schools is telling by itself. One can assuredly say that private schools are delivering more than government schools (which does not necessarily mean much). It is also true that some teachers indicated that government/aided schools at the secondary level preferred children from private primary schools, and this is a valid achievement test for parents.

School achievement is a complex area, where school input combines with parental support and the willingness/aptitude of the individual child. Private school input is regular but not, as we see, of high quality. The family background of private school children is generally socially and economically stronger than that of government school children, as we can see from Table 2.7. At the same time, it is not clear if parents with children in private schools are giving them much extra support. From Table 2.5 one can see that even in private schools, only around 50 per cent of the sample children received help with their homework. Tuition was not much a part of the culture, except in urban Dhaulpur and urban Rampur, where it impacted both government and private school children.

TABLE 2.5: Availability of Home Support in Different Areas by School Type

Proportion of Children Enrolled in*	*Urban*			*Rural*		
	Bhiwani	*Dhaulpur*	*Rampur*	*Bhiwani*	*Dhaulpur*	*Rampur*
Government schools with families:						
With literate adult females	33	41	41	11	19	17
Who help with homework	22	36	59	44	23	6
Who have arranged private tuition	0	23	41	6	15	3
Private schools with families:						
With literate adult females	55	50	51	44	52	10
Who help with homework	41	47	60	61	44	45
Who have arranged private tuition	10	50	49	6	23	0

Note: *Responses were with respect to selected children from sample households.

Cost

Fees increased with progress up the schooling ladder, with the pre-primary level (this could be two to three years) costing the least. The new schools added one more layer of stratification to an already stratified system. Urban areas showed a gap between schooling for the less privileged and for the even less privileged in its most acute form. There were a large number of schools where fees ranged from Rs 15–50, but there were a few prized schools in the range of Rs 150 per month. Rural parents, possibly, had lower paying capacity: schools had a much smaller range of fees—in fact, in our poorest area, rural Rampur, parents were often unable to even pay the monthly school fees of Rs 15–20, for months at a time. Even the most prosperous rural area—rural Bhiwani—had fees ranging between Rs 30–80 per month.

To study the cost of schooling, children were divided into four categories; those enrolled in government schools, low-fee private schools, medium-fee private schools and high-fee private schools. Since the cost of schooling seemed to increase as one went up the schooling ladder, the primary and upper-primary levels were looked at separately. As expected, children in government primary schools have the lowest expenditure (Rs 500), and the expenditure involved rises sharply for each category of private primary school. There is also a rough proportionality between fee and non-fee expenditure. In other words, schools that charge high fees also require proportionately higher non-fee expenditure. This also explains why it is only parents from a less disadvantaged socio-economic background who can send their children to high-fee schools.

The total number of children attending school at the upper-primary level was much smaller. Cost may be an excluding factor, since fees are higher, whatever the type of school. In fact, the expenditure on a child in a private school with fees below Rs 1,200 was only 25 per cent more than that involved for a child in a government school (Table 2.6). Dropout rates are also high because of high and increasing indirect costs, lack of home support and poor teaching at the primary level. More

TABLE 2.6: Annual Household Expenditure Per Child on Schooling

(Rs)

	School Fees Per Annum	*Total Expenditure on Schooling*
Primary level: for a child enrolled in government school	47	499
Private (fees below Rs 600) school	420	1373
Private (fees between Rs 600 and Rs 1,200) school	857	2,427
Private (fees greater than Rs 1,200) school	2,733	6,124
Upper-primary level: for a child enrolled in government school	107	1,579
Private (fees below Rs 1,200) school	753	1,967
Private (fees greater than Rs 1,200) school	3,480	5,924

Notes: Total expenditure includes school fees, expenditure on stationery, textbooks, uniform, transport, private tuition and other costs associated with schooling. These were parents' estimates with respect to selected children in sample households.

children go to government schools at the upper-primary level and the very low-fee private schools do not exist at all, possibly because they are not sustainable. Private schools accessed at this level can be analysed in two groups: annual fees below Rs 1,200 and above Rs 1,200. Some explanation for this completely different scenario at the upper-primary level seems possible. Government schools usually had the upper-primary section as part of the secondary schools, and therefore presented a more attractive option. Private upper-primary schools had perforce to function better if they were to attract their clientele.

Clientele—Class, Caste and Gender, and Choice

The asset-ownership position confirms that private school children come from somewhat better-off families. Associated with this are all the advantages of better health, nutrition, self-esteem and awareness. The government primary school clientele appears most disadvantaged, whereas those in government secondary schools are accessing a good which is in short supply and often of better quality as well. Table 2.7 shows this. The latter group (includes all levels in government schools) are much closer to those in private schools. Obviously, the groups overlap. Some of those currently enrolled in government secondary schools may well have gone to private schools earlier.

TABLE 2.7: Characteristics of Sample Households

	Families with Children Enrolled in		
	Government Primary Schools	*All Government Schools*	*Private Schools*
Proportion (%) of families whose main earning activity is:			
Wage labour (agricultural / non-agricultural)	45	33	18
Employment (temporary / permanent)	9	19	36
Proportion (%) of families owning:			
TV	29	44	69
Refrigerator	0	6	27
Motorcycle	5	7	17
Proportion (%) of families who are:			
SC	38	34	20
OBC	17	15	14
Other Hindus	15	22	39
Muslims	29	28	27
From other religions	1	1	Negligible

Note: Sample households had at least one child currently enrolled between Classes I–VIII.

Macro-level data indicates that going to a private school is a mark of social privilege and that, for example, rural SC females are very unlikely to find themselves in a private school. Some change has taken place with the new type of schools, as we see in Table 2.7. If we look at the occupation and caste distribution of private school clientele, we find that 18 per cent of private school parents were wage labourers and 20 per cent were Scheduled Caste. In other words, there are private schools which are being accessed by a significant number of these very disadvantaged groups. The gender problem requires special discussion. Putting both qualitative data and quantitative data (Table 2.8) together, it is possible to make a few suggestions.

TABLE 2.8: Enrolled Children from Sample Households by School Management, Gender and Location

	Proportion (%) of Children Enrolled in:			
	Classes I–V		*Classes VI–VIII*	
	Boys	*Girls*	*Boys*	*Girls*
Urban areas				
Government school	29.1	27.4	27.5	55.6
Private school	70.9	72.6	72.5	44.4
Rural areas				
Government school	55.0	57.7	41.2	71.9
Private school	45.0	42.3	58.8	28.1

Note: Sample households had at least one child currently enrolled between Classes I–VIII.

If children were enrolled in school, then it was common to find all children of a household enrolled in the chosen school. However, there were isolated examples of what seemed like clear gender bias, with the boy in private school and the girl in government school. Gender bias was much clearer at the level of deciding whether or not to enrol the child in any school at all. This was the case in the poorest region: rural Rampur. It was very common to find girls who were never enrolled, even among families which had a currently enrolled boy (sometimes in private school).

For one thing, many more girls than boys dropped out by primary level, usually because of parental pressure. Second, at this stage a higher proportion of girls was in government schools.[5] The bias was even stronger in rural areas, with the majority of girls in government schools and most boys in private schools.

Very vulnerable families who were trying private schools at the bottom-end of the spectrum often initially sent all their children to government school. When they found they were making little progress, they might take one or more children out and put them in private schools. The privileged ones were often boys.

Few parents could access what they felt was 'a good school': one with good infrastructure, different activities, playing facilities and committed and encouraging teachers. It appears that parents are looking for a school of decent quality and affordable fees within a reasonable distance (Table 2.9 and 2.10). Interestingly, English, which private schools looked on as their main USP, seems to hold less importance than the promise of better achievement held out by their teaching activity.

TABLE 2.9: Criteria for Choice of School in Sample Households

(Per cent)

Proportion of Parents who Considered the Following as Important Criterion for Choice of School:	*Urban*	*Rural*
Distance from home	50	34
Reputation of the school or teachers	50	49
Cost of schooling	50	46
Teach English	14	15
Availability of extra-curricular activity	15	14
Board results	13	13

Notes: The options are not mutually exclusive.
The responses of parents are with respect to the selected child in the sample households.

TABLE 2.10: Proportion (Per Cent) of Non-Enrolled Children among Sample Households

Non-enrolled Children in:	*Urban*			*Rural*		
	Bhiwani	*Dhaulpur*	*Rampur*	*Bhiwani*	*Dhaulpur*	*Rampur*
6–10 age-group						
Boys	9	2	7	9	3	19
Girls	4	13	8	9	11	46
11–14 age-group						
Boys	11	15	25	16	12	6
Girls	16	12	6	24	17	79

Note: Sample households had at least one child currently enrolled between Classes I–VIII.

Parents face a difficult choice between low-quality and no quality at the primary level and enrolment in the new schools is mainly at this level. Government schools could be absent (urban areas), or dysfunctional (rural Rampur), or just casual. Parents often helplessly observe while their child struggles through government primary school and, after two or three years of such struggle, they put him in the nursery class of a (possibly low-quality) private school, out of desperation. Often the government school parents have little idea that their child has not learned much. Of course, it is only fair to point out that there were also cases where parents were disillusioned with private schools and moved helplessly from one to the other, and even went back to the government school. Second, poaching from government schools and from other private schools is also actively pursued by private school entrepreneurs.

The cost of private schooling is still an excluding factor, both for access and for sustaining the enterprise and those who choose private schools in spite of low and uncertain earning capacity may be sacrificing a lot. In urban Rampur and urban Dhaulpur, which seemed fairly alert about educational support, private tuition was also a significant part of the cost for many families. An unpleasant aspect of the non-fee expenditure (Table 2.6) was that it often comprised items like belts and ties and shoes and socks. Sometimes, many textbooks were prescribed even for younger students. In addition, there were hidden costs like, for example, the cost of a picnic or field trip in the more ambitious private schools.

Factors Leading to Increased Presence of these Schools

As suggested by earlier studies the new schools are responding to an increased demand for education and for schooling from low-income groups. This demand has been stimulated by the widespread understanding that education is linked with employment opportunities and upward mobility. But it is partly also a creation of state sponsored schemes like literacy campaigns, NFE schemes and new incentives like dry rations, etc. The poor quality (and even poor availability in urban areas) of government primary schooling has frustrated this demand (the exception was rural Bhiwani, where government school infrastructure was reasonably good). In contrast to government schools, private schools provided a serious atmosphere and concentrated on teaching. These schools were able to show indicators of achievement. This could range from a smattering of English nursery rhymes, knowledge of the alphabet, and some literacy and numeracy. Even the schooling readiness provided by pre-primary schools was desired by parents. Private school children had a better chance of accessing the restricted supply of better quality government/aided schooling at higher levels.

Rampant educated unemployment created the willing supply factor. The supply of such schools is in fact so abundant that, in many cases, it seems to be creating the demand. We came across a schooling situation of great fluidity: entrepreneurs wooing poor parents, schools breaking up or closing down because of manipulation among this group or because of over-supply. In rural areas, the prospect of opening a private school is exciting for the local notables, including the sarpanch. At the primary level, little investment is needed and regulations seem to be easily flouted. The government has greatly diluted norms for schooling and is, at least in Rajasthan, coaxing private parties to open schools. The supply of teachers willing to work for a pittance is also abundant.

At higher levels of schooling, neither demand nor supply factors are currently strong enough to create the same phenomenon. For one thing, many children do not survive primary schooling. Also, the cost of schooling for parents rises sharply even in government schools. Second, government schools at the upper-primary/secondary level, though in short supply, enjoy higher state subsidy, which makes for better infrastructure. They also have a better teaching and learning environment. Since the upper-primary level is integrated with the senior/senior secondary level for the most part, parents have a less expensive opportunity to reach the secondary level. (Aided schools in the sample had similar advantages.) All things considered, parents would therefore stand to lose much more if they abandon government schooling for upper-primary classes in the unaided sector. On the supply side, the level of investment now involved in order to set up a private school, is higher (norms are more demanding), and there is an inbuilt accountability mechanism in the Board results. More rooms, better teachers, better facilities, all lead to increased costs.

Recognition Norms and Quality Schooling

The recognition system has a strong influence on the quality of schooling, but it is the recognised secondary schools that are comparatively better. These are generally for a more advantaged group.

The government has tried to foster privatisation in different ways—commonly by diluting the norms. In Dhaulpur, the norms were so 'dilute' as to be almost non-existent. However, for the elementary level, the system has failed due to many contributory factors: private school owners find compliance a difficult task due to difficult conditions as well as bureaucratic harassment. Education officers complained that the owners are dishonest, as for example non-existent schools were also shown in premises that were not owned by the promoters. Chances are that schools often function at a level beyond that for which they have received recognition. At least this seemed to be the case with two recognised schools in rural Bhiwani, which had begun to call themselves secondary schools. The schools did not even have the infrastructure said to be mandatory at the upper-primary level, such as playground, laboratory, etc. Unrecognised schools had an understanding with recognised schools, so they too could satisfactorily survive at a price by sending their students for exams at the recognised school.

However, the norms do appear to be supplying some benchmark against which schools can measure themselves, if only for the recognition badge that enables them to send children for the school-leaving examinations, or to other recognised schools at this or higher stage. The unrecognised schools appear to be using the recognised schools as a standard. This benchmark function is vital, particularly because government schools themselves are not working according to norms. Interestingly, low-cost private schools concentrate on giving good teaching time, rather than good infrastructure. They can invest only to a limited extent in infrastructure.

One complication in rural Bhiwani was the involvement of the sarpanch. 'How can the sarpanch look after the performance of government school teachers when he is running the biggest private school in the village?', asked the local DPEP representative.

New Development and UEE

The new schools add more tracks to the schooling system, this time among the less-privileged. The development reinforces the duality and elitism inherent in private schooling, without ensuring quality or coverage. Although the government welcomes the sharing of its burden, it must be remembered that while the sharing of the management burden is done by the entrepreneur, it is the disadvantaged parent who bears the costs. This is a difficult and often unsustainable burden. In the new schools, it is commerce and not philanthropy that is the driving force. The quality of schools is likely to be low, proportional to the limited input from disadvantaged parents, in terms of fees, etc., and in terms of home support.

In all three urban samples, access to school in urban areas is largely through private schools, especially those of the new variety. This has been precipitated by the retreat of government schools in the area. But even in rural areas, poorly monitored government schools have created a good field for the new private schools. However, cost remains an excluding factor for private schooling. The very poor are dependent on government schools and, in fact, can generally access only the government primary schools that are seen to be the worst in the sector. This, too, is a cause for concern. It is also important to note that it is not only the very poor, but also the majority of families who are dependent on the government for upper-primary schooling. The supply of these schools is woefully inadequate and is crucial for UEE (Universalisation of Elementary Education).

The survey concentrated on district headquarters and rural areas with private school development (all were accessible). Even in this limited sample of families already motivated for schooling—all have at least one child enrolled in elementary classes—and notwithstanding the wooing of private entrepreneurs, the number of out-of-school children remains sizeable. Girls are especially at risk in this region of high gender bias. Notice that the figures for out-of-school girls in rural Rampur are close to 80 per cent in the older age-group, and around 50 per cent in the younger age-group. Prosperous rural Bhiwani, with its comparatively well-developed government and private school system, also had around one-fourth of its girls in the older age-group out of school. Older boys are also heavily at risk.

The picture would have been more dismal had we included in the sample families where all children were non-enrolled. This is a definite indication, if such was needed, of the inadvisability of relying on private initiatives of this type for UEE. These market-driven ventures will not, for example, be battling the inertia of poor parents who are dependent on the wages or the household help of boys and especially girls, or the vested interests of employers of child labour. This is one of the major challenges of UEE. There are a few (relative to the enormity of the task) education initiatives run by NGOs in difficult urban areas and in remote unserved rural areas, which are doing such tasks. They rely on mainstreaming children into the government schooling system.

Retention issues are crucial for UEE. Qualitative data indicates that children from the better private schools are better able to access the next level of schooling. However, as the survey indicates, there is segmentation in the new private schools. It is possible that the many deprived children are exposed to barely competent teaching and their families cannot support their schooling either. Aided schools are too few to be making an impact.

The regulatory mechanism of 'recognition norms' has failed to ensure a minimum acceptable norm of quality schooling, even though norms have been diluted to an almost poverty-line level. Market forces dictate that if the government schools functioned at a reasonable level, private schools would be forced to follow suit or be forced out of business. This is, in fact, indicated by rural Bhiwani, which had the best functioning government school system and the best functioning private school system as well.

In terms of learning achievement, no miracles can be expected from this sector. The usual curriculum, with all its decontextualised as well as heavy content, remains the curriculum for private schools. In fact, much time is devoted to English teaching—the showpiece of private schools—and again, it appears to be through rote learning, grammatical exercises, etc. In spite of pre-primary schooling for two to three years, we met many children who were lost in the maze of movement from government to private, or even from one private school to another.[6]

Given the shortage of government schools, the enormity of the task, and the tremendous need for quality, there is no real advantage to be gained from allowing government schools to rot—in any case a slow, cumbersome and wasteful procedure. The government could also harness the energies and enthusiasm of the new entrepreneurs in the cause of schooling, with adequate assistance and regulation. The system should also be more transparent for parents. Raising the quality of schools in both sectors will give parents a more meaningful set of choices and contribute to UEE.

NOTES

†All tables included in this chapter are author-generated and are based on the authors' own data.

1. See Introduction above, which stresses that sample areas were chosen for the concentration of private schools.

2. All six were in urban Bhiwani and were more advantaged households. Fees ranged from Rs 350 to Rs 500 per month. The only new elite private school found was in rural Rampur, the poorest area. Fees were Rs 250 per month. Parents here found Rs 15 to Rs 20 difficult to sustain.

3. Aided schools have the benefit of private management. Since government pays teachers' salaries, fees are supposed to be pegged at government school level. Unaided schools qualify for 'recognition' by the department of education, if they follow certain minimum standards of quality laid down by the department.

4. Quantitative information on infrastructure makes these schools sound better than they actually are, since claims were often exaggerated or are downright untruths.

5. The few government secondary schools for girls were good and were beneficial for the enrolment of girls.

6. Bashir (1994) researching in a state where government schooling on the whole is better than that in northern states—and therefore the new private schools can be expected to be better—finds that learning achievement amounts to basic literacy and numeracy.

REFERENCES

Bashir, Sajitha. 1994. 'Public versus private in primary education: comparisons of school effectiveness and costs in Tamil Nadu', unpublished PhD thesis, London School of Economics.

De, A., M. Majumdar, C. Noronha, and M. Samson. 2002. 'Private Schools and Universal Elementary Education'. In R, Govinda, ed. *India Education Report*. New Delhi: Oxford University Press.

3

Education and Girlhood*

Krishna Kumar

Why Girlhood?

In this chapter, I choose to talk about girlhood rather than girls. There are two interrelated reasons for this choice. One reason has to do with my understanding of girls' upbringing. The other has to do with the difficulties that the term 'childhood' presents, when applied in reference to girls. The considerable body of scholarship that now exists on girls' upbringing in India and my own attempt to study this subject have convinced me that the concept of socialisation does not convey the intensity with which girls are conditioned, in the routine course of their upbringing, to behave in a certain way. By intensity, I mean the determination with which social institutions, such as the family and kinship networks, act to mould girls to fit a predefined role. Leela Dube (2001) uses the term 'inescapability' to describe the process by which a girl prepares for her destined life as a woman. The metaphor of metal casting comes to mind. In the lost-wax method, the malleable wax is crafted by expert hands to imprint a chosen design on clay that, once fired, will serve as a mould for metal casting. The term 'girlhood' refers to this mould, shaped through culture over the ages, that imprints on the mind of the female child from the earliest stages of development. The idea of imprinting helps us recognise the difficulties we might encounter if we use the term 'childhood' to describe the early part of a woman's life. It goes without saying that we are referring here to a pattern rather than to individual lives, among which there may be many exceptions to the norm.

To use 'childhood' in reference to this early stage of life is to evoke the normative meanings this term has acquired. Childhood, as a concept, originated in eighteenth century Europe, but its normative connotations, especially the idea that childhood is an innocent time to be protected, has spread across the globe since the mid-twentieth century (Kumar 2016). The normative idea that childhood should be a period of freedom, especially freedom from fear, arises from the general theory of citizenship, and in particular, from the idea of child rights. Such an idea is irreconcilable with

* This chapter was first delivered as a lecture in memory of J. P. Naik, at the Centre for Women's Development Studies, New Delhi, 24 April 2016.

the pattern we notice when we study the everyday lives of small girls. The cultural metallurgy I mentioned earlier ensures that girls internalise knowledge about the lived experience that is exclusive to them.

WHAT IS EDUCATION?

We will return to the subject of girlhood, but let us first talk about education and ask a direct question: What is education? I will attempt an answer by drawing on a corpus of knowledge that has developed, over the twentieth century, on the nature and growth of the human mind. Of course, this corpus is not without its debates and ambiguities, but there are topics on which consensus has been established, especially in the understanding of how children think and learn. Based on the literature, we can give the following answer: education is a means to obtain entry into the social world while ensuring existence in the physical. The 'physical' and the 'social' are not simply two dimensions of the milieu into which a child is born; rather, they are two forms that the milieu takes. The key difference between them is that the physical milieu is visible or tangible, while the social milieu is not. In its physical form, the milieu can be perceived by the senses. But in its social form, the milieu has to be discovered, and this discovery requires knowledge and skills. Human children must understand for themselves how the social milieu impinges on them and their lives.

Why do the two milieus differ in this manner? The reason is that the physical milieu exists and is composed of elements living in the present, whereas the social milieu is composed of elements that have been shaped by a past that borders the present. No one can see the past, or how the social milieu was shaped right up to the present moment in which the child stands. Only with the help of an imagination trained to notice and understand the shaping of the social milieu can the child discover and grasp it. This is the task that education must accomplish if it is to be distinct from socialisation. Socialisation takes place without the child's mind being specifically aware that it is being inducted into the social world. Education, on the other hand, subjects the entrant to all the demands that consciousness makes on cognition. The process of education can, thus, diminish the ineluctability of the social world, by revealing to the learner's eye that the social world has a long past in which it evolved by virtue of human effort.

TENSION BETWEEN HOME AND SCHOOL

This analysis points to a necessary tension between socialisation at home and education at school. While the home provides knowledge necessary for the child's induction into the social world and their adjustment to it, the school deals with different domains and kinds of knowledge that are not necessarily consistent with the knowledge acquired at home. While some kinds of knowledge acquired at school may promote acceptance—or even an appreciation—of the social world that the family presents, other kinds may sow seeds of dissatisfaction and questioning, thereby undermining the family's role in preparing the child to adjust to the social world, along with its norms and values. We are not interested just now in the quality of education that a school might provide under certain systemic conditions. We are referring to the school as an institution, to which society has assigned the task of empowering the young to access knowledge in different fields and understand it. At times, curricula show signs of having been designed to indoctrinate.

Often, the knowledge or subjects covered in curricula have messages or ideas that might unsettle young minds because they contradict what is taught at home. This is one reason why education sometimes has unanticipated consequences. Our definition of education suggests that the process of educating children's imaginations and intellectual energies will be able to attain its true potential only if the school enjoys a certain degree of autonomy in its functioning. I am referring to the autonomy with which teachers interpret knowledge, the methods they use to teach and assess and the resources that the school provides. The greater the autonomy, the greater the chances that the school will educate, in the sense indicated by our earlier discussion.

State's Instinct and Role

In modern times, the school functions as an institution of the state. The particular kind of state is irrelevant; regardless, all present-day societies seem to have delegated the task of education to the state. For instance, if we consider the historical origins of the state in India, we recognise the unmistakable stamp of colonialism. As discussed in *Politics of Education in Colonial India* (Kumar 2013a), colonialism is both an ideology and a set of practices. As an ideology, it entails a particular kind of relationship between rulers and the people they rule. The colonial state apparatus was designed to maintain law and order and to speedily re-establish it when it broke down. This remains the primary function of the Indian state, even as other functions have emerged and accrued over time. These other functions arise from the value framework of the Constitution and are generative in nature.

There is a gap between these generative functions and the older, dominant functions. For this reason, the Indian state behaves as a psychologically split organism, divided between instinct and consciously made choices. The primary instinct is to control; this powerful instinct makes the state chronically apprehensive that ordinary people might leave its control. The colonial perception of the 'native' population has shaped the state's view of the so-called masses. This perception exacerbates the state's apprehension of losing its control. The conscious part of the state's decision-making processes is motivated by more benign feelings towards ordinary people and operates with a differentiated view of the population. These benign feelings include the awareness that ordinary people are capable of behaving like responsible citizens. The idea of a citizen who has a stake in the state's functioning has acquired a kind of half-life: it drives the political side of democracy, while governance remains an exercise in control.

The state's difficulty in engaging with people's cultures arises out of this split. Historically, 1857 is considered the landmark moment when the colonial state decided to distance itself from cultural matters. In the following 90 years before Independence, the colonial state handled social policy with restraint and caution; laws that dealt with cultural practices like child marriage were vaguely worded and difficult to implement. The use of the term 'child' in the phrase 'child marriage' carries a wider connotation, not necessarily of colonial origin. The tendency is to equate boys with girls, both being children, thereby overlooking the vast differences between their lived experiences, in the context of their social existence in the family and community. The M. V. Joshi Committee (1928–29), which examined the consequences of child marriage, presented a vast amount of medical and other evidence, demonstrating how painful and horrific little girls' experiences of marriage can be (Rathbone 1934). We can hardly compare these experiences with those of boys who are married during childhood.

The gender neutrality of this law arose more from the colonial state's sense of its own limitations. Colonial relations between the state and society, in particular in matters dealing with women, were characterised by a specific and studied caution. The argument for this caution was that women represent the core of culture. However, such a perception allowed public policy to essentialise women's lives and matters pertaining to women. In effect, the state adopted the male perspective and left the patriarchy undisturbed, to be reinforced in new forms under the regime of modernity. In education, the cautionary stance—on matters designated as culturally sensitive—meant promoting girl-specific curriculum policies. A strong continuity between home and school came to be regarded as a prerequisite for spreading girls' education. Under this approach, the school would not do anything that might weaken the norms, knowledge, and self-identity cultivated through socialisation at home.

Today, this approach remains a tacit policy and a common perspective. Non-discrimination between boys and girls means overlooking the lives that girls lead at home and the reality of their daily experience of negotiating the distance between home and school. The girl who walks through the school gates wearing her uniform does not leave behind the girl whose life at home is defined by custom and ritual and the demands and expectations of her family and community. The two girls inhabit the same body, but they lead contrasting mental lives. The secular knowledge dispensed by the school to both boys and girls acquires different meanings for the two sexes, reconstructed by their gendered selves to serve their culturally assigned roles in life. It is imprinted on the girl's awareness that her body must serve as her primary form of agency, both instrumentally and symbolically. The meaning that school knowledge acquires for a boy cannot be compared with what it might mean to a girl, who has already internalised culturally approved perceptions of her body's primacy and instrumentality.

Levels of Fear

Fear and preparedness for submission are deeply etched in socially-sanctioned girlhood. Fear must be located within the broader framework of a desirable female life to be lived under the patriarchy. This broader perspective enables us to distinguish three levels of fear. In my recent book, *Choori Bazaar Mein Larki* (Kumar 2013b), I attempted to map the archaeology of fear in a girl's mind using these three levels. On the surface, fear operates in terms of injuries to the body that might deface it. This is important for us to grasp because of the implication it has for infancy and early childhood, especially in the context of play. The power of play to absorb the young in the joy of sheer physicality loses its relevance if the parental gaze conveys anxiety about the distant consequences of an injury caused by vigorous play. Girlhood means learning to be afraid of these consequences with reference to matrimony. Mahadevi Verma (1999) used the metaphor of merchandise to describe a girl's body. The merchandise must stay intact while it awaits a customer.

At the next level, fear manifests in sexuality. Internalising the fear of being violated takes many forms and requires the communicative gaze of the adult but, in this domain, the gaze is surrounded and assisted by the vast and varied powers of mythology, its representation and celebration. The helplessness experienced by Draupadi and, under different circumstances, Sita's ordeal, are among the powerful mythological depictions of fear that girls must internalise in their journeys towards becoming acceptable women. The mythical representation of fear reiterates its importance and postulates that it can be managed by accepting a dependence on men. This lesson is relevant to the third level of fear, which refers to a fear of independence and freedom. Fear of freedom ensures that the self is fully merged with or dissolved into socially authorised identities. The absence or weak presence of a personal self (Gupta 2015) has significant consequences for the motivation to pursue and sustain personal goals.

These consequences of early or primary socialisation at home present a formidable problem for education; however, the problem never translates into a challenge. This is because the state—as the custodian and manager of education—is historically conditioned to practise reluctance whenever it is required to engage with culture (Kumar 2010). For the state, equality between the sexes means the balanced presence of boys and girls in the classroom. Their differing experiences of education are not acknowledged in the state's documents. Thus, in an arithmetical sense, equality has been achieved. In matters related to curricula, textbooks, and teacher preparation, the state has made a certain effort to focus on girls without addressing girlhood, that is, the culturally constructed life of girls. Neither male nor female teachers are equipped to deal with the conflicts and contradictions that arise in the annual calendar and in everyday school life between the aims of education and girlhood. While education implies the pursuit of aims chosen by a girl, girlhood implies the pursuit of matrimony and motherhood as the highest aims of a woman's life. The school has little interest in a girl's life at home. By practising neutrality or non-discrimination between boys and girls, the school overlooks the consequences of the lives they lead at home. It also ignores the layers of fear—including terror—sculpted into girls' inner, mental worlds by cultural imprinting using mythological and folk narratives, customs and rituals. The small number of girls who either escape this imprinting or manage to use their education to gain freedom quite often find themselves in the role of Abhimanyu, the young hero of the *Mahabharata*, who had to fight a battle by himself. Girls' education can take credit for producing a few thousand Abhimanyus, who have symbolic, inspirational value for many others. For the vast majority, education is a pleasant memory, of a time inside the walls of a school or college where girls experienced freedom from terror during the day.

A New Alliance

The role of education may shrink and be tougher to implement in the foreseeable future, on account of a growing alliance between custom and capital. This alliance between market and culture is tightening its grip on girls' lives, thereby giving new strength to girlhood. Socialising the girl into an acceptable woman by facilitating her internalisation of the body project is an agenda shared by market and custom. From the market side, partners include the various industries involved in producing body-merchandise and electronic media, where this merchandise is advertised and promoted. Television and cinema are also involved in seeking girls' cooperation and active participation—by exercising her agency—in the body project. Assertive consumption of objects and services associated with the body reinforces the culture of girlhood. It is a travesty, not unusual for our times, that girls' co-option in the body project is interpreted in certain quarters as evidence of their agency.

The parents of a little girl in an elementary school have bought a dressing table for her. She has learnt to use eyeliner and knows how to choose the right colour of lipstick to match her dress. With peach-pink blush on her cheeks, she preens as she looks at herself in the mirror. Her parents watch admiringly as she totters towards them in her high-heeled shoes. Many of her classmates wear similar attire in an annual event at her nursery. Thus, her long educational journey has begun.

References

Dube, Leela. 2001. *Anthropological Explorations in Gender: Intersecting Fields*. New Delhi: Sage.

Gupta, Latika. 2015. *Education, Poverty and Gender*. New Delhi: Routledge.

Kumar, Krishna. 2010. 'Culture, State and Girls: An Educational Perspective'. *Economic & Political Weekly* 45 (17): 75–84.

———. 2013a. *Politics of Education in Colonial India*. New Delhi: Routledge.

———. 2013b. *Choori Bazaar Mein Larki*. New Delhi: Rajkamal.

———. 2016. 'Studying Childhood in India'. *Economic & Political Weekly* 51 (23): 12–14.

Rathbone, E. A. 1934. *Child Marriage: The Indian Minotaur*. London: George Allen and Unwin.

Verma, Mahadevi. 1999 [1937]. *Srinkhala Ki Kariyan*. New Delhi: Rajkamal Prakashan.

4

Is Equality an Outdated Concern in Education?

Sadhna Saxena

In the post-Independence period, girls' and women's education received much-needed comprehensive attention in the National Policy on Education (NPE) 1986 (Poonacha and Gopal 2004; National Focus Group 2007b). The persistent unequal participation of girls in schools, the pressure of rising women's awareness and movements in India, and international compulsions and commitments compelled national and state governments to formulate compensatory schemes for enhancing girls' participation in education. Some of these schemes cover all girls, while others target girls from disadvantaged communities only. Such schemes may seem in contradiction to the equal educational opportunity and the meritocracy principle or doctrine that the 1966 Kothari Commission and NPE 1986 had affirmed. However, as 'social classes do not come to the market as equals' (Halsey et al. 1997: 257), mere equal educational opportunities do not ensure a level playing field. Compensatory policy decisions seem necessary for the pursuit of equality and justice. Such decisions are 'grounded in an awareness of deep-rooted inequalities and injustices...stem from a history of oppression' (Velaskar 2010: 63). It is generally accepted that in a society like India, which is patriarchal and stratified on caste, class, religious and ethnic lines, girls, especially those from the subordinated groups, would require compensatory measures for inclusion in formal education.

Briefly, the present compensatory schemes include distribution of free uniforms and textbooks to all the girls up to elementary levels, various scholarships on a merit basis up to the secondary and higher secondary levels, and special scholarships for all Scheduled Caste (SC) and Scheduled Tribe (ST) girls. Additionally, there is the mid-day meal scheme and free schooling up to elementary levels for all children. Madhya Pradesh and Bihar have been providing bicycles to SC and ST girls who have to travel long distances for their next level of schooling.

The state of Delhi has also introduced a conditional cash-transfer scheme called Ladli Yojna for girls from Below Poverty Line (BPL) families. A fixed cash amount is deposited annually in the girl's bank account. This scheme has been introduced to encourage higher education among girls and the amount is given on completion of schooling, after the girl is 18 years old. In addition to all these schemes, the state governments also run hostels for SC and ST girls and boys.

The Kasturba Gandhi Balika Vidyalayas (KGBVs), which aim to offer quality education to girls from SC, ST, Other Backward Classes (OBCs), minority and BPL communities of the Educationally Backward Blocks (EBB), also comprise a significant central government scheme, which has generally been appreciated and hailed by educationists. The scheme was launched in 2004 and has been expanded to more than 3,000 blocks so far. The need for such a scheme has been justified on the basis of the lack of participation of girls from these communities in education, reflected in the below national average female literacy rates, high dropout rates and higher gender literacy gaps. However, since the scheme is only for EBB and for not more than 100 girls per block within EBB, it raises concerns about the impact on the larger issue of low participation of girls in education at the national levels.

POLICY FORMULATION AND TRANSLATION

These state policies could be analysed from two perspectives: the implementation perspective, which is the transaction of policy at the field level, and by looking at the policy itself in a larger context. Drawing a distinction between policy formulation and actual 'translation' at the ground level, Ball (Mainardes and Marcondes 2009) describes the negotiation from the 'word' mode to the 'action' mode, which is another level of policy analysis.

Velaskar (2010), on the other hand, emphasises inadequacies in the field of policy research, which is largely confined to examining policy implementation and measuring its effects in terms of goals and targets set by the policy-maker and financier—in other words, by the state. Typically, conventional policy research in India rarely engages with the articulation of the problem in the policy, the nature of the state, the political context and the policy framework as such. As Velaskar argues, policy discourses and processes are deeply political phenomena, 'and hence the production of policy must be located within the dynamics of social structural power relations in specific historical contexts' (Olssen et al. 2004, as quoted in Velaskar 2010: 60). This chapter reviews the KGBV scheme, an important compensatory policy intervention from the above two perspectives—the translation of the policy and in the larger educational context, a critical engagement with the policy itself.

Based on the Government of India (GOI)-commissioned National Evaluation Reports (Sarva Shiksha Abhiyan [SSA] 2007, 2008 b), a state-level United Nations International Children's Emergency Fund (UNICEF 2010) study, direct observation of KGBVs and other writings on the subject, the first part of the chapter provides an insight into the translation of policy. It includes a review of the infrastructure and other facilities, such as human resources, the process for the selection of students, their positive experiences, alienation and problems of adjustment due to the clash of worldviews between the middle-class functionaries and girls' own lives, quality of teaching and learning, working conditions of residential teachers, issues related to their autonomy and their relationship with local authorities, etc. Also, the review underlines the need for deeper insight into classroom transactions, teachers' academic preparedness and learning outcomes, given the quality thrust of the scheme.

The second part of the chapter reviews the contribution of this policy towards equality and equity, within the context of debates on equal educational opportunity and substantive equality. This section briefly notes the debates on the dialectical relationship between education and social change and argues that such schemes further confirm the abandonment of equal educational opportunity, thus weakening the justice goal. It seeks to engage with questions such as the following: What has been the nature of the policy shift in the last five to six decades, from the policy doctrine of equal educational opportunity and compensatory measures, to special schemes for a few? Why have KGBV-type minimalist policy interventions not provoked discussion about the government sidestepping its proclaimed and much-publicised aim of providing quality schooling to all the children? Why are facilities in all state-run schools, where the majority of girls go, not at par either with the Navodaya Vidyalayas or model schools or KGBV schools? Most importantly, does the focus on and visibility of such special schemes camouflage the appalling condition of the majority of government schools?

Policy Implementation

The policy of opening residential schools and hostels has always been perceived as a solution to unequal access of potential rural students residing in remote areas. Tribal and social welfare (now social justice) departments of the state run ashram-*shalas* (residential schools) and SC/ST hostels for children of these communities. Various SC/ST commissions, committee reports and research studies have provided crucial insight into the functioning of these schools and hostels. Detailed observations of *ashram* schools document the appalling living conditions, bad management, inefficiency, nepotism, corruption and poor standards of education. The hostels are also afflicted by similar problems, including overcrowding, unhygienic living conditions, poor quality of food, prevalence of diseases, malnourishment and absence of medical facilities for the residents (National Focus Group 2007a).

The UNICEF (2010) abridged report, based on a study of the status of girls' education in Madhya Pradesh, also documents the lack of decent living conditions in seven randomly selected girls' SC/ST hostels. The detailed report on the above study (Saxena et al. 2009) states that all the seven hostels had acute problems of overcrowding, dilapidated buildings and the complete absence of sanitation, security and medical care. There were no proper cooking facilities, the quality of food was bad and the quantity woefully inadequate. The abysmally low-paid hostel staffs indulged in pilferage that further deteriorated the quality of food and other facilities. In almost all the seven hostels, there were 50–100 girls residing in one or two small rooms with leaking roofs, with only two or three shared bathrooms and toilets, without water and electricity. For example, in one of the hostels, the study reported that (ibid. 2009: 158):

> The roof of the building leaks and girls are protected only by tarpaulin during monsoons. There were buckets all over the room to collect rainwater from the leaking roof. There was only one bathroom for 100 girls. Since the hostel doesn't have a boundary wall, drunken men often enter the hostel, abuse the girls and ask for money.

In another hostel (ibid.):

> For 77 girls, there was only one room. It was a dark and dingy room with girls' luggage, mattresses, pillows and sheets scattered all over. The room had one bulb and one fan. ... These girls were from 7 villages located 3–7 km away, all of them were from BPL families and belonged to ST, SC and OBC categories...There were only two functional latrines and two bathrooms....

Ironically, many reports and studies have also documented that these hostels are in demand due to the shortage and inaccessibility of schools. However, the appalling living conditions are not conducive to a learning environment, defeating the very purpose.

Against this backdrop, KGBV, a flagship scheme of the GOI, is perhaps a refreshing and welcome idea. Though the scheme was launched in 2004, in 2007 it was included in the Sarva Shiksha Abhiyan (SSA) programme as a separate component. The scheme claims to offer a second chance for mainstreaming rural girls from deprived backgrounds, in particular those who could not continue their education beyond Class V or dropped out even earlier and require extra academic support to return to formal education. Under this scheme, such girls are enrolled in Class VI and offered bridging courses to cope with the academic requirements of that class. The central government bears all the expenses for setting up and running the KGBVs, including living and educational expenses of students up to Class VIII.

There are three models for KGBVs—hostel-cum-school for 100 girls (Model I), hostel-cum-school for 50 girls (Model II) and hostel for 50 girls, with teaching arrangements in a nearby middle school (Model III). The scheme provides for opening one school per selected block. The block selection is based on backwardness in terms of education indicators, like below national-level female literacy rates and adverse female school-dropout rates.

Funds are provided for the construction of the building and other infrastructure, like furniture for classrooms, office, library and living rooms, including pillows, mattresses, sheets and blankets; kitchen equipment, including refrigerator, utensils, cookers, gas stoves, storage vessels; and for clothes, stationery and books for all the residents. Compared to ordinary government schools and SC/ST hostels, KGBV schools are much better endowed, though they are not at par with the Navodaya Vidyalayas. Kumar and Gupta (2008) are critical of KGBVs' secondary status compared to Navodaya Vidyalayas, in terms of budgetary allocations, and express concern about the curriculum, content, pedagogy and the status of teachers appointed.

INFRASTRUCTURE AND OTHER RESOURCES

The Ministry of Human Resource Development (MHRD)-commissioned National Evaluation Reports (SSA 2007, 2008b) on the KGBV scheme, based on field visits to 12 states, are very informative. Though the reports seem laudatory and have commented only on the implementation aspects, without reflecting on the policy, they do throw light on the functioning of these institutions and underline the unevenness in operationalisation on the ground. The reports document issues regarding resources, facilities and infrastructure, such as living conditions and learning ambience, which range from excellent to appalling. For example, there are KGBVs with inadequate space for sleeping, cooking and teaching. The study records that sometimes three classes are held in the same room; girls sleep on the floor as either there are no beds or no space to keep beds. There is a shortage of bathrooms, toilets and water, which is reported from almost every KGBV, except Punjab.

The reports also document the problem of girls' alienation, homesickness, breakdowns, hysteria and isolation. On the health front, the reports are disconcerting, to say the least. During the visits, many girls were found to be suffering from scabies (skin) and gastrointestinal diseases, due to shortage of space and water, unhygienic living conditions and the lack of nutritious food. The situation had worsened because most KGBVs lack access to adequate medical and security facilities.

These reports also discuss issues related to lack of warden autonomy, routine teaching methods, untrained or inadequately trained teachers and reinforcement of gender stereotypes through extracurricular activities like sewing, pickle-making, embroidery, tailoring, etc. Some of the reports have recorded evidence of the strengthening of gender stereotypes and Hinduisation through the recitation of mantras before meals, in some of the KGBVs.

The Madhya Pradesh UNICEF report (Saxena et al. 2009) documented the experience of five randomly selected KGBVs across five districts. *Sanchalan Nirdesh 2007–08*,[1] the government guidelines for running KGBVs in Madhya Pradesh, have laid down elaborate preconditions for opening a KGBV. These include close access to medical facilities, adequate residential facilities with electricity for all the residents, including separate facilities for the hostel staff; at least four bathrooms and four toilets for the girls, tank for storing water and motor and pump for lifting water; library, telephone, computers, internet connection, laboratory and sports materials; provision of beds, mattresses, sheets, blankets, clothes, sweaters, towels, undergarments, sleepers, comb, school bags, books, stationery, etc., for every girl.

However, shockingly, the learning ambience and living conditions in these KGBVs were not very different from the SC/ST hostels in the state. The KGBVs were located either in panchayat *bhawans* or in dilapidated school buildings with broken doors and leaking roofs, or in small dingy rented rooms. All these buildings were without ventilation, adequate sanitary facilities and security staff. Contrary to the guidelines, none had regular water supply, electricity and access to medical facilities. Acute shortage of basic facilities like water, toilets and bathrooms forced girls to either bathe only once in a while, or for four to five girls to bathe together, or bathe in the open. For defecation, they had to use an open drain (*nala*). In all the KGBVs, 50–100 girls managed in two-three small rooms, without any arrangements for keeping their belongings, including their study materials. All such items were either scattered or piled up on one table in most of the KGBVs. Due to shortage of space, the same rooms are used for dining, for holding classes and sleeping. Either there were only a few cots, forcing two-three girls to share one cot, or there were none, forcing girls to sleep on the floor. The following excerpts from two KGBVs perhaps sum up the fate of the residents (Saxena et al. 2009: 154):

> For 88 girls, there were only two toilets with attached bathrooms. The doors were broken and rugs were tied for privacy. There was no sweeper and therefore the toilets were never cleaned. Even the bathing space and the space between the two bathrooms was used as urinals.... The girls used open space for washing clothes and utensils and since there was no drainage, the dirty water collected there...There was a make-shift arrangement for the kitchen in the open...Due to acute water shortage water had to be purchased and so the girls were able to bathe only twice in a week even during summer months.

In another KGBV, the study reported that (Saxena et al. 2009: 154):

> There was no electricity. There were four bathrooms and toilets, but without any taps. There were no beds or mattresses for the girls and so they had to sleep on floor even during rainy season, under leaking roof. There was water logging in the playground where scorpions were found. One girl was bitten by a scorpion and the warden called a tantric for Jhad-phoonk.

Interestingly, based on government guidelines, better buildings were constructed for all seven KGBVs, but these were not handed over to them due to the wrangling between the Public Works Department (PWD) and the Education Department. Meanwhile, the condition of some of these buildings has deteriorated beyond repair.

Contrary to this, both the KGBVs in Rajasthan had excellent infrastructure and beautiful campuses, with segregated and well-demarcated spaces for residential blocks, classrooms, library, kitchen, dining room, warden and other staff's residence, etc. These too, however, did not ensure quality education. There were serious problems with the selection procedures. This and other related issues are discussed in the latter part of the chapter.

EMOLUMENTS FOR TEACHERS AND OTHER STAFF

Despite the commendable objectives of the KGBVs, 'to ensure access and quality education to the girls of disadvantaged groups of society' (SSA 2008a:1), it is clear from the National Evaluation Reports (SSA 2007, 2008b), Saxena et al. (2009) and Saxena (2011) that across states, the teachers—the main providers of quality education—and the non-teaching staff of KGBVs are paid pittances for their services, violating even the minimum wage rules. Even this low wages/honorarium is not paid on time as the National Evaluation Report and Madhya Pradesh study records. In some of the KGBVs, teachers and other staff were not paid for months.

All the above documents, as well as Kumar and Gupta (2008) and the Fifteenth Joint Review Mission (JRM) Report 2012, express serious concern about the teachers' low emoluments (SSA 2012). Yet, curiously, the case of KGBV teachers has never been discussed in the context of the larger reality of changing teacher recruitment policies across states. In fact, in the past two decades, under neo-liberal conditionalities, many states in India have been employing contractual teachers on a large scale, against permanent posts. By not locating the status of teachers in a KGBV in the larger context of World Bank conditionalities (Welmond 2002), not problematising this in the context of the increasing thrust on privatisation, demonising teachers and breaking up their unions in anticipation of possible stiff resistance (Ayers and Ayers 2011) and ignoring the international discourse (Brown et al. 1997; Whitty 1997), an immense disservice is being done to the teaching profession.

The recent large-scale protests by contract teachers who were lathi-charged in Chhattisgarh (covered by ETV Chhattisgarh channel on 5 November 2011) and in Punjab (covered by NDTV on 5 December 2011)[2] highlight the grim reality of the service conditions of KGBV teachers across states. There has been enough evidence of turmoil in this sector for the past two decades, which rarely draws the kind of attention it deserves (Saxena and Mahendroo 2004).

In accordance with this policy, the KGBV wardens, with round-the-clock duty hours and posts equivalent to the head of middle school, are surviving on meagre salaries of Rs 4,000 to Rs 5,000 per month, on contract basis! The wardens of both KGBVs of Rajasthan were paid much higher emoluments, Rs 9,000 per month, yet this was still far lower than the regular salary. Both these wardens said that their contracts may not be renewed and they may have to leave soon after having worked hard to establish these institutions, even at the cost of neglecting their own families. They wondered if it was at all worthwhile to invest so much energy into setting up institutions that did not offer any job security or continuity.

Incidentally, the warden is the highest-paid employee of KGBVs. The cooks and watchmen are paid between Rs 1,500 and Rs 2,500 a month! In the name of providing opportunity to girls of the subjugated groups, these professionals are facing the worst kind of inequality.

Quality of Education

More importantly, there is no evidence that these KGBVs are providing quality education. The lack of thrust on academic aspects at policy levels is evident from the low or no priority given to teachers' professional development, to help them handle the multiple academic challenges that they encounter. The greatest challenge is to bring the girls, who left school a few years ago, up to Class VI level through a bridge course. Sometimes, the girls who come to KGBV have forgotten even the basic literacy skills, according to the National Evaluation Report.

These reports and other documents that have been referred to have expressed serious concern about the curriculum, books and the routine pedagogy followed in the classrooms. Even excellent infrastructure and dedicated teachers and wardens could not ensure better teaching in the Rajasthan KGBVs. Class observations in the two KGBVs in Rajasthan clearly showed the teachers' lack of academic competence, as they were unable to handle Classes VI–VIII Social Science, Science and Mathematics. They also seemed unsure while handling girls who had forgotten even their basic literacy skills. These preliminary observations clearly underline the urgent need for a systematic review of the teaching and learning processes in KGBVs.

THE NEO-LIBERAL CONTEXT, PATRIARCHY AND ALIENATION

The scheme has also generated a debate regarding efforts that amount to state surveillance of girls of subordinated classes. There is silence on the critical interrogation of linkages between the increased attention towards girls' enrolment and schooling, neo-liberal economic policies and their impact on land and livelihood issues, and the 'oppressive social and economic hierarchies that these children's communities inhabit' (Balagopalan 2010: 297). Issues such as the alienation of girls from their communities, the imposition of middle-class values at the cost of undermining their own values, the focus on gendered life skills rather than on liberal education, etc., have also been cause for serious concern amongst some educationists. Commenting on the KGBV scheme, Balagopalan (ibid.) is also critical of the fact that the state constructs children as easily isolatable from the poverty of their families and communities and shifts the blame for their not attending schools on the families and the traditions of communities, thus signalling the 'progressive nature of its efforts' (ibid.: 299).

The state obviously cannot be allowed such an escape. However, the family and community as upholders of patriarchal values that obstruct girls' education should also not be overlooked. Girls enjoy living in hostels, as this opportunity is perceived as an escape from the oppressive family and community patriarchy, but they also feel alienated and homesick. Several government and non-government reports on education also claim that access to education raises the age of marriage. However, helping them avoid child marriage does not necessarily empower girls to challenge the authority and structures of inequality. Also, there is little knowledge about which new 'patriarchies' the girls encounter in hostels. In all probability, one kind of authority is replaced by newer forms. Therefore, alienation, isolation, freedom and newer forms of patriarchal control constitute the complex reality of the girls residing in hostels. Have KGBV institutional processes been able to challenge or even acknowledge these structures of authority that are responsible for persisting gender inequality? That is the moot question that demands critical interrogation.

SELECTION CRITERIA OR THEIR ABSENCE

Looking at the residential and other facilities (not necessarily the quality of teaching) at this KGBV, many parents said that they would also like to send their daughters there, but have no idea who gets selected and how (Saxena 2011).[3]

Of the 9,245 girls enrolled in KGBV hostels in MP, only 57 were from the Muslim community, due to the bias the community faces (UNICEF 2010: 58).

The National Evaluation Report also expresses deep concern about the bias in the selection process. The reports record that in most districts where the fieldwork was conducted, there seemed to be no way of reaching out to the out-of-school girls and there was little effort to include girls from Dalit, minority and BPL categories. In many of the KGBVs, girls were either from the same or nearby villages. Many were not even school dropouts, but regular students.

Most importantly, there were very few minority and BPL students and in many KGBVs there were few SC/ST students, disproportionate to their percentage in the general population. For example, in one block where the KGBV is being run by a Christian non-governmental organisation (NGO), there were only Christian girls. Similarly, in both the KGBVs of Rajasthan, there were only ST girls, though there were SC and minority populations in both blocks. Wardens of both KGBVs were evasive about the selection process and, after much prodding, said that girls are selected through awareness campaigns. On being asked how and by whom these campaigns were organised and how people from remote tribal areas came to know about these, the wardens did not offer any direct reply. However, they gave indications of their complete lack of autonomy and the block educations officers' total control over every decision, including the selection of girls. Barring a few exceptions, girls in these two KGBVs were also from nearby villages. Given the policy of privileging and planning for a small percentage of girls per block, at the cost of excluding the majority living under similar conditions, the selection process is bound to be non-transparent.

NGO vs. Government

Finally, according to the JRM 2012 (SSA 2012: A11), there are about 3,435 running KGBVs and total enrolment is about 3.18 lakh. The JRM 2012 report also appreciated the efforts of CARE and Mahila Samakhya in running the KGBVs in some of the states. While the UNICEF (2010) documents the miserable living conditions and learning environment in five randomly selected KGBVs of MP, all run by the MP Education Department under SSA, Saxena (2011) discusses the excellent physical infrastructure and other facilities in the KGBVs of two blocks in Rajasthan that are run by NGOs. The National Evaluation Report also gives indications that NGO-run KGBVs have better infrastructure.

All of this may not constitute adequate evidence to arrive at the general conclusion that NGO-run KGBVs are better managed, but all the same, there are indications to suggest that. Does this mean that the government department is not competent to run such institutes? According to KGBV guidelines (SSA 2008a: 2), there is a provision for corporate groups to adopt these residential schools, for which separate guidelines are to be issued. Considering the fact that such initiatives have serious implications for the government school system, a thorough discussion is warranted, but that is beyond the scope of the present chapter.

KGBV and Inequality

There are two issues that are looked at in this section. The possible implications of the KGBV scheme on the equality agenda is the first, which is discussed from the perspective of the dialectical relationship between school education and social transformation. The second issue entails examining the emergence of the KGBV type of scheme within the framework of the history of education and major policy deviations in the last five decades. In this context, the KGBV goals, as reflected in the guidelines, are also analysed.

Education and Social Transformation

Equality of educational access—through expansion, equal opportunity and positive discrimination—and the possibility of achieving social equality through education, have been issues of sociological engagement from the middle of the twentieth century (Karabel and Halsey 1977; Shukla and Kumar 1985; Velaskar 2010). In this context, the fundamental issue of whether education is a potent tool to challenge and change structural inequalities, or if it can only reproduce and strengthen the dominant ideologies and social and economic inequalities, has also been intensely debated. According to Halsey (1985: 82), 'a society of equals has to be created by economic and political reform and that the role of education must largely be to maintain such a society once it has been attained'.

But does this imply that in modern times, schools can be ignored in struggles for equality? In Karabel and Halsey (1977), there is discussion of the 1972 *Inequality* report by Christopher Jencks. They agreed with Jencks that the economy is the key arena of struggle, but also emphasised that '[S]chools do not turn "inputs" into "outputs" but instead shape the personalities who pass through them'; therefore, the report is, 'mechanistic rather than dialectical in its relegation of schools to marginality' (1977: 26).

Commenting further on the report, they said:

> Though it brilliantly demolished the peculiarly American myth that school reform can serve as a substitute for more fundamental social change, Inequality may unfortunately have replaced it with another equally destructive myth: that a viable strategy for social equality can afford to ignore the schools (ibid.).

The emergence of critical and conflict theories that challenged the mere reproductive role of education further emphasised the complex but critical relationship between social change and education.

However, abandonment of the equal educational opportunity, along with compensatory measures, may subvert any potential of social change through education. A universal demand for quality-for-all may gradually be replaced with competition for gaining entry into the special schools. Thus KGBVs, on the one hand, divide the children of the deprived and subordinated groups into KGBV and non-KGBV groups. But the scheme also introduces another level of opacity by subverting the selection process, as discussed in the policy implementation section. By introducing competition and divisions, instead of addressing the quality concerns of all the children, the link between education and struggle for justice may be seriously endangered.

Displacing Equal Educational Opportunity

The Constitution of independent India was rooted in liberal ideology and committed to the values of liberty, justice and equality. In the context of education, this meant following the principle of equal educational opportunity for all and additional compensatory measures for communities that were historically oppressed and exploited. As stated in the beginning, the basis for such state action was rooted in the recognition of the deep injustices and inequalities that these communities had faced for generations, due to which they enter the education system with multiple inequalities and disadvantages.

However, despite Constitutional Directives for educating all children up to the age of 14 and special care for children of the weaker sections, in concrete terms, elementary education remained a neglected area till the Education Commission (EC) was constituted in 1964. To accomplish the vision of equal educational opportunity, a two-pronged strategy was recommended: massive expansion of state-run, free, lower-primary and upper-primary schools and the establishment of a common school system.

Interestingly, although there was an overt endorsement, the actual translation of this vision of the EC into policy and action, especially the common school system, met with stiff resistance from the upper-caste and class leadership. The only acceptable form of equal educational opportunity was a free, state-run system of elementary education and its expansion. Further cementing the two-tier system, what emerged were government-run free schools for the subordinated people and an elite private system for the powerful. Due to non-allocation of adequate resources for elementary education, the expansion was inadequate in numbers and quality. Therefore, with limited and declining budgetary allocations, in a vast and unevenly developing country like India, the expansion of the state-run and free school system also took a widely divergent path, resulting in inequality, imbalance and inadequate expansion (Velaskar 2010).

The beginning of liberalisation in education, in the context of the opening of the Indian economy, started with the NPE 1986, which laid the ground for external dependence. Its thrust towards privatisation, inadequate allocation of resources for expansion and opening of Navodaya Vidyalayas for the rural elite resulted in further stratification of the government school system, making it more inegalitarian and multi-layered. The unequal and parallel system created for the Adivasis, Dalits, the children of the migrant populations and people living in rural areas, included the setting up of alternative schools. The revival of the much discredited non-formal education centres, as part of the expansion strategy, further exacerbated inequality. The NPE 1986 policy was the beginning of the abandonment of equal educational opportunity, one of the main strategies for achieving equality and justice through education, argues Velaskar (2010). Further, schemes for the establishment of the model district schools, for nurturing the talent of rural disadvantaged children, meant that 'quality for some' gained precedence over 'quality for all', in line with the demands of the rural elite (Kumar 1985).

With the downsizing of the welfare state and the focus on markets in India in the 1990s, the Indian state collaborated with international funding agencies, who changed the political economy of education. The government implemented education reforms that followed the conditions laid down by global actors. The decade was marked by the launch of a new World Bank-funded programme of elementary education, called the District Primary Education Programme (DPEP), which further marginalised the equal opportunity agenda in terms of its objectives. The DPEP guidelines, a very carefully worded GOI publication, clearly stated that the DPEP was the 'operationalisation of NPE 1986' based on 'national experience'. It was a time-bound (five years) specific intervention programme. The programme aimed to reduce the dropout rate and gender disparity in achievement and enrolment, but was not committed to the creation of equal educational opportunity and did not aim for universalisation (Kumar et al. 2001).

Post-DPEP, the inegalitarian school system has been further stratified by creating more layers of schools, including education guarantee schools, budget private schools and in the name of quality, district-level model schools and KGBVs for a chosen few, as opposed to expanding quality government schools for all the children. There is also a further policy thrust on promoting privatisation through public-private partnerships and a voucher system, in the name of choice (Saxena 2010). Commenting on these developments, Velaskar (2010) writes that, with a rise in the number of substandard schools, access may have gone up, but the experience of meaningful learning has gone down for disadvantaged people.

Clearly, over the past six decades, the doctrine of equal educational opportunity and compensatory measures for marginalised communities has been replaced by a multi-layered, inegalitarian school system and an increase in resource-starved government schools, in addition to special schemes that are based on the principle of exclusion of most children. A clear subversion of the constitutional commitment to equality and justice is evident here.

The KGBV scheme is an illusionary measure that tries to cover up such policy subversions by expressing concern about girls' education and the rhetoric of quality. More importantly, it is illusionary because special attention for a few is disguised by statements on the general problem of quality and participation of all girls. These efforts, too, remain minimal. The implementation clearly shows that there is a world of difference between the 'word' mode and the 'action' mode.

KGBV Guidelines

The KGBV guidelines are an acknowledgement of two problems: First, there are areas where a large number of girls are out of school: 'there remain significant gaps in the enrolment of girls at the elementary level as compared to boys, especially at the upper primary levels' (SSA 2008a: 1). And second, 'gender disparities still persist in rural areas and among disadvantaged communities' (ibid.). The guidelines also emphasise that the objective of KGBV is 'to ensure access and quality education to the girls of disadvantaged groups of society by setting up residential schools with boarding facilities at elementary level'.

The objective seems to voice concern for all girls from educationally backward blocks, not a select few, though the policy of opening KGBVs in selected blocks and only for 50–100 girls per block belie such a hope. There seems no convincing rationale or logic behind formulating a scheme privileging a chosen few over thousands of out-of-school girls. For instance, according to the Block Education Officer's report, the number of school dropout girls at the elementary levels in Jhadol block of Rajasthan, which boasts of one well-equipped KGBV, was 6,336 in the year 2009–10 (Saxena 2011).

Similarly, the detailed state-level evaluation reports, on which the National Evaluation Reports (2007, 2008) are based, record that Bankura district of West Bengal has 13 blocks. Even if each block has a Model I KGBV, not more than 1,300 girls could be enrolled in these. The number of school dropout girls in the district was 19,693 in the year 2006–07. Similarly, Purulia district with 20 blocks had 39,711 dropout girls. In the 15 educationally backward blocks of the eight districts of Assam, there were 11,162 dropout girls in 2006–07. Assam had adopted Model II of KGBV and under the best of circumstances, there could not have been more than 750 girls in these KGBVs.

With such staggering numbers and limited seats, the selection process is bound to be non-transparent and bring added distortions in the pursuit of equality. In reality, the KGBV is not a scheme that is trying to make the government system egalitarian and accountable. KGBVs are actually meant for privileging a few and ignoring the rest—the majority of the girls from the communities it proclaims to benefit. Can exclusivity and equality go hand in hand? Is not the policy itself exacerbating inequality amongst the deprived? Do such schemes not turn the equality in education debate on its head and instead encourage inegalitarianism, competition and exclusivity amongst these communities?

Unlike Navodaya Vidyalayas, the privileging here is not even based on 'merit', which too is problematic. Instead, in all probability, it is based on patronage. The visibility and glamour for a few poor girls, who constitute a small fraction of the total number of out-of-school girls, with access to hostels, clean environment, and 'quality education' obfuscates the issue of equal educational opportunity by rendering the majority of the dropout girls invisible. It is time that educationists see beyond the glamour of all such schemes that cater to a minuscule population of the disadvantaged and demand expansion, better facilities and quality education in all the government schools.

As discussed above, the relationship between education and social justice or substantive equality is a complex one. Therefore, it is important to understand how inadequate educational opportunities further erode the possibility of equality and justice.

Conclusions

When there is a policy that addresses the quality and access concern of a select few, excluding the majority, there are bound to be distortions. For quality improvement in schools, one cannot depend on selective criteria, because they tend to take the focus away from the general state of affairs. Does that mean that in principle, the state should never be formulating the schemes for setting up 'model schools'? The answer is both 'yes' and 'no', depending on the long-term goals. If such schools are run with the objective of experimenting with innovative ideas and are based on experience and mainstreaming these ideas, then maybe yes. No, if the objective is to run a few quality schools based on the principle of exclusion, which diffuses the larger reality.

Additionally, the struggle for demanding quality government schools, with adequate infrastructure and qualified teachers for all, has to be relentless and such starry policies/schemes diffuse the focus. Otherwise, there is the danger of a patronising narrative—of at least some children receiving access to better facilities—overtaking the rights discourse.

NOTES

1. See 'Kasturba Gandhi Sanchalan Nirdesh Varsh 2007–08' by the Rajya Shiksha Kendra, Bhopal.

2. During a protest march in district Mukhtsar by contractual teachers calling for regularisation of their services, a woman teacher, Barinder Pal Kaur (from Bhatinda district), was slapped by a male sarpanch of the ruling Akali Dal.

3. Saxena (2011) is an unpublished report based on the study of two KGBVs in Rajasthan in September 2011. This small study was facilitated by the Udaipur-based organisation Seva Mandir.

REFERENCES

Ayers, Bill, and Rick Ayers. 2011. 'Education under Fire: Introduction'. *Monthly Review* 63 (3). http://monthlyreview.org/2011/07/01/education-under-fire-introduction. Accessed on 11 November 2011.

Balagopalan, Sarada. 2010. 'Rationalising Seclusion: A Preliminary Analysis of a Residential Schooling Scheme for Poor Girls in India'. *Feminist Theory* 11 (3): 295–308.

Brown, Phillip, A. H. Halsey, Hugh Lauder, and Amy Stuart Wells. 1997. 'The Transformation of Education and Society: An Introduction'. In A. H. Halsey, Phillip Brown, Hugh Lauder, and Amy Stuart Wells, eds, *Education: Culture, Economy, and Society*, pp. 1–44. New York: Oxford University Press.

Halsey, A. H. 1985. 'Sociology and the Equality Debate'. In Sureshchandra Shukla, and Krishna Kumar, eds, *Sociological Perspectives in Education*, pp. 80–101. New Delhi: Chanakya Publications.

Halsey, A. H., Hugh Lauder, Philip Brown, and Amy Stuart Wells. 1997. *Education: Culture, Economy, and Society*. New York: Oxford University Press.

Karabel, Jerome, and A. H. Halsey. 1977. *Power and Ideology in Education*. New York: Oxford University Press.

Kothari Commission. 1966. 'Report of the Education Commission 1964–66: Education and National Development'. New Delhi: Ministry of Education.

Kumar, Krishna. 1985. 'Quality over Access: Responding to the Demand of the Elite'. *Economic & Political Weekly* 20 (22): 948–49.

Kumar, Krishna, Manisha Priyam, and Sadhna Saxena. 2001. 'Looking behind the Smokescreen: DPEP and Primary Education in India'. *Economic & Political Weekly* 36 (7): 560–68.

Kumar, Krishna, and Latika Gupta. 2008. 'What is Missing in Girls' Empowerment?'. *Economic & Political Weekly* 43 (26–27): 19–24.

Mainardes, Jefferson, and Maria Ines Marcondes. 2009. 'Interview Stephen J Ball: A Dialogue about Social Justice, Research and Education Policy'. *Educação and Sociedade* 30 (106). http://www.scielo.br/scielo.php?pid=S0101-73302009000100015&script=sci_arttext&tlng=en. Accessed online on 8 October 2012.

National Focus Group. 2007a. 'Problems of Scheduled Caste and Scheduled Tribe Children'. Position Paper 3.1, National Council of Educational Research and Training (NCERT), New Delhi.

———. 2007 b. 'Gender Issues in Education'. Position Paper 3.2, NCERT, New Delhi.

Olssen, M., J. Codd, and A. O'Neil. 2004 *Education Policy: Globalisation, Citizenship, Democracy*. London: Sage Publications.

Poonacha, Veena, and Meena Gopal. 2004. *Women and Science: An Examination of Women's Access to and Retention in Scientific Career*. Mumbai: Research Centre for Women's Studies.

Saxena, Sadhna. 2010. 'Para Teachers, Education Guarantee Scheme, and PPP: Road to Dismantling the Public Education System'. In Manoranjan Mohanty, ed. *India Social Development Report 2010: The Land Question and the Marginalised*, pp. 88–100. New Delhi: Oxford University Press.

Saxena, Sadhna, and Kamal Mahendroo. 2004. 'Changing Profiles of School Teachers'. Presented at National Seminar on Strategies and Dynamics of Change in Indian Education, jointly organised by CARE India and the Institute of Applied Manpower Research, 25–27 November, New Delhi.

Saxena, Sadhna, et al. 2009. 'Status of Girls' Education in Madhya Pradesh', unpublished report, UNICEF, Bhopal.

———. 2011. 'Report on Field Visit to Two KGBVs in Rajasthan'. Udaipur: Seva Mandir.

SSA. 2007. 'National Evaluation Report on Kasturba Gandhi Balika Vidyalaya'. New Delhi: MHRD.

———. 2008a. 'Revised Guidelines for Implementation of Kasturba Gandhi Balika Vidyalayas (KGBVs)'. Department of School Education and Literacy, MHRD, New Delhi. http://ssa.nic.in/girls-education/6_FCEED7DF.pdf/view. Retrieved on 25 October 2012.

———. 2008b. 'National Evaluation Report on Kasturba Gandhi Balika Vidyalaya'. MHRD, New Delhi.

———. 2012. 'Fifteenth Joint Review Mission, 16th–30th January 2012: Aide Memoire'. http://ssa.nic.in/monitoring/jointreview-mission-ssa-1/joint-review-mission-ssa. Retrieved on 25 October 2012.

Shukla, Sureshchandra, and Krishna Kumar, ed. 1985. *Sociological Perspective in Education: A Reader*. New Delhi: Sage.

UNICEF. 2010. *Girls Education: A Sociological Perspective*. Bhopal: UNICEF.

Velaskar, Padma. 2010. 'Quality and Inequality in Indian Education: Some Critical Policy Concerns'. *Contemporary Education Dialogue* 7 (1): 58–93.

Welmond, Michel. 2002. 'Globalisation Viewed from the Periphery: The Dynamic of Teacher Identity in the Republic of Benin'. *Comparative Education Review* 46 (1): 37–65.

Whitty, Geoffrey. 1997. 'Marketisation, State and the Re-formation of the Teaching Profession'. In A. H. Halsey, Phillip Brown, Hugh Lauder and Amy Stuart Wells, ed. *Education: Culture, Economy, and Society*, 299–310. New York: Oxford University Press.

5

THE NEW SEGREGATION

*Reflections on Gender and Equity in Primary Education**

VIMALA RAMACHANDRAN AND AARTI SAIHJEE

It is commonly believed that the 1990s was one of the most productive decades in primary education—a decade not only of tremendous churning, but also one where the country made a significant leap in literacy rates. While India still has a long way to go before we are able to ensure good quality basic education for all children up to the age of 14, even the worst of the sceptics will agree that the decade was one of optimism: the 2001 Census revealed that 65.4 per cent people (75.85 among men and 54.16 among women) are now literate and that, for the first time, the absolute number of illiterates actually went down. It also revealed a decadal jump of 11.8 in the literacy rate among men and 15.00 among women; Chhattisgarh recorded a jump of 24.87 in literacy levels among women, Madhya Pradesh a 20.93 jump in female literacy and Rajasthan a jump of 21.47 (M) and 23.90 (F) in literacy levels. A number of programmes were initiated during this period, most notably the DPEP (District Primary Education Programme), and the government mobilised considerable external funds for primary education.[1]

While all this is indeed credit-worthy, dissenting voices tell us that all is not well. Primary education is not only about formal access and literacy rates. It may be recalled that the National Policy of Education (NPE 1986) stressed that the central issue was 'removal of disparities and to equalise educational opportunity by attending to the specific needs of those who have been denied equality so far'. The focus was both on education and social equality. The Programme of Action (POA 1992) correctly highlighted the intervening and empowering role of education in

---

* This chapter is based on a published research study: Vimala Ramachandran, ed., *Gender and Social Equity in Primary Education Hierarchies of Access*. New Delhi: Sage Publications, 2002. The study on which this book is based was funded by the European Commission office in New Delhi, in 2002–2003. We are grateful for their support. At the time of writing this paper, Aarti Saihjee worked with the Educational Resource Unit (Jaipur and Delhi).

people's struggles for equality and justice. The question before us now is whether the decade of the 1990s has made a difference to those who have been left out or pushed out of the education system.

This chapter, based on a study on the experience of the DPEP titled 'Hierarchies of Access: Gender and Social Equity in Primary Education' (Ramachandran 2004), attempts to capture the impact of primary education programmes on the ground. The study started by acknowledging the historical baggage of social and economic inequalities that has reinforced educational disparities for over 50 years in India. Ploughing through data generated through the Census (1991 and 2001) and National Sample Surveys on the one hand and education department statistics (EMIS and PMIS of DPEP) on the other, we realised that most data fail to capture social and gender gaps in education. Our research team took on board the problems associated with relying on gross enrolment data, particularly from schools and the education department, since they are marked by a tendency to over-report. Instead, we tried to look at net enrolment, retention, transition and average years of schooling data disaggregated by gender, social grouping and type of school (unfortunately not always available), so as to assess the effectiveness of policies. We tried, wherever possible, to complement this data with information on dropouts and on those who have never attended school (Visaria and Ramachandran 2002).

Our hunch about the inadequacy of existing data was confirmed and we further observed that even the DPEP's own gender and social equity indices seemed to be caught in a quantitative warp, and was hence unable to adequately reflect the existing gender and social disparities in education across the length and breadth of the country. We decided to supplement the desk review of the DPEP data and project information with six qualitative micro-studies, to explore in-depth the underlying motivations, feelings, values, attitudes and perceptions of ordinary parents, teachers, children as well as the community regarding primary schooling and the impact of the DPEP in transforming them. We examined if gender and equity issues had been 'mainstreamed', or whether they remained sporadic and localised. This led us to analyse if and how equity strategies were positioned in the programme and whether EGS/AS (Education Guarantee Scheme schools/Alternative Schools) is fast emerging as the vehicle to bridge the equity gap—especially with respect to children from disadvantaged communities and in scattered habitations. An important focus of our research related to a subtle but nevertheless discernible hierarchy of access in education, resulting in new forms of segregation in primary schools.

This chapter is based on our findings from the desk review of DPEP and qualitative micro-studies in six DPEP states—Madhya Pradesh, Chhattisgarh, Andhra Pradesh, Haryana, Karnataka, and Tamil Nadu (Ramachandran 2004). The introductory section briefly focusses on the DPEP, especially with regard to its strategy to achieve gender and social equity in primary education. Section II reviews the available statistical data on primary education and maps out the success and failures of the last decade in primary education, with special emphasis on girls and other marginal groups. Section III, on the basis of the statistical review as well as other documented evidence, introduces the emergent concept of 'hierarchies of access' to describe the new segregation occurring in primary education; whereby a child's caste, class, and gender seem to be defining the nature of the school they attend—government primary schools, AS/EGS, or private schools—and its implications for the process of teaching and learning, as well as achieving the larger stated objectives of gender and social equity. Section IV further unravels the 'hierarchies of access', by shifting the focus onto the micro-studies and extensively documenting the tangible and intangible dimensions of gender and social equity, which frame the implementation of the DPEP at the village and panchayat level. It specifically focusses on the persistent inequalities of gender, caste, class and community that often define educational outcomes in their varied guises—often old and sometimes new—even as universal primary education becomes a reality, as opposed to a dream. The penultimate section draws from both the desk study and the micro studies and suggests ways to reverse the trend of segregation, in order to move ahead and make universal primary education a substantive reality. The last section, by way of a conclusion, is a summing-up exercise and highlights the social and gender equity dimensions that frame primary education today.

DISTRICT PRIMARY EDUCATION PROGRAMME

The DPEP was initiated as a part of the larger Social Safety Net Credit Adjustment Loan, under the Structural Adjustment Programme of the World Bank to India, in 1991. Taking off from the policy guidelines in NPE 1986 and drawing upon the experience of a range of primary education programmes, the DPEP Guidelines of 1994 state that holistic planning and management are necessary to achieve universal primary education and that it 'should incorporate a gender perspective in all aspects of the planning and implementation process'. It recognises the importance of mainstreaming gender and making it an integral part of the DPEP, the need for gender focus in tackling the problem of access, retention and achievement levels, and the importance of reaching out to children from the most disadvantaged groups/communities. Educationally backward districts, with female literacy below the national average, were taken as the priority districts. Equally, the project stressed education for socially disadvantaged groups. The goals set by the DPEP are:

- Reduce differences in enrolment, dropout and learning achievements between gender and social groups to less than 5 per cent;
- Reduce overall primary dropout rates for all students to less than 10 per cent;
- Raise average achievement levels by at least 25 per cent over measured baseline levels, by ensuring achievement of basic literacy and numeracy competencies and a minimum of 40 per cent achievement levels in other competencies for all primary school children; and
- Provide access for all children to primary schooling or its equivalent non-formal education.

These goals bring out the programme's intent to increase coverage of girls, improve their academic achievements and reduce gender disparities with respect to enrolment, retention and learning achievements (DPEP 2000c). Essentially,

DPEP adopted a two-pronged strategy to meet the gender and social equity goals, namely:

- Make the education system more responsive to the needs and constraints of girls and children from disadvantaged communities, and
- Create community demand for girls' education and enabling conditions for greater participation.

In pursuance of these objectives, DPEP created monitoring systems and structures to track gender and equity issues. The information and monitoring system of DPEP consisted of the following:

- Project management information system (PMIS) to capture inputs—teacher deployment, civil works, training, research completed, expenditure and reimbursement—thereby tracking both physical and financial information;
- District information system for education (DISE) to capture enrolment, teacher deployment, classroom and performance indicators like Gross Enrolment Ratio, Net Enrolment Ratio, repetition rates, student classroom ratio and pupil-teacher ratio. The data was to be disaggregated by gender and SC/ST; and
- Bi-annual joint review missions, research studies and, most recently, household surveys to estimate the number of out-of-school children, to enable the government and donor partners to assess progress towards short-term, medium-term and long-term development objectives.
- The DPEP MIS cell, based in NIEPA, developed the Index of Gender Equity and Index of Social Equity to track the progress towards gender and social equity objectives, and this continues to be a mandatory exercise in reporting on progress.

DPEP is currently operational in 18 states and 271 districts, after taking into account recent bifurcations and trifurcations in districts and the carving out of three new states. Twenty-three districts of Gujarat, Orissa and Rajasthan were included very recently, that is after April 2001.

Overwhelming Finding

The overwhelming finding that emerged from the desk review of reports and data on education in the 1990s is that there has been a significant increase in overall literacy rates and school participation rates across the country. Gender disparities have declined, with an overall increase in school attendance.[2] This is more than confirmed by the Census 2001 data and also the recent NFHS-II (1998–99) data. Perhaps the most significant change that has taken place in the 1990s is the increase in the demand for primary education across the country. Intensive campaigns, enrolment drives, and the changing social and economic situation have contributed to an appreciable increase in the demand for schooling.

There has been a decline in the proportion of never enrolled children. Data also reveal an increase in the number of schools across the country—AS, EGS, and private-aided and private-unaided schools. DPEP was initiated in low female literacy areas, and it is encouraging to note that very low female literacy districts have shown the maximum gains in literacy levels—especially in MP, Chhattisgarh and Rajasthan (Census 2001). The share of girls to total enrolment, in very low female literacy districts, increased from 43.8 per cent in 1995–96 to 46.7 per cent in 1998–99 (Aggarwal 2000a and 2000b).

While this is indeed an encouraging trend, the data also indicates that we still have a long way to go before gender and social gaps are bridged. As Yash Aggarwal (2000a) points out:

> While household enumeration has been conducted in many DPEP districts/state to identify out-of-school children, the findings are not available in most of the cases... The NSS estimates (52nd round data, 1995–96) indicate that 31 per cent of children in the 6–11 age group were not attending school... availability of schooling facility even within the habitation does not offer any guarantee that all children in the eligible age group attend school.

This observation is reinforced by Vaidyanathan and Nair (2001): 'While the narrowing of spatial disparities suggests that educationally poor areas have experienced, in general, relatively rapid improvements, scrutiny at a more disaggregated level (talukas and villages) reveals the existence of pockets of persistent educational backwardness.'

A large number of children belonging to disadvantaged communities, working children and children with special needs have not yet been covered (coverage of AS and EGS schools is limited to some regions of the country). DPEP data reveals that this is particularly true of Phase II districts, where participation levels are still very low. Similarly, children living in urban slums and peripheral areas have largely remained outside the reach of DPEP. Without addressing the concerns of urban out-of-school children, the goal of universalisation of primary education (UPE) cannot be achieved in its entirety. Household surveys coordinated in 1997–98 by Vaidyanathan and Nair (2001) further confirm that 'literacy rate variations across space and between gender and caste groups are highly correlated; and that higher overall literacy goes with lower disparities between these groups'. Hence, the more educationally backward the region, the greater are the social and gender inequalities (see Table 5.1).

However, we have yet to generate adequate data on the educational access of disadvantaged groups. While NSS, NFHS, and other sample survey data provide a macro picture, intra-regional and intra-community diversities as such are not captured in such surveys. Further, given the time-lag in the publication of detailed Census 2001 tables, most researchers are still relying on 1991 Census data, which is outdated, particularly in the light of preliminary Census 2001 data that reveals a significant jump in literacy levels. Some specific studies (mostly done before 1993) have addressed the issue of access and performance of marginal social groups. The NCAER data (Table 5.1) indicates the wide fluctuations between the literacy rates for men and women belonging to landless families and Scheduled Tribe and Scheduled Caste households in selected states. For instance, in UP, the overall literacy rates for men and women are 62 and 28 per cent, respectively, and these figures sharply contrast with 38.20 and 7.40 per cent among landless families and 48.10 and 13.80 per cent among the Scheduled Castes.

Table 5.1: Educational Indicators of Select States

Indicator	*Kerala*	*Tamil Nadu*	*Uttar Pradesh*	*Rajasthan*	*West Bengal*	*Maharashtra*	*Orissa*	*Haryana*	*Madhya Pradesh*
Literacy rate (7+)									
Male	93.00	75.00	62.00	60.00	66.00	71.00	68.00	70.00	59.00
Female	87.00	53.00	28.00	19.00	50.00	47.00	41.00	38.00	27.00
Net enrolment rate (6–14)									
Male	99.00	91.00	73.00	78.00	67.00	88.00	79.00	84.00	69.00
Female	98.00	84.00	53.00	42.00	65.00	82.00	63.00	72.00	56.00
Discontinuation rate (6–14)									
Male	1.50	7.50	3.30	3.10	5.90	5.90	6.20	3.90	7.00
Female	2.00	14.80	5.60	6.60	6.90	8.40	9.30	4.60	9.00
Literacy rate of landless wage-earners									
Male	86.50	60.50	38.20	44.00	43.60	54.60	43.00	52.50	40.10
Female	77.90	41.40	7.40	5.60	27.50	29.20	15.70	24.20	14.10
Literacy rate of medium-sized landholders									
Male	98.40	89.30	80.50	63.70	83.80	70.1	85.90	72.50	64.20
Female	92.70	49.70	41.60	19.80	68.60	49.40	55.70	39.10	28.20
Literacy rate of large landholders									
Male	98.60	87.80	83.10	65.90	93.40	84.20	87.10	72.80	73.00
Female	100.00	61.10	53.80	21.40	84.30	51.40	64.20	45.30	37.60
Literacy rate of STs									
Male	–	–	–	39.10	–	52.90	40.70	–	42.80
Female	–	–	–	7.50	–	25.20	15.60	–	16.80

(Contd)

Table 5.1 (Contd)

Indicator	*Kerala*	*Tamil Nadu*	*Uttar Pradesh*	*Rajasthan*	*West Bengal*	*Maharashtra*	*Orissa*	*Haryana*	*Madhya Pradesh*
Literacy rate of SCs									
Male	82.60	57.30	48.10	51.80	62.50	60.50	60.40	60.10	47.40
Female	72.20	37.40	13.80	9.10	46.00	34.40	29.80	28.90	17.50
Literacy rate of dominant minority									
Male	94.00	85.80	47.10	45.90	59.30	75.60	73.60	84.50	67.10
Female	89.40	67.90	20.20	7.80	44.40	52.10	41.50	59.70	30.30
Literacy rate of other Hindus									
Male	95.00	80.60	70.80	66.40	75.50	76.80	78.40.5	74.00	69.10
Female	87.40	57.90	35.60	23.90	58.80	51.50	2.40	43.10	34.50
Ever enrolment rate of landless wage-earners									
Male	98.40	88.40	52.70	63.10	51.10	77.10	62.20	69.10	54.10
Female	100.00	76.80	25.80	15.20	45.50	72.50	32.20	50.00	39.30
Discontinuation rate of landless wage-earners									
Male	1.70	9.50	5.20	4.10	3.50	6.00	11.40	4.60	9.20
Female	6.10	17.40	4.40	17.20	16.20	12.30	19.80	4.40	13.40

Source: Shariff and Sudarshan (1996).

Researchers have pointed out that 50 per cent of Dalit children who enter primary school leave by Class V, with a majority dropping out before they reach Class III (Nambissan 2001). According to the MODE/UNICEF Report 1995:

> The socioeconomic profile appears to be a barrier to enrolment directly or indirectly. SC/ST families tend to live in colonies removed by a kilometre or more from the main village. A school within walking distance for the families in the main village would still be at a distance to these children. Secondly, a feeling of alienation from the rest of the village and consequent fears (real or otherwise) of discrimination in school may keep these children away from school. At an indirect level, the high incidence of non-enrolment in SC/ST families almost 'legitimises' not going to school and makes it the norm rather that the exception in the community...

The learning environment, attitude of teachers, backstopping support from home/ parents, and the sheer economics of school participation for extremely poor/ landless families—all these factors tend to push children out of school.[3] Dominant perceptions about the mental abilities of Dalit or tribal children, coupled with stereotypes about certain communities, lead to subtle and sometimes even blatant discrimination against some children.[4]

What about girls? Girls' enrolment has made considerable progress and, as revealed in Census 2001, in the more backward regions like Madhya Pradesh, Rajasthan and Chhattisgarh, many more girls are in school than ever before. However, the situation of girls in poor households, among disadvantaged groups, remains a cause for concern. Education may be technically free, but it is not so in reality. Given the quality of government schools, parents also incur some expenditure on tuitions—even though this is more prevalent among children going to private-unaided and aided schools. This has many implications for girls' participation (Bashir 2000; De et al. 2001). While gender is a determining factor at the time of decision-making by parents on whether and where to enrol, independent research studies and DPEP studies reveal that gender inequities and gender bias were not significant among enrolled girl children (De et al. 2001).

Administrators, educational researchers and development practitioners agree that discrimination inside the school continues to be a major barrier in school participation for girls and other marginal groups (Madan 2002). Unfortunately, without the availability of adequate data, it is not possible to make generalisations on push and pull factors in DPEP. With the exception of recent household survey data from Karnataka, the project has not generated any kind of textured micro-data. This continues to be an important lacuna in the DPEP information system.

These extant issues of access and social equity in government formal schools are overwhelming and need to be given constant priority. Issues of equity in education seem to have taken on more complex overtones within the emergent context of declining enrolment in formal government schools, the growth of private schools across the nation and the opening of state-sponsored Alternative Schools and Education Guarantee schemes in some parts of the country. This new development seems to be reinforcing the existing stratification evident in our educational system in rural areas (which so far has been a defining feature of urban areas). Further, what is significant is that it is giving rise to a new trend of 'hierarchies of access', whereby, paradoxically, the democratisation of access to schools seems to be accompanied by a reaffirmation of a child's caste, community and gender in defining which school she or he attends.

To add to the complexity, the accumulating empirical evidence illustrates that while most teachers in private schools are untrained and work under adverse conditions, teachers in the extant government schools or the AS/EGS are ill-equipped to address the needs of first-generation learners. In addition to concerns of quality and standards, what is disturbing is that there is no consistent policy vis-à-vis unrecognised schools. The remainder of this chapter is devoted to exploring the variety of factors that frame these emerging dynamics of 'hierarchies of access' and their implications for issues of equity.

HIERARCHIES OF ACCESS: DEFINING THE PROBLEM

A significant revelation in recent years has been the documentation of a gradual decline in Class I enrolment. As Yash Aggarwal points out:

> Over the years, the enrolment in formal schools has shown declining trends... It is observed that the states, which witnessed slower growth in formal school enrolment, registered faster increase if the enrolment of formal and alternative modes is combined. This is particularly true of Madhya Pradesh... For the 1998–99 and 1999–00 period, as many as 14 districts (out of a total of 40) showed a decline of more than 5 per cent in Grade I enrolment... The decline in enrolment of class I is more alarming for the educationally backward states like Orissa and Assam....A pertinent question at this stage is, where are the children going? (Aggarwal 2000a).

Further, DPEP data also reveals that after a spurt of enrolment in 1995–96 and 1996–97 in DPEP I, Class I enrolment is declining. At the national level, enrolment has remained steady at 110 million for some time now.

While enrolment in government schools has remained stagnant, there is growing evidence of a large number of out-of-school children on the one hand and growth of and enrolment in private schools on the other. This is indeed a disturbing trend—especially in educationally backward regions of the country. Table 5.2 documents that private schools constitute anywhere between 5 per cent and 10 per cent of primary schools in Karnataka, Haryana and UP (and the share increases with higher education), along with AP, MP, and Maharashtra as well. Research studies reveal that while there is a rising demand for primary education across the country and a sharp reduction in children who have never enrolled, there has been a steady growth in the number of private schools, in both rural and urban areas[5] (Aggarwal 2000a; Bashir 1994, quoted in De et al. 2001[6]; Krishnaji 2001[7]; Srivastava 2001). Six per cent of rural children and 19 per cent of urban children, at the primary stage, are studying in private-unaided schools; this proportion goes up when we include the 31 per cent children who are studying in private-aided schools (World Bank 2001).

Among the reasons for the growth of private schools is the reported decline in government school quality (poor infrastructure, shortage of teachers, lack of

TABLE 5.2: Distribution of Primary Schools by Management, 1998–99

Stat	*Government*			*Private*			*Data not Available*
	Department of Education	*Tribal Welfare*	*Local Body*	*Aided*	*Unaided*	*Others*	
Andhra Pradesh	78.11	8.37	4.42	8.69	0.04	0.02	0.36
Assam	96.44	0.87	1.15	0.20	0.13	0.26	0.95
Bihar	97.63	0.21	0.06	1.19	0.04	0.06	0.82
Gujarat	9.86	6.69	79.54	1.88	0.82	0.40	0.81
Haryana	90.83	0.65	0.39	1.27	3.60	0.21	3.05
Himachal Pradesh	97.98	0.28	0.14	0.07	0.07	0.57	0.89
Karnataka	87.05	0.47	1.16	3.43	6.30	0.15	1.44
Kerala	45.01	0.25	3.54	49.86	0.14	0.46	0.74
Madhya Pradesh	66.46	22.43	1.48	1.17	5.32	1.23	1.91
Maharashtra	0.93	1.85	78.53	14.57	3.58	0.13	0.41
Orissa	93.78	3.69	0.55	0.32	0.52	0.28	0.86
Tamil Nadu	13.78	4.36	71.27	10.00	0.16	0.12	0.30
Uttar Pradesh	92.08	0.38	1.23	1.90	2.79	0.57	1.04
West Bengal	8.21	0.23	90.42	0.18	0.03	0.09	0.81
DPEP States	62.43	10.34	19.06	3.96	2.65	0.43	1.14

Source: Aggarwal (2000b).

accountability of government schools, leading to teacher absenteeism and negligence). This gives way to a positive preference for private schools—even though they may have a relatively poor infrastructure, less qualified teachers and are definitely more expensive (Aggarwal 2000a and b; De et al. 2001; PROBE 1999; Vaidyanathan and Nair 2001). The DPEP studies reveal that parents are becoming disillusioned with the overcrowding and poor quality of instruction in government schools and are opting to send their children to private, fee-charging schools. The free education offered by government schools is no longer an attraction (DPEP October 2000). One of the reasons for the disenchantment with government schools is the indifferent attitude of the teachers towards teaching/learning and an uncaring approach to the social and economic hardships faced by students from poor and vulnerable families. These issues are relevant, as 30–40 per cent of the population in educationally backward areas is barely able to meet their survival needs (Aggarwal 2000b). Between 1986 and 1993, the enrolment in private-unaided (recognised) schools increased at a compound growth rate of 9.5 per cent per annum. The corresponding increase in enrolment in government schools was 1.4 per cent per annum. While the contribution of private schools to universalisation of elementary education (UEE) is significant, it raises a whole range of equity issues.

IMPLICATIONS FOR GENDER AND SOCIAL EQUITY

In the last 10 years, there has been growing evidence on a hierarchy of access to primary education—between states, between communities and groups, and between different types of schools. DPEP focusses on improving the access and participation of children in the 6–10 age-group, so that all such children, irrespective of their place of origin or socio-economic background, are able to complete at least five years of reasonably good quality primary education. However, a few recent independent studies that have explored gender and equity questions (De et al. 2001; PROBE Report 1999; Vaidyanathan and Nair 2001) reveal a disturbing picture. Dysfunctional government schools continue to be an area of concern in the more underdeveloped regions of the country. Where children of the more powerful groups shift to private schools, the pressure on government schools declines sharply. While there is a growing demand for primary education, even in UP, Bihar, Orissa and Rajasthan, the ability of the government schools to respond has not been demonstrated as yet. Madhya Pradesh and Andhra Pradesh have shown strong political will to ensure universal access to elementary education, but the same cannot be said for other educationally backward states.

The most compelling evidence has been thrown up in reviews and research studies done under the aegis of DPEP. Yash Aggarwal points out that while there was a rapid increase in enrolment in the formal system in the first two years of the DPEP (phase I districts), 'subsequently most of the increase in enrolment is accounted for in the alternative school system'. Several states also report a gradual decline in Class I enrolment—partly explained by a slowdown in population growth, improvement in the internal efficiency of the system and the increasing preference for private schooling in some parts of the country. Despite the rapid growth in private and aided schools in many areas of the country, it has been noted that the proportion of girls is higher in government schools as compared to private schools. 'The proportion of girls in unrecognised schools was very low as compared to their share in the government schools. The gender bias in school choice by parents is quite evident. Many villagers report that girls are sent to government schools because they are entitled to various types of incentives' (Aggarwal 2000a). Researchers and administrators have also noted the prevalence of discrimination between girls and boys in the choice of schools (Sharma 1999).

As seen in Table 5.3, SC and ST populations are more concentrated in the low female literacy districts and the share of SC/ST enrolment to total enrolment has increased. However, Aggarwal (2000a) cautions: 'Taken together with evidence of increasing enrolment in private unaided (recognised) schools and increasing enrolment in AS/EGS schools, this increase in SC/ST enrolment may not be as encouraging as it seems.' Evidence shows that it is the poor who access government schools—and SC and ST populations are amongst the poorest. Among the poor, it is the most disadvantaged and those living in remote habitations who opt for Alternative Schools. Given that the hardest to reach are the most likely to enrol in government primary schools and that the better-off (at least in most parts of the country) opt for private schools, the *raison de etre* of a government programme should ideally be to respond to the educational needs of the poor. However, as Manabi Majumdar (2001: 384) argues:

> The recent phenomenon (of growing private schools) is obviously an outcome of unfulfilled educational demand of certain relatively affluent sections of society and their dissatisfaction with the low quality of instruction imparted in government and aided schools. The question, therefore, is not about permitting the private sector in education but about promoting it. Is there a case for encouraging the expansion of the private sector at the elementary level?

Such expansion may further accentuate existing social divisions and reduce commitment towards quality improvement in government schools.[8]

TABLE 5.3: Changes in the Share of SC/ST Enrolment by Levels of Literacy

Category of District	*Per Cent Share of SC/ST Enrolment to Total Enrolment by Category*			
	SC		*ST*	
	1995–96	*1998–99*	*1995–96*	*1998–99*
Very low female literacy	15.8	16.7	20.3	23.9
Low female literacy	16.3	17.4	17.2	20.4
Moderate female literacy	22.3	22.9	9.3	11.7
High female literacy	8.9	7.6	3.8	3.0
Average for DPEP I	18.6	19.4	13.4	15.9

Source: Aggarwal (2000a).

CONSEQUENCES FOR TEACHING AND LEARNING

The emerging dynamics of 'hierarchies of access' have important consequences for the process of teaching and learning in the classroom, as it is also defined and created by the larger politics of teacher recruitment, appointment and training. According to Aggarwal (2000a):

> The large share of SC and ST population in DPEP II districts is also associated with low literacy rates in these districts....out of a total of 30 districts in which the ST population was more than 5 per cent, as many as 11 districts showed less than 10 per cent female ST literacy (1991 Census)... In the 66 districts where share of SC population was more than 5 per cent, as many as 29 districts had female literacy varying between 10 and 25 per cent.....Thus most of the school-going children, especially the girls, in these districts will be first generation learners.

Given that the proportion of government schools with a larger concentration of SC and ST students has been steadily increasing, such schools invariably have large numbers of first-generation learners and require more experienced teachers.

An overwhelming message emanating from DPEP studies and the Joint Review Mission (JRM) reports is that many states continue to face a shortage of teachers. This is more than evident in data on the proportion of single-teacher schools, especially in Phase II districts. In the DPEP Phase I districts, the overall share of single-teacher schools has declined from 18.5 per cent in 1995–96 to 14.3 per cent in 1999–2000. But in the DPEP Phase II districts, the proportion of single-teacher schools increased from 14.3 per cent in 1995–96 to 19.1 per cent in 1999–2000 (Aggarwal 2000a).

If the shortage of teachers in general and the proportion of single-teacher schools in particular is analysed in the context of the teacher-student ratio, the emerging picture does not auger well, especially in educationally backward states. On the one hand, according to DPEP data, Himachal Pradesh, Karnataka, Madhya Pradesh and Orissa show a high percentage of schools with less than 20 students per class (the situation is different in multi-grade classrooms/single teacher schools). On the other hand, in states like West Bengal, Assam and Uttar Pradesh, the share of schools with more than 90 students per classroom is high, at times with states like Assam having only one-room schools. According to Aggarwal (2000b), 'There were about 25,553 schools with an estimated enrolment of 6.12 million students for which the Student Classroom Ration (SCR) was more than 90.'[9] Another related issue that is integral to social equity is that most of the single-teacher schools, especially the AS/EGS schools, are primarily frequented by children belonging to the SC and ST community (see Ghosh 2002).

Among the strategies adopted by DPEP to promote girls' participation is the recruitment of female teachers. DPEP data reveals that one-third of the teachers are women (33 per cent or more in Gujarat, Haryana, HP, Karnataka, Kerala and Tamil Nadu; 27 per cent in Maharashtra, 26 per cent in Assam and UP, 25 per cent in MP, 23 per cent in Orissa, 22 per cent in Bihar, 17 per cent in West Bengal and 34 per cent female teachers in MP's DPEP districts). However, given the large number of single-teacher schools, the low distribution of women teachers in such schools is indeed worrisome; in addition, 72 per cent of two-teacher schools are without female teachers. For example, in Tamil Nadu, 86.8 per cent and 89.4 per cent single-teacher schools do not have any female teachers in Phase I and Phase II districts, respectively. However, the picture seems to be slightly better in Alternative Schools, where reports indicate that Assam has 50 per cent, Bihar 100 per cent, Karnataka 10 per cent, Tamil Nadu 25 per cent, UP 62 per cent and West Bengal 25 per cent single-teacher schools, where the teacher is female (DPEP 2000a). Though the presence of female teachers does have an impact on girls' participation, it emerges that functionality of schools is a far more critical factor for participation. Studies reveal that more than the gender of the teacher, it is dysfunctional schools and teacher absenteeism that have a negative impact, as parents are not happy about leaving their daughters unsupervised in school (Srivastava 2001).

FIELD EVIDENCE

The micro-studies conducted in Madhya Pradesh, Chhattisgarh, Tamil Nadu, Andhra Pradesh, Karnataka and Haryana have been instrumental in generating rich data, which highlights the importance of the local context (political, social and economic) within which the DPEP initiatives are implemented and imparts a more textured and nuanced understanding of 'education' in rural India. The methodology adopted for these micro-studies is primarily qualitative and interpretive in nature; it attempts to capture the local dynamics that frame social and gender equity issues in primary schooling in the DPEP districts across the state. The districts were selected by virtue of being the DPEP Phase I districts (with the exception of Andhra Pradesh), as well as for having a sizeable SC/ST population, so as to be able to reflect the social complexity of local contexts. Similar criteria have been used to select the research block as well as panchayat. The selection was done in tandem with state and district authorities; however, the choice of the panchayat was left to the discretion of the principal researcher (with the exception of Madhya Pradesh), so as to preclude any obvious bias (Table 5.4).[10]

TABLE 5.4: Distribution of Schools by Share of SC/ST Children to Total Enrolment

Phase I

State	*60–80 (1999–2000)*	*Above 80 (1999–2000)*
Assam	8.1	30.0
Haryana	7.7	2.8
Karnataka	6.6	5.7
Madhya Pradesh	11.4	15.7
Maharashtra	12.3	14.1
Tamil Nadu	9.2	10.6

Phase II

State	*Above 80 (1999–2000)*
Assam	42.7
Gujarat	28.9
Himachal Pradesh	15.8
Madhya Pradesh	15.4
Maharashtra	23.5
Orissa	23.0
West Bengal	15.7

Source: Aggarwal (2000b).

The studies traverse a broad canvas of experiences in primary schooling that lie between the two extremes mirrored by the ubiquity of dismal statistics in Chhattisgarh and the 'wonderland' of primary education in MP. It is observed that while, at times, the identified issues are played out in a similar manner across diverse contexts, in other instances, the same issues take on completely different hues with different social consequences. It needs to be qualified at this point that although the issues discussed here impact all children to some extent, some children—by virtue of being girls or belonging to certain social groups—experience these events differently and often with severe social consequences. Some of these important issues are as given below:

Prioritising Education

A tangible impact of DPEP has been the accompanying social processes by which 'education' has been lodged firmly in the rural agenda in DPEP districts. All six micro-studies clearly indicate that the local demand for children's education is growing by leaps and bounds. This is not to say that the demand did not exist before, but rather that DPEP, especially through its LSA in MP and Chhattisgarh, as well as similar surveys in AP and Karnataka, has been able to practically isolate the 'out-of-school' children, shine the spotlight on them and in the process tried to convince the larger community of its collective responsibility to educate children, as opposed to letting the burden fall on individual families. Thus, it is not surprising to find that while peer pressure seems to work as an effective mechanism to ensure enrolment and attendance in school in MP, the Chhattisgarh study contrarily observes that 'the increasing emphasis laid on education and on sending children to school by the different government functionaries has made the community "silent" on this aspect (non-attendance), so it even becomes difficult to assess the reasons behind children not attending school'.

Unpacking Access—the New Segregation

Physical access to a functioning school, at least on the surface, has emerged as a non-issue in all the studies except Chhattisgarh, where it is still relevant because of extant dysfunctional GPS (Government Primary School), as opposed to a lack of schools. In large part, access has been eased by the introduction of new GPS' and private schools in the south (TN, AP and Karnataka), as opposed to burgeoning private schools in Haryana and EGS schools in Chhattisgrah and MP. However, there is an urgent need to unpack the term 'access' to schools, since it glosses over several important issues. One such issue is that, within the larger context of universal access, there is an emerging trend whereby children belonging to different social backgrounds are attending different schools. In AP, there is a divide between the Dalit *basti* GPS and the main hamlet GPS and only SC students attend the former school, while the latter has very few SC students. The youth in the SC colony in the AP study were categorical that even if children from the SC colony try to seek admission in the other GPS, they are discouraged and told to attend the school in their own colony. A similar divide is observed in TN, which is made all the more significant by the glaring disparities between the infrastructure of the two schools in favour of the non-Dalit school. In both these studies, local private schools are also vying for students and most of the children who go to these schools are from relatively well-off families, as well as Backward Caste (BC) and Forward Caste (FC) families. In AP, there was no clear information regarding 155 children between the ages of six and 14; according to the *mandal* resource person, they are probably in private schools outside the village. This seems to be a valid assumption, given the fact that six private school buses ply in the research village.

There seems to be a strong belief in rural India that private schools instil discipline, are better organised since each class has a teacher and their main advantage is that the child learns English. Despite evidence to the contrary and the high fees charged, the belief and perception of private schools offering 'quality' education seems to be strengthening and is best illustrated by the situation in Haryana. Enrolment in private schools in the research panchayat reveals the exclusivity of its children in terms of social status as well as a large gender divide. While the village has almost an equal ratio of SC to OBC and forward caste population, more than 90 per cent children in the government school are from the SC community and more than 90 per cent private school-going children are from OBC and forward castes. Despite this high number, the proportion of forward-caste girls is extremely low in all the schools, partly because of a low sex ratio in the age-specific population of the village. This is particularly noteworthy among the forward castes—Bishnoi, Jat Sikhs (*jat*) and Mehta (*bania*) communities. It is now well-documented that sex ratios among the forward communities in Haryana are particularly skewed against girls. According to Mahajan, the phenomenon of the missing FC girls from village schools can also be attributed to their enrolment in 'convent' private schools of the nearby town, which have a transport pick-up facility. The Karnataka study too highlights the growing lure of private schools and yet, at the same time, also captures the struggle between the schools to establish their credibility in the community, especially when the local GPS can boast of similar or more facilities than the private school and is supported by the village power elite.

A different manifestation of the new dynamics of school segregation is evident in MP where the newly introduced EGS schools are primarily attended by the ST community, while the locally dominant Kurmi community (OBC) sends its children to the GPS. The issue of segregated schools is also further complicated by the presence of a separate girls' primary school (a consequence of the political negotiations by the Kurmi community), which not only reinforces the parallel school systems in the village, but also reflects the socio-cultural attitudes of the different social groups. The segregated GPS' mainly cater to the OBC community and allow for the education of Kurmi girls, while the co-educational classes of the EGS/AS are more reflective of the relaxed gender norms evident in tribal communities. Despite the lack of tangible evidence regarding the 'performance' of the different schools, local perceptions and opinion clearly consider the GPS to impart 'quality' education in comparison to the EGS, and as more 'suited' to the needs of the OBC children. In an interesting turn of events, the Chhattisgarh study turns the dichotomy evident in MP on its head; the EGS schools here are monopolised by the OBC and the tribal elite, whereas the dysfunctional local GPS' have been transformed into the preserve of the poor tribal population.

Given the above empirical evidence, it is becoming apparent that the democratisation of access to schools is ironically being accompanied by a reification of a child's caste, community and gender in defining which school he or she attends. This development has considerable equity implications since it seems to be further reinforcing the stratification already extant in the Indian educational system. What is of particular concern is that in the absence of objective criteria to actually rank these schools (with the probable exception of Chhattisgarh), the emerging social ranking seems to reflect larger social divisions in society and are primarily contingent on 'who goes to school where'.

Reaching the Hardest to Reach

Despite universalising access, several special groups of children still remain hard to reach and constitute the majority of school children. These groups are identified in the different studies as child workers, special needs children and adolescent girls. The child workers have been targeted primarily through the concept of Alternative Schools, with the intention of mainstreaming them in existing formal structures. These groups are most prominent in AP, Haryana and Chhattisgarh and actually fall in the category of 'indentured labour'. In AP, it is observed that most of the boys who are out of school are part of a system of bonded child labour called '*jeetagallu*', where the boys are bonded to well-off families for agricultural work. The boys work at home, grazing livestock. According to Jandhyala, 'The use of the term of out-of-school children has tended to gloss over the issue of the existence of bonded children in the village. It is when we spoke to teachers and community that the problem came to light.' Although the AP government has identified strategies to mainstream out-of-school children by running bridge classes through non-residential centres at the habitation level, residential bridge camps, community campaigns and drives and a closer monitoring at the village level of the out-of-school children, it is observed that the *jeetagallu* consistently fall through the cracks. For instance, the cohort analysis reveals that among boys, there are five dropouts. Of these dropouts, two have gone back to being bonded labour. At the time of writing, the researcher was informed that there are still about 32 children in the SC colony who are out of school. They include eight girls and 26 boys, 21 of whom are bonded labour. What makes the issue more complicated is the fact that the practice is not exclusively observed in inter-community relations and is also documented between SC families. One of the reasons why the issue of bonded labour is not able to draw special attention is that it is seen as the responsibility of the mobiliser attached to Non-Residential Bridge Course (NRBC) and not the primary schoolteacher. Since the current mobiliser is wearing multiple hats at the moment (he is the designated teacher at the NRBC and also teaches the lower classes in the primary school), he is unable to do anything about it.

Similar experiences are reported from Haryana. Vandana Mahajan observes that there is a clearly visible practice of child labour, which has not been addressed at all by the school, Village Education Committee (VEC) or the Cluster Resource Centres (CRC) and Block Resource Centres (BRC). During discussions with the Class V boys in the GPS, the issue of child labour bonded/contracted to local landlords emerged as an important area of concern. Several young boys (in the 11–14 age-group) are given away as Pali to the landlords, on a yearly contract of Rs 3,000 to Rs 5,000 (plus food, some grain and clothes). They do a range of household and farm work and some are enrolled (on paper) in the AS school. Although the teachers in the GPS were at pains to explain that child labour is no longer a problem in their village, there was enough circumstantial evidence of its prevalence, brought out during our interactions with and visit to the poorer and SC communities in the village. According to the head teacher's own rough estimate, presently there are 100–50 '*palis*' in the village. These children are from the SC community and work as *palis* in the landowning GC families in the same village. The Chhattisgarh study also mentions the presence of such a practice, though it does not document it in detail. There is no doubt that the issue of equity takes on a new dimension with the presence of child labour—both within inter- and intra-community interactions.

A glaring absence of strategies to cater to the special needs of children with disabilities is observed in all the research panchayats, with the exception of AP. AP is the only study that highlights the state's acknowledgement of the needs of disabled children. This is primarily because Warangal is one of the districts selected for a pilot initiative for Integrated Education by the DPEP. The IED initiative in the research panchayat started in 1999 and a survey was undertaken to identify the 'special needs' children (five handicapped children in the SC colony, of which two are hearing impaired, two are mentally challenged [one of whom is also physically handicapped] and one has behavioural problems). Currently, only one hearing impaired girl in Class IV and one mentally challenged boy in Class V are in school, while the physically handicapped boy with learning disabilities is enrolled in the NRBC. For the remaining children, records show that they are enrolled, but are not attending school. While the identification has been done and aids provided, especially to the hearing impaired and physically disabled children, teachers are not equipped to deal with the special needs of these children, especially those with learning difficulties. Despite this, these children seem comfortable and well-integrated in regular classrooms and it was observed that other children interact comfortably with them. There was little evidence of any support provided from the *mandal* resource group that was formed to help and assist the teachers to deal with these special needs; the effort being made was primarily an individual choice, facilitated by the fact that the current headmistress has a daughter with a speech impediment and hence was sensitive to the issue. This is a far cry from MP where, despite the initiatives at the district level, the concept of disability itself is unclear, or Chhattisgarh, where the discourse on special needs is absent.

Infrastructure

The DPEP's gender and equity strategies included improvement of school infrastructure and provision of toilets for teachers and students. It was argued that improving school infrastructure could have a positive impact on enrolment and retention of children in school. The six micro-studies confirmed that overall improvement in school infrastructure and facilities does make a difference. Conversely, lack of proper infrastructure—like the broken-down building of the GPS in Chhattisgarh—exerted a negative influence on teachers, students and the community. Low attendance, lack of interest among teachers and indifference of the community were linked to the crumbling school building. In Tamil Nadu, poor facilities (one-room thatched building) of the school in the Dalit hamlet were cited as proof of discrimination. A dirty swamp surrounded even the new building, constructed recently by the Adi Dravida Welfare Board. The hand-pump and toilet were right in the middle of a cesspool. These differences between schools within the same village raise doubts in the minds of the poor about the government's intention to provide equal opportunities to all, irrespective of caste, community or economic status.

Another interesting thread that runs through the six micro-studies is the issue of toilets. In almost all the schools, availability of toilets was perceived as being unimportant, at least at the primary stage, for children (girls and boys). Toilets in schools were mostly used by the teachers. Discussions with children revealed that they do not see toilet facilities as an encouraging or inhibiting factor in school attendance. On the other hand, availability of drinking water was an important issue—hand-pump, well or access to water from a bore-well. In Chhattisgarh, the EGS school children fetched water from a well that was considered 'dirty' and a few children were sent to the primary school (about a kilometre away from the EGS school) to fetch water from the hand-pump for the teachers. In all six panchayats, children in government primary schools did not bring any water bottle with them, but almost all the children attending private schools (observed in Haryana, Tamil Nadu and Karnataka) were seen carrying water bottles and lunch-boxes with them.

Inside the Classroom

Classroom processes, child-centred learning and pedagogic renewal are issues that have received a considerable amount of attention in DPEP. While a considerable amount of work has been done in this area, a coordinated and multi-dimensional approach (simultaneous work on curriculum, textbooks, teacher attitudes, pedagogic renewal, teacher-pupil ratio) has not been followed evenly in all DPEP I districts. This unevenness is clearly reflected in the six micro-studies.

While almost all the teachers interviewed in the course of the micro-studies have participated in DPEP training workshops, not all of them are convinced about the value of child-centred pedagogy. Many of them have not internalised the spirit of the new approach and seem to apply 'techniques' mechanically. For example, in Tamil Nadu, the teachers were familiar with the new approach, but were not convinced—one of them used his cane to order children to sing! A few continued to use the stick. In Karnataka, the teachers' familiarity with the vocabulary and techniques did not always lead to change in classroom processes, but corporal punishment has definitely come down and there was little fear associated with school. This was also the case in Haryana and Madhya Pradesh. There was no evidence of impact in Chhattisgarh.

In most of the panchayats visited, there was not much change in teacher attitudes towards girls and children from very poor/socially disadvantaged groups. It is not that teachers discriminated against all girls—social class, cleanliness and performance also influenced behaviour. There was a clear bias in favour of the better performers and relatively better-off children (it must be noted that most of the children coming to government schools are from poor communities). The double impact of gender and social status was evident in the attention given to children by the teachers, allocation of work in the school, seating and in classroom interaction.

Discussions with teachers in all the six panchayats revealed that there was not much understanding of the family circumstances and special needs of first-generation learners. Similarly, teachers have little appreciation for the work burden of children and their inability to devote time to studies when they get back home. In particular, the teachers were not sensitive to the predicament of girls putting in several hours of work in the house, or the problem of boys who graze cattle before coming to school. They seem to dismiss such children as low performers or bad students.

Discussions with the teachers did not reveal periodic or ongoing academic support given by the block, cluster or *mandal* resource centres. For example, in Andhra Pradesh, the *mandal* resource person is engaged in checking enrolment in the school and non-residential centre—thereby playing an inspectorial role, rather than an academic one. In Chhattisgarh, the BRC and CRC were guardians of data and records and again did not seem to provide sustained or regular academic inputs.

Another interesting revelation was the minimal use (if any) of Teaching Learning Materials (TLM) in the classroom. In some areas, funds for TLM have been discontinued in the academic year 1999–2000.

VEC and Community Participation

Community participation has been an integral part of DPEP vocabulary. However, all six micro-studies reveal that it is synonymous with the VEC or SBC (or any other formal committee instituted for Alternative Schools). These committees are the primary interface between the school and community, and evidence from the field indicates that they either do not function, or seem to function with a mechanical intensity, rather than a genuine sense of participation and commitment. The VEC is dysfunctional in Chhattisgarh; the last meeting had been held more than a year ago, and the records do not include signatures of members. The resolution, which was supposed to have been approved in previous meetings to repair the school building, has not been carried out. In Haryana, the functioning and responsibilities of the VEC are restricted to the occasional get-together and celebration of national days like Independence Day and Republic Day. School-related issues are apparently not discussed in any of the village forums, whether it is the VEC or the *gram* panchayat and *gram sabha* or the village development committee. According to Vandana Mahajan, seven VEC members (out of 12) participated in discussions with the field study team, along with three special invitees. Children of only two members were studying in the government primary school. The children of the remaining members were either going to private schools or were below the age of six. They admitted that the VEC does not meet regularly—not surprising, given that the children of most of the members attend private schools. In this year, it has met only once, to give approval for the auctioning of trees inside the school campus that had fallen during a storm.

Further, despite the mandated composition of VEC to ensure gender and social equity, in reality, the VECs seem to uphold the interests of the dominant group. As per DPEP Haryana norms, the VEC of this village should have representation from the SC community, women and two parents of children studying in the GPS, with the Head Teacher of the GPS as its member secretary. However, in reality, the official VEC has been 'replaced' by another VEC that has been constituted by the block office of the education department, resulting in a local power tussle. Membership of the Village Education Construction Committee (VECC), which is formed out of the VEC, is sought after because of the substantial funds transferred to VECC for the proposed school building:

> It was quite shocking to see that members of the VEC were openly discussing the possibility of misappropriation of school building funds in front of the research team. In the view of the VEC members, its functioning and role is limited by the local level politics of using these bodies to exert influence, extract benefits and distribute patronage. Participation of the women members on the VEC was also not evident. Most of its members had no knowledge of their role and importance of the VEC to address issues related to children's education (Ramachandran and Saihjee 2004: 182).

Such politics tend to create a hierarchy between the various schools' committees, based on the political clout they wield. In AP, the teachers of the GPS in the Dalit *basti* were aware of the play of caste and class factors in determining facilities for the school. They were unequivocal in stating that the school in the main village stands to gain by being in the proximity of the high school and having a majority of children from the dominant BC social group of the village. Consequently, their school committee is stronger and therefore able to lobby for more benefits, better infrastructure, space, etc. This view was expressed during the discussions with the community in the SC colony as well. Similarly in MP, caste identities were reflected in the school committees, with the VEC representing the OBC and the SMC representing the ST, and the latter lacking resources to demand facilities for its school.

In Karnataka, the existing VEC was considered very active and efficient, claiming a high level of community participation. In reality, the community here is reduced to a few elites who, according to Vani Periodi (2004: 283–303), 'participate, take decisions and implement according to their wish and others follow'. She further adds that though there are young people who are active and vocal in the SC community, their voice is not heard by the VEC. When they speak out in the *gram sabha*, or in front of visiting officials, the elders are called and warned by the village elite. At the time of study, however, the state government had withdrawn the VEC and introduced a School Development and Monitoring Committee (SDMC), comprised of parents of children attending the school. This new committee has not yet been constituted and is already a source of much concern and friction in the community. The VEC was rather critical of this development as it challenged their authority. They were blunt in expressing their displeasure about ordinary people occupying the same position as them.

In the case of the Village-Level Committee (VLC) in Tamil Nadu, the situation is even more polarised. The committee hardly meets, as some members live and work in Chennai. The headmaster is keen to have an operational VLC and keep the members informed about the school's needs, concerns and events. He admitted that convening a meeting was difficult. He meets each member of the VLC, writes a report in the format of a meeting and circulates it among the members for their signature. He meets the members again to get their views on the draft and transcribes the minutes to a book. Each member is expected to sign and pass it on to the others. The interesting aspect of the TN study is not the in-absentia functioning of the VLC; it is the only case study which actually documents genuine community participation by women's self-help groups and local Dalit activists. Their participation is neither mechanical nor bureaucratised. Often, it is a highly political activism, especially in relation to the school in the Dalit area. According to Rathnam, this is due to the presence of a village unit of the Dalit Panthers of India. Young Dalit men spend time in the local school and take a few classes, so that the teacher can concentrate on another class. Their participation in teaching has helped the teacher cope with a multi-grade classroom. They pitch in for extra-curricular activities and provide continuous moral support to the teacher.

The teachers of both schools reported that the women's groups should be credited for the high rate of enrolment and retention at the primary level. They have been enthusiastic participants in enrolment campaigns at the beginning of every academic year for the past four years. Women's self-help groups (SHGs) are not only active, but are very clear about their role—they see themselves as the support structure for the school. They keep in touch with the headmaster throughout the year and their engagement with the school ranges from leading a procession of students for enrolment, supplying sweets during school functions, persuading parents to make extra efforts to enhance their wards' academic performance, to demanding improved facilities for the school in panchayat meetings. Those who live close by allow the girls of the school to use the toilets in their houses. They provide drinking water to the students and also persuade reluctant neighbours into extending these facilities to the children. The TN experience also clearly marks the emergence of women's voices and the growing recognition that they are major players in the enterprise of getting children to school. But apart from TN, we did not see any concrete evidence of DPEP efforts to encourage women to be more active at the local level, through the creation of MTAs, holding of mother-daughter fairs and one-third reservation in the VEC (also reinforced by the PRIs). The situation on the ground, at least in the six panchayats covered, does not suggest active community participation.

A mechanical interpretation of community participation and equating it to an officially constituted VEC has not fostered the genuine participation of families of children who attend government schools. Karnataka has made a beginning by dissolving the VEC and replacing it with a school betterment and management committee, comprising of parents of the children. It remains to be seen whether this new committee will have the teeth to monitor the regular functioning of the school.

Competing Inequalities

The undeniable fact is that people, be they parents, teachers, children or community members, do not have one homogeneous identity and hence cannot be subsumed in a generic category of 'the community'. While there are distinct social and economic groups like SC, ST or OBC, these categories also need to be further broken down in each specific context. Similarly, though gender is no doubt a source of stratification, it is also stratified along the lines of caste, class and community. Thus, the experiences of a poor ST girl will be qualitatively different from that of an OBC girl, and so on. In fact, the situation of girls in some forward communities could be worse in some areas. Similarly, in areas where boys migrate for work (like in the hotel belt of Karnataka), girls may have greater access, by virtue of the fact that they remain in the village while boys are often compelled to drop out from school and leave for the city. It is observed that DPEP's emphasis on broad categories of social stratification actually tends to render invisible the competing inequalities that define children's lives and their experiences of primary schooling. A primary source of inequality that is overlooked is the social and economic geographies of marginal settlements, within the context of the larger panchayat and its impact on access to 'functional' schools. All studies point to this fact and elaborate upon the consequences of this spatial organisation.

Another issue that is overlooked is that all members of a social group do not necessarily share the same economic standing and there may be differences within the community. For instance, the practice of bonded labour occurs within the SC community across families—with some children working in the homes of richer SC families in the same village. There is also a local perception that the relatively better-off SCs, who live on the periphery of the main settlement in the AP study and whose children attend the main GPS, are of a different sub-caste and hence different from the rest. Similarly, the Majhwars in Chhattisgarh are classified as ST, as are the Kunwars. However, the similarity ends here, with the latter exhibiting a very high rate of literacy, while the Majhwars are the landless labourers and barely 5 per cent of their children make it to school. The situation of children from Valmiki households is different from other SC groups in Haryana. Among the Sikh community, the social and economic situation of Jat Sikhs is far better than that of the Mazhabi Sikhs (SC community) living in the same village.

Reversing the Trend

At the outset, it needs to be reiterated that, with the exception of Chhattisgarh, almost universal enrolment in primary schools is a reality. The number of never enrolled children—girls and boys—is almost negligible. The presence of a functional upper-primary and secondary school exerts a significant influence on children's and parents' motivation to continue their education. The cohort analysis reveals that the dropout rate at the primary level is very small and almost all children go up to Class IV (in Andhra Pradesh) and Class V (in other areas). The problem begins at the last stage of the primary and post-primary level. Hence, the availability of and accessibility to middle and high schools could dramatically change the educational scenario in rural India. This is of greater importance for girls and children from very poor families. The micro-studies reinforce this very significant finding of desk research.

The micro-studies also reveal that while the better-off have the resources to send their children outside the village, it is the poor who are left behind. However, the quality issue remains a challenge in almost all areas—learning achievements, pedagogic renewal, gender and social class sensitive classrooms, teacher attitudes—these need a lot more work, if we are to ensure good quality education. Further, decentralised micro-planning under the DPEP is expected to address context-specific issues and tailor the programme to reach out to the hardest-to-reach. However, the six micro-studies reveal that this is not happening, even where village-level surveys have been done—like in Madhya Pradesh, Karnataka and Andhra Pradesh. Further, these were undertaken by the teacher and other DPEP functionaries (like the social mobiliser in Andhra Pradesh). The overwhelming finding of the six micro-studies is the need for panchayat level micro-planning, to meet the educational needs of the most deprived in the area. The VEC and/or school betterment and management committee has not been mandated to actively participate in planning, nor do they have any decision-making power. Given the composition of the VEC, the children of most VEC members do not go to the government primary school. The members, thus, have little interest in the school or the marginalised groups in the village. The composition and the role of the VEC need to be reviewed (as it has been done in Karnataka) and these committees need to be given more teeth.

Thus, the immediate need of the hour is to contain this trend, whereby the universalisation of primary education is accompanied by the emergence of segregated schools based on caste and community identity. The initial evidence seems to indicate that 'hierarchies of access' are becoming an inevitable feature of UEE and this does not portend well for a democracy defined by multiple social identities and voices. The DPEP needs to keep this in mind and focus on steps that will strengthen the existing infrastructure, as well as introduce new interventions that will make primary education truly democratic.

Essentially, research studies and reports on DPEP during the past five years confirm an increased demand for schooling among all sections of the population and also point to a significant increase in the supply of schools. Though gender inequalities have been shrinking and the prognosis for the future is positive, the persistence of regional, social and economic inequalities, particularly with respect to access to functioning schools of a reasonable quality, remains an area of concern—more so in educationally backward districts of the country and especially for first-generation learners.

Who has a stake in improving primary schools? The PROBE report and other studies of the late 1990s reveal that states like Himachal Pradesh, Tamil Nadu and, to a certain degree Kerala, have achieved universal elementary education mainly through government schools and private-aided schools. In particular, children of almost all the important social and economic groups depend primarily on government schools. As a result, they have a stake not only in ensuring that schools function, but also in improving quality. It is rare to come across children in Class V who cannot read or write. However, recent micro-studies done in Uttar Pradesh (Srivastava 2001) and the micro-study (see n3, this chapter) done under this project in Chhattisgarh reveal that several children who emerge from primary schools are barely literate! Making sure that schools work (according to the stipulated timing and calendar) and teachers teach has to become a non-negotiable agenda. While DPEP Education–Management Information System (EMIS) data from educationally backward districts suggest a sharp increase in enrolment, we still have no any reliable information on functionality and quality.

We also have very little information on the functioning of VECs/school betterment committees/parent-teacher's associations. What we do have in the form of qualitative micro-studies (see n3) is not very heartening. All the studies clearly indicate that strengthening mechanisms for community participation without ensuring the participation of parents is often counterproductive. Village leaders whose children do not go to government schools have no stake in it.

Elimination of gender, caste and community bias inside the classroom, especially among teachers, remains a challenge. The bias persists and is reflected through:

- Attitudes of teachers and even educational administrators towards children from first-generation learner families;
- Stereotypes about tribal children (especially the more disadvantaged among tribal groups, for example Pahadi Korba, Majhwar, Pando and Kodaku in Chhattisgarh);
- Students from disadvantaged Dalit communities (Valmiki, Rohit, Adi Dravida and other communities who were part of the erstwhile untouchable groups).

The indicators point to a much deeper malaise in our society. These have been reflected in extensive reporting on the situation of Dalits by journalist P. Sainath (in *The Hindu*) and reports of Dalit organisations struggling against the persistence of caste prejudices (proceedings of the World Conference against Racism, Racial Discrimination, Xenophobia and Related Intolerance in Durban, South Africa in September 2001).While acknowledging that the teachers are as much a part of society as anyone else, it becomes more than evident that the government has to play a positive interventionist role to ensure a bias-free and prejudice-free classroom. This unfortunately has not happened in DPEP. While gender issues have been brought centre-stage, the same cannot be said for caste, community and other social prejudices.

A related issue is the pressing need to critically interrogate generic social categories like SC, ST and minorities and further break them down into more region-specific sub-groups, in order to address their needs more effectively. The most glaring example comes from Chhattisgarh, where there are vast differences among the STs, with some being on the margins of the marginalised. The situation of Oraon or even Gond tribes is far better than that of the Pahadi Korba and Majhwars, among whom it is difficult to find even one literate adult. Recent press reports on starvation deaths among Pahadi Korba tribes and other marginalised sub-groups among SC and ST communities further reinforce the fact that these need micro-level and context-specific strategies, since they remain the hardest to reach.

DPEP studies and reports argue that the first and most obvious implication of these hierarchies is for teacher training. Apart from the social sensitisation mentioned above, special training would be necessary to handle first-generation learners, especially from socially and economically vulnerable groups. The second implication is for more focussed and ongoing support from Block Resource Centres (BRC) and Cluster Resource Centres (CRC), with respect to pedagogic renewal. Third, these schools need to be placed on a special watch-list. Given that existing mechanisms for community involvement, including VEC, are weak and strife-ridden, a far greater effort would be necessary on the part of the teacher to reach out. Teachers with commitment and aptitude would have to be posted in such schools. While the government has acknowledged the importance of this issue, specific strategies are yet to be developed to meet the changing composition of government schools. Similarly, the pedagogical implications of this changing composition are yet to be explored.

Finally, there is unanimity among researchers and administrators about the need to increase children's access to upper-primary and middle schools. The absence of post-primary educational opportunities continues to create greater inequalities in the system. Gender bias is more pronounced at this stage—many more girls drop out after the primary level because of lack of meaningful access to upper-primary schools. Social inequalities in access are also more pronounced at the upper-primary stage, with a smaller proportion of children from SC and ST families studying in private-aided and unaided schools. At this stage, it is the poor who depend more on government schools.

A recent World Bank report on the subject revealed that 72 per cent of children in the 11–13 age-group attend school; only 43 per cent of them attend upper-primary, the rest are in primary school.[11] This information, derived from NSSO 52nd Round, Sixth Educational Survey (1993) and other DPEP reports, reveals that the demand for upper-primary education has been increasing exponentially in almost all areas, both rural and urban. Equally, given the wide variations in the quality of primary education, 61 per cent students (56 per cent girls) who enter Class I complete the primary cycle. This national picture hides wide regional differences. However, what is encouraging is that most of the children who complete the primary cycle are eager to move on to the upper-primary level. Our micro-studies also confirm that the presence of an upper-primary and/or high school in the village is the most important factor affecting transition from primary to upper-primary. This is particularly true for girls and for children from poor families.

Summing Up

The six micro-studies reinforce many of the findings of the desk review. DPEP has made a good beginning and has definitely placed primary education on the priority list. Yet, it has a long way to go before inequalities are addressed and the most deprived children have meaningful access to schooling. No single programme or project, however extensive it may be, can hope to correct decades of educational imbalances and inequalities. While acknowledging that the DPEP is perhaps the most ambitious primary education initiative in independent India, eight years is indeed a short time to bring about radical changes and turn the system upside down. This chapter acknowledges that the social and economic dynamics that frame educational access are not the creation of any programme, but a historical baggage—a product of over five decades of social development and educational planning. DPEP may not be able to directly provide solutions to the gender and social inequalities that define every aspect of the Indian social, economic and political fabric. Yet, its success is inextricably entwined with its ability to critically engage in dialogue with the larger weave of Indian society, and thus it must constantly ensure that its programme is designed to do just that.

What is disturbing is that we, as a nation, are becoming more insensitive as the years roll by. The two-glass system is not only confined to teashops, it has permeated all social structures and institutions—including our schools, the real 'temples' of modern India.[12] A new kind of segregation is clearly discernible at different levels and not all of it has been captured in DPEP data and research studies. At one level, children from clearly different social and economic groups attend different types of school—private-unaided, private-aided, government primary schools, EGS schools, Alternative Schools. Even within government primary schools, there is some evidence of sharp difference in quality—physical facilities, community participation, allocation of funds—as illustrated in the micro-studies as well as other reports and research papers (Majumdar 2001; Nambissan 1996, 2001; Ramachandran and Sethi 2001). Single-teacher schools, multi-grade situations (especially when the teachers are not trained to handle it), poorly trained para-teachers—all these have a greater impact on children from disadvantaged groups, as such children have no other options (private schools, tuitions) and their parents cannot support them at home.

General household characteristics like income, caste, occupation and the educational level of parents continue to determine access, attendance, completion and learning achievements. Children from rural families with substantial land, non-agricultural occupations and educational level have greater access than children from landless, agricultural wage-earning families and migrating groups. In some regions of the country, for example Uttaranchal, researchers have found a strong positive correlation between distance of forest and water source and non-enrolment and dropout rate of girls, and even boys in specific age groups (Pande 2001). Children-women ratio was found to be an influencing factor in the enrolment and continuation of girls in school and the work participation rate influenced the enrolment of boys in Andhra Pradesh (Krishnaji 2001). Similarly, in many areas, the number of animals to graze and manage also exerts influence on school participation, as parents cite grazing as an important reason for irregular attendance or non-enrolment. This is referred to as dependency ratio—'the larger the number of infants and old people in the household (i.e., the higher the "dependency burden" on the household), the smaller are the chances of children getting enrolled in school' (Vaidyanathan and Nair 2001). However, NGOs, especially those who are part of a nationwide campaign against child labour, argue that the motivation of parents, coupled with the mobilisation of working children to get back to school, can overcome this challenge. Ravi Srivastava's (2001) study in UP reveals that the burden of dependency is generally borne by adult women and is not necessarily passed on to small children. It may, however, be of greater significance at the upper-primary and middle-school level, particularly for girls.

Since completing of the fieldwork for the micro-studies, we have had the opportunity to travel to Udupi, North Kanara, Bellary and Davanagere districts of Karnataka—three of them being non-DPEP districts.[13] The overwhelming impression we gathered was that, at least in the villages we visited in Karnataka, there is a negligible number of out-of-school children in the 6–11 age-group. Primary schools were functioning and teachers were regular in attending school. However, what disturbed us was meeting a large number of working children in the 11–14 age-group and an even larger number of them in the 15–18 age-group. Discussions revealed that many of them had dropped out after Class IV, V or VI, with poverty and need for work cited as reasons for dropping out, even in the more educationally forward districts of Udupi and Uttara Kannada. Relevance of education (especially beyond the primary stage), lack of employable or self-employment related skills, insecurity about the future and economic pressures continue to push children out of school and into work. This observation is certainly quite different from the situation in Bijapur, Raichur and Koppal, where a recent household survey reveals a large proportion of out-of-school children in the six to 11 age-group. But it is interesting to note that even when a district (like Udupi and Uttara Kannada) achieves universal enrolment and participation at the primary stage, ensuring eight years of basic education poses a major challenge.

Similarly, prior to beginning of this research, a team of researchers was involved in documenting backward and forward linkages that strengthen primary education.[14] We covered two districts in Karnataka, Uttar Pradesh and Rajasthan, one in Orissa, and the cities of Hyderabad, Mumbai and Kolkata. Again, the overwhelming impression gathered was that parents recognise the value of primary education and, notwithstanding their economic situation, are eager to send their children to primary schools. In the more educationally backward areas of the country, availability of a functional primary school remains a problem. In urban areas, accessibility of schooling for children in difficult circumstances and from migrant families continues to pose a major challenge. In almost all these areas, a significant number of children drop out at the primary stage—with an overwhelming number of girls dropping out after Class IV or V. Again, accessibility to and availability of post-primary education remain a problem in many areas.

Notwithstanding prevalent social and economic barriers to schooling, the overwhelming message emanating from DPEP schools is that the presence of a good quality government school, which functions regularly, can indeed surmount many obstacles. Special strategies would, however, be necessary to reach out to the hard core, most of whom are people who not only belong to the most deprived subgroups of Scheduled Castes and Tribes, but are also the people with almost no voice in society.

The challenge for DPEP is reaching out to this hardest-to-reach group with good quality education. We can no longer look at gender disparities in isolation—the intermeshing of geographic location, social status, economic position, gender, occupation and displacement/migration has resulted in new forms of disparities and disempowerment. Ensuring equal quality of access remains a big issue. Reaching out to the most deprived demands more resources, more human resource inputs and a great deal of commitment from the government. Low-cost options will not do; they will merely accentuate existing cleavages in society.

The lesson from a range of research studies done in the past 10 years reiterates that there are no shortcuts or magic formulae to address fundamental problems of access, equity and gender disparity on the one hand, and quality, content and relevance on the other. Education has to be perceived as an integral part of people's survival and their fight for a life of dignity and self-respect. Different components like physical access, mobilisation, quality, teacher management and pedagogic renewal need to be addressed simultaneously—ensuring confluence and synergy. An integrated approach is necessary for meaningful change and lasting/sustainable impact. Also, just five years of primary education—Classes I–V, ages six to11—is insufficient to ensure significant value addition and, in many cases, even retention of basic literacy and numeracy, particularly for groups that have historically been denied education. Eight years of basic education are essential, and this needs to be recognised as the basic minimum and taken on as non-negotiable.

Primary education is not a stand-alone activity and the government has to acknowledge the importance of looking back and looking forward. Pre-school is a critical input into primary education and, conversely, upper-primary education is necessary to encourage and motivate children and their families to send children to primary schools. Moving one step forward, the availability of relevant and good quality vocational and life skill educational opportunities is essential to generate the necessary momentum for primary and upper-primary education. The age-span we are looking at is three to 18, with one level feeding into the other and higher levels creating the necessary suction effect for earlier stages.

There is a consensus that the primary responsibility of basic education has to be shouldered by the government because it alone has the mandate, the ability and the wherewithal to respond to the educational needs of the poor. This study—like several others—shows that the rich have walked away from government schools in urban areas and all indications are that rural India is not far behind (with notable exceptions like Himachal Pradesh). It is the very poor who go to government schools. Enhancing their capabilities and providing them with the tools to negotiate this unequal world from a position of strength requires political commitment and societal support. Investing in the development and growth of those who need it most is the need of the hour. DPEP has indeed made a beginning with respect to primary education; the question is whether this momentum will be sustained at higher levels and for another decade. If it is, India may well be able to achieve the goal of Universal Elementary Education by the year 2010.

NOTES

1. Discussing the spurt in elementary education spending in 1995–96, Sajita Bashir points out, 'After deducting the expenditure on these two programmes (DPEP and Lok Jumbish), real plan expenditure (domestic) for elementary education has grown at the rate of 22 per cent p a, compared to 27 per cent p a when external funds are included. Thus, the increase in domestic funding has been the main factor in raising Plan expenditure on elementary education' (Bashir 2000: 12).

2. 'Across states, districts and even villages, the literacy rates of females and scheduled castes and tribes (SC/ST), though much below average, are highly correlated with overall literacy rates. Also, inter-group disparities tend to decline as the average literacy rate increases. In other words, as we move up the scale of overall literacy, females and SC/STs are found to be more literate. Also gender gaps as well as the differences between socially disadvantaged and other caste groups become narrower...' (Vaidyanathan and Nair 2001).

3. Schools in 46 districts in eight states were surveyed as part of the District Primary Education Programme of the Ministry of Human Resource Development. The learning levels of over 50,000 students were assessed. It was found that in none of the 46 districts surveyed did primary school students achieve an average score of 80 per cent in the basic letter and word reading tests that were administered to assess their learning levels. In many districts students could barely read five to eight words correctly. Children also fared poorly in basic numerical skills' (*The Times of India* [1994], quoted in Geeta Nambissan [2001]).

4. P. Sainath, a noted journalist, has documented the situation of Dalits across the country from 1999 onwards. Articles appearing in *The Hindu* reveal persistent social discrimination inside the school. Certain specific groups among the Dalits, like Valmiki, Rohit, Thoti, Chamar and, in tribal areas, the non-dominant tribes and denotified tribes (classified as criminal tribes by the British), are not only discriminated against by the forward castes, but also by other Dalits, who consider them untouchable.

5. 'It is estimated that the enrolment in unrecognised schools is doubling every five years. *The proportion of girls in unrecognised schools was very low as compared to their share in the government schools. The gender bias in school choice by the parents is quite evident....* What we need is that the government schools should compete with private schools in terms of quality of access, efficiency and performance standards and both sectors supplement each other's effort to achieve the goal of universal primary education' (Aggarwal 2000a; emphasis mine).

6. Sajita Bashir's study in Tamil Nadu, in 1994, revealed that pupils in private-unaided schools came from relatively well-off backgrounds, with only 10 per cent being SC, while in government schools, the proportion of SC children is 26 per cent in rural areas and 46 per cent in urban areas. She also discussed the educational status of parents from private-unaided schools and aided schools as being very different, with more first-generation learners enrolled in government schools (Bashir, quoted in De et al. [2001]).

7. 'Less than 10 per cent of poor families have their children in private schools as against nearly 30 per cent of middle income families and 45 per cent of well-to-do families' (Krishnaji, quoted on in De et al [2001]: 12).

8. 'This differentiation accentuates the precarious position of the disadvantaged groups in terms of access to basic education both quantitatively and qualitatively. This tendency, if allowed to continue, will further aggravate the already serious inequality in access to higher education, thus making a mockery of the notion that education is the most potent instrument for achieving greater equality of opportunity'(Vaidyanathan and Nair [2001: 25]).

9. 'West Bengal has recorded the lowest share of female teachers—merely 15.8 per cent as compared to 73.6 per cent in Kerala. As a first priority, the share of female teachers needs to be improved in single and two-teacher schools...Despite significant moves and gender sensitive recruitment policies, the position with respect to the availability and deployment of female teachers is less than satisfactory... Serious concerns about deployment prevail, as the number of male teacher schools is exceptionally large...The trends indicate a stagnating share of SC/ST teachers in phase I' (Aggarwal [2000a]: Ch. 6).

10. For details of the methodology adopted for the micro-studies, please refer to the original study. Before proceeding further, a caveat is also necessary here. The objective of this exercise is not to pronounce generalisations on the basis of these micro-studies; rather, it is to provide insight into the underlying issues most pertinent to the topic under study. Hence, all comments and observations should be taken in the spirit in which they are intended.

11. 'Across the total population aged 15 years and above in 1995–96, 32 per cent had completed at least an upper-primary schooling. There were major differences by gender and income group. For urban males the completion rate was 63.6 per cent and for rural females the rate was 14.6 per cent. While just over half of the members of the wealthiest 20 per cent of households had completed this level of schooling, the rate for the poorest 20 per cent was under 15 per cent' (World Bank, 2001. *India Expanding and Improving Upper Primary Education in India,* March. Washington DC: World Bank: iii).

12. The two glass system is a practice where hotels and eating shacks keep a separate set of cups for Dalits and other erstwhile untouchable communities, and another set for the use of all other customers.

13. Vimala Ramachandran and Aarti Saihjee travelled in the project areas of The Concerned for Working Children, between 24 September and 1 October 2001.

14. Educational Resource Unit was engaged in a DFID/GOI-supported research project to document experiences of 10 primary education programmes in India. In 2003, it was published as a book, titled *Getting Children Back to School: Case Studies in Primary Education (2000–2001).* New Delhi: Sage Publications.

REFERENCES

Aggarwal, Yash. 2000a. November. 'An Assessment of Trends in Access and Retention'. New Delhi: National Institute of Educational Planning and Administration.

———. (2000b). March. 'How Many Pupils Complete Primary Education in Five Years'. New Delhi: NIEPA.

Bashir, Sajita. 2000. *Government Expenditure on Elementary Education in the Nineties.* New Delhi: The European Commission.

Census of India 2001. 2001. New Delhi: Government of India. Available at http://censusindia.gov.in/2011-prov-results/paper2/data_files/india/paper2_1.pdf [Government of India website].

De, Anuradha, Claire Noronha, and Meera Samson. 2001. *India: Primary Schools and Universal Elementary Education,* India Education Team Report No 3. New Delhi: World Bank.

DPEP. 1999. *Bringing Girls Centrestage*: Strategies and Interventions for Girls Education in DPEP. New Delhi: Gender Unit, EdCIL: Government of India.

———. 2000a. *Study of Declining Enrolment in Class I in Uttar Pradesh, Maharashtra and Tamil Nadu—A Synthesis Report,* October. New Delhi, NIEPA: Government of India.

DPEP. 2000b. *District Primary Education Programme.* Part 1 and 2. 11th Joint Review Mission, April. New Delhi: Government of India.

——. 2000c. *District Primary Education Programme.* Part 1, 2 and 3. 12th Joint Review Mission, November. New Delhi: Government of India.

——. 2001. *District Primary Education Programme.* Part 1, 2 and 3. 13th Joint Review Mission, April–May. New Delhi: Government of India.

Ghosh, Avik. 2002. 'Alternative Schools and Education Guarantee Scheme'. In Vimala Ramachandran, ed. *Gender and Social Equity in Primary Education: Hierarchies of Access.* New Delhi: Sage Publications.

Government of India. 1992. *National Policy on Education—Programme of Action 1992.*New Delhi: GOI.

Krishnaji, N. 2001. 'Poverty, Gender and Schooling: A Study of Two Districts in Andhra Pradesh'. In A. Vaidyanathan and P. R. Gopinathan Nair, eds, *Elementary Education in Rural India—A Grass Roots View.* New Delhi: Sage Publications.

Madan, Vandana. 2002. 'Inside the Classroom: Content Analysis of Classroom Processess Study Done in Eight State'. In Vimala Ramachandran, ed. *Gender and Social Equity in Primary Education: Hierarchies of Access.* New Delhi: Sage Publications.

Mahajan, Vandana. 2004. 'The Hidden Picture: A Case Study from Hisar District, Haryana'. In Vimala Ramachandran, ed, *Gender and Social Equity in Primary Education: Hierarchies of Access.* New Delhi: Sage Publications: 250–282.

Majumdar, Manabi. 2001. 'Educational Opportunities in Rajasthan and Tamil Nadu: Despair and Hope'. In A. Vaidyanathan and P. R. Gopinathan Nair, eds, *Elementary Education in Rural India—A Grass Roots View.* New Delhi: Sage Publications.

Mode and UNICEF. 1995. MODE Research: Attitudes Study on Elementary Education in India—A Consolidated Report, New Delhi.

Nambissan, Geeta. 1996. 'Equity in Education? Schooling of Dalit Children in India'. *Economic and Political Weekly* 31 (16 and 17) 20–27 April: 1011–24.

——. 2000. 'Identity, Exclusion and the Education of Tribal Communities'. In Rekha Wazir, ed, *The Gender Gap in Basic Education: NGOs as Change Agents.* New Delhi: Sage Publications.

——. 2001. 'Social Diversity and Regional Disparity in Schooling: A Study of Rural Rajasthan'. In A. Vaidyanathan and P. R. Gopiathan Nair, eds, *Elementary Education in Rural India—A Grass Roots View.* New Delhi: Sage Publications.

Pande, Anuradha. 2001. 'Uttar Pradesh' in A. Vaidyanathan and P. R. Gopinathan Nair, eds, *Elementary Education in Rural India—A Grass Roots View.* New Delhi: Sage Publications.

Periodi, Vani. 2004. 'Second Generation Issues in Equity and Education: Learning from Kolar District, Karnataka'. In Vimala Ramachandran, ed. *Gender and Social Equity in Primary Education: Hierarchies of Access.* New Delhi: Sage Publications: 283–303.

PROBE Report. 1999. *Public Report on Basic Education in India.* Delhi: Oxford University Press.

Ramachandran, Vimala. 2003. *Getting Children Back to School: Case Studies in Primary Education.* New Delhi: Sage Publications.

——. ed. 2004. *Hierarchies of Access: Gender and Social Equity in Primary Education.* New Delhi: Sage Publications.

Ramachandran, Vimala, and Aarti Saihjee. 2004. 'An Overview of Micro-Studies'. In Vimala Ramachandran, ed. *Hierarchies of Access: Gender and Social Equity in Primary Education.* New Delhi: Sage Publications.

Ramachandran, Vimala, and Harsh Sethi. 2001. *Rajasthan Shiksha Karmi Project—An Overall Appraisal.* Stockholm: Swedish International Development Cooperation Agency (SIDA).

Shariff, Abusaleh, and Ratna Sudarshan. 1996. 'Elementary Education and Health in Rural India—Some Indicators'. In N. Rao, L. Rurup, and R. Sudarshan, eds, *Sites of Change—The Structural Context for Women's Empowerment in India.* New Delhi: FES and UNDP.

Sharma, Rashmi. 1999. 'What Manner of Teacher: Some Lessons from MP'. *Economic and Political Weekly* 34 (35) 19–25 June: 1597–1607.

Srivastava, Ravi. 2001. 'Access to Basic Education in Rural Uttar Pradesh.' in A Vaidyanathan and P. R. Gopinathan Nair, eds, *Elementary Education in Rural India—A Grass Roots View.* New Delhi: Sage Publications.

Vaidyanathan, A., and P. R. Gopinathan Nair, eds, 2001. *Elementary Education in Rural India—A Grass Roots View: Strategies in Human Development.* New Delhi: Sage Publications.

Visaria, Leela, and Vimala Ramachandran. 2002. 'What DPEP and Other Data Sources Reveal'. In Vimala Ramachandran, ed. *Gender and Social Equity in Primary Education: Hierarchies of Access* New Delhi: Sage Publications.

World Bank. 2001. *India Expanding and Improving Upper Primary Education in India.* Washington DC: World Bank.

6

Gendered Inequality in Educational Transitions

Divya Vaid[†]

Introduction

Schooling has innumerable benefits, and yet a vast majority of Indian children, especially girls, are deprived of these. Despite the various measures undertaken by the government and local bodies to reduce the inequality in education between genders, castes, classes and religions, this inequality still persists. The aim of this chapter is twofold. First to highlight the factors responsible for this inequality for both boys and girls from socially deprived origins, and second, to highlight in particular the inequality faced by girls at each educational transition stage. In order to tackle the issues at hand, I begin this chapter with a brief overview of the persisting inequality in education in India and a summary of past research. This is followed by a section on the aims of the present chapter and a discussion of the major hypothesis. I then lay down the methods employed to study this inequality and the data and variables used in this research. This is followed by an explanation of the models used and the results obtained. I end the chapter with a discussion of these results and a summary conclusion.

> The state shall endeavour to provide, within a period of ten years from the commencement of this Constitution, for free and compulsory education for all children until they complete the age of fourteen years.
>
> Art 45, Part IV, Directive Principles of State Policy,
> The Constitution of India, 1951

A far cry from the provisions of the Constitution, India, a land of more than a billion people, has slightly less than one-third of the world's non-literate population aged 15 years and above.[1] The goal of universal education, as set out in the Constitution, seems elusive even after nearly seven decades. The original period of 10 years to achieve this goal was extended to 16 years after the government failed to meet its target. The Education Commission, in its report in 1966, regretted this failure on the part of the government and pushed the date back further. The new target date was 1985. In 1986, the National Policy on Education extended the date by another

10 years. In 1993, the Department of Education, in its report 'Education For All', set the date at 2001 (MHRD 1993).[2]

Despite the government's apparent failure in meeting its goals,[3] a preliminary review of the 2001 Census data reveals that the 1990s saw a phenomenal rise in literacy rates in India, especially for women (Ramachandran and Saihjee 2002).

Table 6.1 depicts the literacy rate in India by gender. A cursory glance at these official figures seems to show that the literacy rates have increased for both men and women, but this is not enough to study how the disparity in educational attainment or the 'inequality of opportunity' between men and women has changed over the years. This is because marginal changes, such as the expansion of the education system or other structural changes in the education system could confound the picture.

TABLE 6.1: Literacy Percentage 1901–2001[4]

*Year**	*Males per cent of Total Male Population*	*Females per cent of Total Female Population*	*Odds Ratio***
1901	9.83	0.60	18:1
1911	10.56	1.05	11:1
1921	12.21	1.81	7:1
1931	15.59	2.93	6:1
1941	24.90	7.30	4.2:1
1951	24.95	7.93	3.9:1
1961	34.44	12.95	3.5:1
1971	39.45	18.69	2.8:1
1981	56.50	29.85	3:1
1991	52.74	32.17	2.8:1
2001	63.24	45.15	2.6:1

Notes: * 1901–41 figures are for undivided India, 1991 figures exclude the state of Jammu and Kashmir, where the census was not conducted.
** Odds Ratios calculated from the official government figures.

Source: Statement 21- Crude Literacy Rate by Sex, p. 103; Provisional Population Totals, http://censusindia.gov.in/2011-prov-results/data_files/india/Final_PPT_2011_chapter6.pdf [accessed July 2016].

In absolute terms, looking at Table 6.1, the gender gap would appear to have increased. But in order to see the real change minus these marginal changes, i.e., to study the relative chances of women and men, one needs to look at the odds ratios. Odds ratios are the ratios of the odds of a woman being literate as compared to a man. A comparison of the odds ratios would help to see if and how the relative chances of literacy have decreased between the two sexes, after allowing for the marginal changes.

Figure 6.1 is a graphical description of the odds ratios presented in Table 6.1. The odds of a man having greater access to education as compared to a woman have clearly declined, indicating a decline in inequality between the two genders, though in 2001, the odds still stood at 2.7:1.

Figure 6.1: Odds Ratios for Male and Female Literacy 1901–2001

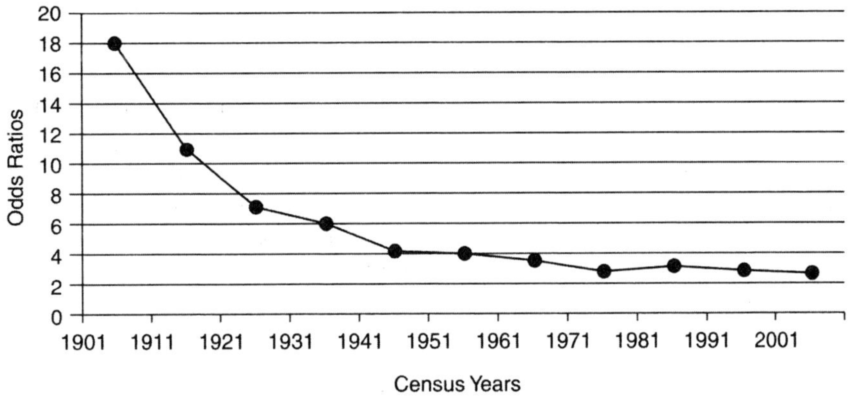

Source: Table in Appendix 6.1.

The relative gender inequality in rural/urban literacy too has declined over the decades, as can be seen in Figure 6.2 (see Appendix 6.1 for the table). The odds-ratio for the rural gender gap has fallen from 4.6 in 1951 to 2.82 in 1997. But interestingly, the gap seems to have fallen and then increased in the urban areas and it has reverted to its 1951 level of 2.85. This has left the gap in the rural and urban areas at approximately the same level, thus going against the widely held belief that the gender gap is higher in rural areas.

Figure 6.2: Odds Ratios for Men and Women in Urban and Rural Areas 1951–97

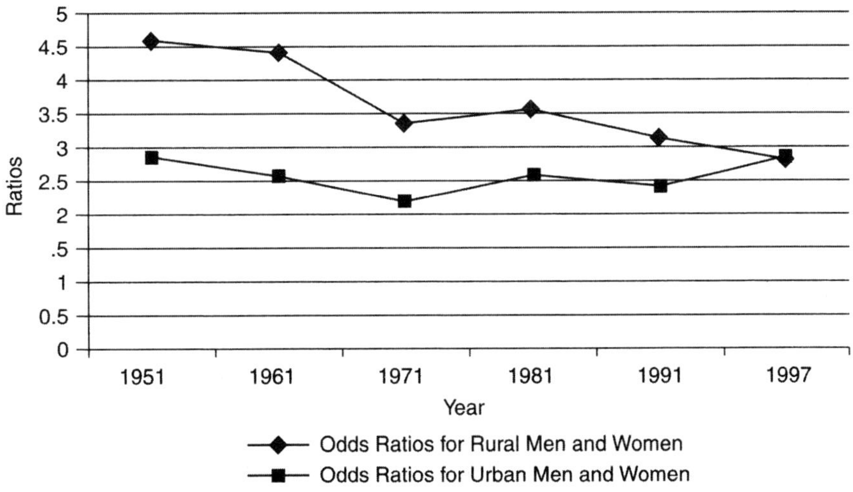

Source: Table in Appendix 6.1.

Figure 6.1 then reveals that since the beginning of the twentieth century, gender inequality in literacy has declined, but more importantly, what it also reveals is that the relative chances of women and men have remained fairly stable in the past few decades. What this means, then, is that despite the rapid expansion of the educational system and other government policies, the gender inequality seems to be persisting.

Inequality in educational opportunities is not only a 'gender' problem in India. The presence of the Scheduled Caste (SC) and Scheduled Tribe (ST) groups,[5] who are historically deprived both socially and economically, makes the situation quite complex. Official figures for the SCs and STs reveal that they consistently lag behind the general category. The literacy rates for SC's and STs (combined) were 56 per cent in 1991, as compared to 76 per cent for the other castes,[6] that is, an odds ratio of 2.5:1.

WHY THIS 'PERSISTENT INEQUALITY' IN EDUCATION?[7]

The benefits of schooling are unquestionable. According to the human capital theory, labour productivity is a direct function of the amount of schooling received. Higher schooling is expected to increase cognitive development and leads to economic modernisation (Colclough 1982). The individual and social returns from women's education are believed to be exceptionally high, especially where the lowering of fertility and infant and child mortality rate are concerned (Kingdon 1999; World Bank 1997). In addition, rising levels of education of women leads to improvements in nutrition and health care facilities and the improvement of children's educational achievements (Colclough 1982; Sengupta and Guha 2002).

Despite the fact that the non-monetary returns to schooling appear to be quite high (Colclough 1982), many parents still don't send their children especially their daughters to school. Several reasons have been put forth for this. Using Indian household data, Rosenzweig and Schultz (1982) find that children who are expected to be more economically productive as adults receive a larger share of family resources. Sathar and Lloyd (1994) seem to agree and conclude that parents decide the amount of education a child receives on the basis of present and future anticipated costs and returns.

> Returns to educational investments in girls are likely to be seen by parents as lower than in boys because of their more limited opportunities in the labour market and the near certainty that they will marry out of the family and devote their future time and earnings to their husband's family (Sathar and Lloyd 1994: 113–14).[8]

In India, a predominantly agrarian country,[9] a substantial number of girls are expected to contribute to the family income by their own labour, or to look after their younger siblings (Aggarwal 1987). The opportunity cost of educating girls is thus especially large in rural and low-income families (Sengupta and Guha 2002).

The National Committee on the Status of Women in India (1975) accepted that poverty plays a major role in the attitude towards girls' education, especially for people below subsistence-level.[10] Prejudice against the education of girls has a strong detrimental effect on the amount of schooling they receive. This prejudice exists, according to Sopher (1980), because an exclusively domestic role is seen as an ideal for a woman. Men, in his opinion, believe that education 'un-suits' women for that role, because an educated female, and he quotes Krishnan and Shyam (1973), '.... may become a doubtful character, or may not be capable of adjusting in the joint family system, or may not participate in obligatory agricultural operations, or may not remain under the control of her husband' (Sopher 1980: 138).

Certain other background factors are believed to affect enrolment and dropout rates in school and are believed to be magnified in the case of girls. Ramachandran and Saihjee (2002), in a study of the District Primary Education Programmes (DPEP), have found that 'general household characteristics like income, caste, occupation and educational level of parents continue to determine access, attendance, completion and learning achievements' (ibid.: 1611). According to Sengupta and Guha (2002) in a study of girl children in West Bengal, the strongest factors with regard to school participation, enrolment and dropout were household factors such as parental, especially maternal schooling, household income and the father's occupation. They also found that caste and religion were important determinants of schooling. Muslim girls, they found (irrespective of whether they lived in a rural or urban area), received less schooling than other religious communities. According to their results, residing in an urban area had strong positive effects on the education of girls.[11] The National Committee on the Status of Women in India (1975) also accepted that apart from the slow growth of women's literacy, there were 'several imbalances in educational development between advanced and backward classes and between regions'.[12]

Present Study

The persisting inequality in opportunity where education is concerned thus becomes apparent through an analysis of official figures, as well as through a study of past research. Several factors such as caste, class, religion, and parental characteristics emerge as important determinants of educational inequality.

However, what most past research seems to be lacking is a holistic view of the interplay of all these social and economic forces together. For example, not many researchers seem to have looked at how gender could magnify other social inequalities, leading to an even worse position of the women from those deprived communities. One researcher who does mention this issue, albeit theoretically and with little empirical analysis, is Raju (1991). Through her analysis of literacy data, Raju (1991) shows that non-Scheduled Caste urban females emerge as a better-off group as compared to the rural males of all categories, including non-Scheduled Caste males. What she suggests, then, is that a distinction needs to be made between women as well and research on women cannot ignore social-class relations in various spheres, in which males are as integral a part as women.

In light of the above, the purpose of the present chapter is twofold. First, I aim to empirically test the factors responsible for the inequality of educational opportunities, for both boys and girls from socially deprived origins. Second, I would emphasise in particular the inequality faced by girls as compared to boys from the same origins, at each stage of the education process.

HYPOTHESES

This section lays down some of the hypotheses that I will test in order to identify the factors that could effect the inequality in educational transitions.

I begin by testing what I call the poverty hypothesis. For this hypothesis to hold, two results should emerge. First, the effect of the father's class on educational transitions should be significant and the results should show that both boys and girls from higher classes are more likely to make a transition to the next educational stage, as compared to those who come from lower classes. But in addition, girls from lower classes should not only do worse than the boys and girls from the higher classes, they should also do worse than the boys from these same lower classes. This is because parents are expected to invest in their sons more than their daughters, especially when resources are low (Sengupta and Guha 2002). In other words, there should emerge an interaction effect between gender and class, which would show that the gender gap is the least at higher levels of the class schema, as parents have more resources to invest in their daughters. The opposite should hold for girls from the lower classes.

Second, community characteristics such as caste and religion are expected to adversely affect the relative chances of children from deprived backgrounds in achieving the same levels of education as the children from more advantaged communities. Some social scientists (Raju 1991; Sengupta and Guha 2002) believe that both religion and caste should interact with gender and lead to a greater inequality for women from the depressed communities. Higher-caste as well as Hindu girls should be in a better position than lower-caste and Muslim girls where transitions to the next stage of the educational process are concerned. I call this the community hypothesis.

Third, I will test the household resources hypothesis or the family background hypothesis. This hypothesis posits that other family characteristics, such as the mother and father's literacy, should prove to be important determinants of the educational decisions made by their children (Burney and Irfan 1991; Sathar and Lloyd 1994; Sengupta and Guha 2002). Thus, parental literacy must emerge as a strong determinant of the likelihood of a child making the next educational transition. In addition, there should also emerge a strong relationship between gender and the mother's education. According to Sathar and Lloyd (1994), mother's literacy has a larger effect on the enrolment of children and this effect is especially larger for girls. In order to test this, the interaction of mother's literacy and gender should emerge stronger than that for father's literacy and gender.

Fourth, under the regional variation hypothesis, two aspects will be studied. These are the rural/urban aspect and the state aspect. There should be lower levels of gender discrimination in urban areas (Raju 1991), as well as in the states that have traditionally had an above average level of literacy. This is because the traditional investment in education for girls, as well as the social acceptance of girls' education, should be higher in these regions (for example Kerala, the state with the highest level of literacy, especially for women).[13] The opposite should hold for states like Bihar and Rajasthan, which have historically lagged behind the national average rate of literacy for girls. The transitions to later stages of education should be lower in these states for all children and the position of women should be even worse.

And finally, the expansion of the education system as well as recent government initiatives to educate girls should be evident in the *Cohort Effect*. Younger cohorts of both boys and girls are expected to do better than the older ones and girls in these younger cohorts should have a relatively better chance, due to more opportunities available to them (Sengupta and Guha 2002).

In sum, for each hypothesis I will test for the presence of a main and an interaction effect for gender, to study inequalities in educational attainment, not only between communities and classes, but also within the same communities and classes where gender is concerned.

Brief Overview of the Indian Education System

India has two distinct streams of education, the formal education stream and the non-formal one. The formal stream begins at the age of six with primary school (Figure 6.3), which continues from grades I–V. Middle school is from grades VI–VIII.[14] Together, primary and middle school comprise elementary school. High school includes grades IX–XII. In this chapter, I will club all colleges (with and without degrees) together.[15]

Figure 6.3: A Simplified Version of the Indian Education System

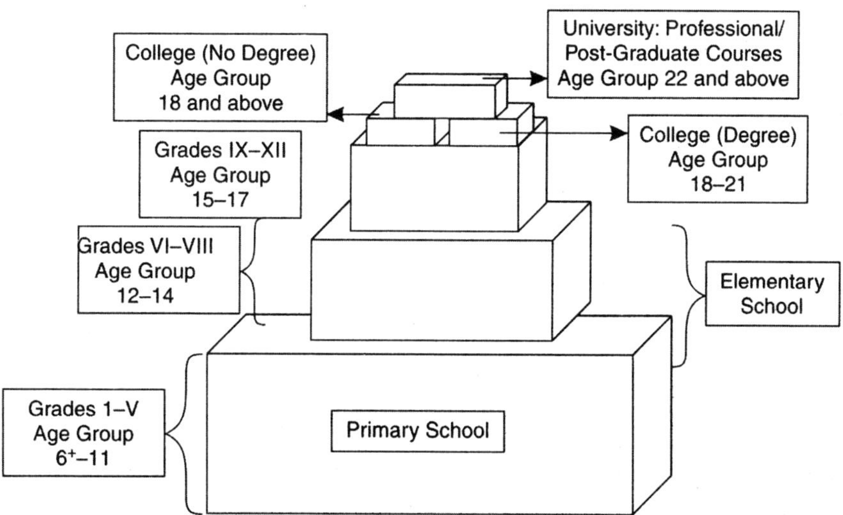

Source: Author's own drawing.

The non-formal stream is expected to provide education to students between the ages of nine and 14. For the government, the non-formal stream is an alternative path to education for children employed in the labour market and deprived of education in the formal stream (Acharya 1994; Aggarwal 1989). But serious doubts remain among theorists (Acharya 1994) about the quality of this kind of education and its relevance in the lives of these children. As there is no information on the non-formal educational stream in the National Election Study Data set that I use, I am unable to deal with these issues.[16] For the purpose of this chapter, I concentrate wholly on the formal stream of education.

METHODS

Ordinary Least Squares regression (or linear regression) and logistic regression are two methods most often used by sociologists to study the effects of socio-economic background variables on educational attainment.[17] The linear regression method treats the highest qualification obtained (measured in the number of school years completed) as the dependent variable and regresses that on the independent background variables, like parental education and father's class. The logistic regression method, on the other hand, treats the outcome as a dichotomous variable and studies whether the background variables have an effect on the likelihood that the subject will make a transition to the next stage of the educational process, given that she has completed the previous stage.

Keeping in mind my initial research questions, for the purpose of the present chapter, I weighed the merits and drawbacks of both these methods. According to Mare (1981), linear models could conceal important social changes by summarising two offsetting trends; 'the univariate dispersion of formal schooling and the multivariate association between school attainment and socioeconomic background characteristics' (ibid.: 83). He goes on to add that 'the parameters of the logistic response model measure—in a sense—'pure' inequality of opportunity because they separate the distribution and allocation of schooling, and measure the latter explicitly' (ibid.: 86).

In light of the possible drawbacks of the OLS regression and the advantage of logistic regression, especially with reference to studying inequality at different transition points, in the present analysis, I decided to use a series of logistic regressions similar to those expressed by Mare (1980, 1981). In these models (henceforth called the Mare Model), I treat 'survival' at different transition points as the dependent variable (Jonsson 1993).

The advantage of this model is that it helps to throw light on the inequality in educational opportunity for boys and girls, without being affected by the degree of educational expansion or contraction (Shavit and Blossfeld 1993). The Mare Model views the educational process as a series of transitions, where at each level, the subject's decision to continue till the next stage or drop out from the educational process is adjusted for in the model.

In order to use the Mare Model, I specified a series of transitions at significant points in the Indian education system. These transitions were:

(a) From illiterate to some primary school
(b) Given some primary school to middle school

(c) Given middle school to high school
(d) Given high school to any college.

The success at each transition is the probability of moving on to a higher transition and was coded as 1.

The first is a broad transition and provides a glimpse of the factors that affect the likelihood of a subject moving from illiteracy to some primary school. Here, I clubbed together the respondents who put down their level of education as literate and those who put down primary school. This was based on the assumption that the 'literate' respondents would have at least enrolled in some sort of primary school (in the formal or the non-formal sector), if not completed it. This transition is an important one in India, where a significant proportion of the children might not have the opportunity to attend primary school. This transition could thus help identify the reasons why some children never make it to school.

The second and third stages look at the transition from one level of school to another and the last transition could help identify the factors that affect the likelihood of a subject making it to college. In the final transition, I clubbed the three categories of 'college no degree, college degree, and professional/postgraduate courses' under 'any' college.

Data and Variables

The data for the present chapter comes from the National Election Study (NES), 1996, conducted by the Centre for the Study of Developing Societies (CSDS), Delhi. The data, collected by a nationally representative and stratified random sample of 9,614 respondents from the electoral rolls, contains roughly the same number of men and women.[18] As the electoral registration rates in India are high and the onus of registration rests with the state, any selection bias in this data-set should thus be minimal.[19]

This NES is a unique data-set and the 1996 data is especially useful for the present study. What sets this data apart from others is the inclusion of detailed background information, not only on the respondent, but also on the respondent's parents' caste, class, education, religion and other background variables.

Success at each of the four educational transitions (mentioned above) was treated as the dependent variable.

Keeping in mind the expected determinants of the likelihood of educational transitions previously laid out in this chapter, the independent variables in this study are gender, father's class, caste, father's education, mother's education, locality (rural/urban) and religion. What has not been looked at in much detail in previous studies is the variation of gender inequality by states. India is a vast country; rural areas steeped in poverty flank highly developed cities. In such a diverse country, the level of education too varies from one region to another. Kottayam in Kerala has one of the highest rates of literacy in the South Asian region, with 95.72 per cent of its population educated. On the other hand, district Jhabua of Madhya Pradesh has the lowest rate of total literacy of 19.01 per cent, according to the 1991 Census.[20]

The gap in literacy between women and men too varies widely by region.[21] Kerala,[22] again, has the highest level of literate women, while Rajasthan has the dubious distinction of having some districts with only 8 per cent educated women.[23] In light of these variations, it becomes essential to study the gender differential in education and its variation by region or state. I now turn to a brief discussion of the explanatory variables used in this study.

Class

A country with more than 60 per cent of its population in the farming and subsistence sector, but with one of the fastest growing IT industries, India is unlike any country in the West. For this reason, to simply apply the class categorisation used in studies in the West to the Indian scenario could provide a skewed and unclear picture. For this purpose, I will be using the class schema developed by Kumar et al. (2002), especially for the Indian case.[24] I use a modified version of their eight-class schema.

Original Classes[25]

(1) Higher salariat = executives, professional, white-collar workers
(2) Lower salariat = Class IV employees
(3) Business = small-scale and large-scale businessmen
(4) Petty business = Small store owners and road-side businesses
(5) Skilled and semi-skilled manual labourer = mechanics, electricians, tailors, weavers, carpenters and craftsmen, and rickshaw puller.
(6) Unskilled manual labourer = manual labourers, excluding those in the agricultural sector (e.g., construction workers, sweepers)
(7) Farmers = owner and tenant cultivators with more than 5 acres of land
(8) Lower agriculturists = less than 5 acres of land, sharecropper, agricultural labourer, landless labourer, tea plantation worker, dairy farmer, fishermen, shepherds, hunters.

Modified Categories:

(1) Class I = higher salariat + business
(2) Class II = lower salariat
(3) Class III = skilled and semi-skilled manual + petty business + farmers
(4) Class IV = unskilled manual labourer + lower agriculturists

Caste

A unique feature of the data-set is its enumeration of caste. The last Indian census to collect data on caste was in 1931. Since then, the census only collects data on the SC (SCs) and the Scheduled Tribes (STs).[26] This procedure has left a conspicuous gap in the data on Other Backward Classes (OBCs) in India, who, like the SCs and the STs, also suffer from numerous inequalities, an important one being access to education. The present data-set thus overcomes this lacuna as it includes variables on the OBCs, SCs, STs, as well as on what have sometimes been referred to as the twice-born castes.

It must be kept in mind at this point that the caste categories I use for the purpose of this chapter are, by necessity, a generalised picture of caste per se in India. Castes are not homogeneous categories and there appears to be stratification within the same caste itself.[27] However, the broad caste categories were considered sufficient for the purpose of this chapter.

Figure 6.4[28] shows the break-up of the castes in this data, with regard to the different educational stages. Due to the small sample size of the STs, which made any analysis difficult, I clubbed the SCs and STs together.

FIGURE 6.4: Castes and their Educational Attainment

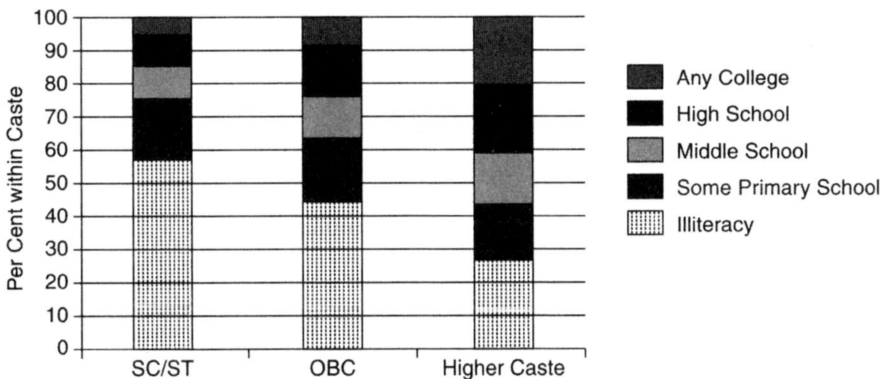

Source: NES 1996, CSDS Data Unit.

Region

In order to study regional disparity, I look at two indicators: the state one belongs to and whether one comes from a rural or from an urban area. Dummy variables were created for each state in the sample (there were originally 21 states, but states with a small N were merged with their nearest large state, leaving me with 15 states).[29] I treated Assam as a 'middling state' (an average state where education and size are concerned) and made that the base category, in order to observe the distribution around it. For rural/urban differences, I coded rural as 0 and urban as 1. Together, these two indicators of state and locality make up the variable of region, which would highlight any impact of regional variation on the educational transitions made.

Parental Characteristics

The data on the respondents' parents' (both mother and father) educational attainment is an important aspect of this data. For both parents, being literate was coded as 1 and being illiterate as 0.

Religion

For the purpose of this chapter, I divided religion into three categories; Hindu, Muslim and 'other'. The 'other' category is quite heterogeneous and includes Christians, Sikhs, Jains, Buddhists and Parsis. Despite this simplification, these religious categories do help in a broad comparison between these communities. I treat Hindu as the base category in the regression, in order to see how these religious minorities fare educationally with regard to the majority Hindu population.

Cohorts

Age-groups were converted into five cohorts, and the base category was taken to be the oldest cohort of respondents born prior to 1940. The youngest cohort was born between 1971 and 1978.

MODELS AND RESULTS

Table 6.2 depicts the models that were constructed using logistic regression at the first transition point. Similar analyses were conducted at each educational transition, but in order to simplify the analysis, these tables for the last three transitions are excluded from the present chapter. Instead of presenting tables for all the four transitions, Table 6.4 brings together the significant models at each of the four transitions.

TABLE 6.2: Mare Model—Logistic Regression Parameters for the Transition to 'Some Primary School from Illiterate'

Independent Variables	*Model*	*Model*	*Model*	*Model*	*Model*	*Model*	*Model*	*Model*	*Model*
	1	2	3	4	5	6	7	8	9
Gender	−1.214	−1.325	−1.387	−1.397	−1.646	−1.709	−1.725	−1.847	−1.947
(Male=0)	(0.048)	(0.051)	(0.053)	(0.053)	(0.061)	(0.062)	(0.063)	(0.066)	(0.081)
Class I		2.909	2.641	2.643	1.583	1.585	1.276	1.362	1.399
		(0.129)	(0.131)	(0.131)	(0.147)	(0.148)	(0.151)	(0.153)	(0.155)
Class II		1.668	1.69	1.704	1.056	1.051	0.763	0.875	0.886
		(0.192)	(0.195)	(0.195)	(0.212)	(0.213)	(0.215)	(0.220)	(0.220)
Class III		0.511	0.479	0.476	0.269	0.262	0.169	0.178	0.185
		(0.053)	(0.054)	(0.054)	(0.061)	(0.062)	(0.063)	(0.068)	(0.068)
Caste (OBC)			0.508	0.547	0.329	0.397	0.408	0.432	0.423
			(0.063)	(0.063)	(0.070)	(0.071)	(0.072)	(0.077)	(0.077)
Caste (Higher)			1.169	1.212	0.776	0.906	0.898	1.075	1.061
			(0.069)	(0.071)	(0.080)	(0.082)	(0.083)	(0.090)	(0.091)

(Contd)

Table 6.2 (Contd)

Independent Variables	*Model*	*Model*	*Model*	*Model*	*Model*	*Model*	*Model*	*Model*	*Model*
	1	2	3	4	5	6	7	8	9
'Other' Religion				0.535	0.442	0.491	0.495	0.308	–0.446
				(0.125)	(0.142)	(0.144)	(0.145)	(0.154)	(0.216)
Muslim				–0.211	–0.186*	–0.276	–0.357	–0.430	–0.430
				(0.089)	(0.099)	(0.101)	(0.103)	(0.108)	(0.109)
Moth. Lit.					1.912	1.875	1.845	1.62	1.596
(Illiterate=0)					(0.138)	(0.139)	(0.140)	(0.144)	(0.144)
Father Lit.					1.668	1.576	1.557	1.458	1.295
(Illiterate=0)					(0.069)	(0.070)	(0.070)	(0.073)	(0.105)
Cohort 1						1.155	1.200	1.356	1.356
(1971–78)						(0.100)	(0.102)	(0.106)	(0.106)
Cohort 2						0.848	0.874	0.959	0.954
(1961–70)						(0.097)	(0.098)	(0.102)	(0.102)
Cohort 3						0.555	0.568	0.641	0.630
(1951–60)						(0.103)	(0.104)	(0.107)	(0.107)
Cohort 4						0.198*	0.185*	0.224*	0.219*
(1941–50)						(0.114)	(0.115)	(0.118)	(0.118)
Locality							0.802	0.738	0.757
(Rural=0)							(0.084)	(0.095)	(0.096)
Bihar								–0.611	–0.636
								(0.176)	(0.175)
Gujarat								1.965	1.949
								(0.274)	(0.275)
Tamil Nadu								0.703	0.664
								(0.189)	(0.189)
Rajasthan								–0.917	–0.579
								(0.201)	(0.225)
Kerala								1.857	1.787
								(0.337)	(0.338)
G * Other Religion									1.357
									(0.287)
G * Father's Lit.									0.317
									(0.139)

(Contd)

Table 6.2 (Contd)

Independent Variables	*Model*	*Model*	*Model*	*Model*	*Model*	*Model*	*Model*	*Model*	*Model*
	1	2	3	4	5	6	7	8	9
G* Rajasthan									−1.111
									(0.294)
Constant	0.957	0.507	0.007*	−0.020*	−0.302	−0.957	−1.034	−1.005	−0.934
	(0.035)	(0.043)	(0.058)	(0.058)	(0.064)	(0.099)	(0.100)	(0.176)	(0.177)
N=7808									
Chi Sq	668.19	1,608.37	1,907.86	1,934.25	3,392.17	3,575.26	3,368.79	3,966.43	4,010.62
	(1 d.f.)	(4 d.f.)	(6 d.f.)	(8 d.f.)	(10 d.f.)	(14 d.f.)	(15 d.f.)	(29 d.f.)	(32 d.f.)

Notes: Standard errors in parenthesis
* Parameter is less than twice its standard error
Omitted Variables: Class IV, Caste (SC/ST), Religion (Hindu), Cohort 5 (those born before 1940), State (Assam). See text for more details.
Interactions are with Gender and are shown as 'G*'.

Source: Authors calculations, based on NES 1996, CSDS Data Unit.

Models 1–8 within Table 6.2 are successive models controlling for additional main-effect background variables. In Model 8, only the significant states have been shown (to make the tables easier to interpret), though all the states were a part of the analysis.[30] Model 8 emerged as the most parsimonious main-effect model and was treated as the baseline model for the addition of interaction effects.

The last column in Table 6.2 depicts the model with interaction terms. This model (Model 9) was derived by adding various interactions, as shown in Table 6.3 (all interactions are with gender). The change in chi-square and the change in degrees of freedom were used to judge the fit of the model. The model with the best fit was deemed the most parsimonious one and was included in Table 6.2 as Model 9.

TABLE 6.3: Deriving the Most Parsimonious Model for the Transition 'Some Primary School from Illiterate'[31]

	Model Chi Sq	*Model d.f.*	*Δ Chi Sq*	*Δ d.f.*
Model 1				
Baseline model	3,966.425	29	–	–
Model 2a				
*Class I	3,966.846	30	0.421	1
Model 2b				
*Class II	3,966.911	30	0.486	1
Model 2c				
*Class III	3,966.519	30	0.094	1
Model 2d				

(Contd)

Table 6.3 (Contd)

	Model Chi Sq	*Model d.f.*	*Δ Chi Sq*	*Δ d.f.*
*Caste (OBC)	3,966.970	30	0.545	1
Model 2e				
*Caste (Higher)	3,966.550	30	0.125	1
Model 2f				
* Religion (Other)	3,989.376	30	22.951	1
Model 3a				
*Other, *Muslim	3,991.547	31	2.171	1
Model 3b				
*Other, *Mother Lit.	3,991.923	31	2.547	1
Model 3c				
*Other, *Father Lit.	3,995.316	31	5.940	1
Model 4a				
*Other, *Father Lit.				
* Cohort 1	3,998.069	32	2.753	1
Model 4b				
*Other, * Father Lit,				
*Cohort 2	3,997.900	32	2.584	1
Model 4c				
*Other, * Father Lit.				
*Cohort 3	3,996.687	32	1.371	1
Model 4d				
*Other, * Father Lit.				
*Cohort 4	3,996.326	32	1.010	1
Model 4e				
*Other, * Father Lit.				
*Locality	3,996.078	32	0.762	1
Model 4f				
*Other, * Father Lit. *Bihar	3,996.299	32	0.983	1
Model 4g				
*Other, * Father Lit.				
*Gujarat	3,996.424	32	1.108	1
Model 4h				
*Other, * Father Lit.				
*Rajasthan	4,010.618	32	15.302	1
Model 5a				
*Other, * Father Lit.				

(Contd)

Table 6.3 (Contd)

	Model Chi Sq	*Model d.f.*	*Δ Chi Sq*	*Δ d.f.*
*Rajasthan, *Tamil Nadu	4,011.648	33	1.030	1
Model 5b				
*Other, * Father Lit.				
*Rajasthan, *Kerala	4,010.618	33	0.000	1

Notes: N=7808.
Standard Errors in parenthesis
* Parameter is less than twice its standard error
The Base Line Model is Model 8 in Table 2. This includes all the main effects, but no interaction terms.
Interactions are with Gender and are shown as 'G*'.
Gender and state interaction is only shown for the states that had a significant main effect parameter.

Source: Authors calculations, based on NES 1996, CSDS Data Unit.

I will begin by explaining the results of the first transition, from illiteracy to some primary school, and in the next section of the chapter, will supplement these results with information from the other transitions. In the final discussion, results will be culled from all four transitions, to provide an overall picture of educational transition decisions and the changing effect of gender and other background variables on these decisions.

The next section provides a detailed explanation of Tables 6.2, 6.3 (see n31) and 6.4. Readers interested solely in the results can turn to the 'discussion' section of this chapter, which puts these results into perspective.

MAIN EFFECTS

Table 6.2 shows the parameter for gender and the other independent variables at the stage of transition to some primary school.[32] The parameter for gender remains negative and highly significant and increases after controlling for additional independent variables. The parameter for father's class is positive and significant and the parameter for Class I is consistently larger than for the other classes. The addition of caste in the model does not change the parameter for class by much. However, belonging to the general non-reserved castes has a stronger parameter than belonging to the Other Backward Classes (OBC), in contrast to the base category of the Scheduled Castes and Tribes. The coefficient for religion is seen to be highly significant. For Muslims, this parameter is negative, while for 'other' religions it is positive, as compared to the base category of Hindus.

The addition of variables for mother and father's literacy leads to a large increase in the parameter for gender, but decreases the parameter for father's class. The parameter for mother's literacy is higher than that for father's literacy, even after adding all the other main effects. A clear cohort effect is visible: the youngest cohort (born between 1971 and 1978) has a strong positive parameter, as compared to the base category of the oldest cohort (respondents born before the 1940s). Similarly regional parameters of locality and state were added to the model. Belonging to an urban area has a positive parameter, even after controlling for the state of the respondent.

Interaction Effects

The above model, with the main effects, assumes that class, caste, parental education, region and religion have the same effects at all levels, for both men and women. Interaction terms help us to see how the effect actually varies across groups. The interactions that were added were for gender and father's class, gender and caste, gender and religion, gender and parents' education, gender and cohort, gender and locality, and gender and state. Each interaction, in turn, was broken up into its subparts, for example: gender * caste (OBC), gender * caste (higher).

At the first transition to some primary school, one can see that the only significant interactions were for gender and 'other' religion, gender and father's literacy and gender and the state of Rajasthan. Controlling for these interactions, one can see that the parameter for gender in Model 9 rises. The other parameters are largely left unchanged, except for other religion, which becomes negative. The parameter for the state of Rajasthan falls, but still remains significantly negative.

These logistic regression parameters do bring out a clear pattern of gender inequality in the likelihood of educational transitions, the effect of background variables and how this inequality varies with the addition of other main and interaction terms. Other interactions were tried as well—for example, caste and class, caste and locality—but were found to be insignificant and have not been included in the tables.

Comparison with Other Transitions

The above was a description of the main and interaction effects for the first transitional stage. As mentioned earlier, similar analyses were conducted at all four transitions. I will now highlight the patterns that emerge through a comparison of the most parsimonious models at each transition level. Table 6.4 puts together all parsimonious models from each transition and helps to interpret how inequality in opportunity varies at each transition stage.

Table 6.4: Logistic Regression Parameters for All Main and Interaction Effects at Each Transition

Independent Variables	*Some Primary School from Illiterate*	*Middle School Given Some Primary School*	*High School Given Middle School*	*College (any) Given High School*
Gender (Male=0)	–1.947	–1.174	–0.781	–0.198*
	(0.081)	(0.122)	(0.163)	(0.155)
Class I	1.399	1.069	0.893	0.762
	(0.155)	(0.138)	(0.137)	(0.147)

(Contd)

Table 6.4 (Contd)

Independent Variables	Some Primary School from Illiterate	Middle School Given Some Primary School	High School Given Middle School	College (any) Given High School
Class II	0.886	0.256*	–0.588	–0.128*
	(0.220)	(0.206)	(0.214)	(0.311)
Class III	0.185	0.254	–0.079*	0.030*
	(0.068)	(0.086)	(0.100)	(0.132)
Caste (OBC)	0.423	0.303	0.018*	0.040*
	(0.077)	(0.102)	(0.124)	(0.163)
Caste (Higher)	1.061	0.866	0.287	0.103*
	(0.091)	(0.127)	(0.125)	(0.157)
Other religion	–0.446	0.380	–0.059*	0.460
	(0.216)	(0.180)	(0.247)	(0.194)
Muslim	–0.430	–0.786	–0.598	–0.520
	(0.109)	(0.123)	(0.138)	(0.180)
Mother Lit. (Illiterate=0)	1.596	0.928	0.605	0.714
	(0.144)	(0.108)	(0.105)	(0.118)
Father Lit. (Illiterate=0)	1.295	0.921	0.551	0.874
	(0.105)	(0.085)	(0.102)	(0.147)
Cohort 1 (1971–78)	1.356	1.725	0.649	0.668
	(0.106)	(0.151)	(0.183)	(0.224)
Cohort 2 (1961–70)	0.954	1.549	0.628	0.527
	(0.102)	(0.136)	(0.175)	(0.222)
Cohort 3 (1951–60)	0.630	1.176	0.348*	0.353*
	(0.107)	(0.142)	(0.184)	(0.234)
Cohort 4 (1941–50)	0.219*	0.762	0.392*	0.262*
	(0.118)	(0.160)	(0.213)	(0.268)
Locality (Rural=0)	0.757	0.530	0.168*	0.111*
	(0.096)	(0.102)	(0.123)	(0.133)
Andhra Pradesh	–	–	–	–
Bihar	–0.636	–	–0.672	–
	(0.175)	–	(0.275)	–

(Contd)

Table 6.4 (Contd)

Independent Variables	*Some Primary School from Illiterate*	*Middle School Given Some Primary School*	*High School Given Middle School*	*College (any) Given High School*
Delhi	–	–	–1.032	–
	–	–	(0.280)	–
Gujarat	1.949	–	–0.790	–0.819
	(0.275)	–	(0.299)	(0.311)
Karnataka	–	–	–	–
Haryana, Himachal Pradesh and Punjab	–	–	–0.825	–
	–	–	(0.333)	–
Orissa	–	–0.914	–	–
		(0.257)	–	–
Maharashtra	–	–	–	–0.555
	–	–	–	(0.270)
Madhya Pradesh	–	–0.624	–1.049	–
	–	(0.233)	(0.293)	–
Tamil Nadu	0.664	–	–0.718	–1.401
	(0.189)	–	(0.270)	(0.296)
Rajasthan	–0.579	–0.791	–1.064	–1.597
	(0.225)	(0.280)	(0.339)	(0.418)
Uttar Pradesh	–	–0.286*	–0.788	–
		(0.217)	(0.253)	–
Kerala	1.787	–	–0.570*	–1.390
	(0.338)	–	(0.291)	(0.306)
West Bengal	–	–0.680	–1.422	–1.022
		(0.220)	(0.267)	(0.293)
G*Higher (Caste)	–	–0.195*	–	–
	–	(0.163)	–	–
G*Other (religion)	1.357	–	0.743	–
	(0.287)	–	(0.356)	–
G*Father's Lit.	0.317	–	–	–
	(0.139)	–	–	–
G*Cohort 1	–	0.464	0.448	–
	–	(0.170)	(0.185)	–

(Contd)

Table 6.4 (Contd)

Independent Variables	*Some Primary School from Illiterate*	*Middle School Given Some Primary School*	*High School Given Middle School*	*College (any) Given High School*
G*Rajasthan	–1.111	–1.301	–1.822	–
	(0.294)	(0.463)	(0.701)	–
G*UP	–	–0.628	–	–
		(0.216)	–	–
G*Locality	–	–	–0.446	–0.688
			(0.186)	(0.217)
Constant	–0.934	–1.346	0.332*	–1.503
	(0.177)	(0.231)	(0.291)	(0.334)
Chi Square	4,010.618	1,238.240	465.288	406.239
	(32 d.f.)	(33 d.f.)	(33 d.f.)	(30 d.f.)
N	7,808	4,554	3,132	2,112

Notes: Standard Errors in parenthesis;
* Parameter is less than twice its standard error;
'–' The insignificant parameters for states and the insignificant interactions with gender are not shown. States that had a significant main-effect parameter but became insignificant with the introduction of interaction effects are shown in the table.
Omitted Variables: Class IV, Caste (SC/ST), Religion (Hindu), Cohort 5 (those born before 1940), State (Assam). See text for more details. Interactions are with Gender and are shown as G*.

Source: Authors calculations, based on NES 1996, CSDS Data Unit.

Controlling for all the background variables, Table 6.4 shows that the impact of gender is negative at all stages, though it declines at later stages, particularly at the stage of moving from high school to college, where the parameter becomes insignificant.

The impact of the father's class, on the other hand, is relatively stable at all transitions. Belonging to Class I (professional, managerial or big business) as compared to Class IV, which is the base category (unskilled manual labour, lower agriculturists), seems to have a positively significant effect on the relative chance of making the next transition. The interaction of gender and class is not significant at any transition.

Belonging to the higher castes has a positive and stronger parameter than OBC. But these caste parameters become insignificant at the last stages. The parameter for caste is weaker than for Class I at each transition stage. The interaction of caste with gender was barely significant at the second stage, but became insignificant after the other interaction terms were added.

With Hindu as the omitted category, one can see the impact of belonging to a Muslim background or belonging to the 'other' religious community. Being a Muslim has a strong negative effect at each stage of educational transition, though the effect is smallest at the first stage. It rises sharply for the transition from some primary to middle school and then falls for the subsequent transitions. What is interesting, though, is the interaction of 'other' religion with gender, which is positive at the first and third transitions. Its main effect, on the other hand, was negative at these transitions.

Mother and father's education too has the expected positive effect on the probability of going to the next level of school. At each level, mother's literacy seems to have a stronger effect on the educational transition of a child than the father's literacy, except at the level of transition to college, given high school completion. Gender and parental literacy interaction is only significant for father's literacy at the first stage. There is a strong cohort effect as expected and the cohort gender interaction is significant at two transitions.

The effect of locality seems to decline and becomes insignificant at the last two transitions. The one state that has a consistently significant parameter at all transitions is the state of Rajasthan. The interaction of gender with Rajasthan too is significant at the first three transitions.

The implications of these findings will now be discussed.

Discussion

The statistical analysis makes it clear that controlling for a host of background variables, the gender inequality in educational transitions still remains, though it does decrease by the last transition, where its parameter becomes insignificant. As already mentioned, the model with the main effects assumes that all background characteristics have the same effects at all levels for both men and women. Interaction terms help us to see how the effect actually varies across groups. The inclusion of interaction effects thus highlights some interesting results. These interactions highlight, in particular, the additional inequality faced by girls while making educational transitions. Figure 6.5 depicts some of the prominent results that have emerged as a part of the analysis.

Figure 6.5: Graphical Description of Selected Parameters

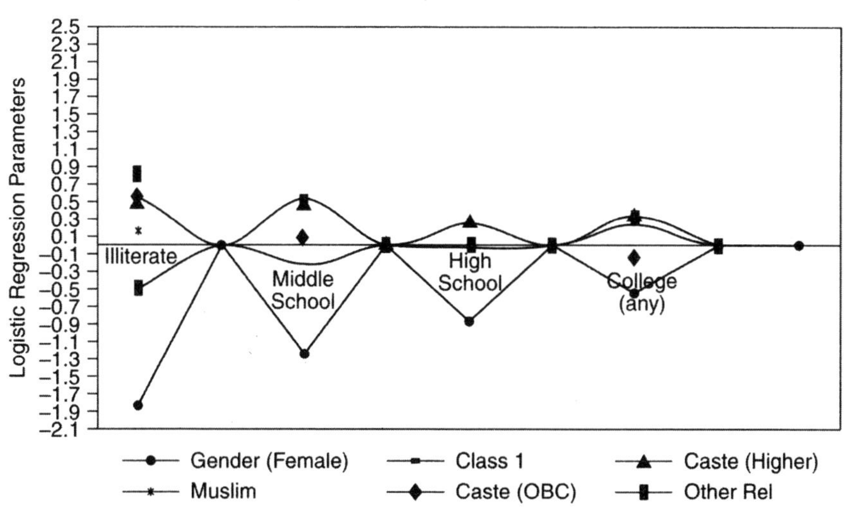

Source: Authors calculations, based on NES 1996, CSDS Data Unit.

In support of the poverty hypothesis (as laid out in an earlier section of this chapter), one finds that father's class, as was expected, plays a decisive role in the transition likelihood of the subject. Father's class has a consistently high parameter at all stages of the educational process. According to the second part of the poverty hypothesis, the effect of gender should vary by class at different transition points. But interestingly, this hypothesis finds no support in my analysis, as the interaction between gender and class was insignificant at each transition stage. Put another way, what emerges is that the gender-odds ratio is the same for all four classes, which refutes the notion of a more egalitarian Indian middle class.

It is observed that higher castes fare better than the backward castes, where education for both boys and girls is concerned, but surprisingly, caste does not appear to play as decisive a role in the decision to make a successive transition, as does father's class. The parameter for caste becomes insignificant in the last transition stages, whereas that for Class I remains positive and significant at all levels. What this means really is that caste no longer distinguishes among the 'survivors' at later stages. In other words, there has already been a kind of natural selection at each stage, in which only the most determined women or men from the backward castes have made it.[33] It is important to note that the interactions that were tried between caste and class were not significant, and the interaction between gender and caste was similarly insignificant.

The second part of the community hypothesis posits that caste and religion should interact with gender; in other words, girls from lower castes, or from religious communities that do not encourage long-term investment in the education of girls, should fare worse than boys sharing the same background. It is believed that particularly among the Muslim community, girls do much worse than the boys (Sengupta and Guha 2002). But contrary to these studies, my analysis refutes this claim, as there emerges no interaction between gender and belonging to the Muslim community. What does emerge, though, is that girls from 'other' religious communities do stand a better relative chance, as the gender and religion interaction parameter is strongly positive for this community. This could be because the 'other' religion category is quite heterogeneous and includes communities like the Christians, Parsis and Jains, who are known to encourage the education of girls (Sopher 1980).

Next, I turn to the household resources hypothesis. I find that mother and father's education both play an important part in the transition likelihood of the subject. A mother being literate has the strongest impact on the child's transition to some primary school from illiteracy, but by the last stage (transition to college), it is the father's education that has a stronger effect. This would seem to support the view that a literate mother would encourage all her children, irrespective of gender, to stay on in school (Sathar and Lloyd 1994), as suggested through the parameter of the main-effect. But here again, I find that there emerges no interaction between mother's literacy and gender. This implies that the belief (ibid.; Sengupta and Guha 2002) that a more educated mother would lead to a higher education for the daughter does not hold. On the other hand, father's literacy and gender interact and have a significant parameter at the first stage, from illiteracy to some primary school.

Under the regional variation hypothesis, support was found for the state aspect, but only partial support was found for the rural/urban aspect. Coming from an urban area has a strongly positive parameter in the first two transitions, which would support the view that an urban background could lead to a higher likelihood of making successive educational transitions, at least till the level of entry into middle school for both boys and girls. But interestingly, the interaction of gender and locality does not have a significant parameter at the first two transitions and reveals a negative parameter at the last two transition stages, which could possibly be due to the selection processes at the later educational stages discussed above.

However, what really stands out with regard to the regional variation hypothesis are the parameters for states, as well as the interaction of gender and states. The state of Kerala has a strong positive parameter and that of Rajasthan a high negative parameter, which seems to empirically support the view that coming from a state with historically high or low levels of literacy could reduce or add to the gender inequality in educational transitions. What needs special attention, however, is the interaction between gender and Rajasthan. The negative and highly significant interaction parameter at the first three stages of the educational transition process throws light on the extreme gender inequality in this state. In addition to the rural/urban effect, then, one also observes a strong regional or state effect. In sum, it emerges that in India, girls have a relatively poorer chance than boys to make successive educational transitions, but in Rajasthan, their chances are even poorer than elsewhere.

Conclusions

Historically, the education of girls in India has lagged behind that of boys (Aggarwal 1987; Agrawal and Aggarwal 1994). In addition, studies have shown that certain communities and classes fare much worse than the others. Recently, some researchers have attempted to lay down the determinants of the inequality in educational attainment for boys and girls. Only a handful of these (Burney and Irfan 1991; Sathar and Lloyd 1994; Sengupta and Guha 2002; Raju 1991)[34] have explicitly looked at the factors responsible for the relative gender inequality in educational attainment. But none of these (except Sathar and Lloyd 1994)[35] deal with the relative chances that girls have vis-à-vis boys, keeping background characteristics constant.

The aim of this chapter has then been twofold: first, to highlight the factors responsible for the inequality in educational opportunities for both boys and girls from socially deprived origins, and second, to highlight in particular the inequality faced by girls at each transition stage. In other words, the aim was not only to see how social background variables effect children's schooling, but keeping all else equal, to study how girls from a particular community or class fared as compared to boys from the same community. This was achieved through interaction effects between gender and all the background variables.

Logistic regression was considered the most appropriate method to conduct the present analysis. The major results of this study seemed to be only partly consistent with previous research. Using the 1996 National Election Study (NES) data, I found that class emerged as a strong determinant of the relative chance of a child continuing in school, but no support was found for an additional class effect where the education of girls is concerned, thus refuting the notion of a more egalitarian middle class. I found only partial and weak support for the effect of caste. Adding caste to the analysis did not appreciably lead to a decline in the parameters of class and it then emerges that, given caste and class together, class seems to have a greater impact on the education that a child receives. This is not to deny the fact that caste has an important part to play in social interaction, especially in blocking certain avenues of education to the minority backward community. But what it does is highlight the fact that, for better or worse, class appears to be an important determinant of who gets ahead and who lags behind.

The effects of other background characteristics, like parental education, religion and region, were found to be important determinants of the likelihood of an educational transition for a child. Parental literacy (especially father's literacy), state (especially the state of Rajasthan) and religion (belonging to the 'other' religion category) had strong interactions with gender.

The decrease in gender inequality, as seen in the West (Shavit and Blossfeld 1993), has not yet come into play in India, where the education of girls is still not considered a necessity (see Table 6.1 and Figure 6.1, which depict the odds-ratios calculated using census figures. These ratios reveal a relatively stable pattern of gender inequality in the past few decades). This could well be due to the dynamics of an agricultural society, where children are an asset on the farms and the opportunity cost of educating them (and doing without their labour) is quite high.

While interpreting the results of the present analysis, one must bear in mind that the method of logistic regression is not without its drawbacks. According to Mare (1993: 352) 'the more that unobservable factors affect school continuation and the greater the degree of selectivity, the more difficult it is to estimate social background effects, and the more important to compare background effects across social contexts.' This problem of unmeasured heterogeneity could be overcome in subsequent studies by the introduction of additional control variables, which are conceptually believed to affect the schooling of girls. These could be the availability of schools, the availability of female teachers, the quality of schools available, the distance of the schools from the village and girls' labour force participation. Even though the present data does not include information on these variables, nevertheless, in my opinion, the data does help to shed light on gender inequality where education is concerned and is a step in the right direction to understand this inequality. A future qualitative field study could also complement the current research and would provide a clearer picture of factors that affect the schooling of girls and boys.

Keeping in mind the results of this study, many avenues for further research emerge. It would be interesting to study if and how caste and class mediate with education to affect the job opportunities for women and men. This could be a good test of the human capital approach (Colclough et al. 1999; Kingdon 1999), which posits that the job opportunity structure could be biased against women, and parents, knowing well that their daughters will not get good enough jobs in the labour market, prefer to invest in the education of their sons instead.

The present chapter is a first step, albeit a small one, to analyse some of the determinants of inequality in educational transitions in India, with particular emphasis on gender inequality.

Appendix 6.1

Table 6.A1: Odds Ratios for Rural Men and Women as well as for Urban Men and Women

This table is for Figure 6.2

Year	*Rural Men per cent of Total Rural Male Sample*	*Rural Women per cent of Total Rural Female Sample*	*Odds Ratios for Rural Men and Women*
1951	19.02	4.87	4.59
1961	29.10	8.55	4.41
1971	33.76	13.17	3.36
1981	49.69	21.77	3.55
1991	57.87	30.62	3.12
1997	68.00	43.00	2.82
Year	*Urban Men per cent of Total Urban Male Sample*	*Urban Women per cent of Total Urban Female Sample*	*Odds Ratios for Urban Men and Women*
1951	45.06	22.33	2.85
1961	57.49	34.51	2.57
1971	61.27	42.14	2.17
1981	76.83	56.37	2.57
1991	81.09	64.05	2.41
1997	88.00	72.00	2.85

Source: Data on Literacy is from Education Statistics, sub-Table X, Department of Education, Government of India website.

Appendix 6.2

Table 6.A2: Number of Respondents by Caste and Education

This table is for Figure 6.4

	Illiteracy	*Some Primary School*	*Middle School*	*High School*	*Any College*	*Total*
SC/ST	1,215	400	212	204	109	2,140
Per cent within caste	56.78	18.69	9.91	9.53	5.09	100
OBC	1,337	558	392	448	261	2,996
Per cent within caste	44.63	18.62	13.08	14.95	8.71	100
Higher	702	464	416	537	553	2,672
Per cent within caste	26.27	17.37	15.57	20.1	20.7	100
Total	3,254	1,422	1,020	1,189	923	7,808
	41.68	18.21	13.06	15.23	11.82	100

Source: NES, 1996, CSDS Data Unit.

APPENDIX 6.3

TABLE 6.A3: Respondents by Final Grouped States

This table is for the section on 'Region' in the text

State	*Respondents*	*Per Cent of Total*
Andhra Pradesh	685	7.1
Assam	337	3.5
Bihar	880	9.2
Delhi	563	5.9
Karnataka	494	5.1
Gujarat	483	5.0
Himachal Pradesh, Haryana, Punjab	425	4.4
Kerala	343	3.6
Madhya Pradesh	707	7.4
Maharashtra	861	9.0
Orissa	373	3.9
Tamil Nadu	723	7.5
Rajasthan	539	5.6
Uttar Pradesh	1,432	14.9
West Bengal	769	8.0
Total	9,614	100.0

Note: This table includes the total number of respondents, including the ones that were later dropped due to missing cases.

Source: NES 1996, CSDS Data Unit.

APPENDIX 6.4

TABLE 6.A4: Mare Model: Logistic Regression Parameters for all Main Effects

Independent Variables	*Some Primary School from Illiterate*	*Middle School Given Some Primary School*	*High School Given Middle School*	*College (any) Given High School*
Gender (Male=0)	–1.847	–1.238	–0.875	–0.536
	(0.066)	(0.084)	(0.093)	(0.113)
Class I	1.362	1.028	0.867	0.770
	(0.153)	(0.135)	(0.135)	(0.146)
Class II	0.875	0.255*	–0.608	–0.134*
	(0.220)	(0.205)	(0.214)	(0.311)
Class III	0.178	0.260	–0.089*	0.024*
	(0.068)	(0.085)	(0.100)	(0.131)

(Contd)

Table 6.A4 (Contd)

Independent Variables	*Some Primary School from Illiterate*	*Middle School Given Some Primary School*	*High School Given Middle School*	*College (any) Given High School*
Caste (OBC)	0.432	0.306	0.007*	0.043*
	(0.077)	(0.102)	(0.124)	(0.162)
Caste (Higher)	1.075	0.762	0.269	0.112*
	(0.090)	(0.108)	(0.125)	(0.157)
Other Rel	0.308	0.374	0.298*	0.452
	(0.154)	(0.179)	(0.185)	(0.193)
Muslim	–0.430	–0.779	–0.583	–0.522
	(0.108)	(0.121)	(0.137)	(0.179)
Mother Lit. (Illiterate=0)	1.620	0.934	0.611	0.712
	(0.144)	(0.108)	(0.104)	(0.117)
Father Lit. (Illiterate=0)	1.458	0.909	0.530	0.865
	(0.073)	(0.084)	(0.101)	(0.147)
Cohort 1 (1971–78)	1.356	1.885	0.778	0.679
	(0.106)	(0.138)	(0.175)	(0.225)
Cohort 2 (1961–70)	0.959	1.506	0.604	0.554
	(0.102)	(0.134)	(0.174)	(0.223)
Cohort 3 (1951–60)	0.641	1.138	0.340	0.389*
	(0.107)	(0.141)	(0.183)	(0.235)
Cohort 4 (1941–50)	0.224*	0.730	0.376*	0.284*
	(0.118)	(0.159)	(0.212)	(0.269)
Locality (Rural=0)	0.738	0.507	0.322	0.317
	(0.095)	(0.101)	(0.104)	(0.116)
Andhra Pradesh	–0.289*	–0.111*	–0.266*	–0.155*
	(0.189)	(0.243)	(0.291)	(0.289)
Bihar	–0.611	0.000*	–0.687	–0.425*
	(0.176)	(0.233)	(0.274)	(0.299)
Delhi	0.004*	–0.039*	–1.038	–0.400*
	(0.224)	(0.258)	(0.279)	(0.282)
Gujarat	1.965	–0.366*	–0.818	–0.797
	(0.274)	(0.251)	(0.298)	(0.310)

(Contd)

Table 6.A4 (Contd)

Independent Variables	*Some Primary School from Illiterate*	*Middle School Given Some Primary School*	*High School Given Middle School*	*College (any) Given High School*
Karnataka	–0.277*	0.230*	–0.307*	–0.329*
	(0.200)	(0.264)	(0.306)	(0.323)
Haryana, Himachal Pradesh and Punjab	0.171*	–0.330*	–0.828	–0.305*
	(0.242)	(0.288)	(0.333)	(0.379)
Orissa	0.097*	–0.912	–0.346*	–0.545*
	(0.217)	(0.257)	(0.338)	(0.337)
Maharashtra	0.248*	–0.142*	–0.459*	–0.568
	(0.183)	(0.223)	(0.265)	(0.269)
Madhya Pradesh	–0.291*	–0.660	–1.049	–0.553*
	(0.179)	(0.233)	(0.292)	(0.344)
Tamil Nadu	0.703	0.050*	–0.747	–1.403
	(0.189)	(0.228)	(0.270)	(0.295)
Rajasthan	–0.917	–1.079	–1.310	–1.615
	(0.201)	(0.263)	(0.326)	(0.419)
Uttar Pradesh	–0.109*	–0.503	–0.789	0.126*
	(0.165)	(0.206)	(0.253)	(0.259)
Kerala	1.857	0.243*	–0.590	–1.409
	(0.337)	(0.268)	(0.290)	(0.305)
West Bengal	–0.122*	–0.677	–1.437	–1.044
	(0.181)	(0.220)	(0.267)	(0.292)
Constant	–1.005	–1.260	0.292*	–1.602
	(0.176)	(0.229)	(0.290)	(0.333)
Chi Square	3966.425	1212.385	444.412	396.082
	(29 d.f.)	(29 d.f.)	(29 d.f.)	(29 d.f.)
N	7,808	4,554	3,132	2,112

Notes: Standard Errors in parenthesis. * Parameter is less than twice its standard error. Omitted Variables: Class IV, Caste (SC/ST), Religion (Hindu), Cohort 5 (those born before 1940), State (Assam). See text for more details.

NOTES

[†]I thank Anthony Heath for his encouragement. I would also like to thank the Data Unit of the Centre for the Study of Developing Societies, Delhi, for permission to use their 1996 National Election Study data set.

1. World Education Report (1998) and the section on *Education Statistics* at the Department of Education (MHRD), Government of India website. Available at http://www.education.nic.in/htmlweb/edusta.htm (accessed in 2002, henceforth DOE website).

2. For a detailed study on the receding goal of universal elementary education, see Acharya (1994); see Agrawal and Aggarwal (1994) for a historical look at policies on education. For a review of the National Policy on Education 1986, see Aggarwal (1989).

3. According to the 1991 Census, only 45 per cent of the total female population aged 6–10 years was in school. In addition only 57 per cent of the male population in the same age-group was enrolled in school. Table 15, *Census of India 1991*. Census Data Online, Government of India website. Available at http://www.censusindia.net/cendat/datatable15.html (accessed in 2002, henceforth Census Data Online).

4. 'The decadal census collects information on literacy. For the purpose of census, a person is considered literate if he or she can read and write with understanding in any language. However, a person who can merely read but cannot write is not literate' (*Education Statistics,* DOE website).

5. Scheduled Castes and Scheduled Tribes are the former 'untouchables' and tribal groups, respectively, who, at the time of the drafting of the Constitution, were included in a constitutional list or 'schedule' and preferential policies for their upliftment were laid out (for details on preferential policies, see Weiner et al. [1981]).

6. Sub-Table XVIII, *Education Statistics,* DOE website.

7. Shavit and Blossfeld (1993), in their cross-national comparison of 13 Western countries, reveal persisting class inequalities. According to their study, the gender inequality seems to have been reversed in the West. This has not happened in India, as this chapter shows.

8. For a discussion on this aspect of girls' schooling, especially with regard to the labour market, see Kingdon (1999), Colclough (1999), Sengupta and Guha (2002).

9. According to the 1991 Census, about 67.7 per cent of the Indian population was engaged in agriculture (Source: Census Data Online).

10. For a discussion on the status of women's education in India, see Aggarwal (1987).

11. Similar studies in the neighbouring country of Pakistan show that household income, parental education and the size of the landholding have a positive impact on a household's decision to send a child to school (Burney and Irfan 1991). Sathar and Lloyd (1994) too, in their study of primary schooling in Pakistan, conclude that 'the basic decisions of children's entry into school and completion of the primary level are largely determined by parent's education, particularly that of mother's and household income' (ibid.: 103). They believe that an important determinant of girls' education seems to be the accessibility of 'appropriate' girls' schools. They conclude that the mother's education far outweighs the father's education, especially where the education of girls was concerned.

12. For a detailed look at basic education in India, see the PROBE team report (1999), and also the World Bank paper on primary education in India (1997). See also Dreze and Kingdon (1999) for a look at factors affecting school participation in rural India.

13. The high rate of literacy of women in Kerala has been attributed to the large Christian missionary community in this state and also to the unique matrilineal structure of society here (see Sopher 1980 for a discussion, especially p. 140).

14. There might be some discrepancy here about the grades, as some schools have their middle school from grades VI–VIII, while others have it till grade IX. For the purpose of this paper, I follow the grades as set out by the National Policy on Education 1986; see Aggarwal (1989) for a discussion. For detailed information on the grade system in different states, see the DOE website.

15. There are various kinds of colleges and vocational education options available to students after completing high school. However, as I will be looking at the determinants of education at different levels and not within a level, for the purpose of this study, it was considered enough to know whether a respondent went to college or not and not what kind of college they went to.

16. See Acharya (1994) for a discussion on the non-formal stream and its weaknesses.

17. Shavit and Blossfeld (1993) present a study of educational inequality in 13 countries using a combination of both these methods.

18. After deleting from the data all the respondents who had missing information on any of the variables used in the study, I was left with a final sample of 7,808 men and women.

19. Though this does not exclude the possibility of official bias while including people on the electoral register, the bias should still be minimal.

20. Sub-Table XI, *Education Statistics*, DOE website.

21. For an interesting discussion on the geographical picture of sex disparity in Indian literacy, see Sopher (1980), in which he studies the reasons why certain regions in India have consistently lagged behind others, as far as equality of educational opportunity is concerned.

22. For a study on what sets Kerala apart from the rest of the country, see Jeffrey (1992).

23. The districts of Barmer and Jalor of Rajasthan have the lowest literacy of 7.68 per cent and 7.76 per cent, respectively. *Census of India 1991*, DOE website.

24. See Kumar et al. (2002) for a discussion of these categories.

25. Father's class is computed from the data on the occupation of the father.

26. For a discussion on the enumeration of caste in the census, see a commentary by Kumar (2000); see also Sundar (2000).

27. For an example of the divisions between the category of 'Dalits' or Scheduled Castes, see Shah (2002).

28. See Appendix 6.2 for the Table corresponding to Figure 6.4.

29. See Appendix 6.3 for a table with the final 15 states.

30. For a comparative picture of all four transitions, see Appendix 6.4, which puts together the most parsimonious models with the main effects, but no interaction terms at each transition point (including the parameters for each state, whether significant or not).

31. Similar procedures were used to derive the most parsimonious model at each transition. The tables for each transition are not included here due to space constraints.

32. The logistic regression coefficients or parameter estimates are the fitted log odds. According to Mare (1981: 83), they 'denote the change in the log odds of grade progression per unit change in an independent variable'. These coefficients are the parameter estimates for each successive transition, given the completion of the previous one.

33. One observes a decline in the background effects on each successive transition, as would be expected under the life-course hypothesis (Shavit and Blossfeld 1993), which posits that background effects should be particularly strong at the lower levels of the education system and should diminish as one moves higher up the education ladder. This could either be because towards the end of the educational career the subject has become independent enough not to depend on parental resources; or what is more likely is that there could have been a kind of a natural selection.

34. Sathar and Lloyd (1994) and Burney and Irfan's (1991) study is based on education in Pakistan.

35. Raju (1991) only mentions the need to deal with this issue, but does not empirically tackle it herself.

REFERENCES

Acharya, P. 1994. 'Universal Elementary Education: Receding Goal'. *Economic and Political Weekly* 29 (1 and 2): 27–30.

Aggarwal, J. C. 1987. *Indian Women: Education and Status*. New Delhi: Arya Book Depot.

———. 1989. *National Policy on Education, 1986: An Appraisal*. Delhi: Doaba House.

Agrawal, S. P., and J. C. Aggarwal. 1994. *Third Historical Survey of Educational Development in India: Select Documents, 1990–1992*. New Delhi: Concept Publishing Company.

Burney, N. A., and M. Irfan. 1991. 'Parental Characteristics, Supply of Schools, and Child School Enrolment in Pakistan'. *The Pakistan Development Review* 30 (1): 21–62.

Census of India 1991. 1991. New Delhi: Government of India. Available at http://www.censusindia.net/cendat/datatable15.html (Census Data Online).

Census of India 2001. 2001. New Delhi: Government of India. http://www.censusindia.net/cendat/datatable15.html (Census Data Online).

Colclough, C. 1982. 'The Impact of Primary Schooling on Economic Development: A Review of the Evidence'. *World Development* 10 (3): 167–85.

Colclough, C., P. Rose, and M. Tembon. 1999. 'Does Poverty Cause Gender Inequality in Schooling?' *Id21 Insights*, Issue 29. Also available at http://www.id21.org/insights/insights29/insights-iss29-art05.html.

Dreze, J., and G. G. Kingdon. 1999. 'School Participation in Rural India'. *Development Economics Discussion Paper Series, No. 18*, Suntory and Toyota International Centre for Economics and Related Disciplines.

Education Commission of India. 1966. *Report of the Education Commission, 1964–66: Education and National Development*. New Delhi: Ministry of Education.

Education Statistics. Department of Education (MHRD), Government of India. Available at http://www.education.nic.in/htmlweb/edusta.htm.

Government of India. 1986. *National Policy on Education, 1986*. New Delhi: Ministry of Human Resource Development.

Jeffrey, R. 1992. *Politics, Women and Well-being: How Kerala Became a 'Model'*. Basingstoke: Macmillan.

Jonsson, J. O. 1993. 'Persisting Inequalities in Sweden'. In Y. Shavit, and H. P. Blossfeld, eds, *Persistent Inequality: Changing Educational Attainment in Thirteen Countries*. Boulder, CO: Westview Press: 101–32.

Kingdon, G. G. 1999. 'Gender Gap in India's Schools: Is the Labour Market a Factor?' *Id21 Insights*, Issue 29. Also available at http://www.id21.org/insights/insights29/insights-iss29-art06.html.

Krishnan, G., and M. Shyam. 1973. 'Spatial Perspective on Progress of Female Literacy in India: 1901–1971'. *Pacific Viewpoint* 14: 203–06.

Kumar, R. 2000. 'Caste Enumeration in Census: Constitutional Imperative'. *Economic and Political Weekly* 35 (35 and 36): 3100–102.

Kumar, S., A. Heath, O. Heath. 2002. 'Determinants of Social Mobility in India'. *Economic and Political Weekly* 37 (29), 20 July: 2983–87.

Mare, R. D. 1980. 'Social Background and School Continuation Decisions', *Journal of the American Statistical Association* 75: 295–305.

——. 1981. 'Change and Stability in Educational Stratification'. *American Sociological Review* 46: 72–87.

——. 1993. 'Educational Stratification on Observed and Unobserved Components of Family Background'. In Y. Shavit, and H. P. Blossfeld, eds, *Persistent Inequality: Changing Educational Attainment in Thirteen Countries*. Boulder, CO: Westview Press: 351–76.

Ministry of Human Resource Development (MHRD). 1993. Education for All, The Indian Scene. New Delhi: Government of India.

National Committee on the Status of Women (India). 1975. *Status of Women in India: A Synopsis of the Report of the National Committee on the Status of Women, 1971–1974*. New Delhi: Indian Council of Social Science Research.

PROBE. 1999. *Public Report on Basic Education in India*. New Delhi: Oxford University Press.

Raju, S. 1991. 'Gender and Deprivation. A Theme Revisited with a Geographical Perspective', *Economic and Political Weekly* 26 (49): 2827–39.

Ramachandran, V., and A. Saihjee 2002. 'The New Segregation: Reflections on Gender and Equity in Primary Education'. *Economic and Political Weekly* 37 (17):1600–13.

Rosenzweig, M. R., and T. P. Schultz. 1982. 'Market Opportunities, Genetic Endowments and the Intra-Family Distribution of Resources: Child Survival in Rural India'. *The American Economic Review* 72 (4): 803–15.

Sathar, Z. A., and C. B. Lloyd. 1994. 'Who Gets Primary Schooling in Pakistan: Inequalities among and within Families'. *The Pakistan Development Review* 33(2): 103–34.

Sengupta, P., and J. Guha. 2002. 'Enrolment, Dropout and Grade Completion of Girl Children in West Bengal'. *Economic and Political Weekly* 37 (17): 1621–37.

Shah, A. M. 2002. 'The 'Dalit' Category and Its Differentiation'. *Economic and Political Weekly* 37 (14): 1317–18.

Shavit, Y., and H. P. Blossfeld, eds. 1993. *Persistent Inequality: Changing Educational Attainment in Thirteen Countries*. Boulder, CO: Westview Press

Sopher, D. E. 1980. 'Sex Disparity in Indian Literacy'. In D. E. Sopher, ed. *An Exploration of India: Geographical Perspectives on Society and Culture*. London: Longman: 130–88.

Sundar, N. 2000. 'Caste as Census Category: Implications for Sociology'. *Current Sociology* 48 (3): 111–26.

UNESCO. 1998. *World Education Report*, United Nations Educational, Scientific and Cultural Organisation, Paris.

Weiner, M., M. F. Katzenstein, and K. V. N. Rao. 1981. *India's Preferential Policies: Migrants, the Middle Classes, and Ethnic Equality*. Chicago: University of Chicago Press.

World Bank. 1997. *Primary Education in India*. Washington, DC: World Bank.

7

Gender Differentials in Education

*Exploring the Capabilities Approach**

Jeemol Unni

The mainstream approach in economics to education is the human capital model. This is based on the concept of maximisation of the utility function. As opposed to this, Amartya Sen and Martha Nussbaum have proposed a capabilities approach to view various states of well-being, including access and use of education. Sen's capabilities approach shifts the conceptual terrain from resources and opportunities as ends in themselves, to focus on the substantive freedom that people have to convert resources into 'valued doings and beings'.

In this chapter, with the help of empirical data, we use the capabilities approach to identify 'conversion factors' that are not typically addressed in the utility approach. We juxtapose the two approaches to examine how institutions such as caste and religion mediate access and returns to education of men and women. The effort is to discuss whether the capabilities approach provides any advantage in addressing questions of inequity that may be mediated through such institutions. The main innovation in this chapter is a comparison between knowledge generated through the use of traditional data sources to measure access and returns to education, with the knowledge about the dynamics of capability formation generated through a mixture of traditional, quantitative and some qualitative data within the capabilities approach.

Utility Approach versus the Capabilities Approach

The term utility is used to mean different things and loosely implies anything having value. Utility has been viewed as 'happiness' as well as 'desire-fulfilment' and both can be taken as guides to a person's well-being. Sen (1987) took exception to the view of utility as a real-valued (that is, numerical) representation of choice. He questioned this approach of the binary relation of choice reflecting the person's well-being: 'an approach that goes back to the origin of the "revealed preference" school'. This approach is deficient in analysing the motivation behind a person's choice. It

* Previously published in *Economic and Political Weekly* 44 (9): 111–17.

makes the heroic assumption that the binary relation underlying choice must be the ordering of the person's own well-being.

Sen (1983) introduced the concept of a person's capabilities to be and to do things of intrinsic worth, i.e., resources adequate to achieve a specified set of functionings. Functionings or 'states of being' could range from elementary states (being nourished, going to school), to complex personal states and activities (participation/appearing without shame). Sen's capability approach emphasised that what mattered to people was 'the actual living that people manage to achieve'. He argued that 'when we make interpersonal comparisons of well-being we should find a measure which incorporates references to functionings, that is what is achieved, but also reflects the intuition that what matters is not merely achieving the functioning but being free to achieve it' (Unterhalter 2003: 2).

> He favoured the capability to function as the criterion for assessing the standard of living, and by implication poverty, rather than the utility that might be derived from using that capability. Thus, Sen eschewed the welfarist approach to poverty with its underlying assumption that the evaluative criterion is the utility that people derive from goods and services. However, he neither offered a practical criterion for evaluating the various capabilities to function nor sought any aggregation of the social values of the separate capabilities (Kingdon and Knight 2003: 5).

Sen shifts the argument from resources and opportunities to achieve functionings, e.g., going to school, to the need to look at the freedom people have to formulate capabilities 'valued doings and beings' and thus convert resources into functionings they value. 'Thus agency and freedom to make up one's mind about schooling as a valued end and convert one's aspirations regarding schooling into valued achievements lie at the heart of Sen's capability approach and distinguish it from other positions' (Unterhalter 2003: 3).

The capability approach to education requires us to think about gendered constraints on functionings and freedoms in educational institutions such as schools. Further, even when girls complete 12 years of schooling, they encounter problems of discrimination in the food they eat, in access to employment and at the workplace, and their contribution to family decision-making or public debate. Measures such as 'years of schooling', used extensively in human capital theory, by no means capture these values. What if women do not claim education, because they reflect what the society expects of them? The approach encourages 'an examination of the ways in which gendered institutions prevent women converting capabilities into functionings' (Unterhalter 2003: 3).

While it is easy to point out the difficulties with the traditional measures of education, it is difficult to visualise a measure using the capabilities approach. As we know, in most multi-ethnic developing societies, certain groups and women are silenced. We attempt to identify 'conversion factors', e.g., institutions of caste and religion that may prevent women from converting resources to 'functioning', in this case education. Further, the intrinsic value of education could be measured as access to media, newspapers, representation in local governments, participation in discussions, freedom from discrimination, etc.

HUMAN CAPITAL APPROACH

The human capital approach has, at its core, the maximisation of utility functions. This is a very popular approach to analysing access and returns to schooling. Traditionally, some of the questions asked through this approach are: who is schooled and what are the returns to education? Also, through the inclusion of independent variables in the participation functions, it seeks to ask whether institutions such as caste and religion affect those who obtain education and, with separate earnings functions, whether there are differences in the returns to education by gender and by these institutions.

The determinants of schooling analysed through this approach begin with a utility function, where parents are assumed to maximise utility, subject to a budget constraint. A demand for schooling function is derived from this maximisation of utility function, which depends on the price or cost of schooling, income and a set of control variables—mainly household, child and parent's characteristics. A probability function of enrolment of a child in school and a grade attainment function help to understand the determinant of schooling. Using this method for Tamil Nadu, Doraisamy (2001) found that parents' education and the household's prosperity emerge as important determinants. The availability of schools and higher adult literacy in the village show better schooling outcomes. A girl's participation in schooling is negatively affected by the presence of young siblings and the number of cattle in the household, while having an educated mother improves her chances. Teacher training had an impact on grade attainment of students.

Juxtaposing the choice, among children, of school enrolment and work participation, Doraisamy (2007) engaged a similar utility maximisation approach and calculated the maximum likelihood probit estimates. While a boy's education was favoured, the parents' education and household income had a positive impact on enrolment over work participation. She concludes that the greater the resources of the household, the higher the demand for children's schooling and less the need for child work to supplement incomes. The influence of institutions like caste and religion is investigated through dummy variables, with children from Scheduled Castes (SCs) and Scheduled Tribes (STs) less likely to attend school. The religion dummy indicates a uniform negative effect for child schooling, compared to the reference category of other religions.

The major limitation of this method is that it assumes that children have choice. The motivation behind the obtained outcome is not investigated, except to say that certain characteristics of the parents and the household can affect the outcome. The actual perception of the child or his/her value for education and the motivation for why SC/ST children are less likely to attend school are not studied in this method.

Another question that the economics of education literature using the utility approach asks is: What are the returns to education? The traditional literature has observed a decreasing returns to education and higher returns to female education (Psacharapoulos 1994). This has been used to justify policies for higher investments in elementary schooling and women's education. However, similar literature in India noted increasing returns to education, or higher level of education had higher returns (Kingdon and Unni 2001; Unni 1996). The returns to female education have been found to be higher than male education in India as well.

Efforts to study the impact of institutions of caste and religion on returns to education using a similar methodology (Unni 2007) found that returns were higher for the SC and ST population, compared to the Muslims. This was attributed to the fact that affirmative action in India has favoured jobs for the SC/ST population, while the Muslim population did not benefit from any such backing.

While these results appear intuitively correct, they fail to answer the question as to why such high returns do not encourage higher female participation in schooling and also greater participation by the SC and ST population, as we shall see later. Again, the critique remains the same as for child schooling. That is, the utility approach concentrates on the outcome of education subject to some constraints, but does not investigate the motivation or whether the person actually has the ability to choose. What are the institutional constraints placed on women, and on particular caste and religious groups, that prevent them from accessing education and jobs with better returns?

In a recent paper, Kingdon and Theopold (2008) have used the human capital utility approach further to ask whether the demand for schooling actually depends on economic returns to education in the local labour market. It is argued that economic returns can have a positive substitution effect, that is, higher return would mean greater participation in schooling. However, economic returns to education could have a negative income effect, due to the higher opportunity cost of labour in the current period. That is, a household may not be willing to forego the extra incomes from the labour of children for longer-term higher returns to education. In India, they noted that higher economic returns had a positive substitution effect for girls, while the negative income effect was stronger for boys in poorer households. They attributed this to the fact that girls' education was substituted by household work, while boys participated in economic activity and earned supplementary incomes for the household.

This result does not appear intuitively correct, nor is it empirically substantiated by the data on school attendance. The higher female returns to schooling should have encouraged greater school attendance among girls, but instead it is the boys who have higher attendance rates. In 2004–05, the attendance of boys in the age groups 5–14 years was 84.7 per cent while for girls it was 79.2 per cent (NSSO 2006). Similarly, the net attendance ratios for 2005–06 in primary school (Classes IV) was 73.2 per cent for boys and 70.5 per cent for girls, while it was 56.8 per cent for middle, secondary and higher secondary scho–ol for boys and 45.6 per cent for girls (NFHS-3 2007).

While the utility approach does provide some broad insights into and direction for the relationships of social and economic constraints on education, it is deficient in explanations for the motivation of the results obtained. It might also lead to a wrong diagnosis for policy, without an understanding of what drives the relationships observed.

CAPABILITIES APPROACH TO EDUCATION

What is it that the capabilities approach allows us to ask or analyse that gives us a better understanding of the economic and social dimensions of education? In the utility approach, it is assumed that people are free to choose, given the constraints of budget. The capabilities approach discusses the ability of the person to choose what he or she values, that is, what is the motivation behind this choice. The argument in the latter approach is shifted from resources and opportunities to acquire education, to discussing the motivation for the choice or the freedom to formulate the capabilities. That is, the focus shifts to how to convert resources into functionings (outcomes) that people value.

The starting point for the capabilities approach is a focus on how the social context sets the conditions for individual freedoms. In the case of education, how free are men and women, boys and girls to access education of their choice, given the institutional dominance of caste and religion in India? The advantage of the capabilities approach is that it invites a wider range of more searching questions with regard to gender equality than just a focus on outcomes.

One of the challenges to the capabilities approach is to devise and measure 'conversion factors'. What variable can define the institutional dominance of caste/religion in the motivation of boys and girls to pursue education? A related issue noted by Sen is the type of data used for assessing well-being, in this case education. He suggests three types of data: market purchase data, responses to questionnaire and non-market observations of personal states (Sen 1987). The utility approach uses market purchase data for a bundle of goods and services that is bought and sold in the market, including education. Non-market items such as fertility, or the choice of having children, are modelled using the non-market observation of personal states, e.g., the number of children.

The third method of responses to questionnaires has been viewed with mistrust in economic literature, on the ground that such information is subjective. However, this method has been increasingly used in recent years, even in the utility approach (for instance, Kingdon and Knight [2003] use it to measure well-being). Non-market state and the questionnaire method are useful types of data to construct variables, to explain the motivations behind the value of education. In the rest of the chapter, we shall attempt to garner some evidence using mainly these two types of data, to better understand whether gender differentials in capabilities in education are mediated through institutions of caste and religion.

INDICATORS OF INSTITUTIONAL MEDIATION BEHIND LOW VALUE PLACED ON EDUCATION

While there could be many reasons for the low value placed on accessing education and the gender bias in it, in spite of high economic returns, in this chapter we focus only on the institution of religion and caste, which operate to restrict freedoms of individuals to choose. The society in India is stratified by social groups, in terms of caste and religion. This system is hierarchical and certain historically vulnerable groups have remained at the bottom of the economic and social pyramid.

In an apparently liberal and democratic society, access to education and capacity to stay within the formal educational system to acquire higher levels of education are limited for the SC/ST and Muslim communities. There is systemic curtailment of freedom by agencies operating on these communities to choose a way out of poverty through education. Besides belonging to the lower castes, the choice of education is further restricted by gender and location. Being a girl/woman living in rural areas, as well as belonging to the SC/ST community ensures that she is triply crippled. While only 15 per cent of boys of the age-group of 5–15 years were out of school, for girls it was nearly 21 per cent. As though the lack of freedom to choose education if one was a girl was not enough, girls living in rural areas (24 per cent) and belonging to SC/ST households (28.5 per cent were out of school) had even more restricted choices (Table 7.1). This discrimination at an early age then becomes a handicap when they enter the labour market, leading to jobs with lower earnings and status. The number of years of schooling that the men and women workers in these groups were able to access reduced systematically from 5.4 years for men to 1.2 for women located in rural areas and belonging to SCs and STs. Compared to men, the choice of having a good education gets progressively worse for women in the unorganised sector, as they carry the triple burden of gender, rural location and belonging to the SC/ST community.

TABLE 7.1: Education and Work by Gender, Location and Social Group (2004–05)

Indicator	*Male*	*Female*	*Rural Female*	*Rural Female SC/ST*
Share of out-of-school children in 5–14 age-group	15.5	20.7	23.5	28.5
Mean years of schooling (all workers)	5.4	2.5	1.9	1.2
Mean years of schooling (unorganised non-agricultural workers)	6.1	3.7	2.9	2.0
Share of all workers up to primary education (including illiterates)	55.6	80.7	85.0	90.7

Source: NCEUS 2007, Table 5.1.

Using the capabilities approach, we look for 'conversion factors' or variables and measures for the motivation behind two questions: (a) why the poor school attendance? (b) why the poor educational attainments?

Reasons for Poor School Attendance

School Infrastructure

While most large villages in India have a primary school, there are many biases in the development of infrastructure mediated through social groups, which are first, more difficult to identify, and then to measure. The Sachar Committee set up by the Government of India to study the social, economic and educational status of Muslims had prepared certain special tabulations for the population Census of 2001, in order to study the availability of infrastructure to the Muslim population. They divided the villages into Muslim population of less than 10 per cent, 10 per cent to 39 per cent and more than 40 per cent, and also by the size of villages. It was found that there was little bias in the availability of primary schools in large villages, but as the size of the village became smaller, it was seen that systematically, the availability of a school in the village with a share of more than 10 per cent and 40 per cent of Muslims went down drastically (Sachar Committee Report 2006: Ch. 7). This would have a clear impact on the choice of children going to school, especially girl children. Parents would hesitate to send young girls to a school located at a distance from the village and this is a gross curtailment of the freedom of persons belonging to this community. The Sachar Committee Report further showed that the availability of roads leading to the village also declined as the village size declined and the share of Muslim population increased. Lack of infrastructure restricts the freedom of choice of parents to send their children to school and acts as a negative 'conversion factor'.

Domestic Work and Child Labour

It is well-known that young girls are engaged in helping their households with domestic duties and the care of siblings. In 2004–05, while nearly 40 per cent (10.8 per cent) and 50 per cent (5.5 per cent) of girls in rural and urban areas, respectively, in the age-group of 5–19 years (10–14 years) were engaged in domestic duties as their major activity, hardly any boys were so engaged (Figure 7.1). This definitely curtailed the freedom of girls to attend school. The boys, more than 50 per cent, if not attending school, were more likely engaged in economic activities compared to girls (27 per cent and 15 per cent in urban and rural areas) in age-groups 5–19 years (NCEUS 2007).

Girls and boys from tribal households and Muslim and SC households were most likely to be out of school, only partly due to being engaged in economic activity (Figure 7.2). Being engaged in economic activity and domestic duties are 'conversion factors' that need to be factored into the choice of children's education.

Further, the level of education of the mother also appears to influence this choice. According to the National Health and Fertility Survey, in 2005–06, children in the age-group of 5–14 years were most likely engaged in paid or unpaid work or household chores for more than 28 hours per week, in households where the mother had no education (NFHS-3 2007: Table 2.21). As the years of mother's education rose, the percentage of children so engaged declined, with hardly any children working in either kinds of work if the mother had more than 12 years of education. While this does show a link between mother's education and perhaps her agency in getting her children into school, it also partly reflects that children from affluent households do not need to work, just as women in such households are most likely to have acquired an education. Further, women from Muslim and SC/ST households were least likely to have studied up to Class VI.

FIGURE 7.1: Share of Boys and Girls in Principal Work, Attending Education and Domestic Duties (Usual Principal Status) by Age-Group, Location and Gender (2004–05)

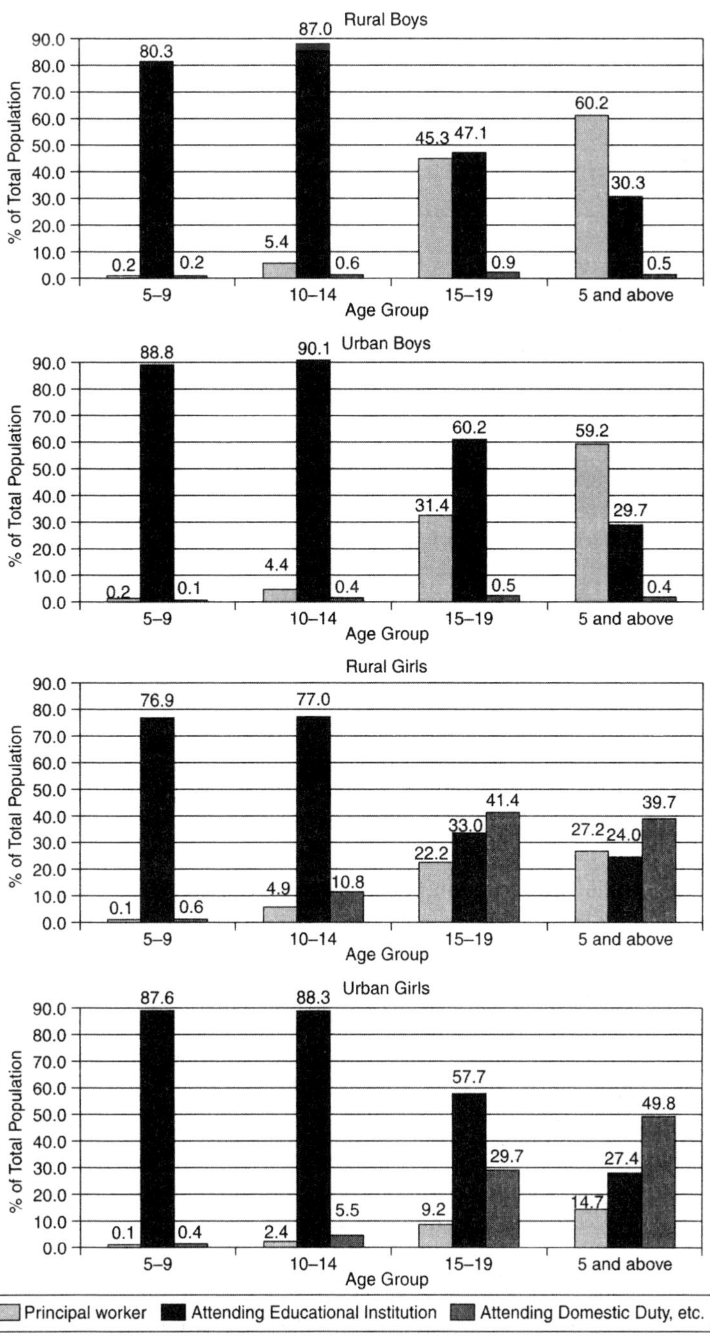

Note: Computed using NSS, unit level data 61st Round on Employment and Unemployment, 2004–05 and adjusted for census population.

Source: NCEUS 2007, Figure 6.3.

FIGURE 7.2: Incidence of Out of School Children and Child Labour (5–14 Years) across Socio-Religious Groups (2004–05)

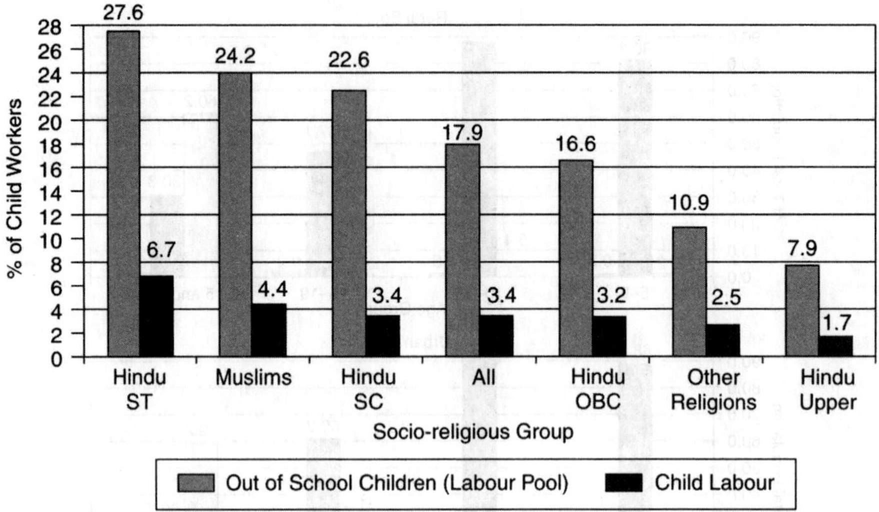

Note: Computed using NSS, unit level data 61st Round on Employment and Unemployment, 2004–05 and adjusted for census population.

Source: NCEUS 2007, Figure 6.2.

Using the questionnaire method, we conducted surveys of 1,236 and 1,407 men and women in rural and urban areas in Gujarat in 2000 and again in 2008, in order to gauge the securities and insecurities they faced in the labour market (henceforth referred to as the GIDR Surveys 2000 and 2008).[1] This was modelled on the basis of the International Labour Organization's (ILO) Socio-economic Security Programme (ILO 2004). In 2008, only about 8 per cent of the households with children in the age-group 5–14 years reported any child as working. The proportion was the highest among Muslim households (18 per cent), followed by Other Backward Classes (OBCs) (nearly 11 per cent), while it was the lowest, about 5 per cent, among upper-caste Hindu households. When the children were engaged in work, nearly 75 per cent of the respondents reported that having them to help was important for the business. Nearly half of the child workers did not attend school and another 20 per cent admitted that child work did interfere with the schooling of children. While this is a further measure of how child work can restrict freedom to study and acquire formal education, the relative differences across communities may be reflecting the fact that Muslims and OBC households are more likely to be self-employed, rather than in salaried jobs. All the same, it helps to understand the motivation behind not sending children to school.

Age at Birth of First Child

The additional burden borne by girls is early marriage and early childbearing, has a negative effect on the chances of the girls completing school and continuing into higher education. In 2005–06, the age at first birth for women in the age-group of

25–29 was the lowest, at 19.1 years, for ST, 19.2 for SC, 19.5 for Muslim, 19.9 for all Hindus (including SC/ST), 21.3 for Christians and the highest was 23.7 for Jain women. Teenage pregnancy (women in ages 15–19 years) was 16 per cent among tribal women, 15.5 per cent among SCs, 12.4 per cent among all Hindus and 11.8 per cent among Muslims (NFHS-3 2007: Tables 4.10 and 4.11). Here again, we see that the institutions of caste and religion bear down on the women in her fertility decisions and curtail her freedom of choice in the sphere of education. Age at marriage and birth of first child are good measures of 'conversion factors'.

Perceptions of Parents with Regard to Children's Education

The questionnaire method can be used to obtain information on the perceptions of people with regard to education and also how and when education and the costs involved become a burden on the households. In Gujarat, in 2000, we noted that the majority of parents viewed the education of children as a source of security for themselves in the future (GIDR Survey 2000, cited in Unni and Rani 2002). When we further queried about the level of education they aspire to for their boys and girls, if they were attending school, we found a gender difference in the responses. The mean level of education for the boys was graduation or above, while for girl children, they only aspired to send them, on average, up to the higher-secondary level. There could be a clear cultural reason for these responses, since most parents expected to live with their male children in their old age.

Poor households live from one crisis to another and have to garner resources to be able to stay alive. This has been clearly brought out in the ILO-based socio-economic security surveys in many countries (ILO 2004: Table 4.5). Some households responded to a financial crisis by pulling their children out of school. In 2008, only about 3 per cent of households with children in the age-group 5–14 years reported that paying for the costs of children's schooling constituted a financial crisis. However, 4.2 per cent of these households said that they had to pull their children out of school in response to a crisis (GIDR Survey 2008, cited in Standing et al. 2010). In most cases, this was due to a serious illness in the household. While the proportion of parents having to resort to this was mercifully small, we noted a gender difference in that girl children were more likely to have to give up schooling. This points to one of the motivations behind poor educational attainment among the poor, and particularly among the girls.

On the positive side, however, the interest of parents to keep children in school was also brought out by another 3.3 per cent of respondents with children of school-going age, who reported that they borrowed money or sold personal assets to keep children in school (GIDR Survey 2008).

Why Poor Educational Attainments

The quantity, level and quality of education in the country are in a deplorable state even today. While communities that are lagging behind need to catch up with their education level, we find that they are falling behind even further. Besides, children are forced to drop out of school for various reasons and also end up having poor quality educational attainments.

Being Left Behind

In the era of globalisation, education and skills are at a premium, and this is crucial for communities if they wish to stay ahead. However, we found that in recent years, the Muslim community was probably getting left behind, with the lowest reduction in illiteracy and growth of graduates as compared to other communities. While the SC/ST reduced illiteracy by 6.9 percentage points and OBCs by 6.5, the Muslims were able to reduce illiteracy only by 4.8 percentage points, from 1999–2000 to 2004–05. Further, the SC/ST and Muslims hardly increased above graduate education (0.3 per cent), while OBCs and the forward communities did so by 1 and 2 percentage points, respectively, from 1999–2000 to 2004–05 (Sengupta et al. 2008).

Dropout Rates

Another feature that indicates the lack of freedom of choice among children to attend school and the low educational attainments is the dropout rates. While there are a number of studies estimating the actual dropout rates, repetition rates, etc., (Mehta 2007) using various secondary and primary sources of data, there are fewer efforts to understand the causes for such poor performance at the primary level.

It is well-known that girls tend to drop out of school after attaining puberty. However, the dropout rate is also mediated through the institutions of caste and religion. The status of children not attending school is of two kinds, those who never attended school and those who did and then dropped out. Nearly 25 per cent of Muslim children in 2004–05 were either never enrolled in school or have dropped out; this was followed by nearly 20 per cent of children from SC/ST households (Sachar Committee Report 2006: Figure 4.8). Less than 5 per cent of children from upper-caste Hindu households suffered this fate.

While quizzed about the main reasons for not attending school or dropping out among children in the age-group of 6–17 years, 36 per cent of the boys and 21 per cent of the girls said they were not interested in studies. It is difficult to interpret the reasons for the lack of interest, but it could reflect the low quality of education, due to which children were unable to cope with the rigours of the educational system, or that they could not see improved prospects of obtaining employment after acquiring education of such low quality. The next major reason given by 18 per cent was that it cost too much. Further, while 15 per cent of the girls said that they were required for household work, 7 per cent of the boys said they were required for work on the family farm or enterprise (NFHS-3 2007: Table 2.10). Thus, economic compulsion in terms of either lack of funds or the need to supplement incomes, or just the perception that it did not improve job prospects, also acts as barriers to acquiring education. Poor educational attainment, due to early dropout from the educational system, needs to be understood in terms of the reasons noted above.

Poor Reading Skills

There is a lot of literature available on the poor quality of education imparted in schools. This further dampens the enthusiasm among poor households to send their children to school, since such education would not provide the children with jobs. *The Annual Status of Education Report* (ASER 2007), based on surveys conducted by Pratham on an annual basis, has come out with startling results. The ASER survey found that 38.4 per cent of children in Class I could not recognise letters in 2006, but this decreased to 31.9 per cent in 2007. Thus, while India's enrolments rates in primary school are close to 90 per cent, the learning achievements, although improving slowly, are a major cause for concern.

The NFHS-3 (2007) data shows that the ability to read varied according to social groups and gender. In the age-group of 15–49 years, the STs fared the worst with 44 per cent of men and 25 per cent of women who were unable to read, despite having completed Class VI. Of the rest, nearly 40 per cent of men and 66 per cent of women could not read at all. The SCs were slightly better off, with 58 per cent and 34 per cent of men and women having completed Class VI, and of the rest, 27 per cent men and 56 per cent women were unable to read at all. The next worst group was of the Muslims, with just a slightly lower percentage of those who could not read at all.

Poor Access to Media and Reading Newspapers

The capabilities approach also helps to understand the nature of the intrinsic good of education by distinguishing those aspects that are linked to achieved functionings, for example, the value of considering a range of different viewpoints from newspapers, television and radio (Unterhalter 2003).

Given the poor reading skills noted above, we do not expect much exposure to newspapers, among the adults in the age-group of 15–49 years. In 2005–06, about 29 per cent of STs, 45 per cent of SCs and Muslims and 54 per cent of all Hindu men reported reading the newspaper or magazines at least once a week, while only 10 per cent, 15 per cent, 18 per cent and 23 per cent of women, respectively, in these social groups read at least once a week (NFHS-3 2007). Among other media such as television, radio and cinema, it was exposure to television that was the highest in India. About 39 per cent and 30 per cent of ST men and women, 59 per cent and 51 per cent of SC, 57 per cent and 45 per cent of Muslim, and 54 per cent and 56 per cent of all Hindu men and women watched the television at least once a week. It is interesting to note that there is much less gender differential in viewing television than in reading of newspapers. This does not require any particular skills. However, even here, the gender differentials exist and are particularly high among Muslims. Other religious groups, particularly the Jains, Sikhs and Christians, were much better-off in their exposure to the print and electronic media. Besides getting exposure, reading the newspapers and viewing television can be considered as empowerment of women and can be used as measures of the 'conversion factor', which might impact on the choice of education.

Role of Governments

As an issue to further social justice, the GIDR Survey (2008) enquired what the government should do to help those who could not meet their basic needs. While the majority of the respondents felt that the government should provide jobs, nearly 20 per cent of the men and 14 per cent of the women respondents thought the government should do something to help meet the basic needs of education of children. The suggestions given included reducing fees, giving bicycles to school-going children and providing high school and degree colleges in the village or in the urban block. The government already has a programme of giving bicycles to girl students in Gujarat and this was perhaps a demand for universalising the scheme. Thus, there was an awareness and demand for schooling and higher education in the community that was so far unfulfilled.

CONCLUSIONS

The capabilities approach is considered superior to the utility approach. While the utility approach assesses the resources and opportunities to achieve functionings, such as going to school, the capabilities approach assesses the motivations and the freedom people have to formulate capabilities. It, therefore, encourages us to ask a wider range of and more probing questions than the utility approach does.

The capabilities approach, however, is still in its infancy when it comes to formal measurement and criteria for evaluation of various capabilities. In the case of education, do people have the freedom to choose, and what motivates it? The starting point for this chapter was that the motivations and freedoms of choice are mediated through institutions of caste and religion. These restrict the freedom, more so of women, and makes them place a low value on education. We explore indicators for the motivation behind poor school attendance and poor educational attainments, based on the institutional context. We note that poor school infrastructure, domestic work, child labour, early marriage and childbirth, and perceptions of parents, motivated through institutions of caste and religion, influence poor attendance of girl children in school. Similarly, caste and religion also motivate poor educational attainments through higher dropout rates, poor reading skills and poor access to media among girls. These explanations for the achieved functionings of schooling by gender help to identify 'conversion factors' not typically addressed in the utility approach. The capabilities approach may have an important public policy role to play, as research on the dynamics of capabilities failure could be used to improve education policy design and, in turn, educational outcomes for girls from disadvantaged caste and religious communities. However, the remedy for poor enrolment and educational attainment of children may not lie in education policy alone, but in a wider set of socio-economic policies.

NOTE

1. The male and female respondents in these surveys were chosen on the basis of stratified random sampling, by the activity status. The areas chosen for study were biased

towards low-income households, since the main theme of the survey was socio-economic security. The urban areas surveyed in both years were in Ahmedabad city. The rural areas surveyed in 2000 were in Ahmedabad district, while in 2008 it was Surendranagar district. The sampling design for the survey of 2000 is presented in Unni and Rani (2002).

References

ASER. 2007. *Annual Status of Education Report.* New Delhi: Pratham. Available athttp://www.pratham.org/aser07/aser2007.php.

Doraisamy, Malathy. 2001. 'Demand for and Access to Schooling in Tamil Nadu'. In A. Vaidyanathan and P. R. G. Nair, eds, *Elementary Schooling in Rural India.* New Delhi: Sage Publications.

———. 2007. 'Child Schooling and Child Work'. In Abusaleh Shariff and Maithreyi Krishnaraj, eds, *State Markets and Inequalities: Human Development in Rural India.* New Delhi: Orient Longman.

ILO. 2004. *Economic Security for a Better World.* ILO Socio-Economic Security Programme. Geneva: International Labour Organisation.

Kingdon, Geeta G., and Jeemol Unni. 2001. 'Education and Women's Labour Market Outcomes in India'. *Education Economics* 9 (2): 173–95.

Kingdon, Geeta G., and John Knight. 2003. 'Well-being Poverty Versus Income Poverty and Capabilities Poverty?'. CSAE WPS/2003-16, Global Poverty Reduction Group, Centre for the Study of African Economies. UK: University of Oxford.

Kingdon, Geeta G., and Nicolas Theopold. 2008. 'Do Returns to Education Matter to Schooling Participation? Evidence from India'. *Education Economics* 16 (4): 329–350.

Mehta, A. C. 2007. *Student Flow at Primary Level – An Analysis Based on DISE Data.* New Delhi: National University of Educational Planning and Administration and Department of School Education and Literacy, Ministry of Human Resource Development, Government of India.

NCEUS. 2007. *Report on Conditions of Work and Promotion of Livelihoods in the Unorganised Sector.* Government of India: National Commission for Enterprises in the Unorganised Sector.

NFHS-3. 2007. *National Family Health Survey, India.* Vol I. Mumbai: International Institute of Population Studies.

NSSO. 2006. 'Status of Education and Vocational Training in India, 2004–05'. 61st Round, Ministry of Statistics and Programme Implementation. New Delhi: Government of India.

Prime Minister's High Level Committee [Sachar Committee], Government of India. 2006. 'Social, Economic and Educational Status of the Muslim Community in India: A Report'. New Delhi: Cabinet Secretariat, Government of India. Available at http://www.minorityaffairs.gov.in/sites/default/files/sachar_comm.pdf.

Psacharapoulos, G. 1994. 'Returns to Investment in Education: A Global Update'. *World Development* 22 (9): 1325–43.

Sen, Amartya. 1983. 'Poor, Relatively Speaking'. *Oxford Economic Papers* 35: 153–69.

———. 1987. *Commodities and Capabilities.* Delhi: Oxford University Press.

Sengupta, Arjun, K. P. Kannan, and G. Raveendran. 2008. 'India's Common People: Who Are They, How Many Are They and How Do They Live?'. *Economic & Political Weekly,* 43 (11): 49–63.

Standing, Guy, J. Unni, R. Jhabyala, and U. Rani. 2010. *Social Income and Insecurity: A Study in Gujarat*. India: Routledge.

Unni, Jeemol. 1996. 'Returns to Education by Gender among Wage Employees in Urban India'. *Journal of Educational Planning and Administration*, April.

——. 2007. 'Earnings and Education among Social Groups'. In A. Shariff and M. Krishnaraj, eds, *State Markets and Inequalities: Human Development in Rural India*. New Delhi: Orient Longman.

Unni, Jeemol, and Uma Rani. 2002. 'Insecurities of Informal Workers in Gujarat, India'. SES Papers 30. Geneva: International Labour Office.

Unterhalter, Elaine. 2003. 'Education, Capabilities and Social Justice'. Background paper prepared for the Education for all Global Meeting Report, 2003–04. *Gender and Education for All: The Leap to Equality*, 2004/ED/EFA/MRT/PI/76, United Nations Educational, Scientific and Cultural Organisation.

8

CONTEMPORARY CHALLENGES TO WOMEN'S EDUCATION

Towards an Elusive Goal?

NANDINI MANJREKAR

In the 1970s, struggles by women around issues of domestic violence, women's employment and livelihoods, communalism, representations in the media, etc., provided the impulse to women's studies, which has been referred to as the 'academic arm' of the women's movement. Critical inquiry into the structural and cultural bases which characterise the maintenance and reproduction of patriarchy in India at the familial, community and state levels have been carried out by women's studies scholars. Women's studies gained well-earned legitimacy within academia, first through state support for its institutionalisation in the 1980s, and more significantly, through the substantial contributions of feminist scholarship to the so-called mainstream disciplines. By questioning the value-neutrality of disciplinary perspectives, pointing to exclusions and invisibility, recovering women's voices and concerns from the margins and often from outside the pages of mainstream academic discourse, and constantly unveiling and exploring the complex relationship between power and knowledge, women's studies have engaged directly with the politics of knowledge.

It is somewhat surprising, then, and worthy of critical attention, that feminist engagements with the politics of knowledge, both in the academic arena and through activism, have bypassed the field of education in a larger sense and school education in particular. The effects of formal education on Indian women, over the so-called silent years between Independence and the early 1970s, were captured in the *Towards Equality* report (GoI 1974), which indicated its role in sharpening class inequalities between women. The findings of the Committee on the Status of Women in India should have alerted the women's movement to the need to interrogate the social character of formal education in India, which has acted to divide women by class, caste and ethnicity. Larger feminist critiques of development policies and paradigms have, unfortunately, overlooked the ways in which formal education, in its organisation and processes, offers a narrow range of subject positions for girls and women, locating and even objectifying them as mere instruments in the narrative of national progress.

The absence of critical thinking on formal education indicates the low status that educational studies hold in the hierarchy of knowledge, even feminist knowledge, in India. Feminist scholars of education in the West have contributed to understanding the relationship between schooling and the reproduction of gender relations in capitalist society. They have examined how race, class and gender intersect in the making of policy, school knowledge, the formation of gendered and raced identities, and modes of resistance from a feminist perspective. This literature is largely what many of those interested in educational issues in India have to refer and draw from, given the paucity of theoretical work in our own contexts. In India, we still do not seem to share a discourse within which to discuss how educational visions have been highly gendered, both within nationalism and in the post-Independence era; or to examine girls' education in relation to issues of their labour and sexuality.

There is, however, a large body of literature from which to construct frameworks to understand these issues in our own context. Feminist perspectives within the different disciplines, as well as the availability of a wide range of sources (women's writings, histories of women's organisations, women's journals, policy documents, NGO reports, etc.) provide a base for the theoretical understanding of gender and education. However, this important work of analysis remains to be done. Meanwhile, those of us who work on education within women's studies and the women's movement will have to continue to nudge and push: for inclusion of gender perspectives in educational fora and the inclusion of educational concerns within the women's movement.

The above discussion is not intended to underplay the significant interventions made by the women's studies movement. In 1986, largely due to the persistence of women's studies scholars, the National Policy on Education (NPE) specifically emphasised the necessity of reorienting education to promote women's equality and envisioned education playing a positive interventionist role in the empowerment of women. The policy recommended the revision of textbooks to eliminate gender bias and stereotyping and the training of teachers towards greater gender sensitivity. The NPE 1986 was a radical policy intervention, in that it placed gender equality through education as a social and political commitment of the state, and it has continued to guide advocacy efforts for women's education. However, even this major intervention at the policy level was limited by the fact that education, and school education in particular, had remained marginal to knowledge-building within the women's movement and women's studies. Thus the NPE Review Committee (NPERC), in its critique of the 1986 policy, noted that gender was markedly absent in the chapter on 'Content and Process of School Education', except for a mention that 'equality of the sexes' is to be one of the 10 core areas (para 6). It also pointed out that the task of addressing gender is fraught with complexity: 'A gender perspective in the content of education means more than the elimination of sexist bias and stereotypes from textbooks....The task of bringing a gender perspective into the curriculum is a complex one and requires research inputs, discussion and debate...' (NPERC 1990: 44).

Gendered access to educational facilities, sexism in school textbooks and stereotyping of curricular choices are issues that have been extensively examined by women's studies scholars. These are extremely important issues in themselves, but are not independent of other processes of schooling. Forms and representation of knowledge in school curricula reflect the discourses of formal education and the pattern of social relations in society—framing, normalising and legitimising social inequalities, processes in which the state plays a critical regulatory role.

We need to critically analyse why education has been peripheral to the concerns of the contemporary women's movement in India, given the legacy of struggle by women to establish their right to education. It is worth considering whether the assumed instrumentalist nature of formal education, particularly in the post-Independence era, has not inhibited more radical interpretations of what formal education means for girls, in terms of self-perceptions as well as materially. The very premise of girls' education, especially education of poor girls—and here it is difficult to disentangle policy rhetoric from popular perceptions—is based on an understanding that education is critical to social development: lower fertility, better child-rearing practices, and so on. On the one hand, these normative positions on the 'benefits' of women's education are persuasive and compelling; on the other, the struggle for the right of girls and women to education gets reduced to issues of access alone. The absence and avoidance of issues of conflict and contestation in mainstream education and curriculum discourse adds to this unidimensional understanding.

It has been easier for women's groups and NGOs to work with girls outside the system of formal education, especially the government system of education, which is notoriously inflexible. It is instructive, at the risk of repeating familiar statistics, to draw a picture of what it means to be schooled in India. There are data to show that the large majority of children, especially poor children, are in government schools. Conditions in most of these schools are hardly conducive to meaningful learning. A minuscule percentage of government schools possess the very basic set of facilities, such as adequate classrooms, toilets and drinking water, teaching-learning materials and libraries. There is evidence to show that physical inaccessibility, irrelevance of curricula, repeated 'failure' and even harsh treatment in schools contribute to children dropping out or never enrolling in school; it has been seen that in the case of girls, the influence of these factors is even more acute (Anandalakshmy 1994: 118, Jalaluddin 1991: 33, PROBE 1999). According to an NSSO (National Sample Survey Office) survey (1995–96), about 26 per cent of those who had dropped out cited reasons other than poverty—unfriendly school environment, doubts about usefulness of schooling and inability to cope with studies. Among girls in rural areas, these factors accounted for over 75 per cent of dropouts (NSSO 1998). Dropout percentages among girls are extremely high in schools: figures for 1997–98 indicate 41 per cent dropout at the primary level, 58 per cent at the middle school level and 72 per cent at the secondary level (GoI 2000 a). Discontinuation rates of rural girls have been found to be twice as high as those of boys (Sudarshan 1998: 19). Literacy and numeracy skills are abysmal among children who attend government schools and are further devalued for poor girls who leave school, most often into environments that do not promote or sustain literacy.

NEW CHALLENGES

Part of the challenge in thinking through our concerns about gender and education lies in uncovering the dialectical linkages between the formal education system and larger social and economic processes, and their influence on girls' and women's lives. In the present context, we are now seeing how an education system, already fragile and alienated from its objectives, is increasingly facing the combined onslaught of right-wing reaction and the market. Both portend the deepening of social divisions and inequalities.

A serious issue affecting girls' education is the appropriation of curriculum discourse by the Hindu Right. The National Curriculum Framework 2000 has a clear-cut position on gender issues, which embodies a break from the rhetoric and approach of earlier policy documents. It seeks to posit women as recipients of a benevolent if not empowering culture, promotes the idea that gender equality is an organic part of our cultural legacy and that the education of girls has a role to play in social cohesion, rather than social transformation. The glorification of women as mothers and the pronouncement that gender equality will be promoted through 'non-adversarial' positions signifies the considerable shift from the NPE 1986 (GoI 1986), which spoke of education as an interventionist agency to promote gender equality in Indian society.

Studies show that privatisation of school education, hitherto restricted to urban centres, has been on the increase in rural areas since the early 1990s. The withdrawal of the state from formal education has been legitimised and endorsed by neo-liberal discourse, most prominently by the Ambani-Birla report (2000), which classifies education as a non-merit good.

Several micro-level studies indicate that families are investing scarce resources in sending their sons to private rather than government schools. There is a perception that English, widely taught in private schools across a wide spectrum, from elite to sub-standard, holds the key to competing for scarce jobs in a shrinking labour market. It is necessary to study the implications of these trends on exacerbating gender divisions and the long-term effects on girls' participation in education. These trends are serious reminders that the women's movement must intensify its engagement with issues concerning women's education.

NATIONAL CURRICULUM FRAMEWORK

The National Curriculum Framework (NCF), officially released in 2000, reflects the efforts of the Hindu Right to seize the opportunity to commandeer the ideological state apparatus of education, to push through its regressive agenda at the national level. The NCF marks a significant departure from earlier frameworks (1975, following the 1968 Education Policy; and 1988, following the 1986 Education Policy), which stressed the inculcation of values of democracy and social justice and national integration, through the appreciation and understanding of the commonalities of different subcultures. The debate on the NCF 2000 and the strong criticism against it (articulated in a petition to the Supreme Court and discussed to some extent in the media) highlight the deeply ideological character of education. Spectacular in its shoddiness and banality, the text of the NCF is an ominous narrative of the Right's educational agenda. It is significant that the framework nowhere addresses the huge deficits in education at all levels.

In the NCF, history holds a key position in the reformulation of social knowledge. Apprehensions expressed by historians, who have been protesting against the framework since 2000, have been vindicated, with textbooks now published (after the vacation of the stay by the Supreme Court) revealing gross distortions of history and a fetishist preoccupation with a glorious Hindu past. Religious education, thinly disguised as education for values, permeates all sections of the NCF. Value education is the main plank for launching the 'spiritual and moral renewal' of India through education:

> Schools can and must strive to restore and sustain the universal and eternal values oriented towards the unity and integration of the people, their moral and spiritual growth enabling them to realise the treasure within. People must realise who they are and what is the ultimate purpose of human life. Self-recognition would come to them through proper value education that would facilitate their spiritual march from the level of sub-consciousness to that of super consciousness through the different intermediary stages. Value based education would help the nation fight against all kinds of fanaticism, ill will, violence, fatalism, dishonesty, avarice, corruption, exploitation and drug abuse (NCERT 2000: 17).

According to the NCF, it is through learning of the 'lives of prophets, saints and the sacred texts' (p. 35) that children can achieve higher SQs (Spiritual Quotients) and EQs (Emotional Quotients) (p. 13). Value education is envisaged to form an integral part of the child's school experience. The child, in the vision of the NCF, is to be immersed in an environment where values, not derived from rules of citizenship in a democratic polity, but from religion, will predominate.

> Value education and education about religions would not form a separate subject of study or examination at any stage. These would be so judiciously integrated with all the subjects of study in the scholastic areas and all the activities and programmes in the co-scholastic areas that the objectives thereof would be directly and indirectly achieved in the classrooms, at the school assembly places, play-grounds, cultural centres and such other places (NCERT 2000: 33).

Quite apart from the dreary drivel it contains, the framework is an enormous setback to the women's movement. It portends a future for women's education which is deeply disempowering. The lack of seriousness with which the NCF approaches social disadvantage can be seen in the manner in which a range of citizens are subsumed within a single disadvantaged category: women, Dalits, Adivasis, along with children with impairments. Valorisation of religious tradition, the leitmotif of the document, negates the essentially oppressive role that tradition plays in women's lives to curb and control their sexuality, labour and individuality. It is not surprising that the NCF, displaying its ideological position on women, includes education of girls in a section titled 'Education for a Cohesive Society'. Here, we get a glimpse of how girls can be educated the 'Right' way. Patriarchal oppression and the struggle for equality and justice are non-issues in a social order in which caste and gender hierarchies are non-conflictual, harmonious elements in the seamless fabric of the great Indian tradition:

> [Besides,] making education accessible to more and more girls, especially rural girls, removing all gender discrimination and gender bias in school curriculum, textbooks and the process of transaction is absolutely necessary. *Moreover, it will be the most appropriate thing to recognise and nurture the best features of each gender in the best Indian tradition. After all, India gave her women the right to vote without any prolonged battle for it unlike in the west. There is a need to develop and implement gender inclusive and gender sensitive curricular strategies to nurture a generation of girls and boys who are equally competent and are sensitive to one another, and grow up in a caring and sharing mode as equals, and not as adversaries* (NCERT 2000: 9, emphasis added).

The 'vision' of the NCF neatly accommodates the pervasive instrumentalist view of education for girls and women, in which women are seen primarily as reproducers.

> Equality of the opportunity [sic] of access to education is necessary if more women are to become the agents of change. Therefore, education of women is an important key to improving health, nutrition and education in the family, and also empowering them to participate in decision-making. Investment, both in formal and non-formal education of young children in general, and of the girl child in particular is expected to yield exceptionally high social and developmental returns (ibid.: 19).

It may be tempting to dismiss the NCF as the usual hocus-pocus that is regularly churned out by the cultural nationalists who command so much media space these days. However, it is important to remember that the framework will influence the ways in which millions of children understand their social worlds and identities through textbooks. Ironically, moreover, the anti-modernity of the NCF's vision of education is entirely compatible with the processes of globalisation. 'Indianising' and 'spiritualising' the curriculum is not antithetical in the least to orienting education to the market. Vocationalisation, a recommendation of the NCF, was originally envisaged as an alternative to college education, which students could opt for after Class XII. It has been a non-starter in Indian education, with less than 5 per cent of students opting for vocational courses (Visaria 1998). Vocational courses for girls are highly gendered—typing, tailoring, etc.—which only allow them entry, if at all, into low-paying jobs in the unorganised sector. The NCF now recommends vocational streaming after Class X. This will only serve to heighten inequalities by caste, class and gender, by further restricting the access of poor girls, Dalits and other marginal groups to higher education and decreasing their representation at this level.

In Gujarat, the crucible of Hindutva, one can see from where documents like the NCF derive their force and purpose. Education has been a key focus of mobilisation by Hindutva organisations over at least the past five years in Gujarat. In Panchmahals, where we happened to do some fieldwork in schools in 2000, government-appointed *vidya sahayaks* were holding *satsangs* in schools and participating in VHP programmes (Manjrekar and Surti 2000). In 1998, a fact-finding team investigating the communal violence visited Sanjeli-Randhikpur in Gujarat, following the marriage of a Muslim youth with an Adivasi girl, and met school teachers who justified the violence against Muslims and supported the actions of the VHP-Bajrang Dal in the area (PUCL report, 1998). With the ascendance of the BJP in elected governance, conflict has been emerging in Gujarat over the running of educational institutions in tribal areas, between Christians and RSS organisations.

By March 2002, the curriculum was already being revised in Gujarat according to the NCF guidelines, paying little heed to the then ongoing Supreme Court case. It is no surprise that RSS-affiliated organisations have been involved in the curriculum revision. Quite in keeping with the NCF guidelines, post-BJP government textbooks are replete with stories of 'the wisdom of our ancient sages'; according to the guidelines, Sanskrit will be taught from Class VI in all schools. The Gujarat education minister stated that a state-level 'campaign' is necessary for implementing the 'National Curriculum' by June 2003, through seminars with principals and teachers (PUCL–Vadodara Shanti Abhiyan 2002 submission to the National Human Rights Commission). It is now slated to be operational from the next academic session.

In this planned saffronisation of education, emphasis on 'value education' derived from religion and 'tradition' replaces the emphasis on social justice, tolerance and plurality. The idea of 'unity in diversity', an educational slogan of the post-Independence era, which had some pedagogic value despite its problems, has been given a quiet burial. This new thrust is of a piece with efforts in other spheres to manufacture a majoritarian view of society, in which the cultural and political space for all marginalised sections, especially minorities, will progressively shrink. What better place to begin than in school? Experience of the present carnage against Muslims in Gujarat begs the question: will a saffronised school curriculum not provide a good setting in which intolerance and further injustices against minorities can be justified? The complex ways in which these distortions will affect the identities of girls of different classes, castes, religions and ethnicities, providing an illusion of empowerment for some and drastically disempowering others, is a cause for concern for the Indian women's movement.

Education and Market

Since the introduction of market reforms in India, there has been a steady attempt to devalue the role of the government in the social sector. Undoubtedly, the Indian state must bear the responsibility for its lack of commitment to constitutional directives, which mandate that all children must be healthy and educated in independent India. However, we need to consider whether privatisation in the education sector is an adequate answer to the government's lack of performance. There is increasing evidence that privatisation is likely to exacerbate existing gender inequalities in education.

In April 2000, the Prime Minister's Council for Trade and Industry submitted a report on a policy framework for reforms in education. The convener and principal member of this 'special subject group' were two leading industrialists. The report outlines, in a succinct manner, the conditions of education in India and talks of the different worlds coexisting side-by-side: the privileged few, the resistance to change from various quarters, the situation of poor children in indefensibly adverse learning conditions. It speaks of raising standards and working to 'create a competitive yet cooperative knowledge-based society'. This report explicitly argues for the necessity of opening up the secondary sector to private initiatives, while maintaining that the primary sector needs the full support of the government, in order to meet the requirements of Article 45 of the Constitution.

The report unequivocally calls for government support to private investment in secondary education in every taluka and a 'user pays' principle, as well as direct foreign investment at the higher education level. The report is profoundly lacking in any reflection on what constitutes learning and what and how children should be learning. It talks of creating 'smart schools', which must be competitive and innovative. Our endeavour, it suggests, should not be the creation of an environment that produces industrial workers and labourers, but one that fosters 'cutting edge' knowledge resources, which can place India in the 'vanguard in the information age' (p. 3).

Several contentious issues in the report need to be debated. First, we must ask ourselves how it is that industry is dictating what national educational priorities must be. Obviously, there is a huge educational market at stake here. A close look at other social sector policies tells us the same story. The *National Population Policy* (GoI 2000 b), for instance, talks of private investment in basic education for girls and the creation of markets at the village level, which will motivate girls to take up vocational training. It is clear that the logic of market intervention in education is related to so-called 'efficiency' and the generation of profit, in the context of education supposedly emerging as a new sector of the global economy. What is frightening, however, is that any educational vision or perspective will be surrendered to this logic. Hence, in the Ambani-Birla report, 'knowledge' and 'information' are viewed as the same, since this justifies entry into the global IT market. However, should we not pause to reflect how this approach, in one imperious sweep, negates the years of struggle and debate on making education relevant and contextual for children, as the best way to sustain their interest in school-based learning? Have we not learned from the available evidence that it is because of an information-loaded curriculum that children find school boring and, in the face of other difficulties, leave early? But the market will demand information, not local knowledge, which children are familiar with and can acquire genuine skills from. We need to contest the report's neo-liberal approach to education on both political and pedagogical grounds.

PRIVATISATION: INTENSIFYING GENDER INEQUALITIES

Given that up to the 1990s, privatisation did not find mention in policy documents, it is quite amazing how fast it has gained ground and seized the imagination of our educational decision-makers. The government's withdrawal from the education sector and the entry of private enterprise is by design, not by default. The failure of the state to provide basic education to all children takes on a different dimension in the context of structural reform of economies. The experiences of other countries attempting such reforms in the name of efficiency tell us that they serve to further marginalise communities who already find themselves on the periphery of formal education.

Although, overall, most children are in government schools, the share of enrolments in private schools out of total enrolment has been steadily increasing, as more and more parents feel that the poor quality of learning offered by state-run schools adds to further disadvantage their children's life chances (Khan and Manjrekar 2002, Sudarshan 1998: 20). There is no regulation or monitoring of most of these private schools, many of which remain unrecognised. Evidence points to the fact that the standards are poor, teachers are underpaid and facilities are lacking. Then why are they still in demand? Most of them have one selling point: the teaching of English. Hence the demand for private schools is largely related to the popular perception that knowledge of English is necessary to survive in the new labour market. It is instructive to see what this means in terms of the actual money spent. The average annual expenditure by families per child, in government schools, is Rs 317, in government-aided schools, it is Rs 391 and in private schools, it is Rs 742 (Sudarshan 1998: 20). Private expenditure has increased as a percentage of consumption expenditure, from 2.5 per cent in the early 1980s to 3.5 per cent in the late 1990s (NSSO 1995–96, cited in *National Human Development Report* 2001: 55–56, 60).

Justified on the basis of returns through employment, increased household expenditure on education will inevitably be discriminatory: boys' education will be favoured over that of girls. There is growing evidence that beyond a certain income level, girls are being sent, if at all, to government schools, whereas their brothers are sent to private schools. For girls, marriageability remains the more critical criterion. Thus, while there is some evidence of increasing demand for girls' education, even in rural areas, the motivation of parents is to seek upwardly mobile marriages to educated salary earners.[1]

Privatisation is unlikely to embody the social understanding and vision that can address the real issues behind the lower participation of girls in education. Recent developments indicate that policies are becoming increasingly gender-blind. One may even venture to say that they are erasing whatever gains have been made towards girls' well-being. We are already witness to drastic reductions in the outlays on the mid-day meal programme, which, with all its problems, has served to ensure some nutrition for poor children, especially girls, and has been shown to have a positive effect on retention in schools (Tilak 1999). The 93rd Amendment Bill, declaring education as a fundamental right, does not include the under-six population from its purview. This effectively means that the entire ICDS programme of early childhood education has been placed in jeopardy. It also means that older girls will have to participate for even longer hours in sibling care. The emphasis on income-generating activities as a priority for educated women bespeaks this myopia. Education for five years, basic literacy and numeracy skills, which can just about sustain these activities, are deemed sufficient for girls. Although economic independence is an important aspect of women's empowerment, it cannot be reduced to income-generating activities, which, more often than not, mean low-paying, insecure jobs, often within the parameters of the traditional domestic roles of women.

It is a telling commentary on our caste, gender and occupational hierarchies that the Kothari Commission's recommendation of neighbourhood schools could never be put into practice. Neighbourhood schools would perhaps have altered the very texture of our society and generated questions missing from the educational agenda today, such as the social contexts of learning and content of curriculum. Despite the claims of privatisation being a great social leveller based on merit alone, for girls, and particularly poor girls, it is likely to be yet another mode of discrimination within the family and economy. As Mary Warnock (1977: 26) puts it: 'There is a world of difference between the equal right to education and the right to equal education'. Class, caste and gender inequalities in education are only going to increase without strong state commitment to equality. That the Indian state has failed to stem these inequalities is not in doubt. However, we should recognise that entrenched privileges of the elites functioning within Indian patriarchal society have contributed to this failure. These interests will continue to influence privatisation as well. We may recall that 25 years ago, J. P. Naik (1979: 177) said that equal opportunity in education cannot be seen in isolation from enhancing opportunity on the political and economic fronts to 'destroy privilege itself'.

WHAT IS TO BE DONE?

Where democratic spaces are increasingly shrinking under the weight of a majoritarian state and the forces of the market, how can the women's movement re-engage with questions of education? In this chapter, I have tried to raise a few issues, which could be addressed as a tentative beginning to this re-engagement. To my mind, there is need for intensive monitoring of new developments which are likely to impact girls' education. Women are central to the contemporary politics of culture, as embodied in the NCF. The struggle for an egalitarian and democratic culture should be extended to a struggle for an education that is critical of received ideologies and can promote such a culture. For this, we may have to work to mainstream gender concerns into alternative educational discourse. Unfortunately, as I have attempted to point out here, there is a gap between those who are part of the more radical debates on education, most of whom are sensitive but hesitant to address gender issues, and women's studies scholars and activists, who do not direct their analysis of gender and society towards questions of educational theory, pedagogy and curriculum.

Many women's rights activists and organisations participate in sessions with teachers, where gender issues are discussed. Teacher training is an important area of intervention, but we should be a little wary of training in isolation from the experience of teachers in schools. At a recent seminar on school education, a participant lamented that a standard response of school administrators to problems of girls' education is to suggest a training course. She said that the idea of training as a solution has become so commonplace that school teachers and even NGOs have unquestioningly accepted it. This brings to mind an interesting experience we had two years ago, while studying social contexts of schooling in Panchmahals district in Gujarat (Manjrekar and Surti 2000). A single teacher managing five classes in a single room (a new room constructed under the District Primary Education Programme (DPEP) lay unused because it was close to collapse) told us that she had learned a great deal from the gender-training course she had received under the DPEP. How do you use some of the ideas in your classroom, we asked. She told us that she made the girls and boys sit together, because in the course she had learned that gender segregation was not a good practice. She added that the arrangement prevented social interaction in the classroom, making it easier for her to teach in that difficult situation. Now, in many co-educational schools, seating girls and boys next to each other, rather than in the more usual segregated manner, is employed as a 'shaming' technique, used by teachers to prevent 'indiscipline' in the classroom. The above example highlights the absurdity of reducing concerns about gender in school education to 'gender training', from which teachers take away what is most practical to their pressing needs in undoubtedly adverse situations.

Privatisation is another area we must keep monitoring. The devaluation of government schooling over the past 20 years or so has been speeded up by market reforms since the early 1990s. Data from urban areas shows that corporation and government schools now mainly have poor girls and very poor children from other marginal communities; in many cities, municipal schools with good infrastructure are lying vacant. It is important to engage with government bodies to see what can be done to improve the quality of schooling, so that more girls can attend these schools and attain an acceptable level of education.

Finally, in the face of multiple pressures, can we debate our—feminist—understanding of what it means to be educated as a girl/woman in contemporary India? Can we put forward an alternate perception of girls' education? Young girls today are facing newer, more complex, forms of regulation. For instance, our experience in an urban context suggests that young school-going girls, under the influence of the market and the media, are experiencing new consumption-related desires, such as the desire to look good. We have also found that poorer girls engage in piece-rate work after school hours to earn enough to fulfil these new needs.

After the violence against Muslims in Gujarat, there have been apprehensions that Muslim girls may be withdrawn from schools. Indeed, this is an issue that came up repeatedly in interactions with victims of the violence, in particular, women and young girls (Panjabi et al. 2002; PUCL–Shanti Abhiyan 2002). A few of us have been meeting young Muslim girls in a school to discuss issues of education. Questions of physical insecurity loom large in these discussions, as can be expected after the trauma that Muslim women and the community as a whole have been through, and the insecurity which continues to loom large over their lives. What has struck us, however, is the determination of many of these girls to continue with education. Many of them said they wanted to be lawyers and teachers. Why, we asked. To fight for our rights and teach girls well, so they can fight too, they said. Can education engender such resistance? Is this the alternate, critical consciousness we have been hoping to articulate as an aim for girls' education? And does it necessarily have to come at so heavy a price? As Brecht said: too many questions.

NOTE

1. The dichotomy that has been set up between boys—superior, private—and girls—inferior, government—has its own tragic consequences for the self-esteem and identity of girls. In my own work, I have spoken to girls who, with considerable anguish, question, but also resign themselves to, this divide that casts them as educationally less deserving than their brothers. This is an important aspect of the social consequences of privatisation and one that needs further study.

REFERENCES

Ambani, M., and K. Birla. 2000. 'Report on a Policy Framework for Reforms in Education'. New Delhi: Prime Minister's Council on Trade and Industry, Government of India.

Anandalakshmy, S. ed. 1994. 'The Girl Child and the Family', Department of Women and Child Development. New Delhi: MHRD, Government of India.

Government of India [GoI]. 1974. *Towards Equality: Report of the Committee on the Status of Women in India*. New Delhi: Ministry of Education and Social Welfare, Department of Social Welfare.

———. 1986. *National Policy on Education*. New Delhi:. Ministry of Human Resource Development, Department of Education.

———. 2000 a. *Annual Report 1999–2000*. New Delhi: Ministry of Human Resource Development, Department of Education.

———. 2000 b [2002]. *National Population Policy*. New Delhi: Government of India, Ministry of Health and Family Welfare. Available at https://mohfw.gov.in/sites/default/files/26953755641410949469%20%281%29.pdf .

———. 2001. *National Human Development Report*. New Delhi: Planning Commission.

Jalaluddin, A. K. 1991. 'Development Imperatives for Universalisation of Basic Education'. In *School Education in the 1990s: Problems and Perspectives*. New Delhi: NCERT.

Khan, F., and N. Manjrekar. 2002. 'Contexts and Constraints of Schooling: Operation Blackboard Ethnographic Studies: A Summary Paper', unpublished.

Manjrekar, N., and T. Surti. 2000. 'Schooling on the Margins of Development: A Study in Shivrajpur, Panchmahals District, Gujarat', unpublished, National Institute of Educational Planning and Administration.

Naik, J. P. 1979. 'Equality, Quality and Quantity: The Elusive Triangle in Indian Education' *International Review of Education* 25 (2/3) Jubilee Number: 167–85.

National Council of Educational Research and Training. 2000. 'National Curriculum Framework', New Delhi: NCERT.

National Policy on Education Review Committee [NPERC]. 1986 [1990]: *Towards an Enlightened and Humane Society*, Acharya Ramamurthi Report, New Delhi.

National Sample Survey Organisation. 1998. *Attending an Educational Institution in India: Its Level, Nature and Cost 1995–96. NSS 52nd Round (1996–97)*, Report No. 439. Government of India: Department of Statistics.

Panjabi, K. K. Bandopadhyay, and B. Gangopadhyay. 2002. *The Next Generation: In the Wake of the Genocide* (A Report by Independent Citizens on the Impact of the Gujarat Pogrom on Children and the Young), supported by Citizen's Initiative, Ahmedabad.

PROBE.1999. *Public Report on Basic Education*. New Delhi: Oxford University Press.

PUCL–Shanti Abhiyan. 2002. *At the Receiving End: Women's Experiences of Violence in Vadodara*. Vadodara: People's Union of Civil Liberties and Vadodra Shanti Abhiyan.

Ramachandran, V. 1998. 'Promises, Promises'. *Seminar* #464 (Right to Education), April: 54–63.

Sahiyar Stree Sanghathan, Gujarat Forum for Women's Studies and Action, NAWO, Movement for Secular Democracy and PUCL. 1998. Fact-finding Reports into Sanjeli-Randhikpur Incidents, August-September.

Sudarshan, R. 1998. 'Where Are We At?' *Seminar* (Right to Education), April: 18–21.

Tilak, J. B. G. 1999. 'National Human Development Initiative: Education in the Union Budget'. *Economic and Political Weekly* 34 (10/11) (March 6–19): 614–20.

Visaria, P. 1998. *Unemployment among Youth in India*, Employment and Training Papers 36. Geneva: International Labour Organisation.

Warnock, M. 1977. *Schools of Thought*. London: Faber and Faber.

9

Why Women Teachers Matter in Secondary Education

Kameshwari Jandhyala and Vimala Ramachandran

There has been no dearth of policy recommendations or specific interventions to advance and increase the pool of women teachers, especially at the school level. No doubt, this concern has always been entwined with larger national goals and the discourse on the development of modern education in India, a significant part of which involves promoting education among women and girls. A focus and thrust on women teachers is not recent; it has been central to much of the educational discourse since the nineteenth century. In a traditional society such as India, where barriers to educating girls in the public domain were circumscribed by caste and religious restrictions, it is not surprising that spaces for training women as teachers opened up fairly early on. Successive Five-Year Plans and commissions made recommendations on the issue of female education and the need to create conditions conducive to increasing the numbers of women teachers.[1] The significance of women teachers was also foregrounded in the efforts to universalise primary and, subsequently, elementary education from the early 1990s. As a result, many state governments introduced reservations for women at the primary school level, in some cases up to 50 per cent, in teacher recruitment policies.

Notwithstanding these measures, in Rajasthan, the percentage of women teachers is far below the national average and it varies from district to district. At the secondary level, the percentage of women teachers across the state is 19 per cent (NUEPA 2012, U-DISE 2011–12). The percentage of women teachers dips to below 9 per cent in educationally backward districts and those that are sparsely populated, such as Jaisalmer, Jalore, and Barmer; while it is more than 40 per cent in Kota, Sri Ganganagar, and Bikaner—districts where education of women has been fairly good for more than five decades now. Low participation of women in secondary and higher education leads to a shortage of women teachers in secondary schools. Acute shortage of women teachers in secondary schools works as a barrier to girls' participation in areas where traditional practices continue and where women's safety is a real problem. The situation not only varies across districts, but also among different social groups, leading to stark differences among different communities.

This chapter, based on qualitative research conducted in three districts of Rajasthan, explores the cumulative impact of the spiral of fewer women teachers and low enrolment of girls in school.

The criteria for selection of the field sample were districts with a high concentration of Scheduled Castes (SC), Scheduled Tribes (ST) and Muslims in the population; urban and rural representation; and the presence of teacher-training institutions and women teachers at the secondary level, higher than the state average, closer to the state average, and lower than the state average. Accordingly, the three sample districts selected were Baran (poor, high ST population); Barmer (geographical and developmental disadvantage and high SC population), and Ajmer (high urban Muslim population). In each district, two blocks were selected, one closer to the district headquarters and another in a remote location. The research study covered six blocks across three districts, six secondary/higher-secondary schools (four for only girls), six government and private undergraduate colleges (three for only girls), and six government and private BEd colleges (one for only girls).

The research tools and methodology included a review of the secondary literature and data, as well as a set of tools for conducting in-depth interviews and focus group discussions (FGD). In-depth interviews were held with state and district-level education department officials and principals of the sample BEd and undergraduate colleges, and with head teachers of the sample secondary and higher-secondary schools. Semi-structured interviews were held with teachers at the collegiate and school levels. Focus group discussions were held with girl students in the sample BEd and undergraduate colleges and in the sample secondary and higher-secondary schools; and at the community level, with parents of girls who dropped out at the secondary level.

The Gross Enrolment Ratios (GER) along the educational continuum, nationally and in Rajasthan, highlight both gender and social gaps quite clearly. Table 9.1 shows that in Rajasthan, as we move from primary (Classes I–V) to higher education, the gender and social gap and dropout rates at each successive level become more significant. As it shows, while the GER at the upper-primary and secondary levels indicate a significant drop, there is sharper drop in GER for girls at the higher education level—14.9 per cent. The lowest higher education GER is for SC girls at 8.5, followed by ST girls at 10.3. This is not surprising, because the share of student enrolment in higher education across all marginalised groups in Rajasthan is less than their proportionate share in the population, which is indicative of the continued persistence of educational backwardness among these communities.

The situation in the sample districts, for instance, presents a similar picture where the gaps in transition to the next higher level of education become sharper. This is true for girls in general, particularly across marginalised social groups like SCs and STs. In Barmer district, in 2012–13, the total enrolment of girls at the secondary and higher-secondary levels was 33.16 per cent and 29.22 per cent. The situation of girls from marginalised communities is a matter of grave concern, with enrolment of SC and ST girls at 13.28 per cent and 1.16 per cent at the secondary level and 11 per cent and 0.79 per cent at the higher-secondary level.[2] Disparities are reflected not only in enrolment, but also at the faculty and staff levels. In Rajasthan, compared to men, women are considerably underrepresented among faculty and staff, in both secondary and at higher education institutions, and this deficit is higher for all marginalised social groups.

TABLE 9.1: Gross Enrolment Ratio in Rajasthan, 2010–11

2010–11	*All*			*Scheduled Castes*			*Scheduled Tribes*		
	Boys	*Girls*	*Total*	*Boys*	*Girls*	*Total*	*Boys*	*Girls*	*Total*
Classes I–V	110.3	109.5	109.9	123.3	124	123.6	135.8	127.8	132
Classes VI–VIII	91	73	82.4	93.7	76.5	85.6	91.1	71.2	81.6
Classes IX–X	72.4	50.1	61.8	64.6	44.8	55.5	58.1	44.3	51.5
Classes XI–XII	61.2	40.8	51.5	53.8	36	45.7	28.7	18.9	23.9
Higher education 18–24 years (2011–12)	20.9	15.2	18.2	13.5	8.5	11.2	15.7	10.3	13

Source: SES GOI 2010–11; higher education data from All India Survey of Higher Education, 2013.

The reduced number of women as one goes up the education ladder is, not surprisingly, reflected in the number of women teachers available at the secondary level, and this remains an important concern in Rajasthan. Overall, the number of women teachers at the secondary level has increased at a very slow pace. In 1990–91, the percentage of women teachers at the secondary and higher-secondary levels (all managements) was 22 per cent and 25 per cent, respectively. In 2011–12, this improved marginally to 28.9 per cent and 29.3 per cent.[3] As Table 9.2 shows, the rural–urban divide is sharp. In the sample districts, except for Ajmer, which has a significantly higher percentage or proportion of women teachers, the situation in backward districts such as Barmer and Baran is poor. The higher percentages of women teachers at the higher-secondary level are also because these schools are generally located in urban and semi-urban areas where road connectivity and transport are not a problem. Further, the higher presence of women teachers in Ajmer district can be explained by the fact that access to higher education is

TABLE 9.2: Women Teachers at the Secondary Level in Government Schools in Sample Districts, 2011–12

District	*Percentage of Women*	
	Secondary Level	*Higher Secondary Level*
Ajmer	39	43.4
Baran	21	18
Barmer	8	16
Rajasthan	21.5	26

Source: *Shiksha ki Pragati*, Board of Secondary Education, Rajasthan, 2011–12.

much better there. Ajmer is one of the seven districts in Rajasthan with a high concentration of higher education institutions.[4] It has 18 BEd colleges, against three in Baran and four in Barmer.

Gaps between social classes, as much as between genders, stand out when gender is intersected with social category. In Rajasthan, at the secondary school level, only 7.7 per cent are SC and 4.8 per cent are ST women teachers and at the higher-secondary level, only 7.44 per cent and 3.73 per cent are SC and ST women teachers, respectively. It may be pertinent to point out that the low representation of SC and ST women teachers is mirrored in the case of SC and ST men as well.

The reasons for this deficit in the representation of marginalised communities, which is further exacerbated in the case of women, are not hard to see. Basant and Sen (2010: 69) make a strong argument for locating the issues of secondary education in the ambit of any strategy looking to enhance participation in higher education. They argue,

> Once persons from underprivileged groups cross the school threshold, the chances of their going to colleges are quite high. Clearly, the constraints on school education must first be fully understood and dealt with so as to enhance participation in higher education. Therefore, even while dealing with the issue of participation, should the higher education policy also focus on ensuring that the threshold (schooling) is crossed?

Quite clearly, any attempt to increase the pool of women teachers would need to have an integrated and organic approach that builds bridges across secondary, collegiate, and teacher-training levels. In the current context, each of these education levels is a discrete and self-contained silo. What is needed is a definite break from such practice, to creatively re-conceptualise the education continuum. This is a tall order and one is not sure that the government and educational bureaucracy are ready for even a dialogue on thinking out of the box.

School Teaching as a Career Option for Women

The FGDs in all the three districts with girl students and women teachers in secondary schools, undergraduate colleges and BEd colleges provided the uniform feedback that teaching, especially in schools, is not a popular or preferred choice. The exception was the feedback from tribal girls in a rural secondary school in Baran district, for whom school teaching as a career held some attraction because of the very limited employment options available. Teaching at the school level, elementary or secondary, is seen as a low-prestige job, and a default option if other avenues, such as the civil services, are closed. Most women became schoolteachers as they felt they could combine their family responsibility with employment. Families also actively support teaching as a career option for women, especially after marriage. One needs to be cautious in applauding this apparent shift in societal attitudes towards women and employment. Growing aspirations for changes in lifestyles require a second income and, therefore, families now want their women to work, as long as it is within the patriarchal framework, where responsibility towards the family predominates. And this balance can be easily maintained if they become schoolteachers.

Gendering of Subject/Stream Specialisations

One of the key issues explored is the possible feminisation of subject specialisation and its implications for the future availability of women teachers in certain subjects. Currently, there is a paucity of women maths and science teachers. Girls, especially from marginalised communities, have limited access to science and maths education, because most government girls' schools (to which most of them go) do not offer these subjects. Further, social perceptions show that maths, in particular, is seen as beyond the inherent capabilities of girls. This deficit in maths and science girl students continues into the college and BEd level and, as a result, very few women science and maths teachers are available.

Nationally, as in Rajasthan, there seem to be growing disparities in enrolment in different academic streams in higher education. Except in the arts stream, in Rajasthan, enrolments are significantly lower in the science and commerce streams than the national averages. Table 9.3 highlights the skewed distribution of women teachers in maths and science at the secondary level in the sample districts. The situation, as far as women maths teachers are concerned, is very grave in the backward districts of Baran and Barmer.

Table 9.3: Percentage of Women Maths and Science Teachers at the Secondary Level in Sample Districts, 2010–11

District	*All Women Teachers*	*Women Maths Teachers*	*Women Science Teachers*
Ajmer	31.8	12.89	30.6
Baran	17.1	4.9	20.2
Barmer	10.3	1.7	14.9
Rajasthan	20.5	7.7	20.8

Source: GOR, Shiksha ki Pragati, Board of Secondary Education, 2011–12.

To understand the roots of this gender imbalance by subject stream among teachers and the poor representation of women in teaching at the secondary level, it is important to trace the story back to the situation at the secondary and collegiate levels.

Issues in Access and Participation

In Rajasthan, where there are no aided institutions, the government remains a significant provider of secondary and higher-secondary education. In 2010–11, 51.81 per cent of secondary schools and 37.16 per cent higher-secondary schools were government schools (Government of Rajasthan 2011–12). Access, however, remains a major challenge in some difficult areas, such as Barmer, where the distribution of schools is in favour of urban and peri-urban areas. In Rajasthan, by and large, higher-secondary schools are known as boys' schools (the term 'boys' school' is used for a co-ed school). Boys' school is a misnomer, because girls are admitted if either a higher-secondary school for only girls is not accessible, or if girls want to pursue specific subjects such as science/maths that are offered only in boys' schools.

The number of girls-only secondary schools is very limited in the state as a whole and this was evident in the sample districts as well. In 2011–12, for instance, there were only 557 girls' only secondary schools against 15,150 for boys in the state. At the higher-secondary level, there were 779 girls-only schools against 7,741 boys' schools. As Table 9.4 shows, the situation in the sample districts is even more skewed, with girls-only secondary schools being as few as five in Barmer district. This issue merits particular attention, especially in a state such as Rajasthan, where girls' education is challenged and obstructed by a traditional society that generally has a not-so-positive view of girls and women.

Discussions with education officials during fieldwork were revealing. We were informed that 'authorities are no longer thinking of separate schools for boys and girls. We are moving in the direction of co-education to foster a change in mindset.'[5] The assumption seems to be that over the past two decades, the whole gamut of gender issues in the elementary sector, including community awareness, access, textbook renewal, teacher sensitisation and so on, have been effectively addressed by achieving gender parity at the elementary level. Hence, at the secondary level, co-education is not a problem. Globally, co-education is being advocated as the direction in which school education needs to move. Even India seems to have accepted this position fairly uncritically.

Table 9.4: Secondary and Higher-Secondary Schools in Sample Districts

	Boys' Secondary Schools	*Girls' Secondary Schools*	*Boys' Higher Secondary Schools*	*Girls' Higher Secondary Schools*
Rajasthan	15,150	537	7,741	699
Ajmer	422	24	221	48
Barmer*	445 (336 government, 109 private	5 (3 government, 2 private)	125 (72 government and 53 private)	12 (all government)
Baran	189	8	64	13

Note: * Field notes.
Source: Directorate of Secondary Education, Bikaner, 2013.

This perspective seems to be short-sighted and fully overlooks persistent social and community-specific barriers to girls' education. The rural co-education senior-secondary school in Barmer had only 18 girls against 451 boys enrolled.[6] Later in this chapter, we discuss the views of various groups on the extent to which co-education, especially at the secondary level, is viable or desirable and the possible adverse effects it may have on girls' participation in secondary education. This also influences higher education and employment opportunities.

Gaps in secondary schooling access, especially among girls, are mirrored at the higher education level as well. An analysis of higher education institutions done by the National Assessment and Accreditation Council (NAAC) in 2008 highlighted the uneven distribution and showed the concentration of higher education institutions in just seven out of the 32 districts in Rajasthan (Sikar, Kota, Ajmer, Dausa, Sri Ganganagar, Jaipur and Jhunjhunu). Further, the concentration in urban and peri-urban areas exacerbates access for poor and marginalised girls in particular.

Teacher education and training in Rajasthan is mainly in the private sector, with the government running very few colleges, most of which are again concentrated in urban areas and in a few districts. In the three sample districts, the variation is vast, with 18 BEd colleges in Ajmer district and Baran and Barmer having just three and four, respectively. The number of seats in teacher-education institutions and their distribution across subjects are fixed, with girls-only colleges having 100 seats and co-ed colleges 125 seats. The stream-wise allocation of seats in favour of arts subjects (at 70 against 20 for commerce and 10 for science) is a clear reflection of the subjects that get offered at the secondary level.

LIMITED ACCESS TO SCIENCE EDUCATION

At the higher-secondary school level, there is poor access to science education, as the number of girls-only schools in Rajasthan is limited and those offering the science stream are few. The consequent feminisation of subjects at the secondary level is only now being recognised. The lack of women teachers has an effect on educational choices for girls, a situation being reported in other parts of the country as well.[7] Girls' schools are often known to offer only humanities and language courses, reflecting, in some senses, the gendered mindset of the education system.

Baran and Ajmer districts provide a clear picture of the skewed access between boys and girls. In Baran, the number of schools offering science is limited, both in government and private schools. Only nine girls-only government schools against 31 co-ed government secondary schools offer the science stream. The sharp disparity is evident in private schools as well, where only five girls' secondary schools against 57 boys' schools offer science. In Ajmer, nine girls' government secondary schools against 31 for boys and seven private girls' schools against 57 for boys, offer the science stream.

Very few students from marginalised groups actually study science or maths at the higher-secondary level. Very few girls (including from forward castes) pursue maths and science and the numbers are minuscule among the marginalised groups. As reported in the FGDs, the science option is seen as an expensive one, as there are costs to be incurred on tuition and laboratory fees. Families are unwilling to incur these costs for girls.

Not surprisingly, the pattern of subjects opted for by students at the undergraduate and later the BEd level is similar to what is chosen at the secondary level. At the college and BEd college level, choices are also circumscribed by the subject streams offered. In Ajmer and Baran, for instance, the undergraduate colleges for girls in the rural blocks offered only arts subjects.

Analysing the situation of women teachers at the secondary level, what comes to the fore is the poor participation, completion rate and transition to the next higher level of education among girls from marginalised communities. Besides class and caste divides, addressing the gender subtext that underpins all aspects of girls' and women's lives is challenging. The manner in which this gender bias plays out is clearly evident in the decisions to choose specific subjects at the secondary level, which do not question the accepted stereotypical roles for women, where family comes before anything else. This aspect also influences the decisions that women teachers take regarding their career prospects and advancement. Often they defer or, in most cases, reject any career advancement if it disturbs their family situation.

Key Challenges

There are no expressly stated systemic barriers faced by women and women from marginalised communities in becoming secondary-level teachers. Despite the host of incentives and reservations in admissions at the collegiate level available for girls, the cumulative burden of poor quality education in government schools, starting from the elementary cycle, contributes to poor achievement and performance at the secondary level, resulting in very low participation in higher education and low success in qualifying examinations. This finally results in very small numbers of women, especially from the marginalised communities, who actually go on to become secondary-level teachers.

The long road of nearly six years after completing secondary schooling to acquire an undergraduate or postgraduate degree and a teacher-training certificate and then clear the state's competitive recruitment examinations to become a secondary-level teacher, is most often a daunting task. This is more so for marginalised girls, who often do not have the resources or support to undertake this journey.

The lack of women teachers at the tertiary level can be traced back to the issue of girls' participation in and completion of secondary education. The number of women science and maths teachers is worrisomely low. This latter problem, in particular, stems from the lack of access to science education at the higher-secondary level.

It is important to note that there has been a perceptible change in community and parental perspectives on girls' education, as our field interactions showed. The thrust on universalisation of elementary education for the past 25 years seems to have yielded some positive outcomes.

The issue is no longer whether girls should be educated, but concerns related to the conditions under which they can continue to the secondary and tertiary levels of education. This is the message from across the spectrum of communities in urban and rural areas that we interacted with. These changed attitudes at the ground level need to be capitalised on and are an important pointer to policymakers. The picture, however, is not sanguine. There are social sub-groups in remote areas among specific communities (such as Rajputs, Muslims, SCs, and STs) that continue to support early marriage for girls and are not keen on secondary education for them. The assumption that a positive environment for girls' education has been created under

Universalisation of Elementary Education (UEE) campaigns and nothing further needs to be done at the community level requires to be critically revisited.

Efforts at universal secondary schooling need to recognise that access to education is not a neutral process. There are several factors that impinge on and influence access to education, especially in traditional cultural contexts. Persistent cultural and traditional constraints on girls' mobility and perceived threats to the safety and security of older girls in general need to be taken on board. The latter issue is emerging as a key constraint and barrier to girls' education at the secondary level. A situation where there are only a very limited number of girls-only schools and a policy that does not expressly promote or support separate schools for girls is a matter of concern. What is worrisome is that there seems to be an unstated government decision that no new girls' schools will be opened, as our field interactions showed. This is a short-sighted approach, to say the least.

The overwhelming demand from the field is for girls-only schools at the secondary and senior-secondary levels. The current policy of ensuring access through an upgradation of upper-primary schools ensures that the deficit at the secondary level continues, as the number of girls-only schools is limited. Often, a shortage of resources is cited for not opening new girls-only schools. This argument flies in the face of the larger national goals of achieving gender and equity in secondary education.

In addition, the importance of hostels cannot be overstated. The overwhelming message from all FGDs with girls in schools, colleges and BEd colleges across all three districts was that hostels are required across the spectrum at the secondary, collegiate and teacher-training levels, especially in rural areas where distances are quite considerable. Family concerns over rising transport costs and safety issues often work as a major deterrent. In far-flung and geographically difficult locations, hostel facilities for girls are necessary, so that even those living in remote areas can participate effectively in secondary education. While opening hostels is part of the overall gender and equity strategy of the Rashtriya Madhyamik Shiksha Abhiyan (RMSA), there does not seem to be any clear approach to strategically locating hostels after mapping local needs.

The need for safe transport has also been pointed out as a major problem. There is a heightened perception of how unsafe it is for girls to travel alone, especially older girls. The issue is critical in rural areas, like in Baran and Barmer, where habitations are dispersed and the nearest secondary school or college may be 10–15 kilometres away. And, even in more urbanised areas like Ajmer, where safety and security concerns are high among Muslims and where the distance to school or college may not be as much, the fear of harassment and teasing has had an adverse effect on girls' higher education.

Our field sample showed that, in general, very few girls and an even smaller number of SC, ST and Muslim girls opt for the science stream. The predominant reason was the non-availability of the science stream in girls-only higher-secondary schools. Hence, girls have to go to co-ed schools for pursuing these subjects, but often cannot, because their families are against co-education. This is particularly true of the Muslim community. Another equally important reason was the additional costs involved in pursuing science. Denying science education to very poor girls from marginalised groups only exacerbates the existing inequities in higher education and employment. In such a context, achieving gender and equity at the secondary level appears very elusive.

It would be pertinent to take a leaf out of efforts to promote agriculture education. In Ajmer district, for instance, we found that a cash incentive given to students who opted for agriculture resulted in many more girls enrolling in this stream. A similar cash incentive could be considered to encourage science and maths education among girls.

A critical and likely major deterrent to girls studying in co-ed institutions is the difficulties of negotiating the social environment in and outside classrooms in institutions at all levels. This was a common thread that ran through all our interactions and discussions with girls in schools and colleges and with women teachers in colleges and teacher-training institutes. Harassment, sexual innuendoes, inadequate physical safety, fear of moving around, even to go to bathrooms within institutions, derisive talk, and so on, were reported as making life in co-ed institutions very stressful. As a girl from a rural secondary school in Ajmer commented, 'It's humiliating. *Man karta hai unko mar dein* (I feel like hitting them).' With very few women teachers in higher-secondary schools and in BEd colleges, both girl students and women teachers feel at a disadvantage. They do not have the safety of numbers, nor the support and solidarity that numbers would have provided. Almost everyone seems to be silent on this issue, so much so that it continues to insidiously gain in strength. This could emerge as the major deterrent to girls' education in general and their participation in higher education in particular.

Addressing These Barriers and Challenges

Recast the Secondary School

There is an urgent need to reconfigure the secondary school. In Rajasthan, the government has two options—either open new girls-only secondary schools, or start girls-only shifts in existing boys' schools. The shift system currently exists in many urban schools and it ensures an optimal use of resources. The state government's current plan to start a higher-secondary school in each *gram panchayat* would address the issue of access to a large extent and introducing separate shifts for girls should not be difficult.

In this context, the importance of distance education in coping with increased demand and poor accessibility cannot be over-emphasised. Its relevance for boys and girls in remote areas goes beyond the elementary level, even to higher education. Further, the distance education mode could also be an option for girls from very orthodox communities that continue to resist sending older girls to school. Our field interactions in the rural sample block in Ajmer district showed that the role of civil society organisations in reaching out to marginalised girls was a key determinant in ensuring the education of older girls beyond the elementary level.

Strategic Provision of Hostels

The mapping of critical locations, where girls would have to travel long distances and where opening a hostel would make a crucial difference, needs to be done expeditiously. The issue of hostels is of equal importance for boys from remote areas and from poor communities.

Another way in which hostels could be provisioned is to locate them within the catchment area of a higher-secondary school, which is an integral part of the Kasturba Gandhi Balika Vidyalaya (KGBV) scheme, for instance. A similar forward linkage is essential, as are provisions made to provide hostels for girls studying in college and for the BEd programme. There needs to be a cooperative and convergent approach between the departments of secondary school education, higher education and SC, ST and minority welfare, to map the provision of hostels for girls, especially from marginalised communities. An immediate step could be to attach a hostel to all BEd colleges in Rajasthan.

Ensuring Safe Travel for Girls

As the state government plans a secondary and higher-secondary school in each *gram panchayat*, it may be useful to provide separate bus services for girls only in rural areas (like the ladies specials used during a fixed time in Delhi, for many years). In urban areas, an escort for groups of girls to go from their homes to school could be considered. This is a strategy that would be welcomed by the Muslim community. This, again, is not a new strategy, as it was used very effectively in the early days of UEE.

Fostering Science Education

A focussed plan to strengthen science and maths education at the upper-primary level needs to be put in place, both to foster interest in science, as well as equip students to confidently opt for science and maths at the secondary level. Every girls-only school (especially in the government sector), or at least a nodal school for a cluster of schools, must offer science and maths at the higher-secondary level. The government could consider providing additional academic support to girls from marginalised groups, especially in Classes IX and XI (this is also important for boys from marginalised social groups). Scholarships for pursuing science and maths at the school level should be introduced with a focus on promoting science among girls. Another enabling intervention could be the creation of science and maths clubs for children in general.

Provision of Career Counselling in Schools and Colleges

The government needs to consider systematic career counselling in schools and later on at the college level, as most students do not receive much guidance from their parents. This would be a positive step, as the majority of students in government secondary schools and colleges are not from economically better-off families. For them, choosing a stream and subjects that could lead to viable employment is crucial.

Creating Sensitivity to Gender and Social Diversities in Educational Institutions

The government, in collaboration with women's organisations, could organise workshops in every secondary and higher-secondary school, to engage students and teachers in a dialogue on the importance of creating a non-discriminatory environment. Given the wealth of evidence, both research-based and media reports, on sexual harassment, caste and community-based discrimination and prevailing social attitudes towards the marginalised, schools and colleges should be positioned as spaces where teachers and students learn and internalise the values of non-discrimination and equality mentioned in the Constitution of India. This could be initiated in a few districts in a time-bound manner, to develop strategies to conduct activities with students and teachers. Interested donor agencies could be brought together to explore how this could be initiated. Making our educational institutions safe spaces is an urgent requirement.

Strategies to Increase the Pool of Women Teachers

The government needs to make a district-wise estimate of the number of women teachers required, if the options of educating girls either through girls-only schools or separate shifts are implemented. Accordingly, seats for women in BEd colleges need to be increased. Equally, the allocation for different academic streams needs to be re examined, to reduce skewed allocations and bottlenecks and to ensure that the numbers of seats for science are increased substantially, from the current 10 per cent to 20 per cent, at least. Perhaps providing an incentive to students who opt for the science stream could be considered. This is important because we noticed that science students opt for the arts stream in BEd colleges. The National Council for Teacher Education (NCTE) and other national regulatory bodies need to be brought on board to work out a strategic plan to enhance the pool of women teachers at the secondary/higher-secondary levels.

Need to Revisit the Strategies for Girls in RMSA

With a daunting goal such as universalisation, it is a matter of some concern that the RMSA adopts a universal strategy, though its stated objective is to bring marginalised groups, especially girls within them, into the ambit of secondary education. The lack of in-depth studies or analysis of the gender situation in different regions and social and economic groups, to inform the development of context-specific interventions that are imperative to address gender inequities, is a major drawback. There are lessons to be learnt from the elementary education sector, where detailed studies on equity across the country became the basis for developing specific strategies and interventions for different contexts and forms of inequity, which resulted in ensuring not only access but also enhanced educational participation and retention of girls, especially those from vulnerable and marginalised social groups.

Further, in the RMSA, increasing the number of women teachers at the secondary and higher-secondary levels is not a core objective. However, under its equity interventions, increasing the number of women teachers is included, along with micro-planning, opening schools in areas with concentrations of marginalised groups, special enrolment drives and constructing separate toilets for girls. As mentioned earlier, education is a state subject and if the central government does not have specific directives on the issue of women teachers, it is left to individual states to decide whether to adopt a targeted approach to the issue of women teachers. If one were to look back again at the experience of the elementary sector, sustained discussion and debate on gender issues at the elementary level, which was facilitated from the national level, resulted in similar processes being initiated at the state level as well. In the absence of a specific gender strategy, particularly for the recruitment of women teachers to address issues of gender at the secondary level, or a specific thrust on increasing the pool of women teachers, there is every chance that gender concerns in secondary education will vanish from government and public debate and discourse.

NOTES

1. Some of the key milestones that emerged over the nineteenth and twentieth centuries are relevant to today's context of trying to achieve gender equity. In 1882, the Indian Education Commission supported women teachers' training through residential programmes and providing financial support to female teacher trainees. Since then, there have been consistent recommendations to increase women's participation in teaching. For example, the Secondary Education Commission of 1952–53 suggested part-time training courses to meet the shortage of women teachers. The First Five-Year Plan suggested part-time teaching for married women who could not get away fully from home responsibilities. The Second Five-Year Plan pointed out that the anticipated expansion of girls' education in the Third Five-Year Plan may not be realised due to an acute shortage of women teachers, which was only 17 per cent (both primary and secondary levels together) in 1953–54. This was one of the first policy documents to point out the provisions and allocations that were needed to generate a conducive and sensitive community environment with situation-specific interventions. The National Commission on Women's Education of 1958 recommended increasing training institutions for women teachers, in addition to condensed courses, fee exemptions for such training, recruiting vulnerable women such as widows for such training, part-time courses, extra coaching classes and placement centres, so that women teacher-graduates were immediately absorbed, among many others. The Education Commission 1964–66, under the chairmanship of D. S. Kothari, made detailed suggestions on the issue of women teachers and specifically established the link between promoting girls' education and the availability of women teachers.

2. Data from the District Educational Office (DEO), Barmer, 2013.

3. GOR, *Shiksha ki Pragati*, Board of Secondary Education.

4. Sikar, Kota, Dausa, Sri Ganganagar, Jaipur and Jhunjhunu, along with Ajmer, are the seven districts with the highest concentration of higher education institutions in Rajasthan. For further details, see NAAC (2008).

5. Field notes, Ajmer district, 2013.

6. Field notes, Barmer district, 2013.

7. Personal communication from Leela Visaria, Gujarat Institute of Development Research (GIDR), Ahmedabad.

REFERENCES

Basant, R., and G. Sen 2010. 'Who Participates in Higher Education in India: Rethinking the Role of Affirmative Action'. *Economic & Political Weekly* 45 (39): 62–70.

Government of Rajasthan. 2011–12. 'Shiksha Ki Pragati' (Progress of Education in Rajasthan). Bikaner: Directorate of Secondary Education.

National Assessment and Accreditation Council. 2008. 'An Analysis of Peer Term Reports of Accredited Institutions of Rajasthan: Issues and Strategies for Quality Enhancement'. Bangalore: NAAC.

NUEPA 2012. U-DISE 2011–12: Teacher's Summary. Rajasthan State Level. New Delhi: NUEPA.

Section II

The Political, Economic, and Social Context

10

'Sisters under the Skin'*

Events of 2002 and Girls' Education in Ahmedabad

Suchitra Balasubrahmanyan and Nina Haeems

The events of 2002 in Gujarat have generally been perceived as acts of state-supported violence directed against Muslims, which included mass murder, sexual abuse and large-scale destruction of property. Without doubt, this was the principal tragedy that left scars on the entire Muslim community. Yet, if we look beyond, the violence has implications for society in Gujarat as a whole, for both Hindus and Muslims, and in particular for the girls of these communities. This chapter looks at the adverse impact of the communal violence of 2002 on the education of Hindu and Muslim girls, focussing primarily on students of two municipal primary schools in two conflict-prone, poor areas of Ahmedabad–Shahpur in the walled city and Rajpur, an industrial suburb.

This chapter is based on data collected as part of an ongoing comparative study of gender-related factors affecting the education of girls at the upper-primary level in municipal schools in Ahmedabad and Mumbai, supported by the Indo-Dutch Programme on Alternatives in Development (IDPAD Phase V). The Municipal Corporation of Ahmedabad provides primary education in nine languages, though for this study three schools were selected—one in the Gujarati medium, which is the principal regional language of the state, one in the Urdu medium, which is increasingly regarded as the main language of the minority community, and the third in the Hindi medium, which is the main language used by migrants to the city. These are also the mediums of instruction that record the highest enrolment on the part of students. Between March and December 2004, we interviewed

* Previously published as Suchitra Sheth and Nina Haeems, '"Sisters under the Skin": Events of 2002 and Girls' Education in Ahmedabad', *Economic and Political Weekly* 41 (17), April 2006: 1708–1712. This is an expanded version of a paper presented at the Indian Association of Women's Studies Conference on 'Sovereignty, Citizenship, and Gender' at Goa, 3–6 May 2005. Additional inputs were provided by Parvin and Hansa. The names of girls and their mothers and teachers have been changed to protect their identity.

150 girls from Classes V, VI and VII and their mothers, belonging to both Hindu and Muslim families. In proportion to the total enrolment in these mediums, 108 girls were selected from the Gujarati-medium schools and 21 each from Urdu and Hindi-medium schools. The Hindi-medium students have not been included in this chapter, as the area in which the selected school is located did not directly experience violence during 2002. The chapter is also informed by the authors' first-hand experience of having lived in Ahmedabad for the past two decades and being eyewitnesses to the events of 2002.

The study uncovered many facets of what it means to be a young girl in Ahmedabad and what it is like to be the mother of a young girl in Ahmedabad. Conversations revealed that despite social and cultural conditioning to think otherwise, mothers did see education for daughters both as a process that would widen their horizons and as a route that could take their families out of the trap of poverty and lack of opportunity. Inspired by the professional women depicted in television serials and the stories about astronaut Kalpana Chawla, girls now aspire to become businesswomen, models, doctors and join the armed forces. Within this picture of hope and ambition, a striking revelation was that for both Muslims and Hindus, deteriorating intercommunity relationships, along with the state's apathy towards restoring security and promoting goodwill between communities, have forced them to not aspire for anything beyond the education offered by the local Urdu or Gujarati-medium municipal primary school. In such circumstances, both mothers and daughters are unable to visualise a future beyond marriage and unskilled, primarily home-based work. And the school, which could be a site for the secular socialisation of future generations, itself becomes an institution for widening the distance between the communities.

HUMAN GEOGRAPHY OF AHMEDABAD

A brief overview of the human geography of Ahmedabad is necessary to better comprehend the post-2002 situation. Shahpur, the first area of focus in this chapter, is located in the old and walled part of the city, established by Sultan Ahmed Shah almost 600 years ago. This walled city is characterised by narrow lanes, flanked on both sides by closely packed houses grouped into '*pols*'. The residents of a *pol* often belong to one caste or community and two adjoining *pols* usually share a common wall. Thus, different castes and communities—Hindus and Muslims, upper and lower castes—live in close proximity in these neighbourhoods. This proximity, however, has also been cause for conflict and it was in the walled city that the communal conflicts usually began and escalated, later spreading to the industrial suburbs.

The industrial suburbs came into existence with the establishment of the textile industry in the late nineteenth century. Ahmedabad expanded on its eastern periphery when mills were set up in the outlying villages, forming an industrial suburb which was gradually subsumed into the city and became part of the Ahmedabad Municipal Corporation (AMC). The workforce, which migrated from neighbouring districts and from other states, settled in *chawls* near the mill compounds. Two-thirds of them were Dalit and Muslim and, like in the old walled city, here too they lived in close proximity. These Dalit-Muslim neighbourhoods, though separate, shared a common 'mill subculture' and their lives were intertwined. Rajpur, the second area selected for the study, is one such former village that was absorbed into Ahmedabad, sometime in the 1930s.

History of Social Conflict

The human geography and social conflict in these areas have shaped each other. Ahmedabad has had a history of Hindu-Muslim tension from the time of Aurangzeb in the seventeenth century. The causes ranged from altercations during Holi celebrations, to provocative behaviour during Muharram or *rath yatra* processions, and even India-Pakistan cricket matches in recent times, which could escalate into full-fledged riots that resulted in destruction of property and loss of lives. Till the 1960s, riots hardly ever left deep scars and the two communities would soon resume business and social interaction. However, the riots of 1969 marked a turning point in Hindu-Muslim relations in Gujarat. A process of ghettoisation set in after these riots and many Muslims moved from mixed neighbourhoods in the walled city to Muslim dominated areas in the industrial suburbs, as well as to areas on the southern periphery of Ahmedabad.

In 1981, upper-caste Hindus began an agitation against the reservation system that gave Dalits and Adivasis access to institutions of higher education and to government jobs. Intense caste violence took place and the clashes between upper-caste Hindus and Dalits, which started in industrial Ahmedabad, escalated into a large-scale caste war. On this occasion, Muslims supported Dalits and protected them when they were attacked. Then came the violence during the second anti-reservation riots of 1985. But this time, it deteriorated into communal riots; the traditional Hindu-Muslim animosity became triangular, with Dalits forming the third vertex. The 1990 riots, precipitated by Lal Krishna Advani's (the then-President of the Bharatiya Janata Party) Rath Yatra, further weakened the frayed social fabric. In 1985, only one high wall came up between a *patidar* and a Muslim neighbourhood in the old city of Ahmedabad; by the end of 1990 the residents of almost all Dalit chawls in the industrial areas had erected high walls around them. At places where Muslims lived side-by-side with Dalits, the dominant sentiment became one of fear and mistrust. The violence sparked by the demolition of the Babri Masjid in 1992 was followed by sustained Hindutva mobilisation, in which the Sangh Parivar systematically wooed the Dalit communities in Gujarat and thus, the communal divide further deepened.

It is against this background that we need to look at the impact of the events of 2002. This time the violence was more brutal, widespread and prolonged and it was marked by the overt and covert partisan role of the state—the elected representatives, law enforcement agencies and the justice system. As a result, hatred, mistrust and fear have intensified between the two communities and the situation appears to have reached a point where relationships cannot be repaired.

URDU SCHOOL IN SHAHPUR

Shahpur, in the walled city, is dominated by Jains, Patels and Muslims. As in many other municipal wards within the walled city, there has been a striking reversal in the population profile since the 1990s. Earlier, Hindus formed 60 per cent of the population and a Muslim candidate could not hope to win a municipal election from this area. Over the last decade, many Hindu families have moved out and today, with Muslims forming over half the population, one of Shahpur's three corporators is a Muslim. AMC runs 90 Urdu-medium primary schools, of which nine are in Shahpur. We interviewed 21 girls from one school which was set up in 1885. Shahpur was directly affected by violence in 2002 and the premises of the school we studied had been converted into a relief camp.

Debate on Medium of Education

A majority of Muslims in Gujarat speak Gujarati at home and the debate on the medium of education for Muslims has been a long-standing one, dating to the nineteenth century. While one section of Gujarati Muslims favoured education in the Gujarati medium, another equally influential section believed that a Muslim's education could be considered complete only when imparted in Urdu, the language of Islamic culture. There were two outcomes of this tension between religious and regional identities. On the one hand, the Muslim community established trusts which set up a few Urdu schools and the AMC too set up Urdu-medium schools. At the same time, there were other Muslim trusts which set up a larger number of Gujarati-medium schools with the reasoning that, from the viewpoint of job prospects, this would be more relevant. Muslim children also attended Gujarati-medium municipal schools.

The events of 2002 seem to have sharpened this debate. Conversations in Shahpur indicate that the recent threat to Muslim religious identity has pushed many members of their community to prefer Urdu-medium schools. As a result, the general declining trend of enrolment of boys and girls in Urdu schools has shown a reversal in 2002. Our enquiries and conversations with parents and the principal of the Urdu school indicate that the reasons behind such enrolment trends are complex. Parents have been taking their boys out of municipal schools and putting them into schools run by Muslim trusts, where, in addition to regular academics, religious teaching is also imparted. They feel that this training will enable their sons to get jobs as '*hafiz*' (religious teacher), in this country and abroad. Parents who dream of non-religious jobs for their sons in the Gulf countries feel that education in Urdu-medium municipal schools is also advantageous. (Others are beginning to prefer Gujarati-medium of education for their boys, as this increases their job prospects within the state.)

'*Mahol*' and '*Mohalla*'

Mothers reveal two possible reasons for the increasing enrolment of girls in Urdu-medium schools. Fatima Bibi, mother of Shahnaz studying in Class VI, revealed one of the reasons: 'The tense "*mahol*" or environment has now become an everyday affair. It is not just restricted to riot times. Hindu boys tease the girls or harass them on the road. I do not want to send Shahnaz far away.' The Urdu-medium school is usually located in Muslim dominated '*mohollas*' or neighbourhoods and mothers prefer to send their girls there. We also found that good-looking girls were confined to the home more than others. The second reason for preferring the Urdu-medium for girls is related to the perception that it strengthens their Muslim identity. Raziya Begum, whose daughter Rubina is in Class VII, felt that 'people prefer the Urdu-medium school for their girls because education in the language of Islam would make their daughter a better Muslim and therefore improve her chances of getting a groom from a "good family"'. When asked why they would not choose the trust-run religious schools as they do for the boys, the reply is that these schools charge fees and while they are prepared to pay for the boys, they are not ready to pay for the girls who are, in any case, not expected to work in the future. Thus, the calculation that investment in boys' education reaps greater economic returns becomes the deciding factor in education matters for girls and boys.

The Urdu-medium municipal schools of Shahpur are only till Class VII. There is only one municipal Urdu high school in far away Asarwa and going there would mean that Parvin would have to travel through Hindu localities. Her mother Hamida Begum admits that learning widens the intellect, but it is unlikely that she will educate her daughter Parvin (who is now in Class V) beyond Class VII. 'I do not want to take the chance when she has "become older"; "something" may happen and her name will get spoilt.' The high schools that are nearer are privately managed and unaffordable. And in any case, reaching these too involves going through 'unsafe' Hindu areas.

It is well-known that it is the poorest communities that opt for municipal schooling and they can scarcely afford private schools for higher education. Many mothers reported that the prolonged curfew in 2002 meant lost wages, living on borrowed money and higher prices for food. Many are in debt and cannot afford education beyond the upper-primary subsidised education available near their *mohollas*.

A more critical deterrent is that the nearby private schools are in the Gujarati medium. As there are very few Urdu-medium secondary and high schools, education beyond upper-primary would involve making a successful transition into the Gujarati medium. This is something few can cope with. The state education system has no support mechanisms for Urdu-medium children interested in pursuing studies beyond Class VII and poor families cannot afford private tuitions.

Being Muslim in Ahmedabad

The study revealed that the Muslim community in general sees education as a futile exercise, because in the vitiated atmosphere of today's Ahmedabad, most people are unwilling to give a Muslim a job. Hamida Begum confesses, 'I would have liked to educate Parvin; if this Urdu school was upgraded to the Xth standard I would send her. She could become a teacher.' She corrected herself, 'But in any case, there is no point in thinking like that because who will give a job to a Muslim? What's the use of studying then?'

Finally, the Urdu-medium schools, where girls outnumber the boys, have become a mirror of the ghetto the girls live in. The increasing ghettoisation of residential spaces has meant that the girls live only among people of their own community. The school is a place which could ideally become a site for secular socialisation of children. But in the context of Gujarat, Urdu is a language used only by Muslims and it is impossible that children in this school will meet children from other communities. Significantly, a Gujarati-medium school is run on the same premises as the Urdu school—on two different floors of the same building, with some classes even having the same timings. Despite this, there is no interaction between the girls of these two schools. Thus, the girls of the Shahpur school live among their '*jamaat*' or caste members at home and at school their fellow students and teachers are other Muslims. The school offers no possibility of exposure to a world beyond their ghetto.

In contrast to the situation for girls, Muslim boys do have the option of going to schools, Urdu or Gujarati, which are further away from their *mohollas*. The *mahol* also does not pose a threat for them as it does for girls, whose gender makes them vulnerable. For the boys, there are possibilities of wider interaction later at their workplace; for the girls there appears to be no future other than marriage. Though most mothers claimed that they entertained marriage proposals only after their daughters turned 18, we observed that the process began soon after the girls started menstruating. And the trend towards early menarche means that such talks start even earlier. Once they get engaged, girls usually drop out. A male teacher in a Muslim trust-run school reported that if engaged girls stay on in school, they are usually more interested in clothes and their looks. As for paid work, both before and after marriage, girls have access only to home-based work in the garment-making, costume jewellery assembly or embroidery sectors. Traders leave raw materials at their homes and come back later to collect the finished goods and make the payment on a piece-rate basis. This system is structured around the general feelings of insecurity about the *mahol* and *moholla* and ensures that girls never need to leave their doorstep.

GUJARATI SCHOOL IN RAJPUR

The situation in Rajpur has to be seen against its own history of once close-knit and shared Dalit-Muslim neighbourhoods, now transformed into antagonistic Hindu-Muslim blocks. This industrial area had a number of flourishing textile mills, which employed Dalits, Muslims and other Hindus mainly from the middle-caste groups, like artisans and farmers (Patels). The decline of the textile mills began in the late 1970s and early 1980s. The non-Dalits slowly began to leave the area in search of better economic opportunities.

This economic downturn coincided with, or was accompanied by, caste riots. Well-to-do Dalits too began to move out in search of security and settled in other parts of Ahmedabad dominated by their own caste-fellows. Rajpur was left with a predominantly poor Dalit and Muslim population. Hindutva mobilisation in the 1990s attracted the Dalits, who saw in it an opportunity for better social status. Increasingly, their self-image also involved a 'Hindu' identity and the amity between an earlier generation of Dalits and Muslims disintegrated. Their *chawls* were separated by high walls and the communal riots accompanying the Ayodhya-centred agitation of the 1990s added to the mutual fear and distrust. Rajpur was also directly affected by the violence in 2002 and camps in the area gave shelter to 6,000 people. Today, it is not surprising to hear frequent anti-Muslim comments from Dalits in Rajpur.

The AMC runs 346 Gujarati-medium schools, of which 16 are in Rajpur. We interviewed over 100 girls in one school, which has been sharing the premises with an Urdu-medium school for the past four years. The Urdu-medium's earlier building was damaged in 2001 by the earthquake. There are almost 500 students in the Rajpur Gujarati-medium school, of whom a little less than 20 per cent are Muslims, while over 80 per cent are poor Dalits. Middle-class Dalits and the few middle and upper castes living in this area send their children to private schools in Rajpur and adjoining areas.

'Border' and '*Bandobast*'

The school is situated in a lane surrounded by residential Dalit *chawls* on three sides. This lane slopes upwards for about a furlong before it meets the main Rajpur road. The area around this intersection is referred to as the 'border' and the Muslim neighbourhoods located beyond this point have been referred to as 'Pakistan', for the past decade at least. The police are always posted in readiness at this border during festivals and religious processions, and even during recent events like the India-Pakistan cricket matches in early 2005. There is police '*bandobast*' (deployment) even when the India-Pakistan matches are played outside Ahmedabad.

How is this *mahol-moholla* situation reflected in the schooling of girls? A point that needs to be highlighted here is that there has been an adverse impact on girls of both communities. A long-standing fear psychosis prevails among both Dalit and Muslim mothers of Rajpur, which has resulted in a reluctance to send girls to schools outside the *moholla*, especially if the route to the school takes them through localities of the 'other' community. Even when the girls go to the nearby municipal school, they feel compelled to escort their daughters. For instance, after the riots of 2002, Ramila accompanied her daughter Bindu to school every day, for months. She says that '*zamana*' (the times) is bad now and she will educate Bindu for only two more years, till she completes Class VII. Mehmuda's daughter Aashiyana is now in Class VI and Mehmuda, like many other mothers, believes that the '*mahol*' has deteriorated. She says, 'If there is trouble, boys can run home, but the girls will get trapped. So it is better not to send them out for too long. In any case, in our community, as soon as the girl "grows up" we will look for a suitable match.' 'Of course,' she adds, 'we will not get her married before she is eighteen, because that's the law.'

Vimla, Manchhi and Dahi were some of the many Dalit women who left Rajpur with their families at the peak of the violence of 2002. They could not go to work in the mills and factories nearby and when their meagre savings ran out, they went to eat at the relief camps. Later, a few went to stay with relatives in other parts of Ahmedabad and some went to their villages. Muslim mothers too shifted, to live with relatives in and outside Ahmedabad. Schools were closed for four months and the girls who relocated missed further months of school. Mayuri, who was doing well academically in Class V, stayed away for many months and when she rejoined, she had to drop the academic year and could not regain her scholastic excellence. She cried in her sleep and was disturbed for many months.

Living in Fear

Anjana reported that she is afraid of the slightest quarrel on the streets. Her mother Hansa says, 'The most insignificant quarrel leads to abusive language and physical violence and people of both communities take to the streets. You too would be nervous if you lived here. It is enough if Anjana completes the VIIth standard.' Anjana can walk through Muslim areas to nearby private schools, like Democratic or Matruchhaya, but Hansa would prefer her to stay at home or come to work with her. Dina, Amba, Kamla and Jyotsna say the same. Unlike Muslim mothers, many Dalit women work in the nearby industrial units and would feel reassured if their daughters stayed at home while they worked. Apart from the housework, for which they needed their daughters' help, they feel anxiety about their daughters being molested on their way to and from a school located far away. Like Muslim girls in Shahpur, many Dalit girls do craft-based work at home, to supplement the family income. A few accompany their mothers to help in work outside the home. On the whole, restrictions on leaving the home are less for Dalit girls, but the *mahol-moholla* factor effectively restricts their access to education beyond the primary level.

There are other complicating dimensions. For instance, Dalit girls in the Gujarati school go home if they need to use the toilet. Of course, the school toilets are in a state of disrepair and there is no water supply, but that is not the reason offered by the girls. They claim that they do not go to the toilets because Muslim boys peek at them from above. And how do they know the boys are Muslim? They answer that the toilets are near the school compound wall and beyond the wall are Muslim *chawls*, so the boys must be Muslims. Not one of the girls has seen the boys and nobody has investigated this story, but all the girls believe it and prefer to go home for a visit to the bathroom. No one among the teachers has made any effort to address this issue or allay the girls' fears and put an end to such interruptions during school hours.

It is not surprising to hear descriptions of feelings of fear and mistrust from Muslim girls and their mothers, given the scale of violence on Muslims in 2002. The significant aspect that seems to go unnoticed is that among the Hindus, too, girls from the marginalised Dalit communities have been equally adversely affected by the fear psychosis resulting from communal hatred.

Presence of Police

This fear of violence erupting at any time exists not just in the women's imagination. The area is considered so sensitive by the administration that the Rajpur Gujarati-medium school is a police point. The first room of the school building has been given over to the police for their use and there is round-the-clock police presence on the school premises. And this has been not just since the 2002 riots. It has existed since the 1980s' anti-reservation stir and the communal riots that followed, except for a few phases in between when the police presence was withdrawn. In fact, for the past 25 years, there has been a uniformed and armed policeman quartered at the school to keep an eye on the locality. Two generations of students have attended school in such circumstances.

In our day-to-day observations during the study period, children did not appear to pay much attention to the policeman on duty. Yet, significantly, during interviews, more Muslim girls reported their fear of the police in general. Farhin of Class VI summed up the sentiments of many Muslim girls when she said that she felt afraid of the policeman. Afsana confessed that, after 2002, she was afraid even of female police personnel because they had conducted home searches at that time. Children, teachers and the administration have internalised the situation to such an extent that no one thinks about whether or not it is appropriate to have the continued presence of uniformed law enforcement personnel in the learning environment of young people.

Interactions between Communities in School

Even if neighbourhoods are antagonistic, one would imagine that the school could be a site for secular socialisation. The Urdu school of Shahpur of course does not offer such a chance, because its students are all Muslims. But we found that the Gujarati school of Rajpur was scarcely different, though it has students from both communities. Teachers reported that the numbers of Muslim girls in the school dropped after the 2002 riots, but they had not made the effort to find out whether they had dropped out altogether or had joined the Urdu school on the floor above. The administrative structure of the municipal school system is such that Urdu schools and Gujarati schools belong to different administrative 'zones'. Their inspectors are different and the teachers in the two mediums of instruction do not formally need to meet each other. Informally, too, the teachers in the two schools keep to themselves and have no more than a nodding acquaintance with each other. The children and teachers in the Gujarati and Urdu-medium school use different entrances to the building and, on the whole, inhabit different worlds.

The teachers prefer not to discuss the events of 2002 in the class. 'It is better we do not remind them of it; it is over and done with,' says Class V teacher, Lakshmiben. 'Of course we tell them that all of us should live together peacefully.' We did not observe partisan behaviour among the children toward the Muslim students, though the classroom interaction we observed was obviously influenced by our presence and could hardly be classified as representative of what normally transpired in the class.

None of the teachers are Muslim, some are Dalits or Dalit-Christians and the others were from the middle Hindu castes. But repeated probing during conversations with the girls revealed that the teachers did not discriminate against Muslim children in any way. Yet, when we left to conduct interviews at the girls' homes, many teachers warned us to be 'careful' when we went to Muslim households.

We asked the girls to name close friends at school and not one Dalit child named a Muslim child and neither did the reverse occur. We found that Muslim children play in their groups and the Hindus in their own. Also, there is no interaction between the Urdu and Gujarati-medium schools, even though their timings are the same and the recess time is the same. The children do not play together, nor do the teachers make any efforts to encourage them to mix. Very few girls manage to transcend these barriers; there are exceptions, such as Bharti in Class VII, who responded poignantly that Niloufer was her friend, but she could not visit her at home. They could only meet and play in school.

ROLE OF THE STATE

As mentioned earlier, in circumstances of widening distance between the two communities, the school is perhaps the only place where children could come together, transcending their religious differences to build bonds of friendship and understanding. Though the creation of a secular society is one of the declared aims of the state, as is the promotion of fraternity, the state in Gujarat has responded to the sharpening of communal identities in a dubious way. Within the two years in which we have been involved in this research, four Urdu schools have been closed down. The administration cites declining enrolment in Urdu schools as the reason for this. On its part, the Muslim community sees it as a motivated move to deprive them of access to education.

Community members and teachers feel that vacancies in Urdu schools are deliberately being left unfilled. This seems quite likely, because Muslim trust-run Gujarati-medium schools (which are aided by government grants) too report that the government has not filled their teacher vacancies. Another complaint is that the administration is withholding granting formal recognition to some newly established schools run by Muslim trusts. All these reports are from Shahpur alone and only a bigger study could reveal how widespread this phenomenon is. The evidence from even this small study suggests that it is a matter for concern. The deliberate insensitivity of the system to the sensibilities and priorities of the Muslim community is revealed by a move in 2004 to introduce Sanskrit as an extra language in Urdu-medium schools. This, again, is perceived by the Muslim community as an antagonistic move.

While families see themselves as 'Hindu' or 'Muslim', the state regards them as Scheduled Castes, Scheduled Tribes, or socially and educationally backward communities. Welfare schemes are conceptualised according to these categories and the differences in schemes for these various groups have added a further dimension to feelings of discrimination and separation. Children belonging to Scheduled Castes and Scheduled Tribes (this second category does not apply to the children covered in the study) receive more money in scholarships than socially and educationally backward communities (Muslims are included in this group). This has led to feelings of discrimination among the Muslims of Rajpur, adding to another cause for discontent.

But the most important fact emerging from this study is that the state is unable to provide the sense of security and safety that is needed for girls of both Muslim and Dalit-Hindu communities to fully access the school system. Girl children are being kept away from anything beyond the upper-primary education offered in their immediate neighbourhoods. As a result, the futures of girls from both communities remain circumscribed by the *moholla*, the *mahol*, puberty and poverty.

11

Gender Gap in Literacy in Uttar Pradesh*

Questions for Decentralised Educational Planning

Lori McDougall†

There is much to praise in India's efforts to tackle high female illiteracy. National female literacy has risen steadily from 7.9 per cent in 1951 to 39.3 per cent in 1991. The gap in literacy attainment between men and women is slowly narrowing, from a 22.1 percentage point difference in 1981 to 20.6 points in 1991. Annual educational spending has increased from 1 per cent of the Gross National Product (GNP) in 1947 to 3.5 per cent (Tilak 1997). And female enrolment jumped by 20 per cent between 1986 and 1993 (World Bank 1997).

However, national statistics disguise vast regional, gender and caste inequities. This theme will be illustrated in a case study of changing spatial patterns in the literacy gender gap within Uttar Pradesh, where the rate of closure has not only failed to keep pace with the national rate, but has also widened by the decade. Using the gender gap in literacy attainment as a proxy for social bias, this case study will show that UP's sharp intra-regional differences support the necessity of a localised approach to educational planning. Meanwhile, a case study on the fast-improving northern hill region of UP shows the importance of social cohesion, political conscientisation and democratic participation in promoting improvements in female literacy—an approach embedded in the Government of India's District Primary Education Programme (DPEP).

Finally, this chapter raises questions for further study about the ability of decentralised planning to promote educational equality. What is the role of the central government in educational planning under decentralised education policies? Does decentralisation allow for both equality and growth? What are the threats to community cohesion? Indeed, increased local participation in governance may

* Previously published in *Economic and Political Weekly* 35 (19), 6–12 May 2000: 1649–58.

allow new opportunities for community cooperation and political accountability, but it also allows more opportunities for wider regional, gender and caste divides because of fewer checks and balances from above. Just as cracks appear larger under a microscope, so do fractures between social groups appear greater under decentralisation. To that end, awareness of social power relations—from the state to the household level—must inform attempts to formulate synergistic public-private relationships.

Causes and Effects of Gender Gap

The liberating potential of education has been extensively discussed by Freire (1972) and others. But in the context of female education in India, researchers in recent years have developed a large body of empirical evidence, demonstrating how education can promote greater capabilities, such as the freedom to participate in political and economic processes; use new technologies; protect oneself against exploitation (legal, economic and sexual); exercise personal mobility; attain higher social status; and increase child and maternal well-being (King and Hill 1993). Indeed, female literacy can have a much more powerful effect than income in boosting social indicators. Uttar Pradesh, for example, has child mortality rates six times higher than those in Kerala, despite the fact that overall poverty head-count ratios are similar in these states (Murthi et al. 1997).

Despite all of the benefits associated with female literacy, perceptions of its risks remain. These risks are both social and economic and are based on household decision-making processes that weigh cost against benefit. At the heart of the gender gap is the fact that many of the benefits of female education are societal—a more productive workforce, lower fertility, lower infant mortality—whereas the costs are private (King and Hill 1993). These can include such tangible costs as tuition fees, uniforms and school supplies, transport and, most importantly, opportunity costs in the shape of foregone child labour.

Yet, parental estimates of educational costs are based both on the quality of services they expect to receive from local schools and on the strength of social norms that discourage female independence. Quality of education is rooted in such factors as the motivation and skill level of teachers and the relevance of the curriculum to local needs and interests, as well as the supply of well-built school buildings within close proximity to the household. However, supply is also clearly linked to demand. Teachers are demoralised by low pupil attendance and poor teaching conditions and so may fail to report for duty—in one study conducted in four districts of Uttar Pradesh, up to two-thirds of teachers in sample primary schools were found to be absent during school hours, while many of those in attendance were acting more as child-minders than teachers (Dreze and Gazdar 1997). School buildings may be left in disrepair because of community scepticism about state action or fear of challenging local elites, who have appropriated the buildings for personal use.

Opportunities for achieving a decent return on household investment in education may also be blocked by social norms that insist on early marriage for girls and mitigate against female employment. For example, many of the poorest households might not be able to afford the social and economic risks of educating girls. In the minds of many parents, allowing girls to go to school unchaperoned creates an unnecessary risk that may later damage the marriage-bargaining process and perhaps even force larger dowries to compensate for loss of reputation. As one mother in rural Karnataka says: 'Who wants to bear the blame? If she talks normally with any man, she is accused unnecessarily that she is flirting, and they make up such stories' (Subrahmanian 1997).

Apart from the possible loss of status, parents often fear that education will make a girl less attentive to household chores and less willing to obey both her parents and her husband. These doubts are institutionalised in hypergamous marriage practices across north India, where parents of educated girls must offer high dowry prices in order to attract a better-educated man.

At the heart of such arrangements is the large-scale inability of educated women to enter the paid workforce and offer reciprocal support to their natal households because of social restrictions on their mobility. Where social norms dictate that girls marry young and live with the husband's family, there is little sense in sacrificing their contribution to family labour and risking a bigger dowry, in order to benefit someone else's household. Though parents may be concerned about their daughter's individual well-being and recognise the benefits of female education, it is difficult to promote voluntary cooperation for the greater good in societies with poor cohesion and few civic networks to promote and safeguard reciprocity (Putnam 1993). This is indeed the case in many parts of UP and other educationally backward states.

Yet, do low economic returns cause the educational gender gap, or is the gap a symptom of entrenched cultural attitudes that discourage aspirations by women and minority communities? For many, little has changed since the Laws of Manu were set down 2,000 years ago: women and minorities are unfit for independence and their education is a threat to the status quo. Such biases may partly explain why India has been so reluctant to implement compulsory primary education—the reasons cannot be entirely economic, as often claimed. Many other low-income countries, including those in sub-Saharan Africa, have managed to do so. Educational change requires political will—the framers of national policy on education dodged the tough task of building consensus for compulsory education and curtailing child labour. Instead, they promoted a massive effort to build a non-formal and night-school system (Weiner 1991).

DISPARITIES IN LITERACY ATTAINMENT

This section presents findings from a study on changes in the female illiteracy rate and the gender gap in Uttar Pradesh, 1971–91.[1] By looking at changes on a district-level basis, rather than a state or national basis, this study aims to reveal certain trends that are invisible at an aggregate level. It is essential that such trends are captured and analysed, as they reflect variations in micro-climates for female education and so have an important bearing on educational planning and management.

This study is based on female and male literacy rates, as reported by Government of India census data collected in 1971, 1981 and 1991.[2] For reasons of simplicity and range, the study analyses total female literacy rates per state and district, comprising both rural and urban rates. UP is a natural subject for this case study because of its size, high female illiteracy and gender gap. If it were a country, its population of 140 million would make it the seventh largest in the world—ahead of both Japan and Nigeria (Government of India 1991a; UN 1998). If it were treated as a separate country in the gender development index, which adjusts the human development index for gender disparity, UP would rank 123rd out of 137 countries. Kerala, by contrast, would rank 80th (UNDP 1996). Simply put, there are more women in UP suffering the indignity of illiteracy than almost any other place on earth—52 million in total, more than double of Indonesia's 20.7 million and almost one-third of China's 185 million (Dreze and Sen 1995; Government of India 1991a).

The disparity that UP represents within India is magnified on a district level. Rural female literacy in UP's Bahraich district, bordering Nepal, was 7.9 per cent in 1991. This is just a fraction of Garhwal's 47.1 per cent rate, located in UP's Himalayan region. This gap is wider than anywhere else in India, including other low-literacy states such as Rajasthan (Government of India 1991a).

Another reason for examining UP is its poor performance in battling the literacy gender gap. After Rajasthan, UP has made the least progress in India in narrowing the male-female literacy gap during the 1971–91 period (Table 11.1). Not only has

TABLE 11.1: Change in Gender Gap, 1971–91 (Percentage Points)

States	*1971–91*	*1981–91*		*1971–81*	
		Gap	*Rank*	*Gap*	*Rank*
Kerala	8.5	4.6	2	3.9	1
Tamil Nadu	8.1	5.2	1	2.9	2
Maharashtra	6.0	4.4	3	1.6	4
Himachal Pradesh	3.4	3.3	4	0.1	6
West Bengal	3.3	2.6	8	0.7	5
Karnataka	2.6	2.6	7	–0.1	7
Punjab	2.3	0.6	10	1.7	3
Gujarat	1.9	2.2	9	–0.3	8
Orissa	1.5	2.9	6	–1.4	10
Haryana	–0.8	3.0	5	–3.8	13
Andhra Pradesh	–1.0	0.3	12	–1.3	9
Madhya Pradesh	–2.4	–0.2	13	–2.2	11
Bihar	–2.6	0.5	11	–3.0	12
Uttar Pradesh	–4.8	–0.2	14	–4.6	14
Rajasthan	–9.3	–3.8	15	–5.6	15
India*	0.7	1.8		–1.0	

Note: * Excluding Assam in 1981; excluding Jammu and Kashmir in 1991.

Source: Census of India.

UP bucked the national trend, which saw the gap close by 0.7 percentage points during this time, its gap has actually widened by 4.8 percentage points. Kerala, by contrast, managed to narrow its gap by 8.5 percentage points.

Maps 11.1 and 11.2 indicate a positive correlation between high female literacy and a low gender gap in 1991; Maps 11.3 and 11.4 demonstrate a similar correlation between rising literacy rates and a declining gender gap over the 1971–91 period. If one takes a longer view, from 1951–91 (Figures 11.1–11.3), this correlation becomes even more evident. For example, as seen in Figure 11.3, Kerala has reduced its gender gap from 18.7 points in 1951 to 5.9 points in 1991 (age 0+). Meanwhile, female literacy has risen by 44 points over that period. Conversely, UP (Figure 11.2) has almost doubled its gender gap, from 13.8 points to 24.9 points (age 0+), while literacy rates have risen by just 16 points (Government of India 1961, 1964, 1971, 1981a, 1991a). Such evidence makes it clear that the most effective way to battle the literacy gender gap is to focus on raising female literacy rates.

NORTHERN PROGRESS, EASTERN STAGNATION

Moving from state-level findings, does the same pattern hold at an intra-state level? This study charted fluctuations in female literacy rates and the gender gap for each district in UP over the 1971–91 period,[3] revealing distinct regional clusters of female literacy and illiteracy.

Maps 11.5 and 11.6 show that, overall, seven of UP's top 10 performing districts in female literacy, 1971–91, are among the top 10 performers in the gender-gap rankings as well. Five of those districts fall within the northern hill region—Almora, Chamoli, Nainital, Dehra Dun, Pithoragarh—while the other two are Lucknow and Etawah. Interestingly, there is zero correspondence between the worst performers in female literacy and the worst performers in the gender gap. The worst literacy performers are clustered along the Nepalese border, just south-east of the hill region, and are led by Bahraich (5.7 points), Budaun (5.8 points) and Rampur (6.7 points). Meanwhile, the worse gender-gap performers form a cluster on the Bihar border, in far-eastern UP, and are led by Etah (–12 points), Ghazipur (–11.7 points) and Pratapgarh (–10.4 points).

Most striking is the consistent growth in female literacy and a narrowing gendergap in the hill region, an area comprising eight districts: Almora, Pithoragarh, Chamoli, Garhwal, Tehri Garhwal, Dehra Dun, Nainital, and Uttarkashi. Female literacy in this region has risen from an estimated 20 per cent in 1971 to 43 per cent in 1991, representing a 23 percentage point increase during this time. Meanwhile, the gender gap has remained constant, at about 33 points.

This contrasts with UP overall, which has seen female literacy rise by just 12.8 points during this time, representing the lowest increase in female literacy among all Indian states, except Rajasthan and Bihar, as well as the lowest performance of the gender-gap, except Rajasthan. The hill region is thus 10.2 points ahead of UP as a whole in female literacy and 4.8 points ahead in the gender gap. Not surprisingly, regional disparities are also evident within this hill region. The high-performing

MAP 11.1: India Female Illiteracy, 1991

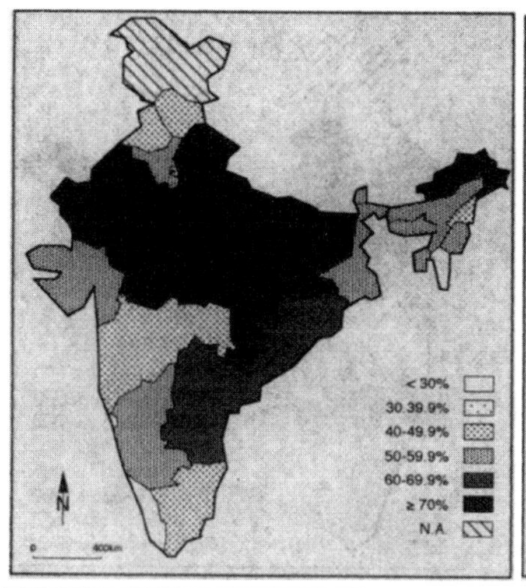

Best Performers		Worst Performers	
1. Kerala	13.8	1. Rajasthan	79.6
2. Mizoram	21.4	2. Bihar	77.1
3. Goa	32.9	3. Uttar Pradesh	74.7
4. Nagaland	45.3	4. Madhya Pradesh	71.2
5. Maharashtra	47.7	5. Arunachal Pradesh	70.3
	India 60.7		

MAP 11.2: India Gender Gap, 1991

< 10
10-14.9
15-19.9
20-24.9
25-29.9
≥ 30
N.A.
(Percentage Points)

Best Performers		Worst Performers	
1. Mizoram	7.0	1. Rajasthan	34.6
2. Kerala	7.4	2. Uttar Pradesh	30.4
3. Meghalaya	8.2	3. Bihar	29.6
4. Nagaland	12.8	4. Madhya Pradesh	29.5
5. Punjab	15.3	5. Haryana	28.6
	India 24.8		

MAP 11.3: India Female Illiteracy, 1971–91

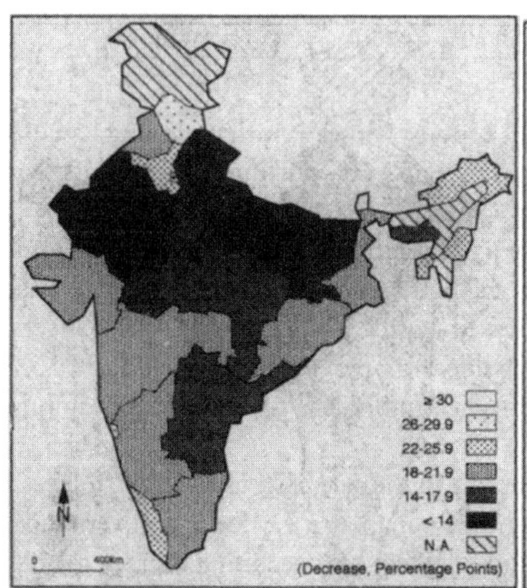

Best Performers		Worst Performers	
1. Sikkim	36.4	1. Rajasthan	10.4
2. Nagaland	33.3	2. Bihar	12.7
3. Himachal Pradesh	28.5	3. Uttar Pradesh	12.9
4. Goa	26.8	4. Andhra Pradesh	14.4
5. Arunachal Pradesh	25.3	5. Meghalaya	15.5
	India 17.3		

MAP 11.4: India Gender Gap, 1971–91

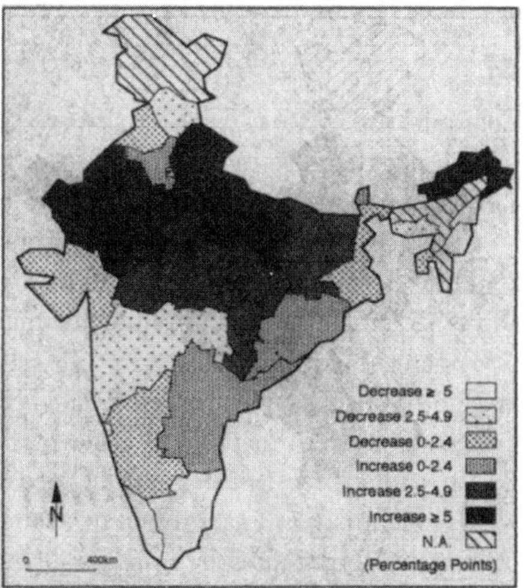

Best Performers		Worst Performers	
1. Kerala	–7.2	1. Rajasthan	+10.8
2. Manipur	–6.8	2. Uttar Pradesh	+6.1
3. Tamil Nadu	–6.1	3. Arunachal Pradesh	+5.6
4. Goa	–5.8	4. Bihar	+4.1
5. Nagaland	–5.3	5. Madhya Pradesh	+3.8
	India +0.8		

MAP 11.5: Uttar Pradesh Female Illiteracy, 1991

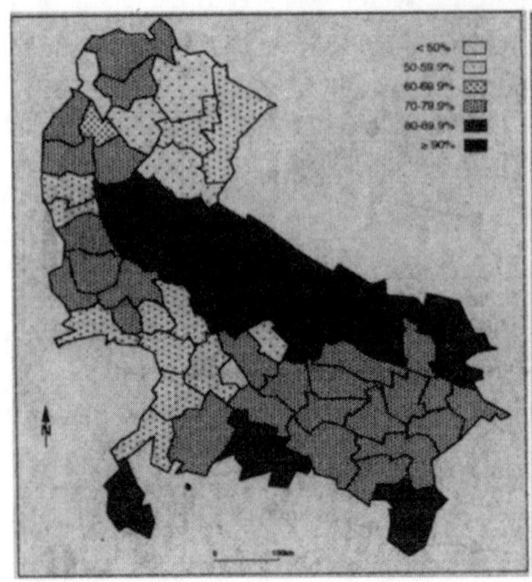

Best Performers				Worst Performers	
1. Dehra Dun	40.7			1. Maharajgaj	89.7
2. Kanpur Nagar	41.2			2. Bahraich	89.3
3. Garhwal	50.6			3. Siddharth-nagar	88.2
4. Lucknow	53.1			4. Gonda	87.4
5. Nainital	56.8			5. Budaun	87.2
6. Chamoli	59.6			6. Rampur	84.7
7. Almora	60.4	*Uttar*		7. Barabanki	84.6
8. Ghaziabad	61.2	*Pradesh*	*74.7*	8. Banda	83.6
9. Pithoragarh	61.6	*Kerala*	*13.8*	9. Kheri	83.6
10. Etawah	61.7	*India*	*60.7*	10. Lalitpur	83.4

MAP 11.6: Uttar Pradesh Gender Gap, 1991

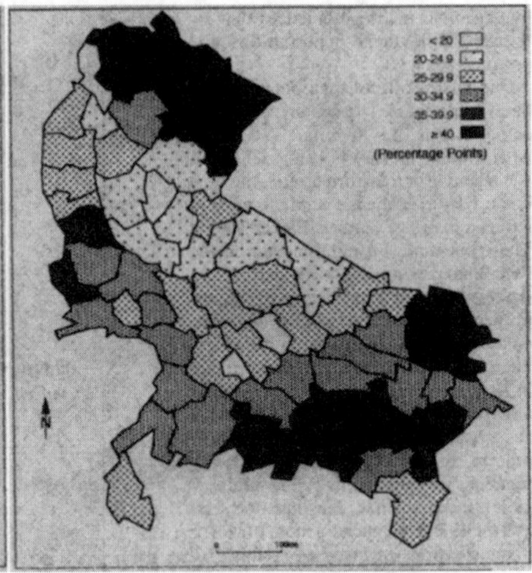

Best Performers				Worst Performers	
1. Kanpur Nagar	17.9			1. Tehri Garhwal	45.7
2. Rampur	18.5			2. Uttarkashi	45.1
3. Dehra Dun	18.7			3. Chamoli	41.6
4. Lucknow	19.6			4. Pithoragarh	41.0
5. Budaun	21.2			5. Almora	40.4
6. Bareilly	23.4			6. Pratapgarh	39.8
7. Moradabad	23.4	*Uttar*		7. Jaunpur	39.8
8. Shahjahanpur	24.1	*Pradesh*	*30.4*	8. Mathura	39.6
9. Kheri	24.2	*Kerala*	*7.4*	9. Bulandshahr	37.7
10. Hardwar	24.6	*India*	*24.8*	10. Ghazipur	37.1

Chamoli district, for instance, shows a 29.4 point increase in female literacy and a 4.4 point decrease in the gender gap during 1971–91, putting it 6.4 points and 4.4 points ahead of the hill region overall.

The performance of the UP hill region parallels that of neighbouring Himachal Pradesh, which has made remarkable progress in raising female literacy over the past 30 years. Female literacy in Himachal increased from 23.7 per cent to 52.1 per cent (28.4 percentage points) during 1971–91, while the gender gap narrowed from 26.7 to 23.3 points (3.4 points). This puts Himachal among the top performers among Indian states over this period (Table 11.1).

In sum, three findings are echoed at the national, state and district levels: (1) regional disparities are inherent to the literacy map at every level of governance; (2) female literacy rates are both a cause and an effect of a declining literacy gender gap; and (3) a widening gender gap is attributable to a multitude of factors, in addition to slow female literacy growth.

These findings suggest that a flexible mix of policy approaches must be employed in accordance with local literacy needs. For example, in areas of increasing literacy, such as UP's hill region, it may be more effective to focus attention on female retention and achievement, rather than access, by increasing the number of female teachers, by creating a more creative and gender-positive curricula and by dedicating specific attention to girls in the classroom. Meanwhile, in slow growth areas of female literacy, such as along the Nepalese border, it may be more important to employ a multi-pronged strategy that seeks to raise household demand for education, alongside greater attention to related needs that can impact demand, such as building more schools in closer proximity to underprivileged villages and providing free learning materials and child-care.

Religion, Urbanisation and Income

What accounts for such strong spatial variations in female literacy and the gender gap? Is it economics or culture, or both? Socio-religious culture is a key determinant of the extent to which women can enter the public sphere via education and employment. For example, most instances of above-average sex and caste disparity occur in rural central and northern India, an area dominated by conservative Hindu mores and rigid caste structures. In a study in UP's Moradabad district, 100 per cent of 14 upper-caste Kayastha males and females were literate, compared with just 4 per cent of 118 Scheduled Caste people, of whom not a single female was literate (Dreze and Saran 1995).

Conversely, in geographically peripheral areas of India, such as coastal Kerala and the far north-east, there is a greater ratio of Muslims and Christians in the population and a smaller proportion of Brahmins and other upper castes. Traditionally, there has also been greater foreign contact via trade and migration, leading to the hypothesis that greater cultural diversity permits more fluid social structures and norms. Indeed, history has shown that regions with high proportions of lower castes and non-Hindus have a dampening effect on conservative Hindu values. For example, nineteenth century Christian missionaries had a significant role in supporting female and lower-caste education in Kerala (Sen 1992).

Meanwhile, Sopher (1980) finds strong evidence that, contrary to popular assumptions, gender-based educational disparity among Muslims is not significantly greater than it is at middle levels of Hindu society. He attributes this to the fact that upper-caste Hindu women face stricter *purdah* norms compared with high-status Muslim women. Specifically, where Indian Muslims do not impose *purdah* within a kin unit and its associates, unmarried Hindu women must generally avoid contact with any member of the opposite sex apart from fathers, brothers and close cousins (Papanek; cited in Sopher 1980). This makes education relatively easier for Muslims than for upper-caste Hindu women.

Cultural values appear to have a profound impact on attitudes toward female employment. For example, urban-dominated districts like Lucknow rank among UP's top 10 performers in female literacy and the gender gap during 1971–91. Yet, Lucknow's female employment rate is just 7.7 per cent—far below averages of the south, where Tamil Nadu and Karnataka register 29.9 per cent and 29.4 per cent, respectively. This is in spite of the fact that Lucknow and the southern states have similar urban female literacy rates: 62.4 per cent for Lucknow, compared with

69.6 per cent and 65.4 per cent for Tamil Nadu and Karnataka (Government of India 1991c). This suggests that urban female literacy in the Hindi heartland may be driven more by cultural values and hypergamous marriage practices than by female employment opportunities and personal agency.

One must be careful, then, not to assume that female literacy is synonymous with empowerment. It is important to consider what kind of literacy is being achieved: is it adaptive or transformative? And how is it used—to challenge gender bias or to attract a marriage partner (Patkar 1995)? These outcomes, in turn, depend on the social and economic arena in which literacy is achieved, such as the degree of support for personal aspirations and the degree of risk a woman faces in raising her voice. Such questions are particularly pertinent in Kerala, where high female literacy has failed to promote female entrepreneurship and greater participation in the political process, or block the spread of dowry practices (Saradamoni 1994; Mathew 1995). Indeed, gender bias must be seen as a multi-layered phenomenon, of which illiteracy is one of many correlates.

Another correlate of the gender gap is population density. Indeed, population density has been found to have a relatively greater impact on raising female literacy rates than male literacy rates. In a study conducted in Karnataka's Bangalore district, Schuth (1980) found that population density was responsible for the greatest amount of variation in female literacy in the districts studied, while local agricultural capability (i.e., land productivity) explained the greatest variance in male literacy in these areas. This was attributed to the fact that girls have less personal mobility than boys to travel outside their village to attend school, so female literacy rates can be expected to rise when schools are closer to home and where there are single-sex study opportunities, as is more likely in an urban setting. It may also be the case that education rises where communication networks are strongest, as the demonstration effect is more visible.

FIGURE 11.1: India Literacy Rate and Gender Gap, 1951–91

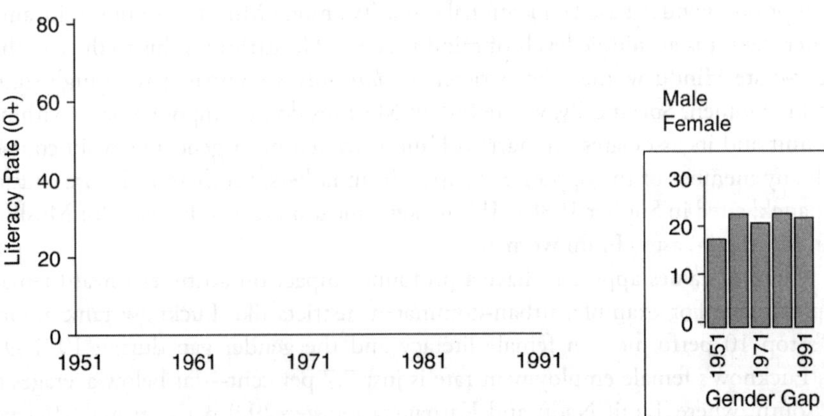

FIGURE 11.2: Uttar Pradesh Literacy Rate and Gender Gap, 1951–91

Literacy Rate (0+)
80
60
40
20
0
1951 1961 1971 1981 1991
Male
Female
30
20
10
0
1951 1971 1991
Gender Gap

FIGURE 11.3: Kerala Literacy Rate and Gender Gap, 1951–91

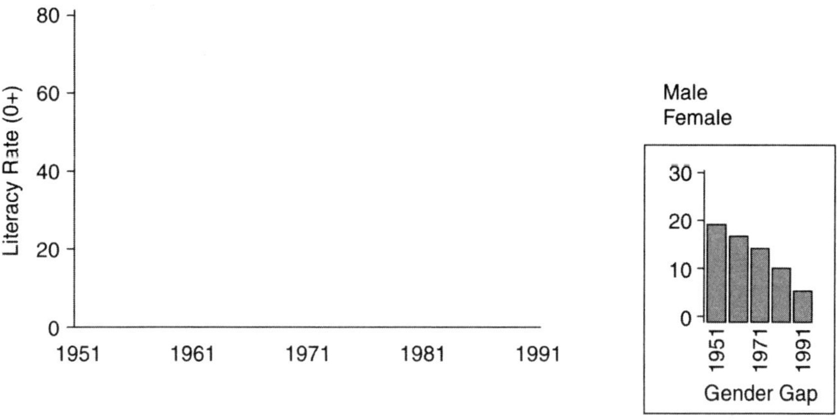

This geographic impact has been confirmed on a national basis by Kundu and Rao (1986), who cite a gender disparity factor of 0.41 in rural areas compared with 0.15 in cities, based on 1981 census data (cited in Raju 1993). Again, population density together with 'urban values' may help explain why Lucknow—UP's most urbanised district, at 62.7 per cent—features on UP's top 10 list of female literacy and gender-gap performers for 1971–91, while the state's least urbanised district, Siddharthnagar (3.5 per cent), features on the list of the poorest gender-gap performers during that time (Government of India 1991c).

Female literacy may well be linked to spatial variations in religion and population density, but evidence is unclear about the correlation of household income with female education. In a study of urban literacy and sex disparity across India, Raju (1993) concludes that 'neither in terms of absolute levels of literacy nor distributive justice, i.e., reduction in gender and caste disparities, does per capita income have any statistically significant positive bearing upon literacy status of states'. Meanwhile, the World Bank concludes that cultural conditions have a greater impact than absolute poverty on the gender gap, while the reverse is true of the caste gap. As a result, it prescribes various demand-linked measures to address the gender gap, such as awareness campaigns, child-care centres and the hiring of more female teachers (World Bank 1997).

Still, a comparison of high and low-performing states shows a definite link between poverty and female illiteracy. Data from the National Family Health Survey, 1992–93, show that only 9.5 per cent of girls from the poorest 40 per cent of households complete Class VIII, while 85 per cent of boys and 80 per cent of girls in the top 20 per cent of households do so (World Bank 1998). Still, it is unclear to what extent this correlation reflects the impact of low income itself, rather than the impact of other variables that are themselves correlated with low income. Indeed, Dreze and Gazdar argue that the importance of poverty as a cause of persistent illiteracy has been inflated and point to recent empirical studies that show that the opportunity cost of child labour is quite low, even among very poor households (Labenne 1995; cited in Dreze and Gazdar 1997). Dreze and Gazdar's (ibid.) own study of primary schools in UP supports this finding that parents' willingness to bear the costs of education depends very much on the quality of the school services received in return.

DEFYING CORRELATIONS: HISTORY, SOCIAL RELATIONS AND POLITICS

An interesting picture emerges when these variables are considered in relation to the UP hill region. Here is an area with a high proportion of upper-caste Hindus: 80 per cent of the population belongs to two upper castes, compared with a national average of 13 per cent (Aggarwal and Agrawal 1995). Population density is extremely low and overwhelmingly rural: 116 persons per square kilometre compared with 473 for UP and 274 for India (Government of India 1991c; Pande 1996). Meanwhile, household income is about 20 per cent below the UP average: one study reports a figure of Rs 1,142 in 1985, with 25 per cent of this remitted by migrant family members (Bora 1996). In other words, many of the characteristics of this mountainous, impoverished region would seem to contradict the correlations discussed above.

Yet, this region is an example of how historical conditions shape current social relations—a point stressed by Putnam and other proponents of social capital theory. Located in the far north of the state, this region has long had a distinct socio-cultural identity, because of its significance in Hindu mythology. As a result, this area has long attracted pilgrims travelling to shrines at Badrinath, Kedarnath and Gangotri. It also attracted a number of upper-caste settlers prior to British colonisation.

The arrival of the British in the early nineteenth century ended the region's long-standing physical separation from the rest of UP, as transport and communication links were established to support administrative activities. The British also sought to mitigate the highly stratified nature of Himalayan UP, with extreme divisions between upper-caste landowners and lower-caste servants. To that end, occupational restrictions were lifted, land rights were conferred on tillers and schools were opened to all who wanted to attend (Sanwal 1976).

The early attention to public education succeeded in raising the aspirations of the peasantry and sparking protests about exploitation by the rest of UP, which many regarded as having a predatory interest in the region's rich forest, mineral and water resources. Pressure began to build after India's Independence in 1947 for the establishment of a separate state to facilitate development and attend to the economic problems caused by the lack of cultivable land, weak infrastructure and state neglect of industrial investment. Lack of jobs and tiny landholdings with low productivity have forced massive migration. Today, as many as 60 per cent of all village households have a male family member working outside of the region, many in Delhi (Bora 1996).

Yet, social cohesion and economic underinvestment may have helped to shape the conditions for high female literacy rates today. The predominance of single-caste settlement patterns, which are remarkably free of caste/class conflict compared with the UP plains (Sanwal 1976), has undoubtedly led to a greater ability to participate equitably in community services, such as education. This effect can be seen in male migrants; 83 per cent in one study had some level of schooling, while 16 per cent were graduates (ibid.).

MAP 11.7: Uttar Pradesh Female Illiteracy, 1971–91

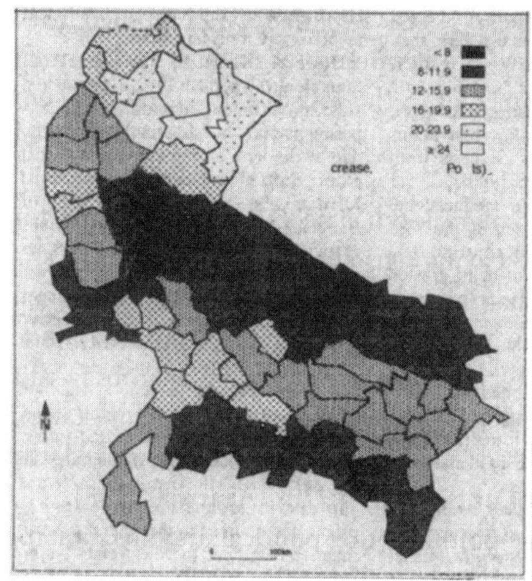

Best Performer			Worst Performers	
1. Garhwal	30.3		1. Bahraich	5.7
2. Chamoli	29 4		2. Budaun	5.8
3. Almora	26.2		3. Rampur	6.7
4. Pithoragarh	21.4		4. Moradabad	6.8
5. Tehri Garhwal	20.7		5. Gonda	7.1
6. Dehra Dun	19.9		6. Bareilly	7.9
7. Nainital	19.0		7. Pilibhit	7.9
8. Lucknow	18.5	*Utt r r 12*	8. Sita ur	8.5
9. Etawah	18.4		9. hen	8.8
10. Uttarkashi	17.5		10. Shahjahanpur	8.8

MAP 11.8: Uttar Pradesh Gender Gap, 1971–91

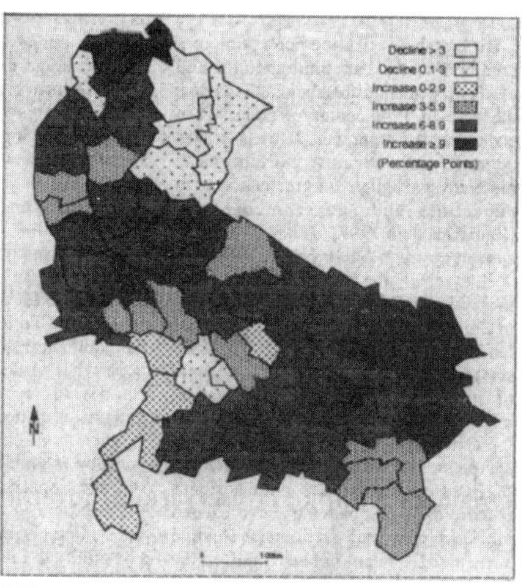

Best Performers				Worst Performers	
1. Chamoli	4.4			1. Etah	–12.0
2. Nainital	2.0			2. Ghazipur	–11.7
3. Almora	0.5			3. Pratapgarh	–10.4
4. Kanpur	0.5			4. Gorakhpur/ Maharajganj	–9.9
5. Pithoragarh	0.4			5. Uttarkashi	–9.5
6. Dehra Dun	0.1			6. Deoria	–9.4
7. Lucknow	–0.3			7. Barabanki	–9.2
8. Etawah	–1.5			8. Basti/ Siddharthnagar	–9.0
9. Jalaun	–1.6	*Uttar Pradesh*	*–4.8*	9. Sultanpur	–9.0
10. Jhansi	–2 5	*Kerala*	*8.5*	10. Mathura	–8.8
		India	*0.7*		

These propitious social conditions have been boosted by state and centre policy attention in recent years. After neighbouring Himachal Pradesh separated from the Punjab and was granted statehood in 1971, UP's hill residents became more conscious of the financial benefits of independence and so agitated more fiercely. As a sop, the UP government introduced separate budgetary provisions for the region in 1974–75 and set up two public corporations to co-ordinate institutional finance and spearhead regional development. Although the region still suffers significant underdevelopment, the influx of state and central funding has created a massive expansion of public services. For instance, there are 166 junior-primary schools per 100,000 people in this region—more than twice the state-level ratio of 65. Similarly, there are 10.5 hospitals and primary health care centres per 100,000 people—almost five times the state-level ratio of 2.7 (Aggarwal and Agrawal 1995). This extensive provision of educational and health care facilities has surely helped boost literacy rates well above the state average.

Second, it can be hypothesised that wives of migrants have gained greater agency, as a result of their new-found responsibilities for household financial management. In Kerala, for example, Gulati (1995) finds that many wives of migrants have gained status and confidence by taking responsibility for household funds and interacting with bank representatives, postal clerks and other officials. This has also tended to encourage a new interest in literacy, as it helps in carrying out these tasks and in communicating with their husbands overseas. These experiences, combined with the traditionally greater freedom of mobility of hill women (Sax 1991) and a much higher incidence of workforce participation than in the rest of UP—25.6 per cent compared with 7.5 per cent (Pande 1996)—also help in explaining the existence of high literacy rates.

Still, it is important to recognise that migration has been a mixed blessing for women, bringing a double burden of low-paying agricultural work and domestic responsibilities. According to a study of Chamoli and Pithoragarh districts, women in migrant households work an extra hour per day, totalling 17.05 hours (Pande 1996). Chores, such as water and fuel-wood collection, are especially onerous in this region, because of the hilly terrain, frequent rain and severe winters. Deforestation from commercial logging has also increased scarcity—an issue that sparked the female-led Chipko conservation movement of the early 1970s (Agarwal 1988).

The Chipko protests were a turning point in the political mobilisation of women in this region. Women helped lead the charge in 1994, when the UP state government announced a 4 per cent increase in reservation quotas for government jobs and college seats for Scheduled Castes, bringing the total to 27 per cent—an inflammatory move in a region with a Scheduled Caste population of just 2 per cent. The intense agitation that followed led to the announcement of a separate Uttaranchal state.

In sum, UP's hill region has been able to boast of increasing female literacy and a declining gender gap, as a result of locally specific characteristics rooted in historical events and conditions. Early expansion of the educational system, a relatively unified social structure, increased state supply of social services, greater socio-economic aspirations and female independence as a result of migration and growing awareness of political rights have created a developmental effect for women that has not been seen elsewhere in UP.

Prospects for Change

History shows that the perception of a common threat can unite people and motivate demands for change. This was the case in nineteenth century Kerala, when economically empowered lower castes began to rebel against extreme caste hierarchy and agitate for greater access to education and government jobs (Ramachandran 1997). This was also the case in post-war South Korea, when the need to rebuild the national economy and to guard against the hegemonic influences of China and Japan helped usher in radical land reforms (Edwards 1992). This also seems to have been the case for the people of Uttaranchal, who have united in protest against exploitation by the state.

Uttaranchal's nascent victory is in sharp contrast to the situation in the rest of UP. Here, caste-based politics dominated by the middle peasantry has fostered anti-developmental factionalism, while vertical social relations have inhibited the formation of the kind of mass civic associations necessary for demanding accountability from political parties and government officials. The result has been rampant corruption, lack of political will and paralysed development, as ideological and developmental goals have been sacrificed in favour of personality politics and factional struggles for power.

This vicious circle helps explain why various central development schemes—from land reforms to the integrated rural development programme to the total literacy campaign—have been remarkably unsuccessful here compared with other states and why state provision of goods and services, such as education, is insufficient and of low quality. In short, there is ample support for the observation that 'the only yardstick of government performance in UP is the successful promotion and protection of specific caste interests' (Aggarwal and Agrawal 1995). Political change may not come quickly to UP, but this does not mitigate the responsibility of the government to supply the provisions necessary for universal primary education and the responsibility of citizens to participate in that process.

Decentralisation and Gender Gap

As seen in the above case study, primary education needs and strengths are highly differentiated, even within a single region. In this case, decentralised educational planning and management are attractive for several reasons: they can promote greater efficiency in communicating local needs and preferences; urge greater responsiveness on the part of elected officials, bureaucrats and teachers; encourage greater levels of participation of local citizens in the democratic process; and create greater scope for experimenting with policy innovations and allowing new leaders to emerge from the grassroots (Wolman 1990).

However, is the recent emphasis on educational decentralisation, as enabled by the 73rd and 74th Panchayati Raj constitutional amendments, in danger of being treated as a panacea for complex socio-economic problems? Can it offer a mechanism for the equitable resolution of conflicts that occur when participation is widened? How can devolution be reconciled with comprehensive national planning? To what extent is this process able to address social and power relations that lie at the heart of educational inequalities?

The extent to which states themselves are willing or able to hand over real responsibility to lower levels of governance—in full or in part—depends very much on the perception of capacity at the lower level, as well as political will and the degree of administrative preparedness. Implementation itself reflects patterns of social relations. For example, early results show that enrolment increases in districts under DPEP (District Primary Education Programme)—an ambitious foreign-funded GOI scheme to reduce the gender and caste gaps in primary enrolment, retention and achievement—have ranged broadly from 4 to 17 percentage points compared with non-DPEP districts, with female enrolment accounting for 51 per cent of this increase (World Bank 1998).

The degree of equality or inequality within a society has a clear impact on what decentralisation can achieve. For example, in 1987, Karnataka embarked on an experiment in decentralisation, establishing elected councils at both the district and sub-district levels and giving councillors clear authority over state bureaucrats and state and central development funds. The results showed a sharp increase in state-society interactions: there was very high voter response in both district and sub-district elections, as elections were perceived to be very fair; women and members of Scheduled Castes developed greater political awareness and participated widely in sub-district elections; party competition grew stronger; and villagers showed increased willingness to contact councillors personally and to get involved in civic associations. As a result, the number of micro-development projects rose dramatically and accountability took a major turn. Overall, 83 per cent of a sample of villagers expressed some satisfaction with both the quantity and quality of government responses (Crook and Manor 1994).

However, Karnataka was not to continue along this path. In 1992, a centralising state government abandoned the experiment and the situation deteriorated, due to the lack of commitment by local elites. Still, Crook and Manor contrast Karnataka's experience with that of Bangladesh to demonstrate the importance of social relations in determining outcomes of decentralisation. In decentralising, Karnataka could build on the advantages of a vigorous freepress and competitive political system, which generated constant pressure on ruling parties to be responsive and honest. Popular perception regarded bureaucrats as accountable to politicians and politicians as accountable to the people.

By contrast, the failure of Bangladeshi villagers to check the vast power of elected sub-district council chairpersons—predicated on links to the central government, rather than the electorate—contributed substantially to the failure of decentralisation. These chairpersons also tended to diminish the power of bureaucrats, who as a result refused to facilitate the decentralisation process. Although the decentralisation process had been well-funded and voter turnout was high, Crook and Manor conclude that a deeply entrenched 'servant-master' mentality in Bangladesh was a key reason why villagers and bureaucrats hesitated to demand better service from higher echelons.

Decentralisation calls for a delicate balance. Neither enhanced conditions for participation nor vast resources can guarantee a positive outcome. Indeed, there is little to suggest that opening up educational structures to greater local participation will yield meaningful input from either parents or panchayat leaders untutored in educational administration (Sharma 1999). The social fractures that existed prior to decentralisation—spatial, caste, and gender—may only be magnified by this process, as dominant groups are given a new forum in which to hold sway and to have their decisions branded as 'consensual'.

In this way, decentralisation may have a negative effect on equity, as it may offer the greatest benefit to those regions that are already blessed with relatively horizontal social relations and strong civic involvement. Regions with wide gaps between social groups may find that the interests of weaker members are increasingly sidelined in actual policymaking and implementation, as more powerful members of society exercise greater power, without being checked by higher levels of governance. In this sense, decentralisation may discourage meaningful participation, more than a centralised system does.

On the contrary, some argue that if regional educational disparities do become wider, this simply reflects the varying importance placed by local populations on educational investments, compared with other development priorities (Carron and Chau 1980). Still, social justice demands that there be some kind of central control and redistribution of resources, to prevent widening regional gaps. Decentralisation should not be an excuse for the centre and state to offload the major funding responsibility to the community, nor can greater local management responsibilities be considered to automatically reduce corruption and increase accountability. Getting the balance right between central and local power is one of the most delicate aspects of decentralisation.

Second, local officials and institutions may lack the capability to plan efficiently. Apart from the problem of the lack of technical skills and training, officials may be hampered by the lack of will of state bodies to devolve funding and support for local planning that may not conform to its own preferences. Crook and Manor found that, in Karnataka, junior bureaucrats felt more threatened by the loss of personal responsibility under decentralisation compared with senior state bureaucrats, who often welcomed greater information flow from rural areas, finding it to be—among other advantages—an effective 'early warning system' against impending rural disasters, such as drought and flood.

On the other hand, even when full control over budgets is given, are local preferences and needs expressed and understood in similar ways? Even when such needs are clearly expressed through participatory processes, this does not guarantee that these preferences will be identical among different sets of people, or that they will be translated into policy in a way that is faithful to the original expression. Policymakers have their own preferences, too, which can lead to the question of whose view prevails if these ideas conflict (Subrahmanian 1999).

Finally, it can be risky to raise public expectations about decentralisation without delivering tangible benefits. This can create greater cynicism about government and the utility of participation. For example, educational equalisation programmes such as DPEP affect access and quality, but cannot guarantee greater household income from participating in education, as this outcome depends on the expansion of the labour market. Though decentralised planning can weigh against this, ensuring that local curricula meet local needs, the prospect of a mismatch between the two can have a distinctly disempowering effect. In the Kerala and UP examples cited earlier, the dearth of jobs for women, or social strictures against female employment, can lead to the instrumental use of education as a commodity in the marriage market. Decentralisation, therefore, must be rooted in a holistic view of the development process, making connections between access, quality and outcomes of education.

CONCLUSIONS

As important as it is to recognise diversity in local educational needs and abilities and to encourage participation, planners must take care not to sell the programme as an easy fix and to remain aware that greater opportunity for participation tends to magnify—not resolve—the conflicts and disharmonies inherent in social relations. In the final analysis, the efficiency gains of decentralised education are dependent on the degree of equity in a community and the scope this allows for collective action.

As Putnam points out, people tend to respond rationally to their social context—this context is determined by history and continues to be reinforced by the degree of reciprocity and civic engagement in society. Kerala, for example, has created dense social ties out of common social struggles and has used this as the basis of strong class-based movements to pursue developmental goals (Heller 1996). Meanwhile, many parts of UP have been in thrall to vertical social relations that have inhibited the scope for trust and mutual cooperation. As Lerche (1995) shows, in a comparative study of agrarian conflict in eastern and western UP, economic patron–client relations are less of a hindrance to class or caste-based activism than new political power structures. Simply put, the balance of power in society sets the framework for action and change.

Will decentralised programmes like DPEP flounder on the rocks of highly unequal social relations? Or can decentralised governance structures provide the first step toward greater civil–state cohesion in a place like UP? This chapter has discussed gender inequity in primary education as an example of unequal social relations rooted in historical events and circumstances. A historical look at changes in literacy attainment in Uttar Pradesh demonstrates the importance of taking a disaggregated approach to this issue, as findings reveal that female literacy is subject to deep regional and sub-regional variations. This underscores the importance of recent policy shifts toward decentralised education programmes.

Yet, in applauding this new sensitivity to the interconnected goals of greater efficiency, governance and equity, one must be careful not to treat decentralisation as an instant tonic for the complex socio-economic problems that perpetuate gender and caste gaps in education. Decentralisation of education invokes both risks and opportunities—including the danger of forced consensus by dominant social groups, as well as the promise of greater public accountability.

Ultimately, decentralisation holds up a mirror to the community it operates in, reflecting both harmony and disharmony, power and marginality. This can create greater unity, or it can create deeper social divisions. But in doing so, the process opens up new opportunities for addressing chronic injustices in female education and allowing greater participation in the structures that set the opportunities and limitations of daily life.

Notes

†I would like to express my gratitude to John Harriss, Jean Dreze, Rene Veron, Ramya Subrahmanian and Roli Asthana for their insightful comments, which contributed much to this chapter. All maps included in this chapter have been generated by the author.

1. For this study, literacy rates were selected as a simple and reliable indicator of the prevalence of gender bias. In calculating the gender gap, this study relies on a percentage-point subtraction method. For example, a 60 per cent male literacy rate and a 35 per cent female literacy rate means a gender difference of 25 percentage points. For the purposes of this study, it was felt that this method is preferable to using sex ratios (i.e., the number of literate females per 1,000 literate males), because in conditions of generally increasing literacy rates, as in UP, sex ratios mask a widening gender gap.

2. This study relies on Census of India 1991 final population totals (1991a), external recalculations of state-level literacy rate (age 7+) for 1981 and 1971 (Jejeebhoy 1991) and the author's own recalculations of district-level data for 1981 (based on Government of India 1981c and 1981d). It was not possible to achieve district-level recalculations of the 1971 data, as age-specific population totals are not available. As a result, the 1971 district-level data used in this study reflects 5+ literacy rates as given by the Government of India (1971) and (1981b). As 5+ literacy rates are slightly lower than 7+ literacy rates, this study may overestimate the increase of literacy at the district level between 1971 and 1991 to a small extent. However, the changed definition of the literacy rate has only a minimal effect on calculations of the gender gap. Longer-term comparisons, covering 1951–91, rely on the crude literacy rate for all decades.

3. Changes in district boundaries in UP have necessitated some minor recalculations. In the 1981 Census, two new districts appeared: Ghaziabad (created from Meerut and Bulandshahr districts) and Lalitpur (carved out from Jhansi district). Similarly, in 1991, seven new districts were created: Hardwar (Muzaffarnagar, Saharanpur, Bijnor); Siddharthnagar (Basti); Sonbhadra (Mirzapur); Maharajganj (Gorakhpur); Kanpur Nagar (Kanpur); Firozabad (Agra, Mainpuri); and Mau (Azamgarh, Ballia) (Government of India 1991b). For decennial comparisons, 1991 data was recalculated to show new districts and their 'parents' as single, unified districts.

REFERENCES

Agarwal, B. 1988. *Structures of Patriarchy: The State, the Community, and the Household.* Delhi: Kali for Women.

Aggarwal, J. C., and S. P. Agrawal. 1995. *Uttarakhand: Past, Present and Future.* Delhi: Concept Publishing.

Bora, R. S. 1996. *Himalayan Migration: A Study of the Hill Region of Uttar Pradesh.* Delhi: Institute of Economic Growth/Sage Publications.

Carron, G., and T. N. Chau, eds. 1980. *Regional Disparities in Educational Development: A Controversial Issue.* Paris: UNESCO

Crook, R., and J. Manor. 1994. *Enhancing Participation and Institutional Performance: Democratic Decentralisation in South Asia and West Africa*, Report to ESCOR/ODA on Phase Two of a Two-Phase Research Project, January.

Dreze, J., and H. Gazdar. 1997. 'Uttar Pradesh: The Burden of Inertia'. In J. Dreze and A. Sen, eds, *Indian Development: Selected Regional Perspectives.* Delhi: Oxford University Press for UNU/WIDER.

Dreze, J., and M. Saran. 1995. 'Primary Education and Economic Development in China and India: Overview and Two Case Studies'. In K. Basu, P. Pattanaik, and K. Suzumura, eds. *Choice, Welfare and Development: A Festschrift in Honour of Amartya K Sen.* Oxford: Clarendon Press Oxford.

Dreze, J., and A. Sen. 1995. *India: Economic Development and Social Opportunity.* Delhi: Oxford University Press.

Edwards, C. 1992. 'Industrialisation in South Korea'. In T. Hewitt, H. Johnson, and D. Wield, eds. *Industrialisation and Development.* Oxford: Oxford University Press/The Open University.

Freire, P. 1972. *Pedagogy of the Oppressed.* London: Penguin.

Government of India. 1961. *Census of India 1961 Union Primary Census Abstracts.* Delhi: Office of the Registrar General.

____. 1964. *1963–64 Statistical Abstract.* Delhi: Office of the Registrar General.

____. 1971. *Census of India 1971 General Report: Uttar Pradesh.* Delhi: Office of the Registrar General.

____. 1981a. *Census of India 1981: A Handbook of Educational and Allied Statistics 1981.* Delhi: Office of the Registrar General.

____. 1981b. *Census of India 1981 Uttar Pradesh: A Portrait of Population.* Delhi: Office of the Registrar General.

____. 1981c. *Census of India 1981 Uttar Pradesh: Social and Cultural Tables.* Delhi: Office of the Registrar General.

____. 1981d. *Comparative Primary Census Abstract 1971 and 1981.* Delhi: Office of the Registrar General.

____. 1991a. *Census of India 1991: Final Population Totals: Brief Analysis of Primary Census Abstract, Paper Two.* Delhi: Office of the Registrar General.

____. 1991b. *Census of India 1991: Provisional Population Totals: Brief Analysis of Primary Census Abstract, Paper Two.* Delhi: Office of the Registrar General.

____. 1991c. *Census of India 1991 Handbook.* Delhi: Office of the Registrar General.

____. 1992. *Revised Policy Formulations and National Programme of Action for Education.* Delhi: Ministry of Human Resource Development.

____. 1993. *Education for All: The Indian Scene.* Delhi: Department of Education.

Government of India. 1997. *Ministry of Human Resource Development Annual Report 1996–97*. Delhi: Ministry of Human Resource Development.

———. 1998. *Economic Survey 1997–98*, cited on www.nic.in, July.

Gulati, L. 1995. 'Migration and Social Change in Kerala'. *India International Centre Quarterly* 22 (2–3): 191–202.

Heller, P. 1996. 'Social Capital as a Product of Class Mobilisation and State Intervention: Industrial Workers in Kerala, India'. *World Development* 24 (6): 1055–71.

Jejeebhoy, S. J. 1991. 'Female Literacy in India: The Situation in 1991'. *The Journal of Family Welfare* 37 (3): 23–34.

King, E. M., and M. A. Hill, eds. 1993. *Women's Education in Developing Countries: Barriers, Benefits, and Policies*. Baltimore and London: The Johns Hopkins University Press for the World Bank.

Lerche, J. 1995. 'Is Bonded Labour a Bound Category? Reconceptualising Agrarian Conflict in India'. *The Journal of Peasant Studies* 22 (3): 484–515.

Mathew, G. 1995. 'The Paradox of Kerala Women's Social Development and Social Leadership'. *India International Centre Quarterly*. 22 (2–3), Summer: 203.

Murthi, M., A. C. Guio, and J. Dreze. 1997. 'Mortality, Fertility and Gender Bias in India: A District-Level Analysis'. In J. Dreze and A. Sen, eds. *Indian Development: Selected Regional Perspectives*. Delhi: Oxford University Press for UNU/WIDER: 357–87.

Pande, P. N. 1996. *Drudgery of the Hill Women*. Delhi: Indus Publishing.

Patkar, A. 1995. 'Socio-Economic Status and Female Literacy in India'. *Educational Development* 15 (4): 401–09.

Putnam, R. 1993. *Making Democracy Work: Civic Traditions in Modern Italy*. Princeton, NJ: Princeton University Press.

Raju, S. 1993. 'Regional Disparities in Female Literacy in Urban India: Problems and Prospects'. In S. C. Nuna, ed. *Regional Disparities in Educational Development*. Delhi: South Asia Publishers/NIEPA: 243–65.

Ramachandran, V. K. 1997. 'On Kerala's Development Achievements'. In J. Dreze and A. Sen, eds. *Indian Development: Selected Regional Perspectives*. Delhi: Oxford University Press for UNU/WIDER.

Sanwal, S. N. 1976. *Social Stratification in Rural Kumaon*. Delhi: Oxford University Press.

Saradamoni, K. 1994. 'Women, Kerala and Some Development Issues'. *Economic and Political Weekly* 29 (9), 26 February: 501–09.

Sax, W. S. 1991. *Mountain Goddess: Gender and Politics in Himalayan Pilgrimage*. Oxford: Oxford University Press.

Schuth, K. 1980. 'Village Literacy and Its Correlates: A Mysore Case Study'. In D. Sopher, ed. *An Exploration of India: Geographical Perspectives on Society and Culture*. Ithaca, NY: Cornell University Press/Longman: 191–212.

Sen, G. 1992. 'Social Needs and Public Accountability: The Case of Kerala'. In M. Wuyts, M. Mackintosh, and T. Hewitt, eds. *Development Policy and Public Action*. Oxford, England: Oxford University Press/The Open University: 253–78.

Sharma, R. 1999. 'What Manner of Teacher: Some Lessons from Madhya Pradesh'. *Economic and Political Weekly*, June 19: 1597–1607.

Sopher, D., ed. 1980. *An Exploration of India: Geographical Perspectives on Society and Culture*. Ithaca, NY: Cornell University Press/Longman.

Subrahmanian, R. 1997. 'If You Build It, Will They Come?: Educational Decision-Making in the Context of Economic Uncertainty and Social Risk'. *IDS Bulletin* 28 (3):101–11.

Subrahmanian, R. 1999. 'Matching Services with Local Preferences: Managing Primary Education Services in a Rural District of India'. *Development in Practice* 9 (1–2): 68–77.

Tilak, J. B. G. 1997. 'Five Decades of Underinvestment in Education in India'. *Economic and Political Weekly* 32 (42), September 6: 2239–41.

United Nations. 1998. *Indicators on Population*. Available at http://www.un.org/depts/unsd/social.poptn/html, 24 August.

United Nations Development Program. 1996. *Common Country Assessment*. Available at http://www.undp.org.in/report/position/cca.html, 24 August, 1998.

Weiner, M. 1991. *The Child and the State in India: Child Labour and Education Policy in Comparative Perspective*. Delhi: Oxford University Press.

Wolman, H. 1990. 'Decentralisation: What It Is and Why We Should Care'. In R. J. Bennett, ed. *Decentralisation, Local Governments and Markets: Towards a Post-Welfare Agenda*. Oxford: Clarendon Press Oxford.

The World Bank. 1997. *India: Achievements and Challenges in Reducing Poverty*. Washington DC: The World Bank.

———. 1998. *Reducing Poverty in India: Options for More Effective State Services*. Washington DC: The World Bank.

12

Community Caretaking and Women Volunteer Teachers in Mumbai Slums*

Anju Saigal

In recent years, the Indian context has seen civil society gain recognition as an important participant in governance. A shift in the perception of the roles of state and civil society has contributed to this salience: good governance has come to be associated with the state playing a facilitative role and markets and society working in collaboration toward the common goal of economic and social development (Archer 1994). Neera Chandhoke notes that from India's Seventh Five-Year Plan (1985–90) onwards, there has been a 'perceptible shift from government to civil society organisations and to the market in matters of service delivery' (Chandhoke 2005: 1). Estimates suggest that there are around 1.2 million non-profit organisations operating in the country, with the voluntary sector engaging 16 million people as part-time or full-time volunteers (Srivastava and Tandon 2005). While India has had a history of active civic engagement (Sen 1998; Tandon and Mohanty 2002), undoubtedly recent policy changes have helped in expanding the role of civil society in governance and creating spaces for citizens' participation. However, how citizens occupy and animate these newly created spaces (cf. Cornwall 2002) and make sense of their participation has received scarce attention. Unarguably, understanding how and why people participate in such spaces for public action would shed light on the forms of citizenship action and render a nuanced reading of people's democratic engagement.

This chapter, drawn from a larger ethnographic study, investigates women volunteers' teaching action in their slum communities in Mumbai. At the time of research, the women were participating with Pratham, a civil society organisation working in partnership with local governments, local slums and village communities across India, toward universalising elementary education. The chapter examines women's meaning-making of their teaching engagement, in their community space.

* Previously published in *Economic and Political Weekly* 43 (42), 18–24 October 2008: 69–75.

It illustrates that the women interpret their teaching roles as community caretaking. Using a feminist reading of the construct of citizenship, the chapter goes on to suggest that such community caretaking may be characterised as an expression of citizenship action. For the women in this study, teaching in their localities is interpreted as an act of care that is both grounded in interpersonal relationships and a desire for social uplift of the disadvantaged. However, such acts of community caretaking are both multi-dimensional and negotiated and challenge simplistic and universalistic notions of citizenship. Far from being autonomous economic and social actors, the women's actions are multi-faceted, rooted in the multiple collectivities of which they are part and the dynamics of the same.

The chapter is divided into five sections. In the first, I describe the study context. In the second, I discuss the theoretical lens used and briefly discuss relevant literature. In the third and fourth sections, I examine women's community-based teaching-caretaking roles: one, as articulated through interpersonal relationships and relational discourses; and two, a desire for social uplift. In the fifth section, I draw conclusions.

THE STUDY CONTEXT

The study was located at Baiganwadi, a sprawling slum area located in north-east Mumbai that spills onto one of Mumbai's solid-waste dumping grounds. The area is Muslim-dominated, with a population of close to 3,00,000 (in two contiguous slum areas, one of which is Baiganwadi). Brutal crimes are commonplace here and the area is generally considered unsafe for women and children. The two government school buildings in the area are overcrowded and cater to the poorest of the population. At the time of data collection, the area had a high incidence of child labour[1] and one of the largest numbers of out-of-school children of school-going age in the city.

The women in this study were working as teachers with Pratham and were part of its 24,000 largely female volunteer-teaching workforce. Pratham was born in 1994, in the wake of the Jomtien Conference on Education for All, where all represented nations pledged universalisation of primary education. Civil society participation was stated as an important strategy for achieving this goal. Pratham began in Mumbai, with the initial seed money from the United Nations International Children's Emergency Fund (UNICEF); today it has a presence in 14 states. Its approach focusses on 'complete coverage' that aims to ensure that every child in the given geographical area has access to education and is learning. At the time of research, Pratham had four programmes, targeted toward the educational needs of children in the age-group of 3–12 years. These included a pre-school programme, a programme to meet the literacy needs of underachieving school-going children, a programme for out-of-school children of school-going age and a library programme for all children in the locality. These programmes were implemented through local women, whom Pratham recruited as teachers to run their programmes for children in their respective localities. Pratham trained the women and also paid them an honorarium; for some programmes, the teachers were also required to charge a fee from students that aimed at partial cost recovery.

For the purposes of this study, data was collected during the period between June 2004 and April 2005. A multi-method approach to data collection (Fontana and Frey 1998) was employed that included a combination of ethnographic methods: secondary data, participant observation and informal interviews, survey data, in-depth interviews and visual methods. Grounded theory methods were used for analysis.

During the period of data collection, Pratham had recruited 64 teachers at Baiganwadi. While most teachers and staff were observed during unstructured observations and many were informally interviewed, 18 teachers were eventually selected through purposeful sampling (Patton 1990) to form the focus of the study. They were selected in order to create a heterogeneous sample group rather than a representative one. Table 12.1 displays the background characteristics of the sample group of teachers.

TABLE 12.1: Profile of Teachers at Baiganwadi: Entire Teaching Group and Sample Group Teachers

	All Teachers	*Sample Group Teachers*
	[N=43]	*[N=18]*
Age:		
16–23 years	39	14
>24 years	4	4
Educational grade completed:[a]		
<Class X	23	9
Class X–XII	17	8
>Class XII	1	1
Marital status:[b]		
Unmarried	38	13
Married	3	3
Separated/divorced	1	2
Religion:		
Muslim	41	16
Hindu	2	2

Notes: [a] Two respondents in the 'All teachers' group did not respond to the question.
[b] One respondent in the 'All teachers' group did not respond to the question.

As indicated in Table 12.1, the typical teacher in this community was unmarried, Muslim and below 23 years. There were a few older, married women, as well as divorced women who worked as teachers. Most of the teachers had an educational completion level that was Class XII or below. Survey questionnaires administered to teachers in similar communities in Mumbai indicated that the teacher profile here was correspondingly similar. In the sample group, the characteristics of most teachers fitted those of the majority in this area.

WOMEN, CITIZENSHIP AND COMMUNITY CARETAKING

In recent years, feminist scholarship has generated extensive literature on the gendered nature of citizenship in liberal democracies (see for example, Foster 1999; Lister 1997; Pateman 1988, 1989; Roy 2005; Walby 1994; Yuval-Davis 1997). Citizenship, as this scholarship argues, is premised on the opposition of the public and private spheres. The underlying assumptions of citizenship are normatively masculine and associated with the public domain. Women, who are both materially and ideologically linked to the private domain, have thus effectively been excluded from attaining full political, civil and social status as citizens. Carole Pateman, for instance, argues that civil freedom is not universal, as the abstract notion of citizenship would seem to suggest; women 'have been incorporated into public life in a different manner from men' (Pateman 1989: 4). Their struggle for inclusion as citizens has been a contested process, one in which 'women have been included as "women"; ...as beings whose sexual embodiment prevents them from enjoying the same political standing as men' (ibid.).

Nira Yuval-Davis (1999) critiques contemporary theorisations on citizenship as being 'westocentric', in the sense of dealing almost exclusively with Western modes of citizenship; further, she argues that this writing assumes a homogeneous notion of 'women', 'moulded in some idealised notion of a white, heterosexual, often middle class western woman' (Yuval-Davis 1999: 120). In order to introduce new frames into the thinking on women and citizenship, she suggests broadening the meaning of citizenship by analytically separating it from the 'nation state' and understanding it as a 'multilayered construct'. As she puts it:

> [C]itizenship needs to be understood as a multilayered construct, in which one's citizenship in collectivities in the different layers – local ethnic, national, state, cross- or trans-state and supra-state – is affected and often at least partly constructed by the relationships and positionings of each layer in specific historic context (ibid.: 122).

Such collectivities could include 'the family, social strata, ethnic and national groupings...as well as institutions like those of education, trade unions and means of communication' (Anthias and Yuval-Davis 1989: 5). Each of these, as Anthias and Yuval-Davis note, produce their own ideologies and are subjected to those of the state as well.

Recent feminist scholarship has sought to explain working-class women's community-based action as 'acts of citizenship' (Mirza and Reay 2000; Naples 1998). However, could such action be considered as a citizenship action? Ruth Lister (1998) addresses this question in her paper based on her research on women's community development activities in low-income neighbourhoods in Northern Ireland. She draws upon the civic republican tradition of citizenship that 'would argue that citizens are supposed to come together to achieve common ends with those different from themselves and in so doing transcend their specific interests and identify with the wider collectivity than with any particular group perspective' (Lister 1998: 230). She points out, though, that the notion of common good is a problematic one. On the one hand, it serves to 'reinforce the position of privileged groups' (ibid.: 230–31);

however, on the other hand, refusal to acknowledge the activism of disadvantaged groups as citizenship action 'is to reinforce the very exclusion that they are fighting in the name of a common good which has subordinated the interests of these communities to those of more powerful groups' (ibid.: 231).

In low-income neighbourhoods, women's community-based action often takes the form of community caretaking. Patricia Hill Collins (2000), for instance, draws attention to the cultural institution of 'othermothering' in African-American communities, where women own responsibility beyond their nuclear families, for children in their kin-group and for those beyond. This cultural institution provides, as she puts it, a 'generalised ethic of caring and accountability among African-American women' (ibid.: 189) and women's experiences as othermothers 'provide the foundation for black women's political activism' (ibid.: 189). In a similar vein, Nancy Naples (1998) characterises the community caretaking roles of Latina and Black community workers in her study as 'activist mothering' that encompassed a broadened definition of actual mothering practices. As she notes: 'The community workers defined "good mothering" to comprise all actions, including social activism, that addressed the needs of their children and community—variously defined as their racial-ethnic group, low income people, or members of a particular neighbourhood' (ibid.: 113). Mirza and Reay (2000) suggest in their study on Black supplementary school women educators in the context of the UK, that the educators' idea of community was a 'pragmatic, conscious construction of a "black home"... They [educators] were not simply a part of the community. They were also engaged in actively constructing it through their work as radical black educators' (Mirza and Ray 2000: 69). Such studies of women's community caretaking roles and actions have highlighted, in Naples' words, the women's 'selfconscious struggles against racism, sexism, and poverty' (Naples 1998: 114). These struggles have often involved, as Gilkes' (1983) study of Black women community organisers points out, an engagement characterised by 'going up for the oppressed', as opposed to the work orientation and 'career patterns associated with the dominant culture notions of professionalism' (ibid.: 136).

In the Indian research scenario, little attention has been paid to analytically examining women's lived experiences as community-based actors. This study therefore takes as its starting point understandings generated through research on low-income women's community-based action, located in the international contexts discussed above. The two sections that follow illustrate how Mumbai's volunteer teachers construct their acts of teaching in their own slum localities through notions of caretaking. In the final section, the chapter suggests framing the women's community caretaking as a citizenship action.

Interpersonal Relationships and Discourses

One way in which this study's participants talked about their teaching engagements was through relational discourses, which were characterised by the actual relationships they shared with their students. Their descriptions of their acts for children's educational inclusion, however, demonstrated a conflicted process, which stemmed from their identities as both women and teachers. As Walkerdine (1990) notes, being a teacher implies legitimacy in the domain of knowledge and power and being a woman implies a lack thereof in the same domains. The teacher narratives discussed in this section reflect the conundrum of being women teachers. They demonstrate women's conflicted legitimacy and the status as 'teacher' in the community space and its resolution, which stemmed from their interpretation of their roles as grounded in interpersonal relations and the relations of care they shared with their students.

Like an 'Older Sister'

Afia consistently talked of her motivation for teaching the '*balwadi*' (preschool class) as stemming from her 'love' for young children and the satisfaction of playing a foundational role in children's education. In order to play this role, Afia spoke of constructing her image as one which was non-threatening to children. While this was a message conveyed to teachers at Pratham, Afia appeared to have reworked it and given it meaning in ways that made sense for her work and teaching role:

> I mingle with the children. I sit among the children, and have them sit around me...I tell them, 'ask me questions and I will answer'...Then I ask children questions and they answer – 'teacher I went here, I saw this, I did that.' Meaning, I found it very easy to be with children...If we are strict with children, they will not be able to do [the task]. If one becomes a child with the children, doing things with children becomes easy. Children will do [the task]...if they know the teacher will not touch me, she will not beat me.... [as a result] children do not consider me a teacher, they think I'm their older sister.

Afia's drawing upon the image of 'older sister' here may be understood as being both gendered and strategic. Older girls in low-income families play the role of nurturing their siblings. Hence, conjuring this image frames her as a nurturer in the context of her teaching role. At the same time, her use of the image is strategic, as it downplays the traditional image of teacher as a figure of authority: it portrays her as non-threatening to the children, which is helpful in creating a child-friendly environment conducive to children's attendance and learning.

Afia was also strategic in her negotiations with parents in order to get their participation, as she knew that the latter was a critical element in ensuring children's attendance. Thus, she talked about using the *balwadi* fees to negotiate children's attendance with parents. Initially, she asked parents not to pay fees, hoping this would eliminate a stumbling block to children's attendance. However, after she began accepting fees, there were many non-paying parents with whom she did not insist on payment of fees. Rationalising her decision, she said: 'because there are mostly Biharis here. Their families are large and they do not even have food to eat. There are a lot of children from whom I do not charge fees.'

While Afia viewed the issue here through the lens of parents' material necessity, she also added that if she were to insist, parents would stop sending their children.

Furthermore, asking parents for fees was implicated in her understanding of her class position. When I probed her about whether she should not expect fees as a matter of her due as teacher, she said: 'I cannot do it. My "abbu" says – "[Even] if there is no food at home, my children are such that they will not go to anyone else's [home] to ask for it."' Evidenced in this is the understanding of her social position and class. Being poor in her context did not command respectability. Asking or insisting on payment of fees would suggest that she, and by extension her family, needed the money for subsistence, which her father as the primary breadwinner, was unable to provide. This would bring disrepute to herself and her family.

When the 'Area *ki ladki*' Becomes a Teacher

When she became a teacher, Nazneen imagined that her 'post' would bring her recognition and respect culturally associated with the teaching profession. However, her everyday interactions with parents highlighted for her a disconnection between perception and reality. Some of her major conflicts with parents had been over the issue of non-payment of fees. Such conflicts sometimes resulted in altercations, because of which she felt insulted: 'I feel like it is a matter of "*jalalat*" [insult]... [T] hat the teacher is fighting over Rs 20. And when they shout at you, you feel bad.' Her conflict with neighbours (who were also parents of children she taught) sometimes become a matter of family dignity, no longer restricted to her. Nazneen's mother got involved in one altercation. After giving the parent a mouthful, Nazneen's mother turned on her and said, as she recounts: 'You do not need to conduct the class, shut it. Do your abbu and your brother not give you money? Do you not get to eat at home?' Implied in her mother's comment was the issue of respectability: in a similar sense as Afia's, Nazneen's asking for fees was tantamount to her family needing her to work for the money and that would be a matter of family disgrace.

Nazneen diagnosed that the reason she did not have 'value', or did not receive the respect of a teacher from the parents in the community was because she was an 'area *ki ladki*' (girl from the locality). She complained about the Pratham staff telling her to talk to the people, to convince them of the importance of sending their child to her class, implying through this that they did not understand the dynamics at play in her social interactions. In a somewhat heated, long monologue, she explained:

> If they [parents] do not send their children, what is our fault? We cannot have authority over others' children. We can explain to them, but we cannot drag them to class... If I were a teacher who came from outside [the locality], had big glasses, wore a sari, I would have had a reputation, I would have had respect. Now I am only a 'ladki' [girl[2]] from the area [locality], so in their eyes, what am I? An area ki ladki. Even if I explain to them from the position of a teacher, from their point of view, I am only from their area, no? So there is no 'value'...Now if I live here, how will they respect me? Even if I have the 'post' of a teacher, the children are from this area.

Nazneen's reference to herself as *ladki* is telling. Age, gender and marital status intersect to produce authority, status and respect. A *ladki* commands the least status in this hierarchy. Thus, Nazneen's reference brings to the fore her lack of authority and status as a young and unmarried girl in her community. This is at odds with the idea of the authority and respect traditionally attributed to a teacher and, in Nazneen's perception, is an important reason for parental non-involvement in the educational programmes she conducted.

It appeared that it was because of these circumstances that Nazneen searched for creative ways of eliciting parental participation. For instance, she attempted to replace the Pratham test instrument (used during surveys to identify low-achieving children) with asking the child to read from her textbook, since she thought this would make a better impact on parental awareness and consequently on their commitment to send their child to her class. However, she understood that parental awareness of a child's low literacy skills was not enough. She would thus use economic and emotional arguments as well. She recounted her arguments to an unwilling parent:

> '*Khala*, tutoring costs a lot. But I'm tutoring at my own home, which will cost you only Rs 20 a month...Your child must be eating [buying snacks] for at least a rupee a day. That adds up to Rs 30 a month. So... if you give Rs 20 here, you are still saving Rs 10.' Some parents understand this and quickly give their names during the survey. ...But when the time comes, [sometimes] the child does not want to attend the class.... So I say, '*Khala*,...This class that we conduct, is it for our benefit, or for yours? ... If someone asks your child to read something and your child does so, how happy will you feel...And if the child is unable [to read], you will begin beating the child....[So] if the child comes to us and learns something, what's the harm?

The work of bringing children to class each day was a challenging one, and a reason why she thought of quitting this work each year. Yet, she had been teaching for the past eight years and when I asked her why she continued, she expressed her motivation in terms of the relationships she had developed with the children and the sense of responsibility she felt toward them. This responsibility was with reference to and rooted in the context in which she taught. Knowing that she was perhaps the only community-based educational resource the children had, she could provide a worthwhile alternative to children, who otherwise would be 'roam[ing] around'. Her attachment to the children then appeared intertwined with her sense of responsibility toward them. As she put it:

> They [children] give me respect. They tell me, teacher, you teach. ...Some say, 'teacher, we will only study with you. We will not go anywhere else'. When I see these children's hearts, their love, I do not feel like shutting down the class. Because they will also suffer....Just for a few children, why should I have the others suffer?

Teaching and Social Upliftment

Viewing their engagement through the lens of the setting within which they worked, women constructed their teaching in terms of working for the underprivileged living in their areas and positioned themselves as caretakers of children who lacked educational resources (Naples 1998). However, their interpretation of their roles was embedded in the gender relations and material circumstances of the population with whom they worked. As the following accounts demonstrate, these women strategically used their status as teachers to negotiate for educational change in their localities.

'*Ilm Bantna*' (Spreading Education)

In Islamic religious philosophy, '*ilm*' roughly refers to true (religious) knowledge, the pursuit and spread of which occupies the highest status. As a teacher, Rubina constructed her role as one with social responsibility, particularly toward parents and children who were not literate. As she put it:

> Our children do not know anything. They are *kore* [blank], they do not know anything. If we do not teach children, if we do not pay attention to them – 'Live the way you live, eat the way you eat', so how will they remain? They will remain *jahil* [uncivilised]. Because they will not know anything. Just work, eat, and live. Alternately, if we know something, ...we [can] work hard to [educate] our children, 'see this is how things are. This is good, this is bad. This is important to study....We give the child as much *ilm* as we have....This is *ilm batna*. Today our children are studying. In the future, they will become somebody and educate others.

Rubina's words echo a modernity discourse, perceiving education as a means for the 'civilisation' of those who were illiterate, to achieve progress and 'become somebody'. She saw her own role as instrumental in this process and sought to use her position as teacher to work towards the same.

While she viewed her role as such, establishing its legitimacy in order to pursue its goals, it was a constant act of negotiation, particularly with parents. This was evidenced in several incidents that she described. One particular incident took place when the staff planned an awareness exercise through organising competitions among children in the community. The teachers were responsible for gathering the children and acting as liaison with the parents. The parents were required to pay a small fee toward the costs. When prizes were awarded only to a few children (who had secured the first three places in every competition), there was an uproar in some localities, particularly that of Rubina's, where parents felt that Pratham had cheated them and taken their money without giving them anything in return. Clearly, this was being said in a context where the poor are regularly cheated and there is a general mistrust of anyone in a position of authority. Rubina, as a representative of the organisation, received the flak. When she heard of this discontent, Rubina refused to visit her locality to distribute the library books, saying: 'They will beat me up'. Slowly, though, she began sending one of her younger nieces, who only came back to report that the parents were demanding to see her. Rubina eventually plucked up the courage to meet the parents because, as she put it, 'this is my work'.

As she recounted it, on meeting with parents, she began questioning them as to why they had been refusing to let the children read, despite the fact that the children loved to do so. The parents, in turn, demanded an explanation regarding the whereabouts of their money. Rubina explained how the money had been used, adding:

> We are working for your benefit. We wanted to see if the children were able to do what they knew. What did they know before and after giving them the story, what have they come to know. Your children will progress in their studies because of this.

Interestingly, Rubina used her symbolic power as a teacher to convert the issue of money, perceived as wrongfully taken, into an issue about the children's educational welfare. The subtext read that she, the teacher, was concerned about and responsible for the children's 'progress', that activities such as those organised would help the children do so and that parents should not stand in the way of the same. Her speaking from the position of a teacher was strategic, in that it both legitimated her authority as a teacher and justified the action she took on behalf of the organisation. Had she positioned herself as an 'area ki *ladki*', to use Nazneen's term, she would have most definitely faced the wrath of parents. The parents were convinced and agreed to participate the next time a programme of this nature was held. As a proof of this, when the programme was held twice thereafter, children from the same locality participated. And, as she told me with pride, she was able to gather the maximum number of children, as compared to other teachers working in her part of the community.

The '*Mahol*' and Teaching Engagement

For many women, their teaching engagement gained meaning through what they referred to as their *mahol* or environment, which in their context suggested deprivation: material, educational, social, security and so forth. Sometimes this meant creating opportunities for children's future; at others, it meant a broader improvement of their localities.

Malika talked of engaging in teaching work because of her '*shauk*' (liking or interest). Her *shauk*, however, appeared conflated with a sense of responsibility toward those who were underprivileged. Malika belonged to a relatively higher socio-economic stratum. She lived in an adjoining slum area and travelled from there to teach in a locality close to the dumping ground. Both she and her older sister taught in a single-room space that belonged to a private school in the vicinity. They rented this space for a few hours each day, paying the rent from their own salaries; they did not receive any help from Pratham in this regard. She chose to come all the way to teach here, since there was dire need for educational work in this area. The low monetary compensation was of little consequence to her, as '[t]he main [thing is] if we begin educating the children from now on, in the future, that child will find the right path. This is why we teach.' She went on:

> Because....we saw the children's *mahol*, that parents just did not want to educate their children. They wanted to extract the maximum work possible from the children. But when we brought our understanding of education [and] sat with the children to teach them, then parents also began to feel that it is right to educate the children. We requested the parents and began calling the children. So the children began attending [the class].

Rooting her role in the social context in which she worked, Malika constructed the image of the parent as that of being poor and, perhaps, ignorant or unknowing, in that they engaged their children in work and not education. As a teacher and therefore educated and aware, she positioned herself as an advocate for children's education, one who made parents realise the worth of educating their children. Like Rubina, she saw herself as an agent whose role was to help parents appreciate the worth of educating their child, which in turn would help the child find the 'right path'.

This 'right path' meant convincing parents not to send their children for garbage collection. She recounted her argument to them:

> See, you have such young children. If at this age you extract work from them, they are illiterate and they will remain illiterate. And they will also be engaged in [nefarious] activities. Then I explained to them the way in which Pratham had trained me.[3]

Perceiving her teaching engagement in terms of creating future opportunities for children, Malika went on to say that when arguments did not work with parents, she would try and coerce the children into attending class. Malika's action with parents and children suggests that she used her legitimacy as teacher to advocate on behalf of the children's education; her position as a teacher gave her legitimacy to seek a change in parental attitudes toward their children's education. Her efforts appeared to receive a fair amount of success, as evidenced by the high levels of children's regular attendance in her class.

Like Malika, Saira used her understanding of the *mahol* to situate her teaching engagement. Aside from perceiving her work as creating educational opportunities for children, Saira interpreted it as that of bringing '*sudhar*' or improvement to her locality. As she explained:

> In this way something can be done about our 'area' [locality]. The condition of our area – that improves [*sudharti hai*]. The children who work in *karkhanas* [small-scale industrial units], ...do not [have the opportunity to] study, ...are able to study.

In speaking about the 'condition of our area', Saira referred to the material and social problems associated with her locality. Her engagement in teaching work contributed to the collective improvement of her locality.

While Malika constructed the parents as ignorant and unknowing, whom she, as a teacher, guided along the 'right path', Saira, in contrast, constructed parents as neglectful ['The parents here are '*lahparwah*' (neglectful)'] and thus herself as one with the responsibility for their children's well-being. As evidence, she pointed to the children's irregular attendance, saying, 'Mothers say, "children do not want to go [to class]—what can we do?" I say, "*arre*, at least (try to) send them. If you send them, only then will they come."' She recounted explaining to them that if they sent their child with a snack, a bag, a slate and if s/he got an opportunity to socialise with other children, then the child would be interested in attending. However, since parents were 'neglectful', 'What can one do? Children do not want to come. They attend *arabi* (madrassas) and that is enough.' As a teacher, Saira saw herself as the one responsibly looking after the children's education, in a social environment detrimental to the children's educational welfare, as opposed to parents who did not give consideration to their children's education beyond their religious learning. In the face of this, she spoke of continuing to persist with parents, exhorting them to understand their 'responsibility' toward their children's education. She recounted telling them often: 'The teacher puts in hard work to teach. She (even) comes (to the locality). It is your responsibility to send the children.'

CONCLUSIONS

Feminist scholarship has long argued that women's collective action in working-class or low-income communities constitutes politics and, consequently, citizenship practice (Ackelsberg 1988; Lister 1998; Morgen and Bookman 1988; Naples 1998). Calling for broadening the notion of politics beyond the arena of formal politics, Morgen and Bookman (1988) define political activity as 'activities that are carried on in the daily lives of ordinary people and are enmeshed in the social institutions and political-economic processes of their society. When there is an attempt to change the social and economic institutions that embody the basic power relations in...society—that is politics' (ibid.: 4). The actions of the women participants in this study are political in this sense: they animate the spaces created by Pratham's entry into local communities as community-based teachers and work toward the collective agenda of educational inclusion of marginalised children. Their citizenship action is expressed through notions of community caretaking, which in turn gains meaning from the challenging socio-economic environment in which women work. The women also have interpersonal relationships with the children, as they work for the social uplift of the most disadvantaged.

However, the women's citizenship acts are multi-faceted and negotiated and they challenge simplistic and universalistic notions of citizenship. For instance, Nazneen traverses her teaching engagement through her dual and contradictory identities as *ladki* and teacher, both of which are tied to her own social location. She is creative regarding her approach with parents and ultimately grounds her work in the relationships she has established with her students. Afia describes constructing relationships with children that would encourage them to attend regularly. In relation to parents, she appears to make strategic use of the issue of fees to ensure their participation. However, the notion of collecting fees goes beyond garnering parental support: as she describes it, it is tied to her own social location and meanings of class and respectability in her context. Rubina characterises her engagement as one stemming from her desire to spread education to disadvantaged children. Parental trust is key to her goal and she ensures the same through strategically using her status as a teacher, rather than positioning herself as belonging to any other collectivity (such as that of women or member of their community). Thus, far from being autonomous economic and social actors, the women's actions are multilayered, rooted in the dynamics of their multiple collectivities (cf. Yuval-Davis 1999).

The women's action gains significance within the larger context of exclusion in which they live. While current discourses on governance have created new spaces for civil society participation and citizen action, the experiences of 'public' (and 'private') differ for different collectivities and for different members of these collectivities (cf. Hill Collins 1994, cited in Mirza and Reay 2000: 69). Multitudes of those who live in poorer slums in Mumbai have little access to services like potable water, sanitation, public health or educational facilities, and face a constant threat of eviction. The women in this study belong to such communities and face exclusions on several fronts, on grounds of their class and gender backgrounds. Their relationship to their own collectivities and to other collectivities, as well as the nature of the relationship of their collectivity to the state, determines the extent and nature of their participation. Belonging to materially deprived contexts and having been excluded from the domain of education, the women today are, paradoxically, engaged in educational change in their localities. For these women, then, their community caretaking acts include their very 'right to have rights' (Dagnino 1998: 48) and reveal the contradictory nature of citizenship.

As the rhetoric of citizen participation grows louder in policy circles, this chapter highlights the need to understand meanings of public action from the standpoint of those who are disadvantaged and working in similar contexts. Along these lines, this chapter has illuminated how women's citizenship action is a complex and negotiated process, which is intersected by gender and class constructs. The study has implicitly emphasised that a view from the grassroots would help reveal the actual terms of people's inclusion and engagement and the relations of power that structure the same (Jones 1997). Any assessment of democratic engagement ought to consider this, in order to illuminate the constraints and resources available to those who participate. An assessment of this nature would undoubtedly point to pathways to strengthen civil society and participatory action.

Notes

1. Since the study, there have been several crackdowns on industrial units employing child labour in this geographic area.
2. Young, unmarried woman.
3. The Pratham rhetoric largely revolved around emphasising the importance of education to parents and the benefits of getting their children educated.

References

Ackelsberg, M. A. 1988. 'Communities, Resistance and Women's Activism: Some Implications for a Democratic Polity'. In A. Bookman and S. Morgen, eds, *Women and the Politics of Empowerment*, 297–313. Philadelphia: Temple University Press.

Anthias, F., and N. Yuval-Davis. 1989. 'Introduction'. In N. Yuval-Davis and F. Anthias, eds, *Woman Nation-State*, 1–15. London: Macmillan.

Archer, R. 1994. 'Markets and Good Government'. In A. Clayton, ed. *Governance, Democracy and Conditionality: What Role for NGOs?* Oxford: INTRAC.

Chandhoke, N. 2005. '"Seeing" the State in India'. *Economic & Political Weekly* 40 (11): 1033–39.

Cornwall, A. 2002. 'Making Spaces, Changing Places: Situating Participation in Development', IDS Working Paper – 170. Brighton: Institute of Development Studies.

Dagnino, E. 1998. 'Culture, Citizenship and Democracy: Changing Discourses and Practices of the Latin American Left'. In S. E. Alvarez, E. Dagnino, and A. Escobar, eds, *Cultures of Politics/Politics of Cultures: Re-visioning Latin American Social Movements*. Boulder: Westview Press.

Fontana, A., and J. H. Frey. 1998. 'Interviewing: The Art of Science'. In N. K. Denzin and Y. S. Lincoln, eds, *Collecting and Interpreting Qualitative Materials*, 47–78. Thousand Oaks: Sage Publications.

Foster, V. 1999. *In Search of the Public: Girls' Status as Learner-Citizens, Global Issues and Local Effects'*, paper presented at the Australian Association for Research in Education.

Gilkes, C. T. 1983. 'Going Up for the Oppressed: The Career Mobility of Black Women Community Workers'. *Journal of Social Issues* 39 (3): 115–39.

Hill, Collins P. 1994. 'Shifting the Centre: Race, Class and Feminist Theorising about Motherhood'. In D. Bassin, M. Honey, and M. Kaplan, eds, *Representations of Motherhood*. New Haven: Yale University Press.

———. 2000. *Black Feminist Thought: Knowledge, Consciousness and the Politics of Empowerment*. Second Edition. New York: Routledge.

Jones, K. 1997. 'Introduction'. *Hypatia* 12 (4): 1–5.

Lister, R. 1997. *Citizenship: Feminist Perspectives*. London: Macmillan.

———. 1998. 'Citizen in Action: Citizenship and Community Development in a Northern Ireland Context'. *Community Development Journal* 33 (3): 226–35.

Mirza, H. S., and D. Reay. 2000. 'Redefining Citizenship: Black Women Educators and "the Third Space"'. In M. Arnot and J. A. Dillabough, eds, *Challenging Democracy: International Perspectives on Gender, Education and Citizenship*, 58–72. London: Routledge/Falmer.

Morgen, S., and A. Bookman. 1988. 'Rethinking Women and Politics: An Introductory Essay'. In A. Bookman and S. Morgen, eds. *Women and the Politics of Empowerment*, 3–32. Philadelphia: Temple University Press.

Naples, N. A. 1998. *Grassroots Warriors: Activist Mothering, Community Work, and the War on Poverty*. New York: Routledge.

Pateman, C. 1988. *The Sexual Contract*. Stanford: Stanford University Press.

———. 1989. *The Disorder of Women: Democracy, Feminism and Political Theory*. Cambridge: Polity Press.

Patton, M. Q. C. 1990. *Qualitative Evaluation and Research Methods*. Second Edition, Thousand Oaks: Sage Publications.

Roy, A. 2005. *Gendered Citizenship: Historical and Conceptual Explorations*. New Delhi: Orient Longman.

Sen, S. 1998. 'The Non-profit Sector in India'. In H. K. Anheier and L. M. Salamon, eds, *The Non-profit Sector in the Developing World: A Comparative Analysis*. New York: Manchester University Press.

Srivastava, S. S., and R. Tandon. 2005. 'How Large Is India's Non-profit Sector?' *Economic & Political Weekly* 40 (19): 1948–52.

Tandon, R., and R. Mohanty 2002. *Civil Society and Governance*. New Delhi: Samskriti.

Walby, S. 1994. 'Is Citizenship Gendered?' *Sociology* 28 (2): 379–95.

Walkerdine, V. 1990. *Schoolgirl Fictions*. London and New York: Verso.

Yuval-Davis, N. 1997. *Gender and Nation*. Thousand Oaks: Sage Publications.

———. 1999. 'The "Multilayered Citizen": Citizenship in the Age of "Glocalisation"'. *International Feminist Journal of Politics* 1 (1): 119–36.

13

Inequality, Gender and Socio-religious Groups*

Balwant Singh Mehta and Megha Shree

Introduction

The track record of post-colonial India presents a mixed picture. On the one hand, the country has made substantial progress in many socio-economic dimensions, but on the other, it has failed to address the problems of marginalised groups, such as women, the Scheduled Castes (SCs), Scheduled Tribes (STs) and Muslims, who have not figured prominently in the mainstream development process for a long time. The government has taken affirmative action in the form of reservations in public-sector jobs and state-funded educational institutions for the uplift of SCs/STs and Other Backward Classes (OBCs) among Hindus. However, there is an ongoing debate among policy-makers and scholars about whether the recent growth and affirmative actions by the government have benefitted only a small section, or whether they have led to changes in inequality in the labour market, among socio-religious groups and genders.

The available literature argues that certain groups in Indian society are discriminated against and this generates inequality in the labour market (Atkinson 1998; Borooa et al. 2005; Kabeer 2000; Madeshwaran and Attewell 2010; Thorat 2008; Thorat and Dubey 2012). This inequality persists in terms of type of work, wage/earnings, and occupations by socio-religious groups and gender (ILER 2014; Kulkarni and Hatekar 2013; Majumdar 2007; Rani 2008).

Some recent studies mention jobless growth during the last decade, while others report improved employment conditions for marginalised groups during the same period, with rising salaries for women and more participation in decent jobs (ILER 2014; Papola 2012; Rustagi and Mehta 2013). However, there is a dearth of studies examining whether inequality among genders and socio-religious groups has increased or declined, despite a recent improvement in the employment conditions

* Previously published in *Economic and Political Weekly* 52 (8), 25 February 2017: 56–60.

of marginalised groups. In addition, it is worth seeing if the affirmative action taken by the government for the improvement of SCs, STs and OBCs has resulted in a reduction of inequality in the labour market.

This chapter explores these questions by analysing the working-age population (15–59 years) from the latest two National Sample Survey (NSS) rounds—the 61st (2004–05) and the 68th (2011–12). Socio-religious groups are formed by combining caste and religion—Hindu SCs, Hindu STs, Hindu OBCs and Hindu upper castes (UCs), Muslims, and other religions. The share of other religions is very small and therefore not discussed much in the analysis. This chapter is divided into four sections: The first presents the background, the second highlights the findings and the third analyses income inequality. The final section concludes the chapter with policy suggestions.

ANALYSIS AND RESULTS

Gender-based Inequality

The share of females in India's total population is almost half, but they constitute less than one-third of the total workforce and contribute only around one-sixth to the total earnings of workers (Figure 13.1). They are also disadvantaged in terms of human capital endowment—only 40 per cent of females are educated up to secondary level, compared to 60 per cent of males.

FIGURE 13.1: Share in Total Population, Education, Employment and Earnings by Gender (15–59 Years), 2011–12 (per cent)

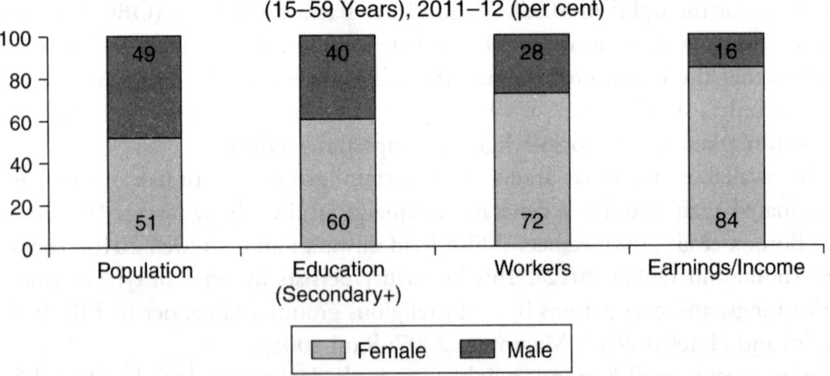

Source: Data calculated from unit-level data CD of NSS 61st and 68th rounds.

The majority of females (70 per cent) are still engaged in casual work, while their share in regular jobs increased from 22 per cent in 2004–05 to 30 per cent in 2011–12. In addition, the share of females (37 per cent) in regular and better-paid government/public-sector jobs increased marginally, by 1 percentage point, which is higher than that of their male counterparts (29 per cent). This confirms that female employment conditions have been improving over the years in the Indian labour market (ILER 2014; Rustagi and Mehta 2013).

The real salary/wages of both regular and casual female workers, as well as those of males, increased from 2004–05 to 2011–12 (Figure 13.2). It increased more for females than for males, narrowing the gender wage-gap over the years. However, the wages/salaries of regular and casual female workers are still 27 per cent and 32 per cent less than that of males. This raises the question: Are females more involved in low-paid occupations and discriminated against in the labour market?

FIGURE 13.2: Average Daily Earning by Gender for Regular and Casual Workers, 2011–12 (15–59 years, in rupees and at constant 2011 prices)

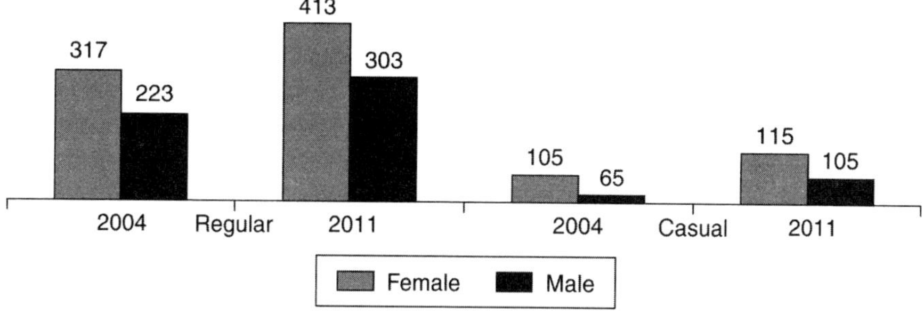

Source: Data calculated from unit-level data CD of NSS 61st and 68th rounds.

The occupational distribution of regular workers by gender confirms that females are relatively more involved in low-paid and less-skilled jobs, such as elementary occupations (domestic helpers, cleaners, street vendors and garbage collectors), services (personal care, housekeeping and salespersons) and office and customer service clerks (Table 13.1).[1] Yet, a substantial proportion of females have also moved to technical (computer professionals) and financial services jobs over the years, which are skilled and better paid (Papola 2012). These jobs are limited to women who are highly educated or skilled.

TABLE 13.1: Occupational Distribution of Regular Workers by Gender (15–59 Years), 2011–12

Occupation	*Workers' Share/Daily Earning (in Rs)*		
	Male	*Female*	*Total*
Senior officials, corporate and general managers and legislators	5 (1,057)	2 (1,000)	4 (1,051)
Professionals in teaching, life science, engineering, health and others	10 (809)	17 (594)	12 (747)
Technicians and associate professionals in teaching, life science, engineering, health and others	11 (554)	23 (341)	14 (482)
Office and customer service clerks	10 (460)	9 (402)	10 (450)
Service workers and shop and market sales workers	16 (285)	14 (147)	16 (260)

(Contd)

Table 13.1 (Contd)

Occupation	Workers' Share/Daily Earning (in Rs)		
	Male	Female	Total
Skilled agricultural and fishery workers	1 (256)	0 (104)	1 (233)
Craft and related trades workers	16 (273)	6 (148)	14 (262)
Plant and machine operators and assemblers	18 (277)	3 (131)	15 (272)
Elementary occupations	12 (217)	24 (113)	14 (183)
Total	100 (413)	100 (303)	100 (392)

Note: Per day salary or earnings are given in brackets.
Source: Data calculated from unit-level data CD of NSS 61st and 68th rounds.

Socio-religious Group-based Inequality

Among socio-religious groups, OBCs are the largest among the working-age population, followed by UCs, SCs, Muslims, STs and other religious groups. Poor human capital endowment among marginalised socio-religious groups is also reflected in their education up to the secondary level and above (Figure 13.3). However, participation in employment shows a reverse pattern, with a higher share of workers from marginalised socio-religious groups. These people cannot afford to remain unemployed and are compelled to work in low-paid informal jobs (World Bank 2011). As a result, their low share in total earnings further increases inequality in socio-religious terms in the labour market.

FIGURE 13.3: Share in Total Population, Employment and Earnings by Socio-religious Groups (15–59 Years), 2011–12

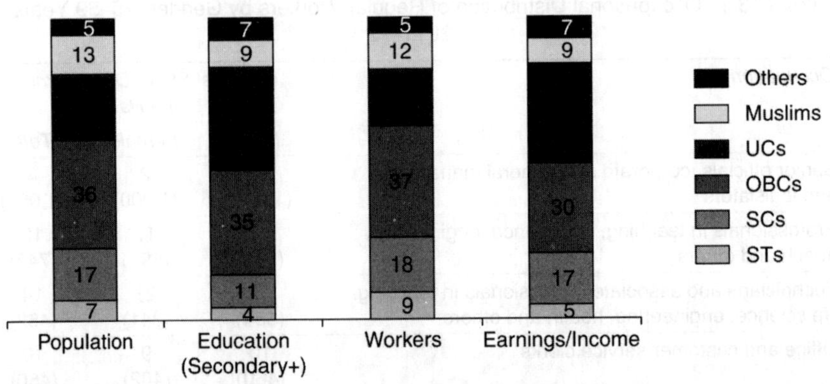

Source: Data calculated from unit-level data CD of NSS 61st and 68th rounds.

The status of employment shows that marginalised socio-religious groups are largely engaged in casual jobs. They do not have any guarantee of work and suffer from uncertainty about earnings (Figure 13.4: 58). Since total earnings depend both on rate of wages and job availability, those with casual jobs earn much less, because jobs are not available for a major part of the week/month/year. This indicates that the predominance of casual workers with no regular work among marginalised socio-religious groups is one of the main reasons for the existing inequality in earnings. As inequality in the labour market leads to disparities in capability formation and ownership of assets, most SCs/STs, OBCs and Muslims are unable to share in the country's growing economic affluence and risk being increasingly marginalised (Mazumdar and Sarkar 2008).

FIGURE 13.4: Distribution of Workers by Status of Employment and Socio-religious Groups (15–59 Years), 2004–05 and 2011–12

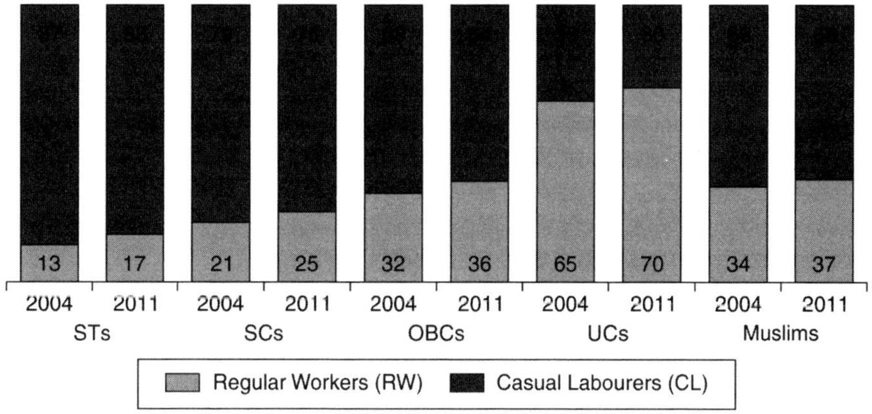

Note: RW-Regular workers; CL-Casual labourers.

Source: Data calculated from unit-level data CD of NSS 61st and 68th rounds.

The low earnings of marginalised socio-religious groups are an outcome of their relatively low average daily earnings (Figure 13.5). Their daily earnings in regular work have increased over the years, but with widening gaps across socio-religious groups. However, the average wage of casual workers is far lower than that of regular workers and there is no visible difference across socio-religious groups. Hence, the inequality analysis is based only on regular workers.

The occupational distribution by socio-religious groups, in Table 13.2, presents a very skewed picture. Marginalised socio-religious groups are more involved in services and elementary occupations, such as personal care, street vending, housekeeping and sales, which require less skill and are low-paid. The services occupations include hairdressers, barbers, sweepers, cleaners and related workers, launderers, dry-cleaners and those ironing clothes. Their per-day earnings confirm that these occupations are low-paid. This supports the hypothesis that people from the Muslim, SC and ST communities are still restricted to menial, low-paying and often socially stigmatised occupations, while upper-caste groups are concentrated in the more preferred occupations (World Bank 2011).

FIGURE 13.5: Average Daily Earning by Socio-religious Groups for Regular and Casual Workers, 2011–12 (15–59 years, in rupees, and at constant 2011–12 prices)

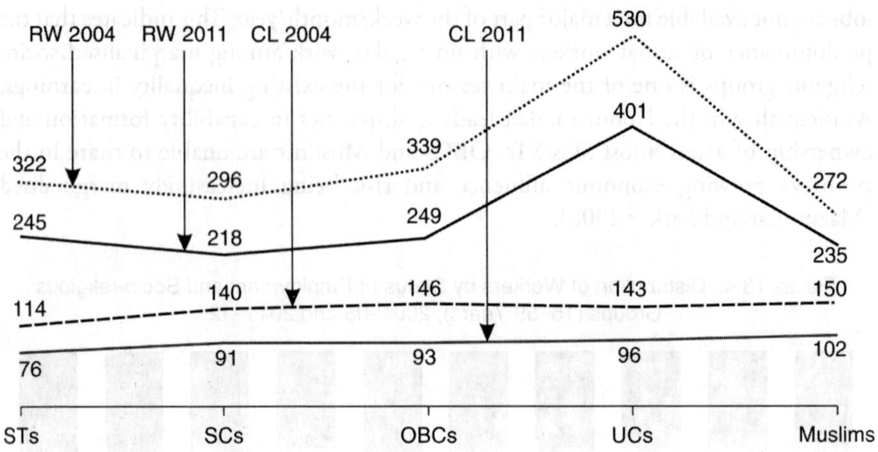

Note: RW-Regular workers; CL-Casual labourers.
Source: Data calculated from unit-level data CD of NSS 61st and 68th rounds.

TABLE 13.2: Occupational Distribution of Regular Workers by Socio-religious Groups (15–59 Years), 2011–12

	STs	*SCs*	*OBCs*	*UCs*	*Muslims*	*Total*
Senior officials, corporate and general managers and legislators	2 (1,182)	2 (641)	3 (726)	8 (1,272)	2 (811)	4 (1,051)
Professionals in teaching, life sciences, engineering, health and others	7 (610)	7 (587)	11 (658)	16 (881)	8 (528)	12 (747)
Technicians and associate professionals in teaching, life sciences, engineering, health	16 (460)	11 (430)	13 (425)	15 (573)	11 (382)	14 (482)
Office and customer service clerks	10 (480)	9 (407)	10 (400)	13 (502)	5 (400)	10 (450)
Service workers and shop and market sales workers	19 (254)	15 (231)	17 (238)	14 (314)	16 (205)	16 (260)
Skilled agricultural and fishery workers	1 (146)	1 (251)	1 (199)	0 (286)	0 (339)	1 (233)
Craft and related trades workers	10 (260)	14 (255)	16 (255)	11 (329)	24 (189)	14 (262)
Plant and machine operators and assemblers	14 (229)	16 (252)	16 (259)	14 (312)	21 (240)	15 (272)
Elementary occupations	20 (147)	25 (182)	13 (177)	9 (199)	13 (182)	14 (183)
Total	(326)	(296)	(337)	(531)	(273)	(392)

Note: Salary/earnings are given in brackets.
Source: Data calculated from unit-level data CD of NSS 61st and 68th rounds.

Whether the government's affirmative actions have benefitted SCs, STs and OBCs can be seen in their rising share in government/public-sector jobs (Figure 13.6). The share in government/public-sector jobs of SCs, STs, and OBCs is almost equal or more than UCs but Muslims, who are not covered under the reservation policy, are an exception.

FIGURE 13.6: Distribution of Workers by Status of Employment and Socio-religious Groups (15–59 Years), 2004–05 and 2011–12

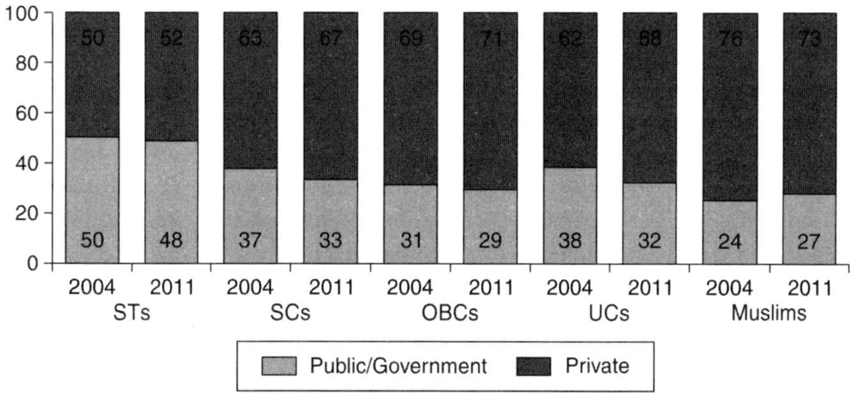

Source: Data calculated from unit-level data CD of NSS 61st and 68th rounds.

However, these groups are vastly overrepresented in the least-skilled occupational categories in government/public-sector jobs. Some studies show that more than 60 per cent of the sweepers in central government ministries were SCs (Desai and Dubey 2011). Some other work also suggests that there is subtle stereotyping in private-sector hiring, with marginalised socio-religious groups facing discrimination in getting past screening questions, such as those on family background, that are asked by prospective employers (Thorat and Attewell 2007). Das and Dutta (2008) propose the notion of glass walls, whereby occupationally slotted socio-groups cannot leave their traditional trades or jobs. They tend to cluster around occupations, whether by choice or compulsion.

Although the reservation policy has benefitted some marginalised socio-religious groups, many of these people are in low-paid and unskilled jobs. The question that arises then is: Has this has resulted in a rise in income inequality or a reduction of it?

INCOME INEQUALITY

Overall income inequality by the Gini coefficient declined from 2004 to 2011, but inequality by earnings of regular workers remained almost stable (Table 13.3: 59). It is noted that inequality in regular workers' earnings in the lower part of the earnings distribution, captured by GE(0) showed a decline, but it increased in the upper part, captured by GE(2), in between 2004–05 and 2011–12.

TABLE 13.3: Income Inequality Overall and Regular Workers (15–59 Years), 2004–05 and 2011–12

	2004				*2011*			
	Gini	*GE(0)*	*GE(1)*	*GE(2)*	*Gini*	*GE(0)*	*GE(1)*	*GE(2)*
Overall	0.55	0.52	0.57	0.98	0.50	0.43	0.48	0.83
Regular workers earnings	0.48	0.43	0.40	0.53	0.48	0.41	0.40	0.55

Note: GE classes of measurements are generalised entropy measures. GE(0) gives more weights to the lower tail of the income distribution, GE(1) gives equal weights and GE(2) gives more weights to the upper tail of income distribution.

Source: Data calculated from unit-level data CD of NSS 61st and 68th rounds.

Income inequality among genders and socio-religious groups also shows a contrasting trend between 2004–05 and 2011–12, at the lower and upper distributions (Table 13.4).[2] At the upper income distribution, the concentration of male and UCs has increased more than the marginalised groups—females, Muslims and SCs/STs. This phenomenon is further examined by the Kernel Density Function (KDF) of income distribution over the years.[3]

TABLE 13.4: Income Inequality by Gender and Socio-religious Groups (15–59 Years), 2004–05 and 2011–12

		GE(0)	*GE(1)*	*GE(2)*
Gender	2004	0.42	0.39	0.52
	2011	0.41	0.40	0.55
Socio-religious group	2004	0.40	0.37	0.50
	2011	0.38	0.37	0.52

Source: Data calculated from unit-level data CD of NSS 61st and 68th rounds.

The KDF graph shows that workers belonging to the marginalised groups, represented as excluded groups (EG),[4] are more concentrated at lower levels of income and other groups, represented as included groups (IG), are concentrated at middle and higher levels of income (Figures 13.7a and 13.7b). The plot largely confirms that excluded groups are less likely to hold better-paying jobs, as the IG lie to the right of the income distribution of the EG. In particular, spikes at the right side of income distribution for females indicate their rising presence in middle and top-level jobs.

An important aspect of income inequality has been a sharp rise in the salaries/earnings of regular workers. A rise is seen with each higher level of education and a steeper increase is observed after the middle level, with the highest for graduates and above (ILER 2014; Sarkar and Mehta 2010). In particular, the salary/wage gap of males and females widened after the middle level, indicating greater gender inequality at higher educational levels in the labour market. A similar pattern was also observed in the case of socio-religious groups. The inequality generated by the discrimination of marginalised groups in the labour market is reflected in the

FIGURE 13.7a: Kernel Density Graph of Weekly Earning of Regular Workers by Gender

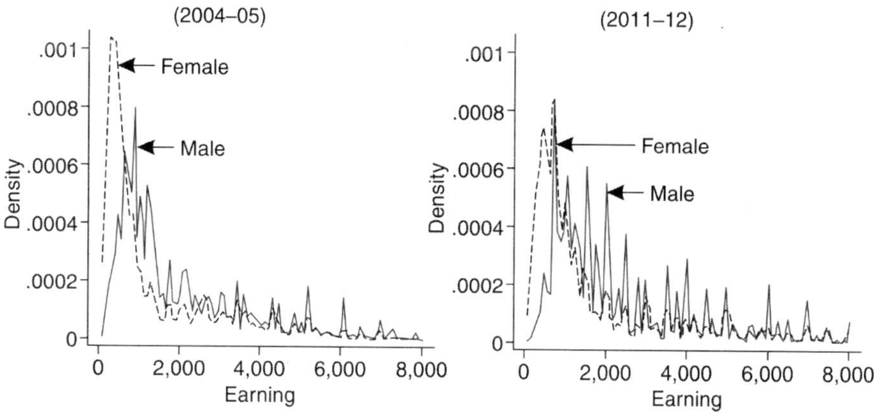

FIGURE 13.7b: Kernel Density Graph of Weekly Earning of Regular Workers by Socio-religious Groups

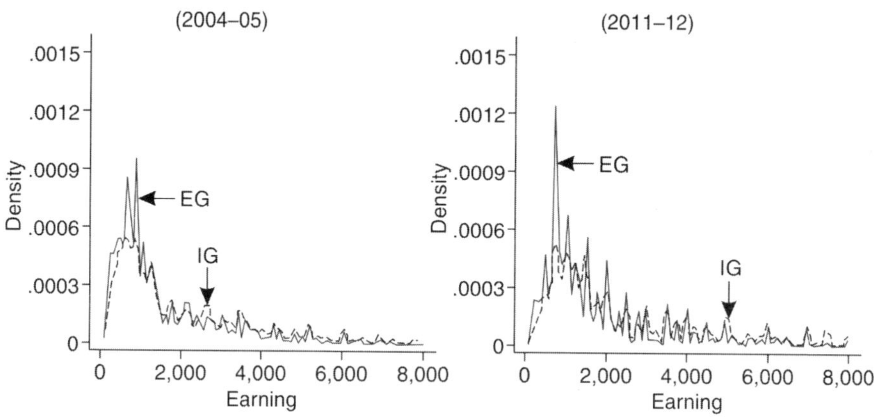

Source: Data calculated from unit-level data CD of NSS 61st and 68th rounds.

significantly lower per-day salary/wage for female graduates (Rs 552 per day) than that for males (Rs 737 per day) with similar qualifications, in 2012–13.

Decomposition Analysis

Apart from gender and socio-religious groups of workers, education or skill level, status of employment, settlement or sector (rural or urban), industry and age (experience) contribute to income inequality. To understand the contribution of each of these attributes, a decomposition analysis has been done by using the Fields approach.[5] Figure 13.8 (60) presents the decomposition of factors (excluding residuals) that contribute to income inequality. The four main factors that contribute to income inequality are educational or skill level, status of work (regular or casual), gender and age or work experience.

FIGURE 13.8: Contribution of Various Factors to Income Inequality

Factor	2004	2011
Status	24	21
Industry	16	6
Education	34	46
Socio-religious Group	3	3
Age	8	9
Gender	11	10
Sector	3	4

Source: Data calculated from unit-level data CD of NSS 61st and 68th rounds.

As discussed earlier, the returns increase with level of qualification and this has been increasing over the years, indicating the rising importance of education in earnings. The second factor, status of employment, also plays an important role, as regular workers are paid for all days in a week whether they work or are on leave, while casual workers are paid only for the days they actually work. The third factor is gender as female, and they are still involved largely in low-skilled and low-paid jobs, but its contribution has been declining over the years due to their rising participation in skilled technical and financial jobs. The important fourth factor, years of experience, also accounts for income inequality and has increased over the years. However, the contribution of socio-religious factors is least in earning inequality, which may possibly be due to two factors—one, the continued concentration of marginalised socio-religious groups in low-paid and low-skilled jobs, and two, low educational levels among these groups.

CONCLUSIONS

The analysis showed rising inequality in the labour market, with widening differences between marginalised groups and others. These marginalised groups earned less in similar type of jobs compared to others and are mostly involved in casual work. They are involved more in low-paid and menial occupations. Over the years, the female presence in high-skilled and better-paid jobs has improved, while the concentration of SCs/STs and Muslims has increased in low-paid jobs.

The main factors that contributed to income inequality in the labour market are educational level, status of work (regular or casual), gender and age or work experience. This is also reflected in the decomposition analysis, where the contribution of gender to income inequality is more than three times that of socio-religious groups. Low educational levels leave socio-religious groups, such as SCs/STs and Muslims, in less skilled and paid occupations even after affirmative policies, while women's participation in better-paid technical and financial jobs is increasing due to rising higher education and skill training among them (Papola 2012).

It is necessary to make marginalised groups employable by making education up to the secondary level universal, so that they can later acquire higher education or skills training. This will help them be employed in better-paid jobs in the formal sector. The increasing availability of corporate social responsibility (CSR) funds could be taken advantage of to lend a helping hand to the marginalised sections, by providing them with relevant skills and employment. If not, the vicious cycle of low human capital and greater participation in employment with less earnings will persist among them for generations to come.

Notes

1. The wages of casual workers are generally low and occupational differences in wages are not much visible. Therefore, only regular workers in relatively better quality jobs with higher payment are analysed in detail.
2. Here, weekly earnings of the regular workers have been taken as a proxy for income.
3. This type of graph gives a visual idea about the nature of inequality. The KDF distribution may be viewed as histograms that have been smoothened to iron out minor irregularity in the observed data (Deaton 1997) and it draws the eye to the essential features of the distribution.
4. For analysis and graphical representation, socio-religious groups are divided into two groups: excluded (SCs, STs, OBCs and Muslims) and included groups (IG or UCs).
5. Fields (2003) developed a new approach that considers, simultaneously, the impact of several characteristics of earnings and allows distinguishing the contribution of each of these characteristics. The approach is useful, as it helps to know the contribution of various factors, including categorical factors that enter as a string of dummy variables (Rani 2008).

References

Atkinson, A. B. 1998. 'Social Exclusion, Poverty and Unemployment'. In A. B. Atkinson and J. Hills, eds, *Exclusion, Employment and Opportunity (CASE Paper 4)*, 1–20. London, LSE: Centre for Analysis of Social Exclusion.

Borooah, V. K., A. Dubey, and S. Iyer. 2005. 'Has Job Reservation Been Effective? Caste, Religion, and Economic Status in India', unpublished manuscript, University of Ulster, Northern Ireland, cited from Takahiro, 2007.

Das, M. B., and P. Dutta. 2008. 'Does Caste Matter for Wages in the Indian Labour Market? Caste Pay Gaps in India,' paper presented at Third Institute for the Study of Labour-World Bank Conference on Employment and Development, Rabat, Morocco, 5–6 May.

Deaton, Angus. 1997. *The Analysis of Household Surveys: A Microeconometric Approach to Development Policy*. Washington: Johns Hopkins Press, World Bank.

Desai, Sonalde, and Amaresh Dubey. 2011. 'Caste in 21st Century India: Competing Narratives'. *Economic & Political Weekly* 46 (11): 40–49.

ILER. 2014. 'Workers in the Era of Globalisation', India Employment Report, Institute for Human Development and Academic Foundation, New Delhi.

Kulkarni, S., and N. Hatekar. 2013. 'Stereotypical Occupational Segregation and Gender Inequality: An Experimental Study'. *Economic & Political Weekly* 48 (32): 112–20.

Fields, G. S. 2003. 'Accounting for Income Inequality and Its Changes: A New Method with Application to the Distribution of Earnings in the United States'. *Research in Labour Economics* 22 (1):1–38.

Kabeer, N. 2000. *The Power to Choose: Bangladeshi Women and Labour Market Decisions in London and Dhaka*. London: Verso.

Madheswaran, S., and Paul Attewell. 2010. 'Wage and Job Discrimination in Indian Urban Labour Market'. In *Blocked by Caste: Economic Discrimination in Modern India*, eds, Sukhadeo Thorat and Katherine S Newman. New Delhi: Oxford University Press.

Majumdar, R. 2007. 'Earning Differentials Across Social Groups: Evidences from India', MPRA paper 12811, University Library of Munich, Germany.

Mazumdar, D., and S. Sarkar. 2008. 'Globalisation, Labour Markets and Inequality in India'. London: Routledge.

Papola, T. S. 2012. 'Social Exclusion and Discrimination in the Labour Market', Working Paper No. 2012/04, New Delhi: Institute for Studies in Industrial Development.

Rani, U. 2008. 'Impact of Changing Work Pattern on Income Inequality,' Discussion Paper No. 193/2008, International Institute of Labour Studies, Geneva.

Rutagi, P. 2005. Understanding Gender Inequality in Wages and Income in India'. *Indian Journal of Labour Economics* 48 (2): 319–34.

Rustagi, P., and B. S. Mehta. 2013. 'Pattern and Structure of Women's Work Participation in India: Changes over time with Globalisation', unpublished paper prepared for ICSSR Research Programme on Globalisation and Labour, Institute for Human Development, New Delhi.

Sarkar, S., and B. S. Mehta. 2010. 'Income Inequality in India: Pre- and Post-reform Periods'. *Economic & Political Weekly* 45 (37): 45–55.

Thorat, S., and P. Attewell. 2007. 'The Legacy of Social Exclusion: A Corresponding Study of Job Discrimination in India'. *Economic & Political Weekly* 42 (1): 4141–45.

Thorat, S. 2008. 'Labour Market Discrimination: Concept, Forms and Remedies in Indian Situation'. *Indian Journal of Labour Economics* 51 (1): 31–52.

Thorat, S., and A. Dubey 2012. 'Has Growth been Socially Inclusive during 1993–94 and 2009–10?'. *Economic & Political Weekly* 47 (10): 43–54.

World Bank. 2011. 'Poverty and Social Exclusion in India'. Washington DC: The World Bank.

14

Globalisation, Higher Education and Gender

*Changing Subject Choices of Indian Women Students**

Karuna Chanana

The changes spearheaded by economic liberalisation and globalisation[1] are having an impact on higher education (HE) worldwide. The relationships between the governments and universities are changing all over the world. Some of the features that characterise this change are: reduction in government funding and the pressure on the universities to raise funds from the industry, the market and the individual student (Bachhi 2001; Clarke 1996; Marginson 2000); universities have been forced to downsize and the language of efficiency and accountability associated with corporate management is being used to run and evaluate universities. All these changes have an impact on pursuing equity issues within the universities because 'a commitment to equity and a commitment to cost-cutting' (Bachhi 2001: 120) may not go hand-in-hand. Several scholars have debated the issue of compatibility between managerialism and equity (Sawer 1989; Yeatman 1990).

There is also a conflict between the traditional image of the university as the place where the pursuit of disinterested scholarship was the main aim and the new image of a corporate university. This conflict is not new. The emerging democracies in industrialising societies in the twentieth century have always expected that universities will reflect the broader social issues and concerns, instead of being just the creators of knowledge. However, the recent shift to a corporate profit culture is in sharp contrast to the image of the university as an agent of social change and social mobility.

* Previously published in *Economic and Political Weekly* 42 (7), 17 February 2007: 590–598. This chapter is adapted from a paper presented at the UNESCO Colloquium on Globalisation, Higher Education and Knowledge, in December 2004, at Paris.

Some of the critical implications of globalisation are: the change in the stratification of disciplines/subjects between arts and science, the expansion of the applied/professional subjects, the private sector as a critical player and shifts in the subject choices of women. Moreover, globalisation is accompanied by an increased focus on techno-sciences which have gendered implications, because women are less likely to be involved in those areas which are frontrunners in the new economy and the market; they are also likely to be at the lower levels; they may also be unable to adjust to the time-space compression that IT demands or fosters (Harvey 1993; Slaughter and Leslie 1997).

The social movements which represent civil society have been questioning the dominance of technology in higher education. They also question the formulation of research agendas around the new technologies and the marginalisation of social issues and the social policy research areas in which the women academic staff and students are generally disproportionately located (McKinnon and Brooks 2001). Do women have the time to join the race for procuring funds for research or for running the departments? How would they fare in the race for promotions if they are linked to funds? Further, wealth creation replaces the traditional concern with the liberal education of undergraduates (Sassen 1998: 37), a majority of whom are women. What are its implications for women, who are part of the gendered system of higher education? (Brooks and Mackinnon 2001; Chanana 2003).

Additionally, women academics involved in feminist critiques are generally located in the humanities and the social sciences and are likely to be affected by the homogenisation of research activity within and across disciplines, which according to Marginson is an effort 'to make the butterflies fly in formation' (2000: 192). According to McKinnon and Brooks, the feminist scholars would wish to disrupt these formations and would like to fly in quite contrary ways (2001: 6).

Globalisation has changed the world into a global market and the direct nexus between the industry, corporate world and higher education has brought a transformation in the skills needed for jobs. There has been a corresponding change in the boundaries between arts and science subjects. While the stratification between arts and science has been further reinforced, the sciences are sub-divided into applied/emerging versus pure sciences. Natural/pure sciences are relegated to a lower position than the applied sciences and professional skills. Again, academic courses related to biosciences, such as molecular biology, microbiology, biochemistry and biophysics, are preferred over biology, physics and chemistry. In this hierarchy of disciplines, new disciplines like management, media and mass communication, fashion technology, etc., have also taken their place towards the higher end of the spectrum. The private institutions are very quick to respond to these demands.

Moreover, the new developments have led to the devaluation of subjects in the humanities and social sciences. Women used to enter colleges and universities mainly in general education or in the arts, humanities and social sciences till the early 1990s—a trend which is continuing. However, they are also entering the professional subjects offered in the public institutions. Simultaneously, they are entering the private self-financing institutions for pursuing their studies in both the new and the traditionally labelled 'masculine' disciplines. The gendered impact of these changes requires attention if the goal of social change and gender equity has to be achieved. The study of gender is, in effect, the study of inequality (Thomas 1990: 2) and social differences are critical to the understanding of women's disciplinary choices.

Women's Subject Choices

Family and educational institutions are the sites of social reproduction and they communicate the binary opposition of femininity and masculinity to little girls and boys through socialisation. Thus, similar ideologies permeate the socialisation process in the family and the home and also underlie the classroom processes, educational structures and organisations.

Feminist sociological perspectives on women's educational experience have highlighted several dimensions, such as their under-participation, underachievement and underrepresentation (Megarry 1984); sex role socialisation and stereotyping of the 'feminine' role and its impact upon the girls' educational situation and the segregation of girls into humanities and arts and boys into science at the school level. Sociologists contended that this imbalance in subjects had to be redressed to remove inequality (Harding 1986; Kelly 1981; Whyte 1986). It was also emphasised that not only should more girls enrol in science in school, but they must also do well. The argument is that girls tend to opt for specific subjects because of their socialisation, which relates feminine roles to feminine subjects. In India, the decision to make science compulsory up to Class X ensured that all girls would read science.

Additionally, subject choice and its relationship to gender in higher education also received attention (Acker 1994; Becher 1981; Harding 1986; Hudson 1972; Keller 1983; Thomas 1990). It is argued that the clustering of women in specific subjects leads to their occupational segregation later in life (Deem 1978; Sharpe 1976; Wolpe 1978). According to Becher (1981), 'academic subjects are not neutral, they are cultures, each with its own way of perceiving and interpreting the world' (quoted in Thomas 1990: 7).

Much has been written on the patriarchal imprint on the subject choices of women in higher education and on the feminine and masculine dichotomy of subjects (Acker 1994; Thomas 1990). Since masculinity and femininity are social constructions (Kellner 1997), the underlying assumptions about subject or disciplinary choices have to be uncovered along with their close connection to women's place in society (Harding 1986). Thomas argues that it is a reflection of the balance of power between the sexes. She mentions three important assumptions (Thomas 1990: 5). The first is that of the demarcation between science and arts or physics and biology. In other words, what is the meaning of science and how are science subjects demarcated? The second relates to the belief that science is more difficult than the humanities and that within science, physics is the most difficult. Why this belief, when the best student in physics may falter in humanities and vice versa? The third assumption relates to the belief that science is good. Thomas says that this is the most debatable and important assumption. This has been falsified recently, in view of the evidence that science has been used for warfare and armaments (Rose 1986). According to Millett (1983), this assumption perpetuates male dominance in science.

Therefore, one should try to understand why certain subjects have become associated with women and others with men. Why is it prestigious to take up science and mathematics? Why are science and mathematics difficult for girls? Moreover, subjects are considered masculine not because of the numerical preponderance of men, rather, it is the other way around, i.e., science is viewed as masculine and therefore more men take it. 'To both scientists and their public, scientific thought is male thought, in ways that painting and writing—also performed largely by men—never have been' (Keller 1983: 188).

CHANGING CONTEXT

There are several dimensions of changes that have taken place since 1991, the most important of which is in the position of the government, reflected in the reduction of state funding to higher education, entry of private players, the increase in the individual cost of higher education, i.e. the self-financing of higher education, the entry of foreign institutions, the large number of Indian students who go abroad on self-financing basis, change in the academic environment of higher educational institutions, impact on the service conditions of teachers, the parameters of efficiency and accountability being transferred from management discourse to educational discourse, the overwhelming dominance of professional and techno-science subjects, etc. All of them need to be looked at and analysed from a gender perspective. However, the expansion of professional education and the changes in disciplinary choices is the most visible.

An attempt is made here to see the influence of the so-called economic liberalisation and the market demand on women's access to higher education and their choices of subjects. There is a perceptible change in the choices of women, especially in the metropolitan cities, where they are enrolling in the new 'professional' courses, such as management, fashion designing, computers, human resource management, etc. Therefore, the question is: How far are these trends reflected at the macro-level and do we have sufficient data to demonstrate the trends?

This chapter seeks to demonstrate the latest trends in the enrolment of women in different faculties and subjects.[2] It is a follow-up of a paper published in 2001, which tried to show the trends in the enrolment of women by discipline. It had also indicated some of the changes in the disciplinary choices of women and tried to infer the reasons for the change. In addition, the data on marginal groups, such as the Dalits and tribals, are also given. Women from these groups suffer the multiple handicaps of gender, caste, tribe and rurality, because these are interlocking systems of domination (Hooks 1989: 22). The regional disparities, too, are as crucial as those of the general population and the marginal groups. Therefore, attention is also given to this dimension, mainly to reflect on trends in the different states of India.

While the disciplinary choices are the main focus, the participation of women at different levels, namely undergraduate, postgraduate and research levels, has also been highlighted. This way, it is possible to focus not only on women's entry into the system of higher education, but also to see what happens to them after they enter the system. What are the chances of their staying on and progressing from one stage of higher education to another?

Access and Equality

Policy Framework

Higher education was entrusted with the responsibility of protecting the constitutional provisions for positive discrimination. The commitment to broaden the student base was reflected in the financial incentives provided to Dalit/Adivasi students, namely hostels, post-matric (high school) scholarships, etc. In addition, special cells/administrative units were set up in universities to monitor the entry/progress of students, staff and teachers from these groups. In the course of time and as a result of political interventions, the reserved categories have been expanded to include people with disabilities and OBCs (Other Backward Classes). There is no gender-based positive discrimination in education or employment, although some provinces or institutions may have made a separate provision for them.[3]

Higher education has occupied a dominant position in independent India, since it was perceived as a promoter of economic growth, technological development and also as an instrument of equal opportunity and upward social mobility. Various commissions and committees have deliberated on its criticality to the social and economic development of the country. Moreover, the expansion of higher education before 1991 also coincided with the centrality of equal opportunities discourses and policies in the public-sector institutions, which provided education and employment. This centrality of equal opportunity reflected the social importance of higher education and the concern of the Indian government to ensure the participation of first-generation students. It was also due to the increasing importance of social justice around the issues of caste, tribe, class and gender.

Moreover, reform in the social situation of women was central to the movement for independence and, therefore, the education of women was included in the Five-Year Plans. The Report of the Committee on the Education of Women, 1959 and the Report of the Committee on the Status of Women, 1974,[4] provided a broader perspective, which led to a shift from a welfare approach to making women active partners in the development process. Later, the National Policy of Education, 1986 underscored the role of education as an instrument of women's equality and empowerment, followed by the National Perspective Plan, 1988–2000. Thus, there has been a careful articulation of education-for-equality for women, which is reflected in the educational policy discourse in post-Independence India.

Due to the twin concern with equality and excellence, higher education in India was fully supported by the federal and provincial governments.[5] However, in spite of very low fees and 'reservations', or the affirmative action, the connection between socio-economic status, merit and elite institutions, the women and the disadvantaged groups have either been excluded from or had a negligible representation in the best public institutions.

However, since 1991, the policies of the government have dramatically changed the seemingly privileged position of higher education. The government began to talk of removing public support to higher education and to make it self-financing while privatising it. Higher education has also become a non-merit good. Private institutions are permitted to be set up on a liberal scale, without a clearly defined policy to regulate the private institutions (Anandkrishnan 2004: 210). The link of universities with the private sector is not new in India, nor is the nexus between higher education and the economy. What is disconcerting is the nature and speed of change, the motives of those who are establishing the private institutions, the ad hoc approach to the new developments and the lack of a considered response from the Indian government.

The policies of the Indian government since 1991 have involved restructuring of the economic institutions and the educational system. At that time, the existing system had become too large and ineffective. It was characterised by a few high-quality institutions at the top, while the majority at the bottom were of poor and indifferent quality. It was also not expanding rapidly enough to meet the rising social demand for higher education, especially of the skill-oriented professional education. The government allowed the private sector to establish fee-paying and self-financing institutions, to meet the increasing demand for higher education and for specific courses.

Prior to this, in the 1980s, the two provinces of Karnataka and Maharashtra allowed the establishment of colleges of engineering and medical education, under the direct political patronage of the state politicians. These colleges filled the unfilled demand for engineers and doctors, and students from all over India flocked to them. While they were affiliated to the universities of the region and were regulated by their statutes, they were also notorious for charging a large amount of money, over and above the tuition fees, etc., fixed by the universities/state governments, for admission. They are widely known as the 'capitation fee' colleges. They remained limited in number and, therefore, did not impact on the system as a whole, in contrast to current developments.

The private institutions levy hefty tuition fees with or without the approval of the state governments. The state governments and the judiciary have had to intervene in the matter of fixation of fees. Increasingly, these colleges have sought the status of deemed universities in order to be autonomous in matters of curriculum and examination/evaluation. Along with the financial exploitation of the students, the quality of their education is also suspect and so are their motivations (Anandkrishnan 2004). Another limitation is that since private institutions get land at subsidised rates, they are expected to reserve seats for the SC/STs, but there is little monitoring of these measures and no statistics are publicly known about reservations.

Simultaneous with the expansion of the private sector, the restructuring of public universities in the post-1991 phase has effectively downsized them, which is likely to exacerbate gender inequalities (Allen and Castleman 2001: 151). The state universities are affected radically by these changes, which are reflecting on the type of academic programmes and subjects introduced by them. In other words, subjects that have a market demand are being introduced. The direct effects of these, coupled with scarce public funding, are reverberating through the public universities. The new programmes in most public universities are also self-funded by the students, thereby increasing the individual cost of education. In fact, since the provincial governments are not increasing funding according to the rise in the cost of running the universities and also according to the demand for new academic subjects, self-financing courses have become a regular source of income for the universities.

Higher Education System

The Indian higher education system is one of the largest in the world. In 2002–03, there were 300 universities. The enrolment was 92,27,833 (about 7–8 per cent of the relevant age-group). There were 4,36,000 teachers in 2002–03, as against 4,57,000 in 2000–01. Of these, nearly 83 per cent are in the affiliated colleges and 17 per cent in the universities. Gender-wise data is not provided by the UGC. However, MHRD (2001–02) provides information on the women teachers in the 12 open universities, which is 18.4 per cent and 21.5 per cent in the institutions offering correspondence courses.

In 2002–03, there were 15,343 affiliated colleges. Of these, 1,650 (10.75) are exclusively for women students. Although the number has gone up, from 1,600 in 2000–01 to 1,650, the proportion has reduced from 12.7 per cent to 10.75 per cent.

Since 1991, a large number of private colleges are being set up on a self-financing basis and their number has increased rapidly. According to Anandkrishnan, the private technical education system in India is the largest in the world and the growth of higher education in the past 15 years has been mainly in the private sector (2004). They seem to fulfil the demand for undergraduate professional courses in engineering/technology, medicine (including dental education and health sciences), management, computer and IT education, mass-media and communication, teacher education, etc. Most of these are in the southern and south-western states of Karnataka, Andhra Pradesh, Tamil Nadu and Maharashtra. Other provinces are following suit. They are quick to respond to the demand for new programmes, though in a limited number of subjects. As a result, their numbers have increased, so much so that they form a majority of the undergraduate colleges in India. For example, in 2002, of 977 undergraduate engineering colleges, 764 (78.2 per cent); of 1,349 medical colleges, 1,028 (76.2 per cent); of 505 management institutions, 324 (64.2 per cent); of 1,521 teacher education colleges, 1,038 (67.4 per cent) were private (Bhattacharya 2004: 177).

The growth of private education has contributed to the increasing undergraduate enrolment in higher education, mainly in the application-oriented science and professional subjects, which are being offered in the colleges of arts and sciences. In fact, they offer what are known as the emerging application-oriented science and management courses in microbiology, biochemistry, business administration and computers.[6] For example, in Tamil Nadu, the number of self-financing colleges in arts and science has increased from 54 in 1993–94 to 247 in 2000-01, while the government colleges increased only from 56 to 60 and aided colleges from 132 to 133 (Bhattacharya 2004: 218). The proportion of women also increased, from 42.89 per cent to –51.07 per cent in the private colleges during this period.

The self-financing engineering colleges in Tamil Nadu increased from 71 in 1996–97 to 212 in 2001–02, while the number of government (7) and aided (3) remained the same. The enrolment in the private colleges increased from 20,250 to 55,500.

WOMEN IN HIGHER EDUCATION

This section provides the data on enrolment (a) of women and men in higher education, (b) of women across faculties/disciplines or subjects, (c) across levels/stages, viz., undergraduate, graduate/postgraduate and doctoral/research level. It also highlights the difference in their enrolment in general and professional education. The period covered is 1950–51 to 2002–03. For specific examples, statistics of 2001–02 have been used, because of the non-availability of data for the later years. The enrolment statistics for the 1990s are the focus of discussion, while the data for the preceding four decades is used to indicate trends and shifts.

Starting from 1950–51, when the proportion of women was 10.9 per cent, to 40.04 per cent in 2002–03, the increase has been significant. In other words, there were 14 women per 100 men in 1950–51, which increased to 67 in 2002–03. Thus, the proportion of women entering higher education today has increased rapidly from 16,85,926 (32 per cent) in 1991–92 to 40 per cent (36,95,964) of all students in 2002–03 (Table 14.1). There have also been shifts in women's choice of disciplines in higher education. There are also wide disparities in enrolment by region, caste, tribe and gender. These differences have an impact on women from the disadvantaged groups.

TABLE 14.1: Enrolment in Higher Education by Gender

(Numbers and percentage)

Year	*Women*		*Men*		
	Number	*Per Cent*	*Number*	*Per Cent*	*Total*
2002–03	36,95,965	40.05	55,31,868	59.05	92,27,833
1995–96	21,91,138	34.1	42,34,486.00	65.9	64,25,624
1991–92	16,85,926	32.0	35,79,960.00	68.0	52,65,886
1980–81	7,48,525	27.2	20,03,912.00	72.8	27,52,437
1970–71	6,55,822	21.9	23,45,470.00	78.1	30,01,292
1960–61	1,70,455	16.2	8,79,409.00	83.8	10,49,864
1950–51	43,126	10.9	3,53,619.00	89.1	3,96,745

Sources: Karuna Chanana (1993; 2000); UGC, University Development in India: Basic Facts and Figures, 1995–96 to 2000–2001; UGC, *Annual Report 2002–03*.

Enrolment in General and Professional Education

The programmes in higher education are divided into those of general subjects, such as the arts (which include social sciences and humanities) and pure sciences on the one hand and the professional courses such as engineering (which includes architecture), medical science, teacher education, agriculture, law, etc. on the other. They are also divided into masculine and feminine disciplines. For example, arts, social sciences, humanities, and teacher education have been viewed as feminine disciplines. On the other hand, commerce, law and engineering are masculine disciplines. Medical science has not been a masculine discipline in India, unlike in Western countries. In India, as in the rest of South Asia, the practice of female seclusion enjoined the treatment of women patients by women doctors. This necessitated training women doctors, thereby enabling women to enter the medical profession (Chanana 1988).

The proportion of women in some of the masculine disciplines was miniscule soon after Independence and remained so till the 1980s, with the exception of commerce (Chanana 2000). For example, the proportion of women in commerce was 0.5 per cent in 1950–51 and increased to 15.9 per cent in 1980–81. Thereafter, it has been going up steadily and now stands at 36.7 per cent in 2002–03 (Table 14.2). In engineering/technical courses, their proportion was 0.2 per cent in 1950–51; 3.8 per cent in 1980–81; and is now 22.3 per cent. In law, their proportion has increased from 2.1 per cent to 20.8 per cent. In education, women were 32.4 per cent even in 1950–51 and are now 50.6 per cent. In medicine, their proportion was 16.3 per cent in 1950–51 and is now 44.7 per cent. The proportion of women in arts, in 2002–03, was 44.2 and has been increasing steadily since 1970–71. The proportion of men, on the other hand, has decreased gradually during the same period, from 83.9 per cent to 54.6 per cent. In teacher education, another feminine discipline, the proportion of women has gone up from 32.4 to 50.6 per cent.

Science, a masculine discipline, provides an interesting insight into the disciplinary choices of young women and men. For example, in science, the proportion of men, which was around 80–90 per cent till 1980–81, has come down to 59.8 per cent in 2002–03. The differential importance of general science for women and men over time has to be understood as a background to shifts in disciplinary choices in the recent past. For example, the proportion of women in science decreased from 33.3 per cent in 1950–51 to 28.8 per cent 1980–81. This was the period when natural science was at a premium, especially physics and chemistry. Till the 1980s, they were the first choice for men students and while competing with men, women were pushed out. It is also possible that science was not, in any case, the first preference for young women whose parents perceived marriage as a priority over higher education. An undergraduate degree of any kind only helped in the marriage market by raising the social status. A science degree required a longer investment of time and other resources and was, therefore, not desirable. The young women were also socialised to perceive higher education from that viewpoint.

Nowadays, research in natural sciences is not preferred by men, because it does not lead to high-salaried professions. It also requires several more years before a job

Table 14.2: Proportion of Men and Women Students to Total Enrolment by Gender and Discipline/Subject (1950–51 to 2002–03)

Faculties	*1950–51*		*1960–61*		*1970–71*		*1980–81*		*1991–92*		*2000–01*		*2002–03*	
	Women	*Men*	*Women*	*Men*	*Women*	*Men*	*Women*	*Men*	*Women*	*Men*	*Women*	*Men*	*Women*	*Men*
Arts	16.1	83.9	24.6	75.4	31.7	68.3	37.7	62.3	41.8	58.2	44.2	55.8	45.4	56.6
Science	7.1	92.9	10.5	89.5	17.8	82.2	28.8	71.2	32.9	67.1	39.4	60.6	40.2	59.9
Commerce	0.6	99.4	0.9	99.1	3.7	96.3	15.9	84.1	22.1	77.9	36.5	63.5	36.7	63.3
Education	32.4	67.6	32.8	67.2	36.5	63.5	47.3	52.7	50.2	49.8	51.2	48.8	50.6	49.4
Engg/Tech	0.2	99.8	0.9	99.1	1.0	99.0	3.8	96.2	7.6	92.4	21.5	78.5	22.3	77.8
Medicine	16.3	83.7	21.9	78.1	22.8	77.2	24.4	75.6	33.2	66.8	44.0	56.0	44.7	55.3
Law	2.1	97.9	3.0	97.0	3.7	96.3	6.9	93.1	11.0	89.0	20.0	80.0	20.8	79.2
Agriculture	5.8	94.2	7.0	93.0	9.5	90.5	13.6	86.4	7.1	92.9	17.4	82.6	20.2	79.8
Veterinary science*									8.0	92.0	20.9	79.1	16.9	83.2
Others									38.3	61.7	37.7	62.3	37.9	62.2

Note: * Agriculture, veterinary science and others are merged for the years 1950–51 to 1980–81.

Sources: UGC, University Development in India: Consolidated Data Statewise, 1988–89 to 1993–94; UGC, University Development in India: Basic Facts and Figures, 1995–96 to 2000–01.

than an engineering, IT, or management degree. Thus, more women are staying on to do research in natural sciences (Bal 2004: 3653) and to fill up the space created by men. Therefore, the percentage distribution of women and men has almost become equal in the 'sciences' during the last decade.

Prior to the 1990s, education and its linkage to the job market early on in life was only for those men who needed jobs and was certainly not for women. These days, young women and men like to earn as soon as they can, even while in school. The revolution in values cuts across the upper and middle strata, who want to begin earning as soon as possible. The daughters of city-based professional parents, especially if they do not have brothers, have really undergone a sea change in their socialisation. The parents are giving the best education to their daughters and are expecting them to be independent and to pursue careers. No doubt, they are in a minority, especially at the macro level. In this changed situation, the priorities of women have also changed. They too want professional education and are, therefore, entering the so-called masculine disciplines. This point is elaborated in a later section. This can be better understood if one were to look at their percentage distribution in different disciplines.

Percentage Distribution in Disciplines/Subjects

The percentage of women as a proportion of the total enrolment of women in higher education is an interesting dimension. In other words, out of every 100 women students who take admission in higher education, how many enrol for which subjects?

It is noteworthy that fewer women per 100 women in higher education are opting for teacher's education or for medicine. For example, in teacher's education, considered a women's profession, the percentage has decreased from 3.1 per cent in 1950–51 to 1.8 per cent in 2002–03 (Table 14.3). In medicine, too, there is a decline from 5.8 per cent to 3.6 per cent. In commerce, the growth chart is interesting. Their percentage has increased from 0.4 per cent in 1950–51 to 11.8 per cent in 1980–81. In fact, most of the expansion seems to have taken place during the 1970s, a period when it begins to become a step-ladder to management, chartered accountancy, etc. After 1980–81, it grows steadily to 16.5 per cent in 2002–03. In engineering and technology, too, there is a significant increase, from less than 1 per cent in 1950–51 to 4.2 per cent in 2002–03 and in law from 0.7 per cent to 4.2 per cent.

Thus, two simultaneous trends of clustering/concentration and dispersal can be seen in the enrolment of men and women in higher education. During the first three decades, while women tended to be clustered in the general disciplines of arts and sciences (nearly 90 per cent); men's participation was characterised by clustering in both arts and science disciplines, but was also significantly dispersed in others such as commerce, engineering/ technical and law. Lately, however, women's participation too is marked by clustering as well as dispersal.

TABLE 14.3: Percentage Distribution by Discipline and Gender: 1951–2003

Discipline	*1950–51*		*1960–61*		*1970–71*		*1980–81*		*1991–92*		*2002–03*	
	Women	*Men*	*Women*	*Men*	*Women*	*Men*	*Women*	*Men*	*Women*	*Men*	*Women*	*Men*
Arts	67.9	43.2	70.2	41.7	64.3	38.7	56.2	34.6	54.2	35.6	51.1	41.0
Science	21.0	33.4	18.6	30.8	25.7	33.2	20.6	19.0	19.8	19.0	19.9	19.8
Commerce	0.4	9.6	0.5	10.2	1.9	14.1	11.8	23.3	14.6	24.3	16.5	19.0
Education	3.1	0.8	3.7	1.5	3.2	1.5	4.5	1.9	3.7	1.8	1.8	1.2
Engg/Tech	0.04	3.4	0.2	5.1	0.1	3.8	0.7	6.2	1.2	6.7	4.2	9.7
Medicine	5.8	3.6	4.5	3.1	3.4	3.2	3.6	4.2	3.5	3.3	3.6	3.0
Law	0.7	3.8	0.5	3.0	0.4	2.9	1.6	8.1	1.8	6.8	1.7	4.3
Agriculture	1.1	2.2	1.8	4.6	0.9	2.5	1.2	2.8	0.3	1.5	0.3	0.8
Veterinary science*									0.1	0.3	0.1	0.2
Others*									0.8	0.7	0.8	0.9
Total												

Note: * Agriculture, veterinary science and others are merged for the years 1950–51 to 1980–81.

Sources: Karuna Chanana (1993); UGC, University Development in India: Consolidated Data Statewise, 1988–89 to 1993–94.; UGC, University Development in India: Basic Facts and Figures, 1995–96 to 2000–2001.

Enrolment by Level/Stage

Once women enter higher education at the undergraduate level, do they move on the next two levels, namely graduate and research? Table 14.4 shows the distribution of men and women by level/stage of education. In 1991–92, 14,79,231 women were enrolled for undergraduate programmes, which increased to 32,85,544 in 2002–03; 1,69,267 women were enrolled for graduate programmes in 1991–92, as compared to 3,55,893 women in 2002–03; and from 19,894 in 1991–92 to 23,609 in 2002–03, for research programmes. During these years, their proportion also increased from 32.8 per cent to 39.9 per cent in undergraduate programmes; from 34.7 per cent to 42 per cent in graduate level programmes; and from 37.1 per cent to 38 per cent in MPhil and PhD programmes. Their proportion was highest at the graduate level, while their proportion in research programmes marginally declined from 39.2 per cent in 1995–96 to 38 per cent in 2002–03. Until 1950–51, only 20.2 per cent women had enrolled for research degrees, which increased in the next three decades to 8,780 in 1980–81 (Chanana 1993: 12). Their number nearly doubled to 15,018 in 1988–89 and in 2002–03, it stood at 23,609. Now it stands at 23,609 in 2002–03.

Table 14.4: Proportion of Women by Level/Stage

Year	*Undergraduate*	*Graduate*	*Researcher*
2002–03	39.93	42.04	38.5
1996–97	34.1	34.0	39.2
1995–96	34.1	34.0	39.2
1994–95	33.6	35.6	38.5
1993–94	33.02	35.4	36.5
1992–93	32.43	35.63	38.4
1991–92	31.8	34.70	37.1
1980–81	27.2	28.2	27.3
1970–71	21.6	25.8	20.7
1960–61	16.2	17.3	15.6
1950–51	10.8	12.1	14.1

Sources: UGC *Annual Reports* for relevant years.

The slightly higher percentage at the graduate level indicates that more women are transiting from undergraduate to the next higher-level courses. It may also have something to do with the popularity of Masters programmes in management, computers and IT, media, advertising, fashion technology, etc., which are popular in the metropolitan cities. However, in the absence of statistics, it is difficult to come to a conclusion.

REGIONAL DISPARITIES

The gendered impact of social, cultural and economic disparities across states (Chanana 1988) has been referred to, time and again, by the official committees and commissions, as well as by the social scientists. These trends are continuing and the enrolment of women varies from province to province. Kerala has had the highest enrolment and even now, it is 60 per cent, i.e., there are more women than men in higher education. The other states where they are more than half the proportion are: Goa (58.5), Punjab (52.68), Andaman and Nicobar Islands (57.77), Chandigarh (55.5) and Pondicherry (52.60). Those with the lowest proportion are also the most backward; namely, Bihar (23.81), Jharkhand (30.40), Chhattisgarh (36.70), Rajasthan (32.33), Uttar Pradesh (38.40) and Madhya Pradesh (37.20). In these provinces, the proportion is less than the all-India average of 40.05 per cent.

The link between state and professional education is very close. For example, variations can also be seen in the growth of engineering and technology courses in the four southern states. In 1991, out of 70,481 students in degree courses, 4,419 (6.3 per cent) were women, which had increased from 3.9 per cent in 1983. A majority of women students were from the southern (1,989) and western (608) regions (Chanana 2000: 1016–17). Even in 2001–02, the enrolment in undergraduate degree programmes BE/BSc (Engg)/BArch was highest in the four states in which the maximum number of private colleges have been established. The number of women is also the highest in states such as Maharashtra (24,710), Karnataka (22,287), Andhra Pradesh (22,615) and Tamil Nadu (10,722), which works out to 20.6, 20.1, 30.4 and 18.7 per cent of total enrolment in the subject.

Similarly, in medicine, Maharashtra has the highest enrolment, followed by Tamil Nadu, Andhra Pradesh, Gujarat and Karnataka. Women's enrolment is also high in these provinces. In Maharashtra, the proportion of women is 48.0 per cent (17,471). It is 38.4 per cent (6,206) in Tamil Nadu, 46.3 (6,066) in Andhra Pradesh, 37.8 (4,173) in Gujarat and 33 per cent (2,367) in Karnataka. Though the number of students pursuing an MBBS degree is nearly the same as in Karnataka, Uttar Pradesh and Bihar, the proportion of women in the last two provinces is lower, at 23.6 and 16.6 per cent, respectively.

In commerce, too, the highest enrolment is in the same states, along with some others.[7] For example, the highest enrolment in commerce is in Maharashtra, West Bengal, Andhra Pradesh, Gujarat, Bihar, Tamil Nadu. The higher enrolment of women is also in the same provinces—39.6 per cent in Maharashtra, 41.7 in Andhra Pradesh, 44.9 in Tamil Nadu and 31.2 per cent in Karnataka. These states add to the increase in the proportion of women at the all-India level. The same is true for the degree programmes in engineering.

The regional differences are due to several factors. One of them is the earlier start of formal education in the southern as compared to the northern region during the colonial period. Moreover, a large number of private engineering colleges have been established here, even in the contemporary period. Third, the socio-cultural practices and positive attitudes of parents towards the higher education of their daughters also impact women's access to professional education. This difference is, to a large extent, due to the practice of female seclusion in the north and its absence in the south (Chanana 1988).

Caste, Class, Gender and Region

It is quite well-known that, in spite of a very well-formulated policy of positive discrimination, the representation of Dalit and Adivasi students is not adequate and the proportion of women among them is negligible. They generally join general education courses and are denied access to elite/courses and institutions. In 2001–02, the proportions of SC/ST students were as follows: Scheduled Castes, 11.5 per cent (10,16,182)—SC men, 8 per cent (7,06,769) and SC women, 3.5 per cent (3,09,813). The ST students constituted 4 per cent (3,51,880) of total enrolment—men, 2.7 per cent (2,40,495) and women, 1.3 per cent (1,14,168). In MPhil/PhD programmes, there were 53,119 students all over the country. Of these, 36.3 per cent (19,299) were women, 5.9 per cent (3,133) SC students and 1.80 (951) were ST students. There were 824 SC women and 344 ST women, i.e., 4.3 per cent and 1.8 per cent, respectively, of all women research students.

Further, they are better represented in states in which women have better representation and in which higher education facilities have expanded in recent years. For example, the proportion of Scheduled Caste women to total SC enrolment is 34.1 per cent in Maharashtra, 39.7 in Tamil Nadu, 32.2 per cent in Andhra Pradesh and 24.5 per cent in Karnataka. Similarly, the Scheduled Tribe women are 29.4 per cent in Maharashtra, 22.6 per cent in Karnataka, 32 per cent in Andhra Pradesh, 41.2 per cent in Gujarat and 33.7 per cent in Madhya Pradesh.[8]

This trend also continues in different disciplines. For example, in 2001–02, the proportion of all women students in BE/BSc Engineering and BArch courses was 24.8 per cent. The proportion of all SC students was 7.4 (38,935) and of STs, 3.5 per cent (18,644). Further, the proportion of SC women was 1.9 per cent of the total and of ST women, 0.4 (2,035). The number of tribal women has increased four-fold since 1995–96, when it was 575. If we look at the proportion of SC/ST women vis-à-vis total number of women in engineering courses, the SC women are 7.5 per cent and ST women are 1.6 per cent.

The proportion of women vis-à-vis the SC/ST students as a whole also reflect the same trend. For example, the proportion of SC women as part of total SC enrolment was 28.2 per cent in Andhra Pradesh, 29.2 per cent in Karnataka, 24.6 per cent in Tamil Nadu and 39.4 per cent in Kerala.[9] Of the SC women students in engineering courses, 61.6 per cent are enrolled in Andhra Pradesh, Karnataka and Tamil Nadu. If only the information had been available for Maharashtra, the proportion would be much higher. Similarly, the proportions of ST women are also high in the same provinces, for example, 23.4 per cent in Karnataka and 18.7 per cent in Andhra Pradesh. If we look at the enrolment in the three states of Karnataka, Tamil Nadu and Andhra Pradesh, 55.3 per cent of women are enrolled in engineering courses in the three provinces.

In medicine, too, the situation is similar, with 60.8 per cent of SC women (4,035 out of 6,637) in medicine in the four states of Maharashtra, Karnataka,

Tamil Nadu and Andhra Pradesh. In medicine, 68.2 per cent (4,577 out of 6,849) ST women are enrolled in Nagaland, a tribal-majority province in north-eastern India. However, the ST students, especially women, are very small in numbers and, therefore, the proportions have to be seen accordingly.

GENDER, SUBJECT CHOICES AND CAREER ASPIRATIONS

The relationship between availability of disciplinary choices and women's ability to access them are not directly related, nor are they dependent on women's academic achievement. In India, girls' academic performance is generally better than or at par with, the boys when they finish school. Every year, newspaper headlines highlight the better performance of girls in the school board examinations in different states. Yet, when they pursue higher studies, it is not necessarily in the subject of their choice.[10]

While the shortage of seats or of intake capacity in specific academic programmes and the lack of success in the entrance tests may be ostensible reasons for the lack of consonance between educational aspirations and disciplinary choices, these do not provide sufficient explanations. The fact is that a large majority of women may be deprived of exercising free options at the school level (for example, being discouraged by family from taking up science subjects by the family) or are not sent to expensive private 'good quality' schools. After schooling, they may not be provided the financial investment in coaching/tuition for entrance tests (for example, there is now an entrance test for coaching classes for IIT entrance tests) because they are very expensive and women, after all, are not socially expected to work and earn before marriage.

Discipline boundaries not only limit choices, but are also dependent on the future options of 'life chances' of women. For example, even though higher education for young women is taken for granted nowadays, among the upper and middle strata in the cities, it is still not viewed as an immediate investment in their careers. Education is, among the majority, an investment to fall back upon, in case the daughter becomes a widow or is deserted (Chanana 1988). Social role expectations affect the aspirations of women in other ways too. For example, in the patriarchal social structure, parents are not expected to use the income of their daughters. Therefore, even educated daughters are not encouraged to work and if they do so, it is for a short period before marriage. It is the right of the groom's family to decide whether she will work or not.

Poor parents have another problem, even though they perceive the significance of education. They expect and need immediate returns from education—something which is possible through professional degrees. But professional education excludes the poor students, because it requires several years of studentship and higher financial investment than general education. General education, although inexpensive, does not assure a job. So general education is useless, while professional education is unaffordable. Besides, there is a lack of role models and socialisation support at home. Women from these social categories are the most affected by the stratification of disciplines, programmes and institutions. Further, the social and economic disparities are reflected not only vis-à-vis caste and tribe, but also at the regional level, i.e., in the different states.

Therefore, for a majority of young women in the academia, higher education is not linked to careers. This is the reason why women, even from well-off homes, join arts and humanities, because they are cheaper, softer and shorter than the professional courses. But we have seen that the number of those who are entering the professional subjects is growing.

In fact, the trends, identified in 2001, of moving away from the general courses to the professional courses which lead to jobs and careers, are being reinforced. One could treat the post-1991 phase as a period that set forth a change, which increased the social demand for a specific kind of professional education, especially skill-oriented undergraduate degrees, which lead to a career and a job. Earlier, an undergraduate degree, except in engineering and medicine, was a step to further higher education and was not a finishing degree. Young men and women were not expected to work and earn soon after finishing undergraduate education. Those who did so belonged to the lower-middle strata and needed to work and earn, to support the family and themselves. The middle and upper strata, on the other hand, could postpone income generation until further education. This was more applicable to most women across strata, i.e., they were not studying in order to earn and to take up jobs. It was an investment in their social status, as well as an additional criterion for marriage.

As mentioned earlier, while this may still be true of a large majority of women and their parents, that is, they do not expect their daughters to earn after receiving a degree, there are changes in the expectations of parents and of young women in big cities. Therefore, parental expectations and young women's aspirations have been push factors in the shift in disciplinary choices in the mid-1990s. More women are enrolling in engineering and law, but the preference for management degrees and computer-related degrees and skills is higher. These subjects are available in the fast-expanding private sector, which responds quickly to the unmet demand for specific skills. Informal discussions with key persons reveal that computer applications and software computer engineering, as compared to other specialisations, are popular among women. Further, HRM (Human Resource Management) requires interaction with the public and there are several others of this kind. In the past few years, women have become visible in the call centres, telemarketing, front-desk jobs in multi-national/private banks, hospitals, hotels, etc. Quite a few of these jobs are short-term and contractual and, therefore, suit the social role expectations of women. It will, therefore, have to be seen if women are getting professional training, which leads to jobs and careers. Moreover, there are several new courses and academic programmes which have not yet found space in the official statistics.

As far as teaching is concerned, it is also anticipated that the public and private institutions which offer contractual, low-paid and short-term jobs may have, in the long run, a substantial number of women faculty, leading to the feminisation of teaching in private higher education (Chanana 2003).

A study of women scientists in biological sciences in central universities and national laboratories also concludes that there are fewer permanent women faculty, in comparison to those who obtain research degrees. It is argued that the researchers join as faculty members when they are in their early 30s, a time when women are either married or have to be married soon. They need a break to raise a family and, after the break, cannot compete with men in research and professional experience. Again, more women than men are holding junior faculty positions (Bal 2004). The presence of women students in technology and engineering has also increased, but a study of women engineers (Parikh and Sukhatme 1992) showed that the most preferred specialisations of women were electronics, electrical and civil engineering. Computer science, chemical and mechanical engineering followed in that order. It also mentioned that there are fewer women students in the elite institutions such as the IITs and the regional colleges of engineering.

Therefore, modern education and skills seem to reinforce tradition for a majority of women students. The new disciplines which are offered in the public and private-sector higher education, though exclusively in the latter, seem to meet the aspirations of only a minority of young women and their parents in metropolises to be professionally qualified, to have a career and to earn to be independent. In their case, gender and class overlap in overcoming the traditional barriers to women's education.

CONCLUSIONS

In spite of the fact that higher education was almost free during the first four decades after Independence, since it was publicly funded, women have not achieved equal access. It has also been either denied to, or almost impossible for, the women from disadvantaged groups to access, because of social and economic reasons. There is a critical need to deconstruct the rhetoric surrounding globalisation and economic liberalisation and their inequitable impact.

Since 1991, a number of private institutions have been established. These private institutions offer market-oriented professional courses and are very expensive. Nevertheless, the private sector has met the unmet demand for specific subjects and increased the intake capacity in the most sought after disciplines. On the other hand, it is at a high individual cost. So the question arises: What would be the impact on women? It is by now quite well-known that a majority of parents are reluctant to invest in the education of their daughters, whose education does not have a production value because their income goes to the groom's family. Therefore, would women be joining them, in what proportions, and in which subjects and specialisations? It is difficult to answer these questions without separate gender-based enrolment data for private and public institutions and for each and every discipline and academic programme separately. Moreover, the issues of social access and equity, or of quality, receive little attention in the private sector. Would parents spend on higher education as well as on the dowries of their daughters?

Additionally, pure sciences, social sciences, arts and humanities, the disciplines preferred by women, remain confined to the public institutions. Has the earlier trend of the concentration of women in these disciplines been reinforced? Again, even though women are enrolling in professional education in larger numbers, which institutions, private or public, are they joining and in what proportions? It has not been possible to answer these questions directly, in the absence of relevant data.[11]

Finally, it is imperative to create a broad-based database on higher education that is gender-sensitive.[12] Information on students, namely their enrolment and outturn by level, discipline, specialisation and institution, are imperative for any understanding of the system. In addition, research on higher education deserves support, so that a quantitative database can be supported by qualitative inputs. It would help in charting out the future course of action and the research policy. It is high time that the government evolved a framework on the role and function of higher education, public and private. For this, it needs a vision which will encompass the issues of access and equity, with a focus on the education of girls and women.

Notes

1. Globalisation means many things to many people. According to some, colonialism was globalisation, while others refer to modernisation as globalisation. I refer to it as the impact of economic liberalisation in my country since 1991 and the impact of it on higher education.

2. It may be noted that the statistics published by the University Grants Commission and Ministry of Human Resource Development are based only on enrolment (which is of uneven quality). For instance, the UGC annual report for 1996–97 merges the enrolment figures for women in agriculture with those of medicine and several other disciplines. I hope to highlight the paucity of statistics on higher education in general and on women in particular.

3. The one measure which the universities have recently been asked to take, in favour of women, is to set up committees against sexual harassment. This directive of the University Grants Commission is fulfilled by some universities. Whether these committees are effectively functioning or not is a moot question.

4. This report was entitled *Towards Equality* and is better known by that title. This committee was appointed by the Government of India, after the declaration of 1975, as the UN Year for Women. The committee submitted its report in December 1974 and covered all aspects of the status of women in post-Independence India. The report was a landmark in that it substantiated a decline in the overall status of Indian women and shook the Indian intelligentsia, political leaders and women out of their complacency. It would be no exaggeration to say that it set the agenda for the contemporary women's movement in India.

5. It may be noted that while higher education was fully state-funded, private schools were allowed to continue, for which the government was criticised, since it allowed the dual system to operate at the school level.

6. This information is given by my colleague, at the Centre for the Study of Regional Development, JNU, New Delhi, India. I think they are run as colleges of arts and sciences in order to circumvent the approval of the All-India Council of Technical Education, which has stringent norms for the approval and establishment of colleges and programmes. They are using a different nomenclature and the universities are allowing them affiliation.

7. Since the cost of setting up institutions in commerce, arts, social sciences and teacher education is not as high as for engineering and medical colleges, many more provinces have started them.

8. The populations of Scheduled Castes and Tribes vary from province to province. Therefore, this is an additional factor that requires attention.

9. The total enrolment was 651, of which 332 were women and 319 men.

10. No doubt, the competition for seats in 'good quality' institutions is high and young women and men have to clear the entrance tests before they can get admission for a subject of their choice. Nonetheless, in the absence of any information about the aspirations of women and men and about how many men and women sit for and succeed in which entrance test, one can only talk about enrolment data which, too, is quite inadequate.

11. The statistics on higher education in India are very poor. The private institutions lack in transparency and do not provide any statistics. The public sector does no better. Even the all-India bodies, such as the UGC, MHRD and AICTE, do not give any statistics on the enrolment of women and men students—institution wise, level wise, discipline wise—and are not gender-sensitive.

12. It is a sad state of affairs that a country which boasts of a very large higher education system should not have considered it necessary to collect data on higher education, which will provide information about students, faculty and staff in the public and private institutions.

REFERENCES

Acker, Sandra. 1994. *Gendered Education: Sociological Reflections on Women, Teaching and Feminism, Modern Educational Thought Series*. Buckingham: Open University Press.

Allen, Margaret, and Tanya Castleman. 2001. 'Fighting the Pipeline Fallacy'. In A. Brooks and A. McInnon, eds, *Gender and the Restructured University*, 151–65. Buckingham: Society for Research into Higher Education & Open University Press.

Anandkrishnan, M. 2004. 'Private Investments in Technical Education'. In K. B. Powar and K. L. Johar, eds, *Private Initiatives in Higher Education*, 202–25. New Delhi: Sneh Prakashan and Amity Foundation for Learning.

Bachhi, Carol. 2001. 'Managing Equity: Mainstreaming and "Diversity" in Australian Universities'. In A. Brooks and A. McInnon, eds, *Gender and the Restructured University: Changing Management and Culture in Higher Education*, 119–35. Buckingham: The Society for Research into Higher Education and Open University Press.

Bal, Vineeta. 2004. 'Women Scientists in India: Nowhere Near the Glass Ceiling'. *Economic and Political Weekly* 7: 3647–53.

Becher, T. 1981. 'Towards a Definition of Disciplinary Cultures'. *Studies in Higher Education* 6 (2): 109–22.

Bhattacharya, Sutanu. 2004. 'Organisation of Higher Education: Moving Towards a System of Uncorporated Universities'. In K. B. Powar and K. L. Johar, eds, *Private Initiatives in Higher Education* 202–25. New Delhi: Sneh Prakashan and Amity Foundation for Learning.

Brooks Ann, and A. Mackinnon. 2001. *Gender and the Restructured University: Changing Management and Culture in Higher Education*. Buckingham: The Society for Research into Higher Education and Open University Press.

Chanana, K. 1988. 'Social Change or Social Reform: The Education of Women in Pre-independence India'. In K. Chanana, ed. *Socialisation, Education and Women: Explorations in Gender Identity*. Delhi: Orient Longman.

Chanana, K. 1993. 'Accessing Higher Education: The Dilemma of Schooling Women, Minorities, Scheduled Castes and Scheduled Tribes in Contemporary India'. In S. Chitnis and Philip G. Altbach, eds, *Higher Education and Social Change in India*, 115–54. New Delhi: Sage.

——. 2000. 'Treading the Hallowed Halls: Women in Higher Education in India'. *Economic and Political Weekly* 35 (12) 18 March: 1012–22.

——. 2003. 'Visibility, Gender and the Careers of Women Faculty in an Indian University'. *McGill Journal of Education* 38 (3) Fall 2003: 381–90.

Clarke, J. R. 1996. 'Educational Equity in Higher Education: An International Perspective'. In G. D. Postle, et al., *Toward Excellence and Diversity: Educational Equity in the Australian Higher Sector in 1995: Status, Trends and Future Directions*. Queensland: USQ Press.

Deem, Rosemary. 1978. *Women and Schooling*. London: Routledge and Kegan Paul.

Government of India. 1974. *Towards Equality: Report of the Committee on the Status of Women*. New Delhi: Ministry of Education and Social Welfare.

——. 2002. *Selected Educational Statistics 2001–02,* Department of Education, Planning, Statistics and Monitoring Division, Ministry of Human Resource Development, New Delhi.

Harding, J. 1986. *Perspectives on Gender and Science*. London: Falmer Press.

Harvey, D. 1993. *The Condition of Post Modernity: An Enquiry into the Origins of Cultural Change*. Oxford: Blackwell.

Hooks, Bell. 1989. *Talking Back*. Boston: Southend Press.

Hudson, L. 1972. *The Cult of the Fact*. London: Cape.

Kaur, Ravinder. 2002. 'Social Framework for Technical Education: Appraisal of Social Issues in Engineering Education', Report, mimeographed.

Keller, E. F. 1983. 'Gender and Science'. In S. Harding and M. B. Hintikka, eds, *Discovering Reality: Feminist Perspectives in Epistemology, Metaphysics, Methodology and Philosophy Science*, 187–206. Reidel: Dordrecht.

Kellner, Douglas. 1997. 'Man Trouble'. In Henry A. Giroux and Patrick Shannon, eds, *Education and Cultural Studies: Toward a Performative Practice*, 79–88. New York: Routledge.

Kelly, A. ed. 1981. *The Missing Half: Girls and Science Education*. Manchester: Manchester University Press.

Marginson, S. 2000. 'Research As a Managed Economy: The Costs'. In T. Coady, ed. *Why Universities Matter: A Conversation about Values, Means and Directions*. Sydney: Allen and Unwin.

Mackinnon, Alison, and A. Brooks. 2001. 'Introduction'. In A. Brooks and A. Macinnon, eds, *Gender and the Restructured University: Changing Management and Culture in Higher Education*, 1–12. Buckingham: The Society for Research into Higher Education and Open University Press.

Megarry, J. 1984. 'Introduction'. In S. Acker, et al., eds, *World Year Book of Education 1984: Women and Education*. London: Kogan Page.

Millett, K. 1983. *Sexual Politics*. London: Virago.

Parikh, P. P., and S. P. Sukhatme. 1992. *Women Engineers in India: A Study on the Participation of Women in Engineering Courses and in the Engineering Profession*, Indian Institute of Technology, Mumbai.

Rose, H. 1986. 'Nothing Less than Half the Labs'. In J. Firich and M. Rustin, eds, *A Degree of Choice*, 226–49. Harmondsworth: Penguin.

Sassen, S. 1998. *Globalisation and Its Discontents: Essays on the New Mobility of People and Money*. New York: The New Press.

Sawer, M. 1989. 'Efficiency, Effectiveness...and Equity?'. In G. Davis, et al., eds, *Corporate Management in Australian Government: Reconciling Accountability and Efficiency*. Melbourne: Macmillan.

Sharpe, Rachel. 1976. *Just Like a Girl*. London: Pelican.

Slaughter, S., and I. I. Leslie. 1997. *Academic Capitalism: Politics, Policies and the Entrepreneurial University*. Baltimore, MD: John Hopkins University Press.

Thomas, Kim. 1990. *Gender and Subject in Higher Education*. Buckingham: The Society for Research into Higher Education and Open University Press.

UGC, University Development in India: Consolidated Data Statewise, 1988–89 to 1993–94. New Delhi: Information and Statistics Bureau.

UGC, University Development in India: Basic Facts and Figures, 1995–96 to 2000–2001. New Delhi: Information and Statistics Bureau.

University Grants Commission. 2003. *Annual Report 2002–03*. University Grants Commission, New Delhi.

Whyte, J. 1986. *Girls into Science and Technology*. London: Routledge and Kegan Paul.

Wolpe, Ann Marie. 1978. 'Education and the Sexual Division of Labour'. In A. Kuhn and A. N. Wolpe, eds, *Feminism and Materialism: Women and Modes of Production*. Boston: Routledge and Kegan Paul.

Yeatman, A. 1990. *Bureaucrats, Technocrats, Femocrats*. Sydney: Allen and Unwin.

15

Do Parents Spread Educational Expenditure Evenly across the Two Genders?

Evidence from Two North Indian States[*]

Kausik Chaudhuri and Susmita Roy[†]

According to the human development report published by the National Council of Applied Economic Research in 1999, gender differences in schooling outcomes are very common to India. The ever-enrolment rate (defined as the proportion of children aged 6–14 years who were ever enrolled in school, at any level, at the time of survey) was only 64.8 per cent for female children, as compared to 77.2 per cent for male children. The discontinuation rate (defined as the percentage of ever-enrolled children who discontinued studies at any time in the age-group of 6–14 years) stood at 7.6 per cent for female children, as compared to 4.8 per cent for male children. The gender gap in literacy, as per the 2001 Census, ranges from 24.6 per cent in rural India to 13.4 per cent in urban India. There are, however, substantial interstate disparities. In the northern part of India, for instance, figures for literacy vary from 27.7 per cent in rural Bihar to 17.5 per cent in urban Bihar, whereas the corresponding figures for Uttar Pradesh are 30.3 per cent for the rural areas and 16.1 per cent for the urban areas. For southern states of India, like Kerala, the gap between the rural and the urban regions is less stark, standing at 6.7 per cent for rural areas and 5.2 per cent for urban areas. The states of Bihar and Uttar Pradesh present an interesting case for exploring the gender dimension in the problem of low levels of educational attainment. As per the National Human Development Report 2002, among the various states of the Indian union, these two states had to cope with not only the lowest levels of enrolment rates in the age-group 6–14, but also the highest levels of dropout rates.

Does the bias against the enrolment of female children, as revealed in the previous paragraph, carry over to the decision of how much to expend on their

* Previously published in *Economic and Political Weekly* 41 (51), 23 December 2006: 5276–82.

schooling, if at all? At the societal level, the expenditure on education comes from two sources: institutional, which can include the expenditure of the state on education, and private, which may consist of the household's own expenditure on education (Tilak 2003). The role of neither of these components can be overemphasised, as they must complement each other to ensure adequacy and equity in education. The Government of India, on its part, is trying to establish a primary school in every village in India. But despite this, many parents are averse to enlisting children and girls, in particular, in any kind of school. On the other hand, the poor quality of the educational services or the absence of the school within the habitat turns away many parents from school, even if they nurture the desire to impart schooling to their children. The outcome is that the poor are left out of the schooling system and only the rich have access to any educational services.

It is a well-known fact that parents in rural India are reluctant to split household resources on education equally across male and female children. The question of interest, however, is whether this reluctance is significantly large, so as to result in a substantial gap in the resources available for the schooling of male and female children. The purpose of this chapter is threefold: to test for both the existence of gender bias in the household expenditure on education, and to determine whether the discrimination is more prominent/likely in certain age-groups and less prominent in others. Second, we also determine whether this discrimination is more likely at the stage of enrolment and less severe for children who are already enrolled, or whether it is a phenomenon that continues to be a significant problem even after conditioning on enrolment. Third, we exploit the rich survey data to estimate an expenditure function at the individual level, to test for the existence of any gender bias that may not have been detected at the household-level equations.

Our estimates of the individual-level expenditure function not only confirm the presence of a gender gap in educational expenditure, but also suggest that this gap becomes more important with a rise in the age of the child. The gap is particularly prominent while making the decision to incur no or zero expenditure versus the decision to incur at least some expenditure. The expenditure wedge is less prominent for those households where parents are already incurring some expenditure, on both the girls and the boys. There can be no claims contested as to the superiority of the individual regressions in detecting gender bias, but it is interesting to note that even our household-level regressions, although not reported, present a picture that mimics the results of the individual-level regressions very closely. The chapter is organised as follows: Section I briefly describes the existing literature; the empirical methodology is introduced in Section II; Section III reports the data along with the descriptive statistics; the empirical results are presented in Section IV; while Section V concludes.

LITERATURE REVIEW

Studies like Das Gupta (1987) and Bardhan (1974) have documented clear evidence of discrimination against females in India (although the explanations put forward by the two authors are quite different)[1] and yet, the empirical evidence on the fact that within the intra-household allocations, a lower level of resources is directed towards the females vis-à-vis the males has been far from satisfactory. The question at hand, however, has important policy implications. If females are indeed allotted fewer resources within the family unit, then such schemes as the mid-day meal programme, etc., assume special significance (Subramaniam 1995). The problem of detecting discrimination at the household level comes from two kinds of limitations: a lack of data on consumption at the individual level and the fact that the lower allocations of one good to the girls, relative to the boys, may be offset by higher allocations of other goods. Deaton (1989) proposes a very useful technique for detecting gender bias at the household level.[2] He applies this technique to test for gender discrimination in Thailand and Cote d' Ivoire. He fails to find any evidence of a significant level of gender bias in Cote d' Ivoire; Thailand, however, evinces some gender discrimination, but the levels of significance are 'not impressive'.

Subramaniam and Deaton (1991) test for gender gaps in the intra-household consumption patterns in Maharashtra using the outlay equivalent/adult good approach. They find that basic foodstuffs were either gender neutral or pro-female. A pro-male preference was also detected for educational and medical expenditures in urban areas. In rural households, discrimination against the girls was confined to the young age-groups. The study, however, did not find any evidence of major gaps in the allocation of resources within the household. Haddad and Reardon (1993) use the same methodology, disaggregated by agro-economical zone (rural versus urban) and income stratum, to test for gender discrimination in Burkina Faso. Their study suggests that there are no significant gaps in the intra-household allocations towards male and female children in Burkina Faso. Subramaniam (1995) applies the outlay equivalent technique for adult goods and educational and medical expenditures for rural areas of five Indian states: Andhra Pradesh, Maharashtra, Punjab, Rajasthan and Tamil Nadu. He fails to find any evidence of gender discrimination in the northern states using the adult goods approach; although Andhra Pradesh and Maharashtra document some evidence of gender discrimination in the 5–9 age-groups. Andhra Pradesh and Rajasthan also depict evidence of gender discrimination in the 10–14 age-groups for educational expenditure, whereas Rajasthan (0–4 age-group) and Punjab (0–4, 5–9 and 10–14 age-group) show evidence of discrimination in medical expenditures. Kingdon (2005) finds significant gaps in the intra-household allocation of educational expenditure for 15 major states of India. The methodology is described in the following section.

Empirical Methodology

In order to estimate individual-level educational expenditure, we modify the Deaton (1989) specification also followed by Subramaniam and Deaton (1991) and Kingdon (2005). The Engel curve approach, based on household-level data, utilises the fact that the budget share of education is likely to change with the composition of the household. This is particularly useful if the data on individual allocation is missing. Individual-level information is not a constraint in the present context, as the survey data provided detailed information on the educational expenditure at the household level. Equations based on expenditure at the individual level may also be more effective in detecting any bias that may not have been detected in the household equations. The empirical counterpart to the household educational Engel curve for the individual level is given by

$$s_{ji} = \alpha + \beta(x_i / n_i) + \gamma \ln n_i + \partial Sex_{ji} + \eta z_i = \varepsilon_i$$

where s_{ji} (the dependent variable) is the total schooling expenditures on the individual children j by household i. The variables n_i, Sex_{ji} and z_i stand for the household size, dummy variables for the gender of the child belonging to a particular age-group in household i and z_i consists of other household and village-level characteristics in the ith household. To estimate the gender gap in individual regressions, we estimate separate regressions for each of the age categories and then look for the significance of the gender dummy in each of these categories. In our case, we model Sex_{ji} as a binary variable taking the value of one, if the jth child is a female belonging to the ith household. In our set-up, we test for the significance of the coefficient associated with the female dummy variable.

Kingdon (2005) points out two potential problems with the OLS (Ordinary Least Squares) approach. The budget share of education may be following a lognormal instead of a normal distribution. The second potential problem is that the aggregation of bias that operates at the stage of decision of whether or not to enrol, with the stage of decision of how much to expend conditional on enrolment, may wipe out the true picture. If, for instance, most of the bias exists at the stage of enrolment, but conditional on enrolment, parents do not discriminate much or in fact direct a higher expenditure towards the girls in the form of their special needs, like travel and clothing, etc., then an aggregation of the two decisions may lead to non-detection of the gender bias, even if significant biases exist. To overcome this problem, she proposes estimation of separate equations for the two decisions, a probit or logit model for the decision of whether or not to invest in education and a conditional OLS for positive educational expenditure. Alternatively, one could also estimate models that allow for the effect of these decisions to vary, for instance, Heckman's sample-selection model.

DATA, VARIABLE DESCRIPTION AND DESCRIPTIVE STATISTICS

We use the 1997–98 Uttar Pradesh-Bihar Survey of Living Conditions (Living Standards Measurement Survey [LSMS]) for our empirical investigation.[3] The dataset covers a total of 2,250 households (120 villages) in rural Uttar Pradesh and Bihar. Respondents provide information on their household demographics, farming and livestock and durable assets. It also contains information on the enrolment status of their children and the type of school attended if enrolled and the current grade at which he/she is enrolled. The data on the cost of schooling (school fees, books, uniform, private tuition and other schooling expenditures) is also available.

The village questionnaire elicits information on anti-poverty programmes in the village and access to facilities like health, education, road and telecommunication.

We selected all children in the age-group of 5–19. Individual information on schooling and gender were subsequently merged with household information like wealth status, religion, caste, parental education and village-level characteristics, like access to facilities and caste composition. The final dataset had 4,104 observations, out of which 2,276 were from Uttar Pradesh and the rest from Bihar.

Description of the Variables Used

Dependent Variable

The dependent variable is the natural logarithm of expenditure incurred on education on individual children. Table 15.1 describes the summary statistics of education expenditure. We also decompose this based on religion and caste. The educational expenditure in an all-female child household in Uttar Pradesh, i.e., where all the children are females, is lower in all the age-groups, as compared to a household where there is at least one boy, although for the age-group of 5–9, individual expenditures on education in all-female households exceed those in the case of households with at least one boy for Bihar. This does not get altered even if we consider only Hindu households. We also observe that this difference gets larger for higher age-groups. Considering only the household belonging to the Scheduled Caste/Tribe, we infer that they spend less on education expenditure of their children; however, the spending pattern across genders remains the same.

Table 15.1: Average Expenditure on Individual Children by Household Type

	Child Age		
	5–9	*10–14*	*15–19*
All households			
Uttar Pradesh			
Household with female child only	160.521	332.726	121.390
Household with male child only	185.777	493.428	493.71
Households with both male and female children	167.783	442.905	468.534
Bihar			
Household with female child only	232.819	293.595	97.272
Household with male child only	246.610	412.190	619.816
Households with both male and female children	197.439	347.521	345.505
Hindu households			
Uttar Pradesh			
Household with female child only	160.429	333.779	121.390
Household with male child only	190.892	508.290	493.710
Households with both male and female children	192.740	448.315	475.451

(Contd)

Table 15.1 (Contd)

	Child Age		
	5–9	*10–14*	*15–19*
Bihar			
Household with female child only	224.508	315.127	104.902
Household with male child only	247.918	446.482	674.050
Households with both male and female children	171.886	369.753	365.651
Scheduled Caste/Tribe households			
Uttar Pradesh			
Household with female child only	87.793	154.370	43.714
Household with male child only	116.977	314.000	267.829
Households with both male and female children	120.069	288.821	250.803
Bihar			
Household with female child only	43.742	62.188	96.833
Household with male child only	120.784	198.132	385.750
Households with both male and female children	66.752	129.324	118.615

Independent Variables

The independent variables included in the set of household-level regressions are the log of per capita total expenditure and its square (total expenditure of household consists of both food and non-food consumption, expenditure on education and expenditure on health), the log of household size and the child-demographic variables captured by a gender dummy. Parental preferences need not always be aligned; for example, mothers may be more compassionate towards daughters, as fathers towards sons. Lillard and Willis (1994) show that in Malaysia, the mother's education has a far larger effect on the daughters' education than on the sons', whereas the reverse holds true for the father's education. Kambhampati and Pal (2001) and Pal (2004) argue that each parent's education may be taken as an indicator of his/her individual preference and suggest that it is the higher level of literacy amongst women that encourages female education in rural Bengal. Keeping this in mind, we introduce a variable that is an index of the level of education attained by the mother and the father. These indices, therefore, serve as a proxy for the parental motivation of educating the children.[4] In the context of intra-household allocation of resources, the existence of a complex interrelation between the household resource constraints and parental preferences cannot also be ruled out. Quisumbing (1993) documents that families that differ with respect to their land constraints also have significantly different patterns of schooling investments and this results in an inequality among the siblings. In order to capture this aspect, we also include the occupational dummies: we consider three dichotomous variables to control for the occupational structure of the household: casual labour, salaried employment and the business class. The base category is own farm activities (sample size 1987) that comprises 48.57 per cent and 'others' (sample size 130) that comprise 4 per cent of the total sample. Given the nature of the job, each of these categories can have different implications for the indirect costs of schooling. The casual labour class, as opposed to the salaried group, for instance, may be less willing to send their children to school when the demand for the labour of their children is high.

We also include dummy variables to control for the religion of the household (1 if Hindu, 0 otherwise) and the caste of the household; either Scheduled Castes and Scheduled Tribes (SC/ST) or Other Backward Castes (OBC) is included, to investigate whether certain schools are preferred or avoided based on extra-quality considerations.[5] The level of village development is captured via dichotomous variables for the presence of electricity (1 if present, otherwise 0) and all-weather roads in the village (1 if present, otherwise 0). Dreze and Kingdon (2001) have also considered the presence of electricity and all-weather roads in the construction of their index for village development.

Finally, we would like to focus on our last variable: the index of caste homogeneity. It is an important indicator of the presence of diversity in interests, or of cultural heterogeneity. Cultural heterogeneity is an important factor that gives rise to the demand for private schools (James 1993). Caste homogeneity also has implications for coordination among the people to press for the provision of public goods and, in particular, for a public school (Dostie and Jayaraman 2003). However, too much homogeneity may not be good, because neighbourhood effects tend to be reinforced. Thus, if households that belong to a particular caste/ tribe have a history of ignoring the education of the females, then such practices are likely to be reinforced in the presence of very low levels of caste heterogeneity, i.e., the presence of a large number of households who think identically makes it more likely that such regressive practices will be continued in the future. The index of caste homogeneity has been constructed in line with the ethno-linguistic fractionalisation index proposed in Paulo (1991). However, since it is a measure of caste homogeneity rather than heterogeneity, it is given by 1-(Ethno-linguistic Fractionalisation Index) $= \sum_i \frac{n_i^2}{N^2}$, where N is the total population and n_i is the population of the ith ethnic group. We have also introduced a district dummy in order to control for district-specific unobserved heterogeneity. We estimate separate equations for Uttar Pradesh and Bihar: the choice being reflected by a likelihood-ratio statistics, comprising of a pooling versus a separate regression.[6]

Empirical Results

At the individual child level, we estimated 24 separate equations (2 states × 3 age-groups × 4 equations). We have not reported estimation from all 24 equations. We have reported in detail the result from the sample selection model in Tables 15.2, 15.3 and 15.4. In Table 15.5, we summarise our findings, in terms of significance of the gender dummy variable. For an expository purpose, we have shown in Figures 15.1 and 15.2 that educational expenditures are better captured using a log normal distribution, rather than a normal distribution. We have split our discussion into parts. In the first part, we discuss the results on the existence of gender discrimination in educational expenditure and in the second, we look at how some other regressors, the village-development indicators and the caste variables, in particular, influence the decisions relating to educational expenditure.

GENDER BIAS IN EDUCATIONAL EXPENDITURE

Table 15.2 corresponds to the individual-level regressions in Uttar Pradesh and Bihar respectively, for the age-group 5–9 for the sample selection model,[7] whereas in Table 15.3 and in Table 15.4, for the age-groups 10–14 and 15–19, respectively. Table 15.2 suggests that the coefficient associated with the female dummy is not significant for both states. Hence, there exists no gender bias for the age-group of 5–9 years. For the 10–14 and the 15–19 age-groups, however, the bias seems to be

TABLE 15.2: Determinants of Household Expenditure on Education (Age 5–9)

	Sample Selection Model			
	Uttar Pradesh		*Bihar*	
	Coefficient	*p-Value*	*Coefficient*	*p-Value*
Log of per capita total expenditure	–2.191	0.291	–5.262	0.074
Square of log of per capita total expenditure	0.145	0.238	0.327	0.062
Log of household size	0.178	0.056	–0.228	0.189
Casual labour	–0.027	0.780	0.003	0.983
Salaried class	0.546	0.000	–0.053	0.782
Business class	0.302	0.009	0.189	0.200
Father's education	–0.441	0.021	–0.431	0.250
Mother's education	1.333	0.000	–0.197	0.640
Hindu household	–0.408	0.016	0.121	0.581
Scheduled Caste/Tribe household	–0.262	0.029	–0.122	0.529
Other Backward Caste household	–0.018	0.857	–0.069	0.632
Female child dummy	0.045	0.508	0.170	0.114
Electricity in village	0.017	0.862	0.245	0.033
All-weather roads	–0.121	0.493	–0.280	0.166
Index of caste				
Homogeneity in the village	0.091	0.715	–0.101	0.782
District dummy	Yes	Yes	Yes	Yes
N	763		658	
Censored N	259		332	
p-Value for Wald Test of Independent Equations (H0: $\rho = 0$)	0.006		0.000	

Note: The dependent variable is the natural logarithm of the share of spending on education. Robust *p* values are reported in parentheses (after adjusting for clustering at the household level).

TABLE 15.3: Determinants of Household Expenditure on Education (Age 10–14 Years)

	Sample Selection Model			
	Uttar Pradesh		*Uttar Pradesh*	
	Coefficient	*Coefficient*	*Coefficient*	*Coefficient*
Log of per capita total expenditure	–3.173	0.235	6.835	0.010
Square of log of per capita total expenditure	0.224	0.161	–0.370	0.017
Log of household size	–0.085	0.462	–0.132	0.353
Casual labour	–0.144	0.189	–0.098	0.524
Salaried class	0.207	0.083	0.108	0.452
Business class	0.108	0.505	0.048	0.714
Father's education	0.651	0.001	0.095	0.806
Mother's education	1.121	0.000	0.078	0.855
Hindu household	–0.243	0.074	0.401	0.094
Scheduled Caste/Tribe household	–0.133	0.304	–0.416	0.010
Other Backward Caste household	–0.098	0.357	–0.015	0.901
Female child dummy	–0.472	0.000	0.071	0.680
Electricity in village	0.059	0.540	0.058	0.620
All-weather roads	0.206	0.275	–0.132	0.499
Index of caste				
Homogeneity in the village	–0.559	0.008	0.493	0.211
District dummy	Yes	Yes	Yes	Yes
N	787		594	
Censored N	209		240	
p-Value for Wald Test of Independent Equations (H0: $\rho = 0$)	0.051		0.052	

Notes: The dependent variable is the natural logarithm of the share of spending on education. Robust *p* values are reported in parentheses (after adjusting for clustering at the household level).

effective for Uttar Pradesh and for the 15–19 age-group in case of Bihar. But does the significance of the gender variable remain the same across different estimations? The answer to this question lies in Table 15.5, where we look at the significance of the coefficient for each of the female dummies across different models.

Let us first look at unconditional OLS.[8] Interestingly, the effect is significant in Uttar Pradesh, but not in the case of Bihar in the 5–9 age-group. However, the effect is present for the other two age-groups. Since unconditional OLS may give misleading results, due to the intermingling of the bias at the two levels, it is also important to look at other methodologies. The probit estimations[9] reveal that the first-level discrimination is important for all the three age-categories in both Uttar Pradesh and Bihar—a result quite different from that of unconditional OLS. The conditional OLS[10] reflects the presence of significant negative coefficient associated with the female dummy, only in the 15–19 age-group for Uttar Pradesh and in the 10–14 age-group for Bihar.

TABLE 15.4: Determinants of Household Expenditure on Education (Age 15–19)

	Sample Selection Model			
	Uttar Pradesh		*Uttar Pradesh*	
	Coefficient	*Coefficient*	*Coefficient*	*Coefficient*
Log of per capita total expenditure	–6.441	0.065	5.893	0.000
Square of log of per capita total expenditure	0.402	0.044	–0.301	0.000
Log of household size	0.120	0.243	0.640	0.103
Casual labour	–0.357	0.043	–0.930	0.011
Salaried class	0.170	0.204	–0.027	0.921
Business class	0.319	0.014	0.047	0.863
Father's education	0.637	0.018	0.289	0.614
Mother's education	0.532	0.070	2.097	0.015
Hindu household	–0.015	0.931	0.268	0.677
Scheduled Caste/Tribe household	–0.078	0.644	0.153	0.701
Other Backward Caste household	0.028	0.809	–0.045	0.889
Female child dummy	–0.318	0.063	–0.753	0.006
Electricity in village	–0.042	0.743	0.168	0.458
All-weather roads	0.546	0.032	–0.873	0.157
Index of caste				
Homogeneity in the village	–0.435	0.221	–0.520	0.558
District dummy	Yes	Yes	Yes	Yes
N	459		350	
Censored N	270		235	
p-Value for Wald Test of Independent Equations (H0: $\rho = 0$)	0.346		0.000	

Notes: The dependent variable is the natural logarithm of the share of spending on education. Robust p values are reported in parentheses (after adjusting for clustering at the household level).

How do these results compare with those at the household level? The result is reported in Table 15.6. Here, we replace the female dummy variable by the size of the jth age-gender class, namely the proportion of female and male children in the age-groups 5–9, 10–14 and 15–19.[11] The basic idea behind detecting a gender bias through the estimation of this equation is the following: the budget share of a child good, like education, is likely to rise with the addition of an additional child in the household. If this increase is higher for the boys, as compared to the girls, then it implies that parents allocate the scarce resources more favourably towards the boys than towards the girls. The test for gender bias in intra-household allocation of educational expenditure in an OLS framework thus boils down to the test for the equality of male and female coefficients for the corresponding age-group. For the other specifications, a difference in the coefficients is a sufficient (not necessary) condition for a difference in the marginal effects. We, therefore, report this as a proxy for a difference in marginal effects.

Table 15.5: Coefficients of the Female Dummy at Individual-Level Regressions

Variable	*Unconditional OLS Model*	*Conditional OLS Model*	*Probit Model*	*Heckman Model*
Uttar Pradesh				
Coefficient on female child of age between 5 and 9 years	–42.751 (0.020)	–0.033 (0.583)	–0.128 (0.000)	0.045 (0.473)
Coefficient on female child of age between 10 and 14 years	–266.104 (0.000)	–0.168 (0.173)	–0.271 (0.000)	–0.472 (0.000)
Coefficient on female child of age between 15 and 19 years	–368.798 (0.000)	–0.333 (0.000)	–0.310 (0.000)	–0.318 (0.063)
Bihar				
Coefficient on female child of age between 5 and 9 years	–17.388 (0.642)	–0.059 (0.4814)	–0.198 (0.000)	0.170 (0.114)
Coefficient on female child of age between 10 and 14 years	–209.504 (0.000)	–0.207 (0.026)	–0.390 (0.000)	0.070 (0.680)
Coefficient on female child of age between 15 and 19 years	–329.421 (0.004)	–0.248 (0.105)	–0.158 (0.009)	–0.753 (0.006)

Note: The figures reported in the parenthesis are the p-values (corrected for clustering at the household level) using a Chi-Square test.

Table 15.6: Differences in the Female-Male Coefficients at Household-Level Regressions

Variable	*Unconditional OLS Model*	*Conditional OLS Model*	*Probit Model*	*Heckman Model*
Uttar Pradesh				
Difference in coefficients of female and male child of age between 5 and 9 years	0.005 (0.717)	0.366 (0.303)	–2.287 (0.019)	0.694 (0.080)
Difference in coefficients of female and male child of age between 10 and 14 years	–0.070 (0.000)	–1.295 (0.000)	–2.539 (0.010)	–0.832 (0.029)
Difference in coefficients of female and male child of age between 15 and 19 years	–0.046 (0.057)	–0.811 (0.160)	–3.712 (0.001)	–0.306 (0.604)
Bihar				
Difference in coefficients of female and male child of age between 5 and 9 years	–0.016 (0.170)	–0.433 (0.414)	–2.077 (0.018)	–0.470 (0.476)
Difference in coefficients of female and male child of age between 10 and 14 years	–0.061 (0.000)	–0.259 (0.583)	–1.506 (0.098)	–0.311 (0.642)
Difference in coefficients of female and male child of age between 15 and 19 years	–0.049 (0.041)	–0.976 (0.166)	–1.310 (0.246)	–1.026 (0.235)

Note: The figures reported in the parenthesis are the p-values (corrected for clustering at the household level) using a Chi-Square test.

Interestingly, in both Uttar Pradesh and Bihar, discrimination in any form seems to be absent in the 5–9 age-group for three models: unconditional OLS, conditional OLS and the Heckman. The probit estimations reveal that the first-level discrimination is important for all the three age-categories in Uttar Pradesh and for the 5–9 and 10–14 age groups in Bihar. Conditional on positive spending, the bias is important in the 10–14 age-group in Uttar Pradesh (the Heckman regression says that the bias is operational even in the 5–9 age-group), but there is no evidence of gender bias in Bihar. Our results also validate the usefulness of using data at the

FIGURE 15.1: Proportion of Educational Expenditure in Uttar Pradesh

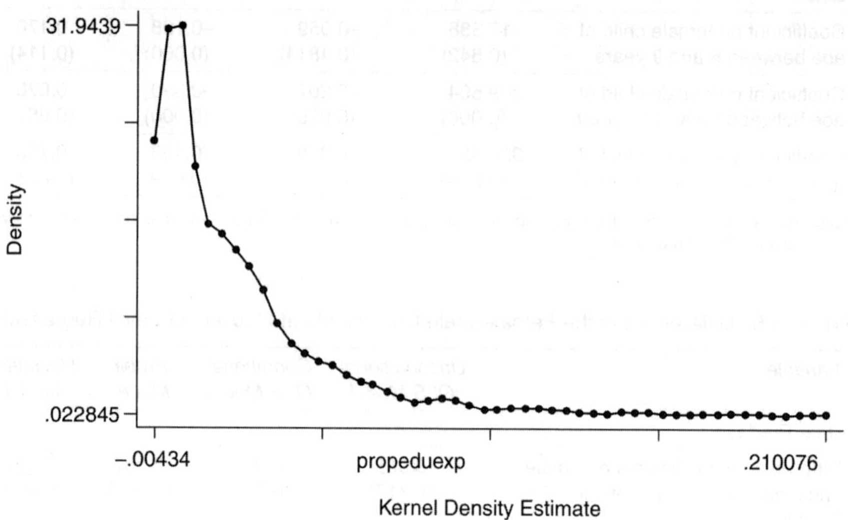

FIGURE 15.2: Log of Proportion of Educational Expenditure in Uttar Pradesh

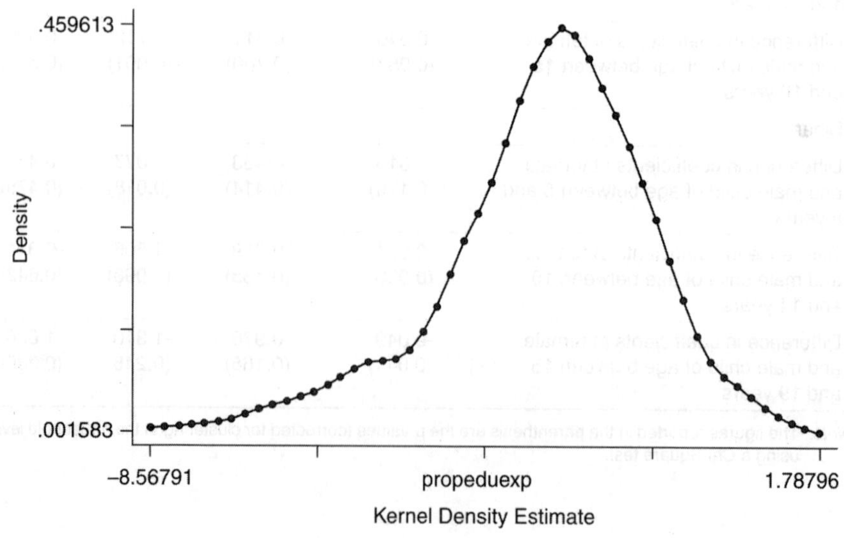

individual level for the 15–19 age-group, where household regressions fail to detect bias in either of the two states, but the individual regressions are able to capture it.

Background of the Household and Village Development

The variables relating to the ethnic group with which the household identifies itself, the caste composition of the village and the indices of village development have their own importance in determining the size and composition (the distribution of the expenditure among the sexes) of the household's choice of educational expenditure. The occupational pattern of the household and the schooling level of the parents are also likely to be important in this context. We, therefore, explore the impact of these variables on the proportion of educational expenditure of the household (i.e., the household-level regressions). Since these may vary widely across states, we compare the results for the two states.

Religion and Caste

In Uttar Pradesh, the budget share of education is higher amongst the Hindus vis-à-vis the Muslims. However, conditional on enrolment, there is a clear evidence of allotting a lower importance to education in the household budget among the Hindus. In Bihar, the scenario is quite different. Conditional on enrolment, the Hindus seem to allocate more vis-à-vis the Muslims. The coefficients associated with SC/ST and OBC households are negative in general. This may be ascribed primarily to the socio-economic disadvantages that these households are subjected to.

Occupational Dummies

Given everything else, we expect that the casual labour and the business-class households have a higher likelihood of not enrolling children, due to the potential child labour earnings. In both Uttar Pradesh and in Bihar, we get the expected results in most cases. However, the effect is insignificant in most cases.

Education of the Parents

The education of the parents, especially of the mothers, has a favourable impact on the educational expenditure in each of the states in most cases. Parental education captures the taste for education and hence we can say that the taste for education is higher among the better-educated households.

Development of the Village

In Uttar Pradesh, as opposed to Bihar, a higher level of caste homogeneity at the village level results in a lower level of expenditure being directed to education in the age-group of 10–14 years. This seems to be driven by the strengthening of the anti-female bias in education, in a society that already has a taste for promoting the education of male children vis-à-vis female children. However, the other infrastructure variable is, in general, insignificant.

CONCLUSIONS

Intra-household allocation of educational expenditure constitutes an important channel through which parental discrimination between the boy and the girl child manifests itself within the family unit. Inappropriate econometric tools may lead to a rejection of gender bias even when it exists and hence give rise to faulty policy recommendations. We use Heckman's sample-selection model. We also argue that Heckman's sample-selection is an appropriate framework in this case. Our results confirm that there are significant gaps in the educational expenditure directed at girls vis-à-vis the boys within the family unit. This discrimination may be either through choice of non-enrolment of girls, or through lower expenditures on her schooling, conditional on enrolment.

In view of the evidence presented in this chapter and Kingdon (2005), programmes like the Integrated Child Development Scheme (ICDS) and the Mid-day Meal Programme, etc., assume special significance. These programmes can enable the government to compensate for the relatively lower allocations directed towards the females within the family unit. Special schemes like the Female Secondary School Scholarships, introduced by the Government of Bangladesh, can also go a long way in ensuring equal opportunities for boys and girls. At the same time, one must acknowledge that the lower allocation of household resources towards the females has its roots in the pro-son attitude that is entrenched in our culture. Governmental interventions can play a complementary role in eradicating this norm. The result, with respect to caste homogeneity in Uttar Pradesh, indicates that the local governments need to play a more active role in eradicating age-old practices, within some dominant communities, of ignoring the education of females. Improving the access to schools through the construction of all-weather roads could also go a long way in bringing children to school. A permanent and effective solution, however, can only come through a greater acceptance and acknowledgement of the important and equal role (vis-à-vis the men) of women in society. Joint efforts by the mass media, the government and non-governmental organisations can help turn this distant dream into a reality (Das Gupta et al. 2003).

NOTES

†The authors would like to thank an anonymous referee for comments that have improved the chapter. All tables included in this chapter are generated by the authors and are based on the authors' own data.

1. While Bardhan offers an economic rationale, that of the lower valuation of female labour in wheat growing areas of north India, vis-à-vis the rice cultivated areas where female labour is highly valued, which gives rise to parental discrimination between girls and boys, Das Gupta argues that such discriminatory tendencies are entrenched in the culture and economic hardships merely aggravate them, rather than giving rise to them.

2. See Deaton (1989) for details.

3. The data can be downloaded from the site: http://www.worldbank.org/ lsms/country/ india/upbhhome.html (accessed June 2019).

4. The indices for parental education are summative indices scaled down to one and capture, whether the parent is illiterate, literate, less than primary, primary, middle school, matriculate, or intermediate-level educated, or is a holder of BA, MA, a professional degree and a diploma. Thus, a literate person would have a score of 1/11 and a professional degree holder would have 10/11 and so on.

5. The two dichotomous variables are constructed as follows: 1 in case of an SC/ST household, 0 otherwise and 1 in case of an OBC household, 0 otherwise, respectively.

6. We did not report these sets of results; however, they are available on request.

7. We report the results for the amount of expenditure conditional on spending. Hence, we allow for the decision of whether to incur any education expenditure to be modelled separately from the decision of how much to spend on education, conditional on spending.

8. In the unconditional OLS, the dependent variable is educational expenditure fitted with all children, including those with zero expenditure.

9. The probit refers to the case where the dependent variable is modelled as a binary variable, taking the value of one when the educational expenditure is positive.

10. In the conditional OLS, the dependent variable is natural logarithm of educational expenditure, fitted only with positive expenditure.

11. The base group is children in the age-groups of 0–4 and >20 years.

References

Bardhan, P. 1974. 'On Life and Death Questions'. *Economic and Political Weekly* 9 (Special Number): 1293–1304.

Das Gupta, M. 1987. 'Selective Discrimination against Female Children in Rural Punjab'. *Population and Development Review* 13 (1): 77–100.

Das Gupta, M., J. Zhenghua, L. Bohua, X. Zhenming, W. Chung, and B. H-Ok. 2003. 'Why is Son Preference So Persistent in East and South Asia? A Cross-Country Study of China, India, and the Republic of Korea'. *Journal of Development Studies* 40 (2): 153–87.

Deaton, A. 1989. 'Looking for Boy-Girl Discrimination in Household Discrimination Data'. *The World Bank Economic Review* 3 (1): 1–15.

Dostie, B., and R. Jayaraman. 2003. 'Determinants of School Attendance in Indian Villages; Do Contextual Effects Matter?'. Available at http://www.econ.nyu.edu/cvstarr/conferences/ESPE/ papers/dostieb.pdf.

Dreze, J., and G. G. Kingdon. 2001. 'School Participation in Rural India'. *Review of Development Economics* 5 (1): 1–24.

James, E. 1993. 'Why Do Different Countries Choose A Different Public-Private Mix of Educational Services?' *The Journal of Human Resources* 28 (3): 571–92.

Haddad, L., and T. Reardon. 1993. 'Bias in the Allocation of Resources within Households in Burkina Faso: A Disaggregated Outlay Equivalent Analysis'. *Journal of Development Studies* 29 (2): 260–76.

Kambhampati, U. S., and S. Pal. 2001. 'Role of Parental Literacy in Explaining Gender Difference: Evidence from Child Schooling in India'. *European Journal of Development Research* 13 (2): 97–119.

Kingdon, G. 2005. 'Where Has All the Bias Gone? Detecting Gender Bias in the Intra-Household Allocation of Educational Expenditure'. *Economic Development and Cultural Change* 53 (2): 409–52.

Lillard, Lee A., and Robert J. Willis. 1994. 'Intergenerational Educational Mobility: Effects of Family and State in Malaysia'. *Journal of Human Resources* 29 (4): 1126–66.

National Council of Applied Economic Research [NCAER]. 1999. Human Development Survey Report. New Delhi: NCAER.

Pal, S. 2004. 'How Much Gender Difference in Child School Enrolment Can Be Explained? Evidence from Rural India'. *Bulletin of Economic Research* 56 (2): 133–58.

Quisumbing, A. R. 1993. 'Intergenerational Transfers in Philippine Rice Villages: Gender Differences in Traditional Inheritance Customs'. *Journal of Development Economics* 43 (2): 167–96.

Subramaniam, S. 1995. 'Gender Discrimination in Intra-Household Allocation in India', mimeograph, Department of Economics, Cornell University.

Subramaniam, S., and A. Deaton. 1991. 'Gender Effects in Indian Consumption Patterns'. *Sarvekshana* 14 (4), April-June: 1–12.

Tilak, J. B. G. 2003. 'Determinants of Household Expenditure on Education in India'. In Jandhyala B. G. Tilak, ed. *Financing Education in India: Current Issues and Changing Perspectives*. New Delhi: National Institute of Educational Planning and Administration.

16

Female Education

Changes and Continuation of Gender Roles in Urban India[*]

Ambika Kohli

The Universal Declaration of Human Rights (UDHR) is a non-legally binding declaration adopted by the United Nations General Assembly in 1948. This declaration recites basic ideals to be upheld by all countries. UDHR defines that all human beings, irrespective of their race, religion, sex, birth status, nationality, property, political thought and language, are equal. The slogan 'women's rights are human rights', given by feminist activists, explains that, in general, women are disadvantaged groups and that gender mainstreaming[1] of human rights is required to raise their status in the quest for gender equality. This will aid women's equal participation in political, social, civil, and economic events, eventually entitling them to basic fundamental human rights in most parts of the world, which is still a distant dream for many. One such right is the right to education, a fundamental human right declared under Article 26 of the UDHR.

The famous Ghanian proverb attributed to the scholar James Emmanuel Kwegyir-Aggrey goes, 'If you educate a man, you educate an individual, but if you educate a woman, you educate a family'. It sheds light on how women were traditionally denied education. The sole purpose behind this saying was to encourage parents to educate their daughters (Burek 2007). This maxim advocates for the creation of new opportunities for women by expanding their social spaces, but within the ideology of traditional gender roles, where men are key breadwinners and women are primary caretakers of their families and children.[2] Interestingly, the aforementioned Ghanian saying was quoted by the United Nations Educational, Scientific and Cultural Organization on its 50th anniversary to promote female education.

This ideology of promoting female education on traditional grounds is evident in various international treaties and conventions. For example, a majority of the

* Previously published in *Economic and Political Weekly* 52 (8), 25 February 2017: 61–66.

educational programmes and international conventions, such as the Convention on the Elimination of All Forms of Discrimination against Women (CEDAW), emphasise women's education in relation to enhanced household nutrition, decline in fertility rate, as well as infant mortality and for improving the health and education of children (Goonesekere and Silva-De-Alwis 2005). On the other hand, these benefits are viewed as effective for the participation of women as agents of change by developing their families and communities (ibid.). However, it is problematic to assert that such an approach to implement human rights will aid women to act as agents of change solely; it may, in fact, reproduce traditional social structures.

This chapter adopts education as a women's human rights approach, in the context of urban, Indian, middle-class, married women of Delhi and Haryana. I have employed the theory of multiple modernities to examine how female education is being used by the women themselves for the purpose of empowerment[3] and/or for accommodating traditional gender roles and social expectations.

PROFILE OF THE PARTICIPANTS

This study was carried out among 45 urban, educated and married middle-class women with children within two states, Delhi and the Yamuna Nagar district in Haryana, during 2010 and 2011. Recruiting educated participants allowed me to examine how educated women use their education, both to challenge patriarchal structures and to reproduce them. I recruited the participants through the technique of snowballing and conducted semi-structured interviews in Hindi. Initially, I approached my acquaintances to ask them if they would be interested in participating (if applicable), or if they could spread the word around regarding my research. Forty-three of the 45 participants were Hindus and two were Muslim. The participants were from different age-groups, ranging from mid-20s to early 60s. Despite being from different religious backgrounds and different age ranges, all of the participants shared the same views regarding the importance of female education for accommodating traditional gender roles and for women's financial independence and personal growth.

I have protected the identity of my participants by using pseudonyms and changing their identification details, such as their field of work or study. Using the snowballing technique to recruit participants means there are high chances that a recruiter reading this might be able to identify any participant through her identification details. Participants were both working and non-working. Those working were either self-employed or working in public or private sectors, in the field of education, medicine and law. Twenty-nine participants were working and 16 were housewives. Most of the participants had more than a basic education; only two participants studied till year five and the remaining either finished their schooling (16 participants) or were highly qualified (27 participants): some of them were doctors, lawyers, government officers, teachers or professors. All the 45 participants, irrespective of their educational background, mentioned female education to be of paramount importance. All of them provided higher education to their daughter or daughters (if they had one); in some cases, daughters were even more educated than the sons.

All participants were from a middle-class background. In this study, middle-class is defined as those who have more than the basic necessities of life (food, clothes and shelter), such as a car, mobile phone, laptop, air conditioner and fridge. In urban areas, middle-class groups are no longer limited to upper-caste Hindus, but consist of people from different religions and castes. Sridharan (2011), based on income earnings, suggests three middle-class groups. These include the elite middle-class (more than Rs 1,40,000 per annum [pa]), expanded middle-class (from Rs 1,05,000 pa) and broadest middle-class (from Rs 35,000 pa). My participants belonged to the expanded middle-class group. Because of their financial status, they were able to provide quality English-medium education to all their children, be it a boy or a girl.

However, it is important to note that class cannot be classified solely on the basis of economic capital; cultural values also play an important role. Practising specific cultural values, such as providing quality education to children (both sons and daughters), maintaining a happy family life and being self-sacrificing mothers are essential features of the urban middle-class group (Kumar 2005; Kumar 2011; Thapan 2009). These features were clearly visible in the interviewees' accounts.

Multiple Modernities in India

Traditions are often seen to be static, conservative, bound, non-Western, communal, uncivilised and backward, as well as ahistoric (Eisenstadt 1972: 1; Spiegel and Boonzaier 1988: 41–44; Wolf 1997: 12). There is no universally accepted definition of modernity. However, modernity[4] in the 1950s articulated notions of 'imperatives of change and progress' and 'universal norms and the promise of a better life' (Misa 2003: 5). Indeed, the classical theories of modernity prevalent in the 1950s, such as those of Max Weber and Karl Marx, stated that over time, the Western European modernity would become universal, by replicating Western social forms throughout the world (Eisenstadt 2000: 1). This dichotomy suggests the Eurocentric view that tradition is inferior and modernity is superior (Wolf 1997).

By contrast, S. N. Eisenstadt (2000) proposed the theory of multiple modernities, which rejects Western hegemony in favour of the idea of universal modernity. Eisenstadt argues that these dominant classical theories of modernisation tend to ignore the huge variations within the West (Casanova 2011; Eisenstadt 2000; Kaviraj 2005). Similar to the West, non-Western countries also reveal distinctive modernities, because non-Western societies have adopted some components of modernity within their local context, without giving up all of their own specific elements of cultural tradition (Casanova 2011; Eisenstadt 2000).

Eisenstadt (2000) explained multiple modernities as a repudiation of the homogenising and hegemonic model of Western modernity in non-Western modernising societies. The European model of modernity spread to the world through military, technological and economic expansion; however, not all aspects of this model of modernity were accepted by non-Western societies (ibid.). Thus, modernity is not homologous to Westernisation, nor is Western modernity the authentic modernity, even if it enjoys historical precedence (ibid.: 3). Modern practices are not plainly new, but they are situated in a historical and social context, as modernity is not written on a 'clean slate' (Kaviraj 2000: 138).

Often modernity, in different settings, is the product of the ongoing interaction between traditional and contemporary cultural traditions, including pre-existing socio-cultural arrangements, and is historically specific (Deshpande 2003: 84; Eisenstadt 2000; Kaviraj 2000, 2005; Thornton 2001). For instance, India had a different colonial experience from Latin America and other Asian countries, because of different socio-cultural settings and histories (Kaviraj 2005). Likewise, contemporary social movements in the non-Western countries are anti-Western and yet modern, since they address current concerns (Eisenstadt 2000). They are culture-specific and shaped in a given society by the traditional values and historical experiences of that society. Similarly, various institutions, such as family, education, economic and political structures, are shaped in the process of modernisation within their given socio-cultural and historical settings, signifying different expressions of modernities, both at the local and national levels (ibid.). Therefore, modernity in different parts of the world is not the product of Western modernity alone.

In contemporary India, for example, the phenomenon of multiple modernities is evident, as modernity took on a much different shape from that of the West. However, Dipankar Gupta (2002), in his book *Mistaken Modernity: India between Worlds*, claimed that India has still not achieved modernity, even though there are definite moves away from tradition. Mistaken modernity suggests that patriarchy and oppression coexist and true modernity could not be achieved without adhering to Western universal norms and ideological change (Basu 2005; Gupta 2002). This theory of mistaken modernity is contrary to the idea of multiple modernities and provides a rigid idea of modernity, as it stresses replicating the Western homogeneous model of modernity. It ignores the fact that each society experiences and reproduces modernity in a distinctive way and that its socio-cultural structures and history cannot be completely eroded while achieving modernity. Therefore, I disagree with Gupta and argue that the Indian modernity is distinctively modern, even though it appears to be greatly influenced by traditional cultural values and historical experiences.

Modernity in India, therefore, cannot simply be understood as countering patriarchal norms, nor is it simply Western and alien (Chaudhuri 2012: 284). The traditional and the modern cannot be simply understood as two distinct parallel categories; instead, they are in a complex interaction, both at macro and micro levels. Multiple modernities suggest that local concerns and interests are also being reconstituted and transformation is not just happening at the macro level of the nation-state, politics and democracy alone, but it is also shaping various institutions (Eisenstadt 2000). Here, changes are evident at both the macro and micro levels. One of the transformations at the macro level is a change in the educational system (Kaviraj 2000, 2005).

Kaviraj (2000) highlights changes within the Indian education institutions, which have the potential to affect people's everyday lives at the micro level. For instance, English-medium education was traditionally limited to males from high social classes, but now, to a large extent, males and females from the urban middle class and, to a lesser extent, the working class, also have access to higher English-medium education. Moreover, in the Brahmanical education system, emphasis was given on memorising, rather than analysing the content. The modern education system introduced during the colonial period has raised awareness of developing critical capacities, in addition to memorising, which is still emphasised (Kaviraj 2005: 517–18).

Multiple modernist theorists place immense importance on the roles of the elite in shaping multiple modernities (Casanova 2011; Eisenstadt 2000; Kaviraj 2000). As Kaviraj (2000) explained, the Bengali elite, who had modern education during the colonial period, shaped the process of political modernity by choosing appropriate Western values and also retained certain traditional Indian values. During the colonial period, the elite could be understood as people belonging to the upper strata of society, such as the upper caste or class, having modern education and having an ability to apply that knowledge within their socio-cultural context (Kaviraj 2000). These traits are quite common among the urban, educated, new middle class in contemporary times, with increasing literacy rates and modern lifestyles (Thapan 2001).

Unlike the old middle class, the new middle-class group does not only consist of upper-caste people, but also constitutes 26 per cent of households in India (Baviskar and Ray 2011: 2; Sridharan 2011: 36). However, similar to the old elite, this group does not constitute a majority, but plays a vital role in the process of social transformation through their practices, such as new forms of commodity consumption, luxurious lifestyles and adhering to modern English education (Brosius 2010). Thus, it could be suggested that the shaping of multiple modernities in India is no longer the preserve of specific groups of elite; rather, the educated, new middle class plays a vital role in this process.

Process of Change

Women's empowerment is a 'process of change', which enables women to access social and material resources, alter structural inequalities, build self-reliance and change the patriarchal ideology (Batliwala 1994; Kabeer 1999: 437). Education is perceived to be one of the most significant tools for women's empowerment (Kabeer 1999; Surarpur 2013). Different organisations have incorporated women's education as central to their welfare programmes, for the development of Southern women. For example, the World Bank, in 1995, prioritised girls' education in its programmes to empower women by lifting poverty, reducing the fertility rate and improving child health (Heward 1999). Education allows women to enter the paid sector and to use their skills and knowledge to ensure financial independence. This suggests that education has the capability to transform unequal structures and is also used to conform to patriarchal socio-cultural mores.

Further, educational programmes are adapted by different government and non-governmental organisations within the local context. This local adaptation is evident within the Indian scenario as well. India, for instance, is a signatory to different human rights treaties, which emphasise the importance of female education for women's empowerment. CEDAW, ratified on 9 July 1993, is one such convention that makes the country liable, under Article 10, to address and eliminate gender disparities in the field of education. Therefore, female education at a political level is viewed through the lens of women's empowerment.

Empowering women through education is the nucleus of Indian policy programmes. An overall increase in the female literacy rate was recorded in the 2011 Census, showing an increase from 53.67 per cent in 2001 to 65.46 per cent in 2011 (Dhar 2011). Further, an increase in female literacy rate is also recorded in Delhi and Haryana. The literacy rate of Delhi is above the national average of 74.04 per cent, i.e., at 86.34 per cent; male literacy is 91.03 per cent and female literacy is 80.93 per cent (Census 2011). Similarly, the literacy rate in Haryana is also above the national average, i.e., 66.77 per cent (Census 2011). This increase is indicative of the success of different state-run programmes advocating female education. As a result, women are now able to enter the paid sector for employment purposes, which enables them to be financially independent; this is a significant societal shift.

The patterns of female education and employment among urban, middle-class Indians are remarkable examples of multiple modernities; both modern and traditional values coexist. For example, the traditional dominant ideology confined women to traditional gender roles, by denying them the right to education (True 2012: 60), or providing education to women only to serve domestic needs (Chaudhuri 2012). This phenomenon has been apparent since the twentieth century, when male social reformers encouraged female education on the grounds that education would aid women to perform their gender roles efficiently. It was argued that the ameliorating measures would help women to be better wives and mothers, and 'better carriers' of traditional values (Chaudhuri 2012: 286; Thapan 2001).

Current female education is not primarily advocated to promote their actualisation as individuals. It aims to increase women's age of marriage and reduce the fertility rate, enhance household nutrition, educate children, reduce child mortality and alleviate poverty (Borkotoky and Unisa 2015; Heward 1999: 1; Jain 2006: 43). The traditional values of women being efficient mothers, wives and primary family caretakers are still prevalent. In no way do I claim to undermine the importance of these goals for women's better lives; these changes mean that girls from the urban middle class now have access to all forms of modern education and a range of choices that were earlier denied to them (Thapan 2001).

It is argued that education is leading towards modernity (Inkeles and Smith 1974 cited in Deshpande 2003: 74) and female education and female employment in paid sectors are modern discourses (Heward 1999: 1), with the central aim to correct women's subordinate position in society. Surprisingly, the increase in female literacy rates and increased employment has resulted in a strong demand by the brides' families to find suitable grooms for the young women. Educated grooms are highly valued and considered a good match in the marriage market;[5] this leads to increased demands for dowry on the educated and employed bride's family (Dalmia and Lawrence 2005; Munshi 2012). Modernisation (female education and employment) has seen a significant increase in dowry practices; this is now rapidly spreading in those areas and communities where it was not prevalent before, or where bride price was practised (Agnihotri 2003; Anderson 2003; Self and Grabowski 2009; Srinivasan and Lee 2004). Women are now entitled to inherit their parents' and grandparents' property, but dowry now seems to be a price for a good match, rather than compensation, or a form of financial support. Earlier, dowry was practised by the upper castes as a form of financial support, as women were restricted from working outside, or as a form of compensation, given that they were not allowed to inherit property like their brothers (Dalmia and Lawrence 2005: 73; Srinivasan and Lee 2004).

Increased female literacy rates and employment rates do not demonstrate that autonomy or individualism have been achieved in India. In light of this, modernity cannot be simply understood as progressive, generating equality or liberating, but is a modern process of change that suits the contemporary nature of society. The interaction of contemporary and traditional practices has led to the alteration and reproduction of elements of social structures, with gender inequality being redefined. Male domination of women remains a lived experience; what differs is the nature of that domination.

Among the urban middle class, female education is given great emphasis. The informants insisted on the importance of female education for their daughters' independence and safe future. Simultaneously, the adoption of the women's education model is also used to accommodate the traditional patriarchal needs, for example, finding a suitable educated marriage alliance for the daughter or the efficient performance of social gender roles.

Findings and Discussions

The first finding is that female education among the urban middle class has resulted in an increase in the marriage age of women. However, the importance of the institution of marriage for women remains unchallenged. For example, those interviewees who got married at a late age, such as in their late 20s or early 30s, discussed how they and their families experienced anxiety and faced social pressure to secure a match. Moreover, in some of the cases, female education could be socially perceived as threatening to patriarchal values, such as the idea of the husband's inherent superiority.

Ria, for instance, a mother of a girl child, was working in a public-sector enterprise. She mentioned that her parents had encouraged her to a postgraduate course, so that she could secure a good job and become independent. But, after finishing her post-graduation, her parents did not allow her to pursue a PhD, as it would have been quite difficult for her parents to find a suitable groom for her if she had such a degree. She managed to find a job based on her Masters' qualification. She said that

> My professor called my parents and said that I should do a PhD as I was quite good at studies. He also said that he would help me in getting my papers published. I wrote a

dissertation in Masters, and I did very well in that. My professor was quite impressed and he tried to convince my family. But, it was not possible as it would have been hard for my parents to find a husband for me.

This statement reflects the dominant patriarchal ideology that marriage is quite crucial for a woman, even more than education. Ria's career was ultimately decided not on the basis of her abilities, but on the basis of her being able to find a potential groom. Finding potential grooms can be a challenging task for parents (Heitzman and Worden 1995). Despite the fact that she was intelligent and capable of finishing a doctorate successfully, Ria made her decision within the patriarchal ideology and acquiesced to the notion that a woman should be educated, but not more so than her man; she should generate income, but not more than her man (Mody 2008), as both of these could pose a threat to masculine structures and male authority.

Another participant, Rama, independently made the decision to break her engagement after a prolonged conflict with her parents, because she was more educated than her fiancé. On several instances, she was told by her parents to stop her studies, as her alliance with her fiancé would be a mismatch. Later, her parents found another match for her, based on her preference, but also within the patriarchal framework, where she was not more educated than her husband. Moreover, some of the participants mentioned that they were never interested in getting married and their aim was to achieve higher education in order to secure a highly paid job, so as to become financially and socially independent. But because of the constant pressure from their extended families, parents and community, they have to get married. This demonstrates that women's education can pose a threat to patriarchal masculine structures and despite their educational status, their identity is reliant on the existence of a man.

The second finding is that the affinal family is vital for women and they tailor their educational skills to meet their family needs and maintain family harmony. Women use their education and employment as an asset for their marital family and not merely for their own individual growth. Some studies with information technology professional women in India share similar results (Devika and Mukherjee 2007; Radhakrishnan 2009).

However, the changing social structures of urban societies, such as women receiving higher education and entering into paid employment, have challenged the essentialist ideas of motherhood for Indian women to some extent (Krishnaraj 2010). For example, these days it is common for urban middle-class women to work full-time, and this indicates a significant social change (Radhakrishnan 2007). This transformation is still not predominant and being a self-sacrificing mother remains central to Indian middle-class values (Radhakrishnan 2009). My research sample, for instance, consisted of urban middle-class women, many of whom were working in influential positions, but they still view motherhood as an essential part of their lives. They ascribed vital importance to their families and children and took breaks from their jobs or left their jobs when their children needed more attention. Or, in some cases, they did not even do any job. For instance, Isha was highly educated and had a child. She admitted that a job could be an empowering experience, but did not find it to be the best option for her. Rather, she shared that working would have been a challenging situation, making it difficult to maintain a balance between work and family.

Participants always prioritised their families over work, as many of them started working to support their families financially. All their contributions were done wholeheartedly to support their families and not to achieve any kind of individual aspiration.

Increasingly, women in urban areas are expected to perform domestic chores, in addition to the income-generating activities they perform (Kumari 2010; Mathu and Jain 2008). But still, they do not tend to pose any major challenges to their husbands' authority. Anu, for example, is highly educated and working at a highly-paid position. She is the mother of one child and has said that educated working women should support their families and husband. She mentioned that: 'One [a woman] should not feel that I have started working and now I can suppress my husband...' Anu's account suggests that women's paid work should be to contribute to the family and support her husband.

Similarly, Yamuna, a mother of three children, mentioned the importance of education for women to be confident wives and educated mothers, who could help their children in their studies. She said that

> We (she and her husband) have never forbidden our daughter from pursuing studies. The elder daughter is working and we provided her high education. The younger one did not want to work, but she wanted to study and we spent lots of money on her education as well. See, either you work or not, but education is very important, and it never gets wasted. Rather, a person's knowledge increases. Both of my daughters can teach their children well and are able to talk with the guests nicely.

Yamuna's account explains that education is not only necessary to secure a good job, but it is also an important tool to allow women to perform their traditional gender roles efficiently.

The above findings and discussions suggest that among the urban middle-class families, female education is gaining popularity. Women are able to address the importance of education in various contexts, for themselves and their daughters. Also, more and more women gaining higher qualifications and entering into paid employment is an expression of women's empowerment, where a change in the patriarchal ideology is evident, since the traditional dominant ideology confined women to traditional gender roles by denying them the right to education (True 2012: 60).

Moreover, through education, women are also able to empower themselves in other aspects, such as being able to lead financially secure lives by accessing different social and material resources and building self-reliance. However, despite these transformations, gender inequality still persists and major changes in traditional patriarchal structures and institutions at the grassroots level are needed. This scenario is a perfect case of multiple modernities, where female education and employment are employed to serve traditional gender roles and modern values and needs. Modernity and tradition are in a complex web of interaction; they are interwoven and are shaping contemporary values and norms in a novel way. Reproduction and transformation of structures are evident at the same time, showing that society is undergoing rapid socio-economic changes.

CONCLUSIONS

Education is a fundamental human right and these days, most contemporary Indian women from the urban middle class have access to this right. This entitlement has aided women to open several socio-cultural and financial avenues for themselves. They have become knowledgeable, been able to access resources and have the ability to build financially secure careers. This indicates that development intervention (in its advocacy of female education) has, to some extent, been a success. This in itself is a major achievement. However, it is important to note that female education alone will not achieve gender equality and the promotion of women's education has been couched in patriarchal values, such as its capacity to make women better and more efficient carriers of tradition and ensure a lower fertility rate.

The social values in contemporary India are complex and sometimes paradoxical: women's empowerment and development are promoted alongside structures which encourage their constant patriarchal subordination (Kohli 2012). This is an excellent demonstration of the ways in which modernity is not universal and carries many meanings and implications within different societies. Modernity is culture-specific and modernity in India cannot be simply understood as countering patriarchal norms, nor is it simply Western and alien (Chaudhuri 2012). Rather, development, oppression, empowerment, equality, inequality and patriarchy exist together. Therefore, it could be concluded that the pursuit of female education has been adapted to fit within the specific values of the local context. Ultimately, the education of girls and women from the urban middle class has the capability to both transform patriarchal structures and entrench patriarchal socio-cultural mores.

NOTES

1. Gender mainstreaming is concerned with creating gender equality, so that women and men can benefit equally and inequality is not perpetuated.

2. A similar pattern of advocating female education on traditional grounds is also evident in the Indian context. This localisation of female education is discussed later in the chapter.

3. Women's empowerment in this chapter is discussed in relation to their access to resources, self-reliance, structural inequalities and changing patriarchal ideology. A detailed discussion will be outlined in the chapter on women's empowerment.

4. It is important to mention that in popular speech, 'modern' refers to the latest, and that is how my participants described it.

5. The term market, as it is used here, highlights the consumerist and capitalist ideology in the institution of marriage in contemporary India.

References

Agnihotri, I. 2003. 'The Expanding Dimensions of Dowry'. *Indian Journal of Gender Studies* 10 (2) June: 307–19.

Anderson, S. 2003. 'Why Dowry Payments Declined with Modernisation in Europe, but Are Rising in India?' *Journal of Political Economy* 111 (2) April: 269–310.

Basu, A. M. 2005. 'Ultramodern Contraception Social Class and Family Planning in India'. *Asian Population Studies* 1 (3) February: 303–23.

Batliwala, S. 1994. 'The Meaning of Women's Empowerment: New Concepts from Action'. In G. Sen, A. Germain, and L. Chen, eds, *Population Policies Reconsidered: Health Empowerment and Rights*, 127–38. Cambridge, Massachusetts: Harvard University Press.

Baviskar, A., and R. Ray. 2011. 'Introduction'. In A. Baviskar and R. Ray, eds, *Elite and Everyman: The Cultural Politics of the Indian Middle Classes*, 1–23. New Delhi: Routledge.

Borkotoky, K., and S. Unisa. 2015. 'Female Education and Its Association with Changes in Socio-demographics Behaviour: Evidence from India'. *Journal of Biosocial Science* 47 (5) September: 687–706.

Brosius, C. 2010. *India's Middle Class: New Forms of Urban Leisure, Consumption and Prosperity*. New Delhi: Routledge.

Burek, C. 2007. 'The Role of Women in Geological Higher Education: Bedford College, London (Catherine Raisin) and Newnham College, Cambridge, UK'. In C. V. Burek and B. Higgs, eds, *The Role of Women in the History of Geology*, 9–38. London: The Geological Society.

Casanova, J. 2011. 'Cosmopolitanism, the Clash of Civilizations and Multiple Modernities'. *Current Sociology* 59 (2) March: 252–67.

Census. 2011. 'Missing...Mapping the Adverse Child Sex-Ratio in India'. Available at http://www.censusindia.gov.in/2011census/missing.pdf (accessed on 14 January 2016).

Chaudhuri, M. 2012. 'Indian "Modernity" and "Tradition" a Gender Analysis'. *Polish Sociological Review* 2 (178): 281–93.

Dalmia, S., and P. G. Lawrence. 2005. 'The Institution of Dowry in India: Why It Continues to Prevail'. *The Journal of Developing Areas* 38 (2) Spring: 71–93.

Deshpande, S. 2003. 'Modernisation'. In V. Das, ed. *The Oxford India Companion to Sociology and Social Anthropology*, 63–98. New Delhi: Oxford University Press.

Devika, J., and A. Mukherjee. 2007. 'Re-forming Women in Malayalee Modernity: A Historical Overview'. In Swapna Mukhopadhyay, ed. *The Enigma of Kerala Women: A Failed Promise of Literacy*, 102–30. New Delhi: Social Science Press.

Dhar, Aarti. 2011. 'Significant Boost in Literacy: 2001 Census—Jump in Female Literacy Rate Trump That of Male Rate'. *The Hindu*, 31 March. Available at http://www.thehindu.com/news/national/significant-boost-in-literacy-2011-census/article1588270.ece (accessed on 15 June 2016).

Eisenstadt, S. N. 1972. 'Post-traditional Societies and the Continuity and Reconstruction of Tradition'. In S N Eisenstadt, ed. *Post-traditional Societies*, 1–27. New York: Norton and Company Inc.

———. 2000. 'Multiple Modernities'. *Daedalus* 129 (1) Winter: 1–39.

Goonesekere, S., and R. Silva-De-Alwis. 2005. *Women's and Children's Rights in a Human Rights-based Approach to Development*. New York: UNICEF.

Gupta, D. 2002. *Mistaken Modernity: India between Worlds*. New Delhi: Harper Collins Publisher.

Heitzman, J., and R. L. Worden. 1995. 'India: A Country Study'. Available at http://countrystudies.us/india (accessed on 11 October 2015).

Heward, C. 1999. 'Introduction'. In C. Heward and S. Bunwaree, eds, *Gender Education and Development: Beyond Access to Empowerment*, 1–14. London and New York: Zed Books.

Jain, A. 2006. *The Saga of Female Foeticide in India*. Delhi: Ascent Publications.

Kabeer, N. 1999. 'Resources, Agency, Achievements: Reflections on the Measurement of Women's Empowerment'. *Development and Change* 30 (3) July: 435–64.

Kaviraj, S. 2000. 'Modernity and Politics in India'. *Daedalus* 129 (1) Winter: 137–62.

———. 2005. 'An Outline of a Revisionist Theory of Modernity'. *European Journal of Sociology* 46 (3) December: 497–526.

Kohli, A. 2012. 'Gang Rapes and Molestation Cases in India: Creating Mores for Eve-teasing'. *Te Awatea Review* 10 (1 and 2) December: 13–17.

Krishnaraj, M. 2010. 'Motherhood, Mothers, Mothering: A Multidimensional Perspective'. In M. Krisnaraj, ed. *Motherhood in India: Glorification without Empowerment?*, 9–43. New Delhi: Routledge.

Kumar, N. 2005. 'Mothers and Non-Mothers: Gendering the Discourse of Education in South Asia'. *Gender & History* 17 (1) April: 154–82.

———. 2011. 'The Middle-class Child: Ruminations on Failure'. In A. Baviskar and R. Ray, eds, *Elite and Everyman: The Cultural Politics of the Indian Middle Classes*, 220–43. New Delhi: Routledge..

Kumari, R. 2010. 'Globalising India and Domestic Violence against Women'. *Dialogue* 11 (3) January-March.

Mathu, A., and A. Jain. 2008. 'Gender Equality in India'. In A. Mathu, ed. *Gender and Development in India the Indian Scenario*, 13–38. Delhi: Kalpaz Publications.

Misa, T. J. 2003. 'The Compelling Tangle of Modernity and Technology'. *Modernity and Technology*, 1–30. London: MIT.

Mody, P. 2008. *The Intimate State: Love Marriage and the Law in Delhi*. New Delhi, UK: Routledge.

Munshi, S. 2012. 'Education and Dowry: An Economic Exploration'. *IIM Kozhikode Society and Management Review* 1 (111): 111–20.

Radhakrishnan, S. 2007. 'Rethinking Knowledge for Development: Transnational Knowledge Professionals and the 'New' India'. *Theory and Society* 36 (2): 141–59.

———. 2009. 'Professional Women, Good Families: Respectable Femininity and the Cultural Politics of a "New" India'. *Qualitative Sociology* 32 (2): 195–212.

Self, S., and R. Grabowski. 2009. 'Modernization, Inter-caste Marriage, and Dowry: An Analytical Perspective'. *Journal of Asian Economics* 20 (1) January: 69–76.

Spiegel, A., and E. Boonzaier. 1988. 'Promoting Tradition: Images of the South African Past'. In E. Boonzaier and J. Sharp, eds, *South African Keywords: The Uses and Abuses of Political Concepts*, 40–57. Cape Town: David Philip.

Sridharan, E. 2011. 'The Growth and Sectoral Composition of India's Middle Classes: Their Impact on the Politics of Economic Liberalization'. In A. Baviskar and R. Ray, eds, *Elite and Everyman: The Cultural Politics of the Indian Middle Classes*, 27–57. New Delhi: Routledge.

Srinivasan, P., and G. R. Lee. 2004. 'The Dowry System in Northern India: Women's Attitudes and Social Change'. *Journal of Marriage and Family* 66 (5): 1108–17.

Surarpur, A. B. 2013. 'Role of Education and Employment in Women's Empowerment'. *Indian Streams Research Journal* 2 (2): 1–4.

Thapan, M. 2001. 'Adolescence, Embodiment and Gender Identity in Contemporary India: Elite Women in a Changing Society'. *Women's Studies International Forum* 24 (3/4): 359–71.

——. 2009. *Living the Body: Embodiment, Womanhood and Identity in Contemporary India*. New Delhi, UK, California, Singapore: Sage.

Thornton, A. 2001. 'The Development Paradigm, Reading History Sideways and Family Change'. *Demography* 38 (4): 449–65.

True, J. 2012. *The Political Economy of Violence Against Women*. Oxford, New York: Oxford University Press.

Wolf, E. R. 1997. *Europe and the People without History*. Berkeley: University of California Press.

17

Does Education Pay Off?

*Subjective Expectations on Education in Rural India**

Annemie Maertens†

Parents invest in the education of their children, as they expect this will increase their own and their children's welfare in the long term. Previous research has shown that the magnitude of this investment depends on many factors, including parental education, social and economic background, work opportunities, village and regional development, school quality, costs and educational subsidies.[1]

I take a different angle in this chapter. Using a detailed child-level data-set, I present some results with regard to the subjective expectations that parents have about the costs and returns to education. I find that the parent of a child is more likely 'to have an idea of the returns to higher education (Class XII)' for this child if (among others) he or she receives more information via media and schools, knows more educated people and is more educated him or herself. Among the parents who 'have an idea of the returns to education', the perceived return differs by region, gender (of the child) and caste, with girls and members of the Scheduled Caste (SC) and the Scheduled Tribe (ST) categories being at a disadvantage. These expectations, and the lack thereof, can be expected to influence parents' investment in education.

I also document that the ideal (i.e., socially acceptable) age of marriage for girls, as perceived by the respondents, is around 18 years, compared to 23 years for boys. In conjunction with the tradition of caretaking responsibility resting with male children, this is likely to result in underinvestment in female education. The role of these gender-based social norms is explored in Maertens (2013).

The remainder of this chapter is structured as follows. Section 1 gives a brief overview of the relevant literature. Section 2 introduces the data. Section 3 presents the results. Section 4 concludes.

* Previously published in *Economic and Political Weekly* 46 (9), 26 February 2011: 58–63.

Background

In India, girls and children belonging to lower castes are less likely to go to school, compared to boys and children from upper castes (Drèze and Kingdon 2000). A part of the explanation for this might be group-based heterogeneity in market returns, due to, for instance, labour market discrimination[2] or imperfect information.

Indeed, in deciding on the education of a child, what will matter to the parents is not the average cost and benefits of education, but what they perceive these cost and benefits to be for their particular child. Attanasio and Kaufmann (2009) find that, in the Mexican context, these subjective returns are significant predictors of college and high school attendance choices (but only for richer individuals). As recent literature has shown that these subjective beliefs can differ substantially from the actual returns to education, measuring and understanding these beliefs becomes critical (Jensen 2010; Nguyen 2008).[3]

In addition to these perceived returns to education, social customs might also influence educational investments, in particular marriage customs. When a girl is in her late teens to early 20s, her parents are often pressured by relatives and friends to get her married. Allowing a girl to continue with higher education, as such, might imply postponing her marriage and lead to criticism, social exclusion and maybe even a higher dowry. After marriage, the bride often moves in with her husband or his parents, a practice known as patrilocality. Once the bride has switched homes, it is commonly socially unacceptable to continue to support her natal family, either financially or in terms of physical care. This implies that expected (net) returns to education, from the perspective of the parents, can be very different for boys versus girls, even if both are earning the same during adulthood.

To my knowledge, two prior papers have looked at these social customs within the South Asian context. Foster and Rosenzweig (2001), using panel data from India, find that the practice of patrilocal exogamy—marriage into families outside of the village—may make parents reluctant to invest in their girls. Field and Ambrus (2008) directly test the hypothesis that women attain less schooling as a result of what they believe to be social and financial pressure to marry young. Using household data from rural Bangladesh, they isolate the causal effect of marriage-timing, using age of menarche as an instrumental variable. They find that delaying marriage results in additional schooling.

Data

I collected the data used for this study in 2007–08 in three villages in India. These three villages were selected in 1975 by the International Crop Research Institute of the Semi-Arid Tropics (ICRISAT) as part of their village level studies (VLS) programme.[4] The programme originally covered six villages in south India, but has expanded recently. At the moment, yearly data are being collected in 18 villages. The data collection I conducted focussed on social networks, aspirations and expectations with regard to education—as the existing ICRISAT-VLS data lacks such information.

TABLE 17.1: Introducing Dokur, Kalman and Shirapur

	Dokur	*Kalman*	*Shirapur*
Distance to nearest town (km)	7	15	12
Number of households in village	530	610	580
Number of households in sample	93	102	144
Number of adults in the sample[a]	294	338	409
Number of young adults in the sample[a]	106	124	145
Number of children in the sample[a]	120	151	189
Number of UC individuals[b]	80	352	430
Number of OBC individuals[b]	417	128	53
Number of SC individuals[b]	23	32	118
Number of ST individuals[b]	0	101	142
Average number of household members	5.59	6.00	5.19
Average *kharif* income (Rs)	44,524	40,713	62,965
Average education level of respondent (in years)[c]	3.60	4.66	5.76

Notes: [a]An adult is defined as an individual over the age of 25, a young adult is defined as an individual between the ages of 15 and 25 and a child is defined as an individual under the age of 15. The adults also include the daughters-in-law under 25, who did not receive their education in the household;
[b]UC = Upper Castes (open category), OBC = Other Backward Castes, SC = Scheduled Castes, ST = Scheduled Tribes;
[c]The respondent is the main decision-maker on the education of children under 25 years in the household.

Table 17.1 introduces the three villages selected. Dokur, with 530 households, is the smallest of the three villages. It is located in the drought-prone, poor Telangana region of Andhra Pradesh. In terms of income, Dokur is situated between the poorer Kalman and richer Shirapur. Kalman and Shirapur, with 610 and 580 households, respectively, are located in the Sholapur district of south-west Maharashtra. At present, Dokur has one public school, which offers education up to Class X. Kalman and Shirapur offer, respectively, up to Class XII and X (Table 17.2).

The ICRISAT-VLS sample includes 93, 102 and 144 households in Dokur, Kalman and Shirapur, respectively, a total of 1,876 individuals. The average size of a household is between five and six members in all three villages. In Dokur, 80 per cent of the individuals are classified as OBC and 15 per cent as upper caste (UC).[5] In the Maharashtra villages, 60 per cent of the individuals belong to UC and between 16 per cent and 19 per cent of the individuals are members of the tribal category.[6]

I interviewed the main decision-maker with regard to the education of the individuals under the age of 26 years. In many cases, the decision-maker is the father of the children, or in some cases, the mother, grandfather or uncle.

The average education level of the respondent is low, especially in Dokur (3.6 years). About 36 per cent of the respondents have not completed first standard and only 6 per cent have received at least one year of higher education. Of the children between the ages of six and 15 years, over 90 per cent are enrolled in school in all three villages (Table 17.2). Of the young adults between the ages of 15 and

25 years, 30 per cent, 36 per cent and 19 per cent, respectively, are enrolled in an educational institute in Dokur, Kalman and Shirapur. There is little gender difference in enrolment up to the age of 15 years, but compared to male young adults, fewer female young adults are enrolled in an educational institute (30 per cent versus 24 per cent). In terms of caste, UC children and young adults are, respectively, up to 10 per cent and 20 per cent more likely to be enrolled in an educational institute, compared to other castes.[7]

TABLE 17.2: Schooling and Education

	Dokur	*Kalman*	*Shirapur*
Number of schools located in the village	1	2	2
Highest grade offered in the village	10	12	10
Children enrolled in school (per cent)*	90	96	91
Young adults enrolled in school (per cent)*	30	36	19

Notes: * See definition in Table 17.1; as a percentage of all individuals within the relevant age-group; children under the age of six were excluded from this calculation.

I elicited current beliefs regarding the returns to education among all 556 individuals, currently enrolled in an educational institute or planning to go to school (for instance, children under the age of seven), using a method inspired by Dominitz and Manski (1996) and Lybbert et al. (2007).[8]

Concretely, I first elicited the minimum and maximum earnings the respondent thought the child would earn (net of direct costs in self-employment), on a monthly basis, when finishing particular schooling milestones, for instance, Class XII.[9] During this exercise, the respondent was asked to imagine the various options possible, i.e., various types of employment, including self-employment, and various locations where the child might live in the future, anticipating the possibility of migration (if applicable in their view). Then, I made three boxes, evenly distributed between this minimum and maximum and I asked the respondent to use 20 identical stones (each stone representing a 5 per cent probability) to form an earnings density function. To ensure that the respondent understood the set-up, I started this game with some simple stone exercises, practising the conversion from stones to percentages/shares. Then, I did two trial games, applied to popular topics (elections, weather, exam success and cricket matches), such as, 'What is the chance it will rain tomorrow?' If the respondent looked confused, put all his stones in one pile, or left an empty box at any of the two ends of the distribution, the question was rephrased. In general, the respondents appeared to have a good understanding of the set-up and I had to repeat the question only a couple of times. This exercise was then repeated for the various levels that the child still had ahead of him/her and could include Class VIII, X, XII, diploma, bachelor's, engineering, medical doctor and master's.[10]

Through this exercise, I basically elicited an estimate of the density function of monthly earnings, unconditional on the nature of the work, but conditional on the child's characteristics, such as gender, caste and perceived ability. During the trial round, I attempted to elicit the function conditional on various jobs, but this appeared a futile exercise due to the many different jobs the respondent had in mind, and the fact that most respondents in the trial round had a sort of trickle-down probability system in mind (the chances of getting job A are x per cent and, if he does not get that job, he will try for job B, etc...). Throughout this chapter, I will refer to these earnings as the perceived 'returns' to education. In addition, for one of the villages (Dokur), I added a similar exercise to elicit the density function of perceived direct costs of education (per level).

In addition to these future earnings, I asked the decision-maker how much he or she expects each of his/her children to contribute to their 'old age pension' and to take care of him/her on a day-to-day basis (in terms of physical care). The respondent was first asked to estimate the total financial contribution of his children on a monthly basis (in Rs)[11] and then asked to rank his children in terms of share contributed. Once the respondent decided on the ranking, I asked to attribute a percentage to each child. The same exercise was repeated in terms of physical care (in terms of days spent per month).

The question with regard to the age of marriage was asked as follows, independent of a particular child, 'What is the ideal age for a girl/boy to get married these days?'

RESULTS

There were several respondents who were unable to reconstruct the future earnings density functions of their children. These respondents answered 'no idea' when asked to reconstruct the density function. From Table 17.3, one can see that the majority of the children for whom the decision-maker does not know the returns to education are located in Dokur. There is no difference between male and female children, indicating that this type of knowledge is household-level knowledge and not child-level knowledge. This is confirmed by comparing knowledge on the returns to education of boys and girls within the same household (results available on request). The percentage of children for whom the respondent states that they

TABLE 17.3: No Idea about Returns to Education (In percentage of total number currently enrolled or planning to go within the relevant age-group)

	Dokur	*Kalman*	*Shirapur*	*Male*	*Female*	*UC*	*OBC*	*SC/ST*
Class VIII	1	1	0	1	0	1	1	0
Class X	2	2	0	2	0	1	2	0
Class XII	18	1	0	5	5	0	14	3
Diploma	41	3	0	12	12	3	33	3
Bachelor's	36	1	0	10	10	1	30	3
Medical doctor	57	1	0	16	16	3	44	3
Engineer	53	1	0	15	15	2	43	4
Master's	59	6	0	17	17	7	46	4

Note: Includes the children under 15 years of age.

have no idea about the returns to education increases as the level (of education) increases. Almost all respondents could answer the question for Class VIII, but only for about 40 per cent of children in Dokur did the decision-maker have some idea of what someone with a master's degree earns.

Table 17.4 shows the results of a regression analysis. The dependent variable is 'whether or not the respondent states "don't know" in the stone game (1 = don't know, 0 = know)'. As in Table 17.3, in order to avoid major issues of selection into the school-going status, I focus on children under the age of 15 (as over 90 per cent go to school within that category). The regression analysis includes Class XII and the higher education choices. Note that network formation is not taken into account and one needs to interpret the coefficients accordingly.

Table 17.4: What Determines Not Knowing Returns to Education

Probit Regression with Dependent Variable:	*Don't Know Returns*	
	Standard	
	Coefficient	*Marginal Effect*
Information received via media, etc.	–0.0887*** (0.0247)	–0.0084*** (0.0023)
Question relates to higher education	0.0661** (0.0295)	–0.0028 (0.0022)
Question relates to Class XII		–0.1166*** (0.0148)
Question relates to higher education	–0.0159***	
* No. of people known in village who received higher education	(0.0057)	–0.0037*** (0.0013)
Question relates to Class XII	–0.0111***	
* No. of people known in village who are educated up to Class XII	(0.004)	–0.0009*** (0.0003)
Question relates to higher education	–0.0931***	
* No. of people known outside of village who received higher education	(0.0277)	–0.0026*** (0.0009)
Question relates to Class XII	–0.1222***	
* No. of people known outside of village who are educated up to Class XII	(0.0211)	–0.0012*** (0.0002)
OBC	0.5412*** (0.1797)	0.0513*** (0.0163)
SC/ST	–0.0486 (0.1947)	–0.0046 (0.0185)
Female child	0.0018 (0.1003)	0.0002 (0.0095)
Age of child (years)	0.0074 (0.011)	0.0007 (0.001)

(Contd)

Table 17.4- (Contd)

Probit Regression with Dependent Variable:	*Don't Know Returns*	
	Standard	
	Coefficient	*Marginal Effect*
Female decision-maker	0.0934 (0.1442)	0.0089 (0.0137)
Age of decision-maker (years)	0.0225** (0.004)	0.0021*** (0.0004)
Education of decision-maker (years)	–0.052*** (0.0189)	–0.0049*** (0.0018)
Highest education level in household (years)	0.0164 (0.0151)	0.0016 (0.0014)
Constant	–3.388 (0.3807)	

Notes: *** p<0.01; ** p<0.05; * p<0.1; robust standard errors are reported in parentheses below the coefficient and average marginal effects estimates.

Controlled for wealth and income effects.

Includes state-fixed effects.

'Information received via media, etc' measures the frequency in which the respondent receives information, from TV, radio, newspapers, internet, magazines and schools, about education and employment. The variable takes a value between 0 (never from any source) and 18 (very often from all sources).

Only includes children under 15 years of age. Only includes Class XII and the higher education choices. N = 2616.

One can see that the respondent is less likely to know the returns to higher education (Class XII) for a particular child if he does not often receive information via the media, is older, received less education himself and knows fewer people, both inside and outside of the village, who completed higher education (Class XII). Note that the variable 'number of people known in the village' includes the people who used to live in the village and migrated out. Knowing the returns appears uncorrelated with the gender and age of the child, but does depend on the caste of the family, with the OBC being at a disadvantage in this regard. This most likely implies that the information variables do not capture all aspects of learning. For instance, one can imagine that just knowing someone with an engineering degree is not sufficient; one also needs to know this person's monthly salary to update one's beliefs with regard to returns to education.

Table 17.5 shows that, on average, respondents believe that medical doctors, engineers and 'postgraduates' (i.e., someone with a master's degree) earn, respectively, Rs 25,985 per month, Rs 18,364 per month and Rs 14,644 per month. With a diploma or bachelor's degree, one is expected to earn (on average) Rs 8,331 per month and Rs 9,528 per month, respectively. Thus, even with a two-year diploma degree, children in these three villages are expected to earn (on average) more than twice as much compared to those who have studied till Class XII.

TABLE 17.5: Expectations with Regard to Earnings (in Rs/month)

By Village:		*Dokur*			*Kalman*			*Shirapur*	
	No.	*Average*	*St Dev*	*No.*	*Average*	*St Dev*	*No.*	*Average*	*St Dev*
Class VIII	116	1,777	679	143	2,680	2,677	180	1,422	599
Class X	131	3,415	4,153	159	3,706	3,948	192	2,090	933
Class XII	119	4,043	1,554	175	5,302	5,825	198	2,911	1,311
Diploma	88	9,172	3,593	187	10,106	10,429	206	6,360	2,233
Bachelor's	95	8,204	2,500	191	10,652	6,841	205	9,094	3,090
Medical doctor	63	29,466	7,896	192	32,257	80,642	206	19,075	8,444
Engineer	69	24,100	7,300	191	20,019	18,201	206	14,908	6,415
Master's	60	17,161	11,282	182	16,701	18,775	205	12,080	4,736
By Gender:		*Total*			*Male*			*Female*	
	No.	*Average*	*St Dev*	*No.*	*Average*	*St Dev*	*No.*	*Average*	*St Dev*
Class VIII	439	1,926	1,699	237	2,039	1,576	202	1,792	1,828
Class X	482	2,983	3,267	262	3,083	3,062	220	2,865	3,498,
Class XII	492	4,035	3,792	271	4,280	4,049	221	3,735	3,435
Diploma	481	8,331	7,046	269	8,704	7,401	212	7,858	6,554
Bachelor's	491	9,528	4,923	273	10,158	5,253	218	8,739	4,361
Medical doctor	461	25,985	52,724	257	27,196	51,131	204	24,460	54,754
Engineer	466	18,364	13,137	260	19,763	13,749	206	16,597	12,126
Master's	447	14,644	13,257	253	15,160	12,909	194	13,971	13,702
By Caste Group:		*UC*			*OBC*			*SC/ST*	
	No.	*Average*	*St Dev*	*No.*	*Average*	*St Dev*	*No.*	*Average*	*St Dev*
Class VIII	196	2,173	2,327	139	1,864	936	104	1,540	758
Class X	222	3,419	4,583	151	2,866	1,342	109	2,260	1,048
Class XII	241	4,291	4,932	142	4,247	2,462	109	3,194	1,572
Diploma	256	8,738	8,895	113	9,285	4,556	112	6,437	2,654
Bachelor's	261	9,788	5,418	118	9,792	4,960	112	8,642	3,356
Medical doctor	256	29,669	70,065	94	25,433	9,641	111	17,956	8,304
Engineer	258	19,244	16,163	97	20,353	8,059	111	14,579	6,543
Master's	244	15,520	15,835	92	16,804	11,498	111	10,927	5,458

Notes: For each individual currently enrolled in an educational institute, the expected average monthly earnings is calculated assuming a step-wise distribution, with the minimum and maximum of the distribution of earnings, as specified by the respondent, for each level/programme of education completed. These earnings are equivalent to the wage in case of wage employment and are earnings net of costs in the case of self-employment.

The numbers presented in this table indicate the simple averages and simple standard deviations of these individual averages.

Includes only children under 15 years of age.

With regard to gender, girls are expected to earn less on a monthly basis, compared to boys, independent of the level of education. This difference is significantly different from zero at the 5 per cent level, only for the bachelor's and engineering degrees. Note that even if there were no systematic difference in perceived ability between girls and boys, this does not imply that the parents anticipate direct wage discrimination for certain jobs, as these expectations also capture the fact that girls might be expected to do different kinds of work.

Compared to OBC and UC, the parents of SC/ST children expect a lower return at all levels of education. The difference with both OBC and UC is significantly different from zero at the 5 per cent level, for all levels of education. UC respondents, on average, expect a lower return to higher education compared to OBC respondents, at most education levels. But the difference is not significantly different from zero at the 5 per cent level.

The perceived direct costs of education, as measured in Dokur village, are significant (compared to the average income). On average, Dokur respondents estimate that a year of education up to Class VIII costs Rs 1,183 per year, Class IX and X cost about Rs 3,183 per year, Class XI and XII cost Rs 5,750 per year. A year of higher education is estimated to cost (on average) Rs 8,482 per year in case of an undergraduate degree, Rs 13,250 per year in case of a diploma, Rs 10,777 per year for a medical degree and Rs 76,832 per year for an engineering degree. These averages need to be taken with a grain of salt, as there is a large amount of variability in these estimated costs. In particular, the actual direct cost will depend on whether or not the child has access to scholarships and the type of educational institute selected (private versus public).

To gain a better understanding of these, between gender and caste differences in perceived returns to education, I run a set of regressions of subjective expected returns to education on (among others) a set of variables capturing various sources of information. Three caveats are in order. First, as the set of variables determining whether a respondent knows the returns are necessarily the same as the set of variables determining his exact beliefs of these returns, one cannot control for the selection effect into the 'knowing status'. This implies that the results are only representative for the people who have already some idea of the returns to education. Second, while the precision of the perceived return is likely to increase with the number of people known, the level of these returns has no obvious relation to the number of people known. Indeed, if both over- and underestimation occur, this relationship might be not be a one-on-one mapping and hence, running a simple regression, as the one below, might make little sense. Ideally, one would need to compare these returns to the returns estimated using nationally representative data, such as NSS. I am leaving this exercise for future research. Third, endogeneity due to omitted variables (such as child ability) and network formation might be present.

Keeping these three caveats in mind, Table 17.6 presents selected results with regard to the engineering degree. One can see that knowing a person from outside of the village with an engineering degree increases the expected returns by (on average) Rs 1,626 per month. Knowing a person from the village with an engineering degree does not have a statistically significant impact on the perceived returns to an engineering degree. The estimated coefficient on SC, 'female child' and 'age of child' is statistically significantly negative. Apart from the coefficient on SC, the signs of these various coefficients are not stable across the various educational choices. This lack of stability suggests that both underestimation and overestimation of the returns is taking place and the specification in Table 17.6 does not fully capture the learning process.

TABLE 17.6: Correlates of Expected Return to Education (Engineering Degree)

Probit Regression with Dependent Variable:	*Expected Return to Education Engineering Degree (in Monthly Earnings in Rs)*	
	Coefficient	
Information received via media, etc.	−78 (747)	−246 (856)
Information received via media, etc. (square)	−45 (37)	−30 (43)
No. of people known outside of the village with such a degree	1,626** (741)	
No. of people known outside of the village with such a degree (square)	−208** (83)	
No. of people known in the village with such a degree	−1921 (1,701)	
No. of people known in the village with such a degree (square)	161 (291)	
No. of people known among non-relatives with such a degree		821 (757)
No. of people known among non-relatives with such a degree (square)		−116 (72)
No. of people known among relatives with such a degree		−253 (1,560)
No. of people known among relatives with such a degree (square)		−197 (196)
OBC	−1174 (1,827)	−1,418 (1,871)
SC/ST	−3,440** (1,580)	−3740** (1,765)
Female child	−3,930*** (1,360)	−3827*** (1,344)
Age of child (years)	−368* (216)	−371* (219)

Notes: *** p<0.01; ** p<0.05; * p<0.1; robust standard errors are reported in parenthesis, below the coefficient and average marginal effects estimates.

Controlled for wealth, income, education of decision-maker, gender and age decision-maker, highest education level in household.

Includes state-fixed effects.

See also notes to Table 17.5.

Note that no control for ability or perceived ability is included, as this variable was not recorded for children under the age of six. N = 375.

Table 17.7 presents the summary statistics with regard to the age of marriage. During the qualitative interviews preceding the questionnaires, many of the respondents mentioned that a family who has an unmarried older daughter at home is often criticised, sometimes compromising the marriage prospects of the other children and resulting in social exclusion of the adult household members. As such, it is in the parents' interest to marry their daughter around the 'ideal age of marriage', i.e., the socially accepted age of marriage. The (average) ideal age of marriage is 18.3 years in the case of girls and 22.7 years in the case of boys. This is a bit higher for both sexes in Dokur, compared to the Maharashtra villages (the difference between Dokur and the Maharashtra villages is significantly different from zero at the 5 per cent level) and a bit lower for SC/ST, compared to the other castes (the difference between SC/ST and the other castes is significantly different from zero at the 5 per cent level).

TABLE 17.7: Ideal Age of Marriage

Total:	*No.*	*Average*	*St Dev*						
Girl's age	338	18.3	1.8						
Boy's age	338	22.7	2.3						
By Village:		*Dokur*			*Kalman*			*Shirapur*	
	No.	*Average*	*St Dev*	*No.*	*Average*	*St Dev*	*No.*	*Average*	*St Dev*
Girl's age	93	19.1	1.5	102	18.0	1.0	143	18.1	2.2
Boy's age	93	24.0	2.2	102	21.7	1.7	143	22.7	2.3
By Caste Group:		*UC*			*OBC*			*SC/ST*	
	No.	*Average*	*St Dev*	*No.*	*Average*	*St Dev*	*No.*	*Average*	*St Dev*
Girl's age	156	18.7	1.9	108	18.5	1.5	74	17.4	1.5
Boy's age	156	22.9	2.4	108	23.0	2.4	74	22.0	1.8

To conclude this section, Table 17.8 presents the financial support and physical care parents expect from their children in old age. With the exception of a handful of respondents who have access to savings or an old-age pension, most respondents reported that they would have to rely on their children. The patrilocal marriage system, as practised in the three villages, in which married couples reside with or near the family of the husband, implies that the (majority) of the returns to education after marriage go to the family-in-law. Table 17.6 shows that, indeed, in all villages and all caste groups, the majority of the care and support is expected from the male children. The difference in support expected from male versus female children is larger in the case of UC and smaller in Dokur. The latter might be due to the phenomenon of cousin marriage in Andhra Pradesh, making the future earnings of daughters more 'accessible' to parents, as she stays within the family.[12]

TABLE 17.8: Support Expected from Children in Old Age

	Total	*Dokur*	*Kalman*	*Shirapur*	*UC*	*OBC*	*SC/ST*
Financial support							
Boys	76	70	74	81	80	72	75
Girls	36	44	31	35	32	44	33
Physical care							
Boys	59	56	63	58	61	59	54
Girls	58	59	46	65	58	60	56

Notes: (Averages, in percentage support expected).

The numbers presented in Table 17.6 are the sample averages of the percentage care/support expected from male/female children.

Note that at a household level, these two percentages add up to 100 per cent, in most cases (except for the case where the respondent has access to savings or a pension); N=273 boys and N=238 girls.

DISCUSSION

Using a detailed child-level data-set collected for this purpose in three villages in Andhra Pradesh and Maharashtra in 2007–08, I present in this chapter a first analysis of subjective returns to education in the Indian context.

I find that the probability that a respondent has some idea of the returns to education for a particular child depends (among others), in a positive manner, on the information received through media and schools, on the number of educated people known and on the respondent's own education. Among the respondents who have some idea of the returns to education, I find that the respondents' expectations with regard to his children's return to education differ by region, gender (of the child) and caste, with girls and members of SC/ST expected to earn less. Whether these caste and gender-based differences reflect labour market discrimination, a systematic difference in perceived ability, or are the result of caste-based information networks, is left as a topic for future research[13]. Note also that these figures are only representative for families with young children (under the age of six) and children currently enrolled in school. Families which have teenage children who are not in school are not being represented and, as such, these figures might underestimate the actual caste and gender-based difference.

In addition, I document that the ideal age of marriage for girls, as perceived by the respondents, is around 18 years (versus about 23 years for boys) and that boys are expected to take financial care of their parents in old age. The latter might reduce the incentive for parents to invest in the education of girls, by reducing the net returns to the parents, while the former might lead to social pressures if a girl is allowed to continue for higher education (and hence, has to postpone marriage). I investigate how these norms impact educational investment in Maertens (2013).

NOTES

†The data for the chapter were gathered in India during 2007–08, in collaboration with the International Crop Research Institute of the Semi-Arid Tropics, and funded through a NSF Doctoral Dissertation Research Improvement Grant, an AAEA McCorkle Fellowship, a Mario Einaudi Center for International Studies International Research Travel Grant, a Cornell University Graduate School Research Travel Grant, an International Student and Scholar Office Grant and funds provided by AEM-CU and Chris Barrett. I thank the research assistants and enumerators on the field: Sanjit Anilesh, Shraavya Bhagavatula, Pramod Bangar, Sana Butool, V. D. Duche, Shital Duche, Madhav Dhere, Nishtha Ghosh, Navika Harshe, Meenal Inamdar, Shilpa Indrakanti, Sapna Kale, Jessica Lebo, Nishita Medha, Ramesh Babu Para, Abhijit Patnaik, Gore Parmeshwar, Arjun Waghmode and Yu Qin. This chapter benefitted from discussions with Cynthia Bantilan, Kaushik Basu, Chris Barrett, A. V. Chari, Steven Coate and George Jakubson. The usual disclaimers apply. All tables included in this chapter are author-generated and based on the author's own data.

1. The literature in economics on education is vast. Rosenzweig (1995) and Schultz (1961, 1989) provide good introductions.

2. Some studies indicate that women and lower-caste groups might suffer from wage discrimination (Ito 2009; Kingdon 1998; Rosenzweig and Schultz 1982). One needs to be careful, however, in interpreting these results. As women in India tend to be found in very different jobs than men, a difference in wages cannot be interpreted as evidence of direct discrimination against women. Once the nature of the job is taken into account, Chakravarty and Somanathan (2007) find no evidence of wage discrimination against women. But then, of course, the question of why women are found in different jobs can be raised.

3. Jensen (2010) finds that measured returns to schooling in the Dominican Republic are high, but the returns perceived by students are extremely low. Nguygen (2008) finds that the median return—as perceived by parents—matches the average return estimated from household survey data in Madagascar. There is, however, a considerable amount of dispersion, in both perception of the average return and of the child's own return. She attributes the latter to heterogeneity in the actual returns and imperfect information.

4. The sample of households selected in each village is representative for each village in terms of landholding size. For an overview of the ICRISAT-VLS programme, see Bantilan et al. (2006), Rao and Charyulu (2007), Singh et al. (1985) and Walker and Ryan (1990).

5. In Andhra Pradesh, next to the SCs and STs, the following socially and educationally backward classes are recognised: Group A (other tribes), Group B (vocational groups), Group C (SC who converted to Christianity), Group D (others), and Group E (Muslims). For the purpose of interstate comparison, I categorised Group C under SC and the other groups under OBC.

6. In Maharashtra, next to the SCs and STs, the following backward classes are recognised: (1) SC converts to Buddhism, (2) STs, including those living outside specified areas, (3) Vimukta Jati and Denotified Tribes, (4) Nomadic Tribes (6) OBCs. For the purpose of interstate comparison, I categorised, Group (6) under OBC, Group (1) under SC and the remainder of the groups under T, referring to tribes.

7. Naturally, enrolment does not imply regular attendance. Of all the children and young adults enrolled in an educational institute, 87 per cent do not miss classes more than 10 per cent of the time. Again, there is some variation between caste groups and gender, with girls being less likely to miss classes and members of lower-caste groups being more likely to miss classes.

8. For an overview on how one can elicit subjective expectations, see Delavande et al. (2010, 2011).

9. In case of seasonal jobs, the respondent was asked to imagine yearly (instead of monthly) earnings, which we then divided by 12.

10. Thus, for a child currently enrolled in Class XI, one was asked to reconstruct the density function for Class XII, diploma, bachelor's, engineering, medical doctor and master's, but not for Class VIII or X.

11. The question was phrased in this manner, as it followed the way the respondents structured their answer to the more open-ended questions on old-age care, during the qualitative data-collection round preceding the trial round.

12. In south India, it is common for Hindu cross-cousins to marry, with matrilateral cross-cousin (mother's brother's daughter) marriages being especially favoured. This southern kinship model prevails in the states of Kerala, Tamil Nadu, Karnataka and Andhra Pradesh. On the cost and benefits of cousin marriages, see Field et al. (2011).

13. Chari and Maertens (2014) provide some suggestive evidence of the second reason and that parents are less attentive to the abilities and qualifications of girl-children.

References

Attanasio, Orazio, and Katja Kaufmann. 2009. 'Educational Choices, Subjective Expectations and Credit Constraints', NBER Working Papers 15087, National Bureau of Economic Research. Available at https://www.nber.org/papers/w15087.pdf.

Bantilan, M. C., S. P. Anand Babu, G. V. Anupama, H. Deepthi, and R. Padmaja. 2006. 'Dryland Agriculture: Dynamic Challenges and Priorities'. *Research Bulletin No. 20*, GT-IMPI (Global Theme on Institutions, Markets, Policy and Impacts), ICRISAT. Available at https://mpra.ub.uni-muenchen.de/16423/1/MPRA_paper_16423.pdf.

Chakravarty, Sujoy, and E. Somanathan. 2007. 'Non-Discrimination in and Elite Labour Market: Job Placements at the Indian Institute of Management—Ahmedabad', paper presented at the International Conference on Comparative Development, Indian Statistical Institute, New Delhi, 18–20 December.

Chari, A. V., and A. Maertens. 2014. 'Gender, Productive Ability and the Perceived Returns to Education: Evidence from Rural India'. *Economics Letters* 122 (2): 253–257.

Delavande, Adeline, Xavier Giné, and David McKenzie. 2011. 'Measuring Subjective Expectations in Developing Countries: A Critical Review and New Evidence'. *Journal of Development Economics* 94 (2): 151–63.

Delavande, Adeline, Xavier Giné, and David McKenzie. 2010. 'Eliciting Probabilistic Expectations with Visual Aids in Developing Countries: How Sensitive are Answers to Variations in Elicitation Design?', Policy Research Working Paper, October, World Bank.

Dominitz, Jeff, and Charles F. Manski. 1996. 'Eliciting Student Expectations of the Returns to Schooling'. *Journal of Human Resources* 31 (1): 1–26.

Drèze, Jean, and Geeta Gandhi Kingdon. 2000. 'School Participation in Rural India'. *Review of Development Economics* 5 (1): 1–24.

Field, Erica, and Attila Ambrus. 2008. 'Early Marriage, Age of Menarche, and Female Schooling Attainment in Bangladesh'. *Journal of Political Economy* 116 (5): 881–929.

Field, E., S. Jayachandran, and M. Al Shafaee. 2011. 'Causes and Consequences of Consanguineous Marriage', Working Paper, July 2011, Duke University.

Foster, Andrew, and Mark R. Rosenzweig. 2001. 'Missing Women, the Marriage Market and Economic Growth', unpublished manuscript. https://sites.hks.harvard.edu/cid/archive/events/cidneudc/papers/sex.pdf.

Ito, Takahiro. 2009. 'Caste Discrimination and Transaction Costs in the Labour Market: Evidence from Rural North India'. *Journal of Development Economics* 88: 292–300.

Jensen, Robert. 2010. 'The Perceived Returns to Education and the Demand for Schooling'. *Quarterly Journal of Economics* 125 (2): 515–48.

Kingdon, Geeta Gandhi. 1998. 'Does the Labour Market Explain Lower Female Schooling in India?'. *Journal of Development Studies* 35 (1): 39–65.

Lybbert, Travis J., Christopher B. Barrett, John G. McPeak, and Winnie K. Luseno. 2007. 'Bayesian Herders: Updating of Rainfall Beliefs in Response to External Forecasts'. *World Development* 35 (3): 480–97.

Maertens, Annemie. 2013. 'Social Norms and Sspirations: Age of Marriage and Education in Rural India'. *World Development* 47: 1–15.

Nguyen, Trang. 2013. *Information, Role Models and Perceived Returns to Education Experimental Evidence from Madagascar (English)*. enGender Impact: the World Bank's Gender Impact Evaluation Database. Washington DC: World Bank. Available at http://documents.worldbank.org/curated/en/655701468053368779/Information-role-models-and-perceived-returns-to-education-experimental-evidence-from-Madagascar

Rao, K. P. C., and D. Kumara Charyulu. 2007. 'Changes in Agriculture and Village Economies'. *Research Bulletin No 21*, GT-IMPI. Andhra Pradesh: ICRISAT.

Rosenzweig, Mark R., and Paul T. Schultz. 1982. 'Market Opportunities, Genetic Endowments, and Intrafamily Resource Distribution: Child Survival in Rural India'. *American Economic Review* 72 (2): 803–15.

Rosenzweig, Mark. 1995. 'Why Are There Returns to Schooling?'. *American Economic Review* 85 (2): 153–58.

Schultz, Paul T. 1989. 'Education Investments and Returns'. In Hollis B. Chenery and T. N. Srinivasan, ed. *Handbook of Development Economics*, 544–630. Amsterdam and Oxford: Elsevier Science.

Schultz, Theodore W. 1961. 'Investment in Human Capital'. *American Economic Review* 51 (1): 1–17.

Singh, R. P., Hans P. Binswanger, and N. S. Jodha. 1985. 'Manual of Instructions for Economic Investigators in ICRISAT's Village Level Studies (Revised)'. GT-IMPI, Andhra Pradesh: ICRISAT.

Walker, Thomas S., and James G. Ryan 1990. *Village and Household Economies in India's Semi-Arid Tropics*. Baltimore and London: John Hopkins University Press.

SECTION III

Pedagogy, Curriculum and Textbooks

18

Education as Trutiya Ratna

Towards Phule-Ambedkarite Feminist Pedagogical Practice[*]

Sharmila Rege[†]

> O learned pandits wind up the selfish prattle of your hollow wisdom and listen to what I have to say.
>
> (Mukta Salve, About the Grief of Mahar and Mangs, 1855)

> Let me ask you something oh Gods!...You are said to be completely impartial. But wasn't it you who created both men and women?
>
> (Tarabai Shinde, A Comparison of Men and Women, 1882)[1]

I begin this chapter with words written by Mukta Salve, a 14-year-old girl student of the Mang caste in Jotiba and Savitribai Phule's school and Tarabai Shinde, a young Maratha woman trained in the Satyashodhak (Society of Truth Seekers) tradition. For these words of fire, with which students talked back to the injustice of their times, are embedded in the writings and practices that addressed the complex relations between culture, knowledge and power and sought not only to include girl students and students from the ex-untouchable castes, but also to democratise the very processes of learning and teaching. This chapter, in many ways, is a collection of 'stories'; of our classrooms, relationships between students and teachers and the political frameworks which constitute these stories. Like all narrators, I have selected some and ignored or postponed other stories, interpreted them in one way rather than another. These stories, I imagine, are a dialogue with fellow teachers on addressing caste and gender in the metropolitan classroom. The present set of stories has been put together from regular diary notes made on teaching, discussions with colleagues and students, notes written by students of their experiences—often in moments of disruptions or departure, comments made on formal course evaluation sheets, the comments they half scratch out from these sheets, questions raised in

* Previously published in *Economic and Political Weekly* 45 (44–45), 30 October 2010: 88–89, and Uma Chakravarti ed. *Thinking Gender, Doing Gender: Feminist Scholarship and Practice Today*, New Delhi: Orient BlackSwan, 2016.

class and those asked hesitantly outside the class, their silences that one rushes past in the business-as-usual mode during peak periods of the semester and gestures that defy narrative expression.

'New times' in the university are marked by narratives that bemoan a 'decline in plurality and standards'. especially in places where a new generation of scholars and students from historically disadvantaged sections in Indian society are posing challenges to the social homogeneity of the classroom, boards of studies and other academic bodies, leading to obvious frictions on issues related to a decline in standards and merit. A new generation of Dalit scholarship, following the Thorat Committee Report on the All India Institute of Medical Sciences, the suicide of Rajani (a Dalit girl student who committed suicide because the banks did not find her creditworthy for a student loan) and Senthil Kumar (a Dalit PhD student whose fellowship was stopped), has raised questions, both about the accessibility of higher education and the limitations in making it enabling for those who struggle to gain entry into it.[2] This has enabled an open debate on the absence of transparency in higher education and the nexus of networks of exclusion that operate, formally and informally, on campuses to reproduce caste inequalities in the metropolitan university.[3]

While there are at present several efforts at 'talking/writing back',[4] I would like to mention a few by way of example: *Insight: Young Voices*, a journal published by students and researchers from Delhi; the work from Hyderabad of young research scholars like Murali Krishna M., who employs his autobiography to theorise educational practices; Indira Jalli, Swathy Margaret and Jenny Rowena, who bring caste to the centre to interrogate feminist practices in the academy; the film *Nageshwar Rao Star*, which starts with reflections on the star/asterisk, the marker of caste identity in the admission list, and moves to reflect on and recover new knowledge on the Tsunduru massacre; *Out-Caste*, an informal, public wall-journal, which looks at caste as a category that structures both exclusion and privilege; discussions on caste on campuses, on several list-serves like Zest-Caste and ongoing MPhil and PhD theses across campuses in India. Closer home, in Pune University, mention may be made of Dilip Chavan's caste-class critique of the debate on reforming the University Grants Commission's (UGC) National Entrance Test (NET), the efforts of the Sajag (conscious) students' research group to reinvent the relationship between social movements and the academia and the 'Research Room Diaries', put together by researchers in women's studies, reflecting on their diverse histories of hidden injuries and privileges experienced as students.[5]

These and several other efforts are seeking to challenge disciplinary regimes of caste, opening up new ways of looking at the present of our disciplines and pedagogical practices and suggesting that critical teachers should be 'listening' rather than bemoaning the loss of better times. I wish to argue that these are 'new times' in the university, the suicides and other forms of 'routine' pedagogical violence notwithstanding. Men and women from excluded castes and classes are entering higher education for the first time and those for long considered 'unteachable' are talking/writing back. This makes it possible to throw back the gaze of the students who have long been 'invisible' and 'nameless' in the classrooms onto disciplinary and pedagogical practices. These new times interrogate the confidence and certainty of the teacher, which comes with acknowledged expertise in an area, outlining how expertise may embed us in certain kinds of arguments, so that we foreclose other possible ways of looking and listening.[6] This chapter is an exercise that is both restitutive and exploratory; reflecting on one's own teaching practices, which ferret out inconsistencies in stories offered by students, I seek to re-listen, reflect and assign new value to the 'stories' and 'voices' ignored and discarded earlier, as also to present recent experiences from the classroom for exploration.

Recently, a Dalit doctoral student and colleague narrated to me his experiences of the school and the university, the ways in which the curricular, extra-curricular and academic success (lesson on Ambedkar in the textbook, elocution competition, becoming a UGC-Junior Research Fellow [JRF] scholar) were all instances that reproduced caste by reducing him to a 'stigmatised particular'.[7] Pointing to a paradox, he asked, 'Why do even sociologists, whose "object of analysis" is caste, believe that caste identities do not matter in academic practices?' I wish to take his question for consideration in the next section, reframing it a little provocatively, to ask: Why are 'we' afraid of 'identity'? Why do we assume neutrality when it comes to identities of caste, ethnicity and gender and presume that they do not affect the content and practice of our discipline? Do we disavow caste, saying that it does not exist in our context and talk of it in other terms and codes, like standards, language and so on? It is common for many of us teaching in state universities and colleges not only to categorise our students into neat categories of English and Marathi-medium, or English and Gujarati-medium, but also reduce these students to this singular identity (for instance, in a local college where I taught, it was customary to ask students to add an EM [English Medium] or MM [Marathi Medium] when they introduced themselves in any gathering). However, we may not always be open to discussing the different and contradictory identities of teachers, students and other players in the social relations of teaching and learning. In the next section, I want to explore this issue of medium of instruction, the 'language question' and fear of identity on the grounds of a more established discipline, namely the practice of sociology, and seek suggestions from this experience for the newly emerging teaching programmes in women's studies.

Hidden in the 'Language Question': Tracing the Fear of Identity[8]

The hierarchy of standards between central and state universities, it might help to recall, draws not only on superior infrastructural facilities, but also on English being the medium of teaching and research in the former, as against the local/regional language in the latter. As teachers in state universities and local colleges, we may counter this logic through an opposition that assumes all social science practised in English to be elitist and that which is practised in the vernacular to be more down to earth. At other times, we may respond to the 'language question' through efforts to find quality reading material in Indian languages and develop English language proficiency through remedial classes. Interestingly, this 'language question' appears quite prominently in some of the discussions that sociologists have had on their discipline being in 'crisis'.

Sociologists, more than other social scientists in India, have, from time to time, described and reflected upon the crisis in the discipline, with a more concentrated debate taking place in the 1970s and 1990s. If we revisit some of the articulations of 'crisis in the discipline' in the 1970s, it is apparent that the 'language question' is strongly implicated in the salient features, causes and solutions suggested to the crisis. The crisis is described in terms of an unrestricted expansion of sociology at the undergraduate level and in Indian languages, market-driven textbooks and takeover of 'pure' pedagogies by politics. The script is one that narrates the story of expansion of sociology at the undergraduate levels and in regional languages as the 'provincialisation' of higher education in general and sociology in particular. Rereading this debate, one is struck by two rather paradoxical anxieties of the sociological community. On the one hand is the angst with academic colonisation (why do we not have 'our own' theories and categories), while on the other is the apprehension about the new and diverse 'expanding public' (what will happen to 'standards' if teaching and learning is no longer to be done in English). The new 'publics' of sociology are denigrated and assumed to be 'residual', those who are in sociology not because they want to be but because of a politically imposed expansion of regional universities/colleges.

The calls of a 'crisis' in the discipline surface again in the 1990s, with comments on the increasing number of students registered in doctoral programmes and their ignorance of elementary facts and concepts. It comes to be argued that both teaching and research are in a deplorable condition because most of our universities and other centres of higher learning have become cockpits for caste, regional and linguistic conflict and intrigue. As the enrolment rates of the 'upper caste',[9] middle-class metropolitan students mark a relative decline and the sociology classroom comes to be more diverse in terms of caste, region and linguistic identities, the anxiety about the expanding 'public' turns into a script of accusation. The accusation operates on two levels; the upsurge of identities in Indian society and politics is seen as causing the demise of merit and any appeal to questions of identity and language on the campus and in the classroom comes to be viewed as part of interest-group politics. In times of Mandal, these narratives of a decline of the discipline from its golden age have to be contextualised as the battle between the pan-Indian English educated elite and the new regional elites moving in on the national scene.

Interestingly, it is practitioners located on the institutional and organisational margins of 'national' sociology who shifted the axis of the debate from standards to questions of equality, inquiring into the legitimacy of sociological knowledge and the pronouncements of decline. Further, the 1990s were marked by prominent 'national' sociologists lending support to the anti-Mandal position, which dominated the middle-class urban perception of the issue. Additionally, the debate on Dalits joining the Durban Conference against discrimination based on race and caste underlined the ways in which sociologists, in the name of objectivity, valued the opinion of experts, while rejecting perspectives emerging from the lived experience of caste and the horror of atrocities. If in the 1970s, as seen earlier, 'national sociology' described the expansion of sociology in regional languages as provincialisation of the discipline, in the 1990s the claims of 'national' sociology stood 'provincialised'. 'National' sociology was 'provincialised' as it failed to say anything beyond popular commonsense on the Mandal controversy, though its identity hinged upon the theorisation of caste; as also because several questions came to be raised about the nation as the 'natural' unit for organising sociological knowledge, and about selective processes that equated happenings in the elite set of institutions in Delhi with Indian sociology.

So if we go back to my colleague's question, with which we began—why do even sociologists assume that these identities have no consequences for the content and practice of their discipline? Why was there an expectation on his part that sociologists would be different from other social scientists? Probably because caste, gender and ethnicity are explicitly stated objects of inquiry and they have been the first to include courses and modules on women, Dalits and tribals in the sociology curriculum? Yet, as we just saw, it is sociologists more than others who seem to be afraid of any claims to caste or gender identities. They appear to assume that avowal of gender and caste identities will lead to feminification of theory or a demise of merit—in other words, to the 'pollution' of academic purity. Here, it might help to focus on the ways in which sociological knowledge and practice are organised by professional bodies and the curriculum. Women, Dalits and Adivasis may be included as substantive research areas of sociology and in optional courses, but this inclusion keeps the cognitive structures of the discipline relatively intact from the challenges posed by Dalit or feminist knowledges.[10] Thus 'good sociology' continues to be defined in terms of the binaries of objectivism/subjectivism, social/political, social world/knower, experience/ knowledge, tradition/modernity and theoretical Brahman/empirical Shudra.

So, every time the problem of expansion of the discipline in Indian languages or the language question comes to be discussed, we gloss over several layers of identities and assume the simplistic binaries of sociology practised in English to be national and rigorous and those in Indian languages as being provincial and simplistic. Alternatively, indigenists and nativists assume the sociology practised in English to be elitist and incapable of grasping 'our culture' and that in regional languages as being down to earth and applicable to 'our culture'. While the former position seeks to resolve the tensions through remedial English courses, translation of textbooks, or a simple commitment to bilingualism, the latter proposes teaching and writing in Indian languages as a 'cultural duty'. These positions, though they seem different, are similar in that they see language only in its communicative aspects, as if separable from power relations and the cultural and symbolic effects of language. In contrast, Dalit imaginations of language wedge open the symbolic and material power of language. In the next section, I shall bring into focus some Dalit imaginations of language, to underline the ways in which caste and gender identities remain hidden in what we discuss as the 'language question'.

DALIT IMAGINATIONS: WEDGING OPEN THE 'LANGUAGE QUESTION'

> Now if you want to know why I am praised – well it's for my knowledge of Sanskrit, my ability to learn it and to teach it. Doesn't anyone ever learn Sanskrit? ...That's not the point. The point is that Sanskrit and the social group I come from don't go together in the Indian mind. Against the background of my caste, the Sanskrit I have learned appears shockingly strange. That a woman from a caste that is the lowest of the low should learn Sanskrit, and not only that, also teach it – is a dreadful anomaly ....
>
> (Kumud Pawade 1981: 21)

> In a word, our alienation from the Telugu textbook was more or less the same as it was from the English textbook in terms of language and content. It is not merely a difference of dialect; there is difference in the very language itself. ...What difference did it make to us whether we had an English textbook which talked about Milton's *Paradise Lost* or *Paradise Regained*, or Shakespeare's *Othello* or *Macbeth* or Wordsworth's poetry about nature in England, or a Telugu textbook which talked about Kalidasa's *Meghasandesham*, Bommera Potanna's *Bhagvtam*....We do not share the content of either; we do not find our lives reflected in their narratives.
>
> (Kancha Ilaiah 1996: 15)

> Through his initiatives, Lord Macaulay was to re-craft a new intellectual order for India which threatened the dominance of the brahmins and questioned the relevance of the *Varna*/caste order. This was to give dalits a large breathing space ... Should we know our past the way we like to, or we know the past as it existed? Or should there be any distinction between History Writing and Story Telling? Those who condemn Lord Macaulay for imposing a 'wrong' education on India do never tell us what kind of education system which Macaulay fought and eventually destroyed.
>
> (Chandra Bhan Prasad 2006: 99 and 115)

> While giving calls of 'Save Marathi', the question I am faced with is 'which' 'Marathi' is to be 'saved'? The Marathi rendered lifeless by the imprisonment of the oral in the standardised written word? The Marathi with its singular aim of 'fixing meaning' which loses rhythm, intonation, emotion, *Rasa*? The Marathi that generates inferiority complex in those speaking 'aani-paani'[11]? The Marathi that forms centres of power through processes of standardisation of language? .... Or the Marathi sans the Word that keeps the bahujan knowledgeable?
>
> (Pragnya Daya Pawar 2004: 45)

......I dream of an english
full of the words of my language.
an english in small letters
an english that shall tire a white man's tongue
an english where small children practise with smooth round pebbles in their mouth to
the spell the right zha
an english where a pregnant woman is simply stomach-child-lady
an english where the magic of black eyes and brown bodies
replaces the glamour of eyes in dishwater blue shades and
the airbrush romance of pink white cherry blossom skins
....

an english that doesn't belittle brown or black men and women
an english of tasting with five fingers...

(Meena Kandasamy 2006: 21)[12]

Kumud Pawade's story of her Sanskrit, Kancha Ilaiah's comment on the sameness of the English and Telegu textbook, Chandra Bhan Prasad's counter commemoration of Macaulay, Pragnya Daya Pawar's interrogation of the power of the printed word over the spoken word and Meena Kandasamy's dream of a global English in small letters offer immense possibilities for wedging open the 'language question'.

Kumud Pawade, a Dalit feminist intellectual, in her testimonio 'Thoughtful Outburst' (1981), reflects on her journey into Sanskrit, teasing out, in the process, the complex character of the 'language question' in our academia. She foregrounds memories of her schoolteacher Gokhale Guruji, a prototypical Brahman dressed in a *dhoti*, full shirt, a black cap and the vermilion mark on his forehead, who she expected would refuse to teach her Sanskrit. However, expected responses stand interrogated, as he not only taught her, but also became a major influence in her life. People in her own community often discouraged her from pursuing a master's degree in Sanskrit, arguing that success at matriculation need not embolden her to this extent. At college the peons, as also the higher-up officials, usually commented on how 'they' were taking strides because of government money and how this had made them too big for their boots. At the university, the head of the department, a famous scholar, took great pleasure in taunting her. She would find herself comparing this man, apparently modern in his ways, to Gokhale Guruji.

However, on successfully completing her master's in Sanskrit and achieving a place in the merit list, her dreams of teaching Sanskrit received a rude shock, as she could overhear the laughter and ridicule in the interview room about people like her being 'government-sponsored' Brahmans. Those passing these comments, she recalls, were not all Brahmans, many of them were from the Bahujan Samaj, who thought of themselves as Brahman-haters and even traced their lineage to Mahatma Phule, and yet, the idea of a Mahar girl who was a part of this Bahujan Samaj teaching Sanskrit made them restless. After two years of meritorious performance at the master's level, unemployment and her marriage to Motiram Pawade, a Kunbi Maratha, she finally got an appointment as an assistant lecturer in a government college and, in later years, went on to become a professor in her alma mater. However, a thought continues to trouble her—it was 'Kumud Pawade' and not 'Kumud Somkuvar' who got the job. Pawade's critical work of memory unfolds the complex gender and caste parameters in the 'language question' and lays bare the dynamics of a Dalit woman acquiring an authorised tongue. Importantly, she underlines the operation of language as a marker of subordination and exclusion in our academia and, thus, the impossibility of viewing the 'language question' as a matter of communication, separable from power relationships and cultural and symbolic effects of language.

Ilaiah comments on the sameness of Kalidasa and Shakespeare, despite the former appearing in the Telugu textbook and the latter in the English. He draws attention to the difference between Brahmanical Telugu and the Bahujan renderings, locating the difference in the latter's emergence from production-based communication. He argues:

> The communists and nationalists spoke and wrote in the language of the *purohit*. Their culture was basically sanskritised; we were not part of that culture. For good or ill, no one talked about us. They never realised that our language is also language, that is understood by one and all in our communities...
>
> (Ilaiah 1996: 14)

Ilaiah further underlines the sameness of the English and Telugu books in being 'alien' to the Bahujan; their only difference being that one was written with 26 letters and the other with 56. Ilaiah's reflections problematise the secular-vernacularist position, underlining the complete domination of Hindu scriptures and Sanskritic cultures in vernacular education. Any easy equation between English as alien and Telugu as 'our language', yielding 'our categories' of analysis, stands interrogated. Further, Ilaiah suggests that the question of culture mediates between the axis of equality and academia and the 'language' in which education takes place is an epistemological issue, more than a matter of mere instruction.

Prasad's celebration, since 25 October 2006, of Macaulay's birthday and installation of a 'Dalit goddess of English' to underscore the turn away from tradition, has often been brushed aside as an attention seeking gimmick. This counter-commemoration of Macaulay has significance for destabilising the hegemonic memory of him as the 'villain' who declared that a single shelf of Shakespeare was worth more than all the Sanskrit and Arabic literature of the East. Prasad rereads 'Minutes on Education' to underline Macaulay's argument about the British having to give scholarships to children to study in Sanskrit and Arabic, even when they were ready to pay for English education. This rereading disrupts the ongoing processes of collective remembrance of language and education in colonial India. Prasad's act of counter-commemoration renders Macaulay's argument as not directed against the vernaculars, but against the outmoded literature of the Vedas and Upanishads and thus, as an important moment in the history of Dalit access to education. It is important to note Prasad's comments on discovering the top secrets of the language politics of Macaulay, in his explorations of the tensions between history writing and storytelling, which thereby suggest that an engagement with the 'language question' is also essentially an engagement with 'reinventing the archive'—the very methods of knowledge.

Pragnya Daya Pawar (2004) talks back to those giving calls in Maharashtra to 'save Marathi', asking them the pertinent question, 'which Marathi?' and teasing out the collusion of state and elites in framing the 'language question'. Interrogating the processes of standardisation of the language, she points to the homogenisation of meaning constituted by the processes of standardisation. She draws attention to the efforts of Maharashtra state to empower Marathi as a language for science and technology, which freeze and deroot the diversity of words into the singular 'Word'. Standardisation on the one hand brutalises/ marginalises/fails the Dalit Bahujan, who brings into the system the 'non-standardised' language practices. On the other hand, more violently, it wipes away the epistemic value of all oral forms of knowing of the Bahujan. She recalls that the dictum of the liberal humanists that 'society will improve when its people gain wisdom from education', was first called into crisis in India by Jotiba Phule. That a Bahujan struggling against all forms of cultural colonisation should have been the first to call this liberal agenda into question, 'is logical and not coincidental' in her observation. The 'language question' thus opened up, she traces the politics of internal fragmentation and hierarchisation of the vernacular in post-colonial Indian states and sees these processes as inseparable from those that monitor the differential epistemic status of different knowledges—particularly the printed and oral.

Meena Kandasamy in 'Mulligatawny Dreams' dreams of an 'English' that is full of words selected from her language, an 'English' that challenges both the purity of standardised vernaculars and the hegemony of English. It is an 'english' in small letters, a language that resists imperialist racism and casteism of both English and the vernacular. Such hybrid formations of language are seen as enriching English by opening it up to appreciate brown bodies, black eyes and eating with five fingers. English as the language of modernisation is disrupted, suggesting that in the present conjuncture, the spread of English has gone beyond the worldwide elite, thus opening up the possibilities of challenging the hegemony of imperialist English with many resisting 'Englishes'. Further, 'the dreams of English' point to the limitations of framing the language question in terms of proficiency in English language, which leaves little space for playful radical innovations in pedagogy.

It is not coincidental that Dalit imaginations engage with the power relations that are glossed over in debates on the 'language question' discussed earlier, and thus wedge open and interrogate not only the right-wing and state agendas of the 'language question', but also that of the liberal humanists. We can see that the liberal humanist fear of identity, of decline in standards, comes from a commitment to a particular idea of democracy. It is not as if those who complain of a decline in standards are opposed to including 'all others' in their system of knowledges, be it the university or the cognitive structures of the discipline. Within this idea of a democratic university, the masses will have to wait until they receive a degree of formal training (learn to 'speak like us') to comprehend the requirements of a plural and democratic university. However, since the 1990s, those considered incapable of comprehending democratic requirements have come to the fore to defend democracy, even as it pertains to the knowledge of democracy, while the imagined champions of democracy began moving away from processes that inform it.[13] 'All others' are entering the university with new vocabularies and moral economy, and, as the Dalit imaginations on language suggest, are interrogating the assumed hierarchy of different knowledges, archives and methods of knowledge. For critical researchers and teachers, fear of identity and the masses can no longer be an option, as the radical instability of the many languages of the subaltern citizens of mass democracy calls for careful 'listening'. If we, as teachers, are to participate in the 'new times', exercises in reimagining the content and methods of knowledge become inseparable from those of reinventing pedagogical practices. In the next section, I argue for reinventing pedagogies through Phule-Ambedkarite-Feminist (PAF) perspectives, asking why these perspectives came to be excluded in debates on education in post-colonial India.

PHULE-AMBEDKARITE-FEMINIST PEDAGOGIES: LOCATION AND EXCLUSION

Having neither the expertise nor the intention to draw a set of guidelines for PAF pedagogies, what I seek to do in this section is to historically map the 'difference' of Phule-Ambedkarite perspectives on the project of education and the probable reasons for the exclusion of these from imaginations of 'alternative' perspectives on learning and teaching. If, following Paulo Freiere (1973),[14] we see critical pedagogy as contesting the logic and practices of the 'banking method' for a more dialogical and transformative project of education, then PAF pedagogies, simply put, may be seen historically as constituting one school of critical pedagogy. Historically, we can read in the colonialist and nationalist discourses on Indian society a battle over the function and nature of knowledge. While the colonialist project represented India as the spirit of Hindu civilisation and therefore distinct and disjunct from the West, the regime of classification and categorisation of 'Indian tradition' created norms for colonial rule, enhancing the status of Brahmans as indigenous intellectuals. While colonial knowledges were structured on binaries that distinguished India from the West, the Orient from the Occident; the nationalists imagined alternate knowledges by reversing the claims of superiority of the West, locating the superiority in the Vedas. Thus, though the colonialists and nationalists contested the function of knowledge in colonial India, for both, the nature of the knowledge of India was essentially Hindu and Brahmanical. After World War II, social science discourse refashioned the binaries of Orient/Occident through the tradition/modernity thesis or indigenous approaches, both of which, glossing over the structural inequalities in Indian society, normalised the idea of knowledge and the educational project of/in India as Hindu and Brahmanical.[15]

Phule and Ambedkar, in different ways, by weaving together the emancipatory non-Vedic materialist traditions (Lokayata, Buddha and Kabir) and new Western ideas (Thomas Paine, John Dewey and Karl Marx, for instance), had challenged the binaries of Western modernity/Indian tradition, private caste-gender/public nation and sought to refashion modernity[16] and, thereby, its project of education. Phule and Ambedkar, in several writings and speeches, but more particularly the former in *Gulamgiri* (1873) and the latter in *Annihilation of Caste* (1936), *Riddles in Hinduism* (compiled and published in 1987) and *The Buddha and His Dhamma* (1957), undertook a rational engagement with the core analytical categories emerging from Hindu metaphysics, which had been normalised as 'Indian culture and science'.[17]

Throughout the text of *Gulamgiri*, Phule stresses that Hindu religion is indefensible, mainly because it violates the rights and dignity of human beings. He turns the 'false books' of the Brahmans on their head by reinterpreting the 'Dashavataara' of Vishnu to rewrite a history of the struggles of the Shudras and Atishudras. He moves swiftly between the power and knowledge nexus in everyday cultural practices, myths and history. In his 'Memorandum Addressed to the Education Commission' (1882) for a more inclusive policy on education and in his popular compositions like the short ballad on 'Brahman Teachers in the Education Department' (1869), Phule demonstrates how state policy and dominant pedagogical practices are intrinsically interlinked. He comments at length on the differential treatment meted to children of different castes and the collusion of interests of the Bombay government school inspectors and teachers. He calls for more plurality in the appointment of teachers and the need to appoint those who are committed to teaching as a truth-seeking exercise. Ambedkar, in *Annihilation of Caste* (1936), argues against the absolute knowledge and holism idealised by Brahmanical Hinduism and critiques the peculiar understanding of nature and its laws (*karma*) in the Shastric texts. Both Phule and Ambedkar underline the preference for truth-enhancing values and methods through an integration of the critical rationality of modern science and the scepticism and self-reflection of ancient non-Vedic materialists and the Buddha. It is clear, both in and through their works, that they see the organisation of knowledge as complexly related to the interlocking connections of different identities. This leads them to value-situated knowledge, such that they do not collapse all experience into knowledge, but do highlight how certain experiences (oppression based on caste and gender) lead people to certain kinds of knowledges.

Phule, in the first modern Marathi Play *Trutiya Ratna*, draws complex linkages between religious-cultural and educational authority and reimagines education, therefore, as the *Trutiya Ratna* (third eye), which has the possibilities to enable the oppressed to understand and to transform the relation between power and knowledge. Ambedkar, in a speech in Nagpur in 1942 at the All India Depressed Classes Conference, advises the gathering to 'Educate-Agitate-Organise' (a motto that became central to the Ambedkarite movement and community), arguing that this was central to the battle for freedom. Phule's conscious adoption of the dialogical form of communication and Ambedkar's insistence, in the Bombay University Act Amendment Bill (1927), to move beyond the examination-oriented patterns of learning and teaching underline their conviction regarding the centrality of dialogue in the project of education. Ambedkar, debating the Bombay University Act Amendment Bill, highlights the linkages between issues otherwise thought to be disjoint, namely understaffing, dictation of notes and the lack of adequate representation of backward castes on administrative bodies, such as the senate. Countering arguments regarding examination-centric education as a safeguard for promotion of standards, he underscores how this exam-centric mode in fact reproduces caste inequalities in the university. He underlines the significance of combining efforts to increase access to education for vulnerable sections with those to reconceptualise administrative and curricular practices of higher education.

Both Phule and Ambedkar, as may be apparent from the discussion above, seek a rational engagement with the pedagogy of culture to see how power works through the production, distribution and consumption of knowledge, within particular contexts, and reimagine a culture of pedagogy based on truth-seeking. The 'difference' of Phule-Ambedkarite pedagogical perspectives lies in a double articulation that conceives education not only in terms of cultures of learning and teaching, but also dissenting against that which is learnt and taught by dominant cultural practices. This entails constituting teachers and students as modern truth-seekers and agents of social transformation, who seek to become 'a light unto themselves'. The methods are those that seek to integrate the principles of *prajna* (critical understanding) with *karuna* (empathetic love) and *samata* (equality). This democratisation of the method of knowledge differentiates Phule-Ambedkarite perspectives from methods based on binaries of reason/emotion, public/private and the assumption of neutral objectivity/celebration of experience, which inform much of our teaching and research. One sees significant intersections with African-American feminist pedagogies that directly link pedagogy with political commitment in envisioning education as the practice of freedom, and thereby seek to challenge the assumed divide between mind/body, public/private and reason and emotion.[18] Why, then, have social scientists in search of alternative pedagogies rarely turned to Phule, Shahu or Ambedkar? Why did the search for alternatives usually end with Gandhi, Aurobindo and Nehru? How might this 'Dalit phobia',[19] or exclusion in the academia and its cognitive structures, be explained?

Baburao Bagul, the revolutionary Dalit writer, has explained the exclusion of this discourse in the formation of knowledges in post-colonial India in terms of the intelligentsia turning the national movement into a form of historical, mythological movement and ancestor worship, thus reducing the other movements to a secondary status.[20] The nationalist labelling of the Dalit discourse as anti-national, ideologically particularistic, specific to certain castes, or as emergent from the British policy of divide and rule, resonated in the practices of higher education in post-colonial India. In the 1970s, the ideology and practices of the Dalit Panthers and Dalit literature, including the compositions of the mud-house cultural activists—the *shahirs* (composers of ballads)—foregrounded the experience of caste to challenge the feudal backwardness of Hinduism normalised in educational practices.[21] This challenge was co-opted in the academia through frames that included Dalits in disciplinary knowledges, while keeping intact the core of disciplinary knowledges. Since the 1990s, as discussed earlier, tensions between different forms of modernities in Indian society are being played out and a new scholarship is making convincing arguments about appeals to caste not being casteism and that claims unmarked by caste, made by the dominant to represent and classify the modern, are situated, local and partial.

Since the 1990s, this 'secular upsurge of caste' at the national level interfaced with local Dalit movements and international contexts, like the UN Conference against Racism, is shaping varied trajectories of Dalit studies in different regions in India.[22] PAF pedagogies are enabled by this conjuncture and the assertion of Dalit feminisms, which has opened up possibilities of new dialogue between Phule-Ambedkarite and feminist perspectives. PAF pedagogical perspectives are critically different from the two much-discussed projects in higher education of the same decade, viz., value education and autonomy. They are different in that they contest the logic of projects based on an essentialist a priori set of morals, or on the neo-liberal rhetoric of choice that comes without freedom. The practice of PAF pedagogies thus seeks to develop cultures of dissent through analyses of the various categories of oppression underlying the structures and organisation of knowledge, but without reducing them to a mere additive mantra of caste, class and gender differences. The practice of PAF obviously needs more than a simple transplantation of the guidelines through which PAF perspectives work to our situations. In the next section, I shall try to grapple with some of the issues that emerge in the practice of PAF pedagogies in our academia.

Interrogating Teacher as God or Saviour: Pedagogy, Authority and Canon

In the present conjuncture, how is the relationship between the teacher and the taught performed? How does the intersection of generational and 'other' differences between them disrupt this relationship? We may, as practitioners of PAF pedagogies, reject the Brahmanic principle of teacher as 'god embodied' (*Guru sakshat paraha brahma*), but then do engaged pedagogies, such as PAF, install teachers as the new 'saviours' of the students? Since the classroom seems to be the best place to start discussing these issues, I would like to consider here two autobiographical notes on disruptions from the classroom,[23] which I believe are situations commonly encountered by teachers. The first refers to the shock, anger, disgust and pain that one recognises in the body language of a student who has just been handed her test paper with the marks or grades. The student often lets some time elapse before contesting the evaluation, probably checking the marks/grades of others in the class, comparing and contrasting, thereby estimating the level of the injustice (imagined and real) done to her.

Three students and, not by coincidence, one from a Nomadic Tribe (NT) and the other two from the Scheduled Tribe (ST) community in Maharashtra and Manipur, mustered enough courage to encounter me and asked, in different ways, if their lower grade had anything to do with the less space they had given in their answer to Phule-Ambedkarite critiques of 'mainstream' perspectives on caste. As a teacher, I had, at that point, at least three options: to respond in terms of some absolutes (it is not really good, you have not covered it all, your expression could have been better), thereby exercising my authority as final judge of the standards, or legitimising my authority as an evaluator by making transparent the parameters of my evaluation. Most difficult of all options seems to be the third one, that of calling into question my juridical authority as a teacher-evaluator, by translating the student's contestation of grade into an opportunity for dialogue. Dialogue here is not suggestive of a strategy of appeasement (of increasing the marks), but of 'listening' to the contestation and reflecting upon and reviewing, in this context, the very parameters of evaluation and, possibly, transforming them. Obviously, these students were raising questions that moved within and outside the classroom; for one, they were raising questions about the possibilities of an evaluation remaining 'fair' in the context of the teachers avowed commitment to a Phule-Ambedkarite politics and about their own alienation from a curriculum which hardly engaged with 'their' histories and experiences.

The second autobiographical narrative relates to the comments of a girl student from the Bhil community in Nandurbar, one of the most underdeveloped regions in Maharashtra, who had opted for three of my courses in consecutive semesters and who I saw as bringing considerable enthusiasm and intensity into the classes. However, at the end of the master's programme, she told me, to my dismay, that the classroom experiences had been profound but troubling, because of the immense loss of 'certitude of definitions' that she had experienced. That sometimes I seemed to her (and probably to many others) like a person who does not know the basics of the discipline (for instance, when I reply to a query with another query, rather than giving a definition/definitive answer). For the student, the unlearning and problematising of much that she had grasped through undergraduate textbooks and excelled in was rendered into a state of confusion. As Phule-Ambedkarite feminist teachers contesting the canons, one has often come up against similar criticism from colleagues who argue that students get confused in 'our' classes, because we introduce critical debates before students have mastered the canons of the discipline.

These cases of students contesting evaluation and efforts at building critical thinking in the classroom, raise questions about the relations between pedagogy, authority, canons and transformation. The second narrative allows us to ask awkward questions: Do we, as teachers of particular disciplines, have a responsibility and accountability to the canon and to initiate the students into the discipline? When is the 'right time' at which the critique can be introduced? In other words, are we saying that, in introducing students to the discourse of caste, 'canons' must be taught before the critical perspectives of Phule, Ambedkar and more contemporary Dalit-Bahujan-feminist critiques of the discourse are introduced? Does such a move not gloss over the ways in which knowledge comes to be categorised and organised into legitimate/canonical and illegitimate/non-canonical, through the design of courses, assignments, lists of prescribed and 'supplementary' readings, selection and elimination of topics as legitimate for classroom discussion? At the level of classroom practice, this would amount to attributing value to the canonical per se and not to the labour of interpretation. Am I then suggesting that the Phule-Ambedkarite feminist teachers do away with the canon? Far from it, the canon to be de-authoricised and demystified must be seen relationally, so that the canonical and the non-canonical emerge in oppositional confrontation, in specific historical conjunctures.

The first narrative pushes us to question the canon built on the conviction of the radical teacher; does she too build a canon to render 'her truth' as natural and beyond the conflictual politics of interpretation? There is a desire for a stable 'saviour' ideology and easily identifiable home,[24] or fixed truth; but as Jenny's account discussed earlier more than bears out, a Phule-Ambedkarite feminist teacher must guard against the exclusions and oppressions which such a desire would entail. The problem, therefore, is not only about teaching the canon, but canonicising whatever we teach, and the challenge is to make the learning process always uncertain and contingent. Often the most difficult challenges for progressive pedagogies like PAF is to retain passion and partnership of the oppressed and yet break through the canonical compulsions that exist at the heart of all pedagogy.[25]

While the relations of power organised by the curriculum and the approaches to the curriculum have been discussed to some extent, those related to the organisation of the college-university classroom as a physical and intellectual space have been relatively unaddressed. Discussing pedagogies requires that we discuss the ways in which power is enmeshed in the discourses and practices of the more mundane and everyday of the classroom. The classroom is a relatively autonomous space, which can both empower the teacher and render her vulnerable. The everyday of this classroom is routinely managed through the regime of timetables and rules published in the handbooks. But on the field, the real questions are: How do we manage the conflictual imperatives of quiet and talk, responsibility and control, risk and safety? Often, these conflicting imperatives mean that classroom learning comes to be achieved through the issuing of threats (to cut marks, freeze on classes), competition and point-scoring (setting groups or individuals against each other, to get them to be responsible) and status consciousness (sanctions for those who talk and interact within given parameters and achieve learning within approved terms). Intentionally or unintentionally, our strategies of getting the immediate done may often conflict with strategies of PAF that seek to encourage collaboration and foster democratic and social justice values. Are there models of progressive pedagogy that may guide us to move beyond these Brahmanical-patriarchal practices of discipline and control in the classroom? In the next section, I will address some of the issues emerging from this question.

Circuitous Relations between Educate-Organise-Agitate: The Risky Paths of Trutiya Ratna

Generally speaking, teachers who believe that learning is linked to social change struggle over identities and meanings and may practise variants and combinations of three possible models of progressive pedagogical practice.[26] The first model is the one in which the PAF teacher believes that she understands the truth/the real relations of power and imparts it to the students. The second model believes in a dialogical mode and making the silenced speak, while in the third, the focus shifts on developing skills, so that students are enabled to understand and intervene in their own history. It is possible that different combinations emerge from these models, for common to all three is a set of similar assumptions. The first model believes that the teacher can and does know the truth, the real interests of different groups brought together in the classroom and has to just impart the truth to them; the second overlooks the real material and social conditions which may disenable some from speaking and others from 'listening to silences'; and the third assumes that the teacher knows and can impart the 'universal skills'. These assumptions become problematic, for, as PAF pedagogues, we agree that students are not cultural dopes who have to be brought to predetermined positions, but this is not to say that the dominant institutions do not seek to dupe them. There is, then, a loss of certainty for the teacher, as she does not have a ready-made mantra to save the world, but this cannot be replaced with a set of relativist celebrations of different voices and experiences.

This kind of a rendering of the PAF pedagogical model, which rejects convincing predefined subjects to adopt the teacher's truth, draws upon not a unilateral but a circuitous understanding of the Phule-Ambedkarite principle of 'Educate, Organise and Agitate'. Education, organising struggles over recognition and redistribution identities, and social transformation related in a circuitous path are constitutive of each other and, as such, the possibilities and constraints on agency, as it intersects with social formation, cannot be predefined. If we look again at Mukta Salve's essay with which we began, it is clear that education becomes '*Trutiya Ratna*' in Jotiba and Savitribai Phule's school, because what was demanded from students was not conformity to some image of political liberation, but gaining understanding of their own involvement in the world and its future. This makes the task of the PAF pedagogues slippery and hazardous, since the focus is on contextual practice, one of multiplying connections between what may seem apparently disjoint things.

This returns us, once again, to the question of authority in the pedagogical process, to ask if the critical pedagogue practising such a model needs to make a difference between abandoning all claims to authority and offering new forms and positions. The teacher still remains responsible for production of knowledge in the classroom, but is required to traverse risky grounds that interrogate the binaries of knowing teacher/ignorant students, public/ private and the rational/emotional. She recognises that often, the students are uninterested in the classroom not because they do not want to work, or because of the difficulties of jargon or theory, but because they do not see reason. Probably the questions being asked and answered are not 'theirs'. This realisation cannot be followed up with a simple dictum that, from now on, students will define the questions. Instead, the challenge is to discover the questions on the terrain of everyday lives and popular cultural practices.

Such a model throws open to question a simple model of authority, one that poses an opposition between mind and body, as also between authority and affection. African-American feminists[27] have underlined the ways in which the body is erased in the process of learning. Entering the classroom is, as if, about giving up to the mind and making the body absent. It is assumed that denial of passion and Eros is a precondition for learning to take place. They remind us that Eros is the moving force that propels life from a state of potentiality to actuality and is, therefore, central to the energy of the classroom. It is often argued that there is no place for the affective in the classroom, because this may affect effective control or neutral evaluation of students. And yet, all of us know that there have always been teachers' favourites, that there have been, and are, affective ties that are exclusive and privatised. The Eklavya narrative is a reminder of the violent consequences of selective and exclusive affective ties between students and teachers.

The pedagogical power in critical practices cannot be wished away by giving up claims to authority and, following feminists like hooks,[28] persuasion of students may be seen as an option. In a diverse classroom, hooks argues that there will always be students who are afraid to assert themselves as critical thinkers. Counter to several feminist claims that the silenced come to voice in an atmosphere of safety and congeniality, she prescribes a 'confrontational' style of dealing with this. This can be very demanding, painful, frightening and never makes the teacher 'instantly popular' or the classes 'fun' to be in. Hooks problematises the rather easy opposition between risk and safety, affect and authority, by centralising the processes of democratic persuasion as crucial to the goal of enabling all students and not just the assertive few in the classroom.

Critical pedagogies do not in themselves constitute a method and micro-level pedagogical implications of PAF, which are crucial to the everyday work of the classroom, need to be discussed and developed through dialogues in and across classrooms. We need to dialogue more on our efforts in the everyday of the classroom to develop different tools, methods and strategies. This dialogue is crucial if we are to combine social critique with skills of doing critical work, in developing new undergraduate and postgraduate teaching programmes in women's studies. In the concluding section, I would like to share some notes on this process, more specifically implementing PAF and collective efforts to develop models, tools and methods.

'Pappu Can Dance....' (?): Possibilities and Limitations of Pedagogical Experiments[29]

Located in a UGC-sponsored Women's Studies Centre in a state university with affiliated colleges, some of us are presently engaged in a project that seeks to reimagine some of the practices in higher education. The project seeks to build new comparative and relational curricula, knowledge resources through 'translation' projects that seek to translate knowledges across locations through inter-institutional models of collaboration, production of innovative resource books and capacity-building workshops for teachers and researchers for 'new times' in the university. The propelling force of the project is pedagogical innovation, operationalised through curricular and co-curricular programmes, such as the Bridge Course, Modular Training and Block Placement Programmes.[30]

The Bridge Course, which runs as a co-curricular course, is distinct from the 'Remedial English Programme' in that it explicitly addresses fractures of English-medium education too.[31] The Block Placement and Internship Programme has evolved through seminars, meetings and focussed dialogue with the state, corporate and non-governmental sector to explore mutually beneficial partnerships, and seeks to introduce students to the critical areas of practice in the fields of development and culture. This programme is closely linked to intensive semester-long training programmes that are integrated in the curriculum through specially designed theme/sector-based modular workshops conducted by professionals. The bridge course, modular workshops and block placement components are integrated as a part of reflexive learning, of seeing the 'field' in the classroom and experiencing the 'classroom' in the field. The project is driven by the need for teachers to 'reinvent' with the changing social composition of our classrooms and changing economy of higher education, wherein we can no longer continue to cultivate students whose futures we imagine will be identical to ours. In what follows, I detail the experience of teaching courses on 'Popular Culture and Modernity in India' and 'Caste and

Gender: History and Memory', not because I, or anyone else involved, imagine it to be a narrative of success, but as a way of opening a dialogue with fellow critical pedagogues on the nuts and bolts of developing pedagogical methods and tools for our present.

The course on 'Popular Culture and Modernity in India' has been floated over three semesters, in classrooms that were socially very diverse and where the co-learners sometimes shared very little in common by way of nationality, caste, region, language and also in terms of their investment in desire and pleasures of what they saw as constituting and constituted by the popular. The course, it was mutually agreed, would be constituted through integrating dialogue, participation and experience,[32] i.e., the important elements of PAF pedagogies. More specifically, the dynamics of learning and teaching were sought to be rethought and reinvented, through a research-based approach to the course. This posed challenges for both the students and the teacher and, in our case, the teaching assistants[33] became very important resources in enhancing dialogue and participation.

The course sought to build in experience, dialogue and participation through a conscious selection of resources materials that came from the everyday/ordinary of students' lives, continuous group-work and intra-group evaluation and developing writing and research as a method of classroom learning. Group-work and evaluation met with considerable resistance, as groups were drawn once by lots and another time by introducing a diversity quotient. Disruptions in dialogue were taken up as an opportunity to view the complex linkages between practice and content; for instance, impatience and tensions between group members (emerging from differences of language, investment in different genres of the popular, access and ease with using audiovisual equipment, ways of reading a text and discussing it) became a ground to reflect on the central theme of the course, namely 'our modernity/ies'.

One batch of students (2007–08) produced a film on 'Cellphone Cultures', which was researched and produced collaboratively. The process involved developing new intellectual, practical and technical skills, as students researched the biography of the product, its travels to different constituencies, SMS (text messaging) as cultural consumption, the perceived dangers and anxieties related to the product, celebrity scandals with camera phones and so on. The film focussed on how cell-phones were organising and conducting students' own lives. The second and third batch of students (2008–09 and 2009–10) wrote and published a collection of researched articles in English and Marathi titled 'Exploring the Popular: Texts, Identities and Politics' and 'Plundering Popular Culture'. The essays not only showcase student writings, but, as Uma Chakravarti comments in the foreword to the collection, '*they* tell us something about why and how we make meaning of life around us and they do so with zest and enthusiasm'.[34]

FOOD AND THE BOUNDARIES

Two controversies centring on 'meat', as served in branded fast-food restaurants and in the student mess, caught the imagination of students opting for the course on

'Caste and Gender: History and Memory'. Arguing that eating habits and food mark the boundaries between the pure and the polluted, the upper and lower classes, male and female, humans and god, students undertook a project that sought to untangle caste, class and gender inequalities on the food plate and in the assumptions that go into the making of national and regional cuisines. The project had its beginnings in the reading of Dalit life narratives, which, as opposed to other life narratives, deal explicitly with the question of food and suggest that food cannot be equated to personal choice and taste. All participants in this project visited bookstores to survey the cookbooks on the shelves and map the history of the cuisines of India therein. Propelled by an analysis of the cookbooks and the tensions in the representation of regional cuisines as national cuisine and 'upper-caste' recipes as regional cuisine, participants in the course produced a collection: 'Is not the plate of Dalit food Indian?'[35] The collection documents the memories of food and recipes in practice in Dalit households, by doing memory-work with 10 Dalit men and women from different castes, arguing thus that the memories of food and the culinary skills and knowledges they make in the process could not be separated.

The students had, in the process of producing the bilingual books, wedged open inequalities hidden in the language question and engaged with the tasks of calling for submissions, reviewing, editing, designing and publishing, and were pleasantly shocked by the quality of the product.[36] Individual and collective research projects not only reinvented the pedagogic space, but helped establish mutually rewarding links with academics, inside and outside the university, and external community groups. The 'social utility' of the several group projects, film, or the collection of essays lies in their capacity for inducing conjectural questioning. However, there could have been more effort on our part to ask significant questions about how these skills of combining critical-thinking with social critique, of writing academic papers, making films and scripting, might transfer to other contexts of collaboration or employment.

The teacher, the teaching assistants and several students often commented on how otherwise 'quiet types', those who rarely spoke in class (those considered '*pappus*') were talking so much in class when it came to engaging with the 'popular' or documenting the 'everyday'. At one level, it appeared as if, contrary to the popular Hindi film song 'Pappu Can't Dance...', investigations into the world of the popular could make '*pappus*' dance. But, at another level, could they really? For as students worked in English, Hindi and Marathi, in different settings, the uneven flow of knowledge and methodologies was more than apparent. The student research projects made apparent how the study of culture has emerged differently in different regions and languages and a question worth asking, but not risked in the classroom, was: How might the course have looked if studies of popular culture did not speak only English but also spoke, for instance, Tamil, Ahirani, Bundeli or Marathi?[37] In a socially diverse classroom there are 'many languages of studying culture' and specific understandings of 'popular' are constituted differently and differentially through them. Our collective efforts at 'dialogue' through research and writing as methods of learning did, to some extent, disrupt established understanding of power and knowledge, but were constrained by the limits set on 'dialogue' by powerful languages.

Lest we prematurely celebrate the 'success' of the dialogue of our PAF pedagogies, the words of Bhujang Meshram, an engaged Adivasi poet who passed away recently, are a reminder of the ways in which power is already enmeshed in dialogue.

The Teacher asked,
'Name any three tribal villages',
So I told.
Slap me if I was wrong
But do tell me do closed doors open without a push?
I only told – Shelti, Varud, and Kondpakhandi'.
The teacher asked,
'For what are these villages famous?'
I only told,
Shelti for Holi,
Varud for the woman – Gowarin Bai,
And Kondpakhandi for the theft of cotton.
The teacher roared and slapped with his hands
He broke a couple of staffs of the Mehendi bushes.
Go get a reference from three people
Or else no entry for you in this school – he said.
That's when I decided to get introduced
to Birsa kaka, Tantya nana and Ambar Singh Maharaj!!
(Bhujang Meshram, *Mala Bhetlelya Kavita* [The Poems I Met] 2007)

Meshram's words, historically grounded in the struggles over resources, identities and meanings, are a reminder that power is never really external to 'dialogue, participation and experience' and that the task of making education '*Trutiya Ratna*' is indeed an arduous long march.

NOTES

†This chapter is a revised version of the NCERT Savitribai Phule Memorial lecture delivered at SNDT, Mumbai in January 2009. I am grateful to the NCERT for deeming me worthy of delivering this lecture, instituted in the memory of Savitribai Phule. I would also like to place on record my sincere thanks to the faculty, staff members and students at Krantijyoti Savitribai Phule Women's Studies Centre and the Department of Sociology at the University of Pune, as also the Phule-Ambedkarite, left and feminist community, for providing meaningful contexts for the practice of critical pedagogies.

1. English Translations of Mukta Salve and Tarabai Shinde's writings were first published in Tharu and Lalita (1991). Vidyut Bhagwat, the regional editor of this section, highlighting the politics of selection and erasure involved in the building of archives, discusses how Tarabai's writing was 'retrieved' in 1975 by S. G. Malshe and that there is no account found of the later writings of Mukta Salve. Scholars like S. G. Mali and Hari Narke have countered the doubts raised about the authorship of writings of Savitribai Phule with historical documents, thus highlighting the erasure of intellection of women, and women particularly of the non-Brahman and Dalit castes, from the processes of established archiving.

2. See Senthilkumar Solidarity Committee 2008: 10–12, as also Kumar 2007: 8–10 and 'Excerpts of Thorat Committee Report' (*Insight*, 2007: 10).

3. See Anveshi Law Collective 2002: 1000–02 and also Palshikar and Patnaik 2002: 1490–91.

4. I use writing back/talking back in the sense post-colonial and Black feminist scholars employ the term; see, for instance, Ashcroft et al. (1989) and bell hooks (1989).

5. See www.insightfoundation.org, Krishna (2004); *IAWS Newsletter* (December 2003); *Nageshwar Rao Star* is a film made by Nikhila Henry, Shonreichon, Rajesh and Nageshwar Rao, a group of mass communication students at HCU, Hyderabad; *Out-Caste* is an informal, public wall-journal started by the Dalit Studies class, under the guidance of course instructor K. Satyanarayana. This is an open forum that engages with the caste question in a specifically Indian context (Out-Caste [blog]). See also Chavan (2008); the Sajag Vidhyarthi Shodharthi Gaat edited issue of *Vatsaru* (2008) and *Research Room Diaries* (2008).

6. The Department of Sociology, University of Pune tried to address this question by organising a two-day national workshop in January 2008 for teachers and students, on Caste in the Curriculum: Documentary Films as Pedagogical Tools'. I am grateful to the speakers, filmmakers and participants in this workshop for suggesting new ways of listening and addressing caste in the curriculum and the classroom.

7. I am grateful to Sanjay Kumar Kamble for the conversations we had on the reproduction of caste inequalities in education, particularly his insights on the renderings of the issue in Marathi cinema, which I hope to pursue in the near future.

8. The debates on the 'Language Question' and the 'Fear of Identity', as they appear in the calls of sociology in crisis, have been detailed in Sharmila Rege (2011). I am thankful to a number of colleagues for their insights from diverse positions and locations on pedagogical practices; to Sujata Patel for continued conversations and discussions on the history and politics of formation of sociology and its implications for the pedagogical; Kushal Deb, Shruti Tambe, Maitrayee Chaudhari and Satish Deshpande for periodic exchanges on the experiences of teaching and 'translating' sociology, to Sadhana Natu and Vaishali Diwakar, for sharing experiences on the diverse and exciting worlds of undergraduate pedagogies in Maharashtra.

9. Words like 'upper castes', 'lower castes' are put into single inverted comma to mark a disagreement with and distance from the ideology in which such linguistic practices emerge.

10. For accounts of this marginalisation, distortion and erasure in cognitive structures of sociology, see Kumar (2005: 514–32), Rodrigues, (2003: 221–58), S. M. Dahiwale (2005) and Sharmila Rege (2004).

11. *Aani Paani* literally means 'and water', but as a phrase, it refers to the Brahmanical colloquial reference to Dalit rendering of Marathi, which is considered 'impure' and technically incorrect.

12. For details, see Ilaiah (1996); Kandasamy (2006); Pawade (1981); Prasad (2006); Pawar (2004).

13. I am drawing this argument from Alam 2004.

14. See Freire (1973).

15. I am drawing this argument from Cohn (1991: 224–54), Patel (2006: 381–95) and Rege (2006 c).

16. For details, see Omvedt (1976), O'Hanlon (1985), Nanda (2002); Guru (2000) and Rege (2006 a).

17. All references to the writings of Phule and Ambedkar are drawn from Y. D. Phadke (1991), volumes, particularly Volume 2, 4, and 11 of Moon (1987) and Khairmode (1992).

18. See, for instance, bell hooks (1989).

19. Prasad (2006).

20. See Bagul, quoted in Arjun Dangle (1992).

21. For details, see Rege (2006 b).

22. For a nuanced and critical review of the local, regional and international contexts of emergence of Dalit studies, see Satyanarayana (2005: 81–95).

23. I am thankful to the several batches (from 1991 to the present) of Masters, MPhil and PhD students at the Department of Sociology and, since 1995, at the Krantijyoti Savitribai Phule Women's Studies Centre, for the collective efforts in building and disrupting the pedagogical space. Their classroom interactions, 'traditional' day celebrations, parties, note and letters of criticism and appreciation, in fact, makes the very exercise of this lecture possible.

24. For a provocative and evocative account of 'home', see Martin and Talpade-Mohanty (1986).

25. This is a question R. Radhakrishnan pursues profoundly in his accounts of cultural politics of parenting and pedagogies in the diaspora (Radhakrishnan 2007).

26. I draw upon and seek to rework the models of progressive pedagogies outlined by Lawrence Grossberg (1994).

27. See hooks (1994: 113–19).

28. For a nuanced discussion on confrontation as against safety in the classroom, see hooks (1989).

29. This draws upon the hit Hindi film song 'Pappu can't dance...', from the film *Jaane Tu Ya Jaane Na* (2008). *Pappu* in the vernacular generally refers to those young people considered 'not so smart or happening', by those who name what is 'in' and 'out'. This section will look at moments in which it seems that 'pappus can also dance – but do they?'.

30. This is a project at the Krantijyoti Savitribai Phule Women's Studies Centre, supported by the Higher Education Initiative of the Navajbai Ratan Tata Trust. Dialogue with Tejaswini Niranjana, Rekha Pappu, Ashish Rajyadhyaksha, Anoop and Ashwin of CSCS, Bangalore, has helped shape this project.

31. See Rege (2010).

32. For more on critical feminist pedagogies of dialogue, participation and experience, see Ngan-Ling Chow, Fleck et al. (2003: 259–75).

33. I would like to thank, for their insights, interventions, energy and affection, Anil Jaybhaye, Nagnath Shelke, Deepa Tak and Tina Aranha, who assisted in teaching the Popular Culture course over the last two semesters.

34. See Uma Chakravarti (2008).

35. See *Isn't This Plate Indian/Hi Thali Bharatiya Nahi Ka? Dalit Histories and Memories of Food*, University of Pune, Krantijyoti Savitribai Phule Women's Studies Centre, April 2009.

36. See Batch of 2005–07 (Course on Dalits and Public Sphere); *Dissonant Democracy*, University of Pune: Department of Sociology, April 2007; Batch of 2006–08 (Course on Popular Culture and Modernity in India); *Sansanati Youth News*: A Short Film on Mobile Cultures Shot on Mobiles, University of Pune: Department Of Sociology, April 2008; Batch of 2007–09 (Course on Gender and Popular Culture in Modern India); *Exploring the Popular: Texts, Identities and Politics*, A bilingual edited volume with a foreword by Uma Chakravarti; University of Pune: Krantijyoti Savitribai Phule Women's Studies Centre, December 2008 and WS 10 Class of 2009 (course on Gender and Caste: History and Memory); *Isn't This Plate Indian/ Hi Thali Bharatiya Nahi Ka? Dalit Histories and Memories of Food*, University Of Pune, Krantijyoti Savitribai Phule Women's Studies Centre, April 2009; and WS 8, Class

of January 2010, 'Plundering Popular Culture'. These documents may be accessed at the libraries of the Department of Sociology, or by writing to wsc@ unipune.ernet.in.

37. I am rephrasing the title of Mariscal's article (Marsical 2006).

References

Alam, Javeed. 2004. *Who Wants Democracy?*. Hyderabad: Orient Longman.

Ambedkar, B. R. 1936. 'Annihilation of Caste', undelivered speech written by Dr. B. R. Ambedkar, Jat Pat Todak Mandal, Lahore.

———. 1957. *The Buddha and His Dhamma*. Mumbai: Siddhartha College Publication.

———. 1987. *Riddles in Hinduism*. Maharashtra: Education Department of Maharashtra.

Anveshi Law Committee. 2002. 'Caste and the Metropolitan University'. *Economic & Political Weekly* 37 (12) March: 1000–02.

Ashcroft, B., G. Griffiths, and H. Tiffin. 1989. *The Empire Writes Back*. London: Routledge.

Chakravarti, Uma. 2008. 'Foreword'. In MA Class of 2008, ed. *Exploring the Popular: Texts, Identities and Politics*. Pune: KSP, Women's Studies Centre, University of Pune.

Chavan, Dilip. 2008. 'Bharatiya Uchh Shikshanatil Gunavattecha Prashna'. *Vatsaru* 8 (4): 16–30 June.

Cohn, Bernard S. 1991. African Models and Indian Histories'. In *An Anthropologist among the Historians and Other Essays*, 224–54. New Delhi: Oxford University Press.

Dahiwale, S. M. ed. 2005. *Understanding Indian Society: The Non-Brahmanic Perspective*. Jaipur: Rawat Publications.

Dangle, Arjun. ed. 1992. *Poisoned Bread: Translation from Modern Marathi Dalit Literature* Hyderabad: Orient Longman.

'Excerpts of Thorat Committee Report'. *Insight* 1 (1): 10.

Freire, Paulo. 1973. *Education for Critical Consciousness*. New York: Continuum.

Grossberg, Lawrence. 1994. 'Identity and Cultural Studies: Is That All There Is?' *Cultural Studies* 8 (1): 87–95.

Guru, Gopal. 2000. 'Dalits in Pursuit of Modernity'. In Romila Thapar, ed. *India: Another Millennium*. New Delhi: Viking.

hooks, bell. 1989. *Talking Back: Thinking Feminist Thinking Black*. Boston: South End Press.

———. 1994. 'Eros, Eroticism, and the Pedagogical Process'. In Henry A. Giroux and Peter McLaren, eds, *Between Borders: Pedagogy and the Politics of Cultural Studies*, 113–19. New York: Routledge.

IAWS Newsletter. 2003. Pune: Women's Studies Centre, December.

Ilaiah, Kancha. 1996. *Why I am Not a Hindu: A Sudra Critique of Hindutva Philosophy, Culture and Political Economy*. Calcutta: Samya.

Isn't This Plate Indian/Hi Thali Bharatiya Nahi Ka? Dalit Histories and Memories of Food. 2009. Student Publication, University of Pune, Krantijyoti Savitribai Phule Women's Studies Centre, April.

Kandasamy, Meena. 2006. *Touch*. Mumbai: Peacock Books.

Khairmode, Changdev. 1992. *Dr Bhimrao Ramji Ambedkar*, Vols. 1–12. Pune: Sugava Prakashan.

Krishna, M. Murli. 2004. Autobiography as a Resource for Educational Theory: A Dalit Life Story, MPhil Dissertation in English Literature, CIEFL, Hyderabad.

Kumar, Anoop. 2007. 'Casteism in Higher Education'. *Insight* 1 (1), September–October: 8–10.

Kumar, Vivek. 2005. 'Situating Dalits in Indian Sociology'. *Sociological Bulletin* 54 (3): 514–32.

Marsical, Jorge. 2006. 'Can Cultural Studies Speak Spanish?'. In Toby Miller, ed. *A Companion to Cultural Studies*. MA: Blackwell Publishers.

Martin, B., and C. Talpade-Mohanty. 1986. 'Feminist Politics: What's Home Got to Do with It?'. In Teresa De Lauretis, ed. *Feminist Studies/Critical Studies*. Bloomington: Indiana University Press.

Meshram. Bhujang. 2007. *Mala Bhetlelya Kavita* [The Poems I Met].

Moon, Vasant. ed. 1987. *Babasaheb Ambedkar Writings and Speeches*, Vols. 2, 4 and 11. Government of Maharashtra: Education Department.

Nanda, Meera. 2002. *Breaking the Spell of Dharma and Other Essays*. New Delhi: Three Essays.

Ngan-Ling Chow, E., Chadveck Fleck, et al. 2003. 'Exploring Critical Feminist Pedagogy: Infusing Dialogue, Participation and Experience in Teaching and Learning'. *Teaching Sociology*, 31 (3) July: 259–75.

O'Hanlon, Rosalind. 1985. *Caste, Conflict and Ideology: Mahatma Jotirao Phule and Low Caste Protest in Nineteenth Century Western India*. Cambridge: Cambridge University Press.

Omvedt, Gail. 1976. *Cultural Revolt in a Colonial Society: The Non-Brahman Movement in Western India: 1873 to 1930*. Bombay: Scientific Socialist Education Trust.

Out-Caste [blog]. 2008. Available at http://out-caste.blogspot.com/2008_02_25_archive.html.

Palshikar, Sanjay, and Arun Kumar Patnaik. 2002. 'Violence in a University: Defending the Indefensible'. *Economic & Political Weekly* 37 (16): 1490–91.

Patel, Sujata. 2006. 'Beyond Binaries: A Case for Self-Reflexive Sociologies'. *Current Sociology* 54 (3): 381–95.

Pawade, Kumud. 1981. *Antasphot*. Aurangabad: Anand Prakashan.

Pawar, Pragnya D. 2004. *Kendra Aani Parigh*. Mumbai: Dimple Prakashan.

Phadke, Y. D. ed. 1991. *Mahatma Phule Samagra Vagmay*. Bombay: Maharashtra Rajya Sahitya Sanskruti Mandal.

Phule, Joteerao Govindrai. 1873. *Gulamgiri* (Hindi edition). Pune: Vani Prakashan.

Prasad, C. B. 2006. *Dalit Phobia: Why Do They Hate Us?*. New Delhi: Vitasta.

Radhakrishnan, R. 2007. *Between Identity and Location: The Cultural Politics of Theory*. Hyderabad: Orient Longman.

Rege, Sharmila. 2004. 'Feminist Challenge to Sociology: Disenchanting Sociology or "For Sociology"?' In Sharmila Rege, ed. *Feminist Sociological Knowledge*. New Delhi: Sage Publications.

———. 2006 a. *Caste, Identity and Public Sphere: Mapping Ambedkarite Counter Publics in Maharashtra*. Kolkata: Samya.

———. 2006 b. 'Dalit Studies a Pedagogical Practice: Claiming More Than a "Little Place" in the Academia'. Malcolm Adiseshiah Memorial Lecture. Chennai: MIDS.

———. 2006 c. *Writing Caste/Writing Gender: Narrating Dalit Women's Testimonios*. New Delhi: Zubaan.

———. ed. 2010. *Building Bridges: On Becoming a Welder: Manual 1*. Pune: KSP, Women's Studies Centre, University of Pune.

———. 2011. 'Exorcising Fear of Identity: Interrogating the "Language Question" in Sociology and Sociological Language'. In Sujata Patel, ed. *Doing Sociology in India: Genealogies, Locations and Practices*. New Delhi: OUP.

Research Room Diaries 2008. Pune Krantijyoti Savitribai Phule Women's Studies Centre, University of Pune.

Rodrigues, Edward. 2003. '"Dalit" Struggle for Recognition within Indian Sociology'. In Maitrayee Chaudhari, ed. *The Practice of Sociology*, 221–58. Hyderabad: Orient Longman.

Satyanarayana, K. 2005. 'Dalit Studies as a New Perspective in the Indian Academia'. In Arun Kumar and Sanjay Kumar, eds, *Dalit Studies in Higher Education: Vision and Challenges*, 81–95. Delhi: Deshkal.

Senthilkumar Solidarity Committee. 2008. 'Caste, Higher Education and Senthil's "Suicide"'. *Economic & Political Weekly* 43 (33) 16–22, August: 10–12.

Tharu, S., and K. Lalita. 1991. *Women Writing in India: 600 BC to the Present.* Vol. 1: 600 B.C. to the Early Twentieth Century. New York: The Feminist Press at the CUNY.

Vatsaru. 2008. 8 (15): 1–15, December, Sajag Vidhyarthi Shodharthi Gaat edited issue.

19

Gender and Curriculum*

Dipta Bhog

The National Curriculum Framework (NCF), introduced by the government on 14 November 2000, has raised considerable debate and controversy regarding the content of social science textbooks. More specifically, the NCF has been accused of adopting a communal and Brahmanical view of history and of seriously undermining the historical method of inquiry through bureaucratic and political interference. While the primary focus has been on the question of history and the deletions that have been mandated by the NCERT, what has not been put under scrutiny is how the NCF jeopardises the government's own commitment to providing gender-just education. Despite its reiterations regarding equality, fundamental rights and quality education for all, a closer reading of the document points to a move towards ensuring that women learn to play out their 'traditional' social roles, as good mothers, wives and daughters, within the family and the nation.

This chapter is divided into two sections. The first looks at how the core thrust of the NCF might impact the likely content of future education. It argues that the emphasis on Indian tradition and the collapsing of value education with religious education puts on hold the possibility of education emerging as an enabling tool for women's empowerment. Comparing the NCF with nineteenth century debates in colonial India about women's education reveals that the new discourse is, in a substantial measure, no more than a restatement of old anxieties and equally antiquated solutions. As a counterpoint to these debates, the second section revisits, albeit briefly, the vision and policy framework of the New Education Policy of 1986, with regard to women's education. More concretely, it analyses the 'trickle-down' effect of progressive policy rhetoric on the actual writing of school textbooks, particularly those relating to language teaching. As the review points out, the decade following the 1986 policy refinements did not produce any significant positive yield, in the manner in which gender was dealt with in the texts. The uptake of this analysis is clear: even as one must critique the NCF for its regressive views on

* Previously published in *Economic and Political Weekly* 37 (17), 27 April–3 May 2002: 1638–42.

women, there is no reason to believe that progressive rhetoric alone can change the entrenched gender stereotypes in school curricula. Unless the policy framework can deal with the issues of actualisation of alternative images and representation for women, no real progress can be made.

Burden of Tradition

As is well known, the nineteenth century saw the emergence of women's education as a significant issue in colonial India. It witnessed the setting up of institutions of learning for women and girls, by social reformers and the British government. Throughout the century, but particularly in the latter half, questions regarding the nature and content of women's education became a subject of heated debate within the broad parameters of a nationalist consciousness—between the so-called liberal-progressive elements on the one hand and the conservative-revivalists on the other. Transcending the differences between the two camps were some common points of agreement. First, both sides concurred that the contemporary absence of education amongst women, regardless of what might have historically contributed to such a situation, was a sign of India's lack of civilisation—an indicator of its low position in the evolutionary spiral that was history. The corollary was straightforward: If India had to catch up with the West in terms of its material achievements, then the nation's women had to be urgently educated. At the same time, this education could not be left to the alien colonial state or the missionaries. Because, if in the process of being educated, the native woman did no more than refashion herself in the image of her white, Western counterpart, then it could create a new crisis of identity for native society or the incipient Indian nation. In formulaic terms, the debate is easily summed up: a resounding yes to women's education, but an equally emphatic no to unregulated Western education.

The anxiety about the content of education was not just in terms of a threat to native identity. It was also powered by fears, based on the rationalist-humanist message of Enlightenment, of a modernist onslaught on the existing social order, overturning hierarchies of power relating to caste, ethnicity or gender and leading to a state of anomie. Not surprisingly, there was an increasing preoccupation with defining the kind of education that would be suitable for Indian women.

Thundered the Mahratta in its comment on the Female High School in Bombay in 1887: 'Nothing can be gained by anglicising our girls or teaching them to ape the ways of men.' Schools must not create an 'aversion to our domestic life'. It was 'most reprehensible' that lessons inculcating the 'high principles of ancient Aryan religious morality were conspicuously absent from the girls' curriculum' and so was 'advice to young women with regard to chaste wifely conduct' (Bhattacharya 2001).

The seemingly 'reactionary' tone of the Mahratta was not exceptional. The most celebrated 'progressive' face of Indian nationalism in the late nineteenth century, Dadabhai Naoroji, voiced the same anxieties in a more sophisticated garb:

> The time will come when natives generally will see the benefit of female education as a great social necessity to rise in civilisation and to advance social happiness and

> progress; and will understand that women had as much right to exercise and enjoy all the rights, privileges, and duties of this world as man, each working towards the common good in her or his respective sphere. *But that time has not come yet... Good and educated mothers only will raise good and educated sons* (quoted in Bhattacharya 2001: 90).

In 1916, K. B. V. Krishna Rao, a zamindar of Cocanada, wrote:

> The education of girls requires to be improved in various directions to suit the conditions of the various classes of girls and make them well equipped so as to enable them to become good housewives and good mothers...it would not be wise to impart such kind of education as would implant in them tastes which they would have no opportunity of gratifying in their after life (quoted in Bhattacharya 2001: 411).

The intent is unambiguous: women's education was not so much an end as it was a means to an end, i.e., the betterment of the family and the nation. While Naoroji does mention that women have the right to enjoy all the rights available to men, there is no mistaking the familiar note of women raising sons for the nation. Nor can one ignore the fear about 'anglicised' Indian women discarding their own culture and tradition and moving towards acquiring 'tastes' that Indian men will be unable to fulfil.

Intrinsic to this creation of a new nationalist patriarchy was the intellectual labour which went into distinguishing Oriental women from Western ones. As Ram Mohan Roy had put it, nearly half a century earlier, Hindu women were 'infinitely more self-sacrificing than men' and their 'exemplifying wifely devotion and spiritual strength' was their distinguishing feature as Oriental women.

The NCF harks back to the nineteenth century. Its overarching concern, too, is to locate the curriculum within a self-evident and unproblematised Indian tradition. In an embarrassingly faithful echo of the earlier debate, the refrain of 'Indianising' the curriculum, so as to maintain the best qualities of Indian womanhood and prevent Anglicisation in the face of technological modernity, runs through the framework document.

Predictably, there is a deep anxiety about contemporary Indian society distancing itself from its 'religio-philosophical ethos':

> However a sizeable segment of the contemporary Indian society, seem to have distanced itself from the religio-philosophical ethos, the awareness of the social design and the understanding of the heritage of the past. Influenced by the alien technological ethos, the parents and the educational institutions emphasise the acquisition of high grade techno-informative knowledge alone. However, the impact of westernisation has been limited to only the elite members of society, leaving the masses unaware of these developments. This has brought into sharp focus the rural-urban, the agrarian-industrial, the affluent-destitute and the literate and the illiterate divides. In this way the structure of the authority of the Indian agrarian society has been disturbed. An individual in the formal work system could exercise authority over those who were otherwise his superiors in age and in societal structure. In the agrarian society, successive generations followed the occupation as well as the goal sets of the family or the caste at large (NCF 2000 b: 3).

In other words, the trope of tradition is invoked to contain the potentially destabilising influence of education. The NCF desires to relocate education where it traditionally belonged—in maintaining and reproducing power relations within traditional caste society. It views contact with Western civilisation as a source of undesirable social conflict and turmoil and singles out Westernisation, defined simply as a challenge to established authority, whether at the level of family or community, as a grave danger. This forms the crux of the fear that pervades the NCF: how to embrace the fruits of 'an alien technological ethos', without abandoning the 'high principles of ancient Aryan religious morality', as desired by the Mahratta.

Needless to say, forgotten in this anxiety is the definition of education as a force for change or liberation. Nowhere in the document does the NCF envision education as a tool for empowerment, or as a means to achieving social mobility or an egalitarian society.

Interestingly, the section on 'Education of Girls' comes under the broad heading of Education for Social Cohesion (rather than, say, change or progress) in the framework document. The dilemma presented is remarkably similar to the one emphasised by Naoroji's statement on women's education. And so is the form; it begins with a large and abstract statement of gender equality and then quickly reduces itself to emphasing gender-specific roles.

> Equality among sexes is a fundamental right under the Constitution of India. Besides making education accessible to more and more girls especially rural girls, removing all gender-discrimination and gender-bias in school curriculum is absolutely necessary .Moreover it will be most appropriate thing to recognise and nurture the best features of each gender in the best Indian tradition.
>
> After all, India gave her women the right to vote without any prolonged battle for it, unlike in the west. There is a need to develop and implement gender inclusive and gender sensitive curricular strategies to nurture a generation of girls and boys who are equally competent and are sensitive to one another, and grow up in a caring and sharing mode as equals and not as adversaries (NCF 2000 b: 9).

Where it differs from Naoroji is in its acute awareness of the potential social conflict that education and notions of gender equality can engender. Hence the conceptual positioning of education for girls under the rubric of social cohesion and the idealised strategic roadmap, which would ostensibly lead to women's equality, beginning with a massive negation of the relevance of agitational politics. Unlike the West, where the demand for women's rights has resulted in the breakdown of the family, women in India need not protest for their rights, because, as in the case of the right to vote, they would be granted their legitimate dues in the natural course by the ever-generous Indian patriarchs. The NCF resonates with facile dichotomies between Western civilisation and the Indian tradition, mistaking secular social trends as a marker of essential cultural difference. Witness, for instance, the following lament: 'In contrast to the joint family and the extended family, the society is now witnessing the phenomenon of nuclear families, single parents, unmarried relationships and so on...'.

The irony is as pathetic as it is profound: Even as the Indian state proclaims its progressive credentials by legislating against domestic violence and sex-selection technologies, it shuts the door on any critique of the family as an institution—something that the women's movement in India has been fighting for long to legitimise.

RELIGIOUS INSTRUCTION AS VALUE EDUCATION

In collapsing the distinction between value education and religious education, the document raises new questions regarding the objectives of educating women and girls in our society.

> Value education and education about religions would not form a separate subject of study or examination at any stage. These would be so judiciously integrated with all the subjects of study in the scholastic areas and all the activities and the programmes in the co-scholastic areas, that the objectives thereof would be directly and indirectly achieved in the classroom, at the school assembly places, play grounds and other such places (NCF 2000 a: 35).

In a society where women have carried the exclusive historical burden of upholding tradition and religious identity, the NCF aims at accentuating the bias. It ignores the subordinate position that women occupy in different religions. Contrast this with the National Education Policy of 1986: 'Education will neutralise the accumulated distortions of the past'. In actual fact, the NCF does worse than going back on the bland promise of its policy predecessor; it expands the agenda of reaffirming religious identities, from the confines of the classroom to the very fabric of social interaction.

What's worse, it introduces a vague and ill-defined concept, that of spiritual quotient or SQ, as an indicator of educational achievement. Not surprisingly, the document remains unconcerned about how this new-fangled intellectual sophistry might be given practical shape. It remains silent on how the SQ will be evaluated and by whom, even assuming it has a determinate and objective content. Could it be that women would have to prove their selfless, sacrificing and devotional qualities in order to score high marks? Alternately, how will those who break with tradition be judged?

The NCF is, without doubt, a huge step backwards from the National Education Policy (1986). The latter saw education as 'an agent of basic change in the status of women'. 'The National Education System,' it argued, 'will play a positive, interventionist role in the empowerment of women.' But we need to assess the impact of its progressive policy rhetoric on the actual making of the textbooks. Did it really 'neutralise the accumulated distortions of the past'? Did gender get portrayed in a manner that was significantly different from past representations of women and girls?

The following is a brief look at the NCERT's language textbooks for Classes III, V and VIII, in the decade following the formulation of NEP.[2] The rationale for focussing on language textbooks is that language is a key issue in feminist pedagogical practice. It is a powerful site for the construction and communication of gender identities and for reinforcing power relations.

Stories/narratives create meaning in all cultures. By ordering and describing our experiences, they enable us to make sense of the world. The power of language derives from its power to reify that which is constructed—precisely at the point where this construction is most questionable—into something that appears natural and self-evident. In short, language serves to naturalise gendered inequalities.

In the preface to the language textbooks, it is claimed that the objective is to expand the horizons of the child, to increase her ability to think and to inculcate values within her. The values that are described in the preface are: determination, helping others, bravery, discipline, timeliness, the importance of hard work, social service and love for the nation.

The preface suggests that the teacher should tackle language teaching through methods that facilitate discussion and interaction in the class as a whole. By encouraging children to undertake role-play, for instance, it is possible to not only elicit the active participation of the students, but also to raise their confidence to communicate. However, the content and the presentation of the lessons leaves one with serious doubt as to whether the teacher would be able to achieve these aims, particularly with regard to the girls in her class. Consider the following statistics, based on a review of 75 lessons from the textbooks mentioned earlier:

- In as many as 34 lessons, i.e. nearly 50 per cent of the aggregate, men and boys were the only actors in the texts. There were no female characters in the narratives.
- In 10 lessons, the presence of women was either mentioned in passing or confined to traditional roles—i.e., as mothers, sisters, etc.
- No fewer than 23 lessons were in the category of information dissemination: didactic pieces on 'the exploding population', the virtues of healthy eating and such like. In this category were also lessons comprising '*dohas*' (couplets) and other poetic forms which might be, prima facie, seen as having no gender bias.
- About one in 10 lessons—eight to be precise—sought to represent women and girls 'in a different light'. Among them, there was one chapter on swimming which included references to women who have achieved excellence in that sport. In another such lesson, a girl writes to a friend about her visit to the zoo. A third describes a sports day celebration which has girls as active participants. In addition, there were three others which made a genuine attempt to represent women in a different light, but even these scanty offerings were not without their own problems. Of the three, two were biographic accounts of Rani Laxmibai and Madame Curie, while the third was an account featuring discrimination experienced by a girl in the village.

They Were Born Great Men!

For the purposes of critique, it is important to look at how men of honour and achievement are represented in these narratives. The texts in question comprise biographical profiles, childhood experiences, letters or anecdotes from the lives of great men. They cover, largely, 'the usual suspects': Mahatama Gandhi, Lal Bahadur Shastri, Rajendra Prasad, Ishwarchandra Vidyasagar, Edison, Chandrashekhar Azad, Vikram Sarabhai, Veer Abhimanyu, Jagdishchandra Basu, Baba Amte and Arjun.

The narratives of their lives and achievements are very much in the public realm. No details are given of their family life or their homes. There is, in Baba Amte's life history, a mention of the impact that his mother had on him, but this is an aspect of the customary supporting role that women have to play in the lives of great men.

Minor events in the lives of the men are imbued with great meaning. For example, in the case of Lal Bahadur Shastri, his stealing a rose from a garden and the consequent words of admonition from the '*mali*' (gardener) are supposed to change his life, motivating him to become a great leader of the future. Apart from the careless myth-making of it, there is something of interest in what the *mali* actually tells the little Lal Bahadur: 'You don't have a father! Your behaviour ought to be unimpeachable. You should try and please everyone – just like this rose.'

Not having the presence of a father in his life would, no doubt, have serious implications for the life of a boy. But does that mean that he has to please everyone? Only if the absence of a father is also understood as an absence of moral authority, not to mention the absence of a credible figure, who might protect the boy against the temptations of the world. Equally, the boy is also expected, in time, to take over the role that his father has prematurely given up; in other words, to assume the mantle of responsible male leadership in the family.

In the minutiae of men's everyday lives—preferably the early years, since the presumption seems to be that you are either born great or achieve greatness first thing in childhood—lie grand moments of revelation, of courage, strength, determination and struggle.

That's What Girls Are For!

Contrast this seamless valorisation with the somewhat muted accounts of the two valiant women who are mentioned in the texts.

The Rani of Jhansi is no doubt a great rider and fighter, but she is vulnerable too—prone to depression (at the death of her son and husband) and doubt (the Rani often finds refuge in prayer and withdrawal from the world). Even when she comes back to fight the British, she has to take recourse to spiritual fortifications—she is said to pray every morning—before commencing on worldly matters. No such doubts plague great men in their lives; they face all challenges with calm assurance and self-certainty.

If it is not doubts that assail women, then there are other, equally important 'distractions'. In the case of Madame Curie, for instance, even as she busies herself in the laboratory, surrounded by chemical fluids, test tubes and complicated experimental equipment, not to mention her scientist-husband, we are informed that, 'Maria used to do all the housework herself. She would clean the house, wash clothes, cook food and wash dishes. After two years of marriage, Maria gave birth to a girl child. This increased the work load on her but did not affect the quality of her work'. Fine words to describe the double burden of women! Apart from making a not-so-subtle case for how it is eminently possible for women, if they so choose, to both work at home and make a 'contribution' to the larger cause of humanity. Ultimately, however, these digressions into the domestic duties of eminent women have a different meaning and purpose. They are meant to be narrative devices that render these women 'normal' for the average reader. In other words, the idea is to 'tame' them, to contain the 'dangers' they pose to the existing order as different women. This provides a stark counterpoint to the lives of great men, where the emphasis is on larger-than-life myth-making and deification, to render the subjects as distant and towering as possible.

The achievements of Rani of Jhansi and Marie Curie need to be reined in, to be 'normalised' through their participation in cooking, washing, cleaning and praying. They are tamed into not being too out of this world, too different, too challenging. Madame Curie's account is strikingly different from the biographies of other male scientists, like Vikram Sarabhai and Jagadish Chandra Bose. Here, the men were not just clear about what they were doing, or what they wanted to achieve—a momentous self-certainty which they share with other great men—but they were also serenely free of any domestic clutter, not to mention any doubt or depression about their chosen vocations in life. The concluding line from the Rani Jhansi story is instructive: 'By her *sacrifice* the Rani proved that *if called upon* [in rather extraordinary circumstances, no doubt], Indian Woman too could give the enemy a tough time'.

Of Boys and Men

This raises questions about the role models that these texts place before the girl child. Her exclusion becomes all the more evident from the way young boys dominate other narratives. Boys are invariably shown as striving for the higher virtues of morality and character—of courage, hard work, grit and determination in the face of all odds (like being blind, parentless) and limitless intellectual inquiry. (But what is the meaning of learning for girls?)

Equally, boys in all three textbooks exhibit greater mobility, travel to various places on their own and, crucially, possess the ability to comment on and describe new experiences. Where women feature in these travels, they are shown to lack in understanding or knowledge. For example, in the lesson '*Tamil Nadu Ki Yatra*', Dinesh is visiting Chennai for the first time. His friend goes to pick him up from the station. Even before they leave the station, Dinesh begins to tell his friend about the geographical details of the state. His friend's wife, Maya, who has lived in Chennai all her life, comments: 'Bhai Sahab, I am hearing these special facts about my state for the first time. How do you know so much?'

We move on further in the travel and Dinesh's wife is shocked at the amount of fish the fishermen have caught in their nets. She exclaims: 'Chi! Chi! O god, how heartless! These fishermen are killing all these fish. What wrong have these fish done to these fishermen!...These mean fishermen catch the fish (at night) while they are asleep.' On hearing her comment, says the narrator, 'We all collapsed with laughter, holding our stomach'.

The question is: Who gets to tell the narrative and to whom? How are women positioned within these narratives, in relation to others?

Despite being a grown woman, Maya is not only lacking in information about a place where she has lived all her life, but her responses are typically naïve and innocent, not to be taken seriously. Throughout the lesson, the voice of the male narrator dominates, to give us all the descriptions about what is worth knowing about Tamil Nadu.

Women as They Are?

Women come in predominantly in their role as mothers; maternal love flows unquestioningly in her in the poem '*Kadamb ka Pedh*'. At other places, they inspire their sons to grow up in the service of the nation, much like the idealised women of the freedom struggle, the mothers of the nation's current and future generations.

But what constitutes the feminine and the masculine emerges most significantly through stories and poems. The feminine is what is close to nature, a matter of habit, while the masculine is cultural, a matter of struggle and accomplishment. For instance, birds are the embodiment of the feminine, when they sing their sweet song and dance with the fairies and buzz around flowers that dance in the garden: soft, tender and vulnerable.

There is a story in the third standard language text, titled 'For the Sparrow', which spells out, for little children, the attributes of masculinity and femininity:

> His name was Balram. The name of his village, Pokhari. His work was farming. The difficulty was that he was not interested in farming. All his ancestral land was lying uncultivated. What ought he to do! He did feel hungry everyday. He would go to the forest and survive on the fruits. When fruits were not available he would collect dried pieces of wood and exchange them in the village for some bread. He would somehow fill his stomach. At times he would consider tilling his ancestral land but farming was not his forte. One day Balram was in the forest collecting firewood. Suddenly his hand came in contact with something very soft. He could hear a faint sound. Balram looked with interest and found a small sparrow there. Balram picked up the sparrow. She was weak and sick. He felt that the bird was saying something to him.
>
> He thought the bird must be thirsty and therefore he gave her a few drops of water. He gave her a fruit to eat. He kept the bird on his shoulder all day long.
>
> In the evening he went to his neighbour and in exchange for the wood he bought back some grain. Balram gave the grain to the bird and said, 'look dear bird, stay in my house. When you are better you can fly away.'
>
> The bird was happy in Balram's house. Everyday she would perch herself on his shoulder and go to the jungle. On the way she would sing him sweet songs. In the evening she would come back with him. Balram would take a lot of care of the sparrow. Now he would go everyday to get wood and from selling this he would get food for himself and the sparrow everyday. Both would chat with each other. Slowly Balram started to love the bird. He found a companion.
>
> As the bird recovered, the possibility of her leaving became real. Finally Balram started to work on his unproductive land. He worked very, very hard. The bird in all this kept flying around him.

> In some time the crop was standing in the field. When the crop ripened then the house was overflowing with grain. Balram showed this to the sparrow and said, "this is all for you. Now you need not go anywhere. Now you stay with me always." On listening to Balram the sparrow started singing with joy!

Is this just a sweet, innocent story about a young boy and a bird becoming friends, or does this communicate something else? The sparrow made an honourable and responsible man out of Balram, while he made sure that she gave up her instinct to fly (away) forever. All she needed was the security of the grain to ensure that she had a reason to stay. Just like a lot of women in their 'marriages', with men as the breadwinners.

In another story involving a black deer being captured by a prince, his companion, the female deer, cries in front of the prince. The prince is so moved by the intensity of the female deer's love for the male deer that he takes the decision to leave the deer. The dramatic strength of the story is parasitic, on the supposedly natural love and affection (*mamta*) that is part of women's nature. Clearly, the women's entreaties to the prince are not in the nature of an achievement. It is in the female deer's nature to cry for her mate. What counts as achievement is something that involves struggle, detachment from conflicting emotions and, finally, perseverance. To wit, the prince, subsuming his desire to catch the deer and, proactively, taking the decision to free the deer, is the real hero. The female deer's emotional outburst pales in contrast to the difficult moral decision that the prince is required to make.

Both stories are indicative of how norms ascribed to men and women can be articulated through seemingly apolitical and innocent descriptions, whether one is talking of nature, or of human relationships with animals, or simply about events that involve an interface between the two.

Conclusions

It is quite clear from the analysis of the language texts that despite an explicit policy commitment from earlier governments to provide an empowering education for women and girls, the situation on the ground did not improve a great deal. Traditional meanings of the masculine and the feminine continued to persist, along with the oppositional, dichotomous categories of active-passive, emotional-rational, nature-culture and dependent-autonomous.

Clearly, gender-sensitive material at the primary and secondary levels require inputs from those who have struggled to bring women's voices, narratives, experiences and worldviews into the academic mainstream. Without this knowledge-base, those charged with rewriting texts will restrict themselves to superficial tinkering: either by increasing the number of times that girls are visually or verbally represented in the books or by facile role-reversals.

The fact that those who have contributed to the creation of knowledge regarding women have had little to do with the writing of text-books might be, in the end, an extremely important reason why we have not, despite a decade-and-a-half of rhetoric, moved beyond the stage of pious policy pronouncements.

Indeed, it might be why, instead of moving ahead, we are in the midst of a severe regression.

NOTE

1. The textbooks in question are *Bal Bharati-Part III* (February 2000), *Bal Bharati-Part V* (1999 [1994]) and *Saras Bharati-Part 20* (2001 [1998]).

REFERENCES

Bhattacharya, S. 2001. 'Introduction'. In Bhattacharya and Bara et al., eds, *Development of Women's Education in India: 1850–1920*. JNU: Kanishka Publication.

National Curriculum Framework. 2000 a. Organization of Curriculum at Elementary and Secondary Stages (Chapter 2), 35. New Delhi: NCERT.

———. 2000 b. Context and Concerns (Chapter 1), 3, 9. New Delhi: NCERT.

20

LITERACY, POWER AND FEMINISM*

MALINI GHOSE

INTRODUCTION

The process of learning to read and write involves considerably more than the acquisition of a skill. For poor rural women, literacy can become an arena where the structures of power encounter the possibilities of contested negotiation and critical reflection—a space inscribed with issues of power—and one where identities and knowledge are constructed, where women's everyday experiences form the basis for understanding and renegotiating the world. It is a matter of recognising and taking power over some aspects of language, literacy and life. In a word: empowerment.

Ironically, while these issues have long been critical for feminists, the politics of literacy and education remains a marginal concern for the women's movement in India. There has been little effort made to address the issues of power that emerge out of and within the practice of education. This is particularly striking in light of the literacy campaigns of the late 1980s and 1990s, which saw a massive mobilisation of women. Similarly, in the ongoing debates around the NCERT National Curriculum Framework 2000, the voices of women's groups have been noticeably absent, even though the framework is clearly antithetical to several issues that have been central to the struggles of the women's movement. Recent policy documents on primary education see women's roles in education as mobilisers—as mothers who must play the role of bringing their children to school. The state's vision of women's education is very apparent, but has not been adequately critiqued. However, when the findings of the Census 2001 announced the increase in female literacy rates and the fact that female literacy rates were rising faster than male, this was widely highlighted as an indicator of an improvement in women's status.

* Previously published in *Economic and Political Weekly* 37 (17), 27 April–3 May 2002: 1615–20.

A version of this chapter has appeared in David Olson and Nancy Torrance, ed. *The Making of Literate Societies*. Oxford: Wiley-Blackwell, 2001.

This is hardly surprising, as the primary focus of groups that do work on education is on access—issues such as increasing enrolment of girls and arresting the drop-out rates. The state, too, responds to this lack by focussing on delivery. Once women and girls have entered the 'public sphere', it is assumed that empowerment will follow implicitly; their life options will expand and they will be in a position to take greater control of their lives. Concerns regarding quality are raised, but are usually limited to improving 'skills' and making the learning environment enjoyable and interactive, so that learning achievements improve. But the reality is that the education spaces themselves create boundaries that limit possibilities and reinforce stereotypes. The curricula, including the content, language, images of textbooks, as well as the perceptions and attitudes of teachers, have the power to strengthen the hold of patriarchal constructs. The educational arena becomes an enclosed space, like the 'domestic sphere', where discriminations are normalised and silenced. The challenge lies in seizing that space, to articulate, critique and renegotiate these discriminations.

This chapter uses the experiences of Nirantar,[1] a resource centre for gender and education, while working with Mahila Samakhya[2] (hereafter MS), a women's empowerment programme in Banda district of Uttar Pradesh, to discuss the reproduction and transformation of power relations in certain literacy learning situations. An examination of how power dynamics play themselves out in literacy programmes, which consciously attempt an empowering and participatory pedagogy, forms the focus of this chapter . The analysis of the power structures and dynamics at play in literacy work is based on reports of three teaching/learning environments: a residential literacy camp, a participatory primer development workshop and a six-month residential educational course for rural women.[3] These are, of course, 'micro' examples, but the issues they throw up certainly have larger implications and I hope this discussion will help to establish the need for the women's movement to engage proactively with education policies at a macro level.

LITERACY AND POWER

Our Approach to Literacy Work

As feminist literacy practitioners, we believe that education is not neutral, nor does our work entail merely delivering certain skills—such as literacy—to women. Our concern has been explicitly with changing power relations at a social and individual level. We are also bound to a pedagogy, which sees process and consequence as part of the same continuum and to a belief that for women to feel empowered as a result of an engagement with education, they must be empowered within the educational practice.

Having said this, we should add that the working understanding of power used in empowerment programmes such as ours draws on dichotomous categories like 'powerful and powerless' and images of 'grabbing power', 'redistributing power' and the like, all of which suggest an understanding of power as a finite commodity. We appreciate the limitations of this approach, but we also find it a valid entry point to discussions, when we are interacting with women who relate to the concept of power as something lacking in their own lives and an asset of their oppressors.

On the other hand, our practice is also informed by a view of power at another level of definition: we see power as a phenomenon of structured but mutable social relationships, in patriarchy for example (Street 1995). This vision of power is elegantly stated by Issac:

> The exercise of power is always contingent, it is chronically negotiated in the course of everyday life...Thus power relations approximate less a model of stimulus and response, and more a model of endemic reciprocity, negotiation, and struggle, with both dominant and subordinate groups mobilising their specific powers and resources (and for the subordinate solidarity is always the greatest resource) (Issac 1986).

Such an analysis of power, which encompasses elements of both approaches, has been at the core of feminism, as have issues of knowledge and representation, authority and subordination, victimhood and agency, construction of subjectivities, and, above all, a concern for the everyday realities of women's lives. The concept of empowerment too, though now a buzzword, has been crucial in problematising the issue of power and bringing a theoretical construct within the realm of practice. Our work has its antecedents in this process.

The complexities and contradictions in the approach to literacy closely resemble our understanding of power, outlined above. Thus, just as on the one hand we accept power as a concrete asset or a lack, we have also found ourselves treating (or being forced to treat) literacy and education as a concrete asset which we must 'deliver' to those lacking it. Then again, we also treat power as a more abstract, contingent and open-ended phenomenon and we try to bring the same openness to our literacy work. The tension between these two broad perspectives of power and education is probably one of the more striking features that emerges in the experiences narrated below. There are, however, other threads running through these episodes. The power dynamics within the programme—between 'us' and 'them', 'teachers' and 'participants' and the power dynamics that are created between the programme and the external environment—between the 'mainstream' and 'alternative' and 'national' and 'local'. This was an area fraught with contradictions, a situation we tried to get past, but also had to accept.

Experiences from the Field

The Context

As the women's issue came to the centre-stage of the 'development' arena in the 1980s in India, a number of empowerment programmes for women were formulated. Some were programmes mooted by the government. The women's movement, through protest, lobbying and critiquing patriarchal structures and institutions, had created an 'alternative space' in the previously forbidden terrain of government programmes. Partnerships between women's groups and government agencies, previously unthinkable, began to be forged. As women's groups attempted to translate feminist constructs into concrete programmes of action, there was a shift, from looking at power as simply a negative or coercive force, to regarding it as a generative, transformative and productive force as well (Batliwala 1993). These programmes became spaces to introduce a different culture of power. MS was a product of this period.

The MS programme works on issues of women's education and empowerment. Banda, the MS district that is the focus of this chapter, is one of the poorest districts in India, with a significant tribal and low-caste population, low literacy levels and a high degree of violence towards women. Women's demand for literacy grew out of their involvement with issues like struggles against landlords and forest contractors, health and water. A particularly innovative effort was training illiterate rural women as hand-pump mechanics. It was born out of a need to redress the water scarcity in the region and a non-functioning government water department. This intervention has had a number of spin-offs—a growing demand for literacy, the acquisition of new skills like masonry and a demand for information. All these efforts have been built on the bedrock of women's understanding of their life situation, their subordination as well as strengths. Literacy was gradually seen as a skill that would enable women to deal with their environment from a position of strength. For the activists at the village level, their new roles as village activists demanded that they interact with the bureaucracy, schools and other mainstream institutions on a regular basis. The women hand-pump mechanics needed literacy for specific reasons: to maintain records of spare parts, other repairs, depths of bores, etc. The demand for literacy was linked to women redefining their lived realities, which now included learning new skills, interacting with mainstream structures of power, greater mobility and self-confidence and the desire for information on a range of issues.

Initially, the articulation of this demand compelled the programme functionaries to quickly get into the act of 'delivering literacy'. The education team consisted of a few '*sahayoginis*'[4] and teachers called '*sahelis*'. The formal schooling levels of the *sahelis*, compared to the educational qualifications of teachers in general, were low, though most had completed their primary education. This is an area where literacy levels for women are abysmally low and it was often difficult to find even a single literate woman in some villages. However, each new intervention led to an evolution of the team's (and our) skills and perspective on education. The group began to consider literacy instrumental to the development of a critical understanding of their life world, their experiences of struggle, of joy, as well as their folklore, language and indigenous ways of knowing. On the other hand, education, for many, continued to be equated with knowledge, power, jobs and the path to a better life.

Politics of Language: An Experience from a Literacy Camp

Literacy camps are residential programmes that initiate women into the world of letters. Through the use of locally relevant keywords, discussion and creation of learner-generated texts, these literacy camps provide a supportive learning atmosphere that helps dispel women's initial lack of confidence about being able to read and write. Since 1990, a number of such camps were held in Banda. A literacy course consisted of a series of three residential camps. Each camp lasted 10 days, with a month-long break between each. Nirantar members were involved in evolving an appropriate teaching/learning methodology and training the local team.

What follows is an experience from one such literacy camp. Two *sahayoginis*, a group of *sahelis* and a facilitator from Nirantar were coordinating this camp.

> Durga (a sahayogini) began writing the names of the months on chart paper. As she wrote 'Chait' the women in her group read out 'Chaiyat'; she wrote 'Baisaakh' they read 'Bayeesaakh'. This continued for a while. I wondered if this was a problem of differences in pronunciation. Or could it be that they were just reading incorrectly.
>
> It soon struck me that the sahelis had written the names of the month in standard Hindi and what the women (even some sahelis) were reading aloud was in Bundeli – the local language – the language of all oral communication in the area. I posed a question to the sahelis – would it not be simpler to write 'Chaiyat' instead?
>
> There were a flood of protests – 'Chaiyat' was not 'proper' or 'correct'. 'But you speak it?' I inquired. One saheli said, "We are teachers, how can we teach them incorrectly? When the women return to their villages their books will be scrutinised by family members and others in the community, like the pradhan (village headman). It will reflect badly on us and the programme". Said another, "Besides they were learning to read and write to be able to access information. All calendars were written in standard Hindi". I was in a quandary.
>
> If 'Chaiyat' is how they say it, how they identify with it, they should write it as such. But in the face of such strong protest, could I push my views, it will not be what they want. But then I thought, 'Chait' for that matter was 'incorrect'; the 'proper' (sanskritised) Hindi word is 'Chaitra'. In fact that is how it is written in most calendars. When I pointed this out to the sahelis, they said that while they were familiar with 'Chaitra' it would be too difficult for the women to learn and pronounce.
>
> On that occasion the women learned to write 'Chait'.
>
> (From the diary of a Nirantar member, November 1993)

The 'Chaiyat', 'Chait', 'Chaitra' incident might appear trivial to some, especially as the words are so close—'Chait' and 'Chaiyat' do not sound very different—but it threw up a number of issues. Questions of power were central to this. Who decides what is 'correct' and what is not? As we had seen, the boundaries between the regional language and standard Hindi were not as clear as we had initially assumed. As 'trainers', we could have pulled rank on the *sahelis* and insisted on Chaitra being taught, or we could have ignored their need to access the mainstream and insisted on their learning the months in the local language—the language they identify with.

Decisions on language policies in the formal education system are made without consulting people, but the issue of language in the non-formal system, where there is flexibility, is not given serious consideration. Decisions are either not taken, implying that the dominant language is used de facto, or at the most a 'transitional approach' is adopted, where the regional or local language is used as a bridge to ultimately take the learner towards learning the mainstream language.

The *sahelis,* despite the local inflections in their own Hindi, saw themselves as 'teachers' representing positions of authority and as providers of information. They were worried that this position would be open to question by other mainstream institutions. They had low levels of education and would not have been accepted as 'teachers' in a formal context. But having become teachers, they had acquired a certain social standing and they quickly stepped into their roles.

The contradiction lies in the fact that they are aware that in other areas of the programme, primacy is given to women's ways of knowing and forms of expression. Yet, when it came to literacy, the *sahelis* became sticklers for formality and purity. They also felt that they needed validation from the community for something as small as writing the names of the months, despite their involvement in processes which question this 'authority' in much more direct and visible ways.

Episodes like this forced us to deal with the issue of language in literacy teaching. While the verbal teaching/learning transaction was done in Bundeli, the actual words being taught and the texts being created were in Hindi. Was this instrumental approach to the local language limiting the women's creativity, inhibiting expression and communication of their thoughts and experiences? Was this approach, thereby, making invisible the women's culture and ways of defining and categorising their life-world? If this was so, then it was our limitation that we did not know the local language. We were Hindi-speaking people. However, the situation was not really all that simple. Hindi symbolised the language of power; the women themselves perceived their language as inferior. It was, they said, a '*dehati*' (rustic), '*lath maar bhasha*' (rough and ready language)—a poor alternative to Hindi. Bundeli had no credibility—a reflection of the inferiority they experience vis-à-vis their caste, class and gender identities.

Three broad categories of power structures came into play in this incident. At a macro level, we see the process through which dominant values, specifically dominant national languages, enforce their hegemony. It is interesting, of course, that literacy lends itself to this process. That is, the norms of correctness are applied to spelling, but not to pronunciation. Second, there is an appeal to the power structures of the educational system. Although this incident occurred in an apparently alternative educational system, expectations of what teachers should teach and learners learn were clearly derived from the mainstream system. Finally, the incident expresses some of the power dynamics between the trainers and the *sahelis*. In this case, the trainers intervened to question the teacher's literacy practice. While we did not enforce any change, the intervention itself opened the issue for negotiation later.

Language, Pedagogy and Knowledge Creation—Process of Developing a Literacy Primer

We decided to develop a new primer for the programme. Having a primer that the women identify with, one that reflected the beliefs of the programme, was felt to be important. A group of 10–12 *sahelis* and *sahayoginis* and members from Nirantar got together to develop a primer through a series of participatory workshops. Developing the primer threw up some important power-related issues of a participatory process of materials production. The incidents described below will highlight the issues around language hierarchies and knowledge creation, between oral and written language, literacy pedagogy and participatory processes.

Tackling language hierarchies

At the outset the following exchange occurred:

Facilitator (F): In what language should your primer be?

The responses of the participants (P) varied, but were unanimously in favour of Hindi:

P: It should not be in the local language.

P: We speak our language, there is nothing new in it, so why teach in Bundeli?

P: If we teach them in their language, they will remain where they are.

P: How will they read other books, if they are taught only in Bundeli?

P: We should teach only the pure and correct form, both in the written and oral mode.

We felt differently. Language in literacy work was not merely a conduit to pass messages from a group of information providers to passive recipients. While we could not disregard the participants' strong notions of and aspirations for mainstream education, we felt that education work in the local language should at least be experimented with. Still, their strong, articulation in favour of Hindi put us in a dilemma. Could we push our agenda? After all, we were committed to a 'participatory' approach. Finally, drawing on the same methodology, we reasoned that it would be unfair if we were not able to find the space to express our views. We thought it necessary to make explicit the issues of power within the question of language.

We decided that a dialogue on the issue was in order. We told the group we wanted to challenge their notions of purity and correctness in the context of language. This proved to be a difficult exercise. We raised with the group issues about the politics of language and the asymmetry of power that exists in the Indian context between the use of standardised (official) languages like Hindi and regional languages and local dialects. We, tried, through numerous illustrations to bring home the point that language was a means to exercise control and domination, as well as self-determination, and a strong cultural expression. While they relate to the concept of 'power' or 'paua' (as they refer to it) and experience it – viz, the landlords, upper castes, and as women, it was difficult for them to do so within the context of language.

Not having made any headway we decided to explore the issue differently rather than drop it completely. To not make explicit the various dimensions of subordination of Bundeli would have been to perpetuate unequal power relations. We undertook an exercise where we developed word lists in Bundeli in certain categories – items found in the house including architectural terms; kinship patterns; different idioms and qualities related to men, women, and children; adjectives used for different types of personalities, jewellery items, etc. The corresponding words in Hindi and English were written alongside. This exercise generated excitement. Every word brought with it an outpouring of stories – intensely personal, but also humorous and satirical; "they used to tell me not to laugh like that ...my mother got these kinds of earrings made when I got married...they used to shout and call him a 'belli' (nut)...the milk used to be hidden in this kind of cupboard..."

Though each story, even around the same word, was different, they all shared a common cultural experience. Experiences, from which we were excluded, but became a part of, in the narration. Our interest somehow seemed to affirm their experiences and the stories kept flowing. (Excerpts from the workshop report, Nirantar 1993)

The process revealed a wealth of indigenous cultural experiences and the richness of the local language, while simultaneously inverting the power dynamics between Nirantar members and the *sahelis*. For instance, the group found that there were words in Bundeli that had no equivalent in Hindi. English was able to capture even fewer nuances. In English, you have only uncle and aunt, in Hindi there are special terms for every kind of uncle or aunt; your father's sister is '*bua*', and mother's sister is '*maasi*'; and Bundeli is even more nuanced. Each term carries connotations of a unique relationship. In other categories too there were Bundeli words that found no place in Hindi. If these words were not within the mainstream language, should they be deleted from our vocabulary as well? Were these words 'incorrect'? As the discussion flowed, the group decided that they would settle for a mix of Hindi and Bundeli.

This exercise brought into focus the following issues. First, that writing, unlike speech, calls for the authorised version. Second, new learners and their teachers are faced with this issue of power and who has the right to say how something will be written.

Participatory Writing Process: The Complexities Involved

So far, so good. But the next day, when we attempted to build on this fruitful exercise, we were in for a surprise.

On the basis of the previous day's exercise, we asked them to select key words and create reading texts. They wrote: 'Minu fetch water', 'Ramu go to the fields', 'Rita cook the food'. Everything was an instruction. The readers were passive receivers.

We took their work and read it back to them. They looked unmoved. We asked them, where was the laughter and animation of the previous day? If we had enjoyed the stories so much, could that not then form part of their primer? They said, 'But then we were "telling" the story. Those kinds of stories are never in books. We never thought they were worth anything much.' 'But then you never wrote books before,' we replied. 'Now you will, so you can put what you want into them.'

It is evident from this incident that there was a sharp distinction in the women's minds between what is appropriate for oral and for written communication. While indigenous language and images find reflection in the oral mode, literacy and the written mode is concerned with instructions, development and information and always reflects the images and perceptions of the mainstream language. We felt we had to intervene again to make the group realise that they had the power to shape the primer as they chose, to include their images and content. The conflicting images of that content, held by teachers and learners, had to be reconciled. It was a realisation of the power they would wield, as well as the potential power to change and redefine what counts as knowledge. To make the alternative possible, we had to first validate their language and cultural experiences and establish that language was central to knowledge creation. And it was not insignificant that the validation was coming from us—people who, to them, represented the mainstream.

How Did We Select What to Include in the Primer?

When it came to making a selection, a majority of the group suggested one of the denial stories, which positioned them as victims. But we felt very strongly that selecting that story would only reinforce the stereotypical relationship between a mother-in-law and a young bride, which is usually portrayed as being tense, strained and one of restriction and denial. Was it not possible to present a more humorous side to women's and young girls' lives?

In the previous day's exercise, they had listed Bundeli words for architectural features within their houses. One such feature was a special cupboard called a '*kimaria*', where all the precious 'goodies', like extra milk or ghee or some sweets, would be stored. Numerous stories had been narrated about the *kimaria*. Most of them had to do with women or young girls being denied access to the *kimaria*. One story was slightly different. It was about how one of the *sahayoginis*, as a young girl, was caught stealing milk from the *kimaria*. It was humorous, used the local idiom and had caused much merriment in its narration. This type of story was finally selected for the primer. Although many of the books available portray young girls as being burdened with work and discriminated against, we emphasised that every time we present a story (written or oral), we are implicated in a particular way of understanding the world and our place in it (Simon 1987). Do we, then, always want to produce narratives that represent women as 'victims—denied, burdened and discriminated against?

Maniya's Story: When Real Events Become Materials for Texts

> As we were working on the primer that evening some women from the office rushed into the room saying, "A young woman, Maniya, has been burnt to death by her husband. A group of us are going to Manikpur (a nearby town) to try and catch him". We all dropped our work and prepared to leave with them. No one needed any prompting.
>
> A group of about 15 women reached Manikpur. We gathered the women of Maniya's neighbourhood and began having a meeting. All of a sudden the dead woman's husband appeared – dressed in white, feigning a deep sense of loss at his wife's death. He thought we had come to pay a condolence visit. But the women were in no mood to be taken in by his deceit. We accused him of the crime. He denied having committed it. The women did not relent. He finally admitted that he was guilty, but with no hint of remorse or shame. We were enraged and started beating him. We painted his face black, made him wear a garland of slippers, and paraded him through the town.
>
> On returning to the workshop everyone started writing out the story as a lesson in the primer. There had been no consultation. The key word selected for the lesson was 'chadchatta' (a deceitful, fraudulent person), a word in Bundeli that had emerged in the previous day's exercise. They were convinced that no other word could describe the man (From Nirantar's workshop report, Nirantar 1993).

The primer workshop experience revealed an interesting sequence of events. Here, the Nirantar members were obviously quite forceful in pushing the women to affirm their local tongue. But after the apparent success in generating a lively discussion on the joys of Bundeli, this momentum floundered the next day because of the deeply ingrained association of literacy with the national language and what is worthy of being in a book. However, it was finally the intervention of 'everyday life', or at least a common tragedy, that shook the women into a realisation of the virtues of their own language. This episode also revealed to us the virtues and limitations of 'classroom exercises'. The classroom discussion, while creative and important, did not seem to have any concrete significance for the women, but after the cathartic experience of punishing Maniya's husband, the women spontaneously drew on their vernacular for what was clearly an empowering act—that of labelling the murderous husband. It is, however, unlikely that this would have happened had the discussions not moved outside the language exercise.

Politics Around Ways of Knowing: Experiences from a Six-Month Residential Course

The women and adolescent girls who had acquired basic literacy skills at the literacy camps and centres articulated a strong demand for further education. A six-month residential course at the Mahila Shikshan Kendra (Women's Learning Centre) began in January 1995, to meet this demand. The example below is drawn from the first course at the Mahila Shikshan Kendra (MSK). It was during this period that the curriculum for the course was developed collaboratively by Nirantar, MS Banda and the 28 participants. How do different belief systems and ways of seeing the world impact upon an educational process? This issue came up starkly in certain sessions, but was an underlying concern throughout.

Are Rivers and the Earth Living or Non-living?

During one of the sessions in the MSK devoted to looking at different ways of categorising, the participants were categorising the world around them into 'living' and 'non-living'. The lesson progressed smoothly, till they came to classifying soil and river. The participants classified both as living. The *sahelis* too believed this. There was a moment of confusion, as the MS resource person present had a niggling feeling of doubt. A science textbook she had read had classified soil as non-living. But the *sahelis* were not persuaded.

That afternoon two members from Nirantar came to the MSK. On hearing about the morning's sessions, they expressed concern; it was factually incorrect to classify river and soil as living. A hasty meeting was convened. The *sahelis* defended their position. They eventually referred to the background material that had been given to them by Nirantar, which said, '*jaise hamare sharer ko hava, pani, aur khana, takat badhane ke liye zaroori hota hain, vaise mitti ko bhi zinda rehne ke liye in sab ki zaroorat hoti hai*' (Just as human beings require air, water and food to stay alive, soil also requires the above). The life-like quality attributed to soil was a turn of phrase and not to be taken literally. For the *sahelis*, it only served to reinforce what they already believed. We defended our position by checking both soil and river against the listed characteristics of living things. They did not fit. Science textbooks were referred to. The *sahelis* fell silent. We decided to reopen the discussion and try and rectify things.

Intervenors (1): Which of you think that soil and rivers are living? All the learners (except one) raised their hands. Why do you think they are living?

Participants (P): River is our '*devi*' (goddess) and '*dharti*' (earth) is our mother.

I: Your real mother is living. Earth and rivers are mother images, not your real mother.
P: They both give life—our grain, plants, forests grow in soil. Rivers give us life-giving water. Our mothers give life.
I: It is true that they are life supporting, but that does not mean they are living themselves. We eat food and grains to live, but the grain itself is not living. They do not grow. They do not procreate.
P: But if soil did not have life it would not produce life. Rivers grow. They grow in the monsoons and shrink in the summers. They do give birth to other rivers.
Chamela, a learner, challenged her colleagues: A river is non-living because rivers dry up in the summer. Something living cannot periodically live and die.
P: River is a mother and mothers can have many children. If one child dies, do we say all other are dead, or that the mother is dead? Earth is our mother and earth drinks water.
I: But a piece of cloth also soaks water, it is not living.
I: What is a river made of?
P: Water
I: Is water living?
P: Water in a glass is not living, but a river is living. A river is living because it flows, it moves, it cuts it own course.
I: You are saying that soil is living, but is this (holding up a lump of soil) living?
P: No, in this form it is not living, but the earth is living. Gods and goddesses give birth to rivers. Earth is a goddess. We pray to them.
I: That is a matter of your belief. Your religion. Other religions or belief systems may not accept this. For instance, scientists believe that they are non-living. Everyone is free to have their own beliefs and that is nice. The logic you put forward holds for the way you look at the world and similarly the logic within the other system is consistent.

This interaction, very early on in the semester, compelled us to reflect on our practice. There was a distinct polarisation between the way we categorised the world and their ways of looking or knowing. The interaction described above pitted one belief system against the other. However, the manner in which the interaction unfolded, with us trying to counter every point they made with a different logic, was not fruitful. The two systems really had no basis for comparison. And though we gave value to their ways of seeing, we did try and uphold a scientific and positivist conception of knowledge. Categories such as living and non-living had been emphasised as 'scientific' and 'logical' and the task of teaching and learning had to do with the acquisition of 'universal' and neutral content.

Yet the situation was not simply about imposing our worldview and disregarding theirs. And the episode, in many ways, was a dialogue among equals. Learners, till the end, were far from convinced that the categorisation we were trying to suggest had any value or validity. Their beliefs that earth and river are 'goddesses', 'life-giving' and 'mother', could not be separated, or broken down into components such as 'river is made of water and water is non-living'. The power and meaning that river and earth hold in their life-world is too great and too integral to their existence. 'Humanising' or giving things human attributes was also integral to the participants' language use—branches are children, sap is blood, when you cut a tree it bleeds and the rustling of the leaves, when a tree or branch is being cut, are cries of pain.

Divorcing this language use, when trying to categorise, is also not possible. Cultural roots are far more resistant and educational interventions cannot wipe these out so quickly or simply. Furthermore, the dangers of negating the learners' life-world are immense. Most education programmes pay little attention, as we did on that occasion, to the connections that exist between knowledge and its practical, cultural and linguistic realities in the learners' lives. Teaching and learning is not simply the acquisition of universal, neutral content; rather, knowledge is an instrument of reflection and insight.

This stalemate was not the last word on the issue of living and non-living; the dialogue resurfaced on another occasion. The same group of women, when discussing how rivers are formed, unhesitatingly declared that they are formed from melting snow of the mountains. This also brought home the fact that people are products of a complex reality, have different 'voices' (Wertsch 1991) and do not necessarily believe in 'one truth'. The voice that argues strongly for the river being a mother, living, a goddess and created by gods, also believes that rivers are born from melting mountain snows. Both voices are equally real.

Some final questions arise: What made us include this in the curriculum? Why try and teach adult women categories like living and non-living? They already had well-defined ways of seeing and categorising. We realised that this decision was unconsciously determined by our own primary-level schooling and not by any carefully thought-out criteria. And indeed, the distinction between living and non-living is one of the first lessons in most school textbooks. But then, if we did not bring in such topics, would we be excluding them from a way of seeing shared with a large section of society? Such questions are important to raise and engage with, to ensure that one's work is constantly evolving.

CONCLUSIONS

The three illustrative examples of teaching/learning activities raise important questions for people who are working in the area of education and literacy. One element that is clearly evident is that by engaging with the politics of language in literacy teaching, one is also engaging with feminist politics. We saw, through the examples, that language plays a critical role in terms of constructing identities, determining what constitutes knowledge, ways of seeing the world and self-expression. We also saw that, by challenging existing power hierarchies, alternatives can be created. The examples also point to the need for greater engagement by women's groups with literacy and education in general, and the politics of language in particular—the politics of standardised and local languages and their gender implications. The perpetuation of the divide between standardised and local language effectively pushes women's knowledge to the margins, and thereby does not weave their life experiences into mainstream knowledge creation. Though the examples in this chapter are limited to women's experiences in a non-formal educational programme, it is not difficult to see that there would be similar issues to grapple with in mainstream school education. There is a need to critically analyse the school textbooks from this perspective and see how language textbooks, for example, reinforce and create gendered identities, or whose experiences find reflection.

The other element that runs through all these experiences is the tension that exists between the mainstream and the creation of an alternative. The experiences demonstrate that in our practice, we cannot do away entirely with the mainstream, nor can we simply construct the 'other' in opposition to the mainstream. Negotiating between the two becomes crucial to the construction of a sustainable literacy intervention, where there is an integrated 'participation' of the two, rather than mere substitution. This brings us back to our understanding of power, where the two notions of power—one as a commodity and the other as generated through structured relationships that are mutable—become part of this negotiation with marginalised groups, who experience power only as a lack.

And lastly, by defining education and literacy as empowering and describing our practice as 'participatory', we often do away with the uncomfortable question of power. In the examples, we attempt to unpack the concept of participation and demonstrate that we are constantly working in situations that are ridden with inequalities. An analysis of power in our daily practice becomes critical, as the teaching/learning situation is not a neutral one. It is a real material site of social relations.

Notes

1. Nirantar, a Gender and Education resource centre, was set up in 1993. Our mandate, very briefly, is to make education an empowering process for women, particularly poor rural women. We work in close collaboration with field-based organisations to plan and implement education strategies, produce alternative curricula and reading material for newly literate adults and conduct gender-sensitisation trainings. We are involved with the autonomous women's movement and attempt to bring these concerns into our education work.

2. Mahila Samakhya or Education for Women's Equality is a central government programme of the Department of Education, Ministry of Human Resources Development. It was launched in 1989 in the states of Karnataka, Gujarat and Uttar Pradesh and has since expanded to cover several other states. Banda is one of the districts in Uttar Pradesh where the programme was first launched. The programme was launched in pursuance of the National Policy on Education in 1986, which was the first policy-level expression of the belief that education can bring about changes in the status of women.

3. Several Nirantar members, including the author, were actively involved in the education work in Banda, from 1991 to 1997. Nirantar's involvement with the gender-training and other aspects of the programme provided the base for building a common understanding on education and women's empowerment with the MS team. The experiences described in this chapter are drawn from our work during the period 1992–95. At the time of writing this chapter, the MS programme in the district was functioning in a limited way in terms of its agenda and staff. The education programme, including the Mahila Shikshan Kendra, is no longer operational.

4. Grassroots workers who coordinated the work of 10 villages.

REFERENCES

Batliwala, S. 1993. *Empowerment of Women in South Asia: Concepts and Practices*. New Delhi: Food and Agriculture Organisation of the United Nations.

Issac, J. 1986. 'Beyond the Three Faces of Power: A Realist Critique'. *Polity* 20 (1): 4–31.

Ministry of Human Resource Development. 1988. *Mahila Samakhya*. New Delhi: Government of India.

Report of Primer Development Workshop, unpublished internal report, Nirantar, New Delhi.

Simon, R. 1987. 'Empowerment as a Pedagogy of Possibility'. *Language Arts* 64 (4), The Issues That Divide Us (April 1987): 370–82.

Street, B. 1995. 'Literacy and Power?', paper presented at the International Seminar on Literacy and Power, Harare.

Wertsch, J. 1991. *Voices of the Mind: A Socio-Cultural Approach to Mediated Action*. Cambridge, Massachusetts: Harvard University Press.

21

Forging a Vocabulary for the Nation

A Feminist Reading of Language Textbooks[*]

Dipta Bhog, Purwa Bharadwaj and Disha Mullick

> The nation is not something alien to me, rather a part of myself that returns to me in the nature of others. Thus, the idea of the nation is bound up with the idea of my ego. If someone slights the nation, they slight me too; if the nation is praised, I have my share in this praise. For the nation is nowhere but in me and my kind.
>
> Otto Bauer (1996: 39–77).

A significant goal that national education systems set out for themselves is the inculcation of 'national character' in children, through schooling: What will enable learners to become ideal citizens? To this purpose, schools play an important role in the communication of ideals and values, through the processes of standardisation and homogenisation (Kumar 2001). Policy documents on education have time and again placed 'national identity', the building of national character and 'patriotism' amongst their core concerns. These concerns implicitly and explicitly mirror the choices that textbook writers make regarding content.

However, defining the ideal national character, or identity, is a matter of political contestation, and so competing visions of nationalism can define the educational curriculum quite differently. The reason why gender is central to this process is because, for historical and other reasons, it is the site where nationalism, especially nationalism in once-colonised societies, defines itself. In the light of this understanding, the theoretical underpinning of our study of textbooks, on which this chapter draws, was to map how the conceptual triad of nation, education and gender is reflected in textbook content. To this purpose, the textbooks were analysed along intersecting rubrics—nation, tradition and modernity, violence, labour, gender and nature. In this chapter, we focus on the analysis of findings from the nation rubric.[1]

* Previously published in *Economic and Political Weekly* 46 (19), 7–13 May 2011: 51–59.

A reading of English, Hindi, Urdu, Sanskrit, Tamil, Gujarati and Bengali language textbooks reveals these books as sites for negotiation on questions of region and nation; of what constitutes an 'Indian' identity; on the moment of the nation's past to be remembered; and who best can represent the values being espoused or promoted as 'ideal'.[2] In this process of searching for and expressing a nationalist self, there is inevitably the idea of the 'other', whether at the level of those who need to be brought in from the margins, or those who exist outside the boundaries of the nation. 'Beneath the modernist notions of liberal constitutionalism, of language of rights, states, citizens, lies embedded a more primordial idea of belongingness to a community and the idea of "foreignness" of the outsider' (Chaudhuri 2001: 81–82). Feminists have seen the community, as well as the whole enterprise of nation, as a masculinist enterprise, where 'masculinised memory, masculinised humiliation and masculinised hope' form the basis of this brotherhood of men (Enloe in Mayer 2000: 6). The question that has been asked is whether women share the same nationalist project as men. It has been long established that women are not only the biological reproducers of the nation, but are also the carriers of culture and tradition (Chakravarti 1993; Sangari and Vaid 1993; Sarkar 2001). And it is this that makes them important signifiers of national difference.

In formulaic terms, if women are the bearers of a nation's identity, it is through the instrumentality of education that they are inducted to assume that role. The process of gender socialisation is mediated through the category (or justification) of the nation. The school is a key arena for the creation and normalisation of specific sets of values, norms and ideals, setting out notions of the ideal citizen, the ideal woman, the ideal family, the ideal worker and so on. At the level of educational policy, the Kothari Commission (1964–66) identified the middle-class woman as the ideal, when it argued for women to share the responsibility of developing the nation equally with men. While being silent on poor women's contribution to productive activity, it mandated 'women' to move out of their homes, to develop careers and contribute to the economy. In the formulation of National Curriculum Framework (NCF) 1975, a clear move was made to link population control with the education of women. The ideal Indian woman was not only one who learnt the alphabet, but also one who limited or controlled her reproductive power to suit the new needs of the state.

This chapter can be broadly divided into two parts: the first explores the historical (and from this, the political) context of the languages and how this influences the vision of nation that particular language textbooks create. The second part (divided into three sections) sees how this historical context is reflected in the physical and emotional landscapes conjured up in the different language textbooks; in the way the other (we focus in this chapter on the Muslim) is constructed; and finally, how patriotism in the present moment acquires flesh and blood through language. A crucial thread through the sections is the way in which gender is manipulated in the evocation of nation, in all the language readers.

STAKING CLAIM TO THE NATION

Questions of Purity

Hindi, Urdu and Sanskrit: The need of the modern nation to define itself by standardising, purifying, and cleansing out others forms a foundation on which to understand the place and politics of Hindi language in the country and its teaching in school. Hindi's claim to the status of national language (which, among other things, necessitates its being the voice of the nation's identity, its history and its culture) result in a continued reliance on a Sanskritised Hindi that gets reiterated as 'pure' or proper Hindi. The focus on writers from the Hindi heartland, the complete absence of translations from other regional languages and the high moral tone of a majority of chapters focussed on building national character, point to a construction of Hindi as a language of values, particularly those expressing the Indian nation.

The emergence of *khari boli* or Harishchandri Hindi, as Veer Bharat Talwar calls it (Talwar 2002), saw, in the late nineteenth century, a conscious inclusion of Sanskrit words and active deletion of Persian and Arabic words. This Sanskritisation of modern Hindi was, according to Rai (2001: 77), also motivated by a desire to claim a 'pedigree' through striking up a relationship with Sanskrit. The claim was that Hindi was the *jyeshtha putri* (eldest daughter) of Sanskrit. Other writers argued that they both were 'sisters'. The passion and clarity with which Hindi school-teachers, in textbook-writing committees, continue to delete words which are Hindustani, or supposedly Urdu, establishes them as the continuing gatekeepers of this *khari boli*.

We can see that an emphasis on maintaining purity comes with the deeper politics of power, hierarchy and ideas of exclusion or inclusion. What is striking in the debate around language in the pre-Independence period was how gendered it was. If the effort was to develop a language which was the language of the new nation, cleansed of foreign and impure influences, Hindi was that pure, good Hindu wife and Urdu was the impure courtesan, beguiling and seductive and uncontrollable (Gupta 2001). Purity of language and emphasis on correctness, thus, is not merely about having a standard register that can be read or understood by a large number of learners from different backgrounds and mother tongues—which is the common argument at the national level. In fact, each language has its own politics of purification: with Hindi, as we see above, it is the Persian influence that is to be purged.

In the case of Tamil, the attempt to emphasise a 'correct' and 'pure' Tamil is located in the distancing of that language from the hundreds of Tamil dialects spoken.[3] Certain words become 'foreign' and, of these, some are allowed, others are ungrammatical and some problematic. Typically, these problematic words are those that have to do with defecation and death. Not only this, Tamil grammar marks certain words as *mangala* or 'auspicious' and differentiates them from inauspicious ones. Here, there is an implicit gendering, where *mangala* is a term usually associated with marriage or god.

In Sanskrit, the purity is vested in the religious or moral history of the language, and so secular literature in Sanskrit is excluded. The interesting point to note in

Sanskrit textbooks today is that there is no difference between the National Council of Educational Research and Training (NCERT) textbooks, state textbooks, private publishers or right-wing publishing houses like Shishu Mandir (Rashtriya Swayamsevak Sangh [RSS]), in terms of the vision/reasons they set out for learning the language. This singularity of purpose that Sanskrit has for education emerges from the claim that Sanskrit makes for itself vis-à-vis the nation: to speak of the *sanskaras* (past conditioning, behaviours, patterns, habits and experiences) that define 'our' common past. 'The land of Bharata is sacred and fragrant like sandalwood. Each and every village is a spiritual site. Each and every girl an image of the goddess, and every child Shri Ram' (from 'Mridapi Ch Chandanam', *Devvani Sanskritam*, Part 3, Shiksha Mandir). Its classical form becomes meaningful to the modern world, through detailing the antiquity and distinctiveness of the nation. Yet, as Sanskrit draws on a Hindu myth to set out the origin of the nation,[4] it also seeks desperately to establish its relevance in a world that rarely utters it as a form of communication. Here, questions of purity become less relevant; the question is one of survival in the education system itself. The new claim that Sanskrit is making is that it is not only a classical language, the well-spring of all our values, but that it is a scientific and modern language too.

The Peculiarities of Urdu and English Language Teaching

If Sanskrit represents a particular cultural context, across publishers and states, Urdu is an interesting foil, representing an amazing diversity, or even lack of singular purpose. Although the Urdu research sample did not cover as many states as the Sanskrit sample, we did see that each publisher's location imprinted its own ideological dynamics in the content of Urdu textbooks.[5] The state-produced textbooks occupied a more nationalist, if not centrist, orientation predictably, while the Jamaat-e-Islami textbooks were at the other end of the spectrum—embracing a religious community and distanced from the national community. Private publishers like Ikra and Maktaba Jamia fall somewhere in between, bringing in both nation and religious community. However, in all these texts, we see that the nation is a fraught space, mostly invisible, or visible through abstract invocations to the *desh* (country/nation) or *qaum* (community)—that has no clear political or geographical boundaries, or markers. Two striking aspects of the Urdu textbooks have been the continued teaching in madrassas, even today, of textbooks written by Ismail Merathi at the turn of the nineteenth century; and the silences that exist in textbooks vis-à-vis minority politics, partition and conflict.

In the case of Urdu language texts that are produced by the state, there is a sense that the assumed reader is a Muslim boy, who is, in all probability, poor. This emerges through the number of Muslim personalities that dot the NCERT books, many of whom have never featured in the English language or Hindi language texts produced by the same organisation. Here, Sir Syed Ahmed Khan and Bi Amma are accorded a significance that they might not have in other texts. (In the national books, those produced by NCERT and Jamia Bureau, they rub shoulders with a galaxy of stars that virtually flood these texts.) Clearly, Muslim *rehnumas* (one who guides the way) are assumed to be of interest to the learner of the language. Given that they are not all in the realm of literature, or writers of the language, it speaks more of the assumption of the textbook writers—that only Muslims learn Urdu in India today.

In the publications used by the madrassas, for instance, the Jamaat books, or even the Merathi texts, the popular perception that they are plagued by political rhetoric of a communal nature turned out to be incorrect. These books are silent on the Partition and on any reference to conflict or riots between religious communities. There is even an absence of any sense of wrong or shortcomings on policies, or welfare activities of the State. What we do find, at times, is an acceptance of the State, as is evident in the poignant rendition of how the madrassas' textbooks locate their learners' future in the nation.

> When you graduate from the madrasa, as a grown up, the country that you will become a part of is a land of sorrow: a country full of bad rituals, torn by division, poverty, hunger and disaster. Yes, a country full of sorrow—yet it is a country that is yours and mine. We have to live and die here, that is why this country is a place that tests you—that measures your love. Do not be frightened when you see all the disaster around you. Do not lose courage.
>
> At this moment our country needs the sweat of our brow. We must work, quietly all the time, with all our heart. This work will take place in the broken-down hut of the farmer, under the smoke-darkened roof of the artisan, in the straw-filled cover of the village madrasa. This work requires our patience.
>
> ('Service of the Nation', Urdu Book 4, Maktaba Jamia).

Ismail Merathi's texts, written at the turn of the nineteenth century, provide a rich description of how the shadow of a shared cultural past still found voice, in a context when Hindustani was being cleaved to give birth to two separate languages. Not only Ahilya Bai, Sita too appears as part of the curriculum for the Urdu text, an impossibility in today's context.

> ...Amongst the Hindus the fame that Ramchandraji's wife Sitaji enjoys, no other woman does. She withstood various tribulations and faced many challenges. She hailed from a family of great position and respect. She was endowed with god-given beauty... Sitaji with complete honesty, good nature, joy and loyalty sowed the seed of limitless love in the heart of her famous husband... thus Sita was an incredible example of purity, loyalty, sobriety, consistency and an unparalleled specimen of a faithful wife.
>
> ('Sitaji', Ismail Merathi Book 4).

These books were written in a time when the medieval age in India was being increasingly articulated as the 'dark ages', a period of tyranny and decadence, by the colonial rulers to justify their own rule. There is no denying that Merathi was attempting to tread the thin line between appreciating the British rulers, while trying to emphasise the bravery and valour of so-called 'Muslim' rulers who governed the country. So, not only are young madrassa learners reading odes to Queen Victoria (Urdu Language Book 4, Merathi: 126–27), they are also learning that an Islamic Sultanate was established with the 'defeat of Hindustan'. At the same time, Merathi is able to highlight aspects in the relations between kings, which did not pivot on axes of religion, but of honour, pride and friendships. As a result, the battle between Prithviraj Chauhan and Mohammed Ghori (Urdu Language Book 4: 93–99) is not tempered with the fire of religious differences.

In the English language readers, the nation in any kind of *real* sense—with its striations of class, caste, religion, region, gender—is absent. In its place is a space of desire, filled by modern gadgets, clothes and aspirations: the space where the identity of the modern Indian child is being constructed. The teaching of English in India has always assumed a certain class of learner. English was historically available to the urban middle class (male) 'native' and it has remained an elite language that few have access to and that connotes a world of power and privilege. The content that contemporary English textbooks include is still reflective of a static sense of history, a history of the language as colonial and alien—still outside the context of many learners' lives. In general, the English textbook includes a regular menu of classic Victorian writers, male and white, dead more often than alive. Wordsworth and Keats are considered sufficiently universal, their landscape, the landscape of English speakers and learners everywhere, assuming a world familiar to only a certain Indian child—middle class, 'upper caste' and fairly well-exposed.

Subsequently, the kind of English language that is taught is most often a stilted, formal English, to be used, again, in a world different from the everyday one of the learner—especially if the learner is not the middle-class one described above. A world where English is a foreign language, which wields great power; one that can be used only in (public) institutions and spaces of power and not to express the feelings and experiences of the (not-elite) child (Geetha 2009). For instance, exercises on conversation in the Tamil Nadu Textbook Corporation (TNTC) Class VI readers are set in official and rigidly hierarchical spaces like the school-room, or a government office. Although English learning and teaching is very much framed by the necessity to move towards modernity, its usage, predominantly in formal spaces of power, also genders its accessibility. Women and girls still have limited access to these spaces, as well as employment in the public sphere, so the formal English taught in school is still inhibiting and deliberately irrelevant. This minimalises the possibility that the learner could see or think of English as her own language—a language organic to her own particular (regional/class/caste) identity—and highlights a tension in the textbook, a constant aspiration for a different identity. The language taught is rigidly functional, almost never creative or colloquial, a language not associated with everyday or casual communication.

Mr Roy: Mr Ali, this is Mr Brown. Mr Brown, please meet Mr Ali.
Mr Brown: How do you do, Mr Ali? I'm John Brown.
Mr Ali: How do you do? It's nice to meet you. Do you live in Kolkata?
Mr Brown: Yes, And where are you from?
Mr Roy: He is from Bangladesh but he lives at Kalyani now.

(An exercise on how to greet people, from a West Bengal Primary English Reader).

The Region and the Nation

As we mentioned earlier, the regional language readers—Tamil, Bengali and Gujarati—are the stage for a play of identities and political interests. Post-Independence, the states negotiate the Indian nation in different ways, depending on their histories. In a way, it is in these regional affirmations and silences, these clashes and merging of interests, that the nation and nationalism seem to take some concrete form.

Paul Brass points to the difference in the way identity-formation unfolded between the north and the south in the nineteenth century (Brass 2004). In the north, the main competition was between the Muslim and Hindu elites. Here, the key marker was religion and it is around this that language and dialect conflicts clustered. However, in the south, it was the rising middle castes who challenged the upper-caste Hindu elites and Brahmins and their Sanskritised culture were the markers of the language debate. The Self-Respect Movement of the early twentieth century in Tamil Nadu sought a cultural and historical departure from the homogenising politics of the north, and politics in the region over the last 80 years have focussed on fashioning a distinct 'Tamil' identity. The study of Tamil Nadu textbooks (Geetha 2009) provides rich insights into how language textbooks 'do' Tamil; it also demonstrates the compromise that is worked out between nation and region. Tamil is so exceptional that it is universal, catholic—this is the hinge on which the negotiation with nation turns. The Tamil language texts set out the determinants of Tamil identity: a sense of literary greatness, its decorous humility, rationality and the secular practice of civility.

Exemplary lives discussed in the Tamil readers also have to do with characteristic ways of 'being Tamil'. Lesson 3 in the Class VIII reader, on the Dalit Tamil scholar Devaneya Paavanar, is a praise essay on his life. His poverty, his self-respect and, most of all, his love for Tamil, are underscored for the child reader—how he argued that Tamil Nadu was where civilisation began and made a case for Tamil being the mother of all languages. In contrast, the story of B. R. Ambedkar's life is told somewhat listlessly (Lesson 7). It does not take recourse to the usual rhetoric of praise, as life stories usually do in Tamil (the text is singularly lacking in adjectives). Since he is not Tamil, the narrative about him does not acknowledge and own up to his heritage. In some cases, as with Paavanar, Tamilness annuls other identities—Paavanar's Dalit identity is not mentioned at all.

However, in this attempt to forge a Tamil identity in the context of the larger nation, the radical caste and gender politics of the Tamil Self-Respect Movement are nowhere to be seen in the textbooks. As we have discussed elsewhere (Bhog et al. 2010), radical politics has no place in the textbook, as this may be disruptive to the maintenance of the status quo, so necessary to the sustenance of the national ideology. The study of Tamil textbooks shows that the ideal of self-respect has come to mean 'honour', particularly 'Tamil honour'. 'This honour is informed not by notions of equality, justice and fraternity, but by a putative ideal of Tamil purity, identified with the valour of Tamil men and the chastity of Tamil women' (Geetha

2009: 6). Consequently, 'safer' pieces are drawn from Tamil literature of the past: there is the chaste wife in the form of Kannagi, seen to represent the 'power of Tamil women', along with the Tamil courtesan, who is the carrier of the much-celebrated culture of dance and music. The '*Ulla*', a form of poetry centred around the passive admiration of women for a king parading around the town, is an interesting reiteration of conventional gender roles through a well-known, classical literary genre (Class TNTC Reader: 138–39).

> A hero walks down a street.
> Everyone is pleased on seeing him.
> A few women who see him thus saunter fall in love with him
> ... Seven different groups of women are possessed with love...

The imperative to link the region with the nation happens in language textbooks in West Bengal (Bengali and English), in the process of constructing the home (Bengal) as the world (both national and global). Communities are represented and/or celebrated through the lens of Bengaliness. Even the national icons chosen pass through a Bengali cultural lens—Derozio, Mother Teresa, for instance. Tagore's 'Jana Gana Mana' is a perfect example of the inclusion of the nation into Bengal—Bengali nationalism, so to speak. In the Bengali textbooks, we see, perhaps most clearly, the self-conscious creation of 'national culture' as a symptom of modernity. They promote Tagore's legacy of enlightenment rationalism and liberalism—also seen in the representations of gender in the textbooks. Women writers like Begum Rokeya communicate the 'woman's question' and the struggle for education, which was at the heart of the debate in the nineteenth century. Mahashweta Devi voices the exploitation of the tribal, part of an accepted critique of the nation. But these allowances, so to speak, are more in the interest of communicating the regional identity as a modern and progressive one, rather than to provide any critique to patriarchal structures, or other hierarchies of power.

Defined and sustained by a male, middle-class sensibility, Bengali language textbooks present an interesting rendering of the nation and region. The essential Bengali identity is the one caught in a nineteenth century moment and its language is a Hindu, *bhadralok* one, rarely informed by the regional, class, cultural and linguistic differences that run through Bengal. Thus, Bengali is articulated as the ubiquitous language of the region, even in the context of Muslim/Urdu-dominated areas. The use of Bengali across communities, then, becomes a way of transacting a (homogeneous, unified) regional identity with the nation and becomes linked to patriotism or nationalism.

LANDSCAPES OF THE NATION

An important objective of history and geography in school is to lay out the nation—its contours, exact boundaries, its bounties, its moments and points of glory and defeat—to the young learner. Language textbooks, too, map out the nation, bringing together its histories and its landscapes in charged and particular ways. Literature has always been instrumental in creating and recreating a desired geography of the nation and also in rousing feelings of patriotic (and other) passion for this geography. The way in which the nation is conjured in literature is almost always gendered—it is a mother, a lover, a wife, its rivers and hills known intimately and from time immemorial and to be protected from foreign touch. In any case, what this study of language textbooks has shown is that, like all literature, textbooks also create and reference a known landscape of the nation, in metaphors that are specific to each language and its own politics.

In the case of Sanskrit and Hindi, the ancient past and its 'sacred' features, or rather, sacred geography, dominate. Similar to geography texts, certain Sanskrit texts too begin with the globe, quickly move to the continent and zoom into the space titled 'Bharatbhoomi', or Aryavarta. Its features are presented to have existed since time immemorial—the lofty Himalayas, holy rivers and so on. The river Sindhu is present in most books, while the river Saraswati is added depending on the ideology of the book. In the post-NCF 2000 NCERT Sanskrit book (Shreyasi Part 2),[6] not only was the river Saraswati included, but proof of its existence was added as well. The National Institute for Open Schooling (NIOS) book, Sanskritam Part 1, goes so far as to outline a map of India at the time of Valmiki. Myths, as a result, become histories and get mapped on to generate a long and continuous geographical existence.

The task that Hindi sets upon itself is to communicate the nation. One of the elements that Hindi nationalist poetry draws on is the sheer antiquity of the nation (primarily north Indian), through its timeless and pure rivers, the Himalayas and Vindhya ranges. In the Tamil Nadu, Hindi Samba reader, this land of Ganga and Yamuna is also the *punyabhoomi* (the land which is pure), *dharmbhoomi* (land of religion, spirituality) and the *janam-sthal* (birthplace) of Raghupati and Sita. Clearly, a corollary of this antiquity argument is that it points in the direction of Hinduism as the origin, and therefore, the core of the Indian nation. In Sohanlal Dwivedi's poem 'Rashtra Devta' (Nation God), which appears in the Tamil Nadu Samba Reader 7, the nation is god, one among the galaxy of gods in Hinduism.

> Greetings to you, my nation god
> Beautiful Himgiri rides on your head
> Ganga and Yamuna adorn your chest
> Constantly extending out to the incomparable seas
> Perfect and imperturbable for ages
>
> From 'Rashtra Devta' (Samba Hindi Reader 7).

Thus, we see a layering in of religio-cultural symbols onto the described terrain, infusing the nation's past with myths and epics that seek a historical status of sorts. Gujarati takes a leaf out of Hindi texts and we see various protective gods on all four sides, demarcating the boundary of Gujarat: Amba Mata in the north, Kali Mata in the east, Kunteshwar Mahadev in the south and Somnath in the west. Thus, the past becomes part of a 'present', where the need to define the boundaries of the state somehow naturalises the logic of its outlines along religious markers. Rivers like Tapti, Narmada and Mahi indicate the prosperity of the land. In fact, the narrative of the river is a genre of writing particular to the Hindi textbooks. The river speaks in the first person, a living proof of the (Hindu) civilisation it carries, flowing to the present, transacting the link between history and geography. Therefore, the origins of both the nation and the river are intertwined and it becomes difficult to say which came first. Here, gender too comes into play as the river, a feminine symbol, informs, or rather, addresses, the reader—the future male citizen—as to how, as a mother, she is willing to be tied down and dammed to nurture the nation; and how his actions have polluted her.

> ...I am your mother. Not only yours, but also the mother of your ancestors. I am Ganga...I desire to serve others incessantly... On my banks, a great civilisation has grown... and I have seen myself as an intrinsic part of this civilisation. This country's culture and I are not separate.
>
> From 'I am Ganga' (Samba Hindi Reader 8).

The Urdu textbooks, in a masterstroke, invoke a *desh* which carries none of this highly Hinduised symbolism or imagery. It carries the sight, sounds and smell of a land one would call one's own. Evoking nature, with a judicious absence of the more specific political grid of the nation, it manages to perform this feat. In fact, the metaphors used to evoke this *desh* are those with regional, rather than religio-cultural, specificity—see how the excerpt from a Maktaba Jamia book uses language that is distinctively north Indian. The geography and the linguistic registers used to evocate this geography is distinctively north Indian—this *watan* or *desh* in the poem could be located anywhere across the north-west frontier to the plains of the north. The poem evokes, as we saw earlier with reference to Bengali, a notion of language not limited by national boundaries.

> Hindostan...the light of our eyes and hearts
> Hindostan...Our country, our beloved
> *Voh savan mei kaali ghata ki bahaar*
> *voh barsaat ki halki halki phuvar*
> (Dark clouds of the monsoon, the seasons of rain
> The drizzle and the light showers of soft pain)
>
> From 'Hamara Watan, Dil ka Pyara Watan' (Maktaba Jamia).

This strategy of tying nostalgia with nature in order to transcend the particular demands of national boundaries, can be seen in the Bengali textbooks too. There, too, the ambiguous term *desh* is used, which was part of Bengali vocabulary in the colonial era. For the present-day reader, it is difficult to say whether the Bangladesh of 1947 or 1971 is part of this *desh*. Here, the nation is ensconced in an emotional symbolism, strongly linked to the sense of being 'at home'. In the Bengali textbook, the landscape of Bangladesh is distilled into the Bengal village, pastoralised and imbued with traditional values of familial love and communal harmony. The analysis of West Bengal textbooks (Chakravarti 2009) points out that the village comes to symbolise a 'timeless borderless idyll, more subjective than real, heavily imbued with the tropes of motherhood. It is a dreamscape protected from the depredation of colonial and feudal oppression, where the male subject of these texts is protected, sustained and loved unconditionally' (ibid: 45). As we can see in Bangla, in the superimposing of nature on the *desh*, the nurturing mother is evoked as the essential component in providing a sense of goodwill and positive affirmation of this abstract idea of all, including the reader, as part of a national community.

The landscape English evokes is one distanced from any 'real' world that the child may know: in terms of economics, geography, history and the specific culture informed by these—language, dress, lifestyle and so on. In comparison to the strenuous nationalism espoused by the Hindi textbooks, or the stratagems in the Tamil textbooks, there is a striking lack of overt political and geographical location in the English textbook. At a microcosmic level, this can be seen in the fact that, more often than not, a selected piece will have no context provided and its meaning is not reflective of the particular time and place it was written in. This, perhaps, is common to all language-teaching in school—the disavowal of any connection between language, literature and the socio-political time it is located in. With English, though, this has the effect of invisibilising the nation and locating the English book in a timeless landscape of meadows (at most, idyllic Himalayan mountains), or a slightly eerie, technology-ridden future. The kind of authors and selections we see in the English textbooks are those which evoke a depoliticised countryside, or a one far from what the reader would recognise (Ruskin Bond's pastoralism is as close the textbook comes to evoking an Indian landscape). As other languages draw on and recreate a history and geography that is desired rather than real, English too evokes a landscape of (mostly Western) rural bliss, or of modern Indian consumerism.

Who Constitutes the Nation: Muslim Identity in the Textbook

Every 'us', whether it be nation or region, includes the idea of the other. The other appears in a variety of ways—perhaps the Muslim, the tribal, the woman or the disabled. As mentioned earlier, the processes of identity formation in Bengal and Tamil Nadu were markedly different from the manner in which they unfolded in the north. Here, it was religion that was both a consolidating and splintering factor, while in the south the anti-Brahmanical movement affected the articulation of politics and ideas of self and community. In this section, we look at how region and political environments reflect the representations of Muslim identity in language readers.

Language as Shared Resource

The West Bengal Madrassa Textbooks: The madrassa board books in West Bengal contrast sharply with the state Bengali books: in the latter, all religious references are erased to present a flattened cultural world, peopled by primarily the *bhadra* Bengali, who is overly secular (perhaps an outcome of left politics), yet represents a Hindu sensibility. Linguistic specificities—the use of Urdu words in the Bengali of Bangladesh, for instance—are also blurred, in the attempt to highlight the fact of a common language. On the other hand, Bengali madrassa books—which are also produced by the state, but only for madrassa schools—draw on both Islamic and Hindu elements, which they clearly see as constituting Bengali culture. The books point to how many famous, present-day Bangladeshi authors were educated in Calcutta University, while all great 'Hindu' poets of the Bengali literary canon were born in what is modern-day Bangladesh. National boundaries and watertight identities based on these thus blur—the notion of an 'Indian' identity is, necessarily, complicated.

A sensitive handling of religious identities, without eulogising or fixing communities into a type, emerges in the madrassa readers, in the shared sense of *desh* across nation and region: this is a community based on a shared language and culture. Whether it is Madhusudan Dutt's 'Banglabhasa', or Kazim-al-Qureshi's 'Bangla Amar', or Nazrul's 'Hindu Musalman', the idea of the common language is stressed. This legacy of a common Bengali language is emphasised through the nationalist poetry of the colonial period, yet it also helps gloss over the Partition.

> Name the country the plight of which causes us the deepest pain
> Name the country the magnificence of which fills us with pride.
> Where our progenitors' memories to be found
> That country is our Bangla Desh, only our Bangla Desh
>
> From 'Bangla Desh', by Satyendranath Dutt (Kishalay 4).

Just as the madrassa books complicate the notion of a Hindu Bengali identity, they also challenge stereotypes of Muslim identity, such as the austerity of the Islamic religion and culture. So, for example, a *hadith* (report of the sayings or actions of Mohammed or his companions) from Hazrat Muhammad, translated by Satyendranath Datta, urges the reader to buy flowers.

> Another such saint cropped up in far away Assam. His name was Shankaradev. His teachings were as open minded as those of the Vaishnava cult. Sanatan Goswami of Gaur was a Hindu sage. He established a new group called 'Darbeshiya' which resembled to a large extent the schools of Vaishnavism and Baul. They used Tasbis and malas like the prominent Hindu cults and flowing Muslim robes or al khalla. Their lyrics included the names of both Allah and Ishwar.
>
> From a piece on Ramakrishna Paramahamsa by Rejaul Karim (Sahitya Path 8, West Bengal Madarsa Board).

Begum Rokeya, an educationist/reformer/writer of the nineteenth century, brings together both the gender and religious identity issue and this partly explains her popularity in the Bengali textbook. She shows progressive Muslim and Bengali identity in the best possible light. Her own struggle to learn Bangla and the setting up of a school by her is a testimony to the change in women's lives in Bengal. The point to consider is whether the identification of Rokeya as promoting women's education (through narratives detailing the problems she faced learning Bangla, or in her fictionalised pieces on the educated housewife, like 'Parabao') make this an issue specific to the Muslim community. There appears to be a need to emphasise that the women's question—and not just in the Bengali books—was resolved at a point in the past and is merely a matter to be relegated to history.

Good Muslim, Bad Muslim: The Hindi Textbooks

The shift between good Muslim and bad Muslim identity is a recurring pattern in the Hindi textbooks. Part of the reason for this is, perhaps, Hindi's own history, its struggle to demarcate itself from Urdu and most importantly, the role that a fervent nationalist history played in defining and strengthening Hindi and the nation. Nationalist history was a reservoir for the heroic literature that emerged as an important feature of Hindi literature. Many of the writers who were part of this 'heroic' literary enterprise also wrote textbooks for schools. Characters like Rani Laxmi Bai, Durgavati, Prithvi Raj Chauhan and Shivaji are classic constructions of this period, who became subjects of plays, novels and poetry and then found their way into the school textbook. Most of these personalities continue to be read and memorised by children in post-Independence India. In these pieces, the *Yavan* appears as a significant presence.[7] A classic characterisation of the invading, marauding Muslim king can be seen in the lesson titled '*Taimur ki Haar*' (the defeat of Taimur), by Ram Kumar Verma (NCERT Bharti Part 2). A little boy challenges Taimur during one of his raids and while adults flee from the invading army, the young boy attempts to attack and kill Taimur. Taimur is so charmed by the fearlessness of the boy that he pardons him. The chapter includes a god-fearing mother, whose primary task is to worry and pray for her son. In a similar vein is Veer Malavji, a young boy who attempts to kill Shivaji. The child is similarly naive, fearless and devoted to his mother—a potent description of an Indian nationalist. Malavji is encouraged by a Yavan to undertake this mission. The boy mirrors the values that Shivaji represents. As a result, devotion to the biological mother, in the case of the boy, mirrors the passion with which Shivaji is meant to be devoted to the 'motherland'.

Incorporating the Other: The Politics of Cohesion

The interesting shift we see in the Hindi textbooks (closer to the end of the 1990s and post-NCF 2000), is that some of the explicit anti-Muslim rhetoric is necessarily replaced. Nationalist pride and fervour are generated in newer ways and, for this, the past is drawn upon yet again. There is a new other—the British. We see an increasing inclusion of personalities in some of the Hindi textbooks, like Tantia Tope, Bismil, Bagha Jatin, and the conflict with the British emerges in vivid accounts of violence, of battle despite defeat and death and where virility and violent resistance are the prime responses. This partly seems to be an effort to rekindle nationalist pride and attachment amongst a new generation of readers. It is no longer easy to continue to represent the Yavans as evil, or as traitors. For now, the safest other is the British and certain selected Yavans are highlighted as allies.

Ibrahim Gardi is the icon featured in the post-1992 New Education Policy initiative.[8] Ibrahim Gardi's loyalty to Shivaji and his definition of a good Muslim are clearly speaking to the present-day anxiety of whether the Muslim is loyal to the nation or to his faith. This question is emphatically answered: Gardi's opponent is caricatured as a corrupt and degenerate man, who is desirous of Gardi's loyalty through force and shared faith. But Gardi is clear that the definition of a good Muslim is one who is loyal to the nation. He speaks to the present more than the past—a believing Muslim, but also a 'secular' one—when he talks of Ram and Rahim as one. The gruesome and violent death he suffers makes his claim to the nation all that more free of doubt or question, given his identity as a Muslim.

Abdul Kalam is a perfect Muslim icon for the textbooks and turns up so frequently that you have to marvel at the writing committees' imagination to stretch the man's qualities as far as they will go. He is among the few Muslims who can be put to productive use in the national textbooks, post-Independence. Kalam is Muslim, yet so aggressively nationalist and secular that he becomes an icon. Poignant stories from his growing years included in the English books show how he struggled against poverty and hardship to study and became the nation's leading scientist (nuclear weapons are mentioned nowhere, of course) and a patriot beyond compare. He also appears in the Tamil books as the perfect Tamil nationalist—holding close ties with his Tamil *taay* (mother), as well as his nation, adept at reading the *Gita* and playing the *veena*.

Festivals in language textbooks become part of the effort to create a national culture that brings its multiple audiences into a collective whole. As a result, Sanskrit's efforts lean towards what can be termed a brotherhood of male citizens. In certain Sanskrit textbooks, particularly the Uttar Pradesh textbooks, there is a mention of Eid and the practices associated with it. However, it emerges as a festival celebrated by the community specifically—members of other communities are not involved. In more recent national Hindi textbooks, festivals like Rakhi, Diwali, Christmas and Eid have come to represent the contours of a homogeneous national space occupied by a citizen who is able to participate in or appreciate these as national events. Yet the purpose of this collective sharing is more to promote a standardised portrayal of 'Unity in Diversity', where even diversity is contained within manageable dimensions.

> Muslim brothers celebrate Id
> Christians sing on Christmas
> Hindus give them both greetings
> Bharat becomes one unit...
>
> (Samba Hindi Reader 4).

The Othered Self

In conclusion, a short note on how this pervasive 'other' in the textbook constructs both itself and its own other—the nation, with its pasts. In Urdu textbooks, we find that the construction of the self, for the Muslim, is primarily of a homogeneous community, with no regional variations or practices. This is evident in the inclusion of only Ed and Bakra-Eid as the two festivals of the community. In the Ikra textbooks and in the Jamaat-i-Islami books, the two festivals are an expression of the religious ideals of Islam. They are not viewed as part of the culture of Muslims in India. As a result, different ways of celebrating Eid find no mention. Also, other festivals that are part of popular culture—for instance, Shab-e-Baraat, Moharram, Barah Wafaat and so on—are not included. Following the main or core teachings, in accordance with the holy book, is the aim of the textbooks. There are there no references to other communities or religions, nor is there an engagement with them.

The Urdu language textbooks are, by and large (with the exception of NCERT and other centrist publications), silent about the nation. In fact, there is also little on Muslims in post-Independence India. There is an attempt to turn the gaze inwards, without any articulation of events that might prove to be uncomfortable for the texts, or impossible for them to discuss, given their position as a minority community in a communally fraught nation. The Partition, the wars with neighbours, the status of Muslims in economic spheres—it is as if a large part of the present and its context is erased in these books.

Patriotism and the Language Textbook

The nation is most stridently visible in the nationalist fervour or patriotism that is communicated as a necessary value in the language books. Different languages 'do' patriotism differently, depending on the relationship they have (or aspire to have) with the nation. Within the ambit of the patriotic story is also the setting up of the ideal patriot: men, women and children. In essence, then, not only do language textbooks tell you how you must feel for your nation, but also provide the physical and moral qualities that being patriotic involves. For instance, Hindi books across states do define and describe what types of ideal women and children are part of this nation, or serve it best. In fact Hindi, in its self-imposed role as 'national' language, articulating a nationalist history and identity, is pre-eminent in defining a patriotism that is adequate for the modern nation.

What is seen as patriotism is deeply gendered and even the present-day language readers communicate an extremely dated version of who is patriotic and in what terms. As feminist scholars on the nation have said (Mayer 2000; Walby 1996), while men carry the prerogative of the nation, women carry the obligation. While men die for the nation, women continue to live, giving birth to others, or betraying male lovers in a show of loyalty to the nation. Their emotion and contribution is always less, somehow, than the desired masculine patriot's. For instance, in a chapter titled '*Meri Maa*' (my mother) in the NCERT Hindi reader, Bharti Part 1, written by the revolutionary Bismil, we see a son writing about the greatness of his mother. After a rather brief sketch of how she was a self-taught, hardworking and nurturing mother, we are provided with a more powerful sense of Bismil and how, as her son, he is able to perform the all-important act of dying for the motherland. Her greatness is in giving birth and nurturing him—although, it is mentioned in passing that she did not agree with the path her son adopted, of violent protest. Bismil promises that, with his martyrdom, his name will be etched in the annals of the history of the nation. Ironically, we are never told what his mother's name is.

The Hindi books also include some classic examples of stories that pit women's love for the nation against their romantic love. In the Tamil Nadu and Gujarat Hindi textbooks, women perform the ultimate sacrifice of handing over their lover (a potential enemy of the king), as proof of their patriotism. However, in one case, the protagonist demands that she too be killed as a reward for bringing in her betraying lover—thus affecting a masterstroke, where her love and loyalty to the nation and her integrity as a woman are both left intact. She sacrifices her love for the nation and her life for her love.

> Vijaya: Hide and seek is played with eyes shut, but this is a different type of play. In this game hands have to be tied. Now give me your hand. (Shreepal puts his hand out, Vijaya ties his hands tight. Jaidev (Vijaya's brother) enters from the other side.)
> Shreepal: (without looking at Jaidev)—Now, what next?
> Vijaya: My brother will play the remaining part of the game (points towards Jaidev).
> Shreepal: Vijaya! That you can practice such deception was beyond my imagination even.
> Vijaya: I am proud that I saved my love from sedition. (...)
> Vijaya: [To Shreepal] My love! I beg your forgiveness for my sin [Taking the necklace from her neck and putting it around his]. This is the final evidence of my love. Today is our *swayambar*. Today I put the wedding garland around the neck of the farmer's son against the tradition of the Maalav race. I have been yours and would remain so.
>
> From 'Maalav Prem', by Harikrishna Premi (Gujarat Hindi Class IX).

Gender and violence, then, become barometers to measure how patriotic one is—and whether patriotic enough. Preetilata Wadekar's story in the Bengali Class V reader (Kishalay) is a dramatic instance of women proving their love for the nation by being imitative of men—in a way, it is the only way that women can be the ideal patriot. The piece shows the common figure of woman as freedom fighter, assistant to '*Masterda*'. Here, the break from the 'normal' woman character—Preeti is active, out in the public and violently fighting for the nation—is made possible by (cross) dressing Preeti in male clothing, to legitimise her transgressive role. Also, as we see in many other instances, the woman is permitted to bend certain traditional and stereotypical rules when she becomes a social activist who is reinforcing dominant values with respect to the nation (for instance, the woman-social activist-*brahmachari* of the Hindi textbooks). As the study of Bengali textbooks (Chakravarti 2009) points out, these bloody instances of women revolutionaries do not really alter gender roles or male narrations of history. They are merely among the many tests women must undergo to prove their patriotism and worthiness and which they never quite pass.

In the case of children, it is in the potential they carry as future actors. The male child, who is the subject of most of the stories, carries the potential and the nation's desire of becoming the ideal patriot. In Hindi language texts, nationalist poetry dominates till middle school: it is invariably the inaugural piece of the book. In the Gujarati books, we see '*Karo Remakda Kuch Kadam*' (Class III), a marching song by Makrand Dave, filled with the thrill of marching boots and advancing armies. An inclusion since the 1970s, it has a child leading a toy army to 'protect Hind desh'. In an interesting way, the nation too, like family property, becomes the inheritance of the male child. Here, a nationalist moment infused with passionate emotion is transposed on a contemporary context, its empowering, rich oratory set to a different tune of the present.[9]

Another pattern that we traced over various language textbooks was the link between civic moral values and a sense of patriotism.[10] In English textbooks, for instance, when the nation is not immediately visible, as such, and patriotism is not directly linked with cries for blood (and so on, as we have seen in Hindi books), patriotism makes itself seen as a moral value. This value is demonstrated by various acts of unspecified 'good' (by this we mean that it is not necessarily explained *why* the act is good)—like planting trees, or showing other forms of concern for the environment; being non-violent and 'tolerant'; by various acts of bravery and uprightness—all of which go into making the model young citizen of the modern nation. As the study of Tamil textbooks (Geetha 2009) mentions, this is also one way in which different regions moor themselves to the idea of a (less abstract) national allegiance.

Conclusions

Language textbooks are a key site in the articulation of national identity, encompassing a range of emotions, values—a sensibility that defines a unique national character and qualities for its citizens. Through a complicated process, gender comes into play to express these emotions, values and so on, giving us crucial insights into how languages forge a national identity. Purity is a key claim made by languages that seek the status of speaking of and for the nation and it is here that gender gets operationalised in multiple ways. For instance, the pure, chaste, *desired* national language—Hindi—and the impure, seductive other—Urdu—are positioned as binaries, to describe what constitutes the core of the nation. Purity is heavily laden with symbolism associated with women's character and morality, and so determines the particular idiom and tenor of different language textbooks. Purity is also claimed by creating distance from the other impure dialects that are marked as having inauspicious and unchaste vocabularies, thereby layering gendered ideas of chastity and honour into what constitutes the standardised language. Maintaining purity of language and of the women of the nation is, therefore, a simultaneous and entangled process—one necessarily defines the other.

The corporeal aspect of this deeply desired purity can be seen in the embedding of desired values and histories on the body-landscape of the nation—always personified as female, passive, sacrificial. Languages adopt different strategies to lay claim to this body; for instance, they may evoke, in a romantic and lyrical language, the emotive relationship to one's 'country'. But the languages with the prerogative over the material and political nation make this claim with the aggressive and male marking of the body of the nation with a certain (Hindu) mythical history. It is here that the nation (the *rashtra*) emerges virtually as a god in its own right, as *rashtra devta*.

In the language of nationalist literature and biography, while ideas of purity and landscape evoke the nation more sublimely, we see a more tangibly articulated 'ideal' in the definition of patriotism: one that is aggressive, violent and male. Here we see, most explicitly, the emergence of the sexed nation, one in which men and women have separate and designated roles. Women, in this nation, whether they betray lovers, sacrifice themselves or kill for the nation—are always already marked as lesser, struggling and incomplete patriots. The patriotism of the Muslim other, too, is always questionable, necessitating deep suffering, violent death and an almost-excessive commitment to the values of the nation.

We need to be mindful, therefore, of the constant tension underlying the efforts to be inclusive of other identities and realities on the one hand and the need of school textbooks to put forth a homogenised 'national' community on the other. What gets included and how and when, are questions that point to the fraught nature of the educational enterprise. Ruptures occur, although rarely, in this seemingly set narrative of nationalism; in glimpses of more nuanced national identities, in characters that question the glorification of violent nationalism, or in pieces that reveal the violence implicit in forging this homogenised national community. The challenge remains to capture these fleeting ruptures and use them to illustrate the fissure between the desired and the much more plural and intersecting national identities that exist.

NOTES

1. To read about the process of developing the research design and the framework of analysis, please see the 'Introduction to Textbook Regimes: A Feminist Analysis of Nation and Identity—Overall Analysis' (Nirantar 2010), available at http://www.nirantar.net/ttgl.htm.

2. Two hundred and twenty three textbooks across seven languages—Urdu, Sanskrit, Hindi, Tamil, Bengali, Gujarati and English—were analysed. Books were published by private and state publishers. In the case of Sanskrit, Hindi and English textbooks, the analysis included books produced by the four states and also those produced at the national level. The time period of the study covers textbooks produced as far back as 1990 in some states, as well as revised publications produced between 1998 and 2005. The study does not include textbooks that were produced under the aegis of NCF 2005 (New Delhi: NCERT). For a detailed list of textbooks, please see Nirantar 2010.

3. Other languages show a similar process of pushing out the local to purify and standardise.

4. Almost all state Sanskrit textbooks claim that India (Bharat) was named after King Dushyanth's son Bharath. Symbolic representations show a 'baby' Bharat counting the teeth of a lion in fearless abandon.

5. The Urdu textbooks analysed included readers used primarily in Deobandi madrassas in Delhi and UP, as well as in private schools. These included books written by Ismail Merathi, private publishers like Ikra and Maktaba Jamia and those written by Jamaat-e-Islami. Ismail Merathi's books are extremely popular, not only in Delhi and UP, but are taught in madarssas all over north India. The sample also included NCERT books, Uttar Pradesh Basic Education books and the books used in the Islamic course for girls (in UP).

6. The National Curriculum Framework 2000 was seen to be a major departure in the approach of NCERT, as it promoted a right-wing, 'Hindu' vision of the Indian nation. The textbooks produced before and after this, especially the history and civics books, have been distinguished in the study as 'pre' and post-NCF 2000—the latter implying books produced in 2002, 2003 and 2004.

7. Yavan originally meant someone from Greece or Yunan. It later came to connote 'foreigner' or 'uncivilised'. In the nineteenth century, it was used to allude to Muslims.

8. Ibrahim Gardi was the Maratha chief who fought Ahmad Shah Abdali in the third Battle of Panipat in 1761. The Marathas lost to Abdali and Gardi was captured and killed.

9. See reference to 'Apna Paraya' by Jainendra Kumar from the Class X Gujarati Hindi textbook, for a rare instance of questioning violence in the name of nationalism in the textbook (Bhog et al. 2010: 117).

10. The formulation of this point owes much to the analysis of English textbooks in the study of Tamil Nadu textbooks (Geetha 2009).

References

Bauer, Otto. 1996. 'The Nation'. In G. Balakrishnan, ed. *Mapping the Nation*. London and New York: Verso.

Bhog, D., P. Bharadwaj, and D. Mullick. 2010. *Textbook Regimes: A Feminist Critique of Nation and Identity—Overall Analysis*. New Delhi: Nirantar.

Bismil. 'Meri Maa' [My Mother]. 2004. *Bharati*, Part I. New Delhi: NCERT.

Brass, Paul. 2004. 'Elite Interests, Popular Passions and Social Power in the Language Politics of India'. *Ethnic and Racial Studies* 27 (3): 353–75.

Chakravarti, Uma. 1993. 'Whatever Happened to the Vedic Dasi'. In Kumkum Sangari and Sudesh Vaid, eds, *Recasting Women: Essays in Colonial History*. Delhi: Kali for Women.

Chakravarti, Paromita. 2009. *Textbook Regimes: A Feminist Critique of Nation and Identity—West Bengal*. New Delhi: Nirantar.

Class VIII Tamil Language Textbook. 2004. Chennai: Tamil Nadu Textbook Corporation [TNTC] Reader.

Chaudhuri, Maitreyi. 2001. 'The Women's Question and Modernity: The Indian Story'. In Abha Avasti and A. K. Srivastava, eds, *Modernity, Feminism and Women Empowerment*. Jaipur: Rawat Publications.

Dutt, Satyendranath. Undated. 'Bangla Desh'. *Kishalay* [Class 4 Reader]. Kolkata: Government of West Bengal Textbook Corporation.

Geetha, V. 2009. *Textbook Regimes: A Feminist Critique of Nation and Identity—Tamil Nadu*. New Delhi: Nirantar.

Gupta, Charu. 2001. *Sexuality, Obscenity, Community: Women, Muslims and the Hindu Public in Colonial India*. Delhi: Permanent Black.

'Humara Watan, Dil ka Pyara Watan'. Undated. *Urdu ki Chauthi Kitab* [Urdu Book 4]. New Delhi: Maktaba Jamia.

'Introduction to Textbook Regimes: A Feminist Analysis of Nation and Identity—Overall Analysis'. 2010. In Dipta Bhog et al. *Textbook Regimes: A Feminist Critique of Nation and Identity—Overall Analysis*. New Delhi: Nirantar. Available at http://www.nirantar.net/ttgl.htm.

Karim, Rejaul. Undated. 'Ramakrishna Paramahamsa'. *Sahitya Path* [Class VIII Reader]. Kolkata: West Bengal Madrasa Board.

Kaviraj, Sudipto. 1998. *The Unhappy Consciousness: Bankimchandra Chattopadhyay and the Formation of Nationalist Discourse in India*. New Delhi: Oxford University Press.

Kumar, Krishna. 2001. *Prejudice and Pride*. New Delhi: Penguin Viking.

Lesson on Mohammed Ghori, *Urdu Zubaan ki Chauthi Kitab* [Urdu Language Book 4]. New Delhi: Ismail Merathi/Farid Book Depot.

Mayer, T. 2000. *Gender Ironies of Nationalism: Sexing the Nation*. London, New York: Routledge.

NCERT. 2003. *Shreyasi*, Part I, II and III. New Delhi: NCERT.

NCF. 2000. 'National Curriculum Framework for School Education'. New Delhi: NCERT.

National Focus Group on Gender Issues in Education (Position Paper). 2006. New Delhi: NCERT.

Premi, Harikrishna. Undated. 'Maalav Prem'. Gujarat Hindi Textbook for Class IX. Ahmedabad: Gujarat State Board of School Textbooks.

Rai, Alok. 2001. *Hindi Nationalism: Tracts for the Times/3*. New Delhi: Orient Longman.

'Rashtra Devta'. 2004. Samba Hindi Reader for Class VII. Chennai: Samba Publishing Company.

'I am Ganga'. 2004. Samba Hindi Reader for Class VIII. Chennai: Samba Publishing Company.

Sangari, Kumkum, and Suresh Vaid, eds, 1993. *Recasting Women: Essays in Colonial History*, 1–26. Delhi: Kali for Women.

Sarkar, Tanika. 2001. *The Hindu Wife and the Hindu Nation: Domesticity and Nationalism in Nineteenth Century Bengal*. Delhi: Permanent Black.

'Service of the Nation'. Undated. *Urdu ki Chauthi Kitab* [Urdu Book 4]. New Delhi: Maktaba Jamia.

'Sitaji'. Undated. *Urdu Zubaan ki Chauthi Kitab* [Urdu Language Book 4]. New Delhi: Ismail Merathi/Farid Book Depot.

Talwar, Veer Bharat. 2002. *Rassakashi: Itihaas Ka Khalnayak aur Hindi Ni Nai Chaal*. New Delhi: Saraansh.

Verma, Ram Kumar. 2004. 'Taimur ki Haar' [The Defeat of Taimur]. *Bharati*, Part II. New Delhi: NCERT.

Wadekar, Preetilata. Undated. Story in *Kishalay* [Bengali Class V Reader]. Kolkata: Government of West Bengal Textbook Corporation.

Walby, Sylvia. 1996. 'Women and the Nation'. In G. Balakrishnan, ed. *Mapping the Nation*. London and New York: Verso.

Notes on the Authors

Aarti Saihjee currently works for UNICEF in Ghana. She was a freelance consultant associated with ERU Consultants, New Delhi, during 1999–2003.

Ambika Kohli has a PhD in Sociology from the University of Canterbury, New Zealand.

Anju Saigal holds a Doctorate in Education from Harvard University. She is the Founder Director of Centre for Equity and Quality in Universal Education, a Mumbai-based non-profit organisation.

Annemie Maertens is a Senior Lecturer at the Department of Economics, University of Sussex, UK.

Anuradha De is a founder member and Director at Collaborative Research and Dissemination, New Delhi.

Balwant Singh Mehta is a Fellow at the Institute for Human Development, New Delhi.

Claire Noronha is a founder member and Trustee, Collaborative Research and Dissemination, New Delhi.

Dipta Bhog is a founder member of Nirantar: Centre for Gender and Education, New Delhi.

Disha Mullick is the Managing Director of Women Media and News Trust, New Delhi.

Divya Vaid is an Assistant Professor at the Centre for the Study of Social Systems, School of Social Sciences, Jawaharlal Nehru University, New Delhi.

Jeemol Unni is Professor of Economics and Public Policy at the Amrut Mody School of Management, Ahmedabad University, Ahmedabad.

Kameshwari Jandhyala is the first Director of Mahila Samakhya Andhra Pradesh and a Consultant to the National Office of Mahila Samakhya at the Department of Education, Government of India. She is currently a Director in ERU Consultants Private Limited, New Delhi, and is based in Hyderabad.

Kausik Chaudhuri is an Associate Professor at Leeds University Business Schools, Leeds, UK.

Karuna Chanana retired as Professor and Chair of the Zakir Husain Centre for Educational Studies, Jawaharlal Nehru University, New Delhi.

Krishna Kumar is a former Director of NCERT and a former Professor of Education at Delhi University. He is currently associated with Punjab University, Chandigarh, as an Honorary Professor.

Lori McDougall is currently a doctoral candidate in the Faculty of Public Health and Policy at the London School of Hygiene and Tropical Medicine, as well as a Coordinator of the Partnership for Maternal, Newborn and Child Health, based at the World Health Organization in Geneva, Switzerland.

Malini Ghose is a founder member of Nirantar: Centre for Gender and Education, New Delhi, and currently works as an independent researcher.

Meera Samson is founder member and Director at Collaborative Research and Dissemination, New Delhi.

Megha Shree works with People Research on India's Consumer Economy (PRICE), New Delhi.

Nandini Manjrekar is Professor at the School of Education, Tata Institute of Social Sciences, Mumbai. She is presently Joint Editor of Contemporary Education Dialogue (Sage), and the Vice-President of the Comparative Education Society of India (CESI).

Nina Haeems taught Sociology and Women's Studies at the undergraduate level in Wilson College, Mumbai, from where she retired in 2001. She was also associated with the Vacha Resource Centre for women and girls in Mumbai, before moving to Ahmedabad.

Purwa Bharadwaj is associated with Nirantar: Centre for Gender and Education, New Delhi.

Sadhna Saxena is a founding member of the Eklavya Foundation. She retired as Professor of Education from Delhi University in 2019.

Sharmila Rege worked in Krantijyoti Savitribai Phule Women's Studies Centre (the department of Gender Studies), University of Pune. She passed away in 2013 at the age of 43.

Suchitra Balasubrahmanyan teaches at the School of Design, Ambedkar University Delhi, New Delhi.

Susmita Roy works for Statistics New Zealand and lives in Wellington, Canterbury, New Zealand.

Vimala Ramachandran was involved in the conceptualisation of Mahila Samakhya (Education for Women's Equality) and served as the first National Project Director (1988–93) at the Ministry of Human Resource Development, Government of India. She established Educational Resource Unit (now known as ERU Consultants Private Limited) in 1998, as a network of researchers and practitioners working on education. She is currently the Managing Director of ERU Consultants Private Limited, and lives in Jaipur.